FREUD, SULLIVAN, MITCHELL, BION, AND THE MULTIPLE VOICES OF INTERNATIONAL PSYCHOANALYSIS

MARCO CONCI

FREUD, SULLIVAN, MITCHELL, BION, AND THE MULTIPLE VOICES OF INTERNATIONAL PSYCHOANALYSIS

MARCO CONCI

IPBOOKS.net
International Psychoanalytic Books

International Psychoanalytic Books (IPBooks)
New York • IPBooks.net

International Psychoanalytic Books (IPBooks)
Queens, New York
Online at: www.IPBooks.net

Book design by Dan Williams

ISBN: 978-1-949093-34-6

Printed in the United States of America

CONTENTS

AN INTERNATIONAL MIND
PREFACE BY STEFANO BOLOGNINI

Today's psychoanalysis consists of and grows through scientific, professional, and training activities that are much more structured and interrelated than they were in the past.

The historically most well-known and well-structured psychoanalytic institution, the International Psychoanalytic Association (IPA), founded by Sigmund Freud in 1910, involves its members and candidates in a remarkable network of conferences, contacts, and collaborations, officially structured through specific committees and task-forces. The members of these are psychoanalysts from various countries (international level) and various continents (interregional level); the most important official language is English, together with Spanish and French, but there are also other groups using other languages in their local meetings.

The major change that took place in the last decade in the analytic community as a whole was in fact a consequence of the multiplication of international and interregional exchanges made possible by new technologies, by increased accessibility via air travel, and by the better knowledge of foreign languages of younger generations of analysts.

On the scientific level, this has meant for many colleagues the possibility of leaving behind the regimes of theoretical-clinical isolation based on the single school of their original enclaves, and the discovery of other conceptual and technical worlds. Much of the merit for bringing about such a great change goes to those colleagues who, in various countries, have been able to build bridges and create a dialogue with the other schools, with other "psychoanalytic families," finding reciprocally comprehensible and acceptable meeting points and common languages that could be shared by many colleagues.

Marco Conci has for many years been an example of this progressive international evolution of the contemporary analyst, and his personal and professional paths unequivocally document this. His very careful attention to North American psychoanalysis, integrating his classical Italian-German training matrix, has been developed through an assiduous and highly active attendance at the congresses in this area of the world, without ever failing to participate in the European ones, and without losing the possibility of meeting the several prominent South American colleagues.

For fifteen years I have had institutional assignments in the psychoanalytic community that obliged me to undertake a great deal of traveling, and I have regularly met Marco (and had the pleasure of talking with him) at meetings across half the world. His is a curious and exploratory mind, developed from his early youth thanks to experiences of study and exchange in foreign countries that his family widely encouraged and supported.

But the peculiarity of Marco Conci's path consists also in another element, an element once atypical and, I would almost say, improbable, but today much more frequent: the passage through and familiarity with different analytic communities outside and inside the IPA, a path that until not long ago meant meeting with and experiencing worlds that were totally separate from each other.

In some ways, Marco was a pioneer of the inclusion of the W.A. White Institute in the American and then in the International Psychoanalytic Association, acquiring familiarity and developing very intense and advantageous collaborations with all those analysts who later also became our very much valued and esteemed colleagues. His experience as coeditor-in-chief of the *International Forum of Psychoanalysis* has made of him one of the most experienced and valued editors of international analytic journals. His admission into and progression inside the German Psychoanalytic Society allowed him to become a member of the IPA, thus successfully completing a long professional journey. Since 2012, Marco Conci has also been a member of the Italian Psychoanalytic Society.

This path through various institutes and institutions is equivalent to a journey through different countries, different communities, different cultures, and, I would dare say, different analytic ethnicities and families; it is easy to imagine how much this might have contributed to the complexity of his training, to the richness of the contributions from which he could benefit, and to the amplitude of his critical, as opposed to "parochial," perspective. In other words, such a cosmopolitan journey has greatly contributed to his culture and to his trust in pluralism as a positive value of our field.

But to understand the path and specificity of Marco Conci the psychoanalyst, it is necessary to refer to another fundamental aspect: he is also a historian, a true, very passionate, and extremely well-informed historian.

His historical interest focuses on both the history of analytic institutions and groups, and the history of some of the protagonists of our history. It has a certain predilection for those who, although having played a scientific and historical role of the utmost importance, seem from a certain point onwards to have been at least partially ignored in (if not definitely "cut" from) the analytic mainstream, from the cultural fashions, and from the idealizing transferential currents that transform some of our authors into monumental figures. These celebrated authors are, of course, not without merits, but they are also the object of substantially parental projections, at the expense of other authors, no less meritorious, who have simply been less lucky in terms of collective transferential fashions and events.

Not only this, but, in addition to appropriately rehabilitating significant but inadequately valued authors of the past, Marco Conci has also chosen to work on the reconstruction of apparently unconnected histories and threads that, conversely, have revealed an unsuspected continuity in the complex context of the history of psychoanalysis. This has very often been on the basis of highly significant but little-known personal relations among the protagonists of its evolution during the past decades.

There are only a few analysts who have dealt in such an accurate, extensive, and authentically respectful way with the periods following the pioneer phase of psychoanalysis, and Marco Conci is one of them. His publications and his activities in this field have rightfully led to an invitation from the IPA to join its "History of Psychoanalysis Committee" as a European Consultant.

The three aspects characterizing Marco that I have briefly mentioned are therefore his *internationality*, the *transinstitutional character of his path*, and his *historical-reconstructive interest* in the analytic community. These are all accompanied by a particular interest in the *"building of bridges"* (among scientific cultures and communities), the *"opening of passages"* (among different training institutions), and the *"shedding of light"* on neglected or partially forgotten but extremely important areas or figures from the history of psychoanalysis.

Marco, with lovely humor and analytic acuity, would probably trace these three aspects back to his family history, given the fact the his father, a civil engineer, built bridges, roads, and tunnels in Trentino-Alto Adige. These facets not only concern a personal specificity of his, but can also be assumed to be models of a possible evolution of the contemporary psychoanalyst: less family-centered, less closed, and less prejudiced toward the other groups (the other families) of our analytic community.

To all of this I want to add a particular mention of another personal trait of Marco's, that is, his natural and active propensity to favor collegiate meetings and contacts, a propensity heading in the opposite direction to the tendency of many colleagues to close themselves after having qualified, and to withdraw from collegiate exchange.

For all these reasons, I am particularly happy to invite readers to immerse themselves in the following pages, accompanied by an author-researcher-colleague who is so good at looking "back" (in terms of our history), "around" (in terms of our international field), "forward" (in terms of the evolution of psychoanalysis as a discipline), and—as all of us working in this field hopefully do—"inside": inside our patients and inside ourselves.

Stefano Bolognini
Former President of the Italian Psychoanalytic Society
(2009–2013) and of the International Psychoanalytic
Association (2013–2017)

ACKNOWLEDGMENTS

With thanks to Routledge, Taylor & Francis group for permission to reproduce previously published material in this anthology. *International Forum of Psychoanalysis* articles: © The International Federation of Psychoanalytic Societies, reprinted by permission of Taylor & Francis Ltd, http://www.tandfonline.com on behalf of The International Federation of Psychoanalytic Societies.

Grateful thanks also go to Margaret Black for kind permission to reproduce Stephen A. Mitchell's letters in Chapter 6.

GENERAL INTRODUCTION

In the spring of 2015, I realized that, in the course of my professional life, I had written and published a whole series of good articles in English that probably deserved to be put together in a book. This is why, at the International Psychoanalytical Association (IPA) Congress held in Boston at the end of July 2015, I asked Peter Rudnytsky for advice, given his experience in the field of publishing. Peter told me that my proposal of a collection of already published papers did not correspond to the editorial policy of most publishers in our field, with the exception of Arnold Richards.

In order to convince myself of the soundness of my idea, I put together, at the beginning of August 2015—while on vacation in Salzburg—a first, provisional table of a book's contents. Having a good relationship with Stefano Bolognini, I had the chance to visit him in Venice around the middle of August, and to discuss with him my project; he told me to be ready for him to write the Preface for the book himself! Having had a frustrating experience with a leading publisher in our field some years before, in connection with the publication of the English version of my book on Harry Stack Sullivan (Conci, 2010, 2012), I discussed the problem with Franco Borgogno, and he confirmed Peter's advice that I should contact Arnold Richards and see if I could publish my book through his new publishing house, International Psychoanalytic Books. Franco associated the excellent idea of preparing and publishing an anthology of papers on Italian psychoanalysis—which became the book *Reading Italian psychoanalysis* (see Borgogno and Luchetti, 2016)—with both Peter's and Arnold's encouragement in this direction. Of course, it took some time for me to make this further step, but in December 2015 I agreed with Arnold Richards that I would meet him in New York at the beginning of January 2016.

My wife Doris accompanied me to my first meeting with Arnold Richards and Arthur Lynch, one of his closest collaborators, which took place on Monday January 11, 2016, around lunchtime, at the Maison Kayser on Third Avenue and 87th Street—a famous restaurant near, as I later learned, Arnie's home and office. This allowed me to share with Doris the excitement of finding a publisher who not only understood and valued my book project, but also accepted it right away, not just on the basis of the limited information I had given him, but also on the basis of the liking that we immediately felt for each other. Doris was also able to take the picture of the three of us that I hope to be able to include in this volume.

From Arnie and Art, I also learned a few things about what the publishing house stood for, for example their readiness to publish anthologies of papers written by their analyst contacts, aiming at reconstructing the latter's scientific contribution to and impact upon contemporary psychoanalysis. In addition, they felt strongly about the right of authors to see their final manuscript printed without any form of censorship or manipulation—for example for commercial reasons. Among other things, I learned about Art's project to help Robert Holt— with whom I am very well acquainted—to edit his correspondence with David Rapaport (1911–1960; see Holt, ed., 2017), a correspondence of unique historical significance that was eventually published in the fall of 2017. In other words, here was a publisher who—at variance with most contemporary publishers of analytic books—had a precise idea of the books he was publishing, and could establish a significant intellectual relationship with his authors beyond the simple commercial aspect of the joint publishing venture. This not only made me very happy, but also gave me the motivation to go on with the book project that we had now agreed upon. Last but not least, while preparing this book, which took more time than I had expected, I also learned several new concepts from Arnold Richards, and I have been able to include these (see below).

The workload of my previous and current obligations—particularly with regard to my input as a co-editor-in-chief of the *International Forum of Psychoanalysis*—was at that point so great that it took me a year to eventually get in contact with Arnold Richards's daughter Tamar and his son-in-law Lawrence Schwartz and talk with them, as I did in January 2017, about how to concretely achieve the publication of my book. Only then did I discover that what they needed from me was not the existing PDF version of the nine articles already published in the *International Forum of Psychoanalysis*, which make up nine of the twelve chapters of the book, but the Word versions. It was only in March 2017 that I was lucky enough to find on my computer my own final Word version of eleven of these twelve chapters, including those in publications other than the *International Forum of Psychoanalysis*—the latter appear in this book as Chapters 4 and 9. It then took me from March 2017 to January 2018 to transform these versions into new final

Word versions, by adding to them the corrections and integrations that had later been made—in the case of the papers from the *International Forum of Psychoanalysis*, by the journal's language editor. Furthermore, I not only homogenized all the references contained in the eleven chapters I had prepared, but also contacted Routledge for permission to publish ten of the twelve chapters. Besides the nine articles already published in the *International Forum of Psychoanalysis*, my work included the contributions that appear as Chapters 4 and 9—the paper in which I presented my book on Harry Stack Sullivan (1892–1949) at the William Alanson White Institute in January 2011, which had been edited at the time by Judit Filc, and the book chapter on the field concept published in *Advances in contemporary field theory. Concept and future developments*, edited in the fall of 2016 by Montana Katz, Roosevelt Cassorla, and Giuseppe Civitarese, whose linguistic refinement had been taken care of by Routledge.

By doing all this work, I was able not only to get my English into very good shape once more, but eventually also to become deeply enough involved in this book project to decide to write its Afterword. I wrote this—directly in English, as I am doing now—between the middle of August and the beginning of November 2017, with the aim of helping the reader better understand, for example, what lies behind the unusual variety of topics I cover in the book itself, the background to the person I have become, and my professional and scientific development. It was not until January 2018 that I started working on Chapter 6, "Stephen A. Mitchell (1946–2000) in Italy"—the only chapter that I wrote specifically for the book. Fortunately, I had the chance to discuss this with Arnold Richards in New York in February 2018, at the yearly conference of the American Psychoanalytic Association (APsaA). He liked it and encouraged me to eventually work at the five Introductions accompanying the chapters, and thus complete my work. So this is what I then aimed for— also taking into account that Stefano Bolognini was in parallel writing the Preface for me. Being in New York to attend the conference was as always an excellent source of inspiration too. There, for example, I conceived the ideas that I am about to formulate concerning the contents and meaning of this book, that is, the messages I would like to convey to the reader through it.

One of the panels I attended at the American conference was on psychoanalytic education and research, at which Otto Kernberg presented the main paper. This allowed him first to mention the anthology of his classical contributions on the topic that had recently come out, with the title *Psychoanalytic education at the crossroads. Reformation, change and the future of psychoanalysis* (Kernberg, 2016). It also gave him chance to repeat his opinion that if the lack of dialogue among competing analytic schools and traditions has recently been replaced by a new reciprocal tolerance, such a tolerance has not grown out of better reciprocal knowledge, but simply from a new political climate, a climate in which colleagues avoid really confronting each other in terms of their theoretical backgrounds. Now, in my experience, such a lack of a real dialogue is the consequence of a lack of knowledge not only of the history of psychoanalysis, but also, more specifically, of the ways in which the main theories we use have been developed by their authors, with particular regard to the relationship between their own lives and characters, and the specific clinical theories they have formulated. In fact, this point of view and the research attitude resulting from it is one of the common denominators of this anthology of papers, centered as it is upon the ways in which the life and personality of Freud, Sullivan, Mitchell, and Bion influenced their clinical priorities, sensibilities, and theories. The same is also true for contemporary authors such as Stefano Bolognini and Horst Kächele, as the reader can see in the interviews I conducted with them, around which Part Four of this book centers. In other words, we not only need to give much more room to the history of psychoanalysis in the training of our candidates, in our ways of looking at our work and of talking about it with our colleagues, but we even need to find a new way of writing about it.

This is what I had already started trying to do in the early 1990s, as the reader can see in the first three chapters of Part One, dedicated to the young Freud's early personal and professional development, with all three contributions entirely based on his letters—to Emil Fluss, Eduard Silberstein, Martha Bernays, and Wilhelm Fliess. In my experience, the dialogical dimension developed by Freud himself in his letters played a fundamental role in the development of psychoanalysis itself as a dialogical experience and discipline. Also for this reason, they should represent an important ingredient of analytic training, as opposed to being almost totally ignored— nowhere in the world have they, I believe, ever received the attention they deserve! The main reason for reforming analytic training in this direction is of course how, through Freud's letters, we can much better understand both the personal background of his theories and the network of influences behind them. In fact, with the eventual publication of the first volume of letters exchanged by the young Freud and his fiancée Martha Bernays— edited in 2011 by Gerhard Fichtner, Ilse Grubrich-Simitis, and Albrecht Hirschmüller—my hypothesis of the interpersonal dimension of Freud's self-analysis was definitively confirmed. The pivotal role played by Martha in the young Freud's psychological growth was a central topic of the opening paper given by Ilse Grubrich-Simitis at the 2011 IPA Congress held in Mexico City (Grubrich-Simitis, 2012). And this is precisely the topic of Chapter 3, "Freud's self-analysis—An interpersonally grounded process," which I originally published in 1998.

In Chapter 2, "Why did Freud choose medical school?" (1996), I try to formulate Freud's choice of medical school in terms not of the influence exerted upon him by Goethe's essay on Nature, as he claimed in his "Autobiographical study" of 1924, but of his attempt to overcome the self-absorption of a lonely adolescent by joining a community of researchers committed to the ideal of scientific progress. As I write in the Afterword, this was also what I discovered to be my own main motivation for choosing medical school. Through the Afterword, the reader can also learn how I spent so much time translating from German—the language of my grandfathers—into Italian, for the journal *Psicoterapia e Scienze Umane*, a series of papers by Johannes Cremerius (1918–2002), in which he extensively quoted from Freud's letters, ending up reading all the volumes of Freud's letters then available in Italian. This allowed me not only to become the editor of the Italian edition of Freud's letters to Eduard Silberstein (Conci, ed., 1991), but also to win the 1991 Candidates Award of the International Federation of Psychoanalytic Societies (IFPS) with the paper reproduced in this book as Chapter 1, "The young Freud's letters to Eduard Silberstein— Early traces of some psychoanalytic concepts." That paper came out in the very first issue of the *International Forum of Psychoanalysis* (1992), edited by Jan Stensson, whose co-editor-in-chief I have been since the summer of 2007.

Further progress in what I am defining as my attempt to find a new way of writing the history of psychoanalysis came from my meeting and association with Stephen Mitchell, which I deal with in the Afterword and specifically in Chapter 6, "S.A. Mitchell (1946–2000) in Italy." Fond as I already was of Harry Stack Sullivan's (1892–1949) work, four of his seven books having been translated into Italian in the 1960s, meeting Stephen

Mitchell in Florence in April 1988 ended up changing my life in terms of making the decision that I would share with Mitchell my passion for Sullivan's work by writing a book on Sullivan aimed at definitively assuring a good reception of his work both in Italy and internationally. If one of the aims of the 1983 book *Object relations in psychoanalytic theory* by Jay Greenberg and Stephen Mitchell (translated into Italian in 1986) had been to reintroduce Sullivan's work into the mainstream of psychoanalysis, it made sense to pursue a similar aim by writing a book on Sullivan in which his work would be revisited in terms of both his own life and the historical and professional context in which he developed it. Although Sullivan's books had been appreciated in Italy in the 1960s, nobody had ever met him, given his untimely death at age fifty-seven, and nothing was known about the context of his work, thus making a real reception of his work and legacy impossible. After publishing *Sullivan rivisitato – La sua rilevanza per la psichiatria, la psicoterapia e la psicoanalisi* in Italian in 2000, I was able to present the (first) English edition of the book at the New York White Institute in January 2011 through the paper reproduced in this book as Chapter 4, "Sullivan revisited: a close look from afar." The book was positively reviewed in the main analytic journals.

On the basis of what I learned from that experience, I think that we should spend much more time—both as candidates and as analysts—closely studying not only the theories, but also the lives and historical and professional contexts of a series of analytic authors—in a way similar to the one adopted by Thomas Ogden in his study of writers like Kafka and Borges (Ogden, 2016). Only by doing this can we in fact talk about the main authors of analytic literature with the level of competence that is necessary to make possible the kind of dialogue whose absence Otto Kernberg deplored in the above-mentioned paper. Last but not least, since I was able to propose—contrary to not only what IPA analysts, but also many White Institute analysts and Sullivan himself thought—that Sullivan's belongs not only to the psychiatric, but also the analytic literature, I think that my work might have contributed to justifying the decision of the American and the International Psychoanalytic Associations to accept the White Institute as a member society in 2015. Sullivan certainly was a pioneer of, for example, the analytic treatment of psychotic patients, those whom Freud had categorized as *übertragungsunfähig*—"incapable of transference"—and who instead represented Sullivan's "favorite patients," as documented in his anthology *Schizophrenia as a human process* (1962). I deal with Sullivan's specific contribution to psychoanalysis, including what he called his "interpersonal theory of psychiatry," in Chapter 5, "Sullivan and the intersubjective tradition."

If what had drawn me to Sullivan from the very beginning was his way of talking about his patients, and the work he did with them, which I found highly inspiring and helpful for my own clinical work, one of my main motivations for working on his legacy was—as I have repeatedly written, and not only in the Afterword here—the possibility of keeping in touch with the life-saving and creative experience that I had had in a suburb of New York City as a high- school exchange student in 1972–1973. As an aside, Gaetano Benedetti (1920–2013), the pioneer of the Italian reception of Sullivan's work and one of my supervisors in Milan (see the Afterword), had also felt drawn to Sullivan because of his unusual clinical competence (Benedetti, 1961). Putting these two dimensions together—language on the one hand, and self-experience on the other—brings to mind the following words formulated by Thomas Ogden to Luca Di Donna: "My interest in language and my interest in psychoanalysis have developed as inextricable parts of a whole" (Ogden, 2016, p. 170). So here is my own way of formulating what such an "inextricable" combination means to me. First, immersed as I was in the American language and culture, I was able to find a new and more positive relationship with myself, thus coming to connect a new and different self with the new language I spoke. Second, if this was true, not only was change possible, but psychoanalysis itself as a source of personal change could also be taken seriously.

If this was the background of my choice of psychoanalysis as a therapy for myself and later as a profession, here are the ways in which I articulate the relationship between language and psychoanalysis today, as a psychoanalyst. If we need a variety of languages to cover the extreme variety of human experiences, we also need a variety of authors and theories to cover, that is, to illuminate the variety of psychopathological experiences of our patients. Going back to Sullivan, I could say that he was able to work well with schizophrenic patients because he had himself gone through and overcome a dissociative crisis (Conci, 2012). In fact, he was also one of the first psychoanalysts to state (as early as 1934; see Sullivan, 1962) that each one of us should understand, given our personality, what types of patients we would work best with—and which patients we would better avoid. From this point of view, our work consists in speaking the language of the patients, in order to put them in contact with those parts of themselves that they are not aware of, or not in contact with. From this point of view, it is clear not only how we ourselves have to be able to understand and speak many languages, but how our capacity to identify with patients is as important as our capacity to interpret the transference. This is what makes of our treatment what Ogden defines as "the experience of talking *with* another person," as opposed to "an experience of talking *to* another person" (Ogden, 2016, p. 175, original emphasis). This is why I believe that the more authors and theories we expose ourselves to and bear in mind, the better we can talk with and help our patients—of course, under the condition that in talking with them we maintain our own unique voice, or the specific voice that we find with each one of them.

It is exactly around this belief that the first chapter, "Freud's 'objects'. Plurality and complexity in the internal world and in the analyst's working self," of Stefano Bolognini's 2009 book *Secret passages. The theory and technique of interpsychic relations* centers: in this he even speaks of the growing international recognition of the "dignity and consultability of the various psychoanalyses" (Bolognini, 2009, p. 22). On the other hand, basing herself on the work of the writer Georges-Arthur Goldschmidt (2006), who showed how the German language was a particularly favorable linguistic ground for the creation of psychoanalysis, the German colleague Anna Ursula Dreher (2016) also formulated the opinion that the variety of languages of contemporary psychoanalysis represents a crucial instrument at our disposal for dealing with the complexity of the psychic life and psychopathological problems of our patients (and ourselves), thus pleading "for giving the potentials *inside Babel* a chance before looking for solutions *beyond Babel*" (Dreher, 2016, p. 310, original emphasis). The pioneer in studying of the relationship between Freud's multilingual background and the creation of psychoanalysis was Didier Anzieu (1923–1999), who in his paper "The place of Germanic language and culture in Freud's discovery of psychoanalysis between 1895 and 1900" wrote:

> Freud was not a man of a single culture but of the interlocking of cultures. This explains why he was able to think in terms of the interlocking aspects of the working of the psyche . . . Even today, it is not possible to become a psychoanalyst without the ability to surpass (while retaining) one's culture of origin and to combine different cultural references. (Anzieu, 1986, p. 222)

Of course, what both Bolognini and Dreher fail to mention is the necessity of introducing into the pluralistic dimension the great value they set on the kind of history of psychoanalysis that I am trying to convey through this book. This is what I tried to do as editor, together with my Munich colleague Wolfgang Mertens, of the German anthology *Psychoanalyse im 20. Jahrhundert. Freuds Nachfolger und ihr Beitrag zur modernen Psychoanalyse* (Conci and Mertens, eds., 2016), aimed at introducing analytic candidates to the major post-Freudian authors. Wolfgang Mertens and I asked the contributors of the single chapters (on Anna Freud, Ferenczi, Klein, Winnnicott, Bion, Bowlby, Lacan, Laplanche, Sullivan, Kohut, Racker, and Alexander Mitscherlich) to first deal with the life and context of the individual authors, and only in the third part of each chapter to cover the theoretical and clinical concepts we owe to them.

It is no wonder that, given such a personal orientation, I felt fascinated by both Jay Greenberg and Stephen Mitchell's 1983 *Object relations in psychoanalytic theory* and Mitchell's 1988 foundation of relational psychoanalysis through his book *Relational concepts in psychoanalysis. An integration*. Both were written in the same analytic climate and tried to deal with the same problems that Robert Wallerstein dealt with in the classical paper "One psychoanalysis or many?" (Wallerstein, 1988), which he presented at the IPA Montreal Congress of 1987. In fact, "multiplicity of voices" is a key concept in Mitchell's relational psychoanalysis, both in terms of the multiplicity of voices (basically Sullivan, Bowlby, Kohut, and Winnicott) that he tried to integrate into his new relational perspective (Mitchell, 1988), and in terms of the multiplicity of voices that he referred to in his attempt to define his clinical work with his patients—as he did in his 1997 *Influence and autonomy in psychoanalysis*. Both books were very good attempts at further developing what at the time was called "comparative psychoanalysis" (see Schafer, 1983; Pine, 1990); they not only allowed Mitchell to formulate a whole series of justified critiques and challenges to Freudian psychoanalysis, but also led him to realize what I perceive as being the "Sullivanian project" of creating a separate "post-Freudian psychoanalysis," that is, the brand of psychoanalysis called "relational psychoanalysis," with its own organization, the International Association of Relational Psychoanalysis and Psychotherapy (IARPP)—of which I am a member.

But my attempt to reconsider Mitchell's legacy represents only the final topic of the chapter, under the title

"Stephen A. Mitchell (1946–2000) in Italy," that I dedicate to him. The first part centers around what I learned from him as a person and as a colleague, and around my own role in the early reception of his work in Italy—the two basic aspects of the letters I received from him between 1988 and 1998—which allows the reader to catch both his style and his ongoing presence. Those readers who have the patience to read the chapter in its entirety will see how complex the problem of his legacy is.

The simplest way to formulate my position is as follows: although I admire and have learned much from both Sullivan's and Mitchell's attempts to go beyond Freud, I cannot conceive a psychoanalysis without Freud. From this point of view, I well agree with Steven Ellman—whose book *When theories touch. A historical and theoretical integration of psychoanalytic thought* I picked up from my library only after having finished writing Chapter 6—inasmuch as he talks of Mitchell as "one overriding influence for the present volume (excluding Freud)" (Ellman, 2010, p. 654). From this point of view, "psychoanalysis as a dialogue" of course starts with Freud—as I have already written—and not with Mitchell, no matter what innovative function was played by his journal *Psychoanalytic Dialogues*. Of course, as I also hypothesize in Chapter 6, my own Freud is not the "North American Freud" or "the APsaA Freud," whom Mitchell was so critical of, but "the Italian Freud" who had nothing against lay analysis, and who—if we take Edoardo Weiss (1889–1970) as "Freud's ambassador to Italy"—was even open and receptive to the Jungian point of view (as we have recently learned from Rita Corsa, 2017). But by adopting such a perspective, we enter another field, the "new field" of "international psychoanalysis," a field that I specifically deal with in Part Four, and which is also still almost totally neglected in analytic training and discourse.

On the other hand, I find it deplorable that in the recent panel "The analyst's use of multiple models in clinical work" published in the October 2017 issue of the *Journal of the American Psychoanalytic Association*, none of the four authors dealing with the subject (Richard Zimmer, Lucy LaFarge, Rachel Blass, and Steven Cooper) ever mentions Stephen Mitchell, whom I consider a pioneer of such a topic. This makes me think that his battle against parochialism in our field is still a valuable battle. On the other hand, and also in connection with the final title of this book, *Freud, Sullivan, Mitchell, Bion, and the multiple voices of international psychoanalysis*, I believe it makes sense to mention the interesting concept of "the analyst's personal core theory of analysis" presented by Lucy LaFarge, which I agree with, inasmuch as I see it as connecting the multiplicity of theories we have at our disposal with our own personal analytic sensibility, priorities, and ways of working. Here are LaFarge's words:

> As I have shown, the theories that reside in the background of the analyst's listening need to be of more than one kind in order for the analyst to work effectively: the fluidity and receptiveness of good analytic thinking require the analyst to draw on multiple and changing part-theories in order to capture the meaning of what she hears; at the same time, analytic work requires a more stable, overarching background theory to serve as a guide as the analyst works and reflects afterward on what she has done. Traditionally this more enduring theory has been identified with the formal model or school to which the analyst subscribes. However, the emergence of post-pluralism in our field highlights the personal nature of each analyst's enduring model, a structure I have called the personal core theory. (LaFarge, 2017, p. 841)

I had already come into contact with Bion's work when I was resident in psychiatry, as the introduction to it written by León Grinberg, Dario Sor, and Elisabeth Tabak de Bianchedi (1977, the English edition) was one of the books I was exposed to at the time (between 1982 and 1986; see also the Afterword). However, Ross Lazar (1945–2017) is the colleague to whom I owe the kind of personal exposure to Bion's world, as both a patient and a supervisee, that allowed me to work scientifically on his life, work, and legacy, as I do in Part Three of this book. Also for this reason, in the Afterword I extensively deal with Lazar—a former supervisee of Donald Meltzer (1922–2004) in the context of his training at the Tavistock Clinic—and with my long, and very constructive relationship with him.

Of course, this personal exposure also stimulated me to get in touch with, and gradually get to know and even become good friends with, Italian colleagues such as Antonino Ferro, Franco Borgogno, Claudio Neri, and Giuseppe Civitarese; to them we owe a whole series of fundamental contributions on Wilfred Bion and his legacy, as well as their active role in organizing its promotion. In fact, all the three chapters comprising Part Three were written for and presented at international meetings in which I participated with them, thus getting to know them better. I presented Chapter 7, "Bion and his first analyst, John Rickman (1891–1951): A revisitation of their relationship in the light of Rickman's personality and scientific production and of Bion's letters to him

(1939–1951)," at the international conference on Bion organized in Boston in July 2009 by Howard Levine and Lawrence Brown. At the previous conference, held in Rome in January 2008, I had presented the paper that appears in this book as Chapter 8, "Bion and Sullivan: An enlightening comparison." Chapter 9, "Analytic field theory—A dialogical approach, a pluralistic perspective, and the attempt at a new definition," represents the chapter I published in the above-mentioned book on the field concept edited by Montana Katz, Roosevelt Cassorla, and Giuseppe Civitarese, which Martin Silverman (himself a contributor to the 2015 panel held in Cambridge and to the book itself) reviewed very positively in a 2017 issue of *Psychoanalytic Quarterly*.

Of course, I will deal at length with all these aspects of my work on Bion in the specific Introduction to Part Three; however, it makes sense to state at this point that the common denominators with Part One and Two are represented not only by the presentation of a collection of letters and their analysis as a way of better understanding Bion's personality and work, but also by the approach to Bion that emerges from the following very eloquent words of Lee Rather, which I discovered while writing this Introduction:

> Bion emphasized that psychoanalytic theories are better recognized as useful models rather than as scientific truths. I say to students that the implications of this viewpoint argue against becoming an orthodox follower of any analytic tradition, and that anyone taking Bion's work seriously would want to consider all psychoanalytic theories as potentially useful models and favor selective integration over orthodoxy. (Rather, 2015, p. 53)

But let me now come to Part Four, and to what I would call the new field of "international psychoanalysis"—this being the title and the topic of this part of the book. The systematic study of Freud's letters, the study of the history of psychoanalysis in terms of the biography of its protagonists, and the serious promotion of a pluralistic point of view are not a regular part of analytic training, and the same is true for what I am calling "international psychoanalysis." I was originally introduced to this relatively new field of studies by the North American sociologist Edith Kurzweil (1924–2016), a Viennese-born scholar whose multilingual competence and interest in psychoanalysis made of her a "participant observer" (to use Sullivan's words) of a variety of analytic communities—not only New York, but also London and Paris, Frankfurt, and Vienna. Around their particular histories and nature she constructed her 1989 book *The*

Freudians. A comparative perspective, which I reviewed in *Psicoterapia e Scienze Umane*, after meeting her in London in July 1990. Here are the opening words of her book:

> Every country creates the psychoanalysis it needs, although it does so unconsciously. For national traditions, interests, beliefs, and institutions influence both the general public and its avant-garde, by conditioning a kind of collective unconscious. . . . This book deals with the roots of these local and national assumptions and with their impact on psychoanalysis itself. (Kurzweil, 1989, p. 1)

My own history is of being an Italian psychoanalyst working mainly in Germany (Munich), but also in Italy (Trento), having worked on the editorial board of the *International Forum of Psychoanalysis* since 1994, and having attended all the meetings of the IFPS since 1989, and those of the American and the International Psychoanalytic Associations since 2007 (see the Afterword for a detailed report). From this, I have learned and can deal with what the bacteriologist and epistemologist Ludwik Fleck (1896–1961) called the "thought style" *(Denkstil)* and the "thought collective" *(Denkkollektiv)* of every analytic community I work in, or work with. And I do this it in a similar way to how I work with my patients, that is, by first trying to learn and speak their languages, before trying to make them familiar with mine, that is, with the language of psychoanalysis that I know and try to speak. But, at variance with the work I do with my patients, I have found up to now only a limited number of colleagues so familiar with the field of "international psychoanalysis" that I could talk about it with them. Certainly, both Stefano Bolognini and Horst Kächele belong to this group, and "international psychoanalysis" is one of the main topics, or "contexts of discourse," of the interviews I conducted with them (in 2005 and in 2013, respectively, the latter together with Ingrid Erhardt), which appear in this book as Chapters 11 and 12. Stefano Bolognini and Horst Kächele talk about Italian and German psychoanalysis, respectively, but as a phenomenon belonging to a much wider scientific and professional context that they have personally experienced and are constantly in contact with. Stefano Bolognini has been the president of the Italian Psychoanalytic Society (2009–2013) and the IPA (2013–2017), while Horst Kächele—together with Helmut Thomä (1921–2013)—is the author of the most translated, and empirically based, handbook of psychoanalysis in three volumes, whose first volume came out in German in 1985 (Thomä and Kächele, 1985–2006).

To this group fortunately also belongs my publisher, Arnold Richards, to whom I am very grateful for having introduced me to the very important and illuminating work of Ludwik Fleck (see Richards, 2017). According to Fleck (whose 1935 book was published in English in 1970 as *Genesis and development of a scientific fact*), we watch things with our eyes, but we see them according to the "thought style" of our group. In other words, this is the reason why so many colleagues have, for example, dismissed the work of Sullivan without having read a line of it, by simply following what Fleck calls "the thought style" of their group. In other words, if we behave in this way, ourselves following the "thought style" of our group of reference, how can we help our patients find their own voice, if we ourselves have so many problems finding our own? Fortunately, the group of colleagues familiar with "international psychoanalysis" also includes German analyst Johannes Cremerius and Italian-Swiss analyst Gaetano Benedetti, and this is also the reason why (back in 1986) I followed the advice of the former (see the Afterword) to do my analytic training at the Milan Scuola di Psicoterapia Psicoanalitica (SPP)—the topic I deal with in Chapter 10, "Gaetano Benedetti, Johannes Cremerius, the Milan ASP, and the future of IFPS."

To give another example of what I mean by "international psychoanalysis," the duration of our analytic sessions varies from fifty minutes (Germany) to forty-five minutes (Italy and some parts of North and South America), and even to a variable duration (France), but only those colleagues familiar with what I call "international psychoanalysis" know about this phenomenon, and about the specific cultural and social reasons behind it. From this point of view, "international psychoanalysis" is for me the subdiscipline created around this kind of data by the community of colleagues who are aware of them. Up to some years ago, analytic meetings centered around the theories and models shared by colleagues from different countries who did not really speak about themselves and what they actually did with their patients. The two interviews in Chapters 11 and 12 are also meant to set the stage for the more personal and concrete exchange between colleagues of different cultures aimed at creating the "international psychoanalysis" we need.

Last but not least, as the historian of medicine Erwin Ackerknecht (1906–1988) suggested in his *Short history of psychiatry* (1959), psychoanalysis itself emerged as— or was made possible by—the form of "international synthesis" that Freud was able to make out of the Viennese neurological tradition (Meynert), the French psychological tradition (Charcot), and the British empirical tradition (Darwin), in the international context of the Hapsburg Empire—to which my native town Trento also belonged until 1918. This international character of psychoanalysis became evident, for example, during World War I, during which the IPA, which had been founded in Nuremberg in 1910, was the only scientific community to maintain its international character (Conci, 2001). If psychoanalysis is to continue as a science and as a profession, as opposed to just a form of psychotherapy—as Freud himself had already stated in 1930, preoccupied as he was with the risk of such a deformation, particularly in North America—such an international character has to be further cultivated and increased. The best way to do this is through small international working groups with concrete projects and a regular exchange of ideas. This is what I myself have been doing as a member of the editorial board of the *International Forum of Psychoanalysis* since 1994—and as member, and then European co-chair, of the International Council of Editors of Psychoanalytic Journals (ICEPJ) since 2007. In my experience, this is a better way of increasing the international character of psychoanalysis than is pursuing the unrealistic goal of agreeing on a uniform number of sessions of training analysis worldwide. This was also the orientation expressed by the IPA Board chaired by Stefano Bolognini and confirmed last July in Buenos Aires.

From my own point of view, I even dare to formulate the fantasy that a truly international institution should allow itself to think of a project like creating an Erasmus exchange program for analytic candidates—following the very positive European experience started in this field in 1987. In other words, this would be a further important ingredient in the creation of the preconditions for that kind of dialogue and exchange whose lack Otto Kernberg deplored in the above-mentioned panel in New York. In my opinion, just as psychiatry can work at its best if taught and practiced as an interdisciplinary field (Conci, 2012), so too can psychoanalysis, in terms of its multilingual essence (Conci, 2009).

Although I began my personal analysis in Trento in September 1983 with Dr. S. Taccani (an Italian psychiatrist who trained in Lausanne as a psychoanalyst in the 1960s, and who also belongs to the above-mentioned group of colleagues familiar with "international psychoanalysis"; see the Afterword for more detail), I became a member of the IPA only in June 2010. This is also why I felt the need to write the very personal Afterword with the title "Why and how I became a psychoanalyst." I wrote this on the one hand to become more aware of what are to be seen as my own personal (conscious, preconscious, and unconscious) reasons for going through such a long odyssey, and, on the other hand, to help the reader better understand how I was able to put together all the chapters of this book. Freud himself had done something similar through his "Autobiographical study" of 1924. This attitude in fact also corresponds to the German concept of *Bildung*, which my publisher sees as the essence of Freud's legacy (Richards, 2017). On the other hand, following Fleck, I could say that we need both a group to work with, and also space to think things through for ourselves.

This is why, in the specific Introductions for the four Parts of the book, I will emphasize—even more than in this General Introduction—my relationship with the colleagues who introduced me to the work of, for example, Freud, Sullivan, Mitchell, and Bion. On the other hand, in writing the Afterword, I was able to become aware of the fact that my priority was never to become a member of, for example, the IPA, but to work with all those colleagues by whom I felt sufficiently inspired and illuminated on my way to finding, or becoming, myself. From this point of view, the common denominator of all this book's chapters is represented by the way in which I systematically try to *interrogare la psicoanalisi*, as I would say in Italian, that is, to question psychoanalysis—*die Psychoanalyse zu hinterfragen*, to put it in German. What can I learn about myself from Freud as an adolescent? What can I learn as a therapist from Sullivan's approach to his patients? What can I learn from Bion in terms of his own approach to psychoanalysis?

If some of these questions run through this book, and are specifically illuminated in the Afterword, I am probably justified in formulating the hypothesis that my own work also belongs—as much as the work of Ferro and Civitarese—to the post-Bionian tradition to which they themselves subscribe. Of course, this is not in terms of the clinical dimension of my work, but in terms of Bion's main priority being similar to the one I have just formulated, that is, to question psychoanalysis, to question it in terms of the various types of knowledge that we can derive from it. From this point of view, at variance with Ferro, I also believe that it is not true that we can call ourselves psychoanalysts only if we are in the presence of a patient (see, for example, Ferro and Nicoli, 2017); in fact, I do believe that what we have personally learned from psychoanalysis as patients is also an important part of it. This is another reason why I wrote the Afterword, that is, to show how psychoanalysis changed my life, and how it became such an integral part of it. From this point of view, I can even formulate the following further proposal for a reform of our training system: that all candidates should be allowed to finish their personal training analysis only once they have written a report on it showing how it has changed them personally as well as their lives. Of course, such a procedure would also enormously enrich our evidence-based archive of the way in which psychoanalysis can change our lives—and the lives of our patients. This, as I realized only once I had finished writing it, was also one of the aims that I was pursuing with the Afterword.

At this point, before closing this General Introduction, let me thank not only Arnold Richards for his trust in my work, but also Stefano Bolognini for his support in this complex enterprise, and Marco Bacciagaluppi, Edith Gould, and Carrie Walker for their editorial work. Furthermore, I am of course very thankful to Sandra Buechler, and Frank Lachmann for their Commentaries to my Afterword. Last but not least, let me thank my wife Doris for her patience and constant support, and also my father Fabio Conci (1920–2003) for having contributed to making my life not only so rich, but also so complicated. Only now, at the age of almost sixty-three, and almost at the end of the process of writing this book, I have the feeling that I have eventually "become myself."

Trento, April 5 2018

REFERENCES

Ackerknecht, E.H. (1959). *A Short History of Psychiatry*. New York: Hafner, 1959. (Original German edition, 1957).

Anzieu, D. (1986). The place of Germanic language and culture in Freud's discovery of psychoanalysis between 1895 and 1900. *International Journal of Psychoanalysis* 67:219–226.

Benedetti, G. (1961). Prefazione all'edizione italiana [Preface to the Italian edition]. In H.S. Sullivan, *La moderna concezione della psichiatria* (pp. vii–xxvii). Milan: Feltrinelli. (Original English edition, 1940).

Bolognini, S. (2009). *Secret Passages. The Theory and Technique of Interpsychic Relations*. London: Routledge. (Original Italian edition, 2008).

Borgogno, F., & Luchetti, A. (2016). General introduction. In F. Borgogno, A. Luchetti, and L. Marino Coe (Eds.), *Reading Italian Psychoanalysis* (pp. 1–6). London: Routledge.

Conci, M. (1990). Review of the book by E. Kurzweil "The Freudians. A comparative perspective", Yale University Press 1989, and of the book by E. Federn "Witnessing psychoanalysis", Karnac Books 1990. *Psicoterapia e Scienze Umane*, 24(4):137–142.

———— (2001). Sigmund Freud, la psicoanalisi e la guerra [Sigmund Freud, psychoanalysis and the war]. In V. Calì, G. Corni, and G. Ferrandi (Eds.), *Gli intellettuali e la Grande Guerra* [The intellectuals and World War I] (pp. 193–207). Bologna: Il Mulino.

———— (2009). A prescription for ideal training. *Contemporary Psychoanalysis* 45:394–405.

———— (2010). *Sullivan Revisited – Life and Work. Harry Stack Sullivan's Relevance for Contemporary Psychiatry, Psychotherapy and Psychoanalysis*. Trento: Tangram. (Original Italian edition, 2000).

———— (2012). *Sullivan Revisited – Life and Work. Harry Stack Sullivan's Relevance for Contemporary Psychiatry, Psychotherapy and Psychoanalysis* (2nd edn). Trento: Tangram. (Original Italian edition, 2000).

Conci, M. (Ed.) (1991). S. Freud, *"Querido amigo . . . ". Lettere della giovinezza ad Eduard Silberstein 1871–1881*. Turin: Bollati Boringhieri. (Original German edition, 1989. English edition, 1991).

Conci, M., & Mertens, W. (Eds.) (2016). *Psychoanalyse im 20. Jahrhundert. Freuds Nachfolger und ihr Beitrag zur modernen Psychoanalyse* [Psychoanalysis in the 20th century. Post-Freudian authors and their contribution to modern psychoanalysis]. Stuttgart: Kohlhammer.

Corsa, R. (2017). *Vanda Shrenger Weiss. La prima psicoanalista in Italia. La psicoanalisi a Roma in epoca fascista* [Vanda Shrenger Weiss. The first Italian psychoanalyst. Psychoanalysis in Rome under Fascism]. Rome: Alpes.

Dreher, A.U. (2016). In Babel. *Forum der Psychoanalyse* 32:299–316.

Ellman, S.J. (2010). *When Theories Touch. A Historical and Theoretical Integration of Psychoanalytic Thought*. London: Karnac.

Ferro, A., & Nicoli, L. (2017). *The New Analyst's Guide to the Galaxy: Questions About Contemporary Psychoanalysis*. London: Routledge.

Fichtner, G., Grubrich-Simitis, I., & Hirschmüller, A. (Eds.) (2011). *S. Freud, M. Bernays, Die Brautbriefe. Band 1. Sei mein, wie ich's mir denke. Juni 1982–Juli 1983* [S. Freud, M. Bernays, The bridal letters. Vol.1. Be mine as I want you. June 1882–July 1883]. Frankfurt: Fischer.

Fleck, L. (1935). *Entstehung und Entwicklung einer wissenschaftlichen Tatsache. Einführung in die Lehre vom Denkstil und Denkkollektiv*. Bâle: Schwabe. (English edition: *Genesis and Development of a Scientific Fact*. Chicago: Chicago University Press, 1970).

Freud, S. (1924). An autobiographical study. *Standard Edition* 20, pp. 3–76.

———— (1930). Introduction to the Special Psychopathology Number of *The Medical Review of reviews. Standard Edition* 21, pp. 254–255.

Goldschmidt, G.-A. (2006). *Freud wartet auf das Wort* [Freud waits for the word]. Zurich: Amman.

Greenberg, J.R., & Mitchell, S.A. (1983). *Object Relations in Psychoanalytic Theory*. Cambridge, MA: Harvard University Press.

Grinberg, L., Sor, D., & Tabak de Bianchedi, E. (1977). *Introduction to the Work of Bion.* Northvale, NJ: Aronson. (Original Spanish edition, 1972).

Grubrich-Simitis, I. (2012). Keime psychoanalytischer Grundkonzepte: Zu den Brautbriefen von Sigmund Freud und Martha Bernays [Seeds of basic analytic concepts: On the bridal letters of Sigmund Freud and Martha Bernays]. *Psyche* 66:385–407.

Holt, R.R. (Ed.) (2017). *The Rapaport–Holt Correspondence 1948–1960.* New York: International Psychoanalytic Books.

Kernberg, O.F. (2016). *Psychoanalytic Education at the Crossroads. Reformation, Change and the Future of Psychoanalytic Training.* London: Routledge.

Kurzweil, E. (1989). *The Freudians. A Comparative Perspective.* New Haven, CT: Yale University Press.

LaFarge, L. (2017). From "either/or" to "and": The analyst's use of multiple models in clinical work. *Journal of the American Psychoanalytic Association* 65:829–844.

Mitchell, S.A. (1988). *Relational Concepts in Psychoanalysis. An Integration.* Cambridge, MA: Harvard University Press.

——— (1997). *Influence and Autonomy in Psychoanalysis.* Hillsdale, NJ: Analytic Press.

Ogden, T.H. (2016). *Reclaiming Unlived Life. Experiences in Psychoanalysis.* London: Routledge.

Pine, F. (1990). *Drive, Ego, Object, and Self. A Synthesis for Clinical Work.* New York: Basic Books.

Rather, L. (2015). Building a "Bion container". In M. Harris Williams (Ed.), *Teaching Bion. Modes and Approaches* (pp. 49–56). London: Karnac.

Richards, A.D. (2017). Sociology and psychoanalysis: The development of scientific knowledge by Jews in the Habsburg Empire – Freud, Brill and Fleck. In A.D. Richards, *Psychoanalysis: Perspectives on Thought Collectives. More Selected Papers by Arnold Richards. Volume 2* (A. Lynch, Ed.; pp. 27–48). New York: International Psychoanalytic Books.

Schafer, R. (1983). *The Analytic Attitude.* New York: Basic Books.

Silverman, M.A. (2017). On the birth and development of psychoanalytic field theory. Part 2. *Psychoanalytic Quarterly* 86:919–932.

Sullivan, H.S. (1934). Psychiatric training as a prerequisite to psychoanalytic practice. In H.S. Sullivan, *Schizophrenia as a Human Process* (H. Swick Perry, Ed.; pp. 309–318). New York: Norton.

——— (1962). *Schizophrenia as a Human Process* (H. Swick Perry, Ed.). New York: Norton.

Thomä, H., & Kächele, H. (1985–2006). *Psychoanalytic Practice.* Vol. 1, *Principles.* Vol. 2, *Clinical Studies.* Vol. 3, *Research.* Berlin: Springer.

Wallerstein, R.S. (1988). One psychoanalysis or many? *International Journal of Psychoanalysis* 69:5–21.

INTRODUCTION TO PART ONE
FREUD

The intellectual background of the three chapters of Part One of this anthology of papers is represented by the following two topics. The first is Freud's letters, that is, Freud in his correspondence in general, and the role this correspondence can play in helping us better understand both his life and his work. The second topic is the specific theme of Freud's letters to Eduard Silberstein, that is, the topic of his specific psychic constitution as an adolescent, and the role it played in his later "discovery" of psychoanalysis. By framing this Introduction in this way, I mean not only to introduce the reader to the three chapters, but also to go beyond them, in the direction of both the preliminary work I had to do at the time I wrote them, and the series of new data that we have now at our disposal on these two topics. In the third and last section of this Introduction, I will direct the reader specifically to each of the three chapters in Part One.

1. SIGMUND FREUD IN HIS
CORRESPONDENCE

Let me start with Freud as a letter writer. As I wrote in the General Introduction, and as the reader can see by taking a look at my Afterword, I owe Johannes Cremerius (1918–2002) my first contact with this chapter of psychoanalysis, that is, in my work as translator of several of Cremerius's papers between 1986 and 1991. In the list I have of all my translations, I have now found indications of having translated seven of his papers from German into Italian, the first being the paper with German title "Spurensicherung. Die 'Psychoanalytische Bewegung' und das Elend der psychoanalytischen Institution," that is, the paper I mention in the Afterword with the Italian title I gave to it: "Alla ricerca di tracce perdute. Il 'Movimento psicoanalitico' e la miseria dell'istituzione psicoanalitica" (Cremerius, 1987). Looking at the Afterword, I can see that I also reported the fact that he had given this paper in Zurich at the end of May 1986.

Cremerius played an important role in both the German and the Italian analytic communities, not only in terms of a series of very good technical papers (Cremerius, 1985), but also with his papers dedicated to a critical appraisal of psychoanalysis as an institution. From this point of view—as I have also written in Chapter 10— he interpreted and proposed psychoanalysis as a legacy of the Enlightenment, and in this regard he was also an important *Gesprächspartner*, that is, an important interlocutor or intellectual partner of Otto Kernberg (Kernberg, personal communication, Bergamo, May 2017). The above-mentioned paper (originally published in the German journal *Psyche* at the end of 1986) is the first of such papers critiquing psychoanalysis as an institution, an institution betraying the spirit of freedom that, according to Cremerius, psychoanalysis originally stood for—and which should always keep guiding it.

Even more famous is the paper by Cremerius on this topic, that is, the topic of how the institution of the training analysis ends up by also becoming a betrayal of psychoanalysis itself, inasmuch as, in itself, it also represents a betrayal of a series of basic analytic principles, starting with the principle of free association. How can our associations really be free in the presence of a training analyst, upon whose evaluation of our mental health depends all our further analytic career? The title of this paper of Cremerius's was "Lehranalyse und Macht," and I also translated this into Italian for *Psicoterapia e Scienze Umane*. Given its originality and highly critical orientation, this paper represents one of the few papers by Cremerius that has been translated into English—it came out in the British journal *Free Associations* in 1990 as "Training analysis and power: The transformation of a method of training and learning into an instrument of power in institutionalized psychoanalysis" (Cremerius, 1989a).

Of course, in this context, I can also add the fact that the relationship I developed with Cremerius not only as a translator, but also as an "analyst in training" at the Milan Institute, the Scuola di Psicoterapia Psicoanalitica (SPP) and as a family friend, influenced my own relationship to the analytic institution and to the specific institution of the training analysis. But I will deal with this topic later in this book, in my Introduction to Part Four. As an aside, for the same issue of *Psicoterapia e Scienze Umane*, I also translated into Italian (Conci, 1989b) the first German review, written by Cremerius himself, of the German edition of Sándor Ferenczi's *Clinical diary* (which came out in1988), which he had published the year before in the journal *Psyche* (Frankfurt). This was my first introduction to the work and legacy of Ferenczi, which was very important for Cremerius, as it keeps being for me.

Going back now to Cremerius's paper on the misery

of the analytic institution, here is the first quotation from a letter of Freud's that I translated, reporting Sigmund Freud's very first formulation of his wish to create an international network of analysts, as he expressed it in his letter to Carl Gustav Jung on January 13, 1910:

> I should like to bring up an idea of mine that has not yet fully ripened: couldn't our supporters affiliate with a larger group working for a practical ideal? An International Fraternity for Ethics and Culture is being organized in pursuit if such ideals. The guiding spirit is a Bern apothecary by the name of Knapp, who has been to see me. Mightn't be a good idea for us to join as a group? (McGuire, ed., 1974, p. 288)

As it turned out, the International Psychoanalytical Association (IPA) was founded only a few weeks later, in the context of the Second International Psychoanalytic Congress held in Nuremberg on March 30th and 31, 1910. But what I want to emphasize by using this quotation, and by the necessity of translating it into Italian, is the sense of receiving a sort of initiation into the "sacred (or secret) books of psychoanalysis"—and who knows how many more secrets they might contain! In other words, this is how I ended up reading the whole volume of *The Freud/Jung letters*, the first ones to have come out in an unabridged form in 1974—edited by William McGuire, the supervising editor of Jung's Collected Works—in a volume that was published at the same time not only in German and English, but also in Italian.

Indeed, the publication of this volume had, back in 1974, been such a major editorial event that I had read about it at the time, and this made me now (in the summer of 1986) even happier because, in connection with my work as a translator, I would eventually be able to devote myself to this fascinating collection of letters. It is still possible, by Googling "Freud/Jung," to find and download the review that Lionel Trilling (1905–1975) wrote about the book in the *New York Times* on April 21, 1974. In addition, while writing this Introduction (on April 4, 2018) and Skyping with Ernst Falzeder (Salzburg, Austria), the main editor of the Freud/Ferenzci letters, we discovered how we were both, as members of that same generation (both born in 1955), fascinated at that time by such correspondence—which Ernst Falzeder also read on his own, as a young university student. One reason for the ongoing fascination of this collection of letters is of course given by the dramatic way in which Freud and Jung's relationship came to an end, that is, in a situation in which the two greatest pioneers of the clinical work on and with the unconscious could no longer understand each other. Apparently, Jung's only possible choice was between remaining a close collaborator of Freud or, let us say, becoming himself! Such a dilemma cost him much pain and work, including a nervous breakdown that lasted some time, but he ended up not only finding his own way, but also later formulating the crucial concepts of "psychological types" and "individuation" (Jung, 1963).

Probably the best-known or most-quoted words from this correspondence are those written by Freud to Jung on June 7, 1910. Here Freud uses for the very first time the word "counter-transference," in response to Jung's having mentioned for the first time the name of Sabina Spielrein (1885–1942) in his letter of three days previously (June 4, 1909). He thus eventually made clear the identity of the difficult patient about whom he had already told Freud, without previously giving her name. Here are Freud's words:

> Such experiences, though painful, are necessary and hard to avoid. Without them we cannot really know life and what we are dealing with. I myself have never been taken in quite so badly, but I have come very close to it a number of times and had a *narrow escape*. I believe that only grim necessities weighing on my work, and the fact that I was ten years older than yourself when I came to psa., have saved me from similar experiences. But no lasting harm is done. They help us to develop the thick skin we need to dominate 'counter-transference', which is after all a permanent problem for us; they teach us to displace our own affects to best advantage. They are a 'blessing in disguise'. (McGuire, ed., 1974, p. 230, original emphasis)

The concept of the countertransference is first mentioned in Freud's published work only nine months later, in the paper "The future prospects of psychoanalytic therapy" that he gave at the above-mentioned Nuremberg Congress in March 1910. In this brief mention there is, however, no trace left of the precise context in which the concept had originally emerged, that is, Freud's supervision—as we can call it today—of Jung's treatment of Sabina Spielrein. Here is how Freud put it at the congress:

> Other innovations in technique relate to the physician himself. We have become aware of the 'counter-transference', which arises in him as a result of the patient's influence on his unconscious feelings, and we are almost inclined to insist that he shall recognize his counter-transference in himself and overcome it. Now that a considerable number of people are practicing psycho-analysis and exchanging their observations with one another, we have noticed that no psycho-analyst goes further than his own complexes and internal resistances permit; and we consequently require that he shall begin his activity with a self-analysis and continually carry it deeper while he is making his observations on his patients. Anyone who fails to produce results in a self-analysis of this kind may

at once give up the idea of being able to treat patients by analysis. (Freud, 1910, pp. 144–145)

Going beyond the fact that I myself am able to learn something much better when I am not just offered a general principle or deduction, but put in touch with the concrete context in which any hypothesis or theory started to emerge, I believe that, also from the point of view of the history of science, it would have been better for Freud to be more transparent about the original context of his discoveries. In fact, reading his letters is the best, or perhaps the only, way to get in touch with this context, which is (almost) systematically omitted from his published work.

Even more eloquent from this point of view is what we can learn about the "discovery" of psychoanalysis from Freud's letters to his best friend and colleague Wilhelm Fliess (1858–1928). The unabridged edition of these letters came out in English in 1985 (the abridged English edition had come out in 1954), with Jeffrey Masson as translator and editor, and this new edition included 133 letters that had been excluded from the 1954 first edition. Only through these letters can we really understand how Freud made himself and his psychological problems the focus of his attention, how he could help his patients only after having learned to help himself, and how he came to write *Die Traumdeutung* (1900), *The interpretation of dreams*, on the basis of the work he did on his own dreams—which represent the very substance of the book. One of the most famous of these letters is that of September 21, 1897, in which Freud gave up the traumatic theory of neuroses in favor of the major role he attributed to people's own fantasies. Much clearer for my purpose, however, are a whole series of letters written by him that same fall. Here, for example, is what he wrote to Fliess on October 3, 1897:

> For the last four days my self-analysis, which I consider indispensable for the clarification of the whole problem, has continued in dreams and has presented me with the most valuable elucidations and clues . . . I can only indicate that . . . in my case the 'prime originator' was an ugly, elderly, but clever woman, who told me a great deal about God Almighty and hell and instilled in me a high opinion of my own capacities; that later (between two and two and a half years) my libido toward *matrem* was awakened, namely on the occasion of a journey with her from Leipzig to Vienna, during which we must have spent the night together and there must have been an opportunity of seeing her *nudam* . . . that I greeted my one-year-younger brother (who died after a few months) with adverse wishes and genuine childhood jealousy; and that his death left the germ of [self-]reproaches in me" (Masson, ed., 1985, p. 268, original emphasis)

And on October 15, 1897, Freud wrote:

Dear Wilhelm,

my self-analysis is in fact the most important thing and promises to become of the greatest value to me if it reaches its end . . . The whole thing is all the more valuable for my purposes, since I have succeeded in finding a few real points of reference for the story. I asked my mother, whether she still remembered the nurse. 'Of course', she said, 'an elderly person, very clever, she was always carrying off to some church . . . During my confinement with Anna (two and a half years younger), it was discovered that she was a thief . . . Your brother Philip himself fetched the policeman; she then was given ten months of prison.' Now look at how this confirms the conclusions of my dream interpretations . . . It is by no means easy. Being totally honest with oneself is a good exercise. A single idea of general value downed on me. I have found, in my own case too, [the phenomenon of] being in love with my mother and jealous of my father, and I now consider it a universal event in early childhood . . . If this is so, we can understand the gripping power of Oedipus Rex . . . the Greek legend seizes upon a compulsion which everyone recognizes because he senses its existence in himself. Everyone in the audience was once a budding Oedipus in fantasy and each recoils in horror from the dream fulfillment here transplanted into reality, with the full quantity of repression which separates his infantile state from his present one. Fleetingly the thought passed through my head that the same thing might be at the bottom of Hamlet as well. (Masson, ed., 1985, pp. 270, 271, 272)

Last but not least, on December 3, 1897, Freud wrote:

My longing for Rome is, by the way, deeply neurotic. It is connected with my high school hero worship of the Semitic Hannibal, and this year in fact I did not reach Rome any more than he did from lake Trasimeno. Since I have been studying the unconscious, I have become so interesting to myself. A pity that one always keeps one's mouth shut about the most intimate things. (Masson, ed., 1985, p. 285)

This is precisely the context of Freud's "discovery" of psychoanalysis, which we do not find in his published work, and which allows us to read his work with new eyes and a much better readiness to also apply it to ourselves. At the same time, such a "discovery" could not have been made without Wilhelm Fliess, whom Didier Anzieu, in his fascinating book on Freud's self-analysis, defines as "the friend, supporter, confidant, sounding-board and amplifier that is vital to any genius embarking, as Freud was, upon a great creative venture" (Anzieu, 1986, p. 114).

A real and very complex relationship covering more than twenty-five years (1908–1933) is the core of the *Correspondence of Sigmund Freud and Sándor Ferenczi*. The same is true of the 1,246 letters contained in the three volumes published in English, by Harvard University Press, between 1992 and 2000, with Ernst Falzeder as

chief editor (and with the collaboration of Eva Brabant
and Patrizia Giampieri-Deutsch), under the supervision
of André Haynal. Published at the same time in German,
French, and Italian, it is probably the most fascinating
of all Freud's correspondence. This correspondence is the
topic of the Discussion Group on "Freud as a letter writer"
that I have been holding together with Henry Zvi Lothane
(2016) and Endre Koritar (2017 and 2018) at the Winter
Meeting of the American Psychoanalytic Association.
I have also organized around it the paper "Freud and
Ferenczi—From psychoanalysis as a 'professional and
personal home' to the creation of a 'psychoanalytic
home' for the patient," which I wrote for the Ferenczi
International Conference that took place in Florence
at the beginning of May, 2018. In this I presented the
point of view that Freud, as Ferenczi's training analyst,
colleague, and friend, played an important role in his later
development of what I call "a psychoanalytic home for
the patient." In fact, as their exchange of letters concretely
documents, Ferenczi found through Freud and through
psychoanalysis his own "professional and personal home."

Here is what Ferenczi wrote to Freud on April 5,
1910, in one of the letters they exchanged after having
successfully carried out the political operation, which they
had conceived together, of founding the IPA, which they
had succeeded in doing in Nuremberg the previous week:

> Your letters always gave me extraordinary satisfaction in
> my intellectual and emotional isolation. This time your letter
> did this to an increased degree; being together for days with
> people of like mind spoiled me – and this evening I caught
> myself singing an Hungarian song with the following text:
> 'On the great ball of earth no one so orphaned as I'. You told
> me once in Berchtesgaden: 'Man must love something'. That
> also could be craft and science. But obviously not exclusively.
> One must also love people if one wants to be happy . . . I have
> to say that Jung is right when he urges me to gather around
> me young men whom I can teach and perhaps also love
> somewhat. (Letter 127; Falzeder, Brabant, and Giampieri-
> Deutsch, 1992–2000, Vol. 1, p. 157)

And here is what Ferenczi wrote to Freud on July 9, 1910,
the day after his thirty-seventh birthday:

> I have already often thanked you for beautifying my
> profession, in fact, my whole life, through the psa. way of
> looking at things. But if I compare my inner psychic existence
> before and after psa. insight, I must regard the most valuable
> thing to be precisely the inner change that you deny. It was
> only through psa. that I became a man from a child. (Letter
> 145; Falzeder et al., 1992–2000, Vol. 1, p. 186)

As we know, this "good attachment" underwent
a first important crisis in Palermo in September 1910,

which Ferenczi, in his letter to Freud of October 3, 1910, attributed to Freud's frustration of his desire "to enjoy the man, not the scholar, in close friendship" and his need for "absolute mutual openness" (see Falzeder et al., 1992–2000, Vol. 1, p. 218). But on April 24, 1911, after a "splendid excursion" of two days to Bozen-Bolzano and Klobenstein am Ritten-Collalbo al Renon, Ferenczi reminded Freud that "I never depart from you without benefit," and this not in terms of "my understanding of mental activity in general, but rather a deepening of insight specifically into my mental life, without which there can be no true knowledge" (Letter 213; Falzeder et al., 1992–2000, Vol. 1, p. 270).

Creating a "psychoanalytic home" for his patients was one of the main themes of Ferenczi's *Clinical diary*, a theme that at the same time runs—not surprisingly— through his whole work. But here is what he wrote on August 13, 1932: "BEING ALONE leads to splitting. The presence of someone with whom one can share and communicate joy and sorrow (love and understanding) can HEAL the trauma. Personality is reassembled 'healed' (like 'glue')" (Ferenczi, 1988, p. 201, original emphasis). As the above-reported quotations document, Ferenczi certainly experienced also with Freud (and not only with, for example, his good friend Georg Groddeck [1866–1934]), the healing power of sharing his experience of loneliness. In other words, we have here a further and very eloquent demonstration of how crucial it is to take the letters written and exchanged by Freud with his main correspondents as what we could analytically call "the primal scene of psychoanalysis," that is, its context of discovery and original elaboration.

But here are the words through which Freud's fourth child Ernst (1892–1970), an architect and the father of the famous artist Lucien Freud (1922–2011), introduced readers of the first general collection of his father's letters to such an important dimension of his father's life as his letter writing:

> As a letter writer, my father was unusually prolific and conscientious. He dealt with his voluminous correspondence unassisted and in longhand. He answered every letter he received, no matter from whom, and as a rule this answer was in the post within twenty-four hours. His evening he devoted to scientific writing, but every spare minute between analysis was dedicated to his correspondence. In the course of his long life strict observance of this routine resulted in the composition of many thousands of letters. (E.L. Freud, 1960, p. vii)

To bring readers into closer contact with Freud's life,

that is, with Freud as a person, before his becoming a medical doctor and a psychoanalyst, the first letter of this important collection is the young Freud's *Maturabrief*, written to his Freiberg friend Emil Fluss (1856–1927) on June 16, 1873, after completing his final high school examinations. In this we can, for example, read the following very interesting self-portrait:

> Finally, my German paper was stamped with an exc. [excellent]. It was a most ethical subject on "Considerations involved in the Choice of a Profession," and I repeated more or less what I wrote to you a couple of weeks ago, although you failed to confirm it with an exc. Incidentally, my professor told me—and he is the first person who has dared to tell me this—that I possess what Herder so nicely calls an *idiotic* style—i.e., a style at once correct and characteristic. (E.L. Freud, ed., 1960, p. 4; original emphasis)

Whenever I told my university students (particularly the ones I taught in Trento, between 2002 and 2011) about this letter, I reminded them of how psychoanalysis itself can be classified as "an idiotic discipline," that is, a discipline "at once correct and characteristic." By this, I of course mean a discipline that specifically tries to integrate the subjective and objective dimensions of human experience. By doing this, I also tried to introduce my students to one of the leading concepts of my approach to Freud as a person, and to his work, that is, what we can call the "iso-morphism" existing between them, an iso-morphism also including the so-called pre-analytic phase of his life. Last but not least, I was able to publish an Italian translation of the young Freud's letters to Emil Fluss in the article I wrote about them for the journal of the Italian Psychoanalytic Society (SPI) (Conci, 2016). Originally published in English in 1969 (see E.L. Freud, ed., 1969), these play a central role in Chapter 2.

After the first publication of the Freud/Fliess letters in 1954 and the above-mentioned anthology of Freud's letters in 1960, the third collection to come out was represented by *Psychoanalysis and faith: The letters of Sigmund Freud and Oskar Pfister*, edited in 1963 by Heinrich Meng (1887–1972) and Ernst Freud. As an aside, Gaetano Benedetti, whose life and work we will specifically deal with in Part Four, left Zurich in 1956 in order to become Meng's successor at the University of Basel, where he spent the rest of his life. But here is the way in which Meng presented the exchange between Freud and Oskar Pfister (1873–1956), again confirming the concept of Freud's letters as a crucial "context of discovery and original elaboration" of psychoanalysis:

> A number of Pfister's works were stimulated by conversation

and correspondence with Freud, and similarly Freud took suggestions from Pfister for his own work. There is, for instance, no doubt that he accepted the most varied suggestions for the technique of child analysis from Pfister's very concrete communications concerning the psycho-analysis of children and young persons at the stage of puberty. (Meng, 1963, pp. 9–10)

This is not to forget the well-known fact that Pfister reacted to Freud's 1927 "The future of an illusion" with his article "The illusion of a future: A friendly disagreement with Prof. Sigmund Freud" (Pfister, 1927); this—according to Meng—"illustrates the personal courage, critical ability, practical skill, as well as respect for Freud's greatness, with which his theologically and psychoanalytically trained colleague opposed his master" (Meng, 1963, p. 9).

In 1965, Karl Abraham's daughter Hilda Abraham (1906–1971) and Ernst Freud edited a first abridged version of the letters between Karl Abraham (1877–1925) and Freud, in which only about two-thirds of the letters were published. We had to wait until 2002 for Ernst Falzeder's edition *The complete correspondence of Sigmund Freud and Karl Abraham 1907–1925*, accompanied by an Introduction written by André Haynal and Falzeder himself. Neither edition has ever been translated into and published in Italian, thus further limiting the impact and importance of the field of the history of psychoanalysis in my country; for example, of the four volumes of the *Minutes of the Vienna Psychoanalytic Society* (edited between 1962 and 1975 by Hermann Nunberg [1884–1970] and Ernst Federn [1914–2007]), only the first volume was ever published in Italian. But before coming back to the 2002 volume of Freud and Abraham, let us go on with the brief synthesis I am making of the historical sequence of publication of the major Freud correspondence.

The next correspondence to come out was *Sigmund Freud and Lou Andreas-Salomé: Letters* (1966), edited by Ernest Pfeiffer (1893–1986), a Göttingen professor who was so close to Lou Andreas-Salomé (1861–1937), the exceptionally gifted pioneer of psychoanalysis, as to not only become her literary executor, but also spend the rest of his life promoting the publication of her work. The Italian edition of this correspondence, which was published in 1983, was accompanied by an Introduction by Mazzino Montinari (1928–1986), the philosophy professor who, together with his teacher Giorgio Colli (1917–1979), collected the works and letters of Friedrich Nietzsche into a first critical edition that became a scholarly standard. In fact, this edition of both works

and letters represented an important model of reference
for a(n) (im)possible future edition of Freud's Complete
works that the Italian historian of psychoanalysis Michele
Ranchetti (1925–2008) often talked about with me when
I visited him in Florence—in his house beyond Piazzale
Michelangelo. In his Introduction, Montinari emphasized
Lou Andreas-Salomé's at the same time deep and
autonomous relationship to Freud (Montinari, 1983, p.
xiii).

The year 1970 saw the publication of not only the
letters exchanged between Freud and Georg Groddeck,
whose German edition was edited by Margaretha
Honegger, but also the only edition of Freud's letters
relevant to the history of psychoanalysis in Italy, that is,
Edoardo Weiss's (1889–1970) volume *Sigmund Freud
as a consultant*. A native of Trieste, at the time the only
harbor of the Hapsburg Empire, and the son of a Jewish
industrialist, Weiss went to Vienna in the fall of 1908
to study medicine, in order to become a psychoanalyst.
This allowed him not only to attend Freud's university
lectures, as he was a medical student, but also to undergo,
upon Freud's personal advice, a training analysis with
Paul Federn (1871–1950). Through this Weiss became a
member of the Vienna Psychoanalytic Society in 1913, a
year before graduating from medical school.

During World War I, in which he served as a medical
officer in the Hapsburg army, he married his fellow student
Vanda Shrenger (1892–1968), an analytically oriented
pediatrician, who later became a Jungian analyst, and
they had two sons (Emilio [b. 1918] and Guido [b. 1928]).
At the end of the war, Weiss went back to Trieste, where
he worked until 1927 at the local psychiatric hospital,
being forced to give up his position after refusing to join
the Fascist Party, and thus continuing to work only as a
psychoanalyst in private practice. In the meantime, he
tried to promote psychoanalysis at national psychological
and psychiatric congresses (for example, Florence, 1923,
and Trieste, 1925), and he was able to help and assist
creative personalities such as the novelist Italo Svevo
(1861–1928) and the poet Umberto Saba (1883–1957).
In Trieste he had also the chance to give the first public
series of introductory lectures on psychoanalysis and to
publish them in 1931 in book form, with the title *Elementi
di psicoanalisi*.

The exchange of letters with Freud clearly documents
how Weiss could consult him on any therapeutic problems
he was having with his patients, as well as how Freud

played an important role in terms of psychological support and professional advice, as Weiss was the only Freudian psychoanalyst practicing in Italy at the time. This enabled Weiss not only to survive in Trieste, but also to move to Rome, which he did in the fall of 1931. Here he was eventually able to give the necessary clinical and didactic substance to the SPI, which had been formally founded in Teramo in 1925, on the initiative of the psychiatrist Marco Levi Bianchini (1875–1961), with Weiss as its only practicing analyst. In Rome Weiss was eventually able to train the two colleagues who would be among the main protagonists of Italian psychoanalysis after World War II, the medical doctor Nicola Perrotti (1897–1970) and the lawyer Emilio Servadio (1904–1995), and to create around himself and his wife Vanda a small analytic group. This is how the Italian Society was in 1935 eventually recognized as a branch society of the IPA.

In 1932 Weiss had also been able to found the *Rivista di Psicoanalisi*, which was then banned by the Fascist Regime in 1934. The journal was re-founded in 1955 by Cesare Musatti (1897–1979), a psychology professor and former university collaborator of the psychologist and pioneer of psychoanalysis Vittorio Benussi (1878–1927), who in his turn had played a fundamental role in the promotion of psychoanalysis in Italy after World War II. Because of the so-called *leggi razziali*, the anti-Jewish laws of 1938, Edoardo Weiss then had to leave Italy; he moved with his family first to Topeka (Kansas), to the Menninger Clinic, and then to Chicago, where he lived and worked until his death in 1970. After having edited Paul Federn's papers on psychoses, *Ego psychology and the psychoses*, in 1952, Weiss published *The structure and dynamics of the human mind* (1960) and *Agoraphobia in the light of ego psychology* (1964).

I greatly value Edoardo Weiss, not only for his having been the first Italian psychoanalyst, and the only one trained in Vienna and familiar with Freud, but also because I share with him what I experience as our common Hapsburg background. In addition I feel particularly attached to him because of the following lucky circumstance. As I report in detail in the Afterword (which I finished writing in the fall of 2017), it was in the context of the conference organized in Trieste by Anna Maria Accerboni (1939–2006) in December 1989 for the hundredth anniversary of Weiss's birth that my career as a historian of psychoanalysis officially started.

Anna Maria Accerboni, a historian of psychoanalysis

whom I had met through Johannes Cremerius, invited me to replace the well-known Viennese psychoanalyst Harald Leupold-Loewenthal (1926–2007), who had suddenly been taken ill. I was already familiar with the young Freud's letters to his friend Eduard Silberstein (1856–1825), which Leupold-Loewenthal was supposed to be introducing his Italian colleagues to with his paper. These letters had just come out in a volume edited by Walter Boehlich (1921–2006)—which I had had the chance to buy in Vienna at the beginning of November; they covered the years 1871–1881 and contained three very interesting letters that Freud had written to Silberstein from Trieste, and whose translation into Italian represented the heart of my paper (see Conci, 1990). This is how I was invited by the Turin publisher Bollati Boringhieri to become the editor of the Italian edition of this collection of letters, which came out in book form in April 1991 (see Conci, ed., 1991), and this work was so stimulating that I was able to extract from it the paper which won the International Federation of Psychoanalytic Societies (IFPS) Candidates Award in Stockholm in August 1991. That paper is published in this anthology as Chapter 1, "The young Freud's letters to Eduard Silberstein—Early traces of some psychoanalytic concepts," which also came out in the very first issue of the *International Forum of Psychoanalysis*, published in the summer of 1992.

Of course, the Trieste conference and the possibility of working as the editor of a collection of Freud's letters also gave me the chance to become a member of the community of historians working on the history of psychoanalysis. By this, I also realized some kind of an adolescent dream—of doing research within a well-respected community of scholars from whom I could learn and further develop myself from a scientific and professional point of view. Since I talk about this in more detail in the Afterword, I will limit myself here to Anna Maria Accerboni and Paul Roazen (1936–2005), both of whom taught me so much about Edoardo Weiss. When Anna Maria died from cancer in 2006, she had not been able to publish the biography of Edoardo Weiss that she had been working on for so many years, and had also been preparing through the publication of a series of articles such as the 1998 article "Vittorio Benussi e Edoardo Weiss a confronto sull'inconscio." My last memory of her is captured by the picture of her I took in June 2004 in front of Weiss's office in Trieste, together with Weiss's son Guido, on the occasion of the erection of a marble plaque in Weiss's memory during the national congress of the Italian Psychoanalytic Society. Fortunately, Anna Maria Accerboni's work has been continued by a former collaborator of hers, the psychoanalyst Rita Corsa, who has recently published two important books (2013, 2017) on Weiss and on his wife Vanda Shrenger Weiss, "the first Italian woman psychoanalyst."

It was even more exciting to talk about Weiss with Paul Roazen, whom I met for the first time in London in July 1990, at the conference on the history of psychoanalysis organized by Alain de Mijolla and his International Association for the History of Psychoanalysis (IAHP), which I write about in the Afterword. A political scientist who graduated from Harvard University, Paul Roazen had become interested in psychoanalysis through the grande dame of psychoanalysis Helene Deutsch (1884–1982), whose biography he wrote in 1985. Roazen's book *Freud and his followers* (1975), based on hours of interviews with Freud's surviving friends, relatives, and colleagues, was a path-breaking influential work that remains a basic reference for historians of psychoanalysis even today. As Paul Roazen personally told me, Edoardo Weiss was the source of some of his best interviews, and from him he received not only the definitive confirmation that it had been Freud who had analyzed his daughter Anna, but also much of the information that allowed him to write one of his most popular books, *Brother animal: The story of Freud and Tausk* (1969)—Viktor Tausk (1879–1919) having been a fellow medical student and a good friend of Weiss. In fact, Roazen ended up dedicating to Weiss his very last book, which came out only a few months before his sudden death in November 2005; I reviewed this book, *Edoardo Weiss: The house that Freud built*, in the *International Forum of Psychoanalysis* (Conci, 2006). In the same review, I also tried to celebrate Roazen's legacy as a historian of psychoanalysis, that is, the first academically trained historian to have devoted his life to our field, making a large contribution in terms of elevating its academic and scientific standards. In fact, this had also been the way in which I had dealt with Roazen's work in my 1996 review of his ground-breaking (1995) book *How Freud worked. First-hand accounts of patients.*

Of course, since all these relationships developed for me only gradually over the years, I remember the work I did as editor of Freud's letters to Silberstein as a rather solitary task. The only author I knew who had tried to give a systematic and very competent overall view of the area of Freud's work represented by his letters was Martin Grotjahn (1904–1990), a psychiatrist who had trained in

Berlin as a psychoanalyst before migrating to the USA
with his Jewish wife Etelka in 1937. Together they also
translated into English the above-mentioned letters
exchanged between Freud and Weiss. I am referring
here to the very long, detailed, and insightful chapter on
"Freuds Briefwechsel," that is, "Freud's correspondence,"
that was published in the volume *Tiefenpsychologie* edited
by Dieter Eicke (1927–2004) in 1976 for the so-called
Psychologie des 20. Jahrhunderts, a very good standard
German work on psychology and psychoanalysis. The 111
pages of this unique contribution include the following
sections: 1—Freud as letter writer; 2—Freud's letters
as an instrument of his self-analysis (Martha Bernays
and Wilhelm Fliess); 3—Freud's correspondence with
the psychoanalytic pioneers (Eugen Bleuler, C.G. Jung,
Ludwig Binswanger, Oskar Pfister, Karl Abraham, Georg
Groddeck, Lou Andreas-Salomé, Theodor Reik, Edoardo
Weiss, James Jackson Putnam); 4—The not yet published
letters to the pioneers of psychoanalysis (Sándor Ferenczi,
Paul Federn, Wilhelm Reich, Otto Rank); 5—The Minutes
of the Vienna Psychoanalytic Society; 6—The Rundbriefe
of the Secret Committee; 7—Freud's correspondence with
artists and scientists (Arthur Schnitzler, Arnold Zweig,
Yvette Guilbert, Romain Rolland, Stefan Zweig, Thomas
Mann, Albert Einstein); 8—Concluding remarks. Not
only is this classification of Freud's correspondence still
valid, but so too is Grotjahn's conclusion: "Only a person
so much rooted in and familiar with his language as
Freud could write such letters" (Grotjahn, 1976, p. 129).
He writes this after having emphasized the great variety
of different tones that we can find in Freud's letters,
depending on the identity of his correspondent.

This was also the impression gained by the second
internationally recognized expert with whom I came in
touch through my work as editor of the Italian edition of
the young Freud's letters to Silberstein, that is, Gerhard
Fichtner (1932–2012), particularly in respect to his
1989 article "Freuds Briefe als historische Quelle." As
I also write in the Afterword, this original contact was
followed by my regular attendance (1997–2007) at the
Symposia on the History of Psychoanalysis that Professor
Fichtner, a historian of medicine, together with his closest
collaborator, Albrecht Hirschmüller, organized once a
year at the University of Tübingen. One of the few persons
capable of reading Freud's handwriting, Gerhard Fichtner
was the world expert on Freud's letters, and a source
of inspiration and support for the whole international
community of analysts and historians working in the field

of Freud studies. Here is how Fichtner completes the picture of Freud's letters formulated by Grotjahn:

> Even the shortest and least important of his letters very well reflects his own language and way of thinking. At the same time, these letters transmit in a very precise way the category to which his correspondent belongs, reflect his nature and adapt themselves to his needs. We can feel this even in the type of correspondence of which only Freud's letters have survived. (Fichtner, 1989, p. 806; my translation)

In his 1989 article, Fichtner speaks of about 8,000 classified letters by and to Freud, and hypothesizes that no less than 20,000 letters must have been written by Freud and probably as many received by him during his lifetime. In his 2007 article "Is there still an unknown Freud? A note on the publications of Freud's texts and on unpublished documents," Ernst Falzeder, based on Fichtner's latest data, gave the following report: "To this date he [Fichtner] has counted 14,147 known letters to and from Freud, of which 'the by far greater number' were written by Freud. When all these letters will have been published, the quantity of Freud's theoretical works will pale in comparison" (Falzeder, 2007, p. 206). Will we ever witness the publication of a new edition of Freud's *Complete works* including all his letters? If Fichtner in 1989 had counted about 400 correspondents of Freud, from whom Freud received and to whom he wrote his letters, we now find "nearly six hundred correspondents" under the heading "General correspondence, 1871–1996" in the description of "Sigmund Freud Papers Collection" at the Library of Congress in Washington DC. This section of the Freud Papers, which has been digitalized and was released online on February 1, 2017, has been described as follows:

> Correspondence including original letters, photocopies, transcripts, translations, and related background material between Sigmund Freud and his friends, professional associates, students, patients, and the public. Arranged alphabetically by name of correspondent and therein chronologically. Unidentified correspondence is filed at the end of the series.
>
> Nearly six hundred correspondents are represented in the series. At times, their correspondence is limited to a single letter to or from Freud. In other cases, the correspondence is extensive, revealing Freud as a prolific correspondent who frequently chastised others for a lack of similar diligence. Included is correspondence with Karl Abraham, Alfred Adler, Franz Alexander, A. A. Brill, M. Eitingon, Sándor Ferenczi, Wilhelm Fliess, Eduard Hitschmann, Ernest Jones, C. G. Jung, Oskar Pfister, Otto Rank, Theodor Reik, Hanns Sachs, Ernst Simmel, Wilhelm Stekel, and Edoardo Weiss, among many others.
>
> Prominent women in the field represented in the series include Lou Andreas-Salomé, Ruth Mack Brunswick, Emma

Eckstein, Jeanne Lampl-de Groot, and Joan Riviere. Notable among Freud's patients with whom he corresponded is Sergius Pankejeff whom Freud referred to as the "Wolf-Man." Other prominent correspondents include Albert Einstein with whom Freud corresponded on the nature of war, Carl Koller who shared Freud's interest in the medical uses of cocaine, and novelist and essayist Thomas Mann. (https://www.loc. gov/collections/sigmund-freud-papers/about-this-collection; April 14, 2018)

Given the importance of this chapter of Freud's work and legacy, I will now briefly go over all the correspondence that came out after the 1989 publication of his letters to Silberstein. This will allow me to give the reader further evidence of the desirability of including this subject in analytic training and analytic discourse, and allow the reader to still better understand the significance of the first three chapters of this anthology—which I originally published in 1992, 1996, and 1998, respectively. Only with the 2011 publication of the first of the planned five volumes of the letters exchanged between the young Freud and his fiancée Martha was the new concept of Freud's self-analysis that I present in Chapter 3 eventually confirmed by an authority in the field, Ilse Grubrich-Simitis (2012). In what follows I rely on both the above-mentioned article by Ernst Falzeder, and the book chapter written on this topic in 2006 by Michael Schröter.

To Gerhard Fichtner we also owe the publication of the letters between Freud and Ludwig Binswanger (1881–1966) that were written between 1908 and 1938, a collection of 190 letters that came out in German in 1992 and in English in 2002 (Fichtner, ed., 2002). The young Binswanger had accompanied C.G. Jung on his first visit to Freud in Vienna in March 1907, a visit he described in his 1956 volume *Erinnerungen an Sigmund Freud* (see Binswanger, 1957). Ludwig Binswanger's grandfather, the psychiatrist Ludwig Binswanger Sr. (1820–1880), had founded the private psychiatric hospital Bellevue in the Swiss town of Kreuzlingen, on Lake Constance. As a young medical doctor, the younger Binswanger spent a year training at the Zurich University Hospital under Eugen Bleuler (1856–1939) and his assistant Jung, who had introduced him to Freud's work. Having become his father Robert Binswanger's successor in 1910, Ludwig Binswanger directed the Bellevue until 1956. He counted many celebrities, for example the art historian Aby Warburg (1866–1929), among his patients, and used psychoanalysis as a way to give every patient the individual attention they required.

Binswanger's   undogmatic   and   philosophical approach to psychiatry made him a follower of the philosophers Edmund Husserl and Martin Heidegger, whose work he tried to integrate into what he called *Daseinsanalyse*, that is, "the analysis of (our) presence, our being-in-the world," and it was to this he dedicated his masterwork of 1942, *Grundformen und Erkenntnis menschlichen Daseins*. In other words, although he moved away from psychoanalysis, his relationship with Freud and the letters they exchanged remained a central ingredient of his life, as we can see from reading the volume edited by Gerhard Fichtner—my colleague and friend Joseph Reppen also confirmed this, in his 2003 article on the topic. Binswanger's most famous case, "Ellen West," was translated into English in 1958 for the volume *Existence: A new dimension in psychiatry and psychology*, edited by Rollo May, Ernest Angel, and Henry Ellenberger, the volume that Irvin Yalom recently celebrated (Yalom, 2017) as one of the books that had most influenced his professional and scientific career. Although Ludwig Binswanger's son Wolfgang (1914–1993, the fourth generation of psychiatrists in the Binswanger family) had to close the Bellevue in 1980 because of financial considerations, its archives were moved to the Institute for the History of Medicine of the University of Tübingen, and this allowed Albrecht Hirschmüller to reconstruct its history in a book that he published in 2004.

The letters exchanged between Sigmund Freud and Ernest Jones (1879–1958) between 1908 and 1939 are totally different in nature; these were edited in 1993 by Canadian historian Andrew Paskauskas into an 836-page volume containing 671 letters, with an Introduction by Riccardo Steiner. Many of these letters in fact center around the compromise reached by the two correspondents between Jones' ambition to become the leader of psychoanalysis in the English-speaking world, and Freud's own concept of and preoccupation with what ideas and positions Jones should have shared with him—their major disagreements were represented by Jones' support of the North American medical monopoly of psychoanalysis, and by how much he helped Melanie Klein (1882–1960) settle in London and establish there her own analytic school. Of course, we cannot think of the psychoanalytic movement without Jones, to whom we also owe the suggestion that Freud found the so-called Secret Committee (1912), as well as (in 1920) the *International Journal of Psychoanalysis*, still the leading analytic journal. From this point of view, we can certainly share Riccardo Steiner's conclusion that:

Nothing keeps one from maintaining that in many of these

letters the reader will be able to feel the still beating, even if
intermittent, pulse of one of the most vital and revolutionary
movements that has characterized the cultural life of our
century. (Steiner, 1993, p. xlix)

If Germany and the German language, as well as
the German-speaking world (including Austria and
Switzerland), remain the center of the reconstruction
and elaboration of the history of psychoanalysis, this has
of course to do with the fact that German was the main
language of psychoanalysis until the end of World War
II. As German was the main language of the so-called
Secret Committee, whose history was reconstructed by
Phyllis Grosskurth in 1991, it is no wonder that Gerhard
Wittenberger and Christfried Tögel were able to edit *Die
Rundbriefe des "Geheimen Komitees,"* that is, the circular
letters exchanged between 1913 and 1927 by its members,
which came out in four very nice volumes through the
Tübingen publishing house Diskord between 1999 and
2006 (Wittenberger and Tögel, eds., 1999–2006). If the
original aim of the circular letters had been to mobilize the
collaborative forces within the Committee, they ended up
making some conflicts more acute, for example the conflict
around Otto Rank (1884–1939), whose consequence was
the provisional end of the Committee's activity. Once the
Committee had been reconstituted in 1924, Anna Freud
replaced Rank in preparing the letters that Freud would
dictate and which she would type and sign herself. In
1927 the life of the Committee came to an end and its
affairs were handled directly by the IPA board, the very
last letter being written by Ernest Jones from London, on
June 20, 1927. The whole history of the Secret Committee
had been already dealt with by one of the two editors,
Gerhard Wittenberger, in a book published in 1995.

Highly instructive for today's candidates and
practicing analysts is *The complete correspondence of
Sigmund Freud and Karl Abraham 1907–1925*, edited
in 2002 by Ernest Falzeder. This is particularly so in
regard to how Freud supervised the first analytic cases
that Abraham started treating in Berlin at the end
of 1907, being at the time the only psychoanalyst in
private practice in the whole country. As he later did
with Edoardo Weiss, Freud not only advised Abraham
on how to promote psychoanalysis in Berlin, whose
leading analyst he remained until his premature death (at
age forty-eight, in December 1925), but also sent him a
series of patients. From a theoretical point of view, the
most important topic on which they worked together was
the problem of the psychogenesis of depression, about

which they both wrote papers that still belong to analytic training and discourse. Here is how André Haynal and Ernest Falzeder introduced the figure of Karl Abraham in their Introduction to the volume:

> Karl Abraham was a central figure in the early history of psychoanalysis. He succeeded in making his own views the prevalent ones, sometimes even against those of Freud, leaving his imprint on the development of psychoanalysis for decades to come. He prevailed over all his opponents and competitors within the movement: Alfred Adler, Wilhelm Stekel, Carl Gustav Jung, Otto Rank, Sándor Ferenczi, Ernest Jones. He succeeded Jung as president of the International Psychoanalytic Association and as editor of its official journal. He contributed important elaborations of Freud's ideas, and he systematized and formulated them in a way that seemed more exact and could more easily be taught to others. He actively sought to establish relations with other disciplines and institutions – sexology, academia, psychiatry, pedagogy, general medicine – or public opinion in general, and in Berlin he developed and implemented, with Max Eitingon and Ernst Simmel, the so-called tripartite model of psychoanalytic training (personal analysis, seminars, supervision) that is still in existence today. Among his pupils and analysands one can mention Helene Deutsch, Edward Glover, James Glover, Melanie Klein, Sándor Rado, and Theodor Reik. (Haynal and Falzeder, 2002, p. xix)

Indeed, the figure of Karl Abraham is so important in Germany that the journal *Luzifer-Amor* produced its third monographic issue on him as Issue No. 61, in 2018. In this, the co-editor Ludger Hermanns published an article (Hermanns, 2018) on the thirty-two letters and post-cards exchanged by Abraham and Jones between 1911 and 1925, which he found, still unpublished, in four archives in the UK and the USA.

In the complete edition of their letters, 225 are letters written by Freud to Abraham, out of a total of 501 for the two correspondents combined. The publication of the letters in 2002 certainly contributed to creating the new interest in the life and work of Karl Abraham that lies behind the recent biographies by the German colleague Karin Zienert-Eilts (2013) and the Dutch colleague Anna Bentnick van Schoonheten (2015). Last but not least, here is the picture of their relationship that Parisian colleague Alain de Mijolla, the founder of the IAHP, formulated in 1997 on the basis of his study of their correspondence:

> Starting at the same time, as we have seen, as the correspondence with Jung and with Ferenczi, the relationship with Karl Abraham remained more distant, despite a number of transient rapprochements concerning the subject of Jewishness or on emerging from institutional crises of which Abraham had rightly seen the first signs. The 'rock of bronze' is a little cold, too reserved, clearly not meschugge enough

for the necessary relational vibration to be established in the long term. I would suggest, moreover, that he was one of the rare people whose affective life or psychoanalytical practice had not been marked by some accident necessitating an appeal to Freud. No adventures with his patients, like Jung or Ferenczi, no sentimental complications, like Jones or Pfister. No opening to new socio-cultural horizons, either, like Lou Andreas-Salomé or Marie Bonaparte. He was a reasonable reasoner whose calming presence was necessary to bring equilibrium to a scenery which was in other respects somewhat in disorder. (de Mijolla, 1997, p. 401)

Of quite another nature are the letters exchanged by Freud and Max Eitingon (1881–1943) between 1906 and 1939, which Michael Schröter edited in two volumes in 2004; these included a total of 821 letters, 365 of which were written by Freud. Eitingon was the first psychiatrist who contacted Freud from Zurich at the beginning of 1907, but their correspondence started becoming regular only in 1918, ending up representing the second most numerous in terms of letters between Freud and his collaborators. As Michael Schröter himself writes in the above-mentioned book chapter, seldom do Freud and Eitingon write about clinical and theoretical topics, their main shared preoccupation instead being administrative and financial points; these concerned the Berlin Psychoanalytic Institute, founded by Eitingon in 1920 and directed by him until 1933, and the IPA, of which Eitingon was the president between 1926 and 1932.

Through their letters, we can see how the international association founded by Freud and Ferenczi in Nuremberg at the end of March 1910 met the growing challenges of a successful international network, including the need to find internationally shared standards of training and the best ways of promoting the publication of the growing analytic literature. Like Otto Rank, Max Eitingon ended up becoming similar to a family member for Freud, whom Freud addressed with the words "Dear Max," at variance with the words "Dear friend" with which he addressed his closest collaborators. This dimension of their relationship is also documented by the large volume of information contained in correspondence concerning family events and Freud's health, especially after the beginning of his struggle with cancer in 1923. This is why Ilse Grubrich-Simitis wrote that these letters bear "the traits of a family correspondence" (Grubrich-Simitis, 2005, p. 270), and how Michel Schröter could qualify them in terms of the only one of Freud's correspondences with his closest collaborators that developed without the emergence of any important conflicts. (Schröter, 2006, p. 223)

Before turning to the letters written to or exchanged between Freud and his family members, let me dwell on the following two further important sets of correspondence: the letters exchanged by Freud and Eugen Bleuler between 1904 and 1937, edited by Michael Schröter in 2012, and the letters exchanged by him and Otto Rank, edited by James Lieberman and Robert Kramer also in 2012.

The publication of the former correspondence represents an important event in the history of Freud's letters, with particular regard to the problem of Freud's relationship to university psychiatry, and to Bleuler's refusal to adhere to Freud's need to organize psychoanalysis in terms of a private association such as the IPA. Franz Alexander and Thomas Selesnick (1965) had already expressed the desire to see this correspondence published in its entirety, in order to better understand the nature of the conflict, which was so full of consequences for the later relationship between psychoanalysis and the university as a scientific institution. The seventy-nine edited letters now at our disposal, twenty-three written by hand by Freud and fifth-six typewritten by Bleuler, eventually show us how their difference of opinion was rooted in the different context of their scientific and professional work, and in Bleuler's ambivalent relationship to Freud. The volume is not only very well edited by Michael Schröter, but also contains a very informative contribution by Swiss psychiatrist Bernhard Küchenhoff (2012) on the opinions exchanged by Freud and Bleuler on the topic of the psychology of the psychoses. In addition, in 1991 Albrecht Hirschmüller wrote an important book on the topic of Freud's "encounter" (*Begegnung* is the German word that he uses) with psychiatry.

At variance with the other correspondence, James Lieberman and Robert Kramer have contextualized the 250 surviving letters exchanged by Freud and Otto Rank in a series of nineteen chapters, through which we can see the whole development of their relationship. James Lieberman had already published, in 1985, an important biography of Rank, *Acts of will. The life and work of Otto Rank*. Of the 250 surviving letters, only about one-fourth are by Freud, and many of them find their place in the first of the five appendixes of the book as "Minor letters," given their character of brief communications. On the other hand, there are about thirty letters by Freud that give us very important keys for a good reconstruction of Freud and Rank's complex relationship, which started in 1905, when the young Rank approached Freud to give him a manuscript with the title "The artist." This was the start of how Rank became the secretary of the Vienna Psychoanalytic Society and how Freud adopted him as some kind of a son, whose university studies he also supported financially.

The crucial change in their relationship coincided with Rank's 1923 publication of *The trauma of birth* (see Rank, 1952), at a time when he was working with Ferenczi on the important and innovative technical book *The development of psychoanalysis*. If we can today revisit Rank's introduction of the concept of the "birth trauma" in terms of an important pioneering illumination of the pre-Oedipal phase of human development, Freud felt not only uneasy about, but even personally attacked for, the secondary role attributed by Rank to the Oedipal phase. In his review of the book in the *Division Review*, Martin Winn underlines the importance of the following words written by Freud to Rank on July 23, 1924 in this regard:

> The exclusion of the father in your theory seems to reveal too much the result of personal influences in your life which I think I recognize, and my suspicion grows that you would not have written this book had you gone through an analysis yourself. (Lieberman and Kramer, eds., 2012, p. 208)

To this he added the following comment: "Among Rank's many enduring contributions to psychoanalysis, an ironic one would be the increased awareness of how central one's own analysis is in the formation of a psychoanalyst" (Winn, 2012, pp. 11–12).

A further merit of Lieberman and Kramer's book is the light they throw on one of the main reasons for the crisis and end of the relationship between Rank and Freud, that is, the negative influence of the debate over Rank's new contributions that came from colleagues in the Secret Committee—a conflict upon which Martin Winn (2012) bases his formulation of the contradictions of psychoanalysis as an institution. Although there have been several important revisitations of the work and legacy of Otto Rank (see, for example, Rudnytsky, 1991), its presentation and exploration in terms of his still relevant contributions to psychoanalysis have never become integrated into the training of our candidates. From this point of view, it certainly makes sense to extend to Otto Rank the critique of the one-sidedness of the theoretical instruction found in our training institutes that was formulated by Paul Roazen in 1990. In the latter's words:

> It is immensely difficult to become well educated in the history of psychoanalysis, and this in large part because of

all the sectarianism that has blinded people over the years. . .
. Not many candidates in training, or even medical students,
ever get anything to read by C.G. Jung, for example, even
though Jung was not only an excellent critic of Freud's but
wrote some pioneering papers in the 1920s on short-term
psychotherapy . . . At the same time it has never been clear
to me how some writers succeed in getting put on the reading
lists of our hospitals and institutes. I suspect that provincial
or national prejudices play a larger role than they might.
Psychoanalytic literature has been accumulating for almost
a century now, and there ought to be more of a consensus
on which papers and books are classics. One does not have
to be a Sullivanian to acknowledge how he pioneered in
the treatment of psychosis or to be a Kleinian to assign, for
instance, her work on depression. (Roazen, 1990, pp. 52–53)

From this point of view, the volume edited by
Lieberman and Kramer certainly contributes to restating
the centrality of Otto Rank for not only the history, but also
the theoretical and technical aspects, of psychoanalysis.

After revisiting Josef Breuer's (1842–1925) life and
work, with particular regard to his contributions to
physiology and psychoanalysis (Hirschmüller, 1978), and
after publishing the above-mentioned books on Freud as
a psychiatrist and on Binswanger's Bellevue Hospital,
Albrecht Hirschmüller edited, in 2005, the first volume
of the so-called Family Letters, to which I will now
turn. This involves the 199 letters exchanged, from 1882
to 1938, by Freud and his sister-in-law Minna Bernays
(1865–1941). Four years younger than her sister Martha
(1861–1951), Minna moved to Vienna in 1896 to live with
Freud's family, and almost half of the letters go back to
the time before Sigmund and Martha's marriage in 1886.
This makes Minna Bernays—together with Wilhelm
Fliess and her sister Martha—Freud's most important
intellectual partner in the so-called period of his "splendid
isolation." But through the publication of these letters,
Hirschmüller is also able to document that it makes no
sense to think of any form of sexual intimacy between
Freud and his sister-in-law, as originally hypothesized
by Peter Swales (1986). Hirschmüller's point of view was
recently confirmed by Henry Zvi Lothane in his 2016
review of two books on the topic written by Barry Gale.
Last but not least, we also owe to Hirschmüller the first
exhaustive reconstruction of the history of the Bernays
family, which we find at the end of the volume. Minna
Bernays was an intelligent, very well-read, humorous,
and dynamic woman who played an essential role in the
life of Freud and his family.

In 2006, the year after Hirschmüller's volume,
Ingeborg Mayer-Palmedo edited all 298 surviving letters

exchanged by Freud and his daughter Anna (1895–1982) between 1904 and 1938; the English edition of this came out in 2014 through Polity Books, with Nick Somers as translator. In 2012, a French edition had in fact been published, but there is still no Italian edition of these letters, this failure being one of the reasons why I am dedicating so much room here to this neglected chapter of the history of psychoanalysis. Anna Freud's biographer Elisabeth Young-Bruehl (1946–2011) had had the chance to use at least some of these letters in her important and very well-written biography of Freud's daughter and heir (Young-Bruehl, 1988). This is in fact one of the main topics that this collection of letters helps us clarify, that is, the way in which Freud was able to tie his daughter to his life and work, and, at the same time, allow her to realize her own life project, with particular regard for her private life. This is also why the historian Hannah Decker concluded her review of the English edition of this volume with the following words: "This correspondence serves as a chronicle of Austrian life a century ago and also offers us a window through which to observe the creation of one of the most famous father-daughter pairs in Western history" (Decker, 2015).

To the Family Letters also belongs the volume of more than 500 letters written by Freud to all his children, except for Anna; this was edited by Michael Schröter in 2010. It includes letters between Freud and his oldest daughter Mathilde (1887–1978) and her husband Robert; his son Martin (1889–1967) and Martin's wife Ernestine; his son Oliver (1891–1969) and his wife Henny; his son Ernst (1892–1970) and his wife Lucie; and his daughter Sophie (1893–1920) and her husband Max. Here is the way in which their editor describes them and assesses their significance in his Introduction to the volume:

> A father writes to his children. He writes to them when they are on vacation somewhere else, when they are at a spa, or when he himself is away for health reasons. He writes to his soldier sons on the front, to his daughter who married abroad, to his children who emigrated abroad, because they had better work chances than at home. After the death of the daughter, he writes to his son-in-law who is under stress because of the education of the two grandchildren, and he writes to a daughter-in-law to thank her for a set of family pictures. He asks his children for some favor, he sends to his grandchildren birthday greetings together with a little sum of money. He organizes meetings, gives advice on financial and health matters, keeps the children informed on the latest family events, and wants them to keep him informed about these events. What is particularly relevant about all this? Why should we read these letters? (Schröter, 2010, p. 7; my translation)

And here is their editor's assessment:

> In conclusion, Freud's letters to his children document his great humanity, and this by itself makes them into a worthwhile document. Furthermore, they allow to ask ourselves to what extent psychoanalysis itself as theory and even more as a therapeutic activity can be retraced back to this very humanity. The same honesty, the same openness in money and sex matters, the same seriousness and the same tolerance in terms of all things human which Freud showed toward his children were also the basic elements of his scientific thinking and of his professional doings. We have no other document at our disposal which allows us to establish this relationship between his person and his work in such an eloquent way as the letters, of a father to his children, printed in this volume. (Schröter, 2010, p. 21; my translation)

This is also precisely the dimension covered by the so-called *Brautbriefe*, that is, the bridal letters that Freud and Martha Bernays wrote to each other between June 1882 and September 1886, the first three volumes of which (out of a total of five) have been already published by the Frankfurt publisher S. Fischer, with Gerhard Fichtner, Albrecht Hirschmüller, and Ilse Grubrich-Simitis as editors. Their publication and the comments they have been receiving (see below) document and confirm what I already wrote in 1998 (see Chapter 3) about the crucial role played by Freud's partner Martha in his self-analysis. Second, they further document the dialogical nature of psychoanalysis and, at the same time, confirm the validity of the dialogical nature of my own book, that is, of the dialogical character of all its chapters. Third, I deal also with the *Brautbriefe* for the same reason I dealt in such a detailed way with all the volumes of Freud's letters that I have presented in this Introduction, that is, the need to bring the reader into contact with a neglected chapter of psychoanalysis, whose cultivation is for linguistic reasons limited to the German-speaking world. Such an operation, of cultural transfer, of course also belongs to the aims and contents of my work, and of this book. And this was the same aim that was pursued by Ilse Grubrich-Simitis in the paper that inaugurated the 2011 IPA Congress held in Mexico City (Grubrich-Simitis, 2012), that is, to inform the analytic community about the eventual publication of this collection of letters in its completeness, and to show the crucial way in which they will change our view of the young Freud, and of the origins of psychoanalysis. The same is true of the very long article (seventy-two pages) reviewing the first volume of this correspondence, which Riccardo Steiner (2013) published in the *International Journal of Psychoanalysis*, and which I will try to briefly summarize here.

Let me start with Grubrich-Simitis' paper, which has the title "Seeds of core psychoanalytic concepts. On the courtship letters of Sigmund Freud and Martha Bernays." This takes as a starting point the 2011 publication of Volume 1, with the title *Sei mein, wie ich mir's denke* (Be mine the way I see it), and covers the time between June 1882 and July 1883. The main topics and considerations formulated by Grubrich-Simitis can be summarized as follows. Compared to the ninety-three letters written by the young Freud to Martha that are contained in the volume of Freud's letters edited by their son Ernst Freud in 1960 (see above), the five volumes—whose full titles Grubrich-Simitis communicates to the reader—contain more than 1,500 letters, all deposited at the US Library of Congress. Their complete publication allows us only now to get in touch with the often dramatic and conflictual dimension of the relationship, with the corresponding crises of jealousy and lack of confidence, and with what the author defines as "a successful reciprocal éducation sentimentale" (Grubrich-Simitis, 2012, p. 386; my translation). Unknown to us—states the author—were also both "the surprising intelligence and independence" of the young Martha, and even more "the intellectual nature of the dialogue" covering many of the letters (see Grubrich-Simitis, 2012). In other words:

> Freud looked for and found in his partner, as he formulated it, 'a collaborator in the most serious matters' (see letter of August 2nd, 1882), meaning his own scientific work. He let Martha participate in his thinking and looked for her critiques. In other words: The unabridged edition of this correspondence – the biggest, most direct and intimate of all the correspondences of Freud – represents . . . something totally new. (Grubrich-Simitis, 2012, pp. 387–388)

After such a premise, the author takes into consideration the whole correspondence in terms of the traces it contains of the main topics of the Mexico City Congress, that is, sexuality, dreams, and the unconscious. In the letters, she finds not only traces of these, but even traces of future concepts such as "countertransference," "analytic method," "free association," and "fundamental rule" (Grubrich-Simitis, 2012, p. 397).

The author concludes her paper by trying to summarize the new portraits of Martha and Freud contained in their correspondence. Given her greater psychological balance and her tenderness, Martha was able to exercise a crucial positive influence on Freud, to the point that their complete correspondence—writes the author—"will from now on permit us to acknowledge and value her role in the original formulation of psychoanalysis – late enough, sixty years after her death" (Grubrich-Simitis, 2102, p. 400). As far as the new portrait of the young Freud that emerges from these letters is concerned, Ilse Grubrich-Simitis underlines what she calls his *Zerrissenheit und Widerpsruchlichhkeit*, that is, his "fragmentation and contradictions" (Grubrich, p. 401), making up a far more complex and pathological neurotic structure than the one emerging from Ernest Jones's biography—as I had myself assumed in the three publications that make up the three first chapters of this book. Last but not least, here is what we can read in the paper in terms of Freud's basic qualities:

> Other traits of the picture of Freud emerging from the bridal letters characterized him for the rest of his life: his deep seriousness, his passionate tenacity and his capacity to lose himself in his scientific work, the extreme openness of his senses, his liberty from prejudices and conventions, the great originality of his thinking and his linguistic talent. To the conditions of his long-lasting and unusually great creativity certainly belonged also the high permeability of his ego boundaries [*die hochgradige Durchlässigkeit seiner Ichgrenzen*], which often represented a danger for his psychological balance. (Grubrich-Simitis, 2012, p. 403; my translation)

Riccardo Steiner was so fascinated by the first volume of the *Brautbriefe* that—as I wrote above—he wrote a seventy-two-page review article on it. In fact, the first ten pages of the review center around the conflict between Jones and Anna Freud and her family concerning the use he wanted to make of these letters in the first volume of the biography, and how he was able to obtain their permission to do it. "Indeed, Anna's sense of discretion . . . meant that Anna did not even allow herself to read some of those *Brautbriefe*," writes Steiner (2013, p. 868) in the first section of the review article. As we learn in the second section, "The 2011 *Brautbriefe* edition," it was only two years before her death (1982) that Anna Freud mentioned to Kurt Eissler (1908–1999), then director of the Freud Archives, that "she did not object to the *Brautbriefe* being published in toto in the future, although not before the year 2000" (Steiner, 2013, p. 874). Furthermore:

> It took more than ten years of the most excruciating, precise and creative philological, historical and exegetic work on the part of the three German scholars to produce what today can be considered probably the masterpiece of research on Freud's private and scientific pre-analytic life. (Steiner, 2013, p. 874)

The third section, "The letters: Freud and Martha," centers around a very detailed summary of what the two partners wrote to each other in the first year of their engagement, with particular regard to their conflicts and the way in which they patiently and lovingly constructed their relationship. "Of the two lovers," writes Steiner in this context, "it was Martha who was the more composed and thoughtful, and the more psychologically aware of their difficulties" (Steiner,2013, p. 907). In the next section, "The *Brautbriefe* and psychoanalysis," the author reviews a whole series of resonances that he finds between Freud's letters to Martha and his later analytic works, and the elaboration of this aspect also contributes to the following conclusion:

> The *Brautbriefe*, in whatever form (I would accept them even in Kindle form if they could find a publisher willing to translate them comparable to the generous Fischer Verlag of Frankfurt), should be a required presence in the library, in the living room or in the consulting room, and be required reading for the young generations of psychoanalysts of today and of the future. (Steiner, 2013, p. 929)

Fortunately, all three volumes of the *Brautbriefe* now published have had a strong resonance in the most important of our journals, and I will thus limit myself to two of them: the *Journal of the American Psychoanalytic Association* and *Psychoanalysis and History*. Christian Maetzner (2012) produced a very informative and well-written review of the first volume (see above), based on the very rich and detailed Introduction that Ilse Grubrich-Simitis wrote for it as an extended version of her Mexico City paper. Here is Maetzner's way of introducing these letters:

> The Freud-Bernays correspondence dates from a time when writing letters, sometimes more than one a day, was the only way to stay in touch. It is thus more than an important historical document. It gives us insight into the hearts and minds of Freud and his soon-to-be wife. Three main themes stand out. One is the struggle of passionate lovers unable to see and talk to each other for long stretches of time. As we know too well from our work, such an arrangement, with delayed or altogether missing input from external reality, gives rise to fantasies that may distort our interpretations of external events. The correspondence contains many instances of this dynamic. A second theme, which many might not have expected, is that Martha, just as much as Sigmund, wrote about these struggles in ways that contain the germs of concepts that would become core ideas of the psychoanalytic model of the mind. And even more, in several instances it was Martha who originated them before Sigmund took them up. A third theme of the correspondence is its documentation of two late adolescents' inner world during the state of being in love. (Maetzner, 2012, p. 1088)

And here is Maetzner's very appropriate final consideration and endorsement:

> In today's fast-paced culture, where condensed and instant

communication via text messaging, e-mail, and twitter have become commonplace, it is refreshing to read the correspondence of two people who took time to reflect about what was on their minds. It is after all what we, as analysts, try to do with our analysands. (Maetzner, 2012, p. 1093)

The second volume of the *Brautbriefe, Unser "Roman in Fortsetzungen"* (Our "novel in installments"), covering the time between July and December 1883, was reviewed at great length in the same journal by Rita Teusch, who also made reference to Katja Behling's (2004) biography of Martha, and summarized the correspondence in great detail. Teusch's concluding remarks are as follows:

Reading these courtship letters was a great pleasure. I was impressed by the depth and the beauty of the couple's love, their ability to express themselves, their sophistication, and their maturity in handling themselves and their relationship, including their painful separation. I highly recommend the book to anyone interested in getting to know Martha Bernays as a warm, intelligent, eloquent and scholarly twenty-one-year old with a natural sense of poise and self-confidence and a wonderful sense of humor. Freud emerges in these letters with an even deeper humanity as he struggles at times with his mood, but overall remains remarkably sensitive and responsive to his betrothed. . . . Freud emerges as deeply relational in these letters, carving for a mutually engaging and unabashedly honest relationship with his fiancée. The letters read like the process of a relational analysis in which both partners work through their transference-countertransference issues and arrive at a more reality-based and empathic understanding of the other. (Teusch, 2014, pp. 342–343)

To Rita Teusch we also owe a detailed review of the third volume of the *Brautbriefe*, covering the time between January and September 1884, whose title she translates into English as "Waiting quietly and with surrender, waiting struggling and with exasperation." As Freud's study of the properties of cocaine was central to this phase of their correspondence, the volume starts with a balanced assessment of this controversial episode written by Albrecht Hirschmüller (2013). But here are the reviewer's final considerations:

It is impossible to convey in a short essay the emotional, intellectual, literary and artistic richness and masterly skill of the correspondence. Upon finishing this volume, I was left again with a profound feeling of admiration for this young couple . . . and their ability to remain deeply committed to each other despite considerable hardship, in the process achieving significant personal and relational maturity and deepening happiness and love. I highly recommend this unique correspondence, as both a literary pleasure and an historical and relational education. (Teusch, 2017, p. 124)

Michael Molnar, the former director of the London Freud Museum has written both reviews of the first two volumes of the *Brautbriefe* that the reader can find in the journal *Psychoanalysis and History*, the journal founded in 1998 by Robert Hinshelwood with Andrea Sabbadini as its first editor—all its volumes can also be found on the PEP-Disk. In order to give the reader a feeling for the way in which such a historically and philologically trained scholar writes about these letters, here is the way in which Molnar begins his second review:

> In my review of the first volume of Sigmund Freud and Martha Bernay's *Brautbriefe*, I sang my praises of its exemplary scholarly apparatus. My review of the second volume begins by marking bis in the margin. The notes and footnoting are excellent as before. And the story that the letters tell continues along the same lines as before. But with some important development and differences.
>
> During the five and a half months covered by this second volume (from 12 July 1883 to 31 December 1883), the couple would write 278 letters. As there were only 231 letters during the entire first year of the correspondence (from 11 June 1882 to 12 July 1883), this means the rate had almost doubled. There was a good reason for that. For most of the previous year Martha was living in Vienna and the couple were able to meet regularly. But in mid-June 1883 'Mama' (Emmeline Bernays) took her daughters back to Hamburg, and the engaged couple would not meet again until September 1884.
>
> This puts us readers in a privileged position. There are no more undocumented personal encounters in this period. Now the entire relationship is there on the pages in front of us. We are almost in their situation, working out the concealed sense of the other's letters. Each of them is defining their new identity as engaged lover by reference to the other's words; each is impeded in this intellectual endeavor by unpredictable emotions welling up through the words. . . . But these respectable lovers can still speak their passion, in fact this is all that is left for them to do. (Molnar, 2015, pp. 121–122)

2. THE YOUNG FREUD IN HIS LETTERS TO EDUARD SILBERSTEIN

Although in Chapter 1 I deal at length with the young Freud's letters to Eduard Silberstein, what I would like to convey in this section is the way I approached them, starting with the above-mentioned paper I gave in Trieste in December 1989 (Conci, 1990). I will then concentrate on the challenging work I did as editor of their Italian edition, which I could only partially refer to in the paper I gave in Stockholm in August 1991, the paper out which Chapter 1 was developed and published in 1992. By this, I also intend to deal with some of the authors and works whose knowledge is indispensable for understanding this early phase of Freud's life and work, and which I merely mention and quote in Chapter 1 without specifically dealing with them. I am referring for example to the work of Kurt Eissler (see 1974a, 1974b, 1978), and Siegfried Bernfeld (1892–1953; see Bernfeld, 1946, 1949, 1951), but not these alone. In this section of the Introduction, I will specifically deal with the way in which I used Freud's letters to Eduard Silberstein to deal with the more general topic of how Freud's psychological constitution might have influenced his conceptualization of the analytic technique. If this was then a crucial topic with which I was confronted as a candidate, it has of course not ceased to interest me. In fact, in this section I also mean to deal with the latest data I have been collecting on it.

The two main themes of the three letters that Freud wrote to Silberstein from Trieste (on March 28, and April 5 and 23, 1876), around whose translation into Italian centered the paper I gave in Trieste on December 8, 1989 (Conci, 1990), were Freud's neurotic defenses against the sexual dimension of life, and its sublimation in terms of his research work on the sexual reproduction of eels. Only later, during my work as editor of the Italian edition of the letters, did the self-analytic aspect, that is, the analytic character of the letters, come to the foreground, as we will see. But here is what the young Freud wrote to Silberstein in his first brief letter from Trieste, in the Spanish language that they had studied together, as translated into English by Arnold Pomerans, who worked on the original German edition edited by Walter Boehlich:

> Dear Berganza, here I am in Trieste. Believe me, your honor, writing would be the silliest thing I could do. I shall tell you all about it by word of mouth. I would like to read some brief lines from you, but do not ask for any from me. Know then, that Trieste is a very beautiful city and that the beasts are very beautiful beasts. (Boehlich, ed., 1990, p. 141)

Whether the young Freud is here speaking of the eels he had worked with or of the human beings he had met in Trieste is not clear, given the way in which he seemed to mix these two categories of living beings in the following letter, a rather long part of which the reader can find in Chapter 1, and from which I will now extract the following, shorter, quotation:

> I would much rather report to you on what I have been able to see of the *bella Italia*, and how I serve the beast-killing science. When . . . I go for an evening stroll after my work, I see precious little of the physiology of the natives of Trieste. Most of what I know I gathered on my first day, when everything was new to me and I found it worthwhile to pay heed to it . . . . The people, finally, are very ugly, with few exceptions. *(By "people" I refer to all living beings who live and work in Trieste.)* The horses and oxen are the same as anywhere else, as are the men, although if anything the

latter are worse . . . . The cats are beautiful and friendly, but the women are especially distinctive. Most of them are true characters in your Leipzig sense, and often have the typical Italian figure, slim, tall, slender-faced, with a longish nose, dark eyebrows, and small raised upper lip. So much for the anatomical features. *Physiologically, all that I know about them is that they like to go for walks* . . . . Unfortunately they are not beautiful in our German sense, *but I remember that on my first day I discovered lovely specimens among the new type which I have not encountered since* . . . . *Since it is not allowed to dissect human beings, I really have nothing to do with them.* (Boehlich, ed., 1990, pp. 142, 144, 146; original emphasis)

As I write in Chapter 1, "this defensive spell gets [only partially, I would add today] broken only two and a half weeks later: during a trip to the sea-village of Muggia, Freud is again able to see nice women around, though in the form of midwives and pregnant women." In fact, as I also report in that chapter, here is what he wrote in his third letter from Trieste, on April 23, 1976:

True, on my first day in Trieste, I felt that the city was inhabited by none but Italian goddesses, *and I was filled with apprehension*, but when I stepped expectantly into the streets on the second day, I could discover no more of these, and ever since a beautiful *donna* [woman] has been one of the rarest things to encounter in the street. In Muggia, however, the women, as I said, are more attractive, mostly blond, oddly enough, which accords with neither Italian nor Jewish descent. (Boehlich, ed., 1990, p. 153; emphasis added)

The character of the young Freud's repression of sexuality—and his tendency to de-animate human beings on the basis of the anatomical and physiological dimensions with which he was so occupied—reminded me of Norbert Hanold, the protagonist of the novel Gradiva by Danish writer Wilhelm Jensen (1837–1911), to which Freud dedicated his fascinating essay of 1907; however, I would not have been able to decipher such a deep neurotic attitude of his had it not been for the help I received from Kurt Eissler. Three long papers by Eissler, described below, at the time exercised—as I am even more aware of now, after rereading them—a very deep influence upon me, and I developed with these a very significant dialogical relationship, one that nourished and sustained me in the work I did not only for Chapter 1, but also for Chapters 2 and 3. These particular papers are "Über Freuds Freundschaft mit Wilhelm Fliess nebst einem Anhang über Freuds Adoleszenz und einer historischen Bemerkung über Freuds Jugendstil" (Eissler, 1974a), "Psychoanalytische Einfälle zu Freuds 'Zerstreute(n) Gedanken'" (Eissler, 1974b; see the references for the translation of the titles), and "Creativity and adolescence.

The role of trauma in Freud's adolescence" (Eissler, 1978). In Chapter 1, immediately after quoting Freud's third letter from Trieste, are the following words, which I extracted from Eissler's 1978 paper; the importance of his contribution to my overall work on Freud's adolescence is so great that I will go over the three papers mentioned above in a way I could not have done in the original paper that makes up Chapter 1. These words deal with the young Freud's renunciation of courting Gisela Fluss as the trauma which he was still defending himself against in Trieste:

> The Gisela experience contributed much to the strengthening of the defensive, repressive apparatus in the youth. *Freud never discarded this apparatus.* One has the impression that he made his discoveries against an inner resistance, that the richness of his accomplishments came to pass against a background of hard labor, the expression of a counterforce which Freud himself intimated when he wrote to Lou Andreas-Salomé about a recent discovery: *'It is a discovery of which one ought almost to be ashamed, for one should have divined these connections from the beginning and not after thirty years.'* (Eissler, 1978, pp. 513–514, emphasis added)

Let me start with the Eissler's 1974a paper, the paper with the longest title. In Chapter 2, I was only able to quote the following words from this paper, without having the chance to say more about the way in which Eissler's approach to the general topic of the young Freud's choice of medical school influenced and enriched my work. It is probably appropriate that I am doing that now in this Introduction. Eissler wrote: "The study of medicine made the satisfaction of the sexual curiosity possible and, at the same time, through the constraint of having to study a large number of ordinary facts, the avoidance of his own fantasies" (1974a, p. 78).

In other words, in this Introduction I believe it is appropriate to introduce the reader not only to Eissler's work on the young Freud, but also to his specific line of thought about it. At variance with the reconstruction of Freud's adolescence offered by both Ernest Jones in the first volume (1953) of his biography of Freud, and by John Gedo and Ernest Wolf (1970), Eissler is not at all of the opinion that Freud's adolescence was relative tranquil; on the contrary, he believes that Freud's neurotic incapacity to court Gisela Fluss (in Freiburg, in the summer of 1872) had a traumatic effect on him, and that even his choice of medical school can be at best explained in this light. Of course, this is also one of the central topics of his 1978 paper, in which, under the heading "Choice of profession," we find for example the following considerations:

> One of the central events in Freud's adolescence that requires psychoanalytic investigation . . . is his decision to study medicine. What really happened was that an adolescent threw his treasure of innate talents to the winds by choosing the study of medicine, which provided for the expression neither of his literary talents nor of his burgeoning imagination. The explanation Freud gave decades later of the puzzling turn of his interests is incorrect and is reminiscent of the legends mighty nations form about their beginning . . . . There is certainly nothing in Goethe's panegyric essay that could induce anybody to study medicine. (Eissler, 1978, pp. 465, 466, 467)

It is exactly in precisely this context that Eissler indicates Freud's letters to Emil Fluss as the key I used in Chapter 2 to come to the formulation of my own, original, hypothesis on Freud's choice of medical school (see below). In fact, he cites Freud's letter to Fluss of May 1, 1873, in which Freud communicates to his friend Emil that he had decided, after having thought about it for a while, to be "a Natural Scientist" (see Eissler, 1978).

Furthermore, I find it appropriate to state in this Introduction how much I learned from Kurt Eissler's work on Freud's "Aphorisms" (Eissler, ed., 1974; Eissler 1974b, 1978) and how much it contributed to the formulation of my new concept of Freud's "self-analysis" as a dimension that was present in his life much earlier than the time of his relationship with Wilhelm Fliess—which I deal with in Chapter 3. As we have seen above, the recent publication of the complete edition of letters exchanged by Freud and Martha goes exactly in the same direction. In other words, although we still use the expression "pre-analytic" for all of Freud's writings that he published between 1877 and 1894, we can today maintain that there is a "self-analytic dimension" running through all his published letters that lies at the roots of psychoanalysis itself, and is worthwhile looking into. This is not to mention the fact that the more we study Freud's "pre-analytic writings," the more connections we are able to establish between them and his analytic work proper, as Manfred Riepe (2016) recently showed through a revisitation of Freud's important work of 1891 on aphasia.

Last but not least, to this Introduction belongs also the following information that I, as an Italian analyst working in Germany, can give to the worldwide community of analysts and historians who are not familiar with German: in 2015, Christfried Tögel, with the collaboration of Urban Zerfass, published the first four volumes of a new *Sigmund Freud Gesamtausgabe*, a new, really complete edition of Freud's collected works whose specific content is represented by all the papers that Freud published between 1877 and 1894 (see the 2015 book review by Johann Georg Reicheneder). Its very first paper is of course the one on the reproduction of eels, on which the twenty-year-old Freud worked in the spring of 1876 at the University of Vienna's Marine Biology Center in Trieste (see Freud, 1877).

Before turning our attention to Eissler's 1978 paper on Freud's adolescence, it is important to add an additional comment to what I just wrote about Freud's "pre-analytic writings," in order to show the reader how complex the whole debate on Freud's life and work still is. It is in fact a peculiar thing that Manfred Riepe published, in the year 2016, a paper in the German journal *Psyche* that showed the crucial role played by Freud's neurological work for the later formulation of the analytic method, but maintaining the concept of Freud's "pre-analytic writings;" in contrast, Ilse Grubrich-Simitis, a member of the editorial board of the same journal, has a different view. In her ground-breaking book of 1993, translated into English in 1997 with the title *Back to Freud's texts: Making silent documents speak*, she proposed, for exactly the same reason, replacing the term "pre-analytic writings" with "early writings." She had even come to the point of speaking of the need to produce a new edition of Freud's *Complete works* containing both categories of Freud's writings (see Chapter 3 in Grubrich-Simitis, 1997). In her opinion, the time is ripe for rejecting the distinction of Freud's writings into "pre-analytic" and "analytic," which Freud himself had introduced for reasons that no longer make sense today. In her own words from the 1993 German edition (pp. 348–349), *"Es ist an der Zeit, Freuds Frühwerk in toto in das Oeuvre zu integrieren . . . . Auch der junge Autor was schliesslich schon Sigmund Freud,"* which can be translated into English as "It is time to integrate the whole early work of Freud into his Oeuvre. After all, the young author was already Sigmund Freud" (my translation).

After having edited the first presentation of Freud's 1871 "Aphorisms" in German (see Eissler, ed., 1974), and having presented his free associations to them (Eissler, 1974b), Eissler dedicated to them the short first section of his 1978 paper, concluding that they "reflect the first stage of his assimilation of classical culture," as I write in Chapter 3 quoting him. Equally short is Eissler's following section, "Choice of profession," which I have already dealt with above, this being the main topic of the paper dealt with in the section "The Gisela episode," to which Eissler dedicates ten pages; he concludes this with the following considerations, which I report here to help the reader better understand the highly condensed work of the first three chapters of this book:

> An outsider well trained in depth psychology ought to have been greatly alarmed in observing that an exceedingly gifted youth turned away from the field of his talents, stayed aloof from girls, objecting even to a kiss, and filled his whole life with academic studies, and all this as a reaction to falling acutely in love for the first time with a girl for a few days.
>
> That the adolescent's passions were intense is evident, nor can there be doubt about the intensity of the defenses. How long would the psychic apparatus be able to withstand the excess of stress and strain such hostility to the drives must create? How would he settle down and prosper in medical studies, having chosen them under the domination of hostility against literature and beauty that had been so close to his heart? (Eissler, 1978, p. 477)

And what do we learn in the longer section that follows, dedicated to the "Student years"? First Eissler reviews the relationship developed by Freud with the professor who had sent him to Trieste, the biology professor Carl Claus (1835–1891), the philosophy professor Franz Brentano (1838–1917), whose lessons he attended between the third and the sixth semesters, and the histology professor Ernst Brücke (1819–1892). We learn how the latter's "monolithic personality" represented "the ideal substitute for a weak father" (Eissler, 1978, p. 484) such as Freud's father was, and how Freud's work at his institute kept him "free of forbidden drives and rendered his defenses impenetrable, an effect that never could have been reached at Claus' Institute" (pp. 488–489). Of course, the time was by then ripe to have Martha enter the scene, and Eissler mirrors this in his next section, centered around the following question: "How did he [Freud] have the stamina to endure the next four stormy and frustrating years of courtship, which caused him to feel without hope that his impecuniousness would ever permit him to attain his passionate desire?" (p. 490). And here is Eissler's answer, that is, his reinterpretation of the previous student phase of medical school:

> What clinically appeared to be a period of repression was in reality evidently a period of silent maturation that made of the youngster who had been tongue-tied at 16 the man more persuasive than Cyrano in the protestations of love, and more successful in attainment, at that. The farewell to an academic career and the falling in love must be interconnected, as Bak (1973) has sensitively pointed out . . . . A remarkable change occurred in the four years of courtship, even though they were even unhappier than the previous decade as a result of the massive frustrations he had to withstand: Freud at least attained the feeling that his life was worthwhile . . . . The

Gisela trauma seemed overcome, and indeed it was, for the
capacity for love fully was attained. (Eissler, 1978, pp. 490,
491, 492)

In other words, the above-reported quotation from
Eissler, which I placed in Chapter 1 directly after quoting
the young Freud's letter of April 23, 1876 from Trieste,
comes only at the end of Eissler's very rich and fascinating
paper, which I highly recommend reading.

A possible alternative to the solution of juxtaposing
these quotations could today be to quote the final
considerations with which North American scholar (a
professor of German literature) Ursula Reidel-Schrewe
concluded her book chapter "Freud's début in the sciences"
(1994), in which she compared the young Freud's letters
from Trieste with the first scientific publication he worked
on:

The juxtaposition of Freud's article on the eels and his letters
from Trieste discussed here reveals a dialectic in Freud's
self-understanding during this early period of his life. His
talents were channeled in two different directions. Letter
writing became a means to stimulate his own imagination,
with personal friends providing a congenial audience. In
the eel article, on the other hand, we confront a document
that reflects the frustration of a young scientist trying to
cope with the expectations of a scrutinizing audience, which
include his immediate superior Carl Claus, the 'challenger'
Simon Syrsky, and the authority of an institution such as
the Academy of Sciences. Freud would continue to immerse
himself in the professional sphere, becoming at times a captive
in the struggle for recognition of his scientific achievements.
At this point, the young Freud did not yet know that he was
capable of creating a work in which his literary and scientific
talent would be closely intertwined, setting in motion a new
understanding of the human psyche. (Reidel-Schrewe, 1994,
p. 16)

A further important research partner during my
self-taught work as editor of the Italian edition of this
fascinating collection of Freud's letters was Siegfried
Bernfeld, whose very instructive papers on Freud's early
life and career (some together with his wife Suzanne
Cassirer Bernfeld [1896–1963]) were collected in German
in an anthology edited by Ilse Grubrich-Simitis (Bernfeld
and Cassirer Bernfeld, 1981). In the first place, Bernfeld's
1951 paper "Sigmund Freud, M.D., 1882–1885," pays
particular regard to his medical studies (1873–1881), the
turning point of 1882 when he left research work with
Professor Brücke and entered the General Hospital to
train as a general physician, and his work on the anatomy
of the medulla oblongata and in the field of clinical
neurology; last but not least, it includes an appendix
containing the "Complete list of the classes in which

Freud registered and paid for." Second, in Bernfeld's 1949 paper on "Freud's scientific beginnings," we learn about the ambivalence with which Freud always looked back at his first scientific paper, due to the fact that he ended up leaving Professor Claus for Professor Brücke, who was able to provide him with the positive fatherly experience that he had lacked in his family. As a result of her personal research in the archives of the University of Vienna, the Vienna psychoanalyst Eva Laible (1993; whom I met in Trieste in December 1989) was able to show how Professor Claus was constantly involved in conflicts with his colleagues and co-workers that poisoned the atmosphere at the Trieste Marin Station, thus better explaining the young Freud's apparent dislike of him, and how he later received from Professor Brücke more support than he had previously known. Finally, there is Bernfeld's famous 1946 paper "An unknown autobiographical fragment by Freud," in which Bernfeld proposed that behind the patient around which Freud centered his 1899 paper "Screen memories" stood for Freud himself—and that Gisela Fluss was the girl he talked about.

Of course, one of the most challenging aspects of my work as editor of *"Querido amigo . . . ". Lettere della giovinezza a Eduard Silberstein 1871–1881* (Conci, ed., 1991) consisted in tracking down, and introducing the reader to, all the books and authors that Freud mentions in his letters, a task which I carried out through a series of footnotes. In the foreground of these letters is also Freud's relationship with philosopher Franz Brentano, which I explored in depth and also reconstructed in the footnotes. Helpful from both points of view were the book chapters "Freud's library and his private reading" by Edward Timms (1988), and Patricia Herzog's "The myth of Freud as anti-philosopher" (1987). The same can be said of two chapters contained in the fascinating anthology *Freud: The fusion of science and humanism*, that is, Harry Trosman's "Freud's cultural background," and John Gedo and Ernest Wolf's "Freud's *Novelas ejemplares*." In this collection of letters, Freud is "Cipion" and Eduard is "Berganza," the names of two dogs taken from one of Miguel de Cervantes' *Novelas ejemplares*; indeed, they often write to each other in Spanish, having studied it together on their own, as I mentioned above.

In terms of assessing the novel aspects of the picture of Freud contained in the letters, what I found very helpful was the detailed presentation of the letters' major themes that was written by the German colleague Günter Gödde (1990) for the journal *Luzifer-Amor*; Gödde treated these in detail in the following sequence: "Close friendship, yes, brotherly community"; "The first secret love – a traumatic experience?"; "We have to avoid to get too greatly involved in politics"; "From 'the desire for philosophical knowledge' to a mistrustful refusal of it"; and "'A clever concealer' of his identity problems in adolescence." Also adding to my attempt to underline in the footnotes possible new aspects of Freud was the close contact I had at the time with Paul Roazen, who formulated his evaluation of this volume of letters in a review published in 1991 in the *American Scholar* with the following words:

> Some people have been tempted to allow themselves to think that everything important about Freud has already essentially been known, and now along comes a set of letters that presents us with a Freud we have not encountered before. He is only fifteen years old at the beginning of this correspondence, and the letters last until the friendship peters out a little more than nine years later. Freud was in the full tide of his youth, and one can be grateful that there is nothing here of the acrimony that one so often finds in his later years . . . . It is startling to find Freud, who in later years claimed to have always abhorred philosophy, here so preoccupied with it . . . . Freud was more devoted to humanistic studies than one might have imagined, although Silberstein does get teased for his commitment to being a social democrat. (Roazen, 1991, pp. 619–620)

As an aside, Robert Holt, whom I had met for the first time in Stockbridge, at the meeting of the Rapaport–Klein Study Group in June 1990 (see the Afterword), at the time I was preparing the Italian edition of the letters, was also impressed by the richness of the new biographical materials they contained. This feeling later found expression in the review Holt wrote on the American edition for Joseph Reppen's journal *Psychoanalytic Books*: "All invaluable source material for an intellectual biography!" (Holt, 1992, p. 243) is what we read at the end of it. On the other hand, Robert Holt did not miss the opportunity to make the following comment on the attitude toward sex that accompanies Freud's three letters from Trieste: "There are many reasons to believe that his own hang-ups and idiosyncrasies show up only slightly transformed in his work" (p. 242).

But even greater was the challenge of classifying these letters as belonging or not belonging to what we can call "the analytic tradition" inaugurated by Freud. In other words, by reading these letters over and over again, I got the feeling that they also belonged to such a tradition, but I of course did not feel I had enough authority—I, an analytic candidate, just thirty-five years old—to state this so openly. Here is the best example of a clear connection between the style of the young Freud's thinking and writing, and the analytic method that he later developed as a psychoanalyst, in the words he wrote to Eduard Silberstein on September 4, 1874:

> Hence my proposal amounts to stipulating that every Sunday each of us, the two sole luminaries of the A.C., send the other a letter that is nothing short of an entire encyclopedia of the past week and that with total veracity reports all our doings, commissions and omissions, and those of all strangers we encounter, in addition to all outstanding thoughts and observations and at least an adumbration, as it were, of the unavoidable emotions . . . . In our letters we shall transmute the six prosaic and unrelenting working days of the week into the pure gold of poetry and may perhaps find that there is enough of interest within us, and in what remains and changes around us, if only we learn to pay attention. (Boehlich, ed., 1990, pp. 57–58)

Fortunately, I had the good luck to come across *Freud as a writer* (1987), by Patrick Mahony, whose approach toward the nature and role of writing in Freud's life and in his discovery of psychoanalysis made it easy for me to include his letters to Eduard Silberstein into the analytic tradition, that is, into the tradition in which such a way of writing was the common denominator as a form of self-cure. This allowed me to conclude my "Presentazione all'edizione italiana" (Conci, 1991), talking of the young Freud's letters to Eduard Silberstein as a form of self-cure through writing, and to implicitly ascribe them (I did not dare to be so explicit then!) to "the so-called analytic tradition" that he later founded.

Before saying a few words on the three chapters in Part One of this book, let me make a further but final step in terms of the definition I had proposed then, back in 1991, that the ongoing and continual self-analytic dimension of Freud's life and work constituted the basic ingredient of "the analytic tradition" we owe to him. I am referring here to the following words confirming my point of view that were written by Elisabeth Young-Bruehl in 1994, which I no longer had in mind when I was writing the paper "Freud's self-analysis: An interpersonally grounded process," found as Chapter 3 of this anthology. The words that follow belong to the final considerations of the important book chapter "A history of Freud's biographies" that Elisabeth Young-Bruehl wrote for the volume *Discovering the history of psychiatry* edited by Mark Micale and Roy Porter in 1994:

> The great weakness in the whole of the Freud biographical literature, in my estimation, is that it is all skewed in the same two ways. First, it is focused on the originary decade

of Freud's science to the neglect of his later work and to the neglect of a sense for the evolving whole of his work; and second, the originary decade is itself constantly read simplistically as a record of or a product of Freud's childhood, which has meant that Freud has not emerged as a character, a man with an adult character, a man who could be portrayed not just analyzed with more or less sophisticated versions of his own theories. Both of these limitations are reflected in the persistent idea that Freud's 'self-analysis' was confined to the period of the Fliess correspondence and *The interpretation of dreams*, whereas *it seems obvious that self-analysis was Freud's constant mode* and that his later work was as deeply indebted to his changing conception of himself as it was to his continued clinical experience. But important self-analytical results from Freud's later years, particularly those concerning his narcissism, have consistently been overlooked by his biographers. (Young-Bruehl, 1994, p. 170, emphasis added)

As you can see, Elisabeth Young-Bruehl (whom I was lucky enough to have the chance to get to know and whose sudden and premature death saddened me greatly) was not only a very good historian, but also a very good clinician. Unfortunately, all the good clinicians who contributed to the otherwise fine anthology on *Self-analysis. Critical inquiries, personal visions* edited by James Barron in 1993 kept identifying "self-analysis" with the work of self-reflection conducted by Freud in his letters to Fliess.

3. THE INDIVIDUAL CHAPTERS

This last section of this Introduction is aimed at introducing the reader to the chapters in Part One, taking as a point of departure the abstracts that accompanied the individual published papers, to which I will add some further notes and comments.

Let me start with the abstract from the original publication of Chapter 1, "The young Freud's letters to Eduard Silberstein—Early traces of some psychoanalytic concepts":

The author, after showing the importance of Freud's letters to E. Silberstein, in terms of retracing the roots of psychoanalysis to the young Freud's inner world, takes into consideration not only the relationship between the two members of the 'Academia Castellana', but also the young Sigmund's emotional vicissitudes in relation to his first love, Gisela Fluss. The hypothesis originally formulated by K. Eissler, according to which sublimation played a major role in the young Freud's psychic balance, finds further confirmation in these letters to Silberstein. This allows the author to bring back to Freud's emotional vicissitudes not only his later concept of female sexuality, but also his conceptualization of the analyst as a "blank screen". On the basis of the route taken in this paper, the author suggests to give more attention to the

relationship between our personal world and the technique
we use with our patients.

It is worth reading Chapter 1 first before coming
back to my notes and comments here. The first thing
that impresses me about this abstract is that the necessity
"to give more attention to the relationship between our
personal world and the technique we use with our patients"
was constantly a major preoccupation of mine. In fact,
this whole book, including the Afterword, represents a
consequence of such an inner necessity and orientation.
Second, I am ready to admit that today I of course find
it somewhat reductive to summarize Freud's concept of
the analyst in terms of the so-called "blank screen." On
the one hand, I have for years been aware of the fact that
Freud's concept of the analyst was and is much more
sophisticated and elastic than that. This conviction has
also arisen through the experience of teaching Freud's
technical papers to candidates, and seeing how much
they can still profit from them. In recent years I have
even had the experience of teaching them in Munich, that
is, the experience of reading and discussing them in the
original German with candidates from Munich Akademie
für Psychoanalyse und Psychotherapie. How well these
papers were and are written is of course easier to see in
the original language. On the other hand, in the last few
years I have also become more and more aware of how
Freud's technical stance was in some ways caricatured
in the interpersonal and relational literature, for reasons
that are not that clear even today.

When I reviewed the anthology dedicated by Ulrike
May and Elke Mühlleitner to a reconstruction of the life
and work of Edith Jacobson (1897–1978), I was very
surprised and impressed to learn that Theodore Jacobs
had experienced her as a supervisee as belonging:

> (together with Marianne Kris and Dora Hartmann) to a group
> of European immigrants who were 'very much engaged with
> and related to their patients', and this to the point that they
> worked 'in a way that resembled the approach employed
> by modern relational analysts' (from Jacobs' original text,
> p.331). (Conci, 2007, p. 120)

The recent biography of Paula Heimann (1899–1982)
published in Germany by Maren Holmes (2017) attests to
the fact that the Berlin-trained pioneer of the concept of
countertransference (see Heimann, 1950) also had a bipersonal concept of the analytic situation.

On the other hand, it was clearly Harry Stack Sullivan
(1892–1949) who formulated the concept of "participant
observation," around which he centered *The interpersonal*

theory of psychiatry (Sullivan, 1953) and constructed the technical approach that he presented in *The psychiatric interview* (Sullivan, 1954). I have dealt with his life and work in my book *Sullivan revisited – Life and work* (Conci, 2012a), and I deal with his work and legacy not only in Chapters 4 and 5, but also in Chapter 9, in which I present him as a pioneer of the "analytic field concept." Of course, I believe that this crucial contribution of his should be more widely known and acknowledged in the analytic community. In fact, it is my feeling that if it is true that we all today work on Freud's shoulders, this is also the case in terms of Sullivan's conceptualization of the clinical situation, that is, in terms of what—outside of the interpersonal tradition—is called "the bi-personal or intersubjective field." For example, Werner Bohleber does not specifically deal with Sullivan's work and legacy in his detailed 2013 review of the concept of intersubjectivity—as I believe he should have.

At the same time, I am very much aware of the fact that our clinical work and the theories we have developed about it, since Freud's time, entertain a very particular relationship with each other: for example, a new way of working very often comes to be adequately formulated only after it has become well established. This is why I, on the one hand, believe that Freud could not have formulated the concept of "transference" if he had not worked as a "participant observer" of his patients' problems, the concept of "participant observation" being a concept that went beyond his way of conceptualizing the analytic situation, and—as we can also say—his epistemology. And this is why I, on the other hand, believe that Sullivan knew and used in his clinical work not only the concept of "countertransference," but even the concept of "projective identification," although neither concept appears in his work. As I also wrote in the first part of this Introduction, the former was introduced by Freud through the paper he gave at the Nuremberg Congress in March 1910, and was not further articulated by him in his later work; the latter was formulated by Melanie Klein only in 1946, that is, many years after Sullivan had shown that he knew what it was all about, as he did through his pioneering work with schizophrenic patients in the 1920s. I am referring here to papers in the anthology *Schizophrenia as a human process* edited by Helen Swick Perry in 1962 (Sullivan, 1962), through which we learn that Sullivan experienced a wordless and regressed schizophrenic patient not as a patient "incapable of transference," as Freud would have classified him, but as a patient who, through his non verbal behavior, was putting the therapist in touch with the loneliness of the patient's internal world.

This is why I personally experience Freud and Sullivan as dialogical partners in a common enterprise, and how I do not have any problem in letting them speak with each other in my own mind. In my opinion, only by such exchanges—made possible by a sophisticated historical reconstruction of the evolution of our field—can our field evolve and create the climate of dialogue and collaboration we need, in order to best help and work with our patients and to come to new and better theories of the ways in which we do it.

I am happy to share this point of view with Henry Zvi Lothane, who in 1997 had already made Freud and Sullivan talk with each other in the paper "Freud and the interpersonal," and then kept working in this direction, formulating the Freudian/interpersonal concept of "dramatology" (see, for example, Lothane, 2009). I share this viewpoint too with Stefano Bolognini, whose book *Secret passages. The theory and technique of interpsychic relations* (2011) also centers around the need to create, not only inside ourselves, but also in the analytic community, a dialogue among a variety of analytic authors, all of whose intuitions, concepts, and feedbacks we need in terms of both our daily clinical work and the evolution of our discipline. In fact, this was also the viewpoint of both Johannes Cremerius and Gaetano Benedetti, who never limited themselves to just practicing what they already knew, but kept trying to reach out to new authors and new theories, and to prove their validity and usefulness. Both of them were, for example, fascinated by how Daniel Stern (1934–2012) could empirically validate Sullivan's interpersonal theory in his now classic book *The interpersonal world of the infant* (1985).

A classic paper on the subject of not only the particular interaction between theory and technique, but also the fictional dialogue between Sullivan and Freud that the author was able to articulate in it, is of course the 1983 paper by Merton Gill (1914–1994) with the title "The interpersonal paradigm and the degree of the therapist's involvement"—which, with Maria Luisa Mantovani, I translated into Italian in the mid-1990s for *Psicoterapia e Scienze Umane*. In it we read these now famous statements:

> I summarize then that while it is a caricature of the Freudian view to say that the analyst is a blank screen or a mirror, it is true that the Freudian view sees the analyst as appropriately participating in only a minor way. I allow myself a verbal play

> by calling the analyst who is considered to be a participant
> in only a minor way the precipitant observer rather than the
> participant observer. (Gill, 1983, p. 210)

And:

> In this respect there is an irony in the difference between
> Sullivan and Freud. Sullivan made the interpersonal
> paradigm explicit while Freud did not, but Sullivan did much
> less to make the transference in the analytic relationship
> explicit than did Freud. (Gill, 1983, pp. 221–222)

Also because of the important clinical perspective it
introduces, I still value the classical paper—mentioned
and referenced in Chapter 1—by the author of *The myth
of mental illness* (1974), Thomas Szasz (1920–2012): "II.
The concept of transference as a defense for the analyst."
In this, he warns against the risk of making such a use
of this concept as "to place the person of the analyst
beyond the reality testing of patients, colleagues, and self"
(Szasz, 1963, p. 443). The same is true for one of the best-
known papers by Edgar Levenson—again mentioned
and referenced in Chapter 1—"Facts or fantasies: On the
nature of psychoanalytic data." Levenson, through other
papers on the topic as well, has greatly contributed to
further developing Sullivan's legacy of a clinically useful
reformulation of the relationship between our internal
work and external reality. In fact, in the last twenty-five
years I have not only kept reading Levenson's work, but
also reviewed his collection of papers *The purloined self*
in the *International Forum of Psychoanalysis* (Conci,
1993). At the time I was writing Chapter 1, I did not yet
personally know Irwin Hirsch, whose paper "Varying
modes of analytic participation" I also mention in the
chapter; Irwin has published since then not only a series
of thoughtful and provocative papers, but also a series
of books, including *Coasting in the countertransference*
(2008), and has been a good friend since we met at the 2006
Ferenczi Conference held in Baden-Baden (Germany).

Last but not least, I am very happy that Marco
Bacciagaluppi, whose help I acknowledge at the end of
Chapter 1, has not only kept accompanying me through
my professional development, but even found the time to
go over all the new pages I wrote for this book, providing
feedback and suggesting a series of corrections. Back in
the fall of 1991, he had helped me reorganize my August
1991 Stockholm paper, whose original title was "Male and
female themes in the letters of S. Freud to E. Silberstein"
into the paper that came out in the first volume of the
International Forum of Psychoanalysis—in which form
the reader can find it here as Chapter 1. To Marco I also
owe my knowledge of some of the authors and papers

I refer to in it, for example Erich Fromm's (1900–1980) important 1935 paper "The social determinants of psychoanalytic therapy"—the English-language title given to it by Ernst Falzeder, who translated it (Fromm, 2000) for a monographic issue of the *International Forum of Psychoanalysis* dedicated to Erich Fromm that I edited. In this paper, Fromm retraced some aspects of Freud's concept of neurosis and analytic therapy to the underlying "patricentric" character of both his personality and his theory, hidden by the bourgeois concept of "tolerance"; he also showed how Ferenczi and Groddeck went much further than Freud in terms of their capacity to identify with and stand behind their patients. One of the greatest joys of our profession of physicians and psychoanalysts has to do with the possibility of keeping in life-long contact with a certain number of colleagues, and this has been the case with Marco and me. Given our familiarity with each other, I was happy to accept his invitation to write a Preface to his 2012 anthology of papers *Paradigms in psychoanalysis – An integration* (Conci, 2012b).

Before coming to the two final topics connected to my presentation of Chapter 1, let me say a few words on how grateful I still am to the late colleague Joseph Barnett (1926–1988), and his late wife Tess Forrest Barnett (1922–2009) for having proposed to the IFPS and financed the Joseph Barnett Candidates Award, which I shared with a woman colleague from New York City at the VIth Scientific Conference of the IFPS held in Stockholm in August 1991, with the title "Male and female themes in psychoanalysis." Receiving this Award changed my whole professional life, firmly connecting it to the *International Forum of Psychoanalysis*, of which I have been a co-editor-in-chief since 2007. Because of how it had changed my life, I proposed to both the IFPS and to the German Psychoanalytic Society (DPG) that they set up similar prizes, which I have financed and which have been assigned every two years since 2014 at the IFPS fora and annually since 2016 at the national congresses of the DPG. The winning papers are published in the *International Forum* and in the German journal *Forum der Psychoanalyse*. It appears that not only the future of psychoanalysis, but even the future of activities such as reading and writing, which have since the beginning accompanied our profession, are at risk today. Reading and writing have always been part of the main vehicles of the kind of self-reflection that our profession stands for, and I hope that the Candidates Award I founded will contribute to keeping these activities and our profession alive—in whatever form this will be.

And now to the last two topics of Chapter 1, which I would like to add some comments to. If in the first part of this section I dealt with the topic of Freud's theory of analytic technique, I also deal in Chapter 1 with the complementary topic of how Freud really worked. A whole series of papers and books on this was produced before and during my training, starting with Samuel Lipton's 1977 paper "The advantages of Freud's technique as shown in the analysis of the Rat Man," continuing with Luciana Nissim Momigliano's 1987 paper "A spell in Vienna – but was Freud a Freudian?," and reaching Paul Roazen's 1995 book *How Freud worked. First-hand accounts of patients*. I would like to deal with this topic because I want to inform the reader about two recent evolutions in our approach to it.

The first of these is connected with the possibility to freely consult the Freud Archives of the Library of Congress, which I mentioned above. The Berlin colleague Ulrike May has done so, and has reported the results of her research in the paper, "Müssen wir unser Bild von Freud verändern? Überlegungen auf der Basis einer neuen Quelle: K.R. Eisslers Interviews mit Patienten und Zeitgenossen Sigmund Freuds" (see the English translation in the References), which she gave in Berlin on Saturday March 2, 2018, in the context of the XXXIst Symposium on the History of Psychoanalysis. Here is her conclusion based on the examination of a series of interviews conducted by Kurt Eissler: that Freud's priority was not represented by his patients, but by his theory, that is, by the confirmation of old and the elaboration of new hypotheses on our unconscious mental functioning, which the work with his patients allowed him to do.

The second new evolution has to do with the recent reconceptualization of the history not only of psychoanalytic technique, but also of psychoanalysis tout court in terms of the history of the analysis of and use of our countertransference. Here is how the historian of psychoanalysis John Forrester (1949–2015), whose untimely death deprived us of a very important source of inspiration in our field, talked about this in a paper delivered at the University of Ghent in May 2000:

> One of the basic worries, basic questions I have asked and I have yet to answer adequately comes from the writings of Jacques Derrida: how can an autobiographical writing, in the abyss of an undetermined self-analysis, give birth to a world-wide institution? (Derrida, 1980, p.324). In other words, how does one go from Freud's self-analysis and its record in *The*

> *interpretation of dreams* – and all of the other analytic acts
> which can legitimately be seen as extensions of Freud's self-
> analysis – to that cultural presence known as 'psychoanalysis'?
>
> A simple psychoanalytic answer to Derrida's question
> might be the following: psychoanalysis is simply the acting-
> out of Freud's countertransference to his patients, his
> colleagues, his family and his culture. (Forrester, 2017, p. 233)

This is precisely the research line pursued for a long
time and eventually presented in all its complexity by
Carlo Bonomi in his book *The cut and the building of
psychoanalysis. Volume 2. Sigmund Freud and Sándor
Ferenczi* (2018a). Carlo Bonomi revisited Ferenczi's
Clinical diary (1932–1933), originally edited in French
by Judit Dupont in 1985, in terms of his elaboration of
the countertransference problems encountered, but not
dealt with, by Freud in the treatment of the traumatic
dimension of his patients' problems. Also from this point
of view, Ferenczi's and Sullivan's clinical research work
developed parallel to each other. But here is the latest
version of this original historical reconstruction, as Carlo
Bonomi presented it in Florence on Friday May 3, 2018,
at the XIIIth International Sándor Ferenczi Conference
that he himself chaired:

> In his meditations Ferenczi went back repeatedly to the
> birth of psychoanalysis, to its taking shape in a new kind of
> space, that, thanks to the intimacy that accompanied a longer
> duration, enabled traumas to emerge not only as memories,
> but also as experiences which could affect the analyst in
> deep ways. In his *Clinical diary*, Ferenczi observed that
> Freud, frightened by this unexpected development, stepped
> back from participation and emotionally abandoned the
> traumatized patient . . . . Ferenczi's view was that Freud
> remained committed to analysis "intellectually but not
> emotionally" (Ferenczi, 1985, p.93). (Bonomi, 2018b, p. 3)

I come now briefly to the final topic of Chapter 1, that
is, the young Freud's apparently traumatic relationship
with Gisela Fluss, and his prolonged incapacity to
develop a close relationship with a woman his age. This
biographical background influenced his later approach to
and elaboration of the basic concepts of an analytically
oriented feminine psychology. I do believe that, in spite of
Freud's prejudices against women, which we can already
find in his letters to Eduard Silberstein, psychoanalysis
can be used for the psychic emancipation not only of
men, but also of women. This was also the point of view
that guided Lisa Appignanesi and John Forrester in the
work of writing their by now classical book on *Freud and
women*, the 2005 Foreword to the paperback edition of
which they concluded with the following words:

> What is clear is that in their encounter with Freud and
> psychoanalysis, as well as in their shaping of what it became,

the women in these pages tested the foundations of what it meant to be woman. Their stories, alongside Freud's, are filled with the bracing air of the beginning of the last century. Sometimes, what now feel like their certainties, as well as their sense of risk, have a naiveté to them. But the adventure of the modern in which they embarked with all its sufferings and turmoil, was what turned a more conventional, prosaic age upside down. Our world is the result. Understanding them helps to unsettle our own certainties. (Appignanesi and Forrester, 2005, p. xxv)

Let us now move to Chapter 2 in the current book. Here is the abstract that accompanied its 1996 publication in the *International Forum of Psychoanalysis*:

After demonstrating the unsatisfactory nature of the reasons Freud gave us for his choice of medical school, the author shows how it is possible to throw new light on it on the basis of his letters to his adolescent friend Emil Fluss. This relationship played a crucial role in forcing Freud to come out of his isolation and the defensive dissection of his feelings that he used to practice, and thus experience an intimate relationship as a better source of self-knowledge and growth. This is the context in which his choice of medical school took place, which can consequently be conceptualized in terms of his unconscious and self-concealed pursuit of a growth-promoting and self-healing agency and experience. It thus was an interpersonal event which compelled him to deviate from his original purpose, i.e. the study of law or the humanities, and take up the "unconscious plan" to soften his defensive apparatus. This is consequently the new meaning we can attach to the experience of "rest and full satisfaction" he made in Brücke's laboratory between 1876 and 1882. What he defines as the "triumph" of his life thus also acquires a new meaning: the possibility to take up again his original interest in psychology not on an exclusively defensive basis any more, but eventually in a constructive way. Such a personal itinerary also represented one of Freud's most convincing experiences of the power of the unconscious, as he formulated it in his book on dreams – and as he articulated it in the new field of psychoanalysis. Since, in the author's opinion, the attempt at self-cure lies at the root of our own choice of our profession, this must have been also Freud's case, at a much earlier time than what is traditionally referred to as his self-analysis. At variance with what Freud himself used to claim, the study of his life remains one of the best keys to the understanding of his intellectual legacy.

Now that I read the article again, I find myself exclaiming: "You have by now given the reader so much background information, in order for them to appreciate the content and the meaning of this chapter, that no more information is needed!" Of course, I am highly relieved by this feeling, after having written such a long Introduction. In fact, it has become longer than I had imagined, not only because in it I have dealt with a topic that I like and am very familiar with, but also because I felt that the reader might only be able to appreciate the first three chapters of this anthology of papers if I helped them become a little familiar with this neglected area of Freud studies as a whole.

On the other hand, reading the abstract of Chapter 2 also made me feel that it was a good idea to write the Afterword I wrote last summer, in which I specifically describe the background of my own choice of medical school. What I wrote in the mid-1990s about Freud, and what I wrote about myself in the Afterword last summer complement and integrate with each other well, and I advise the reader to take a look at the Afterword. In it, there is also the important information that I have already given above about the publication of the Italian edition— that I worked on together with my wife Doris—of the young Freud's letters to Emil Fluss, which appeared in the Italian *Rivista di psicoanalisi* in 2016 (see Conci, 2016), thanks to the interest that its editor-in-chief, Giuseppe Civitarese, showed for them, and to the editorial help I received from Sandro Panizza, the coordinator of the journal's editorial board. As far as the original publication of the 1996 paper is concerned, after its publication in the *International Forum of Psychoanalysis*, it came out (together with the other papers of Issue 2/1996 and all the papers of issue 3/1996) in the volume edited by Patrick Mahony, Carlo Bonomi, and Jan Stensson with the title *Behind the scenes. Freud in correspondence.*

Finally, here is the shorter abstract that accompanied the original 1998 publication of Chapter 3:

On the basis of the assumption that the understanding of Freud's work can gain much from illuminating his own psychological development, the author tries to reconstruct the evolution of his self-analysis. Against the common view of placing it in the context of his relationship with Fliess, the author shows how it actually evolved out of a whole series of experiences and relationships. Freud's self-analysis was initially nourished by his study of the Greek and Latin classics; it acquired the necessary interpersonal dimension through his relationship with Emil Fluss and Eduard Silberstein; it gained a cathartic and thus therapeutic quality through his relationship with Martha; and it eventually became a professional enterprise once his patients forced Freud, with the help of Wilhelm Fliess, to systematically look into himself.

I find this so clear that I do not have anything more to add to it, and this enables me to eventually be able to wish the reader enjoyment of it—and to ask for any comments and feedback readers might have.

REFERENCES

Accerboni, A.M. (1998). Vittorio Benussi e Edoardo Weiss a confronto sull'inconscio [Vittorio Benussi and Edoardo Weiss and their dialogue on the unconscious]. *Rivista di Psicoanalisi* 44:813–833.

Alexander, F., & Selesnick, S.T. (1965). Freud–Bleuler correspondence. *Archives of General Psychiatry* 12:1–9.

Anzieu, D. (1986). *Freud's Self-analysis*. London: Hogarth Press. (Original French edition, 1975).

Appignanesi, L., & Forrester, J. (2005). *Freud and Women* (revised paperback edition). London: Phoenix.

Barron, J.W. (ed.) (1993). *Self-analysis. Critical Inquiries, Personal Visions*. Hillsdale, NJ: Analytic Press.

Behling, K. (2004). *Martha Freud: A Biography*. Cambridge: Polity Press. (Original German edition, 2002).

Bentnick van Schoonheten, A. (2015). *Karl Abraham: Life and Work, a Biography*. London: Karnac.

Bernfeld, S. (1946). An unknown autobiographical fragment by Freud. *American Imago* 4:3–19.

—— (1949). Freud's scientific beginnings. *American Imago* 6:163–196.

—— (1951). Sigmund Freud, M.D., 1882–1885. *International Journal of Psychoanalysis* 32:204–217.

Bernfeld, S., & Cassirer Bernfeld, S. (1981). *Bausteine zur Freud-Biographik* [Foundations of a biographical approach to Freud] (Grubrich-Simitis I, Ed.). Frankfurt: Fischer.

Binswanger, L. (1942). *Grundformen und Erkenntnis menschlichen Daseins* [Basic forms and the realization of human " being-in-the-world"]. Heidelberg: Ansanger, 1993.

—— (1957). *Sigmund Freud: Reminiscences of a Friendship*. New York: Grune & Stratton. (Original German edition, 1956).

Boehlich, W. (Ed.) (1990). *The Letters of Sigmund Freud to Eduard Silberstein* (A.J. Pomerans, Trans.). Cambridge, MA: Harvard University Press. (Original German edition, 1989).

Bohleber, W. (2013). The concept of intersubjectivity in psychoanalysis: Taking critical stock. *International Journal of Psychoanalysis* 94:799–823.

Bolognini, S. (2011). *Secret Passages. The Theory and Technique of Interpsychic Relations*. London,: Routledge. (Original Italian edition, 2008).

Bonomi, C. (2018a). *The Cut and the Building of Psychoanalysis*. Vol. 2, *Sigmund Freud and Sándor Ferenczi*. London: Routledge.

—— (2018b). Ferenczi: Heir of Freud or dissident. A personal view. Paper presented at the XIIIth International Sándor Ferenczi Conference, May 4, 2018, Florence, Italy.

Conci, M. (1990). S. Freud studente a Trieste nelle lettere ad E. Silberstein [S. Freud as a student in Trieste in his letters to E. Silberstein]. *Psicoterapia e Scienze Umane* 25(4):45–60.

—— (1991). Presentazione all'edizione italiana [Introduction to the Italian edition]. In M. Conci (Ed.), *Sigmund Freud – "Querido amigo . . . ". Lettere dell'adolescenza a Eduard Silberstein 1871–1881* (pp. vii–xxxiv). Turin: Bollati Boringhieri.

—— (1992). The young Freud's letters to Eduard Silberstein – Early traces of some psychoanalytic concepts. *International Forum of Psychoanalysis* 1:37–43.

—— (1993). Review of the book by E.A. Levenson "The purloined self. Interpersonal perspectives in psychoanalysis", Contemporary Psychoanalysis Books 1991. *International Forum of Psychoanalysis* 2:193–196.

———— (1996). Review of the book by P. Roazen "How Freud worked. First-hand accounts of patients", Aronson 1995. *International Forum of Psychoanalysis* 5:151–153.

———— (2006). Review of the book by P. Roazen "Edoardo Weiss. The house that Freud built", Aronson 2005. *International Forum of Psychoanalysis* 15:58–64.

———— (2007). Review of the book edited by U. May and E. Mühlleitner "Edith Jacobson. Sie selbst und die Welt ihrer Objekte. Leben, Werk, Erinnerungen" [Edith Jacobson. She herself and the world of her objects. Life, work, memories], Psychosozial-Verlag 2005. *Psychoanalysis and History* 9:111–122.

———— (2012a). *Sullivan Revisited – Life and Work* (2nd edn.). Trento: Tangram. (Original Italian edition, 2000).

———— (2012b). Foreword. In M. Bacciagaluppi, *Paradigms in Psychoanalysis – An Integration* (pp. xiii–xvi). London: Karnac.

———— (2016). Le lettere del giovane Freud a Emil Fluss *(1872–1874)* [The young Freud's letters to Emil Fluss]. *Rivista di Psicoanalisi* 62:1057–1084.

———— (2018). Freud and Ferenczi – From Psychoanalysis as a "professional and personal home" to the creation of a "psychoanalytic home" for the patient. Paper prepared for the XIII International Sándor Ferenczi Conference, May 2018, Florence.

Conci, M. (Ed.) (1991). *Sigmund Freud – "Querido amigo . . . ". Lettere dell'adolescenza a Eduard Silberstein 1871–1881.* Turin: Bollati Boringhieri. (Original German edition, 1989).

Corsa, R. (2013). *Edoardo Weiss a Trieste con Freud. Alle origini della psicoanalisi italiana* [Edoardo Weiss in Trieste with Freud. At the origins of Italian psychoanalysis]. Rome: Alpes.

———— (2017). *Vanda Shrenger Weiss. La prima psicoanalista in Italia. La psicoanalisi a Roma in epoca fascista* [Vanda Shrenger Weiss. The first Italian psychoanalyst. Psychoanalysis in Rome at the time of Fascism]. Rome: Alpes.

Cremerius, J. (1985). *Il mestiere dell'analista* [The analyst's profession]. Turin: Bollati Boringhieri.

———— (1987). Alla ricerca di tracce perdute. Il "Movimento psicoanalitico" e la miseria dell'istituzione psicoanalitica [Looking for lost traces. The "psychoanalytic movement" and the misery of the psychoanalytic institution]. *Psicoterapia e Scienze Umane* 21(3):3–34. (Original German publication, 1986).

———— (1989a). Analisi didattica e potere. *Psicoterapia e Scienze Umane* 23(3):3–28. (Published in English as: Training analysis and power: The transformation of a method of training and learning into an instrument of power in institutionalized psychoanalysis. *Free Associations* 1:114–138, 1990. Original German publication, 1988).

———— (1989b). Review of the book by S. Ferenczi "Clinical diary", Fischer 1988. *Psicoterapia e Scienze Umane* 23(3):121–128. (Original German publication, 1988).

Decker, H. (2015). Review of the book "Sigmund Freud–Anna Freud correspondence, 1904–1938", Polity Books 2014. *Habsburg*, October 2015.

de Mijolla, A. (1997). Images of Freud from his correspondence. In P. Mahony, C. Bonomi, and J. Stensson (Eds.), *Behind the Scenes.*

Freud in Correspondence (pp. 369–412). Oslo: Scandinavian University Press.

Eissler, K.R. (1974a). Über Freuds Freundschaft mit Wilhelm Fliess nebst einem Anhang über Freuds Adoleszenz und einer historischen Bemerkung über Freuds Jugendstil [On Freud's friendship to Wilhelm Fliess and an appendix on Freud's adolescence plus a historical observation on Freud's adolescent style]. In K.R. Eissler, S. Freud., S. Goeppert, and K. Schröter, *Aus Freuds Sprachwelt und andere Beiträge* [From Freud's linguistic world and other contributions] (pp. 39–100). Bern: Huber.

———— (1974b). Psychoanalytische Einfälle zu Freuds "Zerstreute(n) Gedanken" [Analytic free associations to Freud's "Aphorisms"]. In K.R. Eissler, S. Freud, S. Goeppert, and K. Schröter, *Aus Freuds Sprachwelt und andere Beiträge* [From Freud's linguistic world and other contributions] (pp. 103–128). Bern: Huber.

Eissler, K.R. (Ed.) (1974). Sigmund Freud: Zerstreute Gedanken [Sigmund Freud: Aphorisms]. In K.R. Eissler, S. Freud, S. Goeppert, and K. Schröter, *Aus Freuds Sprachwelt und andere Beiträge* [From Freud's linguistic world and other contributions] (p.101). Bern: Huber.

———— (1978). Creativity and adolescence. The effect of trauma in Freud's adolescence. *Psychoanalytic Study of the Child* 33:461–517.

Falzeder, E. (Ed.) (2002). *The Complete Correspondence of Sigmund Freud and Karl Abraham 1907–1925*. London: Karnac.

———— (2007). Is there still an unknown Freud? A note on the publications of Freud's texts and on unpublished documents. *Psychoanalysis and History* 9:201–232.

Falzeder, E., Brabant, E., & Giampieri-Deutsch, P. (Eds.) (1992–2000). *The Correspondence of Sigmund Freud and Sándor Ferenczi*. Vol. 1, *1908–1914*. Vol. 2, *1914–1919*. Vol. 3, *1920–1933*. Cambridge, MA: Harvard University Press. (Original German edition, 1993–2005).

Federn, P. (1952). *Ego Psychology and the Psychoses* (E. Weiss, Ed.). New York: Basic Books.

Ferenczi, S. (1988). *The Clinical Diary* (J. Dupont, Ed.). Cambridge, MA: Harvard University Press. (Original French edition, 1985).

Ferenczi, S., & Rank, O. (1925). *The Development of Psychoanalysis*. New York: Nervous and Mental Disease Publishing. (Original German edition, 1923).

Fichtner, G. (1989). Freuds Briefe als historische Quelle [Freud's letters as historical source]. *Psyche* 43:803–829.

Fichtner. G. (Ed.) (2002). *The Freud–Binswanger correspondence 1908–1938*. New York: Other Press. (Original German edition, 1992).

Fichtner, G., Grubrich-Simitis, I., & Hirschmüller, A. (Eds.) (2011, 2013, 2015). *Die Brautbriefe. Drei Bände* [The bridal letters. Three volumes]. Frankfurt: Fischer.

Forrester, J. (2017). Colleagues, correspondents and the institution – Or: is psychoanalysis without institutions possible? *Psychoanalysis and History* 19:233–237.

Freud, E.L. (1960). Preface. In S. Freud, *The Letters of Sigmund Freud, 1873–1939* (pp. iv–vii). New York: Basic Books.

Freud, E.L., (Ed.) (1960). *The Letters of Sigmund Freud*. New York: Basic Books.

———— (1969). Some early unpublished letters of Freud. *International*

Journal of Psychoanalysis 50:419–427.

Freud, S. (1877). Beobachtungen über Gestaltung und feineren Bau der als Hoden beschriebenen Lappenorgane des Aals (Observations on the form and fine structure of the lobular organs of the eel described as testicles). In C. Tögel (Ed.), with the collaboration of U. Zerfass, *Sigmund Freud Gesamtausgabe. Band 1, 1877–1885* (Sigmund Freud. Complete works. Vol. 1, 1877–1885) (pp. 25–38). Giessen: Psychosozial-Verlag.

——— (1899). Screen memories. *Standard Edition* 3, pp. 299–322.

——— (1900). The interpretation of dreams. *Standard Edition* 4 and 5.

——— (1907). Delusions and dreams in Jensen's Gradiva. *Standard Edition* 9, pp. 1–96.

——— (1910). The future prospects of psychoanalytic therapy. *Standard Edition* 11, pp. 139–151.

——— (1927). The future of an illusion. *Standard Edition* 21, pp. 3–58.

Fromm, E. (2000). The social determinants of psychoanalytic therapy (E. Falzeder, Translator). *International Forum of Psychoanalysis* 9:149–165.

Gedo, J.E., & Wolf, E.S. (1970). The "Ich." letters. In J.E. Gedo and G.H. Pollock (Eds.), *Freud: The Fusion of Science and Humanism* (pp. 71–86). New York: International Universities Press.

——— (1976). Freud's *Novelas ejemplares*. In J.E. Gedo and G. H. Pollock (eds.), *Freud: The Fusion of Science and Humanism* (pp. 87–111). New York: International Universities Press.

Gill, M.N. (1983). The interpersonal paradigm and the degree of the therapist's involvement. *Contemporary Psychoanalysis* 19:200–237.

Gödde, G. (1990). Freuds Adoleszenz im Lichte seiner Briefe an Eduard Silberstein [Freud's adolescence in the light of his letters to Eduard Silberstein]. *Luzifer-Amor*, No. 6:7–26.

Grosskurth, P. (1991). *The Secret Ring. Freud's Inner Circle and the Politics of Psychoanalysis*. London: Cape.

Grotjahn, M. (1976). Freuds Briefwechsel [Freud's correspondence]. In D. Eicke (Ed.), *Psychologie des "20. Jahrhunderts". Tiefenpsychologie. Band 1. Sigmund Freud – Leben und Werk* [Psychology of the 20th century. Deep psychology. Vol. 1, Sigmund Freud – Life and work] (pp. 29–140). Munich: Kindler.

Grubrich-Simitis, I. (1997). *Back to Freud's Texts: Making Silent Documents Speak*. New Haven, CT: Yale University Press. (Original German edition, 1993).

——— (2005). "Wie sieht es mit der Behzieungs- und Beleuchtungsfrage bei Ihnen aus, Herr Professor?". Zum Erscheinen des Freud-Eitingon-Briefwechsels ["How do heat and light work at your house, Professor Freud?" On the publication of the correspondence of Freud and Eitingon]. *Psyche* 59:266–290.

——— (2011). Eine Einführung [An introduction]. In G. Fichtner, I. Grubrich-Simitis, and A. Hirschmüller (Eds.), *Die Brautbriefe. Band 1. Sei mein wie ich mir's denke* [The bridal letters. Vol. 1, Be mine the way I see it] (pp. 12–57). Frankfurt: Fischer.

——— (2012). Keime psychoanalytischer Grundkonzepte. Die Brautbriefe von Sigmund Freud an Martha Bernays [Seeds of core psychoanalytic concepts. On the courtship letters of Sigmund Freud and Martha Bernays]. *Psyche* 66:385–407.

Haynal, A., & Falzeder, E. (2002). Introduction. In E. Falzeder (Ed.), *The Complete Correspondence of Sigmund Freud and Karl Abraham*

1907–1925 (pp. xix–xxx). London: Karnac.

Heimann, P. (1950). On countertransference. *International Journal of Psychoanalysis* 31:81–84.

Hermanns, L. (2018). Karl Abraham – Ernest Jones. Briefwechsel 1911–1925 [Karl Abraham – Ernest Jones. Correspondence 1911–1925]. *Luzifer-Amor*, No. 61:40–91.

Herzog, P. (1987). The myth of Freud as anti-philosopher. In P. Stepansky (Ed.), *Freud: Appraisals and Reappraisals – Contributions to Freud Studies*. Vol. 2 (pp. 163–189). Hillsdale, NJ: Analytic Press.

Hirsch, I. (2008). *Coasting in the Countertransference*. New York: Analytic Press.

Hirschmüller, A. (1978). *Physiologie und Psychoanalyse in Leben und Werk Josef Breuers* [Physiology and psychoanalysis in the life and work of Josef Breuer]. Bern: Huber.

——— (1991). *Freuds Begegnung mit der Psychiatrie. Von der Hirnmythologie zur Neurosenlehre* [Freud's encounter with psychiatry. From brain mythology to the theory of the neuroses]. Tübingen: Diskord.

——— (2004). *Binswangers psychiatrische Klinik Bellevue in Kreuzlingen* [Binswanger's psychiatric hospital Bellevue in Kreuzlingen]. Tübingen: Universität Tübingen.

Hirschmüller, A. (Ed.) (2005). *Sigmund Freud Minna Bernays Briefwechsel 1882–1938* [The correspondence of Sigmund Freud and Minna Bernays 1882–1938]. Tübingen: Diskord.

——— (2013). Kokain: seit Frühjahr 1884 Sigmund Freuds neues Forschungsfeld [Cocain: The new research field of Sigmund Freud since the spring of 1884]. In G. Fichtner, I. Grubrich-Simitis, and A. Hirschmüller (Eds.), *Die Brautbriefe. Band 2* [The bridal letters. Vol. 2] (pp. 11–22). Frankfurt: Fischer.

Holmes, M. (2017). *Paula Heimann – Leben, Werk und Einfluss auf die Psychoanalyse* [Paula Heimann – Life, work and influence upon psychoanalysis]. Giessen: Psychosozial-Verlag.

Holt, R.R. (1992). Review of "The letters of Sigmund Freud to Eduard Silberstein, 1871–1881", Harvard University Press 1990. *Psychoanalytic Books* 3:236–243.

Honegger, M. (Ed.) (1970). *Briefwechsel Georg Groddeck-Sigmund Freud* (The correspondence of Sigmund Freud and Georg Groddeck). Wiesbaden: Limes.

Jones, E. (1953, 1955, 1957). *The life and work of Sigmund Freud. Vol. 1, The Young Freud, 1856–1900. Vol. 2, Years of Maturity, 1901–1919. Vol. 3, The Last Phase, 1919–1939*. New York: Basic Books.

Jung, C.G. (1963). *Memories, Dreams, Reflections*. London: Pantheon Books. (Original German edition, 1962).

Klein, M. (1946). Notes on some schizoid mechanisms. *International Journal of Psychoanalysis* 27:99–110.

Küchenhoff, B. (2012). Zur Psychologie der Psychosen im Briefwechsel zwischen Eugen Bleuler und Sigmund Freud [On the psychology of the psychoses in the correspondence between Eugen Bleuler and Sigmund Freud]. In M. Schröter (Ed.), *Sigmund Freud und Eugen Bleuler. "Ich bin zuversichtlich, wir erobern bald die Psychiatrie". Briefwechsel 1904–1937* [Sigmund Freud and Eugen Blueler. "I am positive that we will soon conquer psychiatry". Correspondence 1904–1937] (pp. 227–242). Basel: Schwabe Verlag.

Laible, E. (1993). "Through privation to knowledge": Unknown documents from Freud's university years. *International Journal of*

Psychoanalysis 74:775–790.

Lieberman, E.J. (1985). *Acts of Will. The Life and Work of Otto Rank.* New York: Free Press.

Lieberman, E.J., & Kramer, R. (Eds.) (2012). *The Letters of Sigmund Freud and Otto Rank. Inside Psychoanalysis.* Baltimore, MD: Johns Hopkins University Press.

Lipton, S.D. (1977). The advantages of Freud's technique as shown in the analysis of the Rat Man. *International Journal of Psychoanalysis* 58:255–273.

Lothane, H.Z. (1997). Freud and the interpersonal. *International Forum of Psychoanalysis* 6:175–184.

———— (2009). Dramatology in life, disorder, and psychoanalytic therapy: A further contribution to interpersonal psychoanalysis. *International Forum of Psychoanalysis* 18:135–148.

———— (2016). Book essay – Freud and Minna: Facts and fictions. *Journal of the American Psychoanalytic Association* 64:1237–1254.

Maetzner, C. (2012). Book review: Sigmund Freud, Martha Bernays: Die Brautbriefe, Band 1. Sei Mein, Wie Ich Mir's Denke, Juni 1882–Juli 1883 [The letters during their engagement, Vol. 1. Be mine the way I see it, June 1882–July 1883]. *Journal of the American Psychoanalytic Association* 60:1087–1093.

Mahony, P. (1987). *Freud as a Writer.* New Haven, CT: International Universities Press.

Mahony, P., Bonomi, C., & Stensson, J. (Eds.) (1997). *Behind the Scenes. Freud in Correspondence.* Oslo: Scandinavian University Press.

Masson, J.M. (Ed.) (1985). *The Complete Letters of Sigmund Freud and Wilhelm Fliess 1887–1904.* Cambridge, MA: Harvard University Press.

May, R., Angel, E., & Ellenberger, H.F. (Eds.) (1958). *Existence: A New Dimension in Psychiatry and Psychology.* New York: Basic Books.

May, U. (2018). Müssen wir unser Bild von Freud verändern? Überlegungen auf der Basis einer neuen Quelle: K.R. Eisslers Interviews mit Patienten und Zeitgenossen Sigmund Freuds [Do we have to change our image of Freud? Reflections on the basis of a new source: K.R. Eissler's interviews with patients and contemporaries of Sigmund Freud]. Paper presented on March 3, 2018, Berlin, Germany.

Mayer-Palmedo, I. (Ed.) (2014). *Sigmund Freud–Anna Freud: Correspondence 1904–1938.* Cambridge, MA: Polity Books. (Original German edition, 2006).

McGuire, W. (Ed.) (1974). *The Freud/Jung letters. The Correspondence between Sigmund Freud and C.G. Jung* (R. Manheim and R.F.C. Hull, Translators) Princeton, NJ: Princeton University Press. (English and Italian editions, 1974).

Meng, H. (1963). Preface. In H. Meng and E.L. Freud (Eds.), *Psychoanalysis and Faith. The Letters Sigmund Freud and Oskar Pfister* (pp. 8–10). London: International Psychoanalytic Library.

Meng, H., & Freud, E.L. (Eds.) (1963). *Psychoanalysis and Faith: The Letters of Sigmund Freud and Oskar Pfister.* London: International Psychoanalytic Library.

Molnar, M. (2015). " . . . But no more romance . . . ". Review of the "*Brautbriefe. Band 2. Unser 'Roman in Fortsetzungen'*". *Psychoanalysis and History* 17:121–138.

Montinari, M. (1983). Introduzione [Introduction]. In E. Pfeiffer (Ed.), *Sigmund Freud–Lou Andreas-Salomé – Eros e conoscenza. Lettere*

1912–1936 (Sigmund Freud and Lou Andreas-Salomé – Eros and knowledge. Letters 1912–1936) (pp. ix–xiv). Turin: Bollati Boringhieri.

Nissim Momigliano, L. (1987). A spell in Vienna – but was Freud a Freudian? An investigation into Freud's technique between 1920 and 1938, based on the public testimony of former analysands. *International Review of Psychoanalysis* 14:373–389.

Nunberg, H., & Federn, E. (Eds.) (1962–1975). *Minutes of the Vienna Psychoanalytic Society. Four volumes, 1906–1918*. New Haven, CT: International Universities Press.

Paskauskas, R.A. (Ed.) (1993). *The Complete Correspondence of Sigmund Freud and Ernest Jones 1908–1939*. Cambridge, MA: Harvard University Press.

Pfeiffer, E. (Ed.) (1966). *Sigmund Freud and Lou Andreas-Salomé: Letters*. London: Hogarth Press.

Pfister, O. (1927). The illusion of a future: A friendly disagreement with Prof. Sigmund Freud. *International Journal of Psychoanalysis* 74:557–579.

Rank, O. (1952). *The Trauma of Birth*. New York: Brunner. (Original German edition, 1924).

Reicheneder, J.G. (2015). Buch-Essay: Sigmund Freuds voranlytische Schriften [Book essay: Sigmund Freud's pre-analytic wrtings]. *Psyche* 70:729–741.

Reidel-Schrewe, U. (1994). Freud's début in the sciences. In S.L. Gilman, J. Birmele, J. Geller, and V.D. Greenberg (Eds.), *Reading Freud's Reading* (pp. 1–22). New York: New York University Press.

Reppen, J.(2003). Ludwig Binswanger and Sigmund Freud: Portrait of a friendship. *Psychoanalytic Review* 90:281–291.

Riepe, M. (2016). Die Zauberkraft der Worte. Von der Neurologie zur Sprache. Freuds voranalytische Schriften und ihre Bedeutung für die analytische Methode [The magic power of words. From neurology to language. Freud's pre-analytic writings and their importance for the analytic method]. *Psyche* 70:705–728.

Roazen, P. (1969). *Brother Animal: The story of Freud and Tausk*. New York: Knopf.

———— (1975). *Freud and his Followers*. New York: Knopf.

———— (1985). *Helene Deutsch: A Psychoanalyst's Life*. New York: Doubleday.

———— (1990). *Encountering Freud. The Politics and Histories of Psychoanalysis*. New Brunswick, NJ: Transaction.

———— (1991). Tampering with the mail. Review of "The letters of Sigmund Freud to Eduard Silberstein, 1871–1881", Harvard University Press 1990. *American Scholar*, Autumn, pp. 613–620.

———— (1995). *How Freud Worked. First-hand Accounts of Patients*. Northvale, NJ: Aronson.

———— (2005). *Edoardo Weiss: The House that Freud Built*. New Brunswick, NJ: Transactions.

Rudnytsky, P. (1991). *The Psychoanalytic Vocation: Rank, Winnicott, and the Legacy of Freud*. New Haven, CT: Yale University Press.

Schröter, M. (2006). Kapitel 12 – Briefe [Chapter 12 – Letters]. In H.-M. Lohmann and J. Pfeiffer (Eds.), *Freud Handbuch – Leben, Werk, Wirkung* [Freud handbook – Life, work, legacy] (pp. 220–231). Stuttgart: J.B. Metzler.

———— (2010). Einleitung [Introduction]. In M. Schröter (Ed.), *Sigmund*

Freud. Unterdess halten wir zusammen. Briefe an die Kinder
[Sigmund Freud. In the meantime we hold together. Letters to the
children] (pp. 7–21). Berlin: Aufbau.

Schröter, M. (Ed.) (2004). *Sigmund Freud und Max Eitingon.
Briefwechsel 1906–1939. Zwei Bände* [Sigmund Freud and Max
Eitingon. Correspondence 1906–1939. Two volumes]. Tübingen:
Diskord.

——— (2010). *Sigmund Freud. Unterdess halten wir zusammen. Briefe
an die Kinder* [Sigmund Freud. In the meantime we hold together.
Letters to the children]. Berlin: Aufbau.

——— (2012). *Sigmund Freud und Eugen Bleuler. "Ich bin
zuversichtlich, wir erobern bald die Psychiatrie". Briefwechsel
1904–1937* [Sigmund Freud and Eugen Blueler. "I am positive that
we will soon conquer psychiatry". Correspondence 1904–1937].
Basel: Schwabe.

Steiner, R. (1993). Introduction. In R.A. Paskauskas (Ed.), *The Complete
Correspondence of Sigmund Freud and Ernest Jones 1908–1939*
(pp. xxi–l). Cambridge, MA: Harvard University Press.

——— (2013). *Die Brautbriefe:* The Freud and Martha correspondence.
International Journal of Psychoanalysis 94:863–935.

Stern, D.N. (1985). *The Interpersonal World of the Infant: A View from
Psychoanalysis and Development*. London: Routledge.

Sullivan, H.S. (1953). *The Interpersonal Theory of Psychiatry* (H. Swick
Perry and M. Ladd Gawel, Eds.). New York: Norton.

——— (1954). *The Psychiatric Interview* (H. Swick Perry and M. Ladd
Gawel, Eds.). New York: Norton.

——— (1962). *Schizophrenia as a Human Process* (H. Swick Perry, Ed.).
New York: Norton.

Swales, P. (1986). Freud, his teacher and the birth of psychoanalysis.
In P.E. Stepansky (Ed.), *Freud: Appraisals and Reappraisals.
Contributions to the History of Psychoanalysis* (pp. 3–82).
Hillsdale, NJ: Analytic Press.

Szasz, T.S. (1974). *The Myth of Mental Illness*. New York: Harper &
Collins.

Teusch, R.K. (2014). Courtship letters of Freud and Martha Bernays.
Review of "Die Brautbriefe. Band 2. Unser 'Roman in
Fortsetzungen'" [The letters during their engagement. Vol. 2. Our
"novel in installments"], Fischer 2013. *Journal of the American
Psychoanalytic Association*, 62:325–343.

——— (2017). More courtship letters of Freud and Martha Bernays.
Review of „Die Brautbriefe. Band 3, Warten in Ruhe und
Ergebung, Warten in Kampf und Erregung" [The letters during
their engagement. "Waiting quietly and with surrender, waiting
struggling and with exasperation"]. *Journal of the American
Psychoanalytic Association* 65:111–125.

Timms, E. (1988). Freud's library and his private reading. In E. Timms
and N. Segal (Eds.), *Freud in Exile: Psychoanalysis and its
Vicissitudes* (pp. 65–79). New Haven, CT: Yale University Press.

Trilling, L. (1974). The Freud/Jung letters. *New York Times*, April 21,
p. 1974.

Trosman, H. (1976). Freud's cultural background. In J.E. Gedo and G.
H. Pollock (Eds.), *Freud: The Fusion of Science and Humanism*
(pp. 46–70). New York: International Universities Press.

Weiss, E. (1931). *Elementi di psicoanalisi* [Elements of psychoanalysis].
Milan: Hoepli.

——— (1960). *The Structure and Dynamics of the Human Mind*. New York: Grune & Stratton.

——— (1964). *Agoraphobia in the Light of Ego Psychology*. New York: Grune & Stratton.

——— (1970). *Sigmund Freud as a Consultant*. New York: Intercontinental Medical Books.

Winn, M. (2012). Birth trauma: The letters of Sigmund Freud and Otto Rank. *Division Review* 6:10–15.

Wittenberger, G. (1995). *Das "Geheime Komitee" Sigmund Freuds. Institutionalisierungsprozesse in der Psychoanalytischen Bewegung zwischen 1912 und 1927* [Sigmund Freud's "Secret Commmitee". Processes of institutionalisation in the Psychoanalytic Movement between 1912 and 1927]. Tübingen: Diskord.

Wittenberger, G., & Tögel, C. (Eds.) (1999–2006). *Die Rundbriefe des "Geheimen Komitees". Vier Bände* [The circular letters of the "Secret Committee". Four volumes]. Tübingen: Diskord.

Yalom, I. (2017). *Becoming Myself*. New York: Basic Books.

Young-Bruehl, E. (1988). *Anna Freud. A Biography*. New York: Summit Books.

——— (1994). A history of Freud biographies. In M.M. Micale and R. Porter (Eds.), *Discovering the History of Psychiatry* (pp. 157–173). Oxford: Oxford University Press.

Zienert-Eilts, K. (2013). *Karl Abraham. Eine Biographie im Kontext der psychoanalytischen Bewegung* [Karl Abraham. A biography in the context of the Psychoanalytic Movement]. Giessen: Psychosozial-Verlag.

CHAPTER 1

THE YOUNG FREUD'S LETTERS TO EDUARD SILBERSTEIN—EARLY TRACES OF SOME PSYCHOANALYTIC CONCEPTS[1]

> "Freud once told his friend and colleague Theodor Reik,
> 'What this world needs are men of strong passions who have
> the ability to control them'. He was speaking of himself, in
> relation to his mother" (Freeman and Strean, 1981, p. 20).

As we all know, S. Freud was a very passionate letter writer. And also a very conscientious one, as his son Ernst testified in 1960 (E.L. Freud, 1960, preface). His letters have in fact become literature. Or, even better, "a major source of literature on the psychoanalytic theory," as Martin Grotjahn put it (Grotjahn, 1976, p. 29). Just think of the letters to C.G. Jung (McGuire, ed., 1974) or to W. Fliess (Masson, ed., 1985). To the 5,039 letters of Freud that have been found and catalogued according to the German historian Gerhard Fichtner (Fichtner, 1989) belong also the letters to S. Ferenczi, the publication of which keeps being postponed (Haynal, 1989).

As regards Freud's letters to his school-friend Eduard Silberstein, which cover the period 1871–1881, it was the Romanian scholar Heinz Stanescu who brought them to light in 1965 (Stanescu, 1966). Bought by the S. Freud Archives at the end of the 1970s (Boehlich, 1990), they were first published in German (Fischer) in 1989. A French (Gallimard) and an English edition (The Belknap Press of Harvard University Press) followed in 1990, and I edited the Italian one (Bollati Boringhieri) in 1991.[2]

Before that, only Freud's seven letters and two postcards to Emil Fluss, edited by Ernst Freud in 1969 (E. Freud, ed., 1969), gave us some knowledge of Freud's adolescence, e.g., his high school final exams (the *Maturabrief* of June 16, 1873), or his choice to give up the study of law and become a natural scientist (letter of May

---

[1] The original version of this article was published in Volume 1 (1992) of the *International Forum of Psychoanalysis*, pp. 37–43. It represents the re-elaboration of the paper presented in Stockholm, in August 1991, at the VIth Scientific Conference of the IFPS.

[2] My work as editor of "*Querido amigo...*," our edition's title, consisted of supervising the translation, writing an introduction, and extending—to a relevant degree—the German editor's notes. This last operation I did with the double aim of helping the common reader to better follow Freud's vicissitudes, and of exploring the possibility of finding important lines of continuity between these letters and his later analytic work.

1, 1873).[3]

As we know from a retrospective account, it was Heinrich Braun, two years older than Freud and his first "best friend," who encouraged him to study law. In 1927 Freud wrote to Braun's widow:

> He directed my interest toward books . . . . I admired him, his energetic behavior, his independent judgement, compared him secretly with a lion and . . . it was understood that I would work with him and never let down his side. Under his influence I also decided at that time to study law at the university. (E. Freud, ed., 1960, p. 379)

But who then was Eduard Silberstein,[4] a year younger than Freud, who took the place of Heinrich in Freud's life during his second year of Gymnasium? Freud wrote to his fiancée Martha on February 7, 1884, commenting on a meeting with Eduard the same day:

> We became friends at a time when one doesn't look upon friendship as a sport or an asset, but when one needs a friend with whom to share things. We used to be together literally every hour of the day that was not spent on the school bench. We learned Spanish together, had our own mythology and secret names, which we took from some dialogues of the great Cervantes. Once in our Spanish primer we found a humorous-philosophical conversation between two dogs which lay peacefully at the door of a hospital, and appropriated their names; in writing as well as in conversation he was known as Berganza, I as Cipion. How often have I written: *Querido Berganza!* and signed myself *Tu fidel Cipion, perro en el hospital de Sevilla!* Together we found a strange scholarly society, the *Academia Castellana* (A.C.), and compiled a great mass of humorous work which must still exist somewhere. (E. Freud, ed., 1960, pp. 96–97, original emphasis)

John Gedo and Ernest Wolf comment on this picture in their 1973 essay "Freud's *Novelas ejemplares*" with the following few words: "Harbinger of Wilhelm Fliess and the International Psychoanalytic Association!" (Gedo and

---

[3] Of course both Ronald Clark (1980) and Peter Gay (1988), having free access to the Washington Archives, made very ample use of Freud's letters to Silberstein, the major written source for their depiction of his adolescence.

[4] Here are the essential biographical data on E. Silberstein: born in Jassy, Romania, in 1857, one of four children of Orthodox Jewish parents, he was sent to Vienna by them for his high-school education. He then studied Law and Philosophy in Vienna and Leipzig. Unfortunately his first wife, Pauline Theiler, treated unsuccessfully by Freud for a major nervous breakdown, committed suicide by throwing herself from a window in his apartment building. With his second wife, Anna Sachs, he settled in Braila, an active commercial harbor town on the Danube, where he became a prominent member of the community. They had an only daughter, Theodora, born in 1895, the mother of Rosita Braunstein Vieyra, whose notes on her grandfather (Boehlich, ed., 1990, pp. 190–194) I am now synthesizing. He died in Braila in 1925.

Wolf, 1976, p. 92).

As a matter of fact, such a comparison, systematically developed by Kurt Eissler in 1974 (Eissler, 1974), was later even more explicitly taken up by León Grinberg and Juan F. Rodriguez at a panel on "Don Quixote, Freud and Cervantes" held at the 1983 Madrid IPA congress:

> Freud-Silberstein or Cipion-Berganza would be the beginning of that fascinating series that would continue with the dialogue of Freud-Martha, Freud-Breuer, Freud-Fliess, to culminate in the great dialogue Freud-Freud, that is self-analysis (Grinberg and Rodriguez, 1984, p. 160).

But let us now go back to Freud, and hear what he writes to Silberstein on September 4, 1874:

> Hence my proposal amounts to stipulating that every Sunday each of us, the two sole luminaries of the A.C., send the other a letter that is nothing short of an entire encyclopedia of the past week and that with total veracity reports all our doings, commissions and omissions, and those of all strangers we encounter, in addition to all outstanding thoughts and observations and at least an adumbration, as it were, of the unavoidable emotions . . . . In our letters we shall transmute the six prosaic and unrelenting working days of the week into the pure gold of poetry and may perhaps find that there is enough of interest within us, and in what remains and changes around us, if only we learn to pay attention. (Boehlich, ed., 1990, pp. 57–58).

Or, on September 18, 1874:

> After all, selfless sympathy with everything that concerns or happens to the other is often the most valuable, indeed the sole, contribution of a friend. (Boehlich, ed., 1990, p. 62)

In other words, it is my contention, which I gave expression in my introduction to the Italian edition of Freud's letters to Silberstein (Conci, 1991), that to the extent to which self-analysis represents the foundation of psychoanalysis, as Didier Anzieu has convincingly demonstrated in 1975 (Anzieu, 1986), these letters to Silberstein contain the original nucleus of our discipline. Or to use Patrick Mahony's words, to the extent to which Freud "conducted his self-analysis predominantly in writing" and "his self-analysis was literally a writing cure" (Mahony, 1987, p. 16), we can look at these letters as an attempt at self-cure.[5]

One of the secrets that this correspondence reveals to us is Freud's passion for Gisela Fluss, that is, the important episode of his life that Siegfried Bernfeld in 1946 was able to bring in connection with the 1899 paper

---

[5] It should not seem strange if self-analysis, Freud's original discovery, has attracted more interest in colleagues like Karen Horney (1942) and Erich Fromm (1989) than inside the orthodox Freudian group.

"Screen memories," revising it in terms of "An unknown autobiographical fragment" (Bernfeld, 1946). Freud writes to Eduard on September 4, 1872 from Freiberg:

> On Wednesday, after I had written to you, she departed . . . I said good-bye sadly and walked to Hochwald, my little paradise, where I spent a most pleasant hour. I have soothed all my turbulent thoughts and only flinch slightly when her mother mentions Gisela's name at the table. The affection appeared like a beautiful spring day, *and only the nonsensical Hamlet in me, my diffidence*, stood in the way of my finding it a refreshing pleasure to converse with the half-naive, half-cultured young lady. (Boehlich, ed., 1990, p. 16, emphasis added)

Only a few lines below, after having expressed his admiration for Gisela's mother, Freud finds an explanation for this peculiar state of mind of his, and a very remarkable explanation: "it would seem that I have *transferred* my esteem for the mother to friendship for the daughter" (Boehlich, ed., 1990, p. 17, emphasis added). Now, since this is the first mention of such a central concept in Freud's work, let me give you also the original German version: "mir scheint, dass ich die Achtung vor der Mutter als Freundschaft auf die Tochter *üebertragen* habe" (Boehlich, ed., 1990, p. 22). As we know, only in "Studies on hysteria" (Freud and Breuer, 1895), more than twenty years later, will the concept of *Üebertragung* attain its first scientific definition.

Of course, everyone who gives credit to the point of view expressed among others by Benjamin Wolstein (1983) (see also Thomas Szasz, 1963, and Leon Chertok and Raymond de Saussure, 1979), who considers "the use of the notion of transference itself as his intellectualized defense against a particular female patient's direct sexual moves towards him" (Wolstein, 1983, p. 287), can find in this statement of Freud's a further—perhaps fundamental—proof in this direction. At the same time, we will later find further evidence of a possible relationship between Freud's emotional vicissitudes and his later development of analytic technique.

It is also true that if we take Freud's reference to Gisela's mother as an unconscious way to deal with his own mother, and with her seductive behavior towards him (see Freeman and Strean, 1981), we can end up sharing Ernest Jones's original hypothesis on the "striking contrast between the rather unflattering picture he revealed to the world concerning his inner life, notably in the analysis of his dreams, and the quite complete reticence on the matter of his love life" (Jones, 1955, p. 409):

> One must suppose that in Freud's earliest years there had

been extremely strong motives for concealing some important
phase of his development—perhaps even from himself. I
would venture to surmise it was his deep love for his mother.
(p. 409)

Of course, we now know that Freud's relationship to
his mother, although he himself had described it, from the
mother's side, as "the most free from ambivalence of all
human relationships" (S. Freud, 1933, p. 133) was much
more complex than Jones let us believe. James Barron et
al. wrote recently:

> his relationship to his mother, fraught with ambivalence and
> early pregenital trauma, provided the motivational source of
> his wish to pursue the secrets of Nature *as a sublimated and
> displaced manner* of dealing with her, and with his love and
> his fear of her. (Barron et al., 1991, p. 161, emphasis added)

And what about Freud and Gisela? In a paper
presented in Bologna in June, 1991, Robert Holt asks
himself:

> we are left with a tantalizing mystery: why did a vigorous
> young, himself attractive enough to the opposite sex, remain
> so distant from Gisela and so uninvolved with girls for another
> decade? . . . . It seems obvious enough where such inhibitions
> might have begun: at home, with the incest taboo. Growing
> up as he did, the big brother in a family of many little sisters,
> Sigi must have had many opportunities and temptations to
> get more or less involved with them. Grinstein (1968) has
> found many evidences, in his dreams and associations, of
> conflict about incestuous desires directed toward sisters as
> well as toward mother . . . it was enough to set up such a
> strong inhibition with respect to girls, that even when he
> was safely away from home and thrown together with as
> attractive and interesting a possibility as Gisela Fluss, he was
> unable even to engage her in any meaningful conversation.
> (Holt, 1991a, pp. 14–15)

And how does Freud further elaborate this "first
passionate storm," as Kurt Eissler defined it in 1978
(Eissler, 1978, p. 472)? In his letters to Silberstein there is
plenty of evidence of the "intensive and extensive defences"
that Kurt Eissler (p. 473) guessed this experience must
have precipitated in him. If we then take into account the
fact that Eduard, aged eighteen, was a more relaxed and
outgoing adolescent, we are ready to hear from Freud the
following harsh and revealing declarations:

> I would very much like to broach a subject that I consider
> serious but that fills me with painful agitation and
> embarrassment on your behalf, for which you will soon
> forgive me. You must know how sincerely I rejoiced at all
> the qualities you possessed and I lacked, your gift of treating
> the world with humor and your poetic genius in dealing with
> life . . . This, and our old friendship, may persuade you to
> grant me the right to pass judgment on your latest affair,
> and encourages me to say straight out that it is very wrong

of you, and causes grave harm to yourself and deep sorrow
to me, to encourage the imprudent affection of a sixteen-year
old girl and—the inevitable outcome—to take advantage
of it . . . What you start with innocent intent, or perhaps no
intent at all, may have the same effect as something that you
pursue with dishonorable intentions from the very beginning.
Yet, I confess, I attach less weight to this consideration than
to another, which I hope will impress you still more. For a
man, in my view, may try and taste many things, may injure
himself and cause himself unhappiness for a time, and yet
do far less harm to himself, on the whole, than a woman or
girl would in similar circumstances. A man seems capable of
tasting passions, of losing himself in wild sentiments, even of
relaxing the reins of morality, for he retains within himself
the principle of his actions, the consciousness of what is good
and what bad. A thinking man is his own legislator, confessor,
and absolver. *But a woman, let alone a girl, has no inherent
ethical standard*; she can act correctly only if she keeps within
the bounds of convention, observing what society deems to
be proper . . . Therefore do not become the cause of the first
transgression of a young girl—one who has barely outgrown
childhood—against a justified moral percept, by arranging
meetings and exchanging letters against her parents' wishes.
For what else can you write or tell her but that you love her,
etc., and what purpose will it serve when you lie yourself into
a passion and she dreams herself into one? . . . *Why then, my
friend, play so dangerous a game with that girl?* (Boehlich, ed.,
1990, pp. 91–94, emphasis added)

In other words, we cannot escape the general
impression that Freud writes to his peer Eduard as if he
were his father!

If we now take this reaction of Freud's in the context
of the Gisela episode, and not as bound to, for example, his
Jewish upbringing, whose influence on him David Bakan
(1990) and Marianne Krüll (1979; see Krüll, 1986) have so
well demonstrated, we can finally catch the personal red
thread which runs through his later "scientific" outlook on
femininity, and which Karen Horney, speaking of man's
flight from womanhood (Horney, 1926) and of man's
dread of woman (Horney, 1942), was the first one to try to
capture. Freud writes in 1925: "Their superego is never so
inexorable, so impersonal, so independent of its emotional
origins as we require it to be in man" (S. Freud, 1925, p.
257).

I agree, then, with Christa Rohde-Dachser's
contention, which she recently thoroughly worked out
in her *Expedition in den dunklen Kontinent* (1991), that
a real liberation of the feminine dimension, through
psychoanalysis, really requires "the patriarchal dimension
of its metatheory to be systematically deconstructed"
(Rohde-Dachser, 1990, p. 49). Also the contributions of
Teresa Corsi Piacentini (1982), Claudia Zanardi (1990),

and Johannes Cremerius (1989), to whom I also owe important stimuli in this regard, go in the same direction.

In the spring of 1876 Freud went to Trieste, which was then the only harbor of the Austrian-Hungarian Empire, to conduct his first scientific research, on the reproductive organs of eels, at the marine biology institute founded by Carl Claus, his biology professor. Dissecting 400 eels (see Eissler, 1978, p. 472) amounted to his first scientific paper: "Observations on the form and finer structure of the lobular organs of the eel, described as testicles" (S. Freud, 1877). It is from his first stay in Italy, which would later become a major source of inspiration for him, that he wrote to Silberstein two of the finest, and most revealing, letters of the whole collection. On April 5, 1876, he writes:

> I would much rather report to you on what I have been able to see of the *bella Italia*, and how I serve the beast-killing science. When . . . I go for an evening stroll after my work, I see precious little of the physiology of the natives of Trieste. Most of what I know I gathered on my first day, when everything was new to me and I found it worthwhile to pay heed to it. I am a person with the unfortunate tendency of finding everything ordinary and becoming used to everything quickly . . . Like the sea, the people and the street names are Italian . . . The people, finally, are very ugly, with few exceptions. *(By "people" I refer to all living beings who live and work in Trieste.)* The horses and oxen are the same as anywhere else, as are the men, although if anything the latter are worse . . . The cats are beautiful and friendly, but the women are especially distinctive. Most of them are true characters in your Leipzig sense, and often have the typical Italian figure, slim, tall, slender-faced, with a longish nose, dark eyebrows, and small raised upper lip. So much for the anatomical features. *Physiologically, all that I know about them is that they like to go for walks* . . . Unfortunately they are not beautiful in our German sense, *but I remember that on my first day I discovered lovely specimens among the new type which I have not encountered since.* For the rest they are paler than they should be, and have, or rather wear, fine heads of hair. Some of them adorn themselves by permitting a lock of hair to hang down their foreheads over one eye. I believe that the extreme forms of this asymmetrical fashion extend to the more dubious classes of society. It is a sort of masonic identification sign. Few small children appear on the streets . . . *Since it is not allowed to dissect human beings, I really have nothing to do with them.* (Boehlich, ed., 1990, pp. 142–146, emphasis on *bella Italia* in the original, other emphases added).

This defensive spell gets broken only two and a half weeks later: during a trip to the sea-village of Muggia, Freud is again able to see nice women around, though in the form of midwives and pregnant women. In his own account to Silberstein:

> True, on my first day in Trieste, I felt that the city was

inhabited by none but Italian goddesses, *and I was filled with apprehension*, but when I stepped expectantly into the streets on the second day, I could discover no more of these, and ever since a beautiful *donna* [woman] has been one of the rarest things to encounter in the street. In Muggia, however, the women, as I said, are more attractive, mostly blonde, oddly enough, which accords with neither Italian nor Jewish descent; the locals are not Slavs either, and do not even speak that tongue. (Boehlich, ed., 1990, p. 153, emphasis on *donna* in the original, other emphases added).

In other words, we can only agree with Eissler's conclusion of his lengthy 1978 essay:

> The Gisela experience contributed much to the strengthening of the defensive, repressive apparatus in the youth. *Freud never discarded this apparatus.* One has the impression that he made his discoveries against an inner resistance, that the richness of his accomplishments came to pass against a background of hard labor, the expression of a counterforce that Freud himself intimated when he wrote to Lou Andreas-Salome about a recent discovery: '*It is a discovery of which one ought almost to be ashamed, for one should have divined these connections from the beginning and not after thirty years*' (1960, p. 331). (Eissler, 1978, pp. 513–514, emphasis added)

Now, before coming to my major point, let me make three further comments. First, it is apparent how Freud's emotional vicissitudes in Trieste recall the crisis undergone by his beloved Norbert Hanold, the protagonist of Wilhelm Jensens's novel (the young archeologist who had fallen in love with an ancient bas-relief, the figure of a graceful woman walking, Gradiva) to which he turned in 1906, composing one of his minor masterpieces (S. Freud, 1907). We can say that he unconsciously must have identified strongly with Norbert Hanold. This is why he loved Jensens' novel so much. Second, the "sublimation hypothesis," originally put forward by Ernest Jones (in 1953), further confirmed by John Gedo and Ernest Wolf (in 1970), and later redefined by Kurt Eissler (see the above conclusion), according to which after his disappointment over his first love, Gisela, Freud withdrew a large part of his libido into sublimation, can be further attested by what we can regard as his identification with Leonardo da Vinci, whose character he depicted in the following way:

> The core of his nature, and the secret of it, would appear to be that after his curiosity had been activated in infancy in the service of sexual interests, *he succeeded in sublimating the greater part of his libido into an urge for research.* (Freud, 1910, p. 83, emphasis added)

Third, as Walter Boehlich remarked in his preface (Boehlich, 1990), the concept of deprivation (the German *Entbehrung*), which represents Freud's solution to his

Trieste anxieties, runs deep through his entire work. In "The future of an illusion" we can for example read, as Boehlich suggests: "The civilization in which he participates imposes some amount of privation on him" (Freud, 1927, p. 16).

I have now come to my major point: does Freud's strategy of sublimation, the effects of which we have seen so heavily at play in his account from Trieste, where his need for human and sexual contact found a sublimated replacement in a scientific endeavor centered around the biology of reproduction, have something to do with his later concept of the analyst as a blank screen (S. Freud, 1912)? Although colleagues like Johannes Cremerius (1981) have been able to show us Freud's freer use of the rigid technique he recommended, Izette De Forest, in her account of "Ferenczi's last visit to Freud" addressed to Erich Fromm, testifies to his insistence, at age seventy-six, of the necessity of "the emotional withdrawal of the analyst" (see De Forest, 1957; this passage from E. Fromm's correspondence is quoted by kind permission of Dr. Rainer Funk, Fromm's literary executor). Or, to put it in other terms: I believe that the new paradigm of the analyst's participation in the patient's experience, the new paradigm which has basically come out of the American interpersonal tradition (see, for example, Gerard Chrzanowski, 1977; Irwin Hoffman, 1983; Irwin Hirsch, 1987; and Stephen Mitchell, 1988), requires us to overcome mere intellectual adherence in favor of a bi-personal field concept, and to go beyond sublimation and control (cf. the opening quotation).

As a matter of fact, the point I am making owes much to the line of research developed by Robert Holt (1987). In one of his most recent papers, "Freud's parental identifications as a source of some contradictions within psychoanalysis," Holt makes the following point:

> My first main thesis is that therapeutic psychoanalysis contains an inner contradiction: on the one hand, the technique is implicitly nonmanipulative, respectful of the patient; it invites him or her to participate actively in struggling against the disorder and finding better ways of living. *On the other hand, it remains prescriptive and controlling in many ways, the analyst's role and techniques being conceived of as forms of sublimated sadism, basically more aggressive than loving, and with great emphasis on neutrality rather than nurturance.* In practice, we know that Freud could occasionally (as in the case of Frink) be astonishingly manipulative, usually to his patient's detriment. *While a variety of historical and other impersonal factors undoubtedly account for this contradictory state of affaires, it seems manifestly grounded in Freud's own personality, specifically in his parental identifications.* (Holt,

1991b, p. 34, emphasis added)

At the same time, it must not be forgotten that Erich Fromm, already in 1935, in comparing S. Ferenczi's "human and friendly approach" with Freud's "patricentric-authoritarian 'tolerance'," emphasized its "essentially hostile nature" (Fromm, 1935), as Marco Bacciagaluppi reports in one of his latest papers (Bacciagaluppi, 1991).

Certainly, a definite solution to the problem I am proposing requires further work and discussion. I will end with two more suggestive and thought-provoking quotations. Edgar Levenson writes in 1981:

> Freud came upon a momentous discovery, the transformational nature of discourse. It is no doubt audacious to say but *he put this discovery to the service of his own neurosis.* Isn't it extraordinary how his later life played out the prophecy of the Irma dream with its leukoplakic spots? No one reading Schur's account of Freud's long tortured course with his mouth cancer can accept the simple explanation that 'sometimes a cigar is just a cigar' or that he had a severe case of nicotine addiction. The suicidal tenacity with which he stuck to the cigars deserves a better explanation. He started by adulating Fliess as a good father and copying him and ended by dying of Fliess's symbolic ministrations, as almost did Irma in reality.
>
> Freud paid a high price for 'closing his eyes', for the point in Sophocles's *Oedipus Rex* is that his father *did* try to kill him . . . .
>
> If one holds to the discovery of discourse as transformation, but shifts the model from the search for distortion to the search for *real experience,* one comes out with a different kind of psychoanalysis, closer to the contemporary search for *interaction,* with the use of *countertransference* as a legitimate tool of therapy, and as a goal a therapy that is not politicized and allows the patient to arrive at his own solutions or even no solution at all. (Levenson, 1981, 498–499, emphasis on *did* in the original, other emphases added)

Michael Friedman writes in 1985: "The point of view of this paper is that psychopathology is, broadly speaking, *the renunciation of normal developmental goals due to considerations of danger*" (Friedman, 1985, p. 530, emphasis added).

In other words, and what follows is my provisional conclusion, Freud's neurosis may be conceptualized in terms of his "renunciation of a normal developmental goal," like courting Gisela Fluss, "due to considerations of danger," variously defined as L. Chertok's and R. de Saussure's "direct sexual moves" or R. Holt's "incest taboo." This led him not only to make use, as an adolescent, of the way out offered by sublimatory processes (K. Eissler), and to later propose a view of women based on his dread of them (K. Horney), but also to advocate a therapeutic stance based both on the analyst's "emotional withdrawal" (I. De Forest) and the neglect of "real experience, interaction, and countertransference" (E. Levenson). Simply put, I am of the opinion that, following the line I developed in Freud's case, the relationship between the persons we are and the technique we use should receive more attention and study. Alan Grey demonstrated this kind of attention in his plenary session paper at the VI Scientific Conference of IFPS (Grey, 1991).

REFERENCES

Anzieu, D. (1986). *Freud's Self-analysis*. London: Hogarth Press. (Original French edition, 1975).

Bacciagaluppi, M. (1991). Ferenczi's influence on Fromm. Unpublished paper.

Bakan, D. (1990). *Sigmund Freud and the Jewish Mystical Tradition*. London: Free Association Books.

Barron, J.W., Beaumont, R., Goldsmith, G.N., Good, M.I., Pyles, R.L., & Rizzuto, A.M. (1991). Sigmund Freud: The secrets of nature and the nature of secrets. *International Review of Psychoanalysis* 18:143–163.

Bernfeld, S. (1946). An unknown autobiographical fragment by Freud. *American Imago* 4:3–19.

Boehlich, W. (1990). Editor's preface. In W. Boehlich (Ed.), *The Letters of Sigmund Freud to Eduard Silberstein, 1871–1881* (pp. vii–ix). Cambridge, MA: Belknap Press of Harvard University Press.

Boelich, W. (Ed.) (1990). *The Letters of Sigmund Freud to Eduard Silberstein, 1871–1881*. Cambridge, MA: Belknap Press of Harvard University Press. A.J. Pomerans, Translator. (Original German edition, 1989).

Chertok, L., & De Saussure, R. (1979). *The Therapeutic Revolution*. New York: Brunner & Mazel. (Original French edition, 1979).

Chrzanowski, G. (1987). *Interpersonal Approach to Psychoanalysis*. New York: Gardner Press.

Clark, R.W. (1980). *Freud, the Man and the Cause*. London: Jonathan Cape.

Conci, M. (1991). Presentazione all'edizione italiana [Presentation of the Italian edition]. In W. Boehlich (Ed.), *"Querido amigo . . ."*. *Lettere della giovinezza a Eduard Silberstein 1871–1881* (pp. vii–xxiv). Turin: Bollati Boringhieri.

Corsi Piacentini, T. (1982). Note sulla sessualità femminile [Notes on female sexuality]. *Psicoterapia e Scienze Umane* 16(2):5–18.

Cremerius, J. (1981). Freud bei der Arbeit über die Schulter geschaut. Seine Technik im Spiegel von Schülern und Patienten [Freud at work, a look from above his shoulders. His technique in the mirror of training analysands and patients]. In U. Ehebald and F.W. Eickhoff (Eds.), *Humanität und Technik in der Psychoanalyse* [Humanity and technique in psychoanalysis] (pp. 150–165). Bern: Huber.

——— (1989). Freuds Konzept der psychosexuellen Entwicklung der Frau schliesst deren autonome Entwicklung in der psychoanalytischen Behandlung im Prinzip aus [Freud's concept of feminine psychosexual development excludes in principle the autonomous development of women in analytic treatment]. In K. Brede (Ed.), *Was will das Weib in mir?* [What does the female in me want?] (pp. 111–129). Freiburg: Kore.

De Forest, I. (1957). Ferenczi's last visit to Professor Freud. Enclosed within a letter to Erich Fromm of February 18, 1957. Tübingen: Erich Fromm Archive.

Eissler, K.R. (1974). Über Freuds Freundschaft mit Wilhelm Fliess nebst einem Anhang über Freuds Adoleszenz und einer historischen Bemerkung über Freuds Jugendstil [On Freud's friendship with Wilhelm Fliess with a note on Freud's adolescence and an historical note on the young Freud's style]. *Jahrbuch der Psychoanalyse* 2:39–100.

——— (1978). Creativity and adolescence. The effect of trauma in Freud's adolescence. *Psychoanalytic Study of the Child* 33:461–517.

Fichtner, G. (1989). Freuds Briefe als historische Quelle. *Psyche* 43:803–829.

Freeman, L., & Strean, H. (1981). *Freud and Women.* New York: Ungar.

Freud, E.L. (1960). Preface. In E.L. Freud (Ed.), *Letters of Sigmund Freud* (pp. vii–viii). New York: Basic Books.

Freud, E.L. (Ed.) (1960). *Letters of Sigmund Freud* (T. and J. Stern, Trans.). New York: Basic Books.

——— (1969). Some early unpublished letters of Freud. *International Journal of Psychoanalysis* 50:419–427.

Freud, S. (1877). Beobachtungen über Gestaltung und feineren Bau der als Hoden beschriebenen Lappenorgane des Aals [Observations on the form and fine structure of the lobulary organs of the eel described as testicles]. *Sitzungsberichte der kaiserlichen Akademie der Wissenschaften, Mathematisch-Naturwissenschaftliche Classe, 1. Abteilung,* 75: 419–443.

——— (1907). Delusions and dreams in Jensen's Gradiva. *Standard Edition* 9, pp. 1–96.

——— (1910). Leonardo da Vinci and a memory of his childhood. *Standard Edition* 11, pp. 57–138.

——— (1912). Recommendations to physicians practising psychoanalysis. *Standard Edition* 12, pp. 109–120.

——— (1925). Some psychical consequences of the anatomical distinctions between the sexes. *Standard Edition* 19, pp. 241–258.

——— (1927). The future of an illusion. *Standard Edition* 21, pp. 1–56.

——— (1933). Lecture XXXIII: Femininity. *Standard Edition* 22, pp. 112–135.

Freud, S., & Breuer, J. (1895). Studies on hysteria. *Standard Edition* 2.

Friedman, M. (1985). Toward a reconceptualization of guilt. *Contemporary Psychoanalysis* 21:501–547.

Fromm, E. (1935). Die gesellschaftliche Bedingtheit der psychoanalytischen Therapie [The social determination of psychoanalytic therapy]. *Zeitschrift für Sozialforschung* 4:36–97.

——— (1989). *Vom Haben zu Sein. Wege und Irrewege der Selbsterfahrung* [From having to being. Ways and mistaken ways of self-experience]. Bâle: Beltz.

Gay, P. (1988). *Freud. A Life for Our Time.* New York: Norton.

Gedo, J.E., & Wolf, E.S. (1976). Freud's *Novelas ejemplares.* In J.E. Gedo and G.H. Pollock (Eds.), *Freud: The Fusion of Science and Humanism* (pp. 87–111). New York: International Universities

Press.

Grey, A. (1991). On being a male analyst: The reluctant discovery of a troublesome goldmine. Paper given in Stockholm at the IFPS VIth Scientific Conference.

Grinberg, L., & Rodriguez, J.F. (1984). The influence of Cervantes on the future creator of psychoanalysis. *International Journal of Psychoanalysis* 65:155–168.

Grotjahn, M. (1976). Freuds Briefwechsel [Freud's correspondence]. In D: Eicke (Ed.), *Die Psychologie des XX. Jahrhunderts, Tiefenpsychologie* [The psychology of the 20th century. Deep psychology] (Vol. 1, pp. 29–140). Bern: Kindler.

Haynal, A. (1989). Brefs aperçus sur l'histoire de la correspondance Freud-Ferenczi [Brief notes on the history of the correspondence between Freud and Ferenczi]. *Revue Internationale d'Histoire de la Psychanalyse* 2:243–254.

Hirsch, I. (1987). Varying modes of analytic participation. *Journal of the American Academy of Psychoanalysis* 15:205–222.

Hoffman, I.Z. (1983). The patient as interpreter of the analyst's experience. *Contemporary Psychoanalysis* 19:389–422.

Holt, R.R. (1987). *Freud Reappraised. A Fresh Look at Psychoanalytic Theory*. New York: Guilford Press.

——— (1991a). Freud's occupational choice and the unconscious reverberations of Goethe's "On nature." Unpublished paper.

——— (1991b). Freud's parental identifications as a source of some contradictions within psychoanalysis. Unpublished paper.

Horney, M. (1926). The flight from womanhood: The masculinity complex in women as viewed by men and women. *International Journal of Psychoanalysis* 7:324–339.

Horney, K. (1942). *Self-analysis*. New York: Norton.

Jones, E. (1955). *Sigmund Freud Life and Work. Volume Two: Years of Maturity, 1901-1919*. New York: Basic Books.

Krüll, M. (1986). *Freud and his Father*. New York: Norton. (Original German edition, 1979).

Levenson, E. (1981). Facts or fantasies: On the nature of psychoanalytic data. *Contemporary Psychoanalysis* 17:486–500.

Mahony, P. (1987). *Freud as a Writer*. New Haven, CT: Yale University Press.

Masson, J.M. (Ed.) (1985). *The Complete Letters of Sigmund Freud to Wilhelm Fliess, 1887–1904*. J.M. Masson, Translator. Cambridge, MA: Belknap Press of Harvard University Press.

McGuire, W. (Ed). (1974). *The Freud/Jung Letters*. R. Mannheim and R.F.C. Hull, Translators. Princeton, NJ: Princeton University Press.

Mitchell, S.A. (1988). *Relational Concepts in Psychoanalysis. An Integration*. Cambridge, MA: Harvard University Press.

Rohde-Dachser, C. (1990). *Weiblichkeits-Paradigmen in der Psychoanalyse* [Paradigms of femininity in psychoanalysis]. *Psyche* 44:30–52.

——— (1991). *Expedition in den dunklen Kontinent* [Expedition in the dark continent]. Berlin: Springer.

Stanescu, H. (1966). Unbekannte Briefe des jungen Sigmund Freud an einen Rumänischen Freund [Unknown letters of the young Sigmund Freud to a Romanian friend]. *Neue Literatur* 16:123–129.

Szasz, T.S. (1963). II. The concept of transference as a defense for the analyst. *International Journal of Psychoanalysis* 44:435–443.

Wolstein, B. (1983). Transference and resistance as psychic experience. *Contemporary Psychoanalysis* 19:276–294.

Zanardi, C. (Ed.) (1990). *Essential Papers on the Psychology of Women*. New York: New York University.

CHAPTER 2

WHY DID FREUD CHOOSE
MEDICAL SCHOOL?[1]

> A ban on fantasy, if declared by the analytic community
> would kill Freud. To keep him spiritually alive means,
> therefore, to invest him with our fantasies (Junker, 1991, p.
> 211; my translation).

In the 1935 Postscript to his "Autobiographical study"
Freud wrote: "Two themes run through these pages: the
story of my life and the history of psycho-analysis. They
are intimately interwoven. This "Autobiographical study"
shows how psychoanalysis came to be the whole content
of my life and rightly assumes that no personal experiences
of mine are of any interest in comparison to my relations
with that science" (Freud, 1935; SE 20, p. 71). Upon careful
rereading, this sounds like a very contradictory statement:
on the one hand, the story of his life is of crucial importance
for the understanding of psychoanalysis and, on the other,
Freud artificially distinguishes between his personal
experiences and his relations with psychoanalysis—
which make up the story of his life. The artificiality of
such a distinction can be easily gathered from the way he
constructed his main work, *The interpretation of dreams*,
in which he introduced his version of the concept of the
unconscious in the light of both his personal experiences
and the story of his life.

Indeed, such a contradiction runs through his entire
work, as we can gather from his identification with
Goethe, who was, in Freud's words, "not only, as a poet,
a great self-revealer, but also, in spite of the abundance
of autobiographical records, a careful concealer" (Freud,
1930; SE 21, p. 212). "We cannot help thinking here," Freud
suggests to the reader, "of the words of Mephistopheles:
'The best of what you know may not, after all, be told to
boys'" (SE 21, p. 212). As we will see, inasmuch as what
we do not seriously try to formulate in words remains
outside our conscious awareness, we can suppose that at
least part of the things which Freud avoided disclosing to
us were also beyond his personal grasp. Concealment thus
becomes self-concealment.

Given such an outlook on his part, it is no wonder that
the way in which he dealt in print with such an important

---

[1] The original version of this article was published in Volume 5 (1996) of
the *International Forum of Psychoanalysis*, pp. 123–132.

turning point of his life as the choice of a profession remains contradictory. Freud does not actually give us a convincing explanation of his choice of medical school—and probably was not able to give it to himself either. The explanations given for his choice remain unsatisfactory. After showing both the character and the unconvincing nature of the claims he made in this regard, on the basis of his letters to his adolescent friend Emil Fluss I will try both to read them in a new key and elaborate a more credible explanation of such a choice. By relying on his postulate of the great role the unconscious plays in our life, it is possible to throw a satisfactory light on such a crucial choice.

Let us start from his "Autobiographical study". After telling us about the lack of "any particular predilection for the career of a doctor" (Freud, 1925; SE 20, p. 8) and the existence in him of "a sort of curiosity, which was, however, directed more towards human concerns than towards natural objects" (SE 20, p. 8), he connects his choice of medical school with the strong attraction exercised upon him by Darwin's theories and with "hearing Goethe's beautiful essay on Nature read aloud at a popular lecture" (SE 20, p. 8). A possible objection to the strength of the first motivation is the fact that he unexpectedly left Carl Claus, the best Viennese representative of Darwinian biology, after writing for him his first scientific paper, on the reproductive biology of eels (Freud, 1877). As far as Goethe's essay goes, from the Fluss letters we know that Freud's choice had not the character of the sudden, unexpected and irresistible event that he wants us to believe—when he states, in the original German edition, that *"der Vortrag von Goethe . . . die Entscheidung gab, dass ich Medizin inskribierte"* (Freud, 1925; GW 14, p. 34).

Given such an ambiguous motivation, it is no wonder that—if we keep reading his "Autobiographical study" — we run across the fact that, on the one hand, he was soon "compelled . . . to make the discovery that . . . 'each man learns only what he can learn' (Goethe)" (Freud, 1925; SE 20, p. 9), and on the other he found in Ernst Brücke's physiological laboratory, between 1876 and 1882, not only "rest and full satisfaction," but "men, too, whom I could respect and take as my models" (SE 20, p. 9). This sequence apparently points in the same direction as Sándor Rado's view of Freud's relationship with Brücke, that is,

> It is obvious that Freud did not perform outstandingly under Bruecke. Freud tried to do a routine type of investigation, every step of which was explained to him; that was hardly a

remarkable accomplishment. He was one of the bricklayers
who helped to build the wall; but he probably did not even
know what the wall was going to be. (see Roazen, 1995, p. 47)

Expanding on his 1927 definition of Brücke as the man
"who carried more weight with me than anyone else in my
whole life" (Freud, 1927; SE 20, p.253), we may formulate
the hypothesis that what Freud was then looking for was
more personal growth than scientific education. Not to
speak of professional medical training, which he never
spontaneously looked for—at least while he was a medical
student. As we will see, this is also the hypothesis that the
Fluss letters drive us towards, that is, the hypothesis of an
unconscious, and always self-concealed, choice on his part
of medical school as a growth-promoting and self-healing
agency and experience.

Indeed, what Freud wrote more than ten years later
in his 1935 "Postscript to an autobiographical study"
points in the same direction. Here is how he explains the
"phase of regressive development," which came about
after his 1923 "The ego and the id" and in which "no
further decisive contributions to psycho-analysis" (Freud,
1935; SE 20, p. 72) were made by him: "My interest, after
making a lifelong *detour* through the natural sciences,
medicine and psychotherapy, returned to the cultural
problems which had fascinated me long before, when I
was a youth scarsely old enough for thinking" (SE 20, p.
72).

In his 1927 "Postscript to 'The question of lay
analysis'", Freud had rationalized such a *detour* in
terms of "the overpowering need" he felt as a youth "to
understand something of the riddles of the world in
which we live and perhaps even to contribute something
to their solution" (Freud, 1927; SE 20, p. 253). Such an
"overpowering need" had made it necessary for him "to
deviate from my original purpose," and "enroll myself in
the medical faculty" (SE 20, p. 253). In my opinion, such
a *detour* cannot be satisfactorily explained in terms of the
personal ambition to contribute something to the solution
of the riddles of the world, but could only be motivated
by a more basic problem, an issue of psychological life
and death. As we will see, this is the direction in which
Freud's letters to Emil Fluss point. As a matter of fact,
the words behind what I just qualified as a rationalization
of his choice in terms of his personal ambition can also be
read in such a new light: in terms of the understandably
"overpowering need" for personal growth and self-healing.

Freud's letters to Fluss center around the following

riddle, "I read Horatian odes, you live them" (see E.L. Freud, ed., 1969, p. 424), which well reflects the significant role sublimation had taken up in the melancholic life the youth conducted (see further documentation below), a problem which Freud certainly had to solve if he was to really grow and become a mature person. Indeed, with such a new key in our hands, Freud's 1935 words may open to new meanings.

In the first place, inasmuch as under the expression "*detour* through" he associates "the natural sciences, medicine and psychotherapy" (Freud, 1935; SE 20, p. 72), and given the well-known, though officially concealed fact that he himself was the first patient of psychoanalysis, we can assume that self-cure might be the common denominator of the three terms. This hypothesis finds a very interesting resonance in the principal phrase of the same 1935 sentence, i.e. "My interest . . . returned to the cultural problems which had fascinated me long before, when I was a youth scarcely old enough for thinking" (SE 20, p. 72), which we can thus read as follows. "Once I had cured myself, i.e. once I had eventually found the solution of my problems somewhere else, I could again come back, with a fresh mind, to those cultural issues which had fascinated me when I was a youth. They had fascinated me to the point of utilizing them to sublimate my own problems, with the risk of substituting *Kultur* for life and entering into a deadly vicious circle." Indeed, as we will see, the awareness of such an impasse in his life is what Freud got out of his exchange of letters with Emil Fluss, that is, what pushed him in the direction of medical school.

Further evidence in support of such a way of looking at Freud's adolescent crisis can be found in the original German version of this same phrase, which—together with the secondary phrase that comes before it—reads as follows: "*Nach dem lebenslangen Umweg über die Naturwissenschaften, Medizin und Psychotherapie war mein Interesse zu jenen kulturellen Problemen zurückgekehrt, die dereinst den kaum zum Denken erwachten Jüngling gefesselt hatten*" (Freud, 1935; GW 16, p. 32). This phrase contains two very important changes, whose tone the Standard Edition does not satisfactorily render, which veer in the direction of supporting the perspective I have just proposed. In the first place, the German "*fesseln*" is etymologically stronger than the English "fascinate"[2]: the corresponding noun, "*die*

---

[2] In Robert Holt's opinion, a better English equivalent is "to enthrall," which carries over the old connotation of "enslave," which is close to

Fessel," literally means "the chain, and the verb "*fesseln*" means in the first place "to chain" and only in a figurative sense "to fascinate," or rather, more exactly, "to enchant, to put under a spell." In the second place, the Standard Edition translation of "*den kaum zum Denken erwachten Jüngling*" is also misleading: these words actually mean "the young adolescent whose capacity for thinking was no more than awakened." What Freud refers to is a condition which does not have to do with chronological age (as the Standard Edition translation, with the word "old," makes us suppose), but with an adolescent's rate of maturation. If we now take both original expressions into consideration, we will have a much better understanding of what Freud actually meant: a young adolescent whose capacity for thinking is barely awakened easily becomes enthralled by cultural problems, which at such an epoch in life are easier to deal with than emotional problems and can easily, through sublimation, become one's "shelter."

We are thus back to the above-mentioned words written to Fluss, "I read Horatian odes, you live them." Or, to give another eloquent reference point, we are reminded of one important, and little explored alter ego of Freud's: Norbert Hanold. The protagonist of Wilhelm Jensens' *Gradiva* came to learn very much about archeology before he was eventually in a position—with the help of Gradiva alias Zoe Bertgang—to start understanding something about life. The fascination archeology exercises easily made a victim of such a fragile adolescent, keeping him for a long time far away from a real solution to his personal problems.

Before turning to the Fluss letters, let us now come to the last bit of information Freud gives us as regards his professional choice. I am of course making reference to the famous words of his 1927 "Postscript to 'The question of lay analysis'", which come after the even more notorious ones; "After forty-one years of medical activity, my self-knowledge tells me that I have never really been a doctor in the proper sense" (Freud, 1927; SE 20, p. 253), that is, "I became a doctor through being compelled to deviate from my original purpose; and the triumph of my life lies in my having, after a long and roundabout journey, found my way back to my earliest path" (SE 20, p. 253). This is a really mysterious sentence. In fact, Freud does not tell us: first, what compelled him to deviate from his original purpose and take a new direction; second, what he means by original purpose; third, what he actually means by triumph; and fourth, in what way he was able to come

"put into chains," and also means "to fascinate, to enchant."

back to his earliest path.

If we look at such questions in terms of what Freud officially stated in print, outside of the 1927 "Postscript", we find an answer only to the second question: "Under the powerful influence of a school friendship with a boy rather my senior who grew up to be a well-known politician," wrote Freud in his "Autobiographical study" , "I developed a wish to study law like him and to engage in social activities" (Freud, 1925; SE 20, p. 8). From his letter of October 30, 1927 to Julie Braun-Vogelstein, we can identify this older boy as Heinrich Braun (1854–1927). Of course, we can imagine that an alternative answer to the same question can be represented by the "sort of curiosity" (SE 20, p. 8), which—in the same context—he qualifies as his earliest interest and motivation. As a matter of fact, such a humanistic and literary orientation might certainly have been reinforced by the fact that, in the context of his *Matura* exam, his professor told him that he had "what Herder so neatly calls a distinctly personal style, i.e. a style at once correct and characteristic" (letter to Fluss of June 16, 1873; see E.L. Freud, ed., 1969, p. 425).

On the other hand, we can hardly accept as a valid and convincing answer to the first question the fact that Freud—in the same context—tells us that, as an adolescent, he had not yet "grasped the importance of observation as one of the best means of gratifying" (Freud, 1925; SE 20, p. 8) his curiosity. At the same time, if we take "observation" to mean "looking out of oneself onto external reality"—as opposed to mere self-observation— and thus as a way of developing a more direct and lively relationship with real life and people, we will have found, in Freud's own words, a further key to the real meaning of his exchange of letters with Emil Fluss. As we will see, such a relationship played a very important role in forcing Freud to come out of his isolation, to partially give up intellectualization as a major defense, and to eventually understand the fundamental role a good friend could play both in one's wellbeing and in the process of self-knowledge.

Freud's letters to Wilhelm Fliess give us a key to at least the second question, that is, the nature of his original purpose. Here is what he wrote to Fliess on May 25, 1895:

> a man like me cannot live without a hobbyhorse, without a consuming passion, without—in Schiller's words—a tyrant. I have found one. In its service I know no limits. It is psychology, which has always been my distant, beckoning goal, and which now, since I have come upon the problem of neurosis, has drawn so much nearer. (Masson, ed., 1985,

p. 129)

And, on January 1, 1896: "I see how, via the detour of medical practice, you are reaching your first ideal of understanding human beings as a physiologist, just as I most secretly nourish the hope of arriving, via these same paths, at my initial goal of philosophy. For that is what I wanted originally, when it was not clear to me to what end I was in the world". (Masson, ed., 1985, p.159). And, on April 2, 1896: "As a young man I knew no longing other than for philosophical knowledge, and now I am about to fulfill it as I move from medicine to psychology. I became a therapist against my will . . ." (Masson, ed., 1985, p.180).

It was also on this basis—and, of course, of his personal knowledge of Freud—that Ernest Jones, following Fritz Wittels' 1924 line of thought,[3] formulated his viewpoint about Freud's choice of medical school. Taking as a starting point Freud's 1927 claim of his "overpowering need to understand something of the riddles of this world," which he genetically justifies in terms of "the puzzling problems of his early family life" (Jones, 1961, p. 23), Jones envisions its satisfaction in one of two ways: "through philosophical speculation or scientific observation" (Jones, 1961, p. 23). After making reference to Freud's personal answer to him about his early interest in philosophy, that is, "As a young man I felt a strong attraction toward speculation and ruthlessly checked it" (Jones, 1961, p. 23), Jones thus formulates his viewpoint about Freud's career choice: "The conflict between giving himself up unrestrainedly to thinking— and doubtless also to the play of phantasy—and the need for the curb of a scientific discipline ended in a decided victory of the latter" (Jones, 1961, p. 25). Indeed, Jones himself, in his psychological constitution, shared Freud's prejudice against philosophy, which, as we will see, Freud developed out of his original defensive use of it.

Although critical of Jones's viewpoint, which he qualifies as "a rationalization at the service of defense" (Eissler, 1974, p. 76), Kurt Eissler, taking as his point of departure the young Freud's sexual inhibition, actually moves along a similar line when he states: "The study of medicine made the satisfaction of the sexual curiosity

---

[3] In Wittels' words: "*Ich verurteilte mich zu Medizin, um mich an den soliden Boden der Tatsachen zu ketten. So war es vielleicht auch bei Freud. Er hat eine harte und langjährige Tatasachenschule durchgemacht*" (1924, pp. 13–14). In my translation: "I condemned myself to medicine, in order to bind myself to the solid ground of facts. This was probably also the case of Freud. He went through a hard and long school of facts."

possible and, at the same time, through the constraint of having to study a large number of ordinary facts, the avoidance of his own fantasies" (Eissler, 1974, p. 78). Indeed, the research project he conducted in Trieste on the reproduction of eels stimulated his sexual fantasies to such an extent that he ended up not seeing any women around town—as we can gather from his letter to Eduard Silberstein of April 5, 1876 (see Boehlich, ed., 1990).

In a paper published in Italian in 1992, Robert Holt on the one hand defines Freud's last year of *Gymnasium*, on the basis of his letters to Fluss, as an "identity crisis" (Erikson), and on the other emphasizes the unconscious activation of his pre-oedipal experience provoked in him by Goethe's (Tobler's) essay on Nature, as conducing to his choice of medical school. James Barron and others have pursued a similar line of thought: "Curiosity, fear and exhilaration came upon him while hearing the essay 'On nature'. There it was—a magnificent opportunity to explore, in *displacement* and *disguise*, the dark and dangerous maternal continent to which he 'owed a death'" (Barron et al., 1991, p. 151).

Freud's letters to Silberstein, from whose study (see Conci, 1992) I derived some of the stimuli conducive to the line of thought developed in this paper, also point in the direction of a deep identity crisis connected to his professional choice. Notwithstanding the fact that "in his first semester, October 1873 to March 1874, Freud signed up for twenty-three hours a week: twelve lectures in anatomy and six in chemistry together with practical work in both" (Jones, 1961, p. 27), here is what he wrote to Eduard on July 17, 1873:

> Of the next, my first university, year, I can give you the news that I shall devote all of it to purely humanistic studies, which have nothing to do with my later field but will not be unprofitable for all that . . . . To this end, I shall be attending the philosophy faculty during my first year. So, if anyone (?) asks me, or you on my behalf, what I intend to be, refrain from giving a definite answer, and simply say: a scientist, a professor, or something like that. (see Boehlich, ed., 1990, p. 24)

And here is Freud's view of the problem the day after the personal visit to Franz Brentano that he made with Joseph Paneth (1857–1890) on March 14, 1875: "When we asked for personal advice, he told us that it was quite feasible and a good idea for us to attempt a doctorate in philosophy as well as in medicine, and that this was not unprecedented – Lotze had done just that and had opted for philosophy" (Boehlich, ed., 1990, pp.102–103).

It was only after his visit to his half-brothers Emanuel (1833–1914) and Philip (1836–1911) and their families in Manchester in the summer of 1875, after his second year of medical school, that he was apparently able to feel relief about and invest some fantasies in his very conflicted choice of the medical profession, that is,:

> Let me confess to you: I now have more than one ideal, a practical one having been added to the theoretical one of the earlier years. Had I been asked last year what was my dearest wish, I would have replied: a laboratory and free time, or a ship on the ocean with all the instruments the scientist needs; now I waver about whether I should not rather say: a large hospital and plenty of money in order to reduce or wipe out some of the ills that affect our body (Boehlich, ed., 1990, p.127)

In other words, around the choice and the attendance of medical school unfolds a gradual reorganization of Freud's personality. Such a process actually seems to have been, also for him, more important than the mere acquisition of the skills necessary for the practice of medicine.

As he disclosed in his 1927 "Postscript to 'The question of lay analysis'", "I took no interest in anything to do with medicine, till the teacher whom I so deeply respected warned me that in view of my impoverished material circumstances I could not possibly take up a theoretical career" (Freud, 1927; SE 20, pp. 253–254). The growth-promoting character of his relationship to his master, as an alternative father figure, comes out clearly in Freud's 1925 report of the same event, that is, "The turning-point came in 1882, when my teacher, for whom I felt the highest possible esteem, corrected my father's generous improvidence by strongly advising me, in view of my bad financial position, to abandon my theoretical career" (Freud, 1925; SE 20, p. 10).

To take a further step forward, let us now look at how the mystified nature of his 1925 account of this episode, his poor reality testing as a medical student, and the corrective character of the emotional experience (a phrase banished from psychoanalysis since Franz Alexander used it!) he underwent under Brücke clearly emerge if we juxtapose his words to Rado's. Here is Freud: "I worked at this Institute [Brücke's], with short interruptions, from 1876 to 1882, and it was generally thought that I was marked out to fill the next post of Assistant that might fall vacant there" (SE 20, p. 10). And here is Rado:

> David Bakan asks a question which Jones raised but never answered; when did Bruecke make this statement to Freud? Bakan traces it to the flare-up of antisemitism that took place

a few years earlier in Austria and Hungary. While this was true, I assure you it was not the answer. The whole system meant that a Jewish boy who was considered to be greedy, hungry for money, should not even dare to go into a laboratory where research work was being done . . . . The assumption was that those people who stayed in the universities came from families with means of their own, just as you could not become a diplomat unless your family could afford it, or else it was misery. (Roazen, 1995, pp. 46–47)

In other words, what we can further gather from such a point of view is that only medical school could offer the possibility Freud eagerly needed not only to find "men whom I could respect and take as my models" (Freud, 1925; SE 20, p. 9), but to develop with them that kind of a growth-promoting experience that only the intensive daily contact unique to a scientific laboratory allows.

Here is what he wrote to Heinrich Braun's widow, Julie Braun-Vogelstein, in 1927: "with the vague perception of youth I guessed that he [Heinrich] possessed something which was more valuable than any success at school and which I have learned since to call 'personality'" (see E.L. Freud, ed., 1960, p. 379). As we will see going over his early letters to Fluss, Freud was then the typical high-achiever in school, with a fragile and rather immature personality, whose intellectual pursuits had basically a defensive quality.

Of course, such a perspective would also throw new light upon Freud's unwillingness to include what are known as his pre-analytic writings in his *Gesammelte Schriften*. Insofar as self-cure was his leading unconscious motivation in putting the former ones together, we can also more easily understand, for example, the lack of clear conclusions of his above-mentioned first scientific paper (Freud, 1877). "Since it is not allowed to dissect human beings, I really have nothing to do with them" (Boehlich, ed., 1990, p. 146), wrote the young scientist to his friend Silberstein-Berganza from Trieste on April 5, 1876. The same might also apply to his incapacity to pursue his studies on cocaine with the scientific rigor shown by his peer—the ophthalmologist—Dr. Koller.

As far as other possible reasons for the choice of medical school are concerned, here are the ones which Freud himself explicitly excluded, in his 1927 "Postscript":

I have no knowledge of having had any craving in my early childhood to help suffering humanity. My innate sadistic disposition was not a very strong one, so that I had no need to develop this one of its derivatives. Nor did I ever play the 'doctor game'; my infantile curiosity evidently chose another path. (Freud, 1927; SE 20, p. 253)

Let us go back now to my attempt to arrive at an alternative formulation about Freud's choice of medical school. I will try to articulate it, with particular regard to his above-reported mysterious 1927 statement, before presenting the evidence pointing in the same direction that I derived from the Fluss letters. Here is my formulation: What compelled Freud to deviate from his original purpose and take a new direction—enrol in medical school—was the change in his perception of himself and in his attitude about life that was imposed upon him by his relationship with both Silberstein and Fluss, and which we find well documented in the Fluss letters. This change he apparently was neither able to consciously articulate in detail nor to make more understandable to us. We are left in the dark even with regard to the measure of the external and internal forces making up such a compulsion. Knowing that Freud's father had "insisted that, in the choice of a profession, I should follow my inclinations alone" (Freud, 1925; SE 20, p. 8), we find it hard to think in terms of an external force acting upon him.

The original German version, *"Ich bin Arzt geworden durch eine mir aufgedrängte Ablenkung meiner urspruenglichen Absicht"* (Freud, 1927; GW 14, p. 290), seems to leave more room for the self-imposed and consequently personally integrated character of a deviation produced interpersonally, that is, by another person or persons, as opposed to a deviation caused by an objective and material cause. This is actually also the direction in which Renata Colorni's Italian translation points: *"Sono diventato medico essendo stato costretto a distogliermi dai miei originari propositi"* (Freud, 1927; OSF 10, p. 418), in which the paradoxical expression *"costretto a distogliermi"* makes the reader think of an unexpected interpersonal event that the subject is capable of integrating into his behavior by actively leaving behind his original purpose. In fact, the more active we are in this latter operation, that is, the less we passively submit to it, the more we are likely to be able, later in life, to find again what we actively turned our back against.

At this point, before turning to the last of the four questions which I presented above, and to which I have just found an important key, let me summarize what we have discovered. The paradoxical expression "being compelled to deviate" represents Freud's condensed evocation of an interpersonal event—such as his relationship with both Eduard and Emil, which exerted upon him an unexpected and positive effect, which he allowed to influence his life to the point of deviating from his original purpose, and which he tried to integrate into his view of himself.

Moving from the first to the last of the four questions I articulated above, this is what I can say: what allowed Freud to find his way back to his earliest path was his own unconscious! By this I not only mean the fact that his earliest path did of course leave such traces in his unconscious as to make it possible for him to find it again. What I really most want to point out is the fundamental role Freud's unconscious played in the whole operation. As we will see, through his relationship with Emil and Eduard he *unconsciously* understood (we are dealing, as we will see, with an *unformulated* kind of comprehension) the defensive, and consequently not particularly productive, nature of his intellectual pursuits (his above-cited "curiosity towards human concerns"). In the second place, Freud *unconsciously* devised the plan[4] to deviate from his original purpose, and try to keep alive the enriching interpersonal and growth-promoting challenge posed by such relationships as the best way to come back to it later. In other words, he unconsciously envisioned the plan to come back to it, to his original purpose, after the process of personal growth—set in motion by his friends and continued through medical school—had made him capable of taking it up again, no longer in a defensive way, but in a constructive way.

After all, how else could we explain such a complex experiential route such as the one which Freud followed and describes to us, if not on the basis of his own postulate of unconscious mental functioning? Has he not placed at the beginning of *The Interpretation of dreams* Virgil's verse "*Flectere si nequeo Superos, Acheronta movebo*"? Does this not mean "If I cannot get along with the conscious mind, I will rely on the unconscious"? As we will see, Freud's reliance on his unconscious as the best guide to his actions was probably the key which he derived, without realizing it, from his relationship with Eduard and Emil and which led him to choose medical school.

At this point, I can easily answer the third question and say that the triumph of Freud's life consisted not only in finding his way in life relying on his unconscious, but,

---

[4] I make use of the concept of "unconscious plan" as developed by Joseph Weiss, Harold Sampson, and the Mount Zion Psychotherapy Research Group in their 1986 book on the psychoanalytic process. According to the higher mental functioning hypothesis developed by the San Francisco group, we may—put simply—unconsciously plan and carry out a variety of behaviors, unconsciously learn from experience, and unconsciously regulate our defensive processes.

even more, in his capacity to unexpectedly make out of such a personal experience the starting point of a new, and revolutionary discipline—psychoanalysis.

Now that I have formulated my answer, I will take up the young Freud's letters to Fluss, and thus both articulate it through them and also integrate all the data I have presented so far in the best possible frame we have at our disposal. The seven letters and two post-cards which make up Freud's earliest correspondence at our disposal cover a time span which goes from September 18, 1872, to April 18, 1874, with the central position occupied by four letters written by Freud between February 1 and June 16, 1873. The latter, the famous "*Maturabrief*," came out in the journal *Imago* in 1941 and was included in the 1960 volume of letters edited by Ernst Freud. The remaining part of the correspondence was found by accident by Masud Kahn in the Freud papers donated to the library of the British Institute of Psychoanalysis and published in the *International Journal of Psycho-Analysis* in 1969.[5] Ilse Grubrich-Simitis wrote in her introduction to their 1971 German edition in book form: "They belong to the earliest documents of Freud, and at the same time contain the origins of psychoanalysis, since they show us, much better than any reconstruction would, those talents which Freud made use of in his discoveries" (Grubrich-Simitis, 1971, pp. 103–104; my translation). I will not present a systematic reading of the letters: it will be enough to show one of the fundamental motifs which runs through them, that is, the parallel we can establish between Freud's growing awareness of the defensive nature of his intellectual pursuits and of the consequent necessity to come out of his isolation, on the one hand, and his choice of medical school on the other.

Such a parallel is revealed very clearly in Freud's letter of May 1, 1873, the letter in which we can read the above-quoted words "I read Horatian odes, you live them" (E.L. Freud, ed., 1969, p. 424). In my opinion, these words capture very well the emotional climate of the whole correspondence, that is, not only Freud's existential dilemma, but also the transferential—and probably also the actual—role which Emil played in the relationship. In the previous paragraph of the same letter his famous words appear;

---

[5] Here is what Paul Roazen communicated to me by letter (December 30, 1995) with regard to the story of the Fluss letters: "It was I who handed over to the librarian of the British Psychoanalytic Society, who in turn contacted Masud Kahn, those letters of Freud to Fluss. I found them in Jones's papers, which Kahn (like others) had never gone through."

I have decided to be a Natural Scientist and herewith release
you from the promise to let me conduct all your law-suits. It is
no longer needed. I shall gain insight into the age-old dossiers
of Nature, perhaps even eavesdrop on her eternal processes,
and share my findings with anyone who wants to learn. (E.L.
Freud, ed., 1969, p. 424)

In the context of this exchange of letters, these
words make Freud's choice of medical school appear
in a new light, which allows us to go beyond retracing
it to his ambition, to his need to keep his speculative
tendency under control, or to the pre-oedipal unconscious
resonance—the maternal dimension—of the study of
nature.

In the previous letter, of March 17, he wrote:

I have a good deal of reading to do on my own account from
the Greek and Latin classics, among them *Oedipus Rex*. You
deprive yourself of much that is edifying if you can't read
all this, but, on the other hand, you retain that cheerfulness
which is so comforting about your letters (E.L. Freud, ed.,
1969, p. 423)

And in the letter of May 1, 1873, in the paragraph
which comes immediately before the one in which he
communicates his fateful decision: "But once you are a
melancholic, you will suck sorrow from anything that
happens" (E.L. Freud, ed., 1969, p. 424). On the basis of
Freud's envy of his friend's cheerfulness and higher level
of personal integration (see below), an alternative reading
of the words he uses to communicate his decision becomes
possible.

Here is my alternative reading: If Freud wants to
come out of his melancholic state, to be able to live an
emotionally richer life, as his peers do, who—at variance
with him—are even able to approach a girl (see below),
he first of all needs to understand the eternal process
that human beings have been always confronted with,
that is, the process of becoming a person, a real person,
as opposed to hiding behind his intellectual pursuits. In
other words, a natural process which he will have more
chance to understand, in this phase of his life, if he tries
to approach it from the point of view of the natural
sciences. Not only because they will give him less of a
chance—so he thinks—to misuse them for defensive
purposes, as happened before with the classics, but also
because natural science research automatically entails
the possibility of sharing and verifying one's findings,
and, for the person who wants to learn, to be helped in
this direction, that is, to be properly instructed—as he
had not really been up till then, given the fact that he
had not even been able to say a few words to a girl he

liked, that is, Emil's sister Gisela. Such a choice would enable him to eventually live without getting lost, as used to happen in the context of the solitary self-exploratory process nourished by Horace, Sophocles, and many other authors! As we will now see in major detail, such a shift in his orientation, with the consequent choice of medical school, can be best understood in the context of Freud's relationship with Emil Fluss.

The very first hint of such a change of direction appears in his letter of March 17, in the form of what he calls "perhaps the most important bit of news in my miserable life" (E.L. Freud, ed., 1969, p. 423), which can not actually be disclosed since "the matter is as yet undecided" (E.L. Freud, ed., 1969, p. 423). In other words, what comes out first is Freud's awareness of the necessity to give a new direction to his life, in relation to which he further states—in between the two sentences just quoted—"If it [my life] will be of any value, it will be thanks to this event." An event, that is, the choice of medical school, which we can rightly suppose not only not to have been made by him yet, but even not yet to be really clear to him.

The necessity to give a new direction to his life is what clearly comes out of the immediately preceding paragraph. "I shall no longer dispute your happiness," writes Freud to Emil, "If, as you say so triumphantly, I was envious, there is now no longer any cause for it" (E.L. Freud, ed., 1969, p. 422). In other words, as I understand it, there will no longer be any cause for envy on Freud's part, if he changes the direction of his life: if he comes out of the sad existence of the lonely student caught up in the unfruitful process of studying himself in isolation and goes in the direction of the possibility of sharing his life with his peers, in a context in which he will have the chance to eventually enjoy the same emotions as they do and thus become a less conflicted person. This is the context which he will later find in medical school—with particular regard to the way in which such an "unconscious plan" found realization in Brücke's laboratory.

Emil Fluss's realization of Freud's unconscious envy came as a consequence of what he was apparently capable of reading into a paragraph of the previous letter, of February 7, 1873. In this letter Freud had taken up Emil's written account of his meeting with Ottilie, that is, "The other day I went ice-skating, and so did she" (E.L. Freud, ed., 1969, p. 422), and had enlarged it into a nice little story, filled up with all the romanticism which he was personally able to imagine but not to actually live in the first person. He had even arrived at the point of concluding it by writing "*You* find Ottilie" (E.L. Freud, ed., 1969, p. 422, original emphasis). In other words, "I read Horatian odes, you live them" (E.L. Freud, ed., 1969, p. 424)!

In my understanding it is as if out of this very episode, of an insight gained not through mere self-observation but as the result of a meaningful interpersonal relation, the young Freud for the first time really understood what he years later confessed to Martha. "In my youth I was never young," he wrote to her on February 2, 1886 from Paris (E.L. Freud, ed., 1960, p. 202); and, before finishing the same letter, "I have always restrained myself" (E.L. Freud, ed., 1960, p. 203). In other words, it was high time to come out of his inhibited isolation and join his peers in some meaningful communal enterprise, that is, go to medical school.

A further confirmation of the perspective I have been developing so far, with particular regard to Freud's realization of both the defensive and unproductive nature of a study of oneself conducted in isolation and of the consequent necessity to give more room to a real exchange with his peers, is actually what we can find in his last two letters to Emil. Whereas at the end of his "*Maturabrief*" (of June 16, 1873) he confesses to Emil that "mercilessly dissect[ing] your feelings . . . does not provide a firm basis for self-knowledge" (E.L. Freud, ed., 1969, p. 426), he ends his letter of March 6, 1874 claiming that the only reason for him to go to listen to a conference by Professor Carl Bruehl would be to utilize it "as an opportunity for a rendezvous with you" (E.L. Freud, ed., 1969, p. 427). In the previous paragraph of this same letter he even comes to the point of confessing to Emil his growing dislike for Bruehl. Of course, we also hear no word about the popular lecture by him, in which he had read aloud Goethe's essay on Nature which "had decided me to become a medical student" (Freud, 1925; SE 20, p. 8)!

As we can see, out of the nature of Freud's choice of medical school we can not only make fruitful use of his theory of the great role the unconscious plays in mental life, but also find the point at which he was able to leave behind the unproductive merciless dissection of his feelings and head towards what is known as his self-analysis, in reality a basically interpersonal process. This was the nature not only of the work he later conducted with Wilhelm Fliess, as documented in detail by Didier

Anzieu (1986), but also of the growth-promoting exchange he developed with Eduard Silberstein, by going the same route he seems to have discovered with Emil. From this point of view, Freud's gradual development of an interpersonally grounded process of self-analysis and his never consciously articulated choice of medical school belong together. On the one hand, they belong to the same period of his life, and on the other they were both ignored and therefore not articulated by him, though they actually represent the very source—in terms of his personal life— from which psychoanalysis originated.

In my opinion, it was the unconscious character of Freud's choice of medical school, with the consequent possibility of taking up psychology again in the Fliess period, and of working on it no longer from an exclusively defensive perspective, but eventually in a constructive way, that actually represented his fundamental personal experience of the positive power of the unconscious. This very experience led him to attribute to dreams, as a manifestation of the unconscious, the function of keeping alive, in a disguised form, our more personal wishes and desires.

To come back to the starting point of this paper, I feel deeply that, notwithstanding his request to others to maintain an artificial separation of his life and personal experiences from his work, the research work we can do on Freud's biographical and subjective dimensions still represents a rich source of our understanding of and familiarization with psychoanalysis. Inasmuch as he was not able to utilize his unconscious choice of medical school as a good piece of evidence for the constructive power of the unconscious, we can actually more easily understand his own identification with Moses, as the man who discovered the New Land without actually setting his foot on it.

At the same time, I do not of course think that any contemporary analyst can derive any advantages from following Freud's own example of keeping his work separated from his life. We all know that we have entered our profession as, in the first place, a means of self-cure. Freud knew it too, but apparently tried to conceal it, thus performing an operation which both we psychoanalysts and our own discipline fortunately no longer need.

ACKNOWLEDGMENT

I wish to acknowledge the encouragement I received in the pursuit of the line of research articulated in this paper from Marco Bacciagaluppi, Ernst Falzeder, Helmut Junker, Henri Zvi Lothane, and Paul Roazen. I am particularly indebted to Robert Holt and Jan Stensson for their very careful reading and valuable suggestions.

REFERENCES

Anzieu, D. (1986). *Freud's Self-analysis*. London: Hogarth Press. (Original French edition, 1975).

Barron, J.W., Beaumont, R., Goldsmith, G.N., Good, M.I., Pyles, R.L., & Rizzuto, A.M. (1991). Sigmund Freud: The secrets of nature and the nature of secrets. *International Review of Psychoanalysis* 18:143–163.

Boehlich, W. (Ed.) (1990). *The Letters of Sigmund Freud to Eduard Silberstein*. A.J. Pomerans, Translator. Cambridge, MA: Belknap Press of Harvard University Press.

Conci, M. (1992). The young Freud's letters to Eduard Silberstein – Early traces of some psychoanalytic concepts. *International Forum of Psychoanalysis* 1:37–43.

Eissler, K.R. (1974). Über Freuds Freundschaft mit Wilhelm Fliess nebst einem Anhang über Freuds Adoleszenz und einer historischen Bemerkung über Freuds Jugendstil [On Freud's friendship with Wilhelm Fliess with a note on Freud's adolescence and an historical note on the young Freud's style]. *Jahrbuch der Psychoanalyse* 2:39–100.

Freud, E.L. (Ed.) (1960). *Letters of Sigmund Freud*. New York: Basic Books.

———— (1969). Some early unpublished letters of Freud. *International Journal of Psychoanalysis* 50:419–427.

Freud, S. (1925). An autobiographical study. *Standard Edition* 20, pp. 1–70. (German: Selbstdarstellung. *Gesammelte Werke* 14, pp. 33–96).

———— (1927). Postscript to "The question of lay analysis." *Standard Edition* 20, pp. 251–258. (German: Nachwort zur "Frage der Laienanalyse." *Gesammelte Werke* 14, pp. 287–296. Italian: Poscritto a "Il problema dell'analisi condotta da non medici." *Opere di Sigmund Freud* 10, pp. 416–423).

———— (1930). Address delivered in the Goethe House at Frankfurt. *Standard Edition* 21, pp. 208–212.

———— (1935). Postscript to an autobiographical study. *Standard Edition* 20, pp. 71–74. (German: Nachschrift 1935. *Gesammelte Werke* 16, pp. 31–34).

Grubrich-Simitis, I. (1971). Jugendbriefe an Emil Fluss. Editorische Hinweise [Youth letters to Emil Fluss. Editorial indications]. In I. Grubrich-Simitis (Ed.), *Schriften von Sigmund Freud zur Geschichte der Psychoanalyse* [Writings of Sigmund Freud on the history of psychoanalysis] (pp. 103–106). Frankfurt: Fischer.

Holt, R.R. (1991). Freud's occupational choice and the unconscious reverberations of Goethe's "On nature." Unpublished paper. Italian: La scelta professionale di Freud e le risonanze inconsce del saggio di Goethe "Sulla natura". *Psicoterapia e Scienze Umane*

26(4):5–32.

Jones, E. (1961). *The Life and Work of Sigmund Freud. Edited and Abridged in One Volume by L. Trilling and S. Marcus.* New York: Basic Books.

Junker, H. (1991). *Von Freud in den Freudianern. Essays* [On Freud in the Freudians. Essays]. Tübingen: Diskord.

Masson, J.M. (Ed.) (1985). *The Complete Letters of Sigmund Freud to Wilhelm Fliess, 1887–1904.* J.M. Masson, Translator. Cambridge, MA: Belknap Press of Harvard University Press.

Roazen, P., & Swerdloff, B. (1995). *Heresy: Sandor Rado and the Psychoanalytic Movement.* Northvale, NJ: Aronson.

Weiss, J., Sampson, H., and the Mount Sinai Psychotherapy Research Group (1986). *The Psychoanalytic Process. Theory, Clinical Observation and Empirical Research.* New York: Guilford.

Wittels, F. (1924). *Sigmund Freud. Der Mann, die Lehre, die Schule* [Sigmund Freud. The man, the doctrine, the school]. Leipzig: E.P. Tal.

CHAPTER 3

FREUD'S SELF-ANALYSIS—AN INTERPERSONALLY GROUNDED PROCESS[1]

> I have destroyed all my notes of the past fourteen years, as
> well as letters, scientific excerpts and all the manuscripts of
> my papers . . . . As for the biographers, let them worry, we
> have no desire to make it too easy for them. Each one of them
> will be right in his opinion of 'The Development of the Hero',
> and I am already looking forward to seeing them go astray.
> (E.L. Freud, ed., 1960, pp. 140–141)

INTRODUCTION

Going against Freud's desire to keep his work separated
from his life—one of whose most explicit expressions is
the one contained in the above-reported words written to
Martha on April 28, 1885—we are today convinced of the
need to familiarize ourselves with his life in order to better
understand his work. This is also the best course we can
follow in order to grasp Freud's "personal equation."
Didier Anzieu defined it in terms of a "hysterophobic
mental structure" (Anzieu, 1986, p. 577) and showed how
it still permeates psychoanalysis; for example as regards
"the Freudian arrangement of psychoanalytic space"
(Anzieu, 1986, p. 580). In their attempt to formulate the
subjective roots of personality theories, George Atwood
and Robert Stolorow showed how:

> Freud's wish to restore and preserve an early idealized image
> of his mother ran through his life like a red thread, influencing
> his reconstructions of his early childhood history, his choice
> of a field of study, his important adult relationships, and his
> theoretical ideas. (Atwood and Stolorow, 1993, p. 59)

How Freud's personal orientation still permeates
psychoanalysis, in the form of the primacy of intellectual
insight and the marginal role of affects as a route to
change, was recently shown by Charles Spezzano (1993).
In my opinion, revisiting the creation of psychoanalysis
in the context of Freud's personal development allows
us not only to grasp better his "personal equation," but
also to show the importance of Harry Stack Sullivan's
(1892–1949) interpersonal theory. One of the major
achievements of Anzieu's reconstruction of Freud's self-
analysis was to reconceptualize it in terms of "a constant

[1] The original version of this article was published in Volume 7 (1998)
of the *International Forum of Psychoanalysis,* pp. 77–84. It represents
the revised version of a paper given in May 1996 at the IFPS Scientific
Conference held in Athens.

dialogue with Fliess" (Anzieu, 1986, p. 569), whose crucial role he convincingly documents. In my opinion, one further element of Freud's "personal equation" is his imperviousness to the interpersonal dimension of human development—including his own.

In a paper I recently contributed to the anthology *Behind the scenes. Freud in correspondence* (Conci, 1996), I tried to find an answer to the question "Why did Freud choose medical school?" in the light of the letters he wrote, between September 18, 1872 and April 18, 1874, to Emil Fluss. These letters allow us to discover both Freud's gradual development of an interpersonally grounded process of self-analysis and the background of his choice of medical school. During the preparation of this paper I also had the chance to take into careful consideration the five aphorisms he composed at age sixteen (see Eissler, ed., 1974), which well reflect a conflicted adolescent's search for self-understanding conducted in isolation, through mere self-observation.

In a paper presented in Bologna in the spring of 1991, Robert Holt proposed the following view of Freud:

> Freud was a far more complex person than the heroic genius of unwavering virtue in whom Jones was so eager to make us believe. I find his extraordinary accomplishments much more credible on the hypothesis that his genius was fired with strong passions, and kept restlessly active by unresolved conflicts. (Holt, 1991, p. 30)

In accordance with the developmental orientation of such a view, I believe that we will eventually have to stop following the official viewpoint promulgated by Ernest Jones, according to which Freud's self-analysis started in response to his father's death and his relationship with Fliess (Jones, 1961, Chapter 14), and instead see it as a continual process running through his entire life. Whereas even such a fine book on self-analysis as the one recently edited by James Barron (Barron, ed., 1993) does not address this problem, more than thirty years ago it had not escaped Marthe Robert that, in his letters to Martha, Freud "was already analysing himself with rare perception" (Robert, 1966, p. 72).

As we will see, Freud's self-analysis was initially nourished by his study of the Greek and Latin classics; it acquired the necessary interpersonal dimension through his relationship with Fluss and Silberstein; it gained a cathartic and thus therapeutic quality through his relationship with Martha; and it eventually became a professional enterprise once his patients forced Freud, with the help of Fliess, to systematically look into himself.

INSPIRATION FROM CLASSICAL STUDIES AND INTROSPECTIVE SELF-ANALYSIS

As we all know, Freud's secondary education took place in the classical *Gymnasium*, with its heavy emphasis on Greek and Latin. As we learn from the so-called *Maturabrief* he wrote to Emil Fluss on June 16, 1873, a Latin translation from Virgil and a Greek translation from Sophocles' *Oedipus Rex* (!) were among the assignments in his final high school exams (E.L. Freud, ed., 1960, p. 4).

In his detailed analysis of Freud's cultural background, Harry Trosman writes:

> The use of Greek names for crucial psychological concepts (Oedipus, Eros and Thanatos, Narcissus), the frequent references to classical myth, the shared values regarding morality and aesthetics, the fascination with Greek and Roman sculpture and archeology, all attest, to the indelible impression of the classical Gymnasium (Trosman, 1976, p. 68)

Freud's classical education "provided a complex substratum against which universals concerning the human mind could be tested" (Trosman, 1976, p. 70).

Twenty years later, Robin Mitchell-Boyask's analysis of "Freud's reading of classical literature" allowed him not only to show "the symbiosis between Freud and classical literature" (Mitchell-Boyask, 1993, p. 27), but to even conclude his essay confirming Frederic Wyatt's 1988 contention that

> the departure of psychoanalysis from Europe during the war brought about a similar impoverishment of psychoanalysis, as the culture which also nourished Freud's thought was lost (Mitchell-Boyask, 1993, p.41).

The five aphorisms that the fifteen-year-old Freud published in 1871 in his school newspaper *Musarion* reflect the first stage of his assimilation of classical culture. According to Kurt Eissler, who edited (Eissler, ed., 1974) and repeatedly dealt with them (see Eissler 1974, 1978), "the keenness of Freud's psychological interest and insight is already visible" (Eissler, 1978, p. 498) in Freud's first literary production known to us. Whereas the first aphorism, "Gold inflates man like air a hog's bladder" (Eissler, 1978, p. 463), reflects—according to Eissler—a precocious adolescent's awareness of man's narcissistic weakness (Eissler, 1978, p. 463), the second, "The most egoistical of all is the man who never considered the possibility that he may be an egoist" (Eissler, 1978, p. 463), gives us important clues to the young Freud's state of mind. Inasmuch as "self-observation and self-judgement are called in as moral agencies that may reduce the gravity of a vice" (Eissler, 1978, p. 463), Eissler ends up bringing this aphorism in connection with a very gifted adolescent's preconscious suspicion that "self-observation [may] be misused as a form of protection against feelings of guilt" (Eissler, 1974, p. 108). It is no wonder that the third aphorism, "Some people are like a rich, never completely explored mine" (Eissler, 1978, p. 463), which is "the earliest picture of man known to us formulated by the young Freud" (Eissler, 1974, p. 112), strikes us "as an anticipation of a basic psychoanalytic theme: man's inexhaustible unconscious, which is not directly accessible to view" (Eissler, 1974, p. 112). On this basis, Eissler brings the fourth aphorism, "Some human beings are minerals, some are yellow biotite and some are white biotite" (my translation of the original German; Eissler, ed., 1974, p. 102), in connection with the fundamental methodological rule of psychoanalysis: do not trust what lies on the surface! (Eissler, 1974, p. 114). This is true inasmuch as biotite shines like a mineral but is worthless. And here comes the fifth and last aphorism, "Any larger animal outdoes man in something, but he outdoes them in everything" (Eissler, 1978, p. 463): "The young pessimist apparently needed some hope," comments Eissler, "just as later, when he was an aged man, he clung to the hope that the voice of intellect wins out in the long run" (Eissler, 1978, p. 463).

From a clinical point of view, it does not escape Eissler that the young Freud's "tendency to speculative generalizations, which we encounter in the aphorisms, might be the expression of a defense against his coercive daydreaming" (Eissler, 1974, p. 118), namely what Jones called his "giving himself up unrestrainedly . . . to the play of phantasy" (Jones, 1961, p. 25). According to Eissler, Freud's preconscious realization of the limits of such a defensive posture is what we can infer from the following words he wrote to Fluss two years later, in the above-cited *Maturabrief* of June 16, 1873: "I am not asking you—should you ever find yourself in the position of doubting yourself—that you mercilessly dissect your feelings; but if you do, you will see how little there is in yourself to be sure of" (E.L. Freud, ed., 1969, p. 426). Inasmuch as "the merciless dissection of his feelings was probably motivated by the attempt to resolve his conflicts through inner processes, namely through insights and not through spontaneous actions" (Eissler, 1974, p. 120), we can also better understand why the sixteen-year-old Freud had not been able to court Gisela Fluss in the summer of 1872. He wrote to Silberstein from Freiberg on September 4, 1872:

"The affection appeared like a beautiful spring day, and only *the nonsensical Hamlet in me, my diffidence,* stood in the way of my finding it a refreshing pleasure to converse with the half-naive, half-cultured young lady" (Boehlich, ed., 1990, p. 16; emphasis added)

Before showing how, through his relationship with Fluss, he was later able to transform a defensive tendency to self-observation into an interpersonally grounded and growth-promoting self-analytic process, let me make a couple of further considerations. In their attempt to integrate psychoanalysis into the history of introspective psychology, John Gedo and Ernest Wolf compared Michel de Montaigne's (1533–1592) system of thought with the body of Freud's theories, and after claiming that "nothing in Montaigne's *Essays* is in disagreement with psychoanalysis" (Gedo and Wolf, 1976a, p. 39), they ended up defining the latter as "the reintegration of the humanist introspective mode into the scientific study of man" (Gedo and Wolf, 1976a, p.45). "Indeed, as a body of knowledge— even as a relevant field of investigation—the patrimony of introspective psychology," claimed Gedo and Wolf, "was excluded from Western science until the intellectual triumph of Freud's ideas within our lifetime" (Gedo and Wolf, 1976a, p. 40). In their description of Montaigne's way of working, they also show us how his basic principle was "Let us only listen; we tell ourselves what we most need" (Gedo and Wolf, 1976a, p.38). On the basis of the line of thought I have been developing, I would say that this type of introspective self-study, which Montaigne developed outside of a meaningful interpersonal exchange, expresses the same mental attitude from which Freud was able to free himself through his relationship with Fluss and Silberstein.

In Paul Kristeller's words (reported by Gedo and Wolf), "When we come to the end of the Renaissance, the subjective and personal character of humanist thought finds its most conscious and consummate philosophical expression in the *Essays* of Michel de Montaigne. The essay, in the form which he created and bequeathed to later centuries, is written in the first person, like the humanist letter, and is equally free in its style and structure: we might call the essay a letter written by the author to himself" (Gedo and Wolf, 1976a, p. 17). And a little below: "What all humanists actually felt but did not express in so many words, he states most bluntly and clearly, namely that he intends to talk primarily about himself and that his own individual self is the chief subject matter of his philosophising" (Gedo and Wolf, 1976a, p. 17).

We also know that the basic ingredients of the era inaugurated by Descartes' 1637 *Discourse on method* were what I would call the interpersonal principles typical of science, namely what Sullivan—in another context—used to call "consensual validation," and what a scientist would address as the necessity to share a common method, and to confront and discuss the results achieved by it.

It is no wonder that the young Freud turned his back on philosophy and classical culture, though they mattered so much to him: he had ended up integrating them into the defensive apparatus which sustained the above-depicted exclusively introspective self-study. By keeping in mind these developmental vicissitudes of the young Freud, we can also better understand what Patricia Herzog has aptly called "The myth of Freud as anti-philosopher," which is usually considered to center around his tenacious attempt to establish the scientific status of psychoanalysis very much at the expense of philosophy (Herzog, 1988, p. 165).

THE SIGNIFICANCE OF FREUD'S RELATION TO EMIL FLUSS

The seven letters and two post-cards that the young Freud addressed to his Freiberg friend Emil Fluss, which represent Freud's earliest correspondence known to us, cover a time span which goes from September 18, 1872 to April 18, 1874, with the central position occupied by four letters written between February 1 and June 16, 1873 (E.L. Freud, ed., 1969). In her introduction to their 1971 German edition in book form, Ilse Grubrich-Simitis wrote:

> They belong to the earliest documents of Freud, and at the same time contain the origins of psychoanalysis, since they show us, much better than any reconstruction would, those talents which Freud made use of in his discoveries. (Grubrich-Simitis, 1971, pp. 103–104)

Their original German publication in 1970 (in the Frankfurt journal *Psyche*) was accompanied by an essay, "The 'Ich.' letters" ("Ich." stands for Ichthyosaura, alias Gisela Fluss), written by John Gedo and Ernest Wolf (Gedo and Wolf, 1976b) from a self-psychological point of view, which deserves to be briefly commented upon.

Apparently taking as their basic point of reference the following words which Freud wrote to Fluss in the *Maturabrief*, " I am sure, [you] have until now not been aware that you are exchanging letters with a German stylist"(E.L. Freud, ed., 1969, p. 425), Gedo and Wolf limit themselves to reconstructing Freud's classical sources

(Horace, the Bible, Shakespeare, Goethe and Heine), whom they reconceptualize as "ideal imago figures for the consolidation of his self-esteem" (Gedo and Wolf, 1976b, p. 85). By placing these letters in Horace's tradition of the epistle, they end up merely considering them as "the externalization of a necessary internal dialogue" (Gedo and Wolf, 1976b, p.81). The real dialogical nature of Freud's letters thus completely vanishes from their view. This is reflected in Gedo's and Pollock's 1976 introduction to this article:

> Kristeller (1965) has designated Montaigne's *Essays* as humanist letters addressed by the author to himself. In this sense, Emil Fluss may be seen as Freud's provincial alter ego, an externalization of Freud's internal audience for the productions of a great German stylist. (Gedo and Pollock, 1976, p.73)

In my opinion, the above-reported words to Fluss can be much better understood in the context of the dialogue with him which takes place in Freud's letters, with particular reference to the following key words contained in the letter of May 1, 1873, namely: "I read Horatian odes, you live them" (E.L. Freud, 1969, p. 424). How well these words capture the emotional climate of the adolescents' exchange is shown by the following passage taken from the letter of March 17, 1873:

> I have a good deal of reading to do on my own account from the Greek and Latin classics, among them Sophocles' Oedipus Rex. You deprive yourself of much that is edifying if you can't read all these, but, on the other hand, you retain that cheerfulness which is so comforting about your letters. (E.L. Freud, 1969, p. 423)

How the seventeen-year-old Freud could really open himself up to his friend Emil, and feel the benefit of his closeness, is further demonstrated by the following words taken from his letter of May 1, 1873: "But once you are a melancholic, you will suck sorrow from anything that happens" (E.L. Freud, 1969, p. 424). At the end of this letter he thus implores his friend: "Only don't again stop writing for months or you will make me consider Mr Emil Fluss in Freiberg an asset lost for me" (E.L. Freud, 1969, p. 424). In my understanding of their exchange, Freud's claim to be "a German stylist" thus reflects his need to compensate his melancholia, and to find a constructive outlet to both his defensive use of Horace and the classics and to his envy as regards Emil's cheerfulness. The above-reported keywords can thus be understood to mean the following: "While I have to limit myself to reading Horace's odes, you can allow yourself to live them in your own life and this makes me envy you."

As the correspondence clearly shows, it was actually through Emil's response to his letter of February 7, 1873 that the young Freud was confronted with his envy for him. "If, as you say so triumphantly, I was envious, there is no longer any cause for it" (E.L. Freud, 1969, p. 422) is what we can read in his next letter of March 17, 1873, in which he apparently starts moving towards the choice of medical school. How Freud's envy surfaces in his letter of February 7 is what we ourselves can experience by patiently examining it. He completely devotes it to "a few comments which came to my mind while reading your letter" (E.L. Freud, 1969, p. 422), thus giving himself the possibility to vicariously experience those very feelings and actions which he had personally avoided going through the previous summer with Emil's sister Gisela. "There is a sentence in your letter"—writes Freud to Emil,

> so unpretentious, plain and simple—but I think it is the profoundest you have ever written: 'The other day I went ice-skating, and so did she'. Can a historian express himself more objectively? But what a story it tells! Allow me to sketch the sequence of events for you. You feel suddenly restless, you can't bear staying at home any longer, a strange presentiment comes over you, almost automatically you pick up your skates; as [if] driven by the force of destiny, you hurry to the fateful place. And there, oh wonderful concatenation of circumstances! *You* find Ottilie. (E.L. Freud, 1969, p. 422, original emphasis)

My contention is that the Fluss letters helped the young Freud to go beyond the kind of introspective self-observation typical of the humanist letter and thus set the stage for the kind of interpersonally grounded self-analysis that he later conducted not only with Fliess, but also, and at a much earlier time, with both Eduard Silberstein and Martha. It is no wonder that his choice of medical school, which in his letter to Emil of May 1, 1873 he defined in terms of the possibility it offered to "share my findings with anyone who wants to learn" (E.L. Freud, 1969, p. 424), can be properly understood in this context. It is also no wonder that such a crucial phase of the young Freud's life can be adequately illuminated in the light of Sullivan's concept of pre-adolescence (Sullivan, 1953, Chapter 16), which he defined in terms of the emergence of a new need, absent in the previous developmental eras, namely the need for "interpersonal intimacy." Such a new need is on the one hand the harbinger of "love" and on the other hand gives rise to the new experience of "collaboration," a big step forward from mere "cooperation," which is typical of the juvenile era. In other words, through his relationship with Emil, Freud apparently entered pre-adolescence, fully experiencing it with Eduard. The extent to which

Eduard took up and expanded Emil's role emerges very clearly from the following words he wrote to him on February 27, 1875:

> You must know how sincerely I rejoiced at all the qualities you possessed and I lacked, your gift of treating the world with humour and your poetic genius in dealing with life, which gives you the right to consider yourself a poet even though you have never turned your hand to rhyme and verse. (Boehlich, ed., 1990, pp. 91–92)

It is no wonder that he had thus introduced Eduard to Martha in his letter to her of February 7, 1884: "We became friends at a time when one does not look upon friendship as a sport or as an asset, but when one needs a friend to share things" (Freud, ed., 1960, p. 96).

EDUARD SILBERSTEIN AND MARTHA

To the interpersonally grounded self-analytic process which the young Freud conducted with Eduard Silberstein we can also ascribe some good therapeutic results. In my opinion, Freud himself preconsciously lived his relationship with him with such an aim in mind. How the melancholia from which he had suffered in the Fluss period disappeared, and how his relationship with Eduard encouraged him to engage in a collaboration to help a friend is what we can learn from the following words he wrote to Silberstein on June 13, 1875, in relation to the depressive condition of their common friend Sigmund Klamper:

> I should naturally make every effort to find time for Klamper, were I to share your view of his condition. Ever since Werther and Faust, every decent 'German man' has experienced a melancholy period of being weary of life without really sharing those heroes' fate. Otherwise, suicide and insanity would be much more prevalent than in fact they are in our half-rational world . . . . Klamper will survive this passing dark mood just as everyone else does . . . . Moreover, your view of his low spirits overlooks the fact that if a person has grounds for complaint at all, then he also feels the need to unburden himself, and he will be most likely to do this with his best friend. And so Klamper pours out his heart to you every week or two with bitter complaints, all the while keeping you in ignorance of what may have pleased him or amused him during this period. I would also ask you to remember that I do not yet enjoy his confidence, and to help me out a little so that in the contacts with him he will feel free to speak of what oppresses him. (Boehlich, ed., 1990, pp. 117–118)

Other researchers (Gedo and Wolf, 1976b) have only stressed the self-analytic aspect and neglected the interpersonal significance of the therapeutic effect of their friendship.

A further key to Freud's preconscious appreciation of the therapeutic quality of his relationship with Silberstein is what we can find in the above-mentioned letter to Martha of February 7, 1884, from which we also learn of a little speech he made in his friend's honor at a time when they were separating to pursue their respective careers. Freud writes:

> Then while we were sitting together in a café . . . I was the first to break the ice and in the name of them all made a speech in which I said he was taking with him my own youth, little realizing how true this was. (E.L. Freud, ed., 1960, p. 97)

If we consider the fact that in his letter from Paris of February 2, 1886, he wrote to Martha "in my youth I was never young" (E.L. Freud, ed., 1960, p. 202), I can suggest the following hypothesis on the therapeutic dimension of both relationships. While Freud's relationship with Eduard helped him to overcome "the nonsensical Hamlet in me" (cf. the above-reported passage of his letter from Freiberg of September 4 ,1872) and to thus eventually court Martha, through his relationship with her he could eventually abreact all the pain and sorrow he had accumulated up to then—to the point of expressing the feeling of never having been young.

As a matter of fact, if we take into careful consideration the first paragraph of this same letter, we can conceive a further interesting hypothesis. Let us listen to Freud again:

> My beloved sweet darling, you write so charmingly and sensibly that every time you speak your mind about something I feel soothed. I don't know how to thank you; I have recently decided to show you a special kind of consideration (you will laugh): by making up my mind not to be ill. For my tiredness is a sort of minor illness; neurasthenia, it is called; produced by the toils, the worries and excitements of these last years, and whenever I have been with you it has always left me as though touched by a magic wand. So I must aim at being with you very soon and for a long time. (E.L. Freud, ed., 1960, p. 200)

Now let us listen to how Jones presented Freud's and Breuer's 1895 "Studies on hysteria": "In the Studies on Hysteria the authors insisted that mere recollection without affective abreaction is of little therapeutic value" (Jones, 1961, p. 178). My hypothesis is that before utilizing the instrument of catharsis with his own patients, Freud had successfully experienced it at the hands of Martha. Of course, I am not oblivious of the fact that any significant love relationship brings about important psychological changes in the two partners; all I want to show is the necessity of first patiently looking into Freud's life, if we really are to understand his work. By this I also mean to imply that Freud's case cannot be different from ours: inasmuch as for most of us the experience of some change in our life was the precondition for us to choose to embark on an analytic experience, this must have also been true of Freud. He must have first experienced some change in his life before trying to devise an instrument which would allow him to help his patients move in the same direction. As we were taught in medical school, medicine is the amplification of nature's healing properties; I believe this to be true also of psychoanalysis. As a matter of fact, Eissler too comes to the point of speaking of Freud's relationship with Martha in terms of "a structural change" (Eissler, 1978, p. 492), whose premises had been laid by the "silent maturation" (Eissler, 1978, p. 490) he had achieved going through medical school.

Indeed, Jones repeatedly hints at Freud's hysteria, but he never puts it in direct connection with his work. Here is an example: "He inferred, from the existence of some hysterical symptoms in his brother and several sisters (not himself: nota bene), that even his own father had to be incriminated" (Jones, 1961, p. 211). In my opinion, we would gain much from rereading Freud's pre-analytic writings and letters trying to figure out how his own attempts at self-cure influenced the development of his ideas—as opposed to merely reconstructing the theoretical path he followed, as Ola Andersson did in 1962 (Andersson, 1962) or Georg Reicheneder in 1990 (Reicheneder, 1990). A fascinating excursion in this direction is contained in Helmut Junker's 1991 book *Von Freud in den Freudianern*, in which he contributes important clues to the construction of Freud's "clinical history."

CONCLUSION

After a very detailed consideration of Freud's adolescence, Eissler could not avoid the conclusion that also in his case "adolescence is the fountainhead of all later creativity" (Eissler, 1978, p. 514). I might not be right in my opinion about what Freud himself called "the development of the hero," but I am sure I have not gone astray by proposing to bridge the gap between his personal development and his development of psychoanalysis. His own self-analysis cannot have been a ready-made instrument, but was probably something he developed in the course of a much longer period of time than merely the Fliess period. In a short essay composed in 1920, "A note on the prehistory of psychoanalytic technique" (Freud, 1920), he himself retraced to his adolescence the roots of the concept of free association. Originally published anonymously, the 1920 note retraces the concept of free association to Ludwig Boerne's 1823 essay "The art of becoming an original writer in three days," which ends up being redefined in terms of "the fragment of cryptomnesia which in so many cases may be suspected to lie behind apparent originality" (Freud, 1920; SE 18, p. 265).

As far as the interpersonal sources are concerned, I would like to point out how Freud himself did not disregard an outlook such as the one later developed by Sullivan. The crucial role of the interpersonal factor clearly stands out in his 1914 short essay "A note on schoolboy psychology":

> My emotion at meeting my old schoolmasters warns me to make a first admission: it is hard to decide whether what affected us more and was of greater importance to us was our concern with the sciences that we were taught or with the personalities of our teachers. It is true, at least, that this second concern was a perpetual undercurrent in all of us, and that in many of us the path to the sciences led only through our teachers. (Freud, 1914; SE 13, p. 242)

In a recent paper entitled "Freud and the interpersonal," Henry Zvi Lothane (1997) has also shown how the point of view we associate with Sullivan's name is not absent from Freud's work.

As a matter of fact, I am of the opinion that the self-analytic work Freud conducted around the above-reported Gisela episode throws much light upon both the interpersonal background of his attempts at self-cure and the evolution of his self-analysis. We can for example read at the end of the third sketch for the "Preliminary communication" of 1893:

> psychical experiences forming the content of hysterical attacks have a characteristic in common. They are all of them impressions which have failed to find adequate discharge, either because the patient refuses to deal with them for fear of distressing mental conflicts, or because (as in the case of sexual impressions) he is forbidden to do so by modesty of social conditions, or, lastly, because he received these impressions in a state in which his nervous system was incapable of fulfilling the task of disposing of them. In this way, we arrive at a definition of a psychical trauma that can be employed in the theory of hysteria: any impression which the nervous system has difficulty in disposing of by means of associative thinking or of motor reaction becomes a psychical trauma. (Freud, 1892, p. 154)

It is possible that all three reasons behind the lack of an adequate discharge were at work in causing the adolescent's trauma bound up with Gisela. Whereas the traumatic effect of Freud's failure to respond to her was articulated by Eissler in 1978, what I have tried to show in this paper is the course Freud took to work it out, ending up, as he did, by making of his life experience the source of a new system of thought.

Only by placing a system of thought in the framework of the life experience of its author can we, in my opinion, really understand it. It was actually the kind of self-analytic work that Freud conducted before what is traditionally considered his self-analysis that allowed him to state in the "Preliminary communication" written together with Breuer:

> The injured person's reaction to the trauma only exercises a completely 'cathartic' effect if it is an adequate reaction—as, for instance, revenge. But language serves as a substitute for action; by its help, an affect can be 'abreacted' almost as effectively. (Breuer and Freud, 1893; SE 2, p. 8)

Although the concepts of unconscious, transference, and resistance, which make up the heart of psychoanalysis were not yet clear in Freud's mind, we can recognize from his words not only an intimate link with his life experience, but also the very essence of psychoanalysis, psychoanalysis as the talking cure we all still practice.

REFERENCES

Andersson, O. (1962). *Studies in the History of Psychoanalysis*. Uppsala: Scandinavian University Books.

Anzieu, D. (1986). *Freud's Self-analysis*. London: Hogarth Press. (Original French edition, 1975.)

Atwood, G.E., & Stolorow, R.D. (1993). *Faces in a Cloud. Intersubjectivity in Personality Theory*. Northvale, NJ: Aronson.

Barron, J.W. (Ed.) (1993). *Self-analysis. Critical Inquiries, Personal Visions*. Hillsdale, NJ: Analytic Press.

Boehlich, W. (Ed.) (1990). *The Letters of Sigmund Freud to Eduard Silberstein*. A.J. Pomerans, Translator. Cambridge, MA: Belknap Press of Harvard University Press.

Breuer, J., & Freud, S. (1893). On the psychical mechanism of the hysterical phenomena. Preliminary communication. *Standard Edition* 2, pp. 1–18.

Conci, M. (1996). Why did Freud choose medical school? *International Forum of Psychoanalysis* 5:123–132.

Eissler, K.R. (1974). Psychoanalytische Einfälle zu Freuds "Zertsreute(n) Gedanken" [Psychoanalytic association to Freud's "free thoughts"]. *Jahrbuch der Psychoanalyse. Beiheft 2. Aus Freuds Sprachwelt und andere Beiträge* (pp. 103–128). Bern: Huber.

Eissler, K. (1978). Creativity and adolescence. The effect of trauma in Freud's adolescence. *Psychoanalytic Study of the Child* 33:461–517.

Eissler, K.R. (Ed.) (1974). Sigmund Freud: Zetrstreute Gedanken

[Sigmund Freud: free thoughts]. *Jahrbuch der Psychoanalyse. Beiheft 2 – Aus Freuds Sprachwelt und andere Beiträge* (p. 102). Bern: Huber.

Freud, E.L. (Ed.) (1960). *Letters of Sigmund Freud*. New York: Basic Books.

—— (1969). Some early unpublished letters of Freud. *International Journal of Psychoanalysis* 50:419–427.

Freud, S. (1892). Sketches for the "Preliminary Communication" of 1893. *Standard Edition* 1, pp. 145–154.

—— (1914). Some reflections on schoolboy psychology. *Standard Edition* 13, pp. 239–244.

—— (1920). A note on the prehistory of psychoanalysis. *Standard Edition* 18, pp. 261–265.

Gedo, J.E., & Pollock, G.H. (1976). Introduction to the "Ich." Letters. In J.E. Gedo and G.H. Pollock (Eds.), *Freud: The Fusion of Science and Humanism. The Intellectual History of Psychoanalysis* (pp. 71–73). New York: International Universities Press.

Gedo, J.E., & Wolf, E.S. (1976a). From the history of introspective psychology: The humanist strain. In J.E. Gedo and G.H. Pollock (Eds.), *Freud: The Fusion of Science and Humanism. The Intellectual History of Psychoanalysis* (pp. 11–45). New York: International Universities Press.

—— (1976b). The "Ich." Letters. In J.E. Gedo and G.H. Pollock (Eds.), *Freud: The Fusion of Science and Humanism. The Intellectual History of Psychoanalysis* (pp. 74–86). New York: International Universities Press.

—— (1976c). Freud's *Novelas ejemplares*. In Gedo J.E. and Pollock G.H. (Eds.), *Freud: The Fusion of Science and Humanism. The intellectual History of Psychoanalysis* (pp. 89–111). New York: International Universities Press.

Grubrich-Simitis, I. (1971). Jugendbriefe an Emil Fluss. Editorische Hinweise [Youth letters to Emil Fluss. Editorial indications]. In I. Grubrich-Simitis (Ed.), *Schriften von Sigmund Freud zur Geschichte der Psychoanalyse* [Freud's writings on the history of psychoanalysis] (pp. 103–106). Frankfurt: Fischer.

Herzog, P. (1988). The myth of Freud as anti-philosopher. In P.E. Stepansky (Ed.), *Freud. Appraisals and Reappraisals. Contributions to Freud Studies*. Vol. 2 (pp. 163–189). Hillsdale, NJ: Analytic Press.

Holt, R.R. (1991). Freud's occupational choice and the unconscious reverberations of Goethe's "On nature." Unpublished paper.

Jones, E. (1961). *The Life and Work of Sigmund Freud. Edited and Abridged in One Volume by L. Trilling and S. Marcus*. New York: Basic Books.

Junker, H. (1991). *Von Freud in den Freudianern. Essays* [On Freud in the Freudians. Essays]. Tübingen: Diskord.

Lothane, H.Z. (1997). Freud and the interpersonal. *International Forum of Psychoanalysis* 6:175–184.

Mitchell-Boyask, R.N. (1993). Freud's reading of classical literature and classical philology. In S.L. Gilman, J. Birmele, J. Galler, and V.D. Greenberg (Eds.), *Reading Freud's Reading* (pp. 23–46). New York: New York University Press.

Reicheneder, G. (1990). *Zum Konstitutionsprozess der Psychoanalyse* [On the origins and development of psychoanalysis]. Stuttgart: Frommann-Holzboog.

Robert, M. (1966). *The Psychoanalytic Revolution. Freud's Life and Achievement.* New York: Harcourt, Brace & World. (Original French edition, 1966).

Spezzano, C. (1993). *Affect in Psychoanalysis. A Clinical Synthesis.* Hillsdale, NJ: Analytic Press.

Sullivan, H.S. (1953). *Interpersonal Theory of Psychiatry* (H. Swick Perry and M. Ladd Gawel, Eds.). New York: Norton.

Trosman, H. (1976). Freud's cultural background. In J.E. Gedo and G.H. Pollock (Eds.), *Freud: The Fusion of Science and Humanism. The Intellectual History of Psychoanalysis* (pp. 46–70). New York: International Universities Press.

INTRODUCTION TO PART TWO—
H.S. SULLIVAN AND S.A. MITCHELL

Of course, there is no need for the Introduction to Part Two to be as long as the Introduction I wrote for Part One, which I felt was necessary to provide the reader with the whole scientific context and background to which the first three chapters of this anthology belong. On the other hand, the three chapters of Part Two have a common denominator that unites them, and that ties them to the three chapters of Part One. I am of course referring to the history of psychoanalysis, and more precisely to the fact that we must rewrite it if we are to better understand both Sullivan's and Mitchell's legacies.

In my book on Sullivan (Conci, 2010, the first, and 2012, the second English edition), I presented him as a psychoanalyst, at variance not only with the more traditional histories of psychoanalysis, but also with both how he ended up presenting himself in the last years of his life, and how he is usually portrayed in the post-Sullivanian literature. In Chapter 6 of this book, which I wrote at the beginning of 2018, I ended up formulating the hypothesis that the medical monopoly of psychoanalysis erroneously established in the USA by the American Psychoanalytic Association in the name of Freud, who was against it, played an important role in what I defined as Stephen Mitchell's post-Sullivanian implicit desire and agenda to found and formulate a purely post-Freudian psychoanalysis. In this Introduction, I will show how the two problems are connected, and how they still await a clear formulation.

As I have already explained in the General Introduction and as the reader can gather from Part One, the chapters of this anthology can be united under the common denominator of psychoanalysis conceived as a dialogue starting with Freud and involving a whole series of authors, a dialogue we need to articulate not only if we want psychoanalysis to further develop itself as a unitary discipline, but also if we wish to work adequately with our patients. Of course, one of the major implications or preconditions of such a dialogue is a careful and respectful revisitation of both the contribution of each one of the authors involved in it, and what we know about their own, personal motives.

A crucial point of departure in developing the point of view I have just formulated is given in the following words with which Elisabeth Young-Bruehl and Murray Schwartz summarized the paper they gave at Yale University in March 2008. This had the title "Why psychoanalysis has no history," and was published in the journal *American Imago* in 2012:

> In this paper we offer a brief history of writing about psychoanalysis' history. We argue that both psychoanalysis and historical writing about it were shaped crucially by the early schisms within psychoanalysis, by Freud's death, and then the diaspora of European psychoanalysis, a trauma history which precipitated a fragmentation or dissociation. We have noted how psychoanalysts have tried to master that trauma with history-writing, and, at certain moments, with a degree of historiographical consciousness. But, we note, psychoanalytic history-writing kept regressing into biography writing, memorializing, or criticizing Freud himself, not the science, and we offer the judgment that even the more historiographically conscious history-writing of the last few years has not yet made psychoanalysis a discipline with a history. It is our assumption that psychoanalysis needs, like a traumatized individual, to be able to tell reflectively the story of the group trauma. (Young-Bruehl and Schwartz, 2012, p. 139)

As the reader can see, in their provocative paper, later published as the first chapter of the 2013 posthumous anthology of Elisabeth Young-Bruehl's papers, with the title *The clinic and the context. Historical essays*, the authors give us a whole series of stimuli, or issues to consider. The first of these points in a complementary direction to the one I dealt with in my Introduction to Part One, in which I showed how the study of Freud's correspondence allows us not only to come to a much more complete picture of Freud's life and work, but also to reconstruct the whole history of the "Psychoanalytic Movement." On the other hand, the historiography of psychoanalysis that Elisabeth Young-Bruehl and Murray Schwartz have in mind is a disciplinary history written in such a way as to help us elaborate and overcome all the traumas that accompanied it, primarily the schisms and conflicts that have produced the fragmentary and theoretically unsatisfactory state of contemporary psychoanalysis. In fact, this is the correct context in which my revisitation of both Sullivan's and Mitchell's work and legacy should be placed. Why did they position themselves outside of Freudian psychoanalysis? Why did they do this even though their production and legacy belong to the new disciplinary dimension "discovered" or originally formulated by Freud? These are the questions that I will try to answer in this Introduction.

Among the books that Young-Bruehl and Schwartz mention as trying to answer the question of why psychoanalysis has no history, let me remind the reader of *Psychoanalysis at the margins*, the intriguing book by Paul Stepansky (2009). In this the author, the former managing director of the Analytic Press (1984–2006), tells the story of a once-cohesive discipline that has split into rivalrous part-fields, each speaking its own language, forming its own institutions, and promulgating its own distinctive version of the psychoanalytic enterprise—as we can read on the book cover. But here is Stepansky's personal testimony concerning how what Freud himself had called "the narcissism of small differences" transformed our field into a conflictual battle-ground with little trace of the kind of professional and scientific collaboration that we need to develop if we are to survive and prosper:

> As Managing Director of The Analytic Press, I experienced the decomposition of American psychoanalysis firsthand. My authors, all psychoanalysts, all men and women of deep insight, all (presumably) doing effective clinical work with their patients – often seemed to live in different professional worlds. Their divergencies were basic and profound. As representatives of one or another psychoanalytic school of thought, they gathered into small enclaves with like-minded colleagues; offered up their own exemplars of great analysts and great analytic work; defined their own standard literature; published their own journals; hosted their own conferences; trained their own successors; and experienced that 'relative fullness of communication' that falls to members of a scientific community. Correspondingly, they expressed, to various degrees and in various combinations, condescension irritation, anger, disapproval, and incomprehension of colleagues who inhabited different psychoanalytic worlds . . . . As an editor and publisher, I came to know and admire American analysts identified with each of the aforementioned schools of thought. But I was frustrated by them as well. Gifted analysts from different walks of professional life never seemed to add up to a collectivity, much less to a community of like-minded professionals with a common body of knowledge. Their disputes, played out at conferences and in the pages of their journals, could and did become personal. (Stepansky, 2009, pp. xi–xii)

Such a sad but realistic portrayal of our community actually allows me to say how I have the feeling that so many of its members are much more interested in what we can define as "the business" they can achieve through their work than they are in making the choice of contributing to and participating in the kind of scientific debate that could allow us, as an analytic community, to attain a more respectable status as a discipline, or the status of a scientific discipline.

In fact, this is a topic that Young-Bruehl and Schwartz also dealt with in the important paper mentioned above, after distinguishing three ways of looking at the past and future of psychoanalysis, and three types of analytic communities centered around them. These are characterized by their incapacity to put together the kind of "reflective trauma story" (see above, and Young-Bruehl and Schwartz, 2012, p. 154) that Young-Bruehl and Schwartz would find appropriate. In their words:

The first of these three commonly heard stories reflects a stance that is depressive. Psychoanalysts drawn to this story acknowledge the fragmentation of their discipline but, rather than look for its cause, they throw up their hands, convinced that Humpty-Dumpty will never be put back together again . . . . A second stance, which is manic, generates a futureward, optimistic story, again without an explanatory past: out of chaos, a new paradigm will certainly come, either a new unifying idea or a clear common ground. Some people of this persuasion will go as far as to announce that the redemptive new psychoanalysis is at hand: object relations theory or attachment theory will embrace all disparate strands; or psychoanalysis will make an alliance with neuroscience that will, finally, dispel any charge that the polyglot psychoanalysis is not scientific. To cite an example, Joseph Schwartz, in his *Cassandra's Daughter* (1999), is a psychoanalyst historian in this vein, who celebrates the triumph of relational psychoanalysis, of which he is a partisan.

Finally, a kind of middle way position, cautious and sometimes obsessional, embraces diversity and tells a very present-oriented story of groups in dialogue, meetings, fruitful pluralism . . . . From the work of Fred Pine, embracing diversity, through Lewis Kirshner's recent *Having a Life: Self-pathology after Lacan* (2004), efforts to negotiate and translate differences have not generated a large following. For practical as well as more deeply rooted psychic reasons, most analysts adhere to and continue the orientation of a local group or subgroup, at least in public. It is difficult for clinicians who do not identify with an orientation to have a presence in such an identity-typed world; they are like stateless people. (Young-Bruehl and Schwartz, 2012, pp. 154, 155, 156)

In other words, this anthology is the product of a "stateless psychoanalyst" trying to revisit and rewrite the history of our field in the light of some of the conflicts, traumas, and group processes that are usually not addressed by the analytic community. As an aside, if I ever wanted to become—let us say—a famous psychoanalyst, Young-Bruehl's words make very clear how this will never be possible, and how, by taking the way I have chosen, the result being the production of this anthology, I have completely missed such a target—a target I never admitted to myself that I was really interested in pursuing. But back to our discourse: Sándor Ferenczi's work and legacy can also be seen in this light, that of a stateless psychoanalyst whose main priority was his analytic research work, and this is the reason why I will shortly deal with him, before turning to Sullivan and Mitchell.

First, however, let me complete my revisitation of the crucial contribution of Elisabeth Young-Bruehl and Murray Schwartz to the way in which we should eventually write the history of psychoanalysis as a discipline. Here, I wish to underline the fact that, since the three modes of approaching the past and future of psychoanalysis described above are "defenses against recognizing the traumatic past," "they all insist that some feature of Freud's legacy must be discarded—and thus they repeat the trauma of splitting and dissociation that has marked psychoanalysis as it banished split-off theories" (Young-Bruehl and Schwartz, 2012, p. 156). According to the authors, colleagues with the first depressive approach discard Freud's structural model; colleagues in the second group jettison Freud's libido theory; and colleagues with the third mode discard Freud's focus on the Oedipus complex. Of course, a similar phenomenon of splitting and discarding is what Sullivan's work and legacy also went through, given the difficulty of understanding it in all its complexity. I will try to elucidate this in the next section.

My aim is to look at the history of psychoanalysis in line with the epistemological perspective developed by Ludwik Fleck (1896–1961), whose work and legacy I have already cited in my General Introduction. I am also very grateful to Arnold Richards for having been the first psychoanalyst to revisit our history in the light of Fleck's point of view (see Chapters 1 and 2 in Richards, 2017). Central to Fleck's contribution is the concept of the "thought collective," which, for our purposes, we can translate as follows: that any candidate undergoing training at any institute of the International Psychoanalytical Association (IPA) is very likely to adopt the one-sided reconstruction of the history of psychoanalysis offered by the institute, and therefore not consider H.S. Sullivan, for example, as a psychoanalyst. In other words, they will follow the "thought collective" to which they, as a candidate, want to belong, as opposed to, for example, finding out autonomously how things really stand, such as in terms of Sullivan's relationship with Freud's legacy and with psychoanalysis as a whole.

This is exactly the direction in which I have always worked and thought, and also exactly the message I want to convey through this anthology. In other words, psychoanalysis should mean that we not only have to find our own voice and help our patients find theirs, but should also find our own way of positioning ourselves in terms of the history and nature of our discipline—as opposed to limiting ourselves to sticking to the "thought collective" of the institute we belong to. How autonomous can we be if we are so little familiar with the kind of autonomous research that psychoanalysis (not only clinically, but also theoretically) should be concerned with? This is how Ludwik Fleck's epistemology, through promoting the need to look at things with our own eyes, goes in the direction of helping us to revisit the history of psychoanalysis in the way I have just described. Elisabeth Young-Bruehl too formulated this dilemma analytically, when she wrote, at the end of her chapter "A history of Freud biographies," that what we need is also a history of Freud as a "transference object." In her own words:

> It is not surprising, of course, that the man who gave
> theoretical formulation to the phenomenon of 'transference'
> . . . should be a 'transference object' for a particular class
> of analyst and non-analyst biographer-historians and more
> generally across our polysemic culture. We need a history of
> this transference object. (Young-Bruehl, 1994, p. 171)

Before dealing with Ferenczi's case, I would like to briefly describe here who Ludwik Fleck was and what his work concerned, having had no room in the General Introduction to do this. Fleck was a Jewish-Polish physician and biologist who was born in Lemberg (Lwóv in Polish, now L'viv, in Ukraine) and carried out important work on epidemic typhus with the Polish biologist Rudolf Weigl (1883–1957)—the inventor of the first effective vaccine against epidemic typhus. In the 1930s, Fleck developed the concepts of *"Denkstil"* [thought style] and *"Denkkollektiv"* [thought collective] (see Fleck, 2011), which help to explain how scientific ideas change over time, much as in Thomas Kuhn's (1922–1996) later notion of "paradigm shift." Having started to collaborate with Weigl as a medical student, Fleck graduated from medical school in 1922 and specialized in bacteriology, the medical research field with which he became most familiar and which later became the starting point and object of his epistemological research, with particular regard to the group and social dynamics behind any scientific progress. In 1927 Fleck spent a year in Vienna working with Rudolf Kraus (1868–1932), a pioneer of laboratory diagnostics, and published his first epistemological paper, "Über einige spezifische Merkmale des ärztlichen Denkens" (Fleck, 1927).

Being very familiar with the German language, he was able in 1935 to publish in Basel his book *Entstehung und Entwicklung einer wissenschaftlichen Tatsache. Einführung in die Lehre vom Denkstil und Denkkollektiv,* published by Chicago University Press in 1979, whose basic ideas anticipated social constructionism and comparative epistemology. According to Fleck, our capacity to perceive and describe any new phenomenon is very much limited by the "thought style" and "thought collective" of the social group to which we belong, with the consequence that any scientific progress becomes possible only after we have helped our research group to first abandon our old ways of looking at things. Such an operation is not easy, exactly because—according to Fleck—every research or thought collective attains over time a specific way of investigating, bringing with it a blindness to alternative ways of observing and conceptualizing. Scientific progress and change becomes easier—according to Fleck—through the collaboration of two different groups, or the combination of their different perspectives. As psychoanalysts, we can certainly feel how Fleck's point of view reminds us of Wilfred Bion (1897–1979) as the author of *Learning from experience* (see Bion, 1962), that is, of his concept of our need to see our ideas confirmed, instead of challenged, and of the anxieties that arise as consequence of anything new and still unfamiliar to us.

After having worked as bacteriologist in several hospitals but mainly in his private laboratory, Fleck was, as a Jew, forced to give up his profession in 1937, which he was able to resume only in 1939, thanks to the Soviet occupation of Poland. When the Germans occupied Lemberg in 1941, Fleck was arrested and could work only under Nazi supervision, then being deported to Auschwitz with his whole family in February 1943. A year later, he was transferred to Buchenwald, where he was able to continue working as a bacteriologist. After the Russian liberation, he had the chance to teach bacteriology and microbiology at various Polish universities, before emigrating to Israel in 1957, where he died on June 5, 1961.

Fleck's 1935 book was reprinted in German through the Frankfurt publisher Suhrkamp in 1980, having been rediscovered by Lothar Schäfer and Thomas Schnelle, and was again republished in 2017. In 2011, Sylvia Werner and Claus Zittel edited a large anthology of 682 pages in which they collected not only all Fleck's papers, but also a whole series of scientific and biographical materials. In their Introduction, we learn not only of the many translations of Fleck's book and papers, but also of the existence of a Ludwik-Fleck Zentrum at the University of Zurich. Here is the new light in which Werner and Zittel place the contemporary reception of Fleck's legacy:

> What Fleck described and formulated in his book was the
> program of an epistemological revolution, which not only
> aimed at understanding the external conditions of scientific
> production, but also to illuminate the role of the unconsciously
> transmitted attitudes coming from tradition and from the
> social milieu . . . . Fleck's radical point is that not only what
> the value of a fact is, but even what a fact is, is the product
> of the decisional process of a specific thought style of a given
> thought collective . . . . Fleck understood much better then
> Kuhn how scientific theory and cultural theory are connected
> to each other . . . . In other words, Fleck's theories have
> eventually emerged from the shadow of Kuhn's theories, and
> have been now recognized as an autonomous epistemological
> position. (Werner and Zittel, 2011, pp. 10, 15–16)

Before we deal with Sullivan and Mitchell, we will consider the very instructive case of Sándor Ferenczi, that is, the most famous case of exclusion from and rediscovery by the analytic community of a psychoanalyst's work and legacy, a psychoanalyst who was for many years Freud's closest and dearest collaborator. The most recent, complete, and trustworthy reconstruction of this complex story is represented by the autobiographical book by Judith Dupont (born 1925) *Au fil du temps . . . Un itinéraire analytique*, which Carlo Bonomi reviewed in the *International Forum of Psychoanalysis* in 2017. Judith Dupont became the literary executor of Ferenczi's posthumously published work after the death of Michael Balint (1896–1970) and we owe to her the 1985 publication in French of Ferenczi's *Clinical diary* and the 1992 publication in French of the first of the three volumes of his correspondence with Freud which I dealt with in the Introduction to Part One.

Judith Dormandi, who in 1952 married Jacques Dupont, was the daughter of the artist Olga Dormandi (1900–1971), born Székely-Kovács and herself the sister of Alice Balint (1898–1939), Michael Balint's first wife. Judith's mother Olga and her aunt Alice were in turn the daughters of one of Ferenczi's most important training analysands, Vilma Kovács (1884–1940), in whose house the analytic group created by Ferenczi used to hold its regular scientific meetings. In 1937 Judith emigrated to France with her parents, and there she later studied medicine and did her training analysis with Daniel Lagache (1903–1972), becoming a member of the French Psychoanalytic Association (APF). In 1969, Judith Dupont founded the journal *Le Coq-Héron*, which played a crucial role in the translation and promotion of Hungarian psychoanalysis in France. No wonder that she was the key person in the rediscovery of Ferenczi's work and legacy, whose beginning we can date to the First International Ferenczi Conference held in New York in 1991, with proceedings edited by Lewis Aron and Adrienne Harris in 1993. Three weeks ago, before writing this Introduction, on Thursday May 3, 2018 in fact, the XIIIth International Sándor Ferenczi Conference, chaired by Carlo Bonomi, was inaugurated in Florence—and it went very well, both scientifically and in terms of the positive human climate experienced by the more than 300 participants.

But here are the main chapters of the sad, dramatic, and traumatic story that probably led to Ferenczi's premature death, on May 22, 1933, at not yet sixty years old, and describes the ways in which his work and legacy for almost sixty years lived a marginal life outside of the so-called analytic mainstream, totally neglected by it. The original clinical research that had characterized *The development of psychoanalysis*, published with Otto Rank in 1924, was continued by Ferenczi in the following years with a series of important papers, starting with "The adaptation of the family to the child" (1927), and culminating in the now very famous paper "Confusion of tongues between adults and the child," which he presented at the IPA Wiesbaden Congress in September 1932. As Ernest Jones wrote in the third volume of his Freud biography, when Ferenczi visited Freud in Vienna before the congress and read his paper aloud to him, Freud reacted very negatively to both the paper and its author, and this was the beginning of the curse that lasted such a long time. But here are Jones' words:

> Without a word of greeting Ferenczi announced on entering the room: 'I want you to read my Congress paper.' Halfway through Brill came in and, since Ferenczi and he had recently talked over the theme, Freud let him stay, though he took no part in the talk. Freud evidently tried his best to bring about some degree of insight, but in vain. A month later Ferenczi wrote to Freud accusing him of having smuggled Brill into the interview to act as judge between them, and also expressing anger at having been asked not to publish his paper for a year. In his reply Freud said the latter suggestion was made solely in Ferenczi's own interest in the hope, which Freud had still clung to, that further reflection might show him the incorrectness of his technique and conclusions. (Jones, 1957, p. 184)

Jones succeeded in preventing Ferenczi's Wiesbaden paper from being published in English until 1949, when it appeared in the *International Journal of Psychoanalysis*. In addition, in the above-mentioned biography of Freud, Jones connected Ferenczi's death with a whole series of negative and unjustified attributions, as we can read in the following quotation:

> The last letter from Ferenczi, written in bed on May 4, was
> a few lines for Freud's birthday . . . . Then there were the
> delusions about Freud's supposed hostility. Towards the
> end came violent paranoiac and even homicidal outbursts,
> which were followed by a sudden death on May 24. That
> was the tragic end of a brilliant, lovable, and distinguished
> personality, someone who had for a quarter of a century been
> Freud's closest friend. The lurking demons within, against
> whom Ferenczi had for years struggled with great distress
> and much success, conquered him at the end, and we learnt
> from this painful experience once more how terrible their
> power can be. (Jones, 1957, p. 190)

In an important review article, Carlo Bonomi (1999)
convincingly demonstrated the lack of foundation of
all Jones's negative allegations and showed how they
contributed to the elimination of Ferenczi's work from
the mainstream of psychoanalysis and from the analytic
literature recommended to candidates in training. But here
is a series of reasons that Judith Dupont formulates in her
book to account for the great resistance that Ferenczi's last
papers caused in his colleagues, starting with Jones himself:
the role assigned by Ferenczi to the concept of trauma,
as opposed to Freud's more or less exclusive emphasis on
our internal fantasies, in the pathogenesis of our patients'
problems; the importance of the personal participation
and involvement of the analyst in the relationship with
the patient, as opposed to Freud's concept of neutrality
or—as we have seen in the Introduction to Part One—
what Merton Gill defines as "minor participation"; the
importance of analyzing our countertransference as a key
to understanding the patient's problems, a point of view
that would start emerging in psychoanalysis only in the
1950s; and, last but not least, the way in which Ferenczi
put his colleagues' narcissism to a hard test, and handled
in a democratic way both analytic training and the life of
psychoanalysis as an institution. As we shall see, Sullivan
had developed a similar clinical perspective and also
suffered from similar problems with his colleagues.

Particularly significant and even moving are the pages
dedicated by Judith Dupont to Ferenczi's *Clinical diary*,
which she proposes as a model of the kind of openness,
honesty, sincerity, and intellectual autonomy that we all
need so that we can best deal with our patients' problems.
To such an assessment Dupont adds also the fact that, in
her experience, no analytic training can really transmit
such a unique attitude, but can only limit itself to helping
the candidates or analysts-in-training find their own
voice, and feel the necessary sense of responsibility for the
patient and the treatment, as opposed to being seduced
into imitating some older colleague. Only such an attitude

can allow us—in Dupont's experience—to perceive and understand the inevitable mistakes we make with our patients, and to find the courage to admit them.

I must admit that I feel particularly in tune with this point of view, which looks at psychoanalysis not only in terms of a very sophisticated intellectual dimension and emotional experience, but also in very simple and down-to-earth human terms. From this point of view, I am ready to define it as the unique situation in which patients can not only say whatever comes to their mind, but also experience a relationship with a level of collaboration and reciprocity that they have never experienced before. To such a dimension also belongs the readiness of the analyst to openly admit and discuss with the patient any mistakes he might have made. From this point of view, human relationships are very simple, that is, they automatically obey a law of reciprocity, according to which, for example, if we are able to excuse ourselves for a mistake, it is very likely that we will be able to promote the same attitude and behavior in the person involved with us in such an exchange. And this is, I believe, the best expression of the analytic principle that we change our relationships by first changing ourselves—or by experiencing a relationship through which we can change. From this point of view, psychoanalysis should also obey the principle that any significant human discovery, if really worthwhile and significant, should imply a complex intellectual work of elaboration, and also be amenable to being explained in very simple, human, terms. Last but not least, the way in which Judith Dupont speaks of analytic training in the light of Ferenczi's *Clinical diary* runs parallel to the type of openness and independence of mind that Ludwik Fleck (and Wilfred Bion) consider necessary for any scientific (or, in our case, emotional) discovery (or, in our case, insight).

In Aron and Harris' 1993 anthology *The legacy of Sándor Ferenczi*, mentioned above, there are at least three chapters of great interest for better understanding Sullivan's case, that is, his professional identity and legacy. The first is Sue Shapiro's "Clara Thompson: Ferenczi's messenger with half a message," in which the author introduces us to the life (1893–1958) and work of this pioneer psychoanalyst, who was in treatment with Ferenczi between 1928 and 1933, and was also Sullivan's successor as director of the W.A. White Institute (1949–1958). Clara Thompson was, in fact, "the patient Dm" in Ferenczi's *Clinical diary*, the one who had spread the rumor that she "could kiss Papa Ferenczi whenever I want," and whom

Ferenczi described as having been "grossly abused by her father, who was out of control" (see Shapiro, 1993, p. 160). Shapiro's chapter centers around the fact that, although Thompson "gave birth to a generation of analysts who, often unknowingly, were deeply immersed in continuing Ferenczi's line of work with countertransference . . . there were several other areas, often very significant, that she neglected to communicate" (p. 159). In other words, for a variety of reasons that the author explores in her chapter (on the one hand, the private nature of the therapeutic work she did with Ferenczi, and, on the other hand, the conservative climate of the 1950s, and the taboo surrounding the mention of Ferenczi's name in the IPA), Thompson explicitly talked so little about Ferenczi, even to her own training analysands, that Ferenczi's role in the development of the interpersonal point of view pioneered by Sullivan started becoming both clear and important only during the 1980s. In her 1982 biography of Sullivan, Helen Swick Perry has a specific chapter on "The influence of Sándor Ferenczi," in which we learn that Sullivan heard Ferenczi lecture at least twice (in December 1926, in New York City, and April 1927 in Washington DC), and that he "persuaded Thompson to go to Budapest and study under Ferenczi so that she could come back and teach him what she had learned" (Swick Perry, 1982, p. 228).

It is no wonder that in the chapter of *The legacy of Sándor Ferenczi* directly following the chapter by Shapiro, Benjamin Wolstein (1922–1998) writes that only with the English publication (1988) of Ferenczi's *Clinical diary* was he eventually able to understand how his clinical focus on "the direct experience between analyst and patient" went back not only to his training analysis with Clara Thompson, but also to her own work with Ferenczi (see Wolstein, 1993, p. 181). Only after he had read Ferenczi's *Clinical diary* was Wolstein able to see and make such a connection explicit, in the article he published in 1989 with the title "Ferenczi, Freud and the origins of American interpersonal relations." This is how Dale Ortmeyer was able to include Ferenczi among the pioneers of interpersonal psychoanalysis in the chapter about its history included in the 1995 *Handbook of interpersonal psychoanalysis*, edited by Marylou Lionells, John Fiscalini, Carola Mann, and Donnel Stern, seventy years after it had begun with Sullivan's psychotherapeutic work with young schizophrenic patients (see Sullivan, 1962).

The third chapter of relevance for what follows is Marco Bacciagaluppi's chapter "Ferenczi's influence on

Fromm," whose first common denominator the author sees in the fact that "because of the originality of their thinking, both endured the ostracism of mainstream psychoanalysis" (Bacciagaluppi, 1993, p. 185). After a detailed analysis of their convergences (for example, the stimulating relationship which both had with Georg Groddeck, 1866–1934) and divergences, Bacciagaluppi comes to the following final considerations:

> There was a deep affinity between Ferenczi and Fromm on certain basic points, such as independence of mind and a loving approach toward the patient. On the other hand, in more ways than one, their contributions may also be regarded as complementary. (1) Both were original thinkers, but whereas Ferenczi never dared to openly challenge Freud's authority, Fromm was very outspoken in his critique of Freud and in his defense of Ferenczi. (2) Both were ostracized by mainstream psychoanalysis. Fromm, however, circumvented this ostracism by reaching out to a much wider public. (3) Fromm could supplement Ferenczi's mostly clinical approach by his wider cultural references . . . . (4) At the clinical level, Fromm's theoretical formulations were very advanced, but Ferenczi seems to have been much more radical in his therapeutic practice. (Bacciagaluppi, 1993, p. 196)

Among other things, Erich Fromm (1900–1980) played an important role in creating the international network that took the initiative of founding, in Amsterdam in 1962, the International Federation of Psychoanalytic Societies (IFPS), which I deal with not only in the Afterword, but also in Chapter 10. Of course, it is a pity that his contribution to psychoanalysis—which I study in detail in my book on Harry Stack Sullivan (Conci, 2010, 2012)—continues to be neglected by the mainstream analytic community. In 2000 I edited a monographic issue of the *International Forum of Psychoanalysis* centered around Fromm's work and legacy (Conci, 2000)—which I have already mentioned in this book, in connection with Ernest Falzeder's translation into English of Fromm's important 1935 paper "The social determinants of analytic therapy."

A final topic that deserves to be briefly mentioned, before dealing with "The case of Sullivan," is the fact that the *International Forum of Psychoanalysis* made an important contribution to what we today can call "The Ferenczi renaissance" by publishing a whole series of papers from several of the twelve International Sándor Ferenczi Conferences held between 1991 (New York) and 2015 (Toronto). This is what Carlo Bonomi and Franco Borgogno deal with in their Editorial introducing Issue 1/2014 of the journal, a monographic issue containing a series of papers given at the XIth Conference, which was held in Budapest at the end of May 2012 (Bonomi and

Borgogno, 2014).

1. THE CASE OF SULLIVAN

In the Prologue to her fascinating biography of Sullivan, Helen Swick Perry speaks of his interpersonal theory as "an American product, raised to the level of science and art through the lonely search and the brilliant observation of a boy growing up in Chenango County at the turn of the century" (Swick Perry, 1982, p. 7). But what was the professional identity of one of the few American-born pioneers of an interdisciplinary and analytically oriented psychiatry? Giving credit to his originality, Sullivan's biographer adopts and documents in her book the peculiar definition proposed by sociologist Dorothy Blitsten in her book *The social theories of Harry Stack Sullivan*, that is, the concept she had developed of him—through many years of contact and collaboration—as "a social scientist whose specialty was psychiatry" (Blitsten, 1953, p. 11).

In fact, Sullivan did not consider himself primarily a psychoanalyst, although he remained a member of the American and International Psychoanalytic Association until his premature death, in Paris, on January 14, 1949. This is what we can read in the encyclopedic *History of psychoanalysis* published in 1979 by Reuben Fine (1914–1993) (Fine, 1979, p. 102). Douglas Noble and Donald Burnham, in their 1989 book chapter on the "History of the Washington–Baltimore Psychoanalytic Society and Institute," wrote that Sullivan became a member of the American Psychoanalytic Association during a meeting held by the Association in Atlantic City, NJ, on June 3, 1924, where he presented the paper "The oral complex" (see Noble and Burnham, 1989, pp. 556–557). As we learn from Helen Swick Perry, the arrival in the USA of the European analysts who had been able to escape from Nazi Germany and Austria changed the composition and the balance of forces of the American Psychoanalytic Association to such a point that Sullivan, whom I consider a "normal American-born psychoanalyst of the first generation," felt the need to stop playing the active role he had played in it for several years, and decided to found and devolve his energies to his own institutions (see below). For example, according to Noble and Burnham (1989, p. 546), on May 31, 1930, as vice-president of the American Psychoanalytic Association, Sullivan presided over the constitutive meeting of the Washington–Baltimore Psychoanalytic Society, which in turn elected Clara Thompson as its first president. The European analysts were much closer to Freud than were their North American colleagues, and many of them even shared Freud's prejudices against America, but this allowed them to take control of the American Psychoanalytic Association. This group also included, on the one hand, Europeans such as Sándor Rado (1899–1981), who in 1931 became the first director of the first North American Institute of Psychoanalysis, the New York Institute; and, on the other hand, those members of the second generation of North American analysts who had gone to Europe (Vienna, Berlin, and London) for training.

Nathan Hale Jr. (1922–2013) describes this delicate phase in the history of the American Psychoanalytic Association in three chapters of his 1995 second volume of the now classical work *Freud in America*: Chapter 6, "Psychoanalytic training: Young Americans abroad;" Chapter 7, "The Depression, schisms, refugees;" and Chapter 8, "The second psychoanalytic civil war and the California case, 1939–1942." In Chapter 10, "Teachers of psychiatry, psychoanalysis and psychosomatic medicine: Adolf Mayer, Harry Stack Sullivan, Flanders Dunbar, Franz Alexander," Hale dedicated several pages to Sullivan, in which we hear the two following versions of his relationship to psychoanalysis. On the one hand, Hale writes:

> Sullivan from the outset made no effort to place his system within orthodox psychoanalytic theory and indeed sharply criticized the psychoanalysts: their tendency to overgeneralize, the dogmatism of some who were filled with the "holy light" of their own personal analyses; the theory that mental disorder resulted from the fixations at past stages; and what he regarded as the projection into infancy and childhood of sexual elements taken from the genital development of adolescence. (Hale, 1995, p. 175).

On the other hand, however, he says: "Sullivan claimed to use what he regarded as the fundamentals of psychoanalysis: interpretation, free association and transference" (Hale, 1995, p. 177).

This is the conflictual context within which Sullivan founded the Washington School of Psychiatry (1936) and the—still existing—journal *Psychiatry* (1938), and in which he left New York City for Washington DC, in order to work as a supervisor and lecturer at the Chestnut Lodge Sanitarium; here he held the lectures out of which Helen Swick Perry edited his posthumous work in the 1950s. *The interpersonal theory of psychiatry* came out in 1953 and *The psychiatric interview* in 1954, but only the first of his seven books available in English, *Conceptions of modern psychiatry* (1940), came out during his lifetime.

In 1943—together with Erich Fromm, Frieda Fromm-Reichmann (1889–1957), Clara Thompson, and Janet (1905–1974) and David Rioch—Sullivan founded the New York Branch of the Washington School of Psychiatry, which in 1946 became the White Institute of Psychiatry, Psychoanalysis and Psychology—still located in the Clara Thompson building on the Upper West Side. As an aside, an important paper by Clara Thompson on "The history of the William Alanson White Institute," the text of a talk she had given in 1955, was published in 2017 in *Contemporary Psychoanalysis*—the journal founded by the White analytic community in 1964. As Swick Perry documented in her book, William Alanson White (1870–1937), the director (1903–1937) of the biggest and most important North American psychiatric hospital, Saint Elisabeth's Hospital in Washington DC, had played a key role in promoting Sullivan's career as both a psychiatrist and a psychoanalyst, ending up occupying an important place in both his heart and mind.

Together with Smith Ely Jelliffe (1866–1945), White founded in 1913 the—still existing—*Psychoanalytic Review*, a psychoanalytic journal that, not having met with Freud's sympathies, as documented by John Burnham (1929–2017) in his important book of 1983 *Jelliffe: American psychoanalyst and physician and his correspondence with S. Freud and C.G. Jung*, has not yet been recognized as "psychoanalytic," that is, as belonging to the psychoanalytic establishment! This is what we can find implied in Henry Smith's 2010 farewell as editor of the *Psychoanalytic Quarterly*, founded in 1934 by a group of "orthodox" members of the American Psychoanalytic Association, when he greeted Jay Greenberg as his successor as editor of "the oldest free-standing psychoanalytic journal in North America" (Smith, 2010, p. 877). How the *Psychoanalytic Review* contributed to the development of psychoanalysis as a scientific discipline is described in Alan Barnett's celebration of the first century of its life, which makes of it not only "the first English-language periodical dedicated to psychoanalysis" but even "the oldest continuously published psychoanalytic journal in the world" (Barnett, 2013, p. 1). As we can see, the conflictual situation out of which Sullivan developed his unique psychoanalytic perspective is somehow still with us, and this is precisely the topic I mean to address in this section, that is, those traumas and wounds of our history that Elisabeth Young-Bruehl and Murray Schwartz believe that we still have to deal with and to heal.

But, coming back to Sullivan and White, I also find

it important to inform the reader of how the Italian-American psychiatrist and psychoanalyst Arcangelo D'Amore, revisiting White's legacy in the book chapter "William Alanson White – Pioneer psychoanalyst," stated that he "made the Saint Elisabeth's Hospital the 'Burghölzli' of the American continent" (D'Amore, 1976, p. 84). This implied a relationship between Sullivan and White similar to the one developed by Jung with Eugen Bleuler (1857–1939), and this allowed him to come to the following conclusive assessment:

> White succeeded, I think, in assimilating, organizing, and popularizing psychoanalysis in the United States in a way that at first aroused Freud's doubts and misgivings but which, in the long run, reflected good judgment and an open-mindedness that contributed to its considerable growth and development during the years White gave nurture to it. (D'Amore, 1976, p. 88)

I am very thankful to D'Amore because his assessment of White shaped my own assessment of Sullivan, as well as my decision to consider his work and his legacy as belonging to the discipline of psychoanalysis. In fact, the same is true for Gaetano Benedetti (1920–2013), whose work and legacy I repeatedly deal with in this anthology (in the Afterword, in Chapter 10, and in the Introduction to Part Four). Benedetti introduced Sullivan's work into Italy (see Benedetti, 1961), and founded in 1956 with Christian Müller (1921–2013) the International Society for the Psychotherapy of Schizophrenia (ISPS), which became closely connected with the Chestnut Lodge tradition inaugurated by Sullivan and further developed by—among others—Harold Searles (1918–2015) and David Feinsilver (1939–1999).

Even more important, however, is the fact that the main reason why Benedetti created in Milan—with Johannes Cremerius (1918–2002)—the analytic group that later founded the Scuola di Psicoterapia Psicoanalitica (SPP) was his not having been allowed to transmit his analytic experience with schizophrenic patients to the candidates of the Swiss Psychoanalytic Society, of which he always remained an associate member and never became a training analyst (Benedetti, 1992; see also Chapter 10, and the Introduction to Part Four). Inasmuch as I have experienced Benedetti as a very good psychoanalyst, I tend to do the same with Sullivan, who was—among other things—also an important model for Benedetti himself, particularly with regard to the need that both felt to be psychoanalysts who would not give up their original identity of psychiatrists, but would instead try to integrate these two identities.

This was also the climate, "between orthodoxy and eclecticism," of "the Washington–Baltimore experience," as described by Donald Burnham in 1978, that is, a dialectical balance that lasted only as long as Sullivan was alive. In 1950, Clara Thompson, Janet Rioch, and Ralph Crowley (1905–1984) were stripped of their role as training analysts of the American Psychoanalytic Association. Thompson applied to it several times on behalf of the White Institute in the following years, but since the American Psychoanalytic Association refused to recognize the White Institute as one of its member societies, Thompson withdrew her application in November 1952 (see Burnham, 1978, p. 101). This was the professional climate in which Janet Rioch, in 1956, became the first president of the newly founded American Academy of Psychoanalysis, as Marianne Horney wrote in her 1978 book chapter "Organizational schisms in American psychoanalysis" (Horney, 1978, pp. 156–157). Italian-American psychiatrist and psychoanalyst Silvano Arieti (1914–1981) became one of the most active protagonists of this, for example as first editor of the *Journal of the American Academy of Psychoanalysis*, which he founded in 1973. Through Arieti, Gaetano Benedetti became a member of the Academy, then through Benedetti, Marco Bacciagaluppi became a member of it in 1979, and then through Bacciagaluppi and his friend Jules Bemporad (1937–2011), I myself became member of the Academy in 1993. In 2015 the White Society and Institute eventually became a member society of the American and International Psychoanalytic Associations, and this eventually created the conditions for new bridges to be constructed between the two analytic networks, which had for many years grown apart from each other. The long and patient work of reconstructing Sullivan's life and work, culminating in the publication of the original Italian edition of my book in the year 2000, had of course also originated in the same dialogical attitude that informs this anthology—and, of course, also the whole work of Gaetano Benedetti, a truly Freudian and, at the same time, interpersonal analyst.

To make a further contribution to such a dialogue, I will now revisit Sullivan's identity and legacy as a psychoanalyst, as I was recently able to do in the Introduction I wrote (Conci, 2017) to the new Italian edition of his *Psychiatric interview*. First published in Italian in 1967, *Il colloquio psichiatrico* had disappeared from the bookshelves of Italian book stores in the mid-1990s, when the publisher Feltrinelli stopped investing in the field of psychoanalysis; the new Italian edition was produced on my advice by the Rome publisher Giovanni Fioriti in the fall of 2017. Whereas contemporaries and students of Sullivan such as Clara Thompson, Mabel Black Cohen (1908–1972), and Otto Allen Will (1910–1993), kept talking of Sullivan as a psychoanalyst, this was no longer the case with the following generations, including, for example, not only Gerard Chrzanowski (1913–2000), but also Stephen Mitchell (1946–2000) and Donnel Stern.

In my Introduction to the Second Part of the anthology I edited in 1997 with Sergio Dazzi and Maria Luisa Mantovani, I had underlined what I at the time considered to be Sullivan's most important legacy, that is, the very good level of integration among the fields of psychiatry, psychotherapy, and psychoanalysis that he had been able to bring about in his work (Conci, 1997). But, of course, as my own identity has in later years shifted in the direction of psychoanalysis, I have become more interested in looking at Sullivan from this specific point of view. To such a change also belongs my initiative of organizing a panel on "H.S. Sullivan, psychoanalyst" at the IPA Congress held in Boston in July 2015, at which Sandra Buechler gave a paper on the subject, followed by a discussion by Henry Zvi Lothane—which will soon come out in the *International Forum of Psychoanalysis*.

Let me start with Clara Thompson and her 1952 book chapter "Sullivan and psychoanalysis," reproduced in 1978 in *Contemporary Psychoanalysis*. From its very beginning, Thompson situates Sullivan as an heir of Freud, the psychiatrist Adolf Meyer (1866–1950), and White, and tells us how "for many years, he devoted his research to an attempt to apply psychoanalytic theory and technique to the therapy of the psychotic" (Thompson, 1952; 1978, p. 488). After introducing the reader to the technical innovations of Wilhelm Reich (1897–1957), Otto Rank, and Sándor Ferenczi, she states how "some of his [Sullivan's] early innovations closely paralleled those developing in Europe" (p. 491). After presenting the specific contributions made by Sullivan through his interpersonal theory, with particular emphasis on the concept of "self-system," and reassessing them in terms of Freud's ego psychology, Thompson concluded her attempt to show both their similarities and their differences with the following concluding remarks:

> Sullivan is greatly indebted to Freud. He undoubtedly stands on Freud's shoulders. It is apparent that most of the concepts of the two were attempts to formulate similar phenomena

observed, and, in a crude way, they can be translated into each other's language. But to do so is misleading in that it overlooks the basically different orientation of the two men, and it is this very difference in orientation that has made it possible for Sullivan to add certain new ideas to psychoanalysis. Freud seeing man more mechanistically, more as an isolated entity in the universe and primarily evolving as a product of his sexual development, was handicapped by his very theory in incorporating many observations he actually made of man's dependency on the approval of his fellow man. Sullivan, by discarding the cumbersome libido concept, was freer to observe the results of the powerful socializing forces on personality. Moreover, Sullivan does much less unverifiable theorizing than Freud. In short, I believe that although Sullivan's thinking is an outgrowth of psychoanalytic thinking and although he is greatly indebted to Freud, he has opened up a new avenue of approach which makes further research into the study of the human personality more possible. (Thompson, 1952; 1978, p. 501)

Also very balanced is the reconstruction of Sullivan and Fromm's contributions that Thompson discusses in a paper included in the anthology of selected papers edited in 1964 by Maurice Green and reprinted in 1979 in *Contemporary Psychoanalysis*:

In short, neither denies the importance of instinctual drives, but each believes they are relatively weak in the human and are not the usual cause of neurotic difficulty. Fromm's idea of the goal of therapy is somewhat more far-reaching than anything Sullivan has stated on the subject. According to Fromm, the goal of therapy is the transformation of the personality. This is achieved when the therapist succeeds in breaking through the defense systems and reaching the true core of the individual. In other words, one has exposed the true self. To roughly contrast the difference in therapeutic approach between Sullivan's methods and Fromm's, I would say that Sullivan concerns himself more with helping the patient to see how his defense machinery (security operations) works to the detriment of effective living, while Fromm attempts to cut through the defenses to communicate with the underlying constructive forces, leaving the security operations to fall by the wayside. (Thompson, 1964; 1979, p. 200)

It is no wonder that an author like Mitchell retraces the birth and original formulation of interpersonal psychoanalysis to Clara Thompson's successful integration of Sullivan and Fromm's different yet complementary legacies, without taking further into consideration, or perhaps with discarding, the former's identity as a psychoanalyst. Here is what Mitchell wrote in this regard in 1997:

Interpersonal psychoanalysis was born of the convergence between Harry Stack Sullivan's home-grown American interpersonal psychiatry and Erich Fromm's Marxist version of Freudian psychoanalysis, which Fromm brought with him as a refugee from war-torn Europe. The person most responsible for brokering this fertile mingling of ideas was Clara Thompson, who had been trained in classical psychoanalysis and analyzed by Ferenczi.

Thompson had a keen sense of the history of psychoanalytic ideas and recognized the strong natural affinity among Ferenczi's rediscovery of the importance of actual trauma and his emphasis on the centrality of the relationship between analyst and patient; Sullivan's innovative approach to schizophrenia as a disorder of family systems; and Fromm's relocation of Freudian libido theory into a broad Marxist perspective emphasizing the importance of culture and history ('humanistic psychoanalysis'). Thompson's vision led to the generation of an ongoing psychoanalytic tradition that emphasizes the importance of interaction since its inception. (Mitchell, 1997, pp. 63–64)

A further step in leaving behind Sullivan as a psychoanalyst is what we find in Donnel Stern's desire to emphasize how radically the post-Sullivanian tradition created by his and by the previous generation of White analysts (in the first place by Edgar Levenson) differs from Sullivan's own perspective. Here is what Stern wrote in the recent book *Relational freedom*:

But those who eventually became the early interpersonal analysts also recognized that Sullivan's thinking was never intended to be psychoanalysis. Sullivan was doing something different. He thought of himself as a psychiatrist, not a psychoanalyst, and, in fact, he actively resisted being labeled as a psychoanalyst. He may very well have believed that his work was an alternative to psychoanalysis; but however much his colleagues and students admired his thinking, those of them who were psychoanalysts, aspired to be, or were interested in psychoanalysis, did not take his views to be sufficient in and of themselves. While these analysts were sometimes quite critical of certain aspects of the dominant psychoanalytic theories of the era, they did not intend simply to replace Freud with Sullivan. What they wanted was to *meld* Sullivan's views with existing psychoanalytic thought. They wanted to create a new *kind* of psychoanalysis, one in which the interpersonal relations they had learned about through Sullivan played a larger and central role. Sadly, although that is what eventually happened, few members of the first two generations of interpersonal analysts lived to see it. (Stern, 2015, p. 52)

This is why, in preparing to write my Introduction to the new edition of Sullivan's *Psychiatric interview*, I preferred to revisit also what Mabel Blake Cohen had written in her 1953 Introduction to Sullivan's *Interpersonal theory of psychiatry*, and what Otto Allen Will had written in his 1954 Introduction to *The psychiatric interview*. They both helped me to revisit Sullivan as a psychoanalytic author, that is, as an author whose discourse belongs—from a purely disciplinary point of view, and wholly independently from what he might have thought about it—to the kind of intellectual discourse inaugurated by Freud.

Before dealing with these two important authors, I must not forget to mention how reading Gerard Chrzanowski's 1977 *Interpersonal approach to psychoanalysis. Contemporary view of Harry Stack Sullivan* had been important in shaping the idea that his most important contribution might have consisted in his interdisciplinary perspective, as I formulated in the above-mentioned Introduction of 1997. Second, I should not overlook how Irwin Hirsch (2016) recently celebrated Sullivan's contribution to the formulation of interpersonal psychoanalytic thinking, which he did in his Introduction to the anthology of his own papers with the title *The interpersonal tradition. The origins of psychoanalytic subjectivity.* Last but not least, I also want the reader to know that, in my own book on Sullivan, I of course specifically dealt with the topic "Sullivan and contemporary psychoanalysis" (Conci, 2012, pp. 425–435), and that, from this point of view, rediscovering the deeply psychoanalytic inspiration of a book like Sullivan's *The psychiatric interview* represented a further step in the research work which this anthology is about. Of course, in the process of writing—as was the case with the Introduction to the new Italian edition of Sullivan's book—I myself also discover new things, as opposed to just stating things I already know.

In what follows you will see how Mabel Blake Cohen summarized what she called "Sullivan's major contributions to psychiatry" (Blake Cohen, 1953, p. xvi), using the word "psychiatry" instead of "psychoanalysis" probably because she was writing at a time when the American Psychoanalytic Association had made the word "psychoanalysis" its own private property, more or less explicitly prohibiting students of Sullivan making use of it themselves. In fact, as you will see, what Blake Cohen attributes to Sullivan is a specific psychoanalytic contribution, or way of working. Here are her words:

> A summing up of Sullivan's major contributions to psychiatry would not be complete if one omitted his clinical work itself. It was in the actual treatment of patients that his theory grew, with a constant return to the therapeutic situation for verification and further development. In fact, it is natural for one who knew and worked with Sullivan to think of him primarily as a clinician, since the teaching of the art and science of psychotherapy was one of his greatest skills. In supervising the work of a student psychiatrist, he would, after listening for an hour or so to the student's stumbling report on a patient, have a grasp of the patient as a person which was astonishing and clarifying. To cite but one example of the application of his theory to the practice of psychotherapy: in working with a patient, Sullivan always

listened to the date with the question in mind, 'Where is the flow of communication being interfered with by the threat of anxiety?' Such a point could be identified by noting where the patient shifted from a presumably significant subject; where the security operations of the patient began to intensify; or where various somatic accompaniments of anxiety began to appear. Having identified such a point of change, a therapist is then in a position to recall, or to inquire about, what was going on just prior to the shift. This technique, when grasped and correctly used, gives a precise and reliable method for identifying and investigating patterns of difficulty in living. (Blake Cohen, 1953, pp. xvi–xvii).

In fact, this kind of work is precisely what psychoanalysis is still about, that is, being able to perceive and find the best words aimed at helping patients understand what is going on in themselves, in order for them to become increasingly aware of their emotions and ways of functioning. This is, at the same time, what Sullivan called "participant observation," and what Freud himself started doing with his patients, thus creating psychoanalysis as a discipline and as a profession— although Freud did not use the expression "participant observation" because his epistemology and his ambition to create an "objective science of pure observation" did not allow him to do it.

The same is true for Otto Allen Will, that is, for the way in which he introduces to the reader Sullivan's work and legacy in his Introduction to his *The psychiatric interview*. In the above-mentioned Introduction to the new Italian edition of *Il colloquio psichiatrico*, I deal in great detail with how much this book can still contribute to helping candidates and analysts-in-training develop a true psychoanalytic identity, and I will limit myself here to one single aspect. It is amazing how well in this book Sullivan captures and coherently pursues what Stefano Bolognini, revisiting the analytic concept of empathy (Bolognini, 2003) started referring to as (in my words) "the complexity of analytic work as an essential aspect of it." But let us see how Will formulated this aspect:

It should be clear that this book does not present a definite schematization of just what the interviewer should do in conducting an interview. It is not intended as an outline guide for action, but rather as a provocative succession of ideas which may prove stimulating to the thinking of anyone who conducts an interview . . . . Sullivan was trying to make some formulation of a process, by which I mean an always progressing, never stable movement of interactions taking place between people . . . . Thus in his consideration of the interview Sullivan reflects a movement in his own thinking toward an operational, field approach to the study of psychiatry, and his writing can be understood best when this developing point of view is kept in mind. (Will, 1954, pp.

xvii–xviii)

And now, in Sullivan's words:

> All psychiatric data arise from participation in the situation that is observed – in other words, by participant observation. Thus instead of 'knowing what one is looking for', one wants to be *alert to the possibilities of the immediate future of the relationship in which one is involved*. This is why I cannot say, 'Here are seventeen tables of events that characterize interviews; now, you memorize all these and then you will always know just what to expect'. No such thing is possible. (Sullivan, 1954, p. 57, original emphasis)

Of course, to my ears, this attitude, an essential asset of analytic work, sounds very similar to Bion's concept of "working without memory and desire," and this is why I, for example, find it easy to have them talk with each other in my mind. And also why I wrote the paper figuring in this anthology as Chapter 8.

2. THE CASE OF MITCHELL

When, in January 2018, I started writing Chapter 6, "S.A. Mitchell (1946–2000) in Italy," I had intended first to reconstruct the personal relationship I had had the chance to develop with him after our first meeting in Florence in April 1988, with particular regard to the role I played in the early phase of reception of his work in Italy, exploring this through a series of letters he wrote to me between April 1988 and September 1998. The second topic I deal with in that chapter is the further reception of his work in Italy. My third focus is an attempt to revisit his work and legacy all together, with particular regard to the crucial topic of his relationship with Freud's work, and with the way in which the American Psychoanalytic Association represented and made use of it, for example in terms of the medical monopoly of psychoanalysis—which Freud actually opposed.

Given the fact that, with my Introduction to Part One and with what I have written so far in this Introduction to Part Two, I have already not limited myself to introducing the reader to the individual chapters, but have also gone beyond them, I will do the same here. From this point of view—as I wrote at a certain point of my Introduction to Part One—I can even advise the reader to read Chapter 6 first, and only after that come back to what I am about to write now. In other words, I intend to use this Introduction to further develop what I wrote in Chapter 6, with particular regard to the history of psychoanalysis, that is, to the history of North American psychoanalysis, as the context in which Mitchell's work has to be placed.

Having made this clear, let me first go to Chapter 6. In this chapter I propose to look at Mitchell not only as a post-Sullivanian author, but as the best possible *continuatore*, as I would say in Italian, of Sullivan's work, that is, as his best follower, meaning the author who at best further articulated and continued his work. In fact, I even refer to the following dimensions of their work in which I find Mitchell following in Sullivan's footsteps: the clinical, the interdisciplinary, the epistemological, and the political. By "political" I mean Sullivan's intention and ambition to create a "post-Freudian psychoanalysis," which Mitchell actually ended up also following and apparently agreeing with. On the other hand, in my reconstruction of Mitchell's formulation of relational psychoanalysis, I stress more what Jay Greenberg suggests as having been Mitchell's desire to unite all psychoanalysts, medical doctors, and psychologists (as well as psychoanalysts coming from other backgrounds), around the discussion of the clinical (and relational) aspects of our work, which the American Psychoanalytic Association had been incapable of doing, as opposed to seeing it as Mitchell's way of creating a post-Freudian psychoanalysis. In fact, in my personal experience of Mitchell, he loved psychoanalysis too much to make it run the risk of undergoing the kind of impoverishment and decadence it might be exposed to if we got rid of Freud's legacy. By "Freud's legacy" I in the first place mean the very sophisticated intellectual dimension which he developed even before he started working with his patients as a psychoanalyst, and which I have placed at the center of this anthology, especially in Part One.

In fact, at variance with Sullivan, Mitchell knew and appreciated Freud's work and legacy much better than Sullivan did. If this is the case, I believe that Mitchell ended up developing relational psychoanalysis in the direction of a post-Freudian version of psychoanalysis, not only because of the personal wound he had experienced as a psychologist whom the American Psychoanalytic Association had as such excluded from the possibility of identifying with Freud's legacy, but also because of the superordinate phenomenon of the ongoing fracture that existed between the American Psychoanalytic Association and all the North American analytic institutes outside it at the time of Mitchell's analytic training. In other words, this is the best path we can take in order to eventually write the history of psychoanalysis, which, according to Elisabeth Young-Bruehl and Murray Schwartz, has not yet been written; this would be a history of the ways in which Freud's and Sullivan's legacies were used more in terms of the power politics these could justify than in terms of the cultivation of their legacy as a scientific discourse.

From this point of view, I even dare to say that if Mitchell had been more aware of such a historical dimension, that is, of the way in which the American Psychoanalytic Association had actually betrayed Freud, he would have been less ready to create such a deep gap between Freudian and relational psychoanalysis. By "betrayal of Freud" I am referring not only to the already-mentioned medical monopoly of psychoanalysis, but also to what can be called its "politically conservative orientation." This is the specific way in which the history of psychoanalysis and its adequate reconstruction can help us again make as our priority psychoanalysis as a scientific discipline—as opposed to a form of power politics or even business.

From this point of view, we can fortunately refer not only to the older work done by Russell Jacoby (1983) in his book *The repression of psychoanalysis. Otto Fenichel and the political Freudians*, but also to the new and original work done by Dagmar Herzog (2017) in her book *Cold War Freud. Psychoanalysis in an age of catastrophes*. Jacoby's book was the very first book I reviewed in *Psicoterapia e Scienze Umane* (Conci, 1987). In addition, Dagmar Herzog is a very good historian, who has recently become the co-editor-in-chief of *Psychoanalysis and History*—and whose brilliance I had the chance of experiencing when I met her in June 2017 in Munich.

"The Americanization of psychoanalysis" is a central chapter of Jacoby's book, and my hypothesis is that if Stephen Mitchell had read it carefully (which he probably did, as I believe he used to do with most of the books he read), and thus understood that "the American Freud" was not "the European Freud" that Otto Fenichel (1897–1946) had assimilated and unsuccessfully tried to keep alive through his *Rundbriefe*, he might not have felt the need to get rid of Freud, but only "the American Freud." Of course, only Jay Greenberg and Margaret Black know how carefully Stephen read Jacoby's book, and why he did not make of it the use I would recommend. From this point of view, as an Italian, I might even say that he was, of course, "a normal North American colleague" who knew Europe only from the literature and from the limited experience of a tourist—not to mention the fact that he only spoke English.

But let me remind you of some of the best statements to be found in Jacoby's book, which still hold true thirty-five years after their original publication. Jacoby's thesis is that the politically oriented psychoanalysis represented by Otto Fenichel, and around which centered many of his "circular letters," did not survive his premature death. He backs this up with a series of facts and statements, including the following examples: "The culture and humanism of Freud's German evaporated in the English translations that sought to validate psychoanalysis as a science" (Jacoby, 1983, p. 140); "The translation of psychoanalysis into a professional and scientific enterprise affected its language, spirit, breadth, and even those attracted to it; fewer and fewer individuals with humanist, intellectual, or political commitments entered the discipline" (p. 141); "The forces that guided Americanization can be roughly identified: professionalization and medicalization; the insecurity of refugee analysts; the gap between American and European culture, and—as cause and effect—the emergence of the neo-Freudians" (p. 142); and the following:

> Few issues provoked Freud more passionately then lay analysis; he relentlessly defended it. His reasoning was simple and prescient: monopolization by medical doctors would degrade psychoanalysis into a specialty. Freud wanted psychoanalysis to contribute to general knowledge and culture; he objected to medical doctors restricting it to therapy .... He called the American resolution against lay analysis 'an attempt at repression.' (Jacoby, 1983, pp. 145–146)

And here is how Russel Jacoby illuminated the historical and social background of the fractured situation out of which the neo-Freudian group emerged: "Inasmuch as the political Freudians did not intrude on the public consciousness, they left a vacancy the neo-Freudians successfully occupied" (Jacoby, 1983, pp. 152–153). Jacoby closed this chapter with these words:

> When Fenichel fled Europe he pledged to himself not to surrender the heart and soul of classical analysis; indeed this was the program of the political Freudians – to hold fast to the raw power of psychoanalysis. This program, these hopes, did not survive Americanization; they sank into the unconscious of the profession. (Jacoby, 1983, p. 160)

Before coming to the way in which Dagmar Herzog describes, in the first part of her book, under the title "Leaving the world outside," the conservative turn of American psychoanalysis that occurred in the 1950s, I will briefly go back to the topic of what I call "international psychoanalysis," that is, the necessary international character of any scientific discipline. By this I mean that the history of psychoanalysis is so complex that only an international network of researchers can reconstruct it as it deserves. I will make this clear through some brief bibliographical notes. Whereas one of the best books on the Frankfurt school of sociology is (for me) still represented by Martin Jay's 1973 book *The dialectical imagination: A history of the Frankfurt school and the Institute of Social Research, 1923–1950*, it has probably escaped most North American colleagues that, in 1998, the Viennese historians Johannes Reichmayr and Elke Mühlleitner edited Fenichel's *Rundbriefe* in two volumes, a German and an English one. The same must be true for the very interesting biography of Fenichel published by Elke Mühlleitner in German in 2008, which has not yet been translated into English. From this point of view, I can also add that one of the great merits of Dagmar Herzog's research work is that it took place in three different linguistic worlds—North America, Germany, and France and Switzerland—and that it also deals with Italy, and with the journal *Psicoterapia e Scienze Umane*. In fact, in his review of the book, Michael Shapira qualifies it as belonging to that new category of books on the history of psychoanalysis that "point to the fact that psychoanalysis should be looked at as knowledge and practice operating in relation to particular sociocultural settings," that is, to the fact that "each country has 'its own psychoanalysis'" (Shapira, 2018, p. 113). And Murray Schwartz defines it as "a major achievement" (Schwartz, 2018, p. 180).

Methodologically a continuation of the pioneering book by Edith Kurzweil *The Freudians. A comparative perspective*, which I mentioned in the General Introduction from the point of view of its contents concerning North America, *Cold War Freud* can actually be seen as a continuation of Jacoby's book. The two chapters of the First Part, "The libido wars" and "Homophobia's durability and the reinvention of psychoanalysis," deal respectively in fact with how conservative North American psychoanalysis became in the 1950s and 1960s, and how conservative it also remained in the 1970s and 1980s:

> It was only in 1991 – we read for example at the end of Chapter 2 – when the American Psychoanalytic Association passed its nondiscrimination declaration, that openly gay or lesbian individuals in the USA could begin to move toward being certified as analysts and only 1993 when they were permitted to become training analysts as well . . . . In other parts of the world it would take yet longer . . . . The matter in the USA had taken years of behind-the-scenes negotiations.

(Herzog, 2017, p. 82)

In fact, in this context Herzog also mentions Stephen Mitchell's 1981 paper on "The psychoanalytic treatment of homosexuality: Some technical considerations" as an important innovative paper on the topic. At the same time it is true that—looking at it again today—I can see that, even at that time, Mitchell did not sufficiently emphasize the fact that Freud was not as prejudiced against homosexuality as those "Freudian analysts" who treated homosexuality as a psychopathological problem, whose "directive-suggestive approach" Mitchell rightly criticized. And what about Chapter 1? This centers around what Herzog defines as "the desexualization of psychoanalysis":

> Chapter 1 explores the complex combination of a deliberate desexualization of post-Freudian psychoanalytic theory with a maintenance of Freudianism's titillating reputation, and positions this within an active rapprochement with mainstream Christianity, Catholic as well as Protestant, a Christianity that was itself at that historical moment in the process of being transformed. Psychoanalysis, I argue, so often shorthanded as 'the Jewish science' might in fact better be described as undergoing a kind of 'Christianization.' (Herzog, 2017, pp. 11–12)

To put it simply, let me formulate my hypothesis as follows: if Mitchell was not able to see how Freud's "liberal legacy," in terms of his position on both lay analysis and homosexuality, was so badly misrepresented and betrayed by the American Psychoanalytic Association, I understand how he might have ended up wanting to give up Freud's legacy altogether. Second, on the basis of the kind of reconstruction of the history of psychoanalysis I have proposed, I believe that the most urgent thing to do would have been to work in the direction of overcoming the trauma of the split between the "orthodox Freudians" and the "neo-Freudians." This may actually have been what Mitchell had in mind when he proposed the new paradigm of relational psychoanalysis, but why drop Freud?

In my opinion Freud is the father of us all from both the disciplinary and the professional point of view, and it is a pity that his "liberal legacy" was so misrepresented in North America. Very instructive from this point of view is the final chapter of Herzog's book, in which she reconstructs the socially critical, progressive, and liberal attitude with which Freud's legacy was kept alive by the Zurich group around Paul Parin (1916–2009), his wife Goldy Parin-Matthèy (1911–1997), and Fritz Morgenthaler (1919–1984)—an important chapter of the history of postwar European psychoanalysis that is still almost totally unknown in the USA. Incidentally, this Zurich group played also a very important role in the identity and evolution of the journal *Psicoterapia e Scienze Umane*.

Last but not least, the polarization of analytic discourse in a "drive model" and a "relational model" around which relational psychoanalysis centers does not seem to have ever become an accepted point of view, if not for the colleagues who strictly adhere to relational psychoanalysis. From this point of view, I agree with the attitude of not only Stefano Bolognini, but also a whole series of contemporary authors who look at these two poles not as paradigms, but as metaphors (see, for example, Wurmser, 1977), that is, as useful metaphors from which we can greatly profit in our daily work. Indeed, today I would speak more of metaphors (see, for example, the volume on the topic edited in 2013 by Montana Katz) than of paradigms. This is also why I agree with the necessity to keep in mind Freud's "drive model" in terms of the connection it creates with the biological dimension of our life. From this point of view, I also agree with Carlo Strenger's position that psychoanalysis must not discard science and human nature (Strenger, 2013). Along the same lines of the attempt to find a new integration between the classical emphasis on self-reflection and the contemporary relational revisitation of it also runs, of course, much of the work of Morris Eagle, with particular regard to his 2011 book *From classical to contemporary psychoanalysis. A critique and integration*.

Finally, in writing this Introduction, I have reread a good article on which Adrienne Harris originally worked with Stephen Mitchell in the summer of 2000, which was published only in 2004 in *Psychoanalytic Dialogues*, as "What's American about American psychoanalysis?" I agree with the authors' suggestion of how well Roy Schafer has been able to find a new balance between the impact of the intrapsychic and the interpersonal dimensions (Mitchell and Harris, 2004), and to reach a very good level of integration between Freud's original orientation and the cultural North American tradition and context in which he operates. In addition, I am in agreement with what Mitchell and Harris call their "perception or prejudice . . . that Europeans are rarely well-grounded in American thought and theory" (Mitchell and Harris, 2004, p. 173). Of course, there is no way of understanding North American psychoanalysis without a good knowledge of North American language, history, society, and culture, and this chapter (as well as this anthology of papers) is of course also a tribute to such a way of dealing with it. In fact, in my experience, some of the best cultural syntheses have come from the integration of the European intellectual tradition of introspection (which Freud represents very well) with the mental attitude resulting from a cultural and social climate open to change, that is, a pragmatic and democratic climate of which the USA has often been, in the course of history, a very good example. Last but not least, this is also one of the major ingredients of my Afterword.

Another very good historian apparently at home in both the Old and the New World is Eli Zaretsky, whose books *Secrets of the soul: A social and cultural history of psychoanalysis* (2004) and *Political Freud* (2017) I recommend to the reader. The following words were taken from Zaretsky's 2011 paper "Why the Freudian century: Reflections on the statue of Athena":

> With the construction of the statue of Athena, the nineteenth-century Viennese bourgeoisie sought to give unity to the great public buildings that they constructed on the *Ringstrasse*: Parliament, the University, the *Rathaus* or City Hall, and the theatre. What was that unity? It was the human mind, implying the advance of rationality in all areas of life. Critical to the linking of psychoanalysis to the statue of Athena was that psychoanalysis synthesized scientific and humanistic (for example, literary) currents in its picture of the mind. What gave this synthesis historical weight was a tradition of thinking about subjective freedom that went back beyond the Enlightenment to the Renaissance and indeed to antiquity. What made it so compelling in its present was the discovery of a new object: the idiosyncratic, meaning-saturated, morally inflected psychical life of the human being and the accompanying assumption that a meaningful life necessitated self-reflection in depth.
>
> The 1960s spelled the disintegration of this synthesis. On the one hand, the scientific lineage of psychoanalysis gave way to neuroscience, brain research, and psychopharmacology, at first in the United States and then, more slowly, elsewhere. These currents conceived of psychology "objectively," as the reflection of material (chemical, electrical, and physiological) interactions. On the other hand, the humanistic and literary lineage of psychoanalysis gave way to cultural studies, feminist theory, "queer" theory, and the study of identity, narrative, and representation. These currents conceived of subjectivity as reflecting collective oppressions, such as racism, sexism, and anti-Semitism. In both cases, the link between introspection and the overall advance of knowledge was threatened, with what disposition we do not at present know. Why this matters can be grasped by remembering why the statue of Athena had been erected in the first place. At every point of history, when confronted by contending, sometimes clamorous, truth claims, the best road to progress has been to redirect attention to the human subjects putting

forth contending claims, in other words to understanding our own nature, including what is in our day most interesting about it—the new possibilities of personal freedom opened up by mass consumption capitalism, by psychoanalysis, and by the radical movements of the 1960s. (Zaretsky, 2011, pp. 686–687)

3. THE INDIVIDUAL CHAPTERS

Chapter 4, "H.S. Sullivan revisited: A close look from afar," is the paper I gave at the White Institute on January 11, 2011—on the invitation of the present director of the Institute, Pasqual Pantone—to present the first American edition of my book *Sullivan revisited – life and work. Harry Stack Sullivan's relevance for contemporary psychiatry, psychotherapy and psychoanalysis* (Conci, 2010). Two years later, with the help of Marco Bacciagaluppi, I produced a second, linguistically revised version of the book (Conci, 2012), with the same title and no changes other than to the language. The book was meant to introduce Sullivan's life and work to all those colleagues and readers interested in coming into contact with and better understanding what we can call "the interpersonal tradition" that he had been able to formulate and promote. The original Italian edition (2000) had been followed by a German edition (2005), and after the two already-mentioned editions in English came a Spanish edition (2012), thanks to the active interest in the book of Rebeca Aramoni (Mexico City) and the generous commitment to it of both the translator (José Manuel Villalaz) and the publisher (Amparo Espinosa Rugarcía).

The best review the book received came out in the *Journal of the American Psychoanalytic Association*, thanks to the book review editor, Rosemary Balsam, and to the very respectful and appreciative attitude developed toward it by the reviewer, Jane Tillman (Tilman, 2012). She understood very well that the aim of my book, "a work of love," was not the promotion of Sullivan's work per se, but the detailed illustration of his fascinating and still challenging research work. To give an example: although Freud's concept of *lapsus* has been widely adopted around the world, this is not yet the case with Sullivan's concept of the "interpersonal situation." In other words, the simplistic tendency to value and judge individuals not on the basis of the interpersonal variables of the single social situation they are involved in, but on the basis of their presupposed intelligence or lack of it, is still very widespread. Sullivan was acutely aware of how our personality differs according to who we are relating to, thus complementing in a very useful way Freud's concept of our tendency to constantly repeat ourselves (in German, *Wiederholungszwang*).

Chapter 5, "Sullivan and the intersubjective tradition," is the only chapter of this Second Part to have already been published; its abstract from the published version in the *International Forum of Psychoanalysis* is as follows:

> The author sees H.S. Sullivan's (1892–1949) interpersonal theory as the best theoretical framework for the contemporary intersubjective perspective in psychoanalysis and presents the former in its pluridimensional articulation. After having extended Freud's therapeutic approach to psychotic patients, Sullivan developed both a developmental psychology and a psychoanalytic and psychotherapeutic technique based on the "interpersonal field" as the basic unit of study. To the pluridimensional character of his theory also belongs its application to the cultural and social aspects of our personal identity. The contemporary psychoanalytic authors who shaped the intersubjective perspective having limited themselves to the clinical dimension, Sullivan's interpersonal theory can still provide the theoretical framework that any psychoanalytic perspective needs.

As the reader can see, this paper—which I originally presented in Athens in October 2010, at the IFPS Forum organized by the Athens group chaired by Professor Grigoris Vaslamatzis—represents an earlier stage of the point of view presented in this Introduction. My aim was to show that although Sullivan tried his best to formulate a new, post-Freudian psychoanalysis, his contribution was not limited to the clinical and therapeutic levels, but went in the direction of creating for psychoanalysis also a new, and highly articulated, intellectual framework—in other words the kind of complex framework lacking in most contemporary intersubjective perspectives, limited as they are to clinical and therapeutic points of view.

Chapter 6, "S.A. Mitchell (1946–2000) in Italy," I have of course already talked about at length above.

REFERENCES

Aron, L., & Harris, A. (Eds.) (1993). *The Legacy of Sándor Ferenczi.* Hillsdale, NJ: Analytic Press.

Bacciagaluppi, M. (1993). Ferenczi's influence on Fromm. In L. Aron and A. Harris (Eds.), *The Legacy of Sándor Ferenczi* (pp. 185–198). Hillsdale, NJ: Analytic Press.

Barnett, A.J. (2013). The Psychoanalytic Review: 100 years of history. *Psychoanalytic Review* 100:1–56.

Benedetti, G. (1961). Prefazione all'edizione italiana [Preface to the Italian edition]. In H.S. Sullivan, *La moderna concezione della psichiatria* (pp. vii–xxvii). Milan: Feltrinelli.

——— (1992). Mein Weg zur Psychoanalyse und zur Psychiatrie [My way to psychoanalysis and to psychiatry]. In L. Hermanns (Ed.), *Die Psychoanalyse in Selbstdarstellungen. Band 2* [Psychoanalysis in the form of self-portraits. Vol. 2] (pp. 11–72). Tübingen: Diskord.

Bion, W.R. (1962). *Learning from Experience*. London: Hogarth Press.

Blake Cohen, M. (1953). Introduction. In H.S. Sullivan, *The Interpersonal Theory of Psychiatry* (pp. xi–xviii). New York: Norton.

Blitsten, D. (1953). *The Social Theories of Harry Stack Sullivan*. New York: William-Frederick Press.

Bolognini, S. (2003). *Psychoanalytic Empathy*. London: Free Association Books. (Original Italian edition, 2002).

Bonomi, C. (1999). Flight into sanity: Jones' allegation of Ferenczi's mental deterioration reconsidered. *International Journal of Psychoanalysis* 80:507–542.

——— (2017). Review of the book by J. Dupont *"Au fil du temps ... Un intinéraire analytique"*, Campagne Première 2015. *International Forum of Psychoanalysis* 26:129–131.

Bonomi, C., & Borgogno, F. (2014). Editorial – The Ferenczi renaissance: Past, present and future. *International Forum of Psychoanalysis* 23:1–2.

Buechler, S. (in press). Sullivan's impact on the clinician's feelings and therapeutic style. Paper given in Boston, in July 2015. *International Forum of Psychoanalysis*.

Burnham, D.L. (1978). Orthodoxy and eclecticism in psychoanalysis: The Washington–Baltimore experience. In J.M. Quen and E.T. Carlson (Eds.), *American Psychoanalysis: Origins and Development. The Adolf Mayer Seminars* (pp. 87–108). New York: Brunner/Mazel.

Burnham, J.C. (1983). *Jelliffe: American Psychoanalyst and Physician and his Correspondence with S. Freud and C.G. Jung Edited by William McGuire*. Chicago: University of Chicago Press.

Chrzanowski, G. (1977). *Interpersonal Approach to Psychoanalysis. Contemporary View of Harry Stack Sullivan*. New York: Gardner Press.

Conci, M. (1987). Review of the book by R. Jacoby "The repression of psychoanalysis. Otto Fenichel and the political Freudians", Basic Books 1983. *Psicoterapia e Scienze Umane*, 21(2):103–111.

——— (1997). Introduzione alla prima parte – Origini e sviluppi [Introduction to the first part – Origins and developments]. In M. Conci, S. Dazzi, and M.L. Mantovani (Eds.), *La tradizione interpersonale in psichiatria, psicoterapia e psicoanalisi* [The interpersonal tradition in psychiatry, psychotherapy and psychoanalysis] (pp. 15–36). Rome: Erre Emme.

——— (2000). Editorial – Erich Fromm, a rediscovered legacy. *International Forum of Psychoanalysis*, 9:141–144.

——— (2010). *Sullivan Revisited – Life and Work. Its Relevance for Contemporary Psychiatry, Psychotherapy and Psychoanalysis*. Trento: Tangram. (Original Italian edition, 2000. German edition, 2005. Spanish edition, 2012).

——— (2012). *Sullivan Revisited – Life and Work. Its Relevance for Contemporary Psychiatry, Psychotherapy and Psychoanalysis* (2nd edn.). Trento: Tangram.

——— (2017). Introduzione alla nuova edizione italiana [Introduction to the new Italian edition]. In H.S. Sullivan, *Il colloquio psichiatrico* [The psychiatric interview] (pp. vii–xl). Rome: Fioriti.

D'Amore, A.R.T. (1976). William Alanson White – Pioneer

psychoanalyst. In A.R.T. D'Amore (Ed.), *William Alanson White: The Washington Years, 1903–1937. The Contributions to Psychiatry, Psychoanalysis and Mental Health by Dr. White while Superintendent of St. Elisabeths Hospital* (pp. 69–91). Washington DC: US Department of Health, Education, and Welfare.

Dupont, J. (2015). *Au fil du temps . . . Un itinéraire analytique* [In the course of time . . . A psychoanalytic itinerary]. Paris: Campagne Première.

Eagle, M.N. (2011). *From Classical to Contemporary Psychoanalysis. A Critique and Integration.* London: Routledge.

Ferenczi, S. (1927). The adaptation of the family to the child. In *Final Contributions to the Problems and Methods of Psycho-analysis* (M. Balint, Ed.; E. Mosbacher, Trans.). (pp. 61–76). London: Karnac, 1994.

———— (1933). Confusion of tongues between the adults and the child. In *Final Contributions to the Problems and Methods of Psycho-analysis* (M. Balint, Ed.; E. Mosbacher, Trans.). (pp. 155–167). London: Karnac, 1986. (Original German publication, 1933).

Ferenczi, S., & Rank, O. (1924). *The Development of Psychoanalysis.* Madison, CT: International Universities Press, 1986.

Fine, R. (1979). *A History of Psychoanalysis.* New York: Columbia University Press.

Fleck, L. (1927). *Über einige spezifische Merkmale des ärtzlichen Denkens* [On some specific characters of medical thinking]. In S. Werner and C. Zittel (Eds.), *Denkstile und Tatsachen. Gesammelte Schriften und Zeugnisse* [Thought styles and facts. Collected papers and documents] (pp. 41–50). Frankfurt: Suhrkamp, 2011.

———— (1979). *Genesis and Development of a Scientific Fact* (T.J. Trenn and R.K. Merton, Eds.). Chicago: University of Chicago Press. (Original German edition, 1935).

———— (2011). *Denkstile und Tatsachen. Gesammelte Schriften und Zeugnisse* [Thought styles and facts. Collected papers and documents] (S. Werner and C. Zittel, Eds.). Frankfurt: Suhrkamp.

Hale, N.G., Jr. (1995). *The Rise and Crisis of Psychoanalysis in the United States. Freud and the Americans, 1917–1985.* Oxford: Oxford University Press.

Herzog, D. (2017). *Cold War Freud. Psychoanalysis in an Age of Catastrophes.* Cambridge: Cambridge University Press.

Hirsch, I. (2016). *The Interpersonal Tradition. The Origins of Psychoanalytic Subjectivity.* London: Routledge.

Horney, M. (1978). Organizational schisms in American psychoanalysis. In J.M. Quen and E.T. Carlson (Eds.), *American Psychoanalysis: Origins and Development. The Adolf Mayer Seminars* (pp.141–161). New York: Brunner/Mazel.

Jacoby, R. (1983). *The Repression of Psychoanalysis. Otto Fenichel and the Political Freudians.* New York: Basic Books.

Jay, M. (1973). *The Dialectical Imagination: A History of the Frankfurt School and the Institute of Social Research, 1923–1950.* Boston: Little, Brown.

Jones, E. (1957). *Sigmund Freud, Life and Work. Volume Three: The Last Phase 1919–1939.* London: Hogarth Press.

Katz, M.S. (Ed.) (2013). *Metaphors and Fields. Common Ground, Common Language and the Future of Psychoanalysis.* London: Routledge.

Kirshner, L. (2004). *Having a Life: Self-pathology After Lacan.* Hillsdale,

NJ: Analytic Press.

Kurzweil, E. (1989). *The Freudians. A Comparative Perspective*. New Haven, CT: Yale University Press.

Lothane, H.Z. (in press). Emotional reality in Freud and Sullivan. Discussion of Dr. Sandra Buechler's paper. Paper given in Boston, in July 2015. *International Forum of Psychoanalysis*.

Mitchell, S.A. (1981). The psychoanalytic treatment of homosexuality. Some technical considerations. *International Review of Psychoanalysis* 8:63–80.

Mitchell, S.A. (1997). *Influence and Autonomy in Psychoanalysis*. Hillsdale, NJ: Analytic Press.

Mitchell, S.A., & Harris, A. (2004). What's American about American psychoanalysis? *Psychoanalytic Dialogues* 14:165–191.

Mühlleitner, E. (2008). *Ich – Fenichel. Das Leben eines Psychoanalytikers im 20. Jahrhundert* [I – Fenichel. The life of a psychoanalyst in the 20th century]. Vienna: Paul Zsolnay.

Noble, D., & Burnham, D.L. (1989). The history of the Washington–Baltimore Psychoanalytic Society and Institute. In A.-L. Silver (Ed.), *Psychoanalysis and Psychosis* (pp. 537–573). Madison, CT: International Universities Press.

Ortmeyer, D.H. (1995). History of the founders of interpersonal psychoanalysis. In M. Lionells, J. Fiscalini, C.H. Mann, and D.B. Stern (Eds.), *Handbook of Interpersonal Psychoanalysis* (pp. 11–27). Hillsdale, NJ: Analytic Press.

Reichmayr, J., & Mühlleitner, E. (Eds.) (1998). *Otto Fenichel: 119 Rundbriefe. 2 Bände* [Otto Fenichel: 119 circular letters. 2 volumes]. Frankfurt: Stroemfeld.

Richards, A.D. (2017). *Psychoanalysis: Perspectives on a Thought Collective. More Selected Papers by Arnold Richard. Volume 2* (A.A. Lynch Ed.). New York: International Psychoanalytic Books.

Schwartz, J. (1999). *Cassandra's Daughter: A History of Psychoanalysis*. New York: Viking Press.

Schwartz, M.M. (2018). Review of the book by D. Herzog "Cold War Freud: Psychoanalysis in an age of catastrophes", Cambridge University Press 2017. *Journal of the American Psychoanalytic Association* 66:172–181.

Shapira, M. (2018). Review of the book by D. Herzog "Cold War Freud. Psychoanalysis in an age of catastrophes", Cambridge University Press, 2017. *Psychoanalysis and History* 20:113–115.

Shapiro, S.A. (1993). Clara Thompson: Ferenczi's messenger with half a message. In L. Aron and A. Harris (Eds.), *The Legacy of Sándor Ferenczi* (pp. 159–173). Hillsdale, NJ: Analytic Press.

Smith, H.F. (2010). Editor's note. *Psychoanalytic Quarterly* 79:877–878.

Stepansky, P.E. (2009). *Psychoanalysis at the Margins*. New York: Other Press.

Stern, D.B. (2015). *Relational Freedom. Emergent Properties of the Relational Field*. London: Routledge.

Strenger, C. (2013). Why psychoanalysis must not discard science and human nature. *Psychoanalytic Dialogues* 23:197–210.

Sullivan, H.S. (1940). *Conceptions of Modern Psychiatry*. Washington DC: Washington School of Psychiatry.

———— (1953). *The Interpersonal Theory of Psychiatry* (H. Swick Perry and M. Ladd Gawel, Eds.). New York: Norton.

———— (1954). *The Psychiatric Interview* (H. Swick Perry and M. Ladd

Gawel, Eds.). New York: Norton.

——— (1962). *Schizophrenia as a Human Process* (H. Swick Perry, Ed.). New York: Norton.

Swick Perry, H. (1982). *Psychiatrist of America. The Life of Harry Stack Sullivan*. Cambridge, MA: Harvard University Press.

Thompson, C. (1952). Sullivan and psychoanalysis. *Contemporary Psychoanalysis* 1978; 14:488–501.

——— (1964). Sullivan and Fromm. *Contemporary Psychoanalysis* 1979; 15:195–200.

——— (2017). The history of the William Alanson White Institute. *Contemporary Psychoanalysis* 53:7–28.

Tilman, J.G. (2012). Review of the book by M. Conci "Sullivan revisited – Life and work", Tangram 2012. *Journal of the American Psychoanalytic Association* 60:615–619.

Werner, S., & Zittel, C. (2011). Einleitung [Introduction]. In S. Werner and C. Zittel (Eds.), *Ludwig Fleck – Denkstile und Tatsachen. Gesammelte Schriften und Zeugnisse* [Ludwig Fleck – Thought styles and facts. Collected papers and documents] (pp. 9–38). Frankfurt: Suhrkamp.

Will, O.A. (1954). Introduction. In H.S. Sullivan, *The Psychiatric Interview* (pp. ix–xxiii). New York: Norton.

Wolstein, B. (1989). Ferenczi, Freud and the origins of American Interpersonal relations. *Contemporary Psychoanalysis* 25:672–676.

——— (1993). Sándor Ferenczi and American Interpersonal relations. Historical and personal reflections. In L. Aron and A. Harris, *The Legacy of Sándor Ferenczi* (pp. 175–183). Hillsdale, NJ: Analytic Press)

Wurmser, L. (1977). A defense of the use of metaphor in analytic theory formation. *Psychoanalytic Quarterly* 46:466–498.

Young-Bruehl, E. (1994). A history of Freud biographies. In M.S. Micale and R. Porter (Eds.), *Discovering the History of Psychiatry* (pp. 157–173). Oxford: Oxford University Press.

——— (2013). *The Clinic and the Context. Historical Essays*. London: Karnac.

Young-Bruehl, E., & Schwartz, M.M. (2012). Psychoanalysis has no history. *American Imago* 69:139–159.

Zaretsky, E. (2004). *Secrets of the Soul: A Social and Cultural History of Psychoanalysis*. New York: Knopf.

——— (2011). Why the Freudian century: Reflections on the statue of Athena. *American Imago* 68:679–688.

——— (2017). *Political Freud: A History*. New York: Columbia University Press.

CHAPTER 4

SULLIVAN REVISITED:
A CLOSE LOOK FROM AFAR[1]

I am very happy to be here with you today. I feel very honored by your invitation. Giving here, at the White Institute, a paper on my work and point of view on H.S. Sullivan represents for me something like the realization of a dream. An old friend from Milan, Marco Bacciagaluppi—whom some of you certainly know—congratulated me on the invitation, but also warned me with the words: "For a European to give a paper on Sullivan at White must be as hard as selling ice to the Eskimos." But after some time I realized that what is most challenging about talking about Sullivan at the White Institute has only partly to do with me, that is, with the fact that I did not train at the White, that I am not American, and that I come from Italy. An even bigger challenge must have to do with the fact that, here at White, each one of you is very much likely to have his or her own Sullivan in mind. I mean by "his or her own private Sullivan" some sort of a "precious possession"—as Sullivan used to define our own individual self—which you do not find easy either to talk about or to define exactly. Considering my topic of today from this point of view, talking about Sullivan at the White Institute is easier for me than for you.

My special thanks go, of course, to Pasqual Pantone. Without his invitation I would not have been forced to dedicate so much energy to successfully completing the process of preparing the American edition of my book on Sullivan. *Sullivan rivisitato*, the original Italian edition, had appeared in 2000, and *Sullivan neu entdecken*, the German edition, in 2005. Thanks to Pasqual's invitation, the American edition is now here: *Sullivan revisited – Life and work. Harry Stack Sullivan's relevance for contemporary psychiatry, psychotherapy and psychoanalysis*. I myself got hold of the first copy of the book last Friday. You will be able to order it through Google in a few weeks.

Second, Pasqual played a crucial role in the choice of the title of the paper I am presenting to you today. My original idea had been "Sullivan revisited: A view from

[1] The original version of this paper was presented at the W.A. White Institute, New York, on Tuesday January 11, 2011. Original linguistic revision by Judit Filc.

Italy." Pasqual reacted with: "Sullivan revisited: A view from afar," which became the intermediary step to the title I ended up formulating and which we agreed upon: "Sullivan revisited: A close view from afar." In other words, this is the best title for capturing the paradox I have already talked about: it is easier to discuss our founding fathers through the view and voice of an outsider—of an informed outsider. In fact, paradox is also one of the central dimensions of psychoanalysis, and of our daily work with our patients. We help them by developing the kind of "close look from afar" that I will be trying to articulate in this paper.

The first aspect of this particular view of mine on Sullivan is easy to identify. Since nobody taught Sullivan to me, the only alternative I was left with was just reading his books. And by this I mean, all seven of his books available in English, five of which have also appeared in Italian, in the time span from 1961 to 1993. In fact, *Conceptions of modern psychiatry* was the first of his books to be published in Italy, by the Milan publisher Feltrinelli in 1961 with an Introduction by Gaetano Benedetti. The fifth one to come out, in 1993 and with a Preface written by me, was *Schizophrenia as a human process. The interpersonal theory of psychiatry*, *The psychiatric interview*, and *Clinical studies in psychiatry* had all come out in the 1960s. It might also interest you to know that, with five out of seven books by Sullivan translated into Italian, Italy has been and is the European country most receptive to his work. Only his *The interpersonal theory of psychiatry* and *The psychiatric interview* were ever translated into German and Spanish, and only *Schizophrenia as a human process* was published in France.

Italy has been and is one of the countries in the world in which the translation of psychoanalytic books has been and keeps being as large and inclusive as possible. Together with Sullivan, Fromm-Reichmann, and Fromm, Heinz Hartmann's, Melanie Klein's, and Jacques Lacan's work also started being translated into Italian in the 1960s. This fact undoubtedly contributed to the constant expansion of psychoanalysis in my country in the last forty years, and to the fact that most psychoanalytic points of view have been well received by different sectors of our psychoanalytic community and/or have had a significant impact on them. This was and is true—as I will later show—also for relational psychoanalysis.

Of such a psychoanalytic climate, the climate in

which psychoanalysis started to develop in Italy in the 1960s and in which my own work on Sullivan began some years later, I can even offer you the personal testimony of such a prominent psychoanalyst as Adam Limentani (1913–1994). An Italian Jew, Limentani left Rome for London just after finishing his medical studies in 1938, and there he not only trained as a psychoanalyst, but also ended up becoming a very influential colleague of the Middle Group and a president of the International Psychoanalytical Association (IPA; 1983–1986). Here is what he wrote in 1989 in a report entitled "Psychoanalysis in Italy: A personal appraisal," published in the catalogue of the exhibition *Italy in psychoanalysis*, in the context of the XXXVIth IPA Congress, held in Rome:

> I recall that when I first visited the Italian Society in 1966 . . . the experience of reading a paper at the Milan Center . . . went beyond my expectations . . . . I soon realized that most of those present were much better read than I was . . . . Living and working in a city like London with the possibility of attending several scientific meetings in the course of a month is not inductive to much reading. Those who work in a so-called psychoanalytically underdeveloped country imbibe foreign and local literature on a very large basis. (Limentani, 1989, p. 26)

In other words, this is the climate of great curiosity for and interest in psychoanalysis that allowed Wilfred Bion (1897–1979) to charm the Italian psychoanalytic community to the point of not only earning him many Italian followers, but also even giving rise to such a strong commitment to the study of his work as to produce a whole series of internationally famous "Bion scholars." The most famous of them is, of course, Antonino Ferro, whom I had the pleasure of introducing to you here last year, on Saturday January 16, 2010. Bion's work was initially translated into Italian at the end of the 1960s, and he himself had had the chance to hold the famous Italian Seminars in the summer of 1977. In fact, his own daughter Parthenope (who had studied philosophy in Florence, trained as an analyst in Rome, and married an Italian musician) translated his work and later contributed to its systematic reception until her untimely death in July 1998, at age 53.

Back to my own work on Sullivan, and before I deal with Gaetano Benedetti's contribution to it, let me tell you that a similar role to the one played by Bion in the case of Ferro and his generation was played in my case and some of my colleagues' by Silvano Arieti's (1914–1981) visits to Italy. In July 1979, when I was a medical student in Florence, I heard Arieti give a lecture on his fascinating

book *Creativity: The magic synthesis*. He had been invited
to the department of psychiatry by Adolfo Pazzagli (an
IPA analyst to whom I owe my first introduction to
psychiatry) while on his way to his summer house in
Sardinia. Arieti had given his first paper in Italian, on
the psychotherapy of schizophrenia, back in 1962, upon
Gaetano Benedetti's and Pier Francesco Galli's invitation.
As some of you certainly know, after finishing his medical
studies in Pisa, Arieti had been forced to leave Italy at the
same time and for the same reason as Adam Limentani.
Thanks to his Italian contacts, not only was the *American
handbook of psychiatry*, edited by him in 1959, becoming
the most widely read psychiatric handbook in Italy in the
1960s and 1970s, but all of his books also found an Italian
publisher, and even an Italian translator, my very good
friend Marco Bacciagaluppi. In the early 1960s, Marco
had been a resident in psychiatry at New York Medical
College together with Arieti's cousin Jules Bemporad,
and Arieti himself had been one of his supervisors. This
is how he became Arieti's Italian translator. And how I
myself ended up reading all his books in Italian.

In Italy we have a famous saying: *il mondo è piccolo*,
meaning "the world is small." Now, not only Silvano
Arieti, but also Gaetano Benedetti made the world smaller,
that is, brought us all closer together—not only in terms
of our countries, Italy and the United States, but also
in terms of bringing us, as psychoanalysts, closer to our
schizophrenic patients. As I wrote in the Afterword to the
Italian edition of his book *Psychotherapie als existentielle
Herausfoderung* (Psychotherapy as existential challenge),
Benedetti's dialogical voice is the central dimension of his
work and legacy—dialogue not only with patients, but
also with colleagues, that is, with the whole international
analytic community. This allowed him both to help his
schizophrenic patients give up their autistic retreat
and enter a shared human dimension, and to introduce
Sullivan and the interpersonal point of view in Italy.
For those who know him, I am also happy to say that he
turned 90 last July and still has a clear mind. He was very
happy to hear about my having been invited to give this
paper here today—and this makes him also spiritually
present among us here now.

But here is the persuasive voice with which Benedetti
presented Sullivan's point of view to Italian readers back
in 1961: "Sullivan's capacity to delineate the dynamics of
mental states was seldom reached by other researchers.
Here the clinically oriented Sullivan penetrates further
into the nature of mental states than the theoretically

oriented Freud—who studied only a limited number of psychiatric patients. What also strikes me is the sense of truthfulness coming from Sullivan's clinical observations, and his moving away from any construction of a purely theoretical nature. Sullivan brings to life in front of us phenomena that in other psychiatric systems look like a lifeless tissue sample. Freud himself sounds rigidly and abstractly mechanical as compared to Sullivan's dynamic phenomenology" (1961, p. xviii; my translation). Only later, when he was my supervisor in Milan, did I discover to what extent Benedetti had actually taken Sullivan as a model, for example with regard to how important it was for him to keep alive the double identity of psychiatrist and psychoanalyst.

In fact, I myself had felt very much fascinated by Sullivan when I discovered his *Interpersonal theory of psychiatry*, the first book by him I read, as a medical student in the spring of 1977. The problem I was then trying to articulate in my mind and for which I found a satisfying answer in Sullivan's book related to the influence of culture and society on the development of one's identity. A few years before, I had been an exchange student in a suburb of New York and, after the usual allergic reaction that every European has toward American culture, I was able to see how much I could profit from the fruitful complementariness of the European and the American concepts of autonomy. As much as I had been able to teach myself to integrate the European concept of "independence of mind" and the American concept of "practical self-reliance," I was later able to find out on my own what Sullivan was all about—and to find him truly fascinating. This experience also brought about the first dimension of my identification with him: the self-taught character of our research.

As I started working as a psychiatrist—it was the spring of 1982—I not only discovered Sullivan's *Conceptions of modern psychiatry* and Benedetti's Preface to it, but also ended up carefully reading and letting myself be guided by his *Psychiatric interview* and his *Clinical studies in psychiatry*. I belonged then to the generation of Italian psychiatrists whose professional choice owed much to the revolution brought about by Franco Basaglia's (1924–1980) *nuova psichiatria* (new psychiatry); this culminated in the 1978 Reform Law which closed down mental hospitals to new admissions and created a whole new network of mental health centers. Nonetheless, as I would soon discover with the help of Sullivan's books, Basaglia's "new psychiatry" was one-sided in its political and social orientation. Many of his followers were giving up the clinical dimension of psychiatry, which was so central to Sullivan's system of thought—as I could gather from my self-taught approach to it. It was here that the reception of Sullivan's ideas by his very first interpreter, Patrick Mullahy, was very helpful:

> The psychiatrist, if he is to function with social effectiveness, can no longer stand aloof. He must, *while maintaining his specialty*, join hands with the other social scientists. This broader point of view – wrote Mullahy – in 1945 requires a new orientation and the perfection of new techniques. (Mullahy, 1953, p. 294, emphasis added)

In other words, guided by the feeling that Sullivan's point of view had not been understood by Italian psychiatrists as it deserved to be, and fascinated as I was by the coherence and the interdisciplinary character of his overall work, in the spring of 1988 I offered a course on "H.S. Sullivan and the meeting of psychiatry with the social sciences" to the philosophy students of the University of Venice. Both Lucio Pinkus (the Venice professor of dynamic psychology with whom I collaborated then), and Pier Francesco Galli (one of Benedetti's first Italian collaborators and the founder of the journal *Psicoterapia e Scienze Umane* in 1967, to which I had started contributing in 1986) were very sympathetic to my point of view. Sullivan's interdisciplinary journal *Psychiatry*, and its attempt to create (back in 1938) a common forum for psychiatry, psychotherapy, and psychoanalysis, had been an important model for Galli's journal, for which I later translated and reviewed some of the most important of Stephen Mitchell's articles and books.

It was exactly at this point of the articulation of my view of Sullivan's work and legacy that I was lucky enough to attend the first Italian workshop given by Stephen Mitchell and Jay Greenberg. It was held at the beginning of April 1988 at the Florence Neo-Freudian institute, which later became the "Sullivan Institute." At the Rio de Janeiro Forum of October 1989, it also became a member society of the International Federation of Psychoanalytic Societies (IFPS). Greenberg and Mitchell's 1983 masterwork *Object relations in psychoanalytic theory* had been translated into Italian in 1986. I had already read it and found it fascinating, and wanted to get to know them. As it turned out, in the workshop given by Mitchell the consecutive translation was not good enough, and so I jumped in as translator. Consequently, Stephen was able to say after some time: "I see that you translate well, since people started laughing at my jokes."

This unique event established a climate of collaboration between us that lasted till his untimely death in December 2000 and whose second important step, that same evening, was represented by the discovery of a common passion: teaching Sullivan. "Why don't you write a book on Sullivan?," Stephen asked me at the end of that evening. I was thus able to start perceiving what I later discovered as being his well-known intellectual generosity, which Jay Greenberg also celebrated in his obituary of 2001.

As you can imagine, Stephen really succeeded in getting me started on this project, and he is, therefore, also spiritually here with us today. The first step was the paper on Sullivan's *Schizophrenia as a human process* that I gave in September 1988 at the IXth Symposium on the Psychotherapy of Schizophrenia organized by Gaetano Benedetti and Pier Maria Furlan in Turin. This paper allowed me to become the editor of the Italian edition of the fifth book by Sullivan to come out in Italian (in 1993). In the Preface I wrote, I formulated one of the conclusions of my self-taught study of Sullivan: that the papers of the 1920s and 1930s, edited by Helen Swick Perry (1911–2001) in the anthology *Schizophrenia as a human process*, stand at the very roots of Sullivan's overall work, and should be the first papers that anyone trying to understand his work and legacy should read!

But let us not run too much ahead of time: a month later, in October 1988, I met Earl Witenberg at a conference held near Florence on the relevance of Sullivan's legacy. This was also the beginning of an important relationship, which lasted many years—among the things I owe Earl is the discovery of the relevance of the book *A Harry Stack Sullivan case seminar. Treatment of a young male schizophrenic*, edited by Roger Kvarnes and Gloria Parloff in 1976.

Even more important, however, was visiting Stephen during the 1988 Christmas vacation in New York, reading and discussing with him *Relational concepts in psychoanalysis: An integration*, and getting ready to become what I would call his "ambassador to Italy." I still remember the excitement of translating into Italian papers like "The intrapsychic and the interpersonal. Different theories, different domains or historical artifacts?" or his papers on the concepts of multiple selves and of analytic interpretation, which he gave during the two subsequent trips to Italy that I organized for him in 1991 and 1996. In 1993 the Italian edition of his 1988 book came out with an Introduction by me, in which I explained to Italian readers who he was, what his background and training had been like, what notion of psychoanalysis he was trying to develop, and what his "relational turn" was about. I had originally reviewed the book in detail in 1990 in the journal *Psicoterapia e Scienze Umane*, and I did the same in 1994 for *Hope and dread in psychoanalysis*. It is no wonder that, given also the interest in his work shown by Italian IPA colleagues, his books not only sold very well, but were also rapidly translated into Italian, until all seven of them were published. I am making reference to *Freud and beyond. A History of modern psychoanalytic thought*, written together with Margaret Black, and to *Influence and autonomy in psychoanalysis*, as well as the two posthumously published books *Relationality: From attachment to intersubjectivity* and *Can love last? The fate of romance over time*. In the PowerPoint presentation I gave at the conference of the International Association for Relational Psychoanalysis and Psychotherapy (IARPP) organized in Rome by Gianni Nebbiosi and Emanuel Berman in June 2005, I presented a whole series of pictures and documents illustrating the topic of "S.A. Mitchell in Italy."

But to Stephen Mitchell I am of course very thankful not only for the admirable passion with which he pursued his psychoanalytic interests and for the generosity of his friendship, but—and here I go back to my own work on Sullivan—for the way in which he himself interpreted H.S. Sullivan and his legacy. As I could show in detail in an unpublished paper I gave at the IFPS Rome Forum in May 2006, Stephen gave me a very important key to the further articulation of my own view of Sullivan in that he had the following four characteristics in common with Sullivan: a great clinical sensibility, a deep interest for the interdisciplinary background of and debate around psychoanalysis, a particular interest for the epistemological and scientific dimensions of psychoanalysis, and—last but not least—a politically informed drive toward the creation of a clearly post-Freudian psychoanalysis.

In fact, both *Object relations in psychoanalytic theory* and *Relational concepts in psychoanalysis* contributed so much to bringing Sullivan's work back into mainstream psychoanalysis that my role as Stephen Mitchell's "Italian ambassador" allowed me to establish a whole series of important contacts with some of the most prominent members of the Italian Psychoanalytic Society. The first one of these was with Luciana Nissim Momigliano (1917–1998), one of the most important influences on Antonino Ferro's work, that is, one of the analysts who most contributed to the growing interest in Bion's work, and whose 1992 book *Continuity and change in psychoanalysis. Letters from Milan* I reviewed in 1995 in Joseph Reppen's journal *Psychoanalytic Books*. In the important book she had edited together with Andreina Robutti in 1992, *Shared experience. The psychoanalytic dialogue*, they had stressed the importance of the "interpersonal moment" (1992, p. 18) and also cited Mitchell's work (1992, p. 17). Since these prestigious analysts did not know much about Sullivan's work or about Mitchell's revisitation of it, the need to contribute to placing his work back into mainstream psychoanalysis became a further motivation for writing a book on Sullivan in Italian. Antonino Ferro himself was one of the co-authors of *Shared experience*, and I was later able to get him interested in your interpersonal tradition, both through my own book on Sullivan and through a whole series of contacts and very fruitful exchanges. Of course, to this chapter of my work also belongs what I learned from him about Wilfred Bion's work, which in 2009 allowed me to publish a paper with the title "Bion and Sullivan: An enlightening comparison."

Before turning to the second part of my paper, that is, the presentation of how I deal with Sullivan's life and work in my own book, let me finish the discussion of the multiple ingredients of my own "close look from afar" by mentioning a couple more episodes of my complex itinerary of "consensual validation" of my own perspective. Upon the invitation of the late David Feinsilver, I was able to participate in the XIth Symposium on the Psychotherapy of Schizophrenia held in Washington DC in June 1994 on the theme "Psychotherapy and Comprehensive Treatment." I gave the paper "The interpersonal tradition in Italy and Europe" at a panel coordinated by John Kafka and with the participation of a whole series of Sullivan's students, such as Donald Burnham, Robert Cohen, and Clarence Schulz, with whom I was also able to compare my view of Sullivan. By the way, in September 1992 I had had the chance to visit the Chestnut Lodge Sanitarium, to take a look at its library together with Anne-Louise Silver, and to be invited by Mauricio Cortina to give the paper "H.S. Sullivan and the training of the psychiatrist" (Conci, 1993c) at the Washington School of Psychiatry. I was also for many years able to conduct an important work of consensual validation of our own views of Sullivan with my very good friend Henry Zvi Lothane, who greatly contributed to bringing Sullivan's point of view back into the analytic mainstream, not only through his masterwork on President Schreber, but also through papers such as "Freud and the interpersonal."

Last but not least, let me just briefly mention those of you who accompanied me in the long process of putting together "my close view of Sullivan from afar" and contributed to shaping it. Let me start with Milt Zaphiropoulos, whose introductory lectures on Sullivan's life and work I had attended in June 1993 together with the present secretary general of IFPS, the Norwegian Agnar Berle. I even remember that Agnar and I were then invited to the party given by Gerard Chrzanowski for his eightieth birthday. Gerard had given me his book *Interpersonal approach to psychoanalysis: Contemporary view of Harry Stack Sullivan* as a gift, and I am also very grateful to him for having initiated the process of recognition of Milan's Associazione di Studi Psicoanalitici (ASP), founded by a group of supervisees of Benedetti and Johannes Cremerius (1918–2002), as a member society of IFPS at the Rio de Janeiro Forum of October 1989. With Carola Mann I have, of course, worked for many years for the IFPS, which your group contributed to founding back in 1962. I very much appreciate your supporting our journal, the *International Forum of Psychoanalysis*, of which I have been co-editor-in-chief since June 2007. Sondra Wilk has always been very kind to me and assisted me in my bibliographic research since I started visiting your institute, back in December 1988. Not only did Earl Witenberg open the doors of your institute for me, but his successors—Marylou Lionells (1992–2000), Joerg Bose (2000–2008), and Jay Kwawer (since 2008)—were also happy to see me around and to let me participate in all your scientific events. I was also lucky enough to get to know Arthur Feiner, who published a paper of mine in 1993 in *Contemporary Psychoanalysis*, and whose work was taken up by Jay Greenberg in 1995 and by Don Stern in 2002, who invited me to join your journal as a corresponding editor. With Mark Blechner we collaborate in the International Council of Editors of Psychoanalytic Journals (ICEPJ), coordinated by Peter Rudnytsky. And then come a whole series of colleagues actively involved in the international exchange that our Federation stands for, like Darlene Ehrenberg, Jack Drescher, and Sandra Buechler. My view of Sullivan was undoubtedly also shaped by the work of Edgar Levenson (which I reviewed in the *International Forum* in 1995), and by the points of view developed in a whole series of papers by Alan Grey, the late John Fiscalini, and Irwin Hirsch.

My report on this chapter of my research journey

would not be complete without mentioning the two Italian colleagues with whom I shared such a long-standing relationship with your institute, that is, Sergio Dazzi and Maria Luisa Mantovani, with whom in 1997 I edited an anthology of the most important contributions of your tradition entitled *La tradizione interpersonale in psichiatria, psicoterapia e psicoanalisi*, whose chapters we ourselves translated into Italian and introduced to Italian readers. Our anthology includes historically relevant papers such as Janet Rioch's 1943 essay "The transference phenomenon in psychoanalytic therapy," Mable Blake Cohen's "Countertransference and anxiety" (1952), and Otto Will's 1959 paper "Human relatedness and the schizophrenic reaction"—all of them originally published in Sullivan's journal *Psychiatry*.

At this point, I cannot but try to satisfy your curiosity as to how—given the ingredients I have discussed so far—I articulated my "close view of Sullivan from afar" in my book *Sullivan revisited – Life and work*. First, the book deals not only with Sullivan's life and work, but also with the historical and scientific context in which his work emerged. What in your tradition of specialization would require a historian, a biographer, and a clinician, in the European tradition I come from can still be performed by a single person—or still could be in my generation. Helen Swick Perry's (1911–2001) unique 1982 biography deals with Sullivan's work only to a certain extent, and the 1996 book by F. Barton Evans III, *Harry Stack Sullivan. Interpersonal theory and psychotherapy*, does not take into consideration the context of Sullivan's work at all—as had also been the case with the earlier monographic book on Sullivan published by A.H. Chapman in 1976. Second, in the two parts that make up the book—"The historical and scientific context of Sullivan's life and work" and "Sullivan's relevance today"—I take into consideration the three fields of psychiatry, psychotherapy, and psychoanalysis, in which I myself trained as a medical doctor specialized in psychiatry. A third important general feature of the book is the fact that it not only reflects the self-taught journey I just described to you in the first part of this paper, but also aims at putting all the data on Sullivan I found at the reader's disposal, as opposed to just articulating my point of view on Sullivan. In other words, I try to stimulate the reader to read Sullivan on his or her own, that is, to embark on a journey through Sullivan's entire oeuvre and through the secondary bibliography that tackles his work and his legacy, as I did. This was also the direction taken by Henry Ellenberger in his 1970 seminal book *The discovery of the unconscious: The history and evolution of dynamic psychiatry*, which, together with Henri Zvi Lothane's book on Schreber (1992), inspired my own work. In fact, we are dealing with a very interpersonally oriented model—a model in line with a book on H.S. Sullivan.

It is thus no wonder that in the first chapter of the book, with the title "Psychotherapy takes hold in North America," I deal with three important figures that gave shape to the context within which Sullivan's work appeared—William James (1842–1911), James Putnam (1848–1918), and Adolf Meyer (1866–1950). Sullivan's interpersonal psychiatry is rooted in James's attempt to integrate subjective experiences and empirical facts. Furthermore, in James's *Principles of psychology* we can even find a definition of the "social self" centered on the fact that "a man has as many social selves as there are groups in which he is interested" (1890, p. 295). This is clearly the source of Sullivan's definition of "personality." From the detailed reconstruction of the life and work of the first American psychoanalyst done by Nathan Hale, Jr., we learn not only of Putnam's anti-reductionist epistemological critique of psychoanalysis, but also of the social orientation he had inherited from the philosopher Royce and the psychologist Baldwin, which allowed him to see "the restoration of social ties" as "an integral part of therapy" (Hale, 1971, p. 52). Already in 1967 John Burnham had spoken about what he called "the social bias" of American psychoanalysis as "present in the earliest years" (1967, p. 208). As far as the Swiss-born Meyer is concerned, he not only promoted (according to George Mora, 1992) two revolutions in American psychiatry (from neuroanatomy to the clinical, and from the clinical to the psychotherapeutic dimension), but was also the first one to articulate the concept of psychiatry as an intellectually challenging and interdisciplinary new field where the psychoanalytic, the social, and the biological dimensions could complement each other in the service of the patient—as Theodore Lidz wrote in 1966.

I can thus come to the second chapter, "Psychoanalysis in the 'New World'," where I present Saul Rosenzweig's 1992 reconstruction of Freud's 1909 trip to the States, I reconstruct Stanley Hall's (1844–1924) motivations for inviting him as well as the "social and behaviorist orientation" of his own psychology, and I analyze Ernest Jones' (1879–1959) model of the "full-time analyst," which was opposite to the one proposed by all the pioneers of American psychoanalysis. Such a conflict is the focus of the central section of this chapter, "Psychoanalysis in North America: Deformation or emancipation," where I show how, by rendering psychoanalysis into an essential part of psychiatry—as Freud had originally asked C.G. Jung to do—the American pioneers of psychoanalysis—starting with Abraham Brill, Trigant Burrow, and Clarence Oberndorf, and including also Smith Ely Jelliffe and William Alanson White—were able to emancipate psychoanalysis from the ambulatory cure of neurotic patients. Already in 1939 Jelliffe had reacted to Freud's criticism of the Americans' "lack of judgment" (1930; SE 21, p. 255) by stating: "Certain superlative natures have been happy to view this enormous extension [of psychoanalysis in the USA] as an expression of American superficiality. It takes a lot of hot fire to have wide-spread irradiations. This is as elementary in psychiatry as it is in physics" (1939, p. 339). Because of the essential role played by Jelliffe (1866–1950), whom I redefined as "the clinician as an intellectual," and by White (1870–1937), with his "healthy American eclecticism," in shaping Sullivan's own approach to psychoanalysis, I conclude the chapter by discussing their life and work in detail—basing myself on John Burnham's precious book on Jelliffe (1983). Here is, for example, what the Italian-American colleague Arcangelo D'Amore wrote of White in 1976, after having stated that he "made of St. Elisabeths Hospital the 'Burghölzli' of the American continent" (1976, p. 84):

> White succeeded, I think, in assimilating, organizing and popularizing psychoanalysis in the United States in a way that at first aroused Freud's doubts and misgivings but which, in the long run, reflected good judgment and an open-mindedness which contributed to its considerable growth and development during the years White gave it nurture. (D'Amore, 1976, p. 88)

Among other things, in 1913 Jelliffe and White had founded *The Psychoanalytic Review*, the first (still existing) American journal of psychoanalysis—at variance with what Henry Smith states in his latest Editor's Note in *The Psychoanalytic Quarterly*.

In the third chapter I present Sullivan's life, based not only on Helen Swick Perry's splendid 1982 biography, but also on the above-cited book by Chapman (1976) and on Kenneth Chatelaine's 1981 book on Sullivan's formative years. There I stress how paradigmatic his life was and is for any of us working in the field of mental health, an activity which requires us to have gone through some deep personal crisis, to have recovered from it through a process of self-reflection (conducted with or without the help of a therapist), and to have been able to redirect our lives correspondingly. This was also Freud's path—notwithstanding Ernest Jones's attempt to downplay Freud's neurosis in his biography. In fact, Sullivan was very Freudian in his orientation, if we just look at the two basic poles of the latter's contribution and not at the techniques he developed. On the one hand, how we can learn to look at ourselves, and see what we do wrong. On the other hand, how we can only get to know ourselves and change accordingly through the eyes of others and thanks to their help. This is what all Freud's letters show us—the laboratory of his discovery of himself and of psychoanalysis, as I demonstrated in 1998 in a paper on his self-analysis and his partners.

Following in C.G. Jung's footsteps, in terms of his application of psychoanalysis to psychiatry, Sullivan tried to apply to the sickest patients what Freud had discovered in working with neurotics, and he proved that it was possible to work with them psychoanalytically, not by just letting them associate freely, but by actively creating a relationship, a bridge of words and deeds. From this point of view, Sullivan is the typical follower who remained faithful to his teacher precisely by going beyond him—by a process of internalization rather than by doing the same as the teacher through imitation. Any one of us can do this as long as we are able to keep listening to ourselves, to keep our capacity for self-teaching activated during our training. And each one of us has to go through such a learning process! Also from this point of view, Sullivan remains, in my opinion, an important example for all of us in the fields of psychiatry, psychotherapy, and psychoanalysis. A.H. Chapman stressed the self-taught dimension of his creativity in a paradoxical way: "If Sullivan had had a standard education he probably would have been an outstanding psychiatrist, but it is doubtful that he would have made his original, revolutionary contributions to psychiatry" (1976, p. 29).

After having shown how Sullivan was a typical American psychoanalyst of the first generation (a member of the American from 1926 till his death in 1949), in Chapter 4, "Sullivan's work and the neo-Freudian turn," I discuss what he soon started perceiving as his professional and scientific priority: the creation, in the footsteps of Meyer and White, of the new field of psychoanalytic psychiatry, that is, "dynamic psychiatry." The first laboratory of such an important project was his first book *Personal psychopathology*, written in 1932 and published only in 1972, which I tackle in the first section of the chapter. In it not only did he demonstrate Freud's mistake in distinguishing between patients "capable and incapable of transference," but he also proposed a systematic classification of our defense mechanisms before Anna Freud, and introduced the adaptive viewpoint before Heinz Hartmann. Having outlined there the basic concepts of his interpersonal theory of psychiatry, he presented a more mature articulation of this theory in his *Conceptions of modern psychiatry*, which I examine in the second section of the chapter. Sullivan's priority here is not the development of psychoanalysis along Freud's predetermined lines, but its application to the highest possible number of patients, and to the sickest of them. "Regardless of the warp incorporated in the self, the psychiatrist," wrote Sullivan in 1939, "given sufficient insight and skill, may expect favorable changes to ensue from his study of the patient's situation" (1953, p. 97). In other words, "one achieves mental health to the extent that one becomes aware of one's interpersonal relations" (Sullivan, 1953, p.207). As we know, Sullivan was not alone in his attempt to rethink psychoanalysis in light of the needs and epistemological horizons of his time when Freud was still alive, as I show in the third section of the chapter.

This is what brought him close to Clara Thompson (1893–1958), Lucile Dooley, and Ernest Hadley, and to European emigrants Erich Fromm (1900–1980) and Karen Horney (1885–1952). In my reconstruction of the evolution of the so-called "Zodiac Group," leading to the psychoanalytic schisms of the 1940s, it was not they who left the ship of American psychoanalysis—but the ship that left them. According to another, very interesting point of view, the atmosphere that led to the American schisms of the 1940s had already started to develop in Berlin with Karl Abraham's death in 1925. As a consequence, Melanie Klein, no longer feeling protected by him, had moved to London, where she found the support of Ernest Jones. From this point of view, I also consider the so-called "neo-Freudian turn" one of the best instances of collaboration between European and American analysts, and/or a demonstration of the fruitful complementariness of their approaches. No wonder I answer the question I advance in the fourth section of the chapter, "Neo-Freudian: is this definition still valid?" by showing, based on the ideas developed by Greenberg and Mitchell and by Morris Eagle (1991), how far ahead of their time they were in their critique of libido theory, in their approach to schizoid and narcissistic patients, and in their attempt to further develop the interdisciplinary dialogue Freud himself had espoused. Not to mention their acceptance—at variance with the American Psychoanalytic Association—of Freud's concept of lay analysis, around which the analytic training offered by your institute (founded back in 1943) was organized.

In the fifth and last section of Chapter 4 I introduce the reader to Sullivan's overall work and to the most important secondary literature concerned with it, with which I specifically deal in the Second Part of the book.

I can now come to the Second Part of the book, "Sullivan's relevance today." In Chapter 5, "The psychotherapy of schizophrenia," I explore Sullivan's pioneering and still relevant contribution to this field in the light of Ronald Laing's assessment of it in his 1963 review of *Schizophrenia as a human process* in the *International Journal of Psychoanalysis*:

> Reading these articles by Sullivan written thirty to forty years ago is a somewhat depressing experience. They are altogether more contemporary than they should be. What were brave and sometimes reckless dicta then, should have become hypotheses, long since confirmed or disconfirmed. Instead, most of the issues are still open, most of the work that Sullivan's vision demanded is still not done. (Laing, 1963, pp. 377–378)

Sullivan's capacity to establish a good communication and even a working relationship with the sickest patients is a resource and asset that lies outside today's training in psychiatry. What is more, even the organizational premises he envisioned and tried to put into practice are still out of reach for an average department of psychiatry. And here I make reference not only to Sullivan's statement that "teamwork by all those concerned in the treatment of the acutely schizophrenic patient is essential" (1962, p. 253), but also to the inability—in any average department of psychiatry—to carry out the necessary selection of "all those concerned."

> "I have come to feel," wrote Sullivan in 1931, "that the personality qualifications of all those with whom the acute schizophrenic patient comes in contact should be the primary consideration of any attempt to achieve good results from treatment. It has been demonstrated again and again that a great deal of good work is easily ruined by even brief contact of the patient with unsuitable personnel" (Sullivan, 1962, p. 253).

In this chapter I also examine C.G. Jung's role as a pioneer of the interpersonal point of view and/or of the establishment of a non-Freudian branch of psychoanalysis; the important influence of the Zurich School on the nature and development of American psychoanalysis, given that pioneers such as Abraham Brill and Trigant Burrow were first introduced to Freud's new discipline there; and the life and work of Frieda Fromm-Reichmann (1889–1957)—making reference to the important volume about her life and legacy edited by Ann-Louise Silver in 1989. Last but not least, as far as *Schizophrenia as a human process* is concerned, I both present in detail every single paper anthologized in it and show how the roots of his later interpersonal theory of psychiatry lie here, not to mention his collaboration with a great number of social scientists.

In Chapter 6, "Sullivan as a social scientist," I articulate in detail Dorothy Blitsten's definition of Sullivan as "a social scientist whose specialty was psychiatry" (1953, p. 11)—originally suggested by Helen Swick Perry in 1982. First of all, I explain what the Chicago School of Sociology was all about, and why George Herbert Mead (1863–1931) and Edward Sapir (1884–1939) were such important sources of inspiration for Sullivan. I then show the high level of scientific exchange which characterized the two "Colloquia on Personality Investigation" organized by Sullivan, White, and the sociologist William Thomas in 1928 and 1929, and illustrate his still noteworthy commitment to the problem of psychiatric training. Very few psychiatrists have ever openly stated that "the preferred doctrine of psychiatric causation is often a *necessary* part of the personality system of the psychiatrist," as he did in the article "The support of psychiatric research and teaching" in 1939 (p. 275), or have formulated with such precision what the study of psychiatry should consist of, as he did in 1947 in "The study of psychiatry: Three orienting lectures." In his own words:

> I would like you to realize that the practical purpose of the study of psychiatry can be formulated as the learning of (1) what actually occurs in interpersonal fields with others; (2) how much and just what in these performances is inadequate and inappropriate to the achievement of satisfactory outcome and the protection of all concerned from unnecessary anxiety; (3) wherefore these inadequacies and inappropriateness of field integration and process still characterize your living; (4) wherein you are inexperienced in living and thus at a disadvantage at integrating, and in influencing the process in interpersonal fields. (1947, p. 367)

Possibly even more instructive is my introduction to the first ten volumes of Sullivan's journal *Psychiatry* in the third section of Chapter 6. This journal's interdisciplinary richness still remains unsurpassed, and is documented in papers like Edward Sapir's "Why cultural anthropology needs the psychiatrist" and Harold Lasswell's "What psychiatrists and political scientists can learn from each other" (see the References in my book). Equally important is my detailed description of the articles by Sullivan edited by Helen Perry in *The fusion of psychiatry and social science* in the following section. This account allows us to follow the evolution of Sullivan's definition of the concepts of psychiatry, interpersonal field, and personality in the light of the research projects in which he actively participated. What follows is an example of how he implicitly uses the notion of "projective identification" in dealing with the white people's image of the African-American:

> The tragedy of the Negro in America seems to be chiefly a matter of culturally determined attitudes in the whites, by the manifestations of which the Negro is generally distorted into a pattern of interracial behavior which permits the continuance of the attitudes without much change. This is a vicious circle, the interruption of which is an undertaking of great difficulty. (1964, p. 106)

It is no surprise that Sullivan also became a pioneer of a branch of psychiatry which did not yet exist at the time, that is, preventive psychiatry. He tried to generalize his psychotherapeutic approach in the direction of what he called "a psychiatry of peoples," which I discuss in the last section of Chapter 6. Here is how he formulated the psychiatrist's task in this regard, in the last section of his *Interpersonal theory of psychiatry*:

> Every constructive effort of the psychiatrist today is a strategy of interpersonal field operations which (1) seeks to map the areas of disjunctive forces that block the efficient collaboration of the patient and others, and (2) seeks to expand the patient's awareness so that this unnecessary blockage can be brought to an end. (1953, p. 376)

In Chapter 7, by the title "From Sullivan's interpersonal theory to the clinical and psychotherapeutic dimensions of his work," I take readers by the hand through the most important chapters of Sullivan's *Interpersonal theory of psychiatry*, assuming that they have the need both to be introduced to them and to patiently go through the whole book by themselves. How rewarding an experience this can be is proved by the fact that its close reading became one of the major sources for the later development of both group and family therapy. "Sullivan's formulations are exceedingly helpful for understanding the group therapeutic process" (1970, p. 17), wrote Irwin Yalom in this regard. The same is true for family therapy, as Richard Gartner amply proved in the chapter he devoted to this topic in the *Handbook of interpersonal psychoanalysis.* Of course, we can also easily say that through the speculative approach of his interpersonal theory Sullivan was able to anticipate most of what Daniel Stern was able to empirically demonstrate forty years later (1985)—as Stern himself confirmed to me in 1994 in Florence. Or, as I wrote in the paper where I compared Sullivan and Bion, it is also true that the former's concept of "maternal tenderness" runs parallel to the latter's concept of "maternal reverie." Not to mention how important Sullivan's notion of pre-adolescence still is and, together with it, the whole chapter of human development centered on peer relations outside the family, as opposed to Freud's concept of what Sullivan himself called "the Jesuitical first seven years" (1953, p. 248).

I also find Sullivan's *Clinical studies in psychiatry* very relevant today, both the first part, "Dynamisms of living and their misuse in mental disorder"—particularly his "interpersonal theory of mental disorders" and his concepts of "selective inattention," "dynamisms of 'emotion',," and "paranoid and schizophrenic dynamism"—and the second part, "Therapeutic approaches to patterns of difficulty—the clinical entities," especially his analysis of hysteria and obsessionalism and his therapeutic strategies in their regard. How much easier it is to understand the inner dynamics of these two groups of patients in terms of their interpersonal relations as opposed to doing so in terms of Freud's psychosexual phases! No wonder that Lorna Smith Benjamin adopted Sullivan's point of view in the creation of her diagnostic and therapeutic system for personality disorders published in 1993. Equally important is the great clinical and therapeutic sensitivity which allows Sullivan to show us how, in the case of obsessional patients, "the obsessional fog" they use as one of their basic defense mechanisms is meant to hide a deep sense of pain that only a long and systematic therapy such as psychoanalysis can heal. As he puts it,

> The relevant part of treatment consists in coming to see that all the conventional sweetness and light was just a veneer; in the process of study, what was mask and what was motive gets itself something clear. This insight is often attended by bitter grieving, in which one of several things might be the case. In general the grieving is over the many opportunities for possible happiness that were wasted because the patient was so puzzled as to whether he was right or wrong about the savage interference of the significant parent. This is true grief. It is the final emancipation from a lost object of desire which has been festering, as it were, in the personality from childhood onward. (1956, p. 268)

Even more stimulating and rewarding is a careful study of Sullivan's *Psychiatric interview*, which I explore in Chapter 8, the last chapter of my book, from the dual point of view of what I call the "common psychotherapeutic language" that he articulated in it and of his own personal technique, which I discuss separately in the first two sections. By "common psychotherapeutic language" I mean Sullivan's successful attempt to create a new language, both indebted to and independent from psychiatry and psychoanalysis, whereby a trained expert, who would not necessarily have to be a psychiatrist or a psychoanalyst, could conduct an interview to find important new data concerning the way of functioning of the patient, who would therefore get an important benefit from it. As you all know, there is nothing similar to be found in Freud's work. For Freud, the basic aim of the preliminary meeting was to establish whether an analytic treatment on the couch (five or four times a week) was indicated (see Freud, 1913). Sullivan's promoting the "psychiatric interview" as an effective means of intervention and offering it to everybody—in or outside the mental health field—who was interested in mastering it, is certainly a very meaningful sign of his professional and political openness—what we could call an "anti-trust move." What is even more noteworthy is that he put the best of his experience—a technique very similar to the one he would use with his own patients—at the disposal of such new experts. A case in point is the use of free association, which he describes as follows: "Thus my way of getting this valuable aspect of personality to work is to induct the patient into the reporting of relatively free-floating thought before giving him any hint that this is a very important method . . . . So the psychiatrist should try to get something to *happen*, that he can refer then to as having happened, instead of telling the patient to say every littlest thing that comes to his mind, or something of the sort" (1954, pp. 84–85, original emphasis).

A further, even more important common denominator between his own technique and the concept of interview he develops in the most widely read of his books, is the complexity of the kind of work concerned, and of the psychotherapeutic work in general. In his own words,

> Thus, instead of 'knowing what one is looking for', one wants to be *alert to the possibilities of the immediate future of the relationship in which one is involved.* This is why I cannot say 'Here are seventeen tables of events that can characterize interviews; now, you memorize all this and then you will always know just what to expect.' (Sullivan, 1954, p. 57, original emphasis)

And what about what I call "Sullivan's technique"? In the second section of this chapter I deal with the secondary literature on this topic produced by all those colleagues who tried to formalize his technique, namely Mary Julian White, Jean Pearce and Saul Newton, A.H. Chapman, and Leston Havens. As a matter of fact, I wrote not only this section, but also the whole chapter with the following words of Stephen Mitchell in mind: "Sullivan's technique has been presented in vastly divergent ways by different interpreters and students of Sullivan" (1997, p. 79). Such complexity is even more evident in the next section, "Sullivan and contemporary psychotherapy," where I take into consideration the following topics: how Sullivan's point of view inspired two handbooks as different in their conception as Hilde Bruch's *Learning psychotherapy* and Lester Luborsky's *Principles of psychoanalytic psychotherapy. A manual for supportive-expressive treatment*; how it was explicitly and systematically developed by Gerald Klerman and his group in the form of their *Interpersonal psychotherapy of depression* (1984); how it lay at the core of the research done by Hans Strupp and Jeffrey Binder and published in their 1984 book *Psychotherapy in a new key: A guide to time-limited dynamic psychotherapy*; Sullivan's influence on the fields of group and family therapy reported above; and such new developments as the one culminating in what is known as the "Society for the Exploration of Psychotherapy Integration," a new field pioneered by Paul Wachtel's *Psychoanalysis and behavior therapy: Toward an integration* (1977), and the one focused on the utilization of Sullivan's ideas in the field of cognitive therapy, as explicitly documented by *Interpersonal process in cognitive therapy*, published in 1990 by Jeremy Safran and Zindel Segal. Even more interesting is the following section, "Sullivan and contemporary psychoanalysis," where I present the perspectives formulated in this regard by Clara Thompson, Ernest Ticho, Jay Greenberg and Steve Mitchell, Alan Grey, Jay Kwawer, Howard Bacal and Kenneth Newman, Philip Bromberg, and Irwin Hoffman. Only in the following section do I tackle "Interpersonal psychoanalysis" in view of its valuable articulation in the *Handbook* edited in 1995 by Marilou Lionells, John Fiscalini, Carola Mann, and Donnel Stern. I conclude the book with Stephen Mitchell's "relational turn," which I have already talked about in the first part of this presentation.

After such a detailed exposition of the contents of my book, and having shown how I depicted the context in which he lived and developed his work as well as the latter's relevance for us today, let me offer you some final considerations regarding my "close view of Sullivan from afar." I will try to go beyond my book and develop yet another dimension. I think that Sullivan's continuing relevance has to do with multiple levels of reference and abstraction. He was among the first psychoanalysts to extend to the sickest patients what Freud had discovered about neurotic patients in terms of the dynamics and treatability of their clinical picture; he was among the first psychoanalysts to treat patients not only on the couch, but also face to face; he was among the first psychoanalysts to use psychoanalytic psychotherapy and to see a continuity—and not a contradiction—between it and psychoanalysis proper; he was among the first psychoanalysts to make us realize the importance of the interaction between analyst and patient for a successful outcome of the treatment; but even more, his self-taught and open-minded orientation allowed him to pose a whole series of questions we must answer every day with each one of our patients. Number one: what is the "right distance" at which to situate ourselves, depending on the patient's problems and the phase of the treatment? Number two: to what extent do we have to be in touch both with the patient and with ourselves? Number three: to what extent can we rely on patients' free associations, and to what extent do we have to provide the new experiences they missed in life, to which no free associations can ever direct them? Number four: to what extent does analytic change follow or precede insight? In this context, we must resort to Janet Rioch's (1969) definition of the perspective offered by Sullivan as "that tradition which does *not* have answers, but which constantly tries to keep questions open" (1986, p. 44).

Another way to apprehend Sullivan's unique voice—the kind of voice we can still profit from if we listen to it while working with our patients—has to do with the unsurpassed way in which he mastered the rhythm of our music. The Sullivan expert Merton Gill (1914–1994) grasped this very well in a comment he made in his famous 1983 article "The interpersonal paradigm and the degree of the therapist's involvement." He referred there to Sullivan's careful choice of words in the following statement taken from his *Psychiatric interview*:

> the experience of the psychiatrist is synthesized into *an aptitude to do nothing exterior to his awareness* which will greatly handicap the development of the interview situation or which will direct its development in an unnecessarily obscure way. (1954, p. 68–69, original emphasis)

Having stated that Sullivan's "emphasis falls on

being aware of what one is doing rather than on what to
do" (1983, p. 211), Gill adds:

> This passage also subtly reveals Sullivan's attitude about
> what even the skillful psychoanalyst is likely not to do and
> is one of the reasons why it is so often a pleasure to read
> him. It is a variant of 'we are all much more simply human
> than otherwise'. He does not say 'will handicap'; he says
> 'will greatly handicap'. He does not say 'in an obscure way';
> he says 'in an unnecessarily obscure way'. He takes it for
> granted that there will be handicapping and obscurity. (Gill,
> 1983, p. 211)

What about calling it "the rhythm of participant
observation"? Such a rhythm is what we can also find in
a quote from Sullivan's 1934 paper "Psychiatric training
as a prerequisite to psychoanalytic practice." Helen Swick
Perry published it in *Schizophrenia as a human process*,
and I believe Gill overlooked it when he wrote the above-
cited paper—which I translated into Italian with Maria
Luisa Mantovani in 1995. But here are Sullivan's words:

> The meaning of the free associational material—the
> formulations that the psychoanalyst can offer to assist
> the patient—in the last analysis come entirely from the
> interpersonal relationship which the physician participates in
> and permits the patient to integrate with him. (1962, p. 314)

Yet what strikes me even more, what fascinates me
about Sullivan once and again, and what makes his voice
accompany me both in my clinical practice and in my
supervising and teaching activities is his highly developed
sense of the complexity of the psychoanalytic situation.
Here is, for example, what follows my previous quote:

> There is nothing else in the activity of man that approximates
> the complexity and subtlety of the psychoanalytic situation.
> No one can know all about this type of relationship as it exists
> today, and it is unthinkable that anyone can delineate the
> psychoanalytic situations that will be integrated with people
> in the future. Culture grows and the human personality is an
> expanding series. Techniques of therapy must grow in the
> same manner. (Sullivan, 1962, pp. 314–315)

And now let me ask you the following question:
does Sullivan's train of thought stop here, does he take it
further, or does he shift it? Not only does he shift his train
of thought in the direction of psychoanalytic training,
but he also touches the dimension of psychoanalysis as
a form of music, as the kind of activity that requires us
to be in tune with it every single work day. Here are his
own words again, in direct continuity with the ones just
quoted above:

> None the less, *admitting that this work is an unending
> quest*, in which the best of us must at times prove opaque
> or inattentive or incapable of grasping a sufficient number

of factors, one can still point out certain failures which are
or should become unpardonable in psychoanalytic practice.
*I refer here to failures of the psychoanalyst to recognize the
transference processes,* the shifting emotional relationships
which spring up in his work with each individual patient.
Any blindness in this field produces great stresses in the
personality undergoing psychoanalysis .... Just as you, before
you had acquired some of the wealth of the Greek and the
Latin languages for creating terminologies, could have read
medical books without much profit, so also in psychoanalysis
until one has learned the signals, the signs and the symptoms
of transference manifestations, by successes and failures, by
tedious trials and errors, *one knows nothing of what is really
psychoanalysis – something which is talked about a great deal,
but is understood only after a long apprenticeship.* (Sullivan,
1962, pp. 315, emphasis added)

Of course, when I feel the need to be more in tune
with my clinical work, I can also resort to some of
Sullivan's shorter formulations, such as the following
two from the book Earl Witenberg recommended to me,
A Harry Stack Sullivan case seminar: "I wish you would
follow patients with extraordinary alertness of what it
means to them and how it can be used" (Kvarnes and
Parloff, 1976, p. 165). And: "The handling of all patients,
that is, the useful handling of all patients, depends on
one's establishing some kind of genuinely communicative
situation" (Kvarnes and Parloff, 1976, p. 201).

Twenty-five years later, Dr. Ryckoff alluded to the
multiplicity of levels Sullivan was able to include in his
working style in the following way:

In many of the . . . passages, he really follows two or three
different tracks simultaneously. One is that very often he
seems to be talking about the necessity of getting facts, of
getting history. But the next thing I feel is that he is not doing
that, that he is using that only as a way of establishing the
important thing, which is a sense of communication and
understanding with the patient. (Kvarnes and Parloff, 1976,
p. 235)

By the way, I think that one of the implicit merits
of the book edited by Roger Kvarnes and Gloria Parloff
is the way in which it introduces the reader to the great
value of group supervision as a training instrument. As
you all know, group supervision is not part of the most
widely used model of psychoanalytic training, namely the
Berlin or Eitingon model, consisting of training analysis,
individual supervision, and seminars. At the Milan
institute, where I trained, group supervision, introduced
by Gaetano Benedetti and Johannes Cremerius, was a very
important and fruitful aspect of training. We already have
so-called "Balint groups," groups of physicians who talk
about their patients with the help of a supervisor, which

were introduced by the English-Hungarian psychoanalyst Michael Balint (1896–1970). Why then not name the instrument of analytic group supervision the "Sullivan group"? I believe he was one of the first psychoanalysts to give so much room to, and to experiment with, this still not sufficiently recognized training tool. The significance of such an instrument in the hands of Gaetano Benedetti for the evolution of our Milan group, the ASP, is what I stressed in my Preface to the publication of a series of audiotaped group supervisions conducted by Benedetti in Milan between 1975 and 1995 and edited in 2010 by Claudia Bartocci. I myself promoted the use of group supervision as the main psychiatric training device when I was assistant professor of psychiatry at the Brescia Medical School, between 1991 and 1997.

In fact, one of the four participants in Ryckoff's seminar, Dr. Jacobson, comes to formulate the hypothesis that Sullivan's notion of group supervision and his way of conducting it may be at the origin of still another tool for ongoing training very much used nowadays, that is, what you call here the "peer supervision group." In German we call it *Intervisionsgruppe*, and in Italian colleagues still refer to it through the periphrasis "discussion group of clinical cases among colleagues." In other words, this is yet another instrument of professional exchange that does not yet have a name—that does not bear the name of its inventor. But here is Dr. Jacobson, back in March 1972:

> The other thing is that I think Sullivan came to feel that probably the greatest learning experience was peer exchange in psychiatry, that there was not enough of it, and that it was particularly worsened at the time by the psychoanalytic model. You go and talk to your therapist and presumably you learn about psychoanalysis from your own analysis, but you and your analyst maintain a certain secrecy about your analysis, so there was a tendency not to have a free exchange of what you and psychiatry are about. I think he was pointing at that. I think time has borne him out. (Kvames and Parloff, 1976, p. 178)

As you can see, what I was able to do in this last part of my paper, in order to bring Sullivan back to life, is different from yet complementary to the way in which I tried to bring him back to life throughout my book, to whose detailed articulation I devoted the second part of this paper. In order to better spell out the significance and the features of this second approach, let me quote Calvin Hall and Gardner Lindzey's and Irwin Yalom's portrayal of Sullivan's legacy. The former authors wrote in 1979:

> Sullivan was much more of an innovator. He was a highly original thinker who attracted a large group of devoted

> disciples and developed what is sometimes called a new
> school of psychiatry. (Hall, Lindzey, 1979, p. 116)

And here is Yalom:

> Sullivan's professional fate has been similar to that of many
> other innovators. The conservative community responded to
> his ideas at first by ignoring them, then by attacking them,
> and finally by so assimilating them that their innovative
> nature is forgotten. (Yalom, 1970, p. 19)

In the context of my effort to bring Sullivan back to life
in terms of the tone of these two definitions of his legacy,
I can say that I believe that today we can go beyond just
celebrating his historical role as a pioneer of contemporary
psychiatry, psychotherapy, and psychoanalysis. This was
not the purpose of my book, or rather, it was not its only
purpose. My goal was and is to allow him to become
eventually what Donnel Stern would call "a partner in
thought," that is, an important ingredient of our analytic
identity.

Fortunately, this has now also become possible for all
those colleagues who, like me, did not train at the White
Institute! I suppose that it was only after the death of
Anna Freud in 1982 that psychoanalysts (who did not
belong to the English Middle Group, which had come
to life around this very same issue some years before)
were able to go beyond the one-sided analytic training
they had received and gradually internalize and resort to
analytic voices and points of view that were not part of
the institute where they had trained. Here is how a good
friend, historian Paul Roazen (1936–2005), dealt with the
educational aspect of this problem in 1990:

> It is extremely difficult to become well educated in the history
> of psychoanalysis, and this is in large part because of all the
> sectarianism that has blinded people over the years . . . .
> Psychoanalytic literature has been accumulating for almost
> a century now, and there ought to be more of a consensus
> on which papers and books are classics. One does not have
> to be a Sullivanian to acknowledge how he pioneered in
> the treatment of psychosis, or to be a Kleinian to assign, for
> instance, her work on depression. (Roazen, 1990, pp. 52–53)

As I told you at the beginning of this presentation,
Italy was so underdeveloped psychoanalytically for
such a long time that we tried to assimilate all the
analytic literature we could translate! When Anna Freud
died, we were thus even more ready than other, more
appropriately trained colleagues, to participate in, and
even to contribute to, the gradual process of creation of
some kind of a "common psychoanalytic language." This
new language makes room for a whole series of authors
and points of view, and facilitates their discussion. This is

the climate in which Robert Wallerstein gave a paper by the title "One psychoanalysis or many?" at the 1987 IPA Congress in Montreal. It is in this pluralistic climate that we Italian psychoanalysts have developed our identity and this has become an important asset for the growing exchange that has been taking place in our international community during the past fifteen years. That is how Antonino Ferro became one of the most appreciated Bion experts worldwide, how Stefano Bolognini is running for president of the IPA, and how I have been able to attempt to perform the following double operation: to make Sullivan, his legacy, and his analytic voice available to my Italian colleagues and to the international community; and to try to help you, colleagues of the White Institute and Society, to look at Sullivan no longer just as your "private possession" but as a very precious asset and resource which the whole analytic community is happy to share with you.

REFERENCES

Arieti, S. (1976). *Creativity: The Magic Synthesis*. New York: Basic Books. (Italian edition: *Creatività. La sintesi magica*. Rome: Il Pensiero Scientifico, 1979).

Arieti, S. (Ed.) (1959). *The American Handbook of Psychiatry. Two Volumes*. New York: Basic Books. (Italian edition: *Manuale di psichiatria. Tre volumi*. Torino, Bollati Boringhieri).

Barton Evans III, F. (1996). *Harry Stack Sullivan. Interpersonal Theory and Psychotherapy*. London: Routledge.

Benedetti, G. (1961). Prefazione all'edizione italiana [Preface to the Italian edition]. In H.S. Sullivan, *La moderna concezione della psichiatria* (pp. vii–xxvii). Milan: Feltrinelli.

——— (1992). *Psychotherapie als existentielle Herausforderung* [Psychotherapy as existential challenge]. Göttingen: Vandenhöck & Ruprecht.

Bion, W.R. (2007). *The Italian Seminars* (P. Bion Talamo, Ed.). London: Karnac. (Original Italian edition, 1985).

Blitsten, D. (1953). *The Social Theories of Harry Stack Sullivan*. New York: William-Fredrick Press.

Bruch, H. (1974). *Learning Psychotherapy*. Cambridge, MA: Harvard University Press. (Italian edition: *Apprendere la psicoterapia*. Torino: Bollati Boringhieri, 1979).

Burnham, J.C. (1967). *Psychoanalysis and American Medicine, 1894–1918: Medicine, Science and Culture*. New York: International Universities Press.

——— (1983). *Jelliffe: American Psychoanalyst and Physician. And his Correspondence with S. Freud and C.G. Jung Edited by William McGuire*. Chicago: Chicago University Press.

Chapman, A.H. (1976). *Harry Stack Sullivan. His Life and his Work*. New York: Putnam's Sons.

Chatelaine, K.L. (1981). *Harry Stack Sullivan: The Formative Years*. Washington DC: University Press of America.

Chrzanowski, G. (1977). *Interpersonal Approach to Psychoanalysis. Contemporary View of Harry Stack Sullivan.* New York: Gardner Press.

Conci, M. (1990). Review of the book by S.A. Mitchell "Relational concepts in psychoanalysis. An integration", Harvard University Press 1988. *Psicoterapia e Scienze Umane* 24(1):124–130.

——— (1993a). Prefazione all'edizione italiana [Preface to the Italian edition]. In H.S. Sullivan, *Scritti sulla schizofrenia* (pp. v–ix). Milan: Feltrinelli.

——— (1993b). Presentazione [Introduction]. In S.A. Mitchell, *Gli orientamenti relazionali in psicoanalisi. Per un modello integrato* (pp. ix–xv). Turin: Bollati Boringhieri.

——— (1993c). H.S. Sullivan and the training of the psychiatrist. *Contemporary Psychoanalysis* 29:530–540.

——— (1993d). Review of the book by E.A. Levenson "The purloined self". *International Forum of Psychoanalysis* 2:193–196.

——— (1994a). Review of the book by S.A. Mitchell "Hope and dread in psychoanalysis". *Psicoterapia e Scienze Umane* 28(4):130–133.

——— (1994b). The Interpersonal Tradition in Italy and Europe. Unpublished paper given at the XIth Symposium on the Psychotherapy of Schizophrenia, June 1994, Washington DC.

——— (1995). Review of the book by L. Nissim Momigliano "Continuity and change in psychoanalysis. Letters from Milan". *Psychoanalytic Books* 6:199–204.

——— (1997). Postfazione [Afterword]. In G. Benedetti, *La psicoterapia come sfida esistenziale* (pp. 295–313). Milan: Cortina.

——— (1998). Freud's self-analysis – An interpersonally grounded process. *International Forum of Psychoanalysis* 7:77–84.

——— (2000a). *Sullivan rivisitato. La sua rilevanza per la psichiatria, la psicoterapia e la psicoanalisi* Bolsena, VT: Massari Editore. (German edition: *Sullivan neu entdecken.* Giessen: Psychosozial-Verlag. English edition: *Sullivan Revisited – Life and Work. Harry Stack Sullivan's Relevance for Contemporary Psychiatry, Psychotherapy and Psychoanalysis.* Trento: Tangram Edizioni Scientifiche, 2010).

——— (2005). Stephen Mitchell in Italy. Unpublished PowerPoint presentation held at the IARPP Conference, June 2005, Rome.

——— (2006). H.S. Sullivan and S.A. Mitchell, a comparison. Unpublished paper given at the IFPS Forum, May 2006, Rome.

——— (2009). Bion and Sullivan: An enlightening comparison. *International Forum of Psychoanalysis* 18:90–99.

——— (2010). Introduzione [Introduction]. In C. Bartocci (Ed.), *Gaetano Benedetti. Una vita accanto alla sofferenza mentale. Seminari clinico-teorici (1973–1996)* [Gaetano Benedetti. A life taking care of human suffering. Clinical-theoretical workshops (1973–1996)] (pp. 13–19). Milan: Angeli.

Conci, M., Dazzi, S., & Mantovani, M.L. (Eds.) (1997a). *La tradizione interpersonale in psichiatria, psicoterapia e psicoanalisi* [The interpersonal tradition in psychiatry, psychotherapy and psychoanalysis]. Rome: Erre Emme.

D'Amore, A.R.T. (1976). William Alanson White, pioneer psychoanalyst. In A.R.T. D'Amore (Ed.), *William Alanson White, the Washington Years 1903–1937* (pp. 69–91). Washington DC: US Department of Health, Education and Welfare.

Eagle, M. (1991). The nature of theoretical change in psychoanalysis.

Paper published in Italian: *La natura del cambiamento teorico in psicoanalisi. Psicoterapia e Scienze Umane* 26(3):5–33. (Translated by M. Conci).

Ellenberger, H.F. (1970). *The Discovery of the Unconscious. The History and Evolution of Dynamic Psychiatry*. New York: Basic Books. (Italian edition: *La scoperta dell'inconscio. Storia ed evoluzione della psichiatria dinamica*. Turin: Bollati Boringhieri, 1972).

Freud, S. (1913). On the beginning of treatment. *Standard Edition* 12, pp. 121–144.

———— (1930). Introduction to the Special Psychopathology Number of "The Medical Review of Reviews". *Standard Edition* 21, pp. 254–255.

Gartner, R.B. (1995). The relationship between interpersonal psychoanalysis and family therapy. In M. Lyonells, J. Fiscalini, C.J. Mann, D.B. Stern (Eds.), *Handbook of Interpersonal Psychoanalysis* (pp. 793–822). Hillsdale, NJ: Analytic Press.

Gill, M.M. (1983). The interpersonal paradigm and the degree of the therapist's involvement. *Contemporary Psychoanalysis* 19:200–237. (Italian translation: *Il paradigma interpersonale e la misura del coinvolgimento del terapeuta. Psicoterapia e Scienze Umane* 29(3): 5–44, 1995. Translated by M. Conci and M.L. Mantovani).

Greenberg, J.R. (2001). Stephen A. Mitchell: 1946–2000. *Contemporary Psychoanalysis* 37:189–191

Greenberg, J.R., & Mitchell, S.A. (1983). *Object Relations in Psychoanalytic Theory*. Cambridge: MA: Harvard University Press. (Italian edition: *Le relazioni oggettuali nella teoria psicoanalitica*. Bologna: il Mulino, 1986. Translated by C. Mattioli).

Hale, N.G., Jr. (1971). *James Jackson Putnam and Psychoanalysis. Letters Between Putnam and Sigmund Freud, Ernest Jones, William James, Sandor Ferenczi and Morton Prince, 1877–1917*. Cambridge, MA: Harvard University Press.

James, W. (1890). *Principles of Psychology*. New York: Holt.

Jelliffe, S.E. (1939). Sigmund Freud and psychiatry. *American Journal of Sociology* 45:326–340.

Jones, E. (1959). *Free Associations. Memories of a Psychoanalyst*. New York: Basic Books. (Italian edition: *Memorie di un psicoanalista*. Roma, Astrolabio, 1974).

Klerman, G.L., Weissmann, M.M., Rounsaville, B.J., & Chevron, E.S. (1984). *Interpersonal Psychotherapy of Depression*. (Italian edition: *Psicoterapia interpersonale della depressione*. Turin: Bollati Boringhieri, 1989).

Kvarnes, R.G., & Parloff, G.H. (Eds.) (1976). *A Harry Stack Sullivan Case Seminar. Treatment of a Young Man Schizophrenic*. New York: Norton.

Laing, R.D. (1963). Review of the book by H.S. Sullivan "Schizophrenia as a human process". *International Journal of Psychoanalysis* 44:376–378.

Lidz, T. (1966). Adolf Mayer and the development of American psychiatry. *American Journal of Psychiatry* 123:320–332.

Limentani, A. (1989). Psychoanalysis in Italy: A personal appraisal. In G.E. Viola and F. Rovigatti (eds.), *L'Italia nella psicoanalisi–Italy in psychoanalysis* (pp. 25–28). Rome: Istituto dell'Enciclopedia Italiana.

Lionells, M., Fiscalini, J., Mann, C.H., & Stern, D.B. (Eds.) (1995). *Handbook of Interpersonal Psychoanalysis*. Hillsdale, NJ: Analytic

Press.

Lothane, H.Z. (1992). *In Defense of Schreber. Soul Murder and Psychiatry*. Hillsdale, NJ: Analytic Press.

———— (1997). Freud and the interpersonal. *International Forum of Psychoanalysis* 6:175–184.

Luborsky, L. (1984). *Principles of Psychoanalytic Psychotherapy. A Manual for Supportive-expressive Treatment*. New York: Basic Books.

Mitchell, S.A. (1988a). *Relational Concepts in Psychoanalysis. An Integration*. Cambridge, MA: Harvard University Press. (Italian edition: *Gli orientamenti relazionali in psicoanalisi. Per un modello integrato*. Turin: Bollati Boringhieri, 1993. Translated by S. Rivolta).

———— (1988b). The intrapsychic and the interpersonal. Different theories, different domains or historical artifacts? *Psychoanalytic Inquiry* 8:472-496 (Italian translation: L'intrapsichico e l'interpersonale. Differenti teorie, ambiti differenti o artefatti storici? *Quaderni dell'ASP*, No. 5:7–26, 1992. Translated by M. Conci).

————(1991). Contemporary perspectives on self: Toward an integration. *Psychoanalytic Dialogues* 1:121–147. (Italian translation: Prospettive contemporanee sul Sé: verso un'integrazione. *Psicoterapia e Scienze Umane* 25(3):3–30, 1991. Translation by M. Conci).

———— (1993). *Hope and Dread in Psychoanalysis*. New York: Basic Books. (Italian edition: *Speranza e timore in psicoanalisi*. Turin: Bollati Boringhieri, 1995. Translated by E. Izard).

———— (1997). *Influence and Autonomy in Psychoanalysis*. Hillsdale, NJ: Analytic Press. (Italian edition: *Influenza e autonomia in psicoanalisi*. Turin: Bollati Boringhieri, 1999. Translated by M. Schepisi).

———— (2000). *Relationality. From Attachment to Intersubjectivity*. Hillsdale, NJ: Analytic Press. (Italian edition: *Il modello relazionale. Dall'attaccamento all'intersoggettività*. Milan: Cortina, 2002. Translated by F. Gazzillo).

———— (2002). *Can Love Last? The Fate of Romance Over Time*. New York: Norton. (Italian edition: *L'amore può durare? Il destino dell'amore romantico*. Milan: Cortina, 2004. Translated by G. Gazzillo).

Mitchell, S.A., & Black, J. M. (1995). *Freud and Beyond. A history of Modern Psychoanalytic Thought*. New York: Basic Books. (Italian edition: *L'esperienza della psicoanalisi*. Turin: Bollati Boringhieri, 1996. Translated by S. Rivolta).

Mora, G. (1992). The history of psychiatry in the United States: Historiographic and theoretical considerations. *History of Psychiatry* 3:187–202.

Mullahy, P. (1945). A theory of interpersonal relations and the evolution of personality. In H.S. Sullivan, *Conceptions of Modern Psychiatry* (pp. 239–294). New York: Norton.

Nissim Momigliano, L., & Robutti, A. (Eds.) (1992). *Shared Experience. The Psychoanalytic Dialogue*. London: Karnac. (Original Italian edition, 1992).

Rioch, J. (1969). Letter to the editor. *W.A. White Newsletter*, Spring 1969.

Roazen, P. (1990). *Encountering Freud. The Politics and the Histories of Psychoanalysis*. New Brunswick: Transactions.

Rosenzweig, S. (1992). *Freud, Jung and Hall the King-maker. The Expedition to America (1909)*. Seattle: Hogrefe & Huber.

Safran, J.D., & Segal, Z.V. (1990). *Interpersonal Process in Cognitive Therapy*. New York: Basic Books. (Italian edition: *Il processo interpersonale nella terapia cognitiva*. Milan: Feltrinelli, 1993).

Silver, A.-L. (Ed.) (1989). *Psychoanalysis and Psychosis*. Madison, CT: International Universities Press.

Smith, H.F. (2010). Editor's note. *Psychoanalytic Quarterly* 79:877–878.

Smith Benjamin, L. (1993). *Interpersonal Diagnosis and Treatment of Personality Disorders*. New York: Guilford.

Stern, D.B. (2009). *Partners in Thought: Working with Unformulated Experience, Dissociation, and Enactment*. New York: Routledge.

Stern, D.N. (1985). *The Interpersonal World of the Infant*. New York: Basic Books. (Italian edition: *Il mondo interpersonale del bambino*. Turin: Bollati Boringhieri, 1987).

Strupp, H.G., & Binder, J.L. (1984). *Psychotherapy in a New Key*. New York: Basic Books.

Sullivan, H.S. (1939). The support of psychiatric research and teaching. *Psychiatry* 2:273–279.

——— (1940). *Conceptions of Modern Psychiatry*. Washington DC: W.A. White Psychiatric Foundation. Reprint: New York, Norton, 1953. (Italian edition: *La moderna concezione della psichiatria*. Milano: Feltrinelli, 1961. Translated by E.D. Mezzacapa).

——— (1947). The study of psychiatry: Three orienting lectures. *Psychiatry* 10:355–371.

——— (1953). *The Interpersonal Theory of Psychiatry* (H. Swick Perry and M. Ladd Gawel Eds.). New York: Norton. (Italian edition: *La teoria interpersonale della psichiatria*. Milan: Feltrinelli, 1962. Translated by E.D. Mezzacapa).

——— (1954). *The Psychiatric Interview* (H. Swick Perry and M. Ladd Gawel Eds.). New York: Norton. (Italian edition: *Il colloquio psichiatrico*. Milan: Feltrinelli, 1967. Translated by I. Fontana).

——— (1956). *Clinical Studies in Psychiatry* (H. Swick Perry Ed.). New York: Norton. (Italian edition: *Studi clinici*. Milan: Feltrinelli, 1965. Translated by E.D. Mezzacapa).

——— (1962). *Schizophrenia as a Human Process* (H. Swick Perry, Ed.). New York: Norton. (Italian edition: *Scritti sulla schizophrenia*. Milan: Feltrinelli, 1993, Translated by E.D. Mezzacapa).

——— (1964). *The Fusion of Psychiatry and Social Science* (H.S. Perry, Ed.). New York: Norton.

——— (1972). *Personal Psychopathology* (H. Swick Perry, Ed.). New York: Norton.

Swick Perry, H. (1982). *Psychiatrist of America. The Life of Harry Stack Sullivan*. Cambridge, MA: Belknap Press of Harvard University Press.

Wachtel, P. (1979). *Psychoanalysis and Behavior Therapy. Toward an Integration*. New York: Basic Books.

Wallerstein, R.S. (1988). One psychoanalysis or many? *International Journal of Psychoanalysis* 69:5–21.

Yalom, I.D. (1970). *The Theory and Practice of Group Psychotherapy*. New York: Basic Books. (Italian edition: *Teoria e pratica della psicoterapia di gruppo*. Turin: Bollati Boringhieri, 1974).

CHAPTER 5

SULLIVAN AND THE INTERSUBJECTIVE PERSPECTIVE[1]

In his 1995 paper "Intersubjectivity in psychoanalysis: A critical review," Jonathan Dunn described the intersubjective tradition as centered around the definition of mind as "striving for connection and communication, rather than discharge and gratification of endogamous instinctual pressures" (Dunn, 1995, p. 724). Following such a metapsychological point of view, intersubjective analysts "see the clinician and the patient co-constructing the clinical data from the interaction of both members' particular psychic qualities and subjective realities" (Dunn, 1995, pp. 723–724). The author furthermore retraces the emergence of the intersubjective paradigm in psychoanalysis to the critique undergone by Freud's concepts of countertransference and of ego function. Although Dunn cites a large number of authors, mostly belonging to the self-psychological and to the interpersonal and relational groups, he does not mention the name and the work of what I consider to be the pioneer of the intersubjective turn in psychoanalysis, that is Harry Stack Sullivan (1892–1949). Since Sullivan's work and legacy are not well enough known, I will take them up again in this paper, in order to show how his point of view can still represent the best theoretical framework for the intersubjective perspective.

Sullivan is one of my favorite psychoanalytic authors. After teaching a course on his life and work at the University of Venice in the spring of 1988, I met the late Stephen Mitchell in Florence on his first trip to Italy with Jay Greenberg, to give lectures and seminars around their book *Object relations in psychoanalytic theory* (Greenberg and Mitchell, 1983) at what later became the Istituto Sullivan, and discovered that Mitchell was also very fond of Sullivan's work. With his encouragement, and thanks to the contribution made by my supervisor Gaetano Benedetti to the introduction of his work into Italy (Benedetti, 1961), I started working on a book on Sullivan's life and work, which was published in Italy in 2000 and in Germany in 2005. Its American edition, *Sullivan revisited – Life and work. Harry Stack Sullivan's*

---

[1] The original version of this article was published in Volume 22 (2013) of the *International Forum of Psychoanalysis*, pp. 10–16. It represents the revised version of a paper given at the XVth Forum of the IFPS held in Athens in October 2010.

relevance for contemporary psychiatry, psychotherapy and psychoanalysis, is, at the time of writing this article, now in print, and will soon be able to be ordered by simply Googling Sullivan's name. Sullivan went beyond Freud not only by extending the latter's new therapeutic approach to psychotic patients, but also by formulating a new clinical point of view, based upon the interaction of analyst and patient.

The aim of this paper is to let you hear Sullivan's voice, to introduce you to his fascinating system of thought, and to show its pluridimensional character. By pluridimensional character, I mean the fact that Sullivan's work includes not only the clinical and the developmental, but also the empirical and the applied or interdisciplinary dimension of psychoanalysis. From this point of view, the pluridimensional character of Freud's own work was certainly an important influence on Sullivan. An essential aspect of such an orientation is also his emphasis on the cultural and social coordinates of our personal identity. This is how Sullivan's interpersonal point of view can still represent the best theoretical framework of the intersubjective perspective—as I defined it above, following Jonathan Dunn.

SULLIVAN'S VOICE

Sullivan's first ground-breaking contribution, which started in the 1920s and is documented in detail in the anthology *Schizophrenia as a human process* edited by Helen Swick Perry in 1962, was to show how wrong Freud was in distinguishing patients into those capable and those incapable of transference. Parallel to such an important paradigmatic change is his critique of Emil Kraepelin's (1856–1926) concept of schizophrenia as being a physical and not a psychological illness—as Jay Greenberg and Stephen Mitchell remind the reader in their above-mentioned book (Greenberg and Mitchell, 1983). Although he seldom mentioned the word "countertransference," Sullivan based his therapeutic work with the sickest patients on his "participation" in their condition, that is, on the subjective resonances evoked by them in him. This was the basis of his therapeutic attitude. He thus went beyond Freud's original and narrow use of the concept, exclusively related to the neurotic component of our reaction to patients, and pioneered the definition of "countertransference" later introduced by Paula Heimann in the 1950s. Here is what Paula Heimann wrote in 1950: "the Analyst's emotional response to his patient within the analytic situation represents one of the most important tools of his work. The analyst's countertransference is an instrument of research into the patient's unconscious" (Heimann, 1950, p. 81).

Indeed, the experience and resolution of the dissociative episode that his biographer Helen Swick Perry documented as having taken place in his life between the spring of 1909 and the fall of 1911 must have allowed Sullivan to much more easily attune himself to the inner world of psychotic patients than the average psychiatrist and psychoanalyst (Swick Perry, 1982). From such a line of work also emerged the interpersonal point of view, whose systematic formulation he developed in the 1940s and which can be found in his book *Interpersonal theory of psychiatry* (1953). In other words, as Freud has used his own psychopathology—which he got in touch with and analyzed in his letters to Wilhelm Fliess—as a key to the therapy that he developed with neurotic patients, so also did Sullivan do this with his psychotic patients. A further similarity between Sullivan and Freud has of course to do with the autodidactic character of the development of their theories, an aspect that I have repeatedly emphasized in my above-mentioned book on Sullivan (Conci, 2010).

But let us now turn to Sullivan, and to his peculiar voice, that is, to how he talked about psychotic patients on the basis of his own personal and professional experience, as he did for example when he presented his clinical work to the social scientists participating in the first of the two "Colloquia on Personality Investigation", which he organized with W.A. White (1870–1937) in 1928 and 1929:

> Aside from perhaps the most significant of my activities – the attending of conferences with social scientists – my attempts at collecting data on personality take the form of living with schizophrenic individuals. In the address from the chair, it was stated that general familiarity with the work of each other would be assumed. As, however, there seems to be no particular consensus even among my psychiatric colleagues as to the connotation of the term schizophrenia, it is perhaps rather of interest for this conference that I say something by way of explanation.
> . . . Some schizophrenics impressed me, years ago, as singularly interesting [says Sullivan after having first presented their clinical picture] in part, because of their striking manifestations of some of my own highly esteemed traits. I refer, of course, to my personal appraisal of my traits. I therefore cultivated them and this gave such complimentary returns to my self-respect and feeling of well-being that I have continued it since, alternating chiefly with attendance upon scientific deliberations and the like.
> I find many such individuals very human indeed, particularly when they have not been exposed for a long

period to a 'good' psychiatric care. It has seemed to me
that in these schizophrenics one finds in almost laboratory
simplicity the manifestations of complex processes which are
combined in the more fortunate of us in such great complexity
that they can scarcely be grasped and subjected to anything
approximating scientific critique . . . . One discovers on
acquaintance with these individuals something different
indeed from the traditional psychiatric picture. (Sullivan,
1928/1962, pp. 218, 220)

As Jung, working with schizophrenic patients, had
ended up renouncing to Freud's libido concept, so Sullivan
ended up considering schizophrenia what we can call a
"personal sickness," that is, the sickness developed by an
individual who does not succeed in becoming a person. I
am of course making reference to those individuals who
cannot easily distinguish between internal and external
reality, and who either retreat silently into themselves or
develop a so-called "productive" symptomatology, with
hallucinations and delusions. It was in this context of
discovery that Sullivan had for the first time utilized the
word "interpersonal" in 1927, at the end of the first section
of the paper "The onset of schizophrenia":

Study of the onset of the disorder in male patients of this hospital
seems to establish two factors preliminary to schizophrenic
psychoses. Firstly, the appearance of the disorder is late in a
long series of subjectively difficult adjustive efforts. Secondly,
it seems never to occur in those who have achieved if only for
a short time a definitely satisfying adjustment to a sex object.
We have not been successful in our effort to identify exactly
the factors which cause milder maladjustive efforts to pass
over into schizophrenia. Neither do we believe we are justified
by accumulated facts, to stress the sex factor as of exclusive
importance. Much more data is needed in regard to the onset
of the malady; at this stage, however, there seems little reason
to doubt that cultural distorsions provided by the home
are of prime importance. We have not seen maladjustment
which was without a foundation of erroneous attitudes
which parents or their equivalent had thrust upon the child.
We have found all sorts of maladjustment in the history of
patients who suffered the grave psychosis, but regardless of
vicious influences subsequently encountered, the sufferer had
acquired the tendency to such an illness while in the home
situation. *Interpersonal factors seem the effective elements
in the psychiatry of schizophrenia.* (Sullivan, 1962, p. 104,
emphasis added)

Published in 1962 in the anthology *Schizophrenia
as a human process*, this paper represents one of the
turning points of Sullivan's overall work. As I wrote in
the Preface to the Italian edition of this anthology (which
came out in 1993 with the title *Scritti sulla schizophrenia*
[Papers on schizophrenia]), we can at best understand
Sullivan's interpersonal theory of psychiatry of the 1940s
as his attempt to give an answer to the questions arisen in

his work on schizophrenia of the 1920s and 1930s, with particular regard to the subtle and complex interpersonal processes which enable a newborn infant to become a healthy human being.

Before taking up some of the key concepts of Sullivan's interpersonal theory, let me propose to you some of the basic conclusions to which he came around 1930, at the end of his first research journey into the nature and treatment of schizophrenia, which he concluded between the fall of 1922 and the summer of 1930 at the Sheppard Pratt Hospital in Maryland.

First:

> The only tools that have shown results that justify any enthusiasm in regard of the treatment of schizophrenia are the *psychoanalytic* procedures and the *socio-psychiatric* program which the writer evolved from them. (Sullivan, 1962, p. 283, original emphasis)

Second:

> In conclusion, it may be restated that, at least in the case of the male, fairly young schizophrenic patients whose divorcement from fairly conventional behavior and thought has been rather abrupt, when received under care before they have progressed either into hebephrenic dilapidation or durable paranoid maladjustments, are to be regarded as of good outlook for recovery and improvement of personality, if they can be treated firstly to the end of socialization, and thereafter by more fundamental reorganization of personality. (Sullivan, 1962, p. 290)

SULLIVAN'S FIELD CONCEPT AND HIS INTERPERSONAL THEORY

No wonder that the most well-known of Sullivan's posthumous works, *Interpersonal theory of psychiatry*, is based on another new important concept pioneered by him, the concept of "interpersonal field," around which his own definition of the field of psychiatry is centered. Psychiatry "arises not from a special kind of data, but from the characteristic actions or operations in which the psychiatrist participates. The actions or operations from which psychiatric information is derived are events in interpersonal fields which include the psychiatrist" (Sullivan, 1953, pp. 13–14).

Having come to the conclusion that schizophrenia has its origin in a disturbed interpersonal field, which the patient reproduces in his relationship with the psychiatrist in his role of "participant observer," Sullivan centered his interpersonal theory around the way in which the interpersonal field influences and shapes the development of the individual.

On the theoretical level, Sullivan derived his field concept from Kurt Lewin's (1890–1947) book *A dynamic theory of personality*, which he explicitly makes reference to in his *Interpersonal theory of psychiatry* (1953). Indeed, this was also one of the theoretical sources of the work of Willy and Madeleine Baranger, who introduced the concept of field in the South American post-Kleinian tradition at the beginning of the 1960s. Here is their own definition of the field concept:

> The analytic situation should be formulated not only as a situation of one person who is confronted by an indefinite and neutral personage . . . but as a situation between two persons . . . involved in a single dynamic process . . . neither member of the couple can be understood without the other. (Baranger and Baranger, 1961/2008, p. 796)[2]

The fact that interpersonal theory centers around not only the horizontal axis of the field concept, but also the vertical axis of development can be at best explained by making reference to how Sullivan himself talks about it in his *Interpersonal theory of psychiatry*. After having emphasized the necessity—originally formulated by W.A. White—of conceiving a psychiatry which not only "attempts to e*xplain* serious mental disorders," but can also be "of some use in living in general" (Sullivan, 1953, p. 4), here is how Sullivan introduced such a new developmental theory in the above-mentioned book:

> How to communicate this particular theory of psychiatry has puzzled me and harassed me for a great many years, and I have finally come to the decision that the only approach is by the developmental route. In other words, if we go with almost microscopic care over how everybody comes to be what he is at chronologic adulthood, then perhaps we can learn a good deal of what is highly probable about living and difficulties in living. (Sullivan, 1953, p. 4)

A central position in such a new theory is of course given by Sullivan (in a way similar to Melanie Klein) to the concept of anxiety, with particular regard to how it arises in the context of the interpersonal field. Here is how Sullivan goes about this:

> Because a great many phenomena in the whole biological field are easier to understand if you trace them from their

---

[2] This connection with the work of Kurt Lewin did not escape Robert Hinshelwood in the paper he gave in Athens (Hinshelwood, 2010), in which he also emphasized Sullivan's important role as pioneer of the intersubjective perspective. In this context, I can also add how exciting it was to hear in Athens also Madeleine Baranger herself, now 90 years old, give a paper on the pioneering work done with her husband Willy in South America.

> beginnings to their most complex manifestations, I would like
> to describe how I think anxiety begins in the infant. I do not
> know how early in life anxiety manifests itself. It is not exactly
> a field that you can get mothers and infants to cooperate in
> exploring . . . . It is demonstrable that the human young in
> the first months of life . . . exhibits disturbed performance
> when the 'mothering one' has an emotional disturbance . . . .
> Whatever the infant was doing at the time will be interrupted
> or handicapped – that is, it will either stop, or will not progress
> as efficiently as before anxiety appeared. Thus anxiety is
> called out by emotional disturbances of certain types in the
> significant person – that is, the person with whom the person
> is doing something. (Sullivan, 1953, pp. 8–9)

In other words, this is how Sullivan came to define
the relational nature of human and mental development,
that is, how he originally formulated what later became
the basis of the intersubjective perspective. From another
point of view, we can also emphasize the fact of how
Sullivan's new point of view, based on both observation
and theoretical speculation, represented the dimension
out of which Daniel Stern much later described what he
called *The interpersonal world of the infant* (1985).[3]

Indeed, Sullivan's theory of the interpersonal genesis
of mind, development, and psychopathology was so
powerful as to allow him to theoretically formulate a series
of consequences or principles which were only later taken
up by authors such as Winnicott, Bion, and Kohut and
eventually confirmed by empirical research. I am making
reference to Winnicott's concept that there is no baby
without a mother, to Bion's concept of maternal reverie,
to Kohut's concept of empathy, and to the empirical
confirmation of Sullivan's so-called "theorem of anxiety,"
that is: *"The tension of anxiety, when present in the
mothering one, induces anxiety in the infant"* (Sullivan,
1953, p. 41, original emphasis).[4]

At this point, before dealing with how Sullivan
specifically articulates the therapeutic dimension of his

[3] The important role played by Sullivan's interpersonal theory in the
development of his own research work was confirmed to me personally
by Daniel Stern during the Athens Forum, at which he himself gave
one of the key note papers.

[4] I dealt with the many similarities between Sullivan's and Bion's life,
personality, and work in my paper "Bion and Sullivan: An enlightening
comparison" (Conci, 2009). In a very good paper with the title "Klein,
Bion, and intersubjectivity: Becoming, transforming, and dreaming"—
which appeared in *Psychoanalytic Dialogues* during the preparation
of this paper for publication—Lawrence Brown also emphasizes the
interpersonal foundation of Bion's concept of alpha function. He
does this with the following words: "*It is important to note that alpha
function is the internalization of a complex intersubjective relationship
between the mother and the infant and not just the internalization of a
maternal function*" (2010, p. 677, original emphasis).

theory in his posthumous book *The psychiatric interview* (1954), here is how he introduced it in the first chapter of his *Interpersonal theory of psychiatry*:

> In attempting to outline this whole system of psychiatry, I want to stress from the very beginning the paralyzing power of anxiety. I believe that it is fairly safe to say that anybody and everybody devotes much of his lifetime, a great deal of his energy – talking loosely – and a good part of his effort in dealing with others, to avoiding more anxiety than he already has and, if possible, to getting rid of his anxiety . . . . For years and years psychiatrists have been struggling to cure this-and-that distortion of living as it came up in patients . . . . But a much more practical psychotherapy seems to be possible when one seeks to find the basic vulnerabilities to anxiety in interpersonal relations, rather than to deal with symptoms called out by anxiety or to avoid anxiety. (Sullivan, 1953, p. 11)

Such a therapeutic approach centers around Sullivan's concept of participant observation, to which we now turn.

SULLIVAN AND PARTICIPANT OBSERVATION

"In the psychiatric interview a great part of the experience which one slowly gains," explains Sullivan in the first chapter of *The psychiatric interview*, "manifests itself in a show of mild interest in the point at which there is a tonal difference" (Sullivan, 1954, p. 7). Thus we may conceive of the voice—rather than the words—as the "mirror of the patient's soul." This kind of listening and participation requires us to also ask very simple questions in order to clarify the meaning of the patient's words, for their meaning may deviate from the meaning we give them. "Thus part of the skill in interviewing," states Sullivan, "comes from a sort of quiet observation all along: 'Does this sentence, this statement, have an unquestionable meaning? Is there any certainty as to what this person means?'" (Sullivan, 1954, p. 8). According to the concept of "consensual validation," efficient communication occurs only if we are able to agree on a common meaning after we have examined what meaning each of us gives to the words. Consensual validation, and its promotion through participant observation, forms the basis of Sullivan's concept of the interview—and of therapy.[5]

Of course, this is also the basis of Sullivan's approach to his patients' anxiety: anxiety is revealed through a

---

[5] It was also in connection with this attitude of Sullivan that Janet Rioch defined the interpersonal tradition he was the founder of as that tradition which "doesn't have answers, but only questions" (1969, p. 156). Not only Bion, but also André Green has often underlined the importance of such a point of view.

change of the patient's voice; our sensitivity to it allows us to point this out to the patient; equally important is our skill in helping the patient become aware of what makes him anxious. Participant observation allows us to be there and experience what the patient feels and, at the same time, to be detached enough from him to help him become aware of his feelings. In Sullivan's words:

> Thus whenever the psychiatrist's attempt to discover what the patient is talking about leads the patient to be somewhat more clear on what the is thinking about or attempting to communicate or conceal, his grasp on life is to some extent enhanced. And no one has grave difficulties in living if he has a very good grasp on what is happening to him. (Sullivan, 1954, pp. 23–24)

Without going into the very articulated way in which Sullivan talks about his clinical work in this book, let us now limit ourselves to seeing how he specifically defines the concept of "participant observation," that is, his own conceptualization of what would later be called countertransference. The psychiatrist as participant observer has "an inescapable, inextricable involvement in all that goes on in the interview; and to the extent to which he is unconscious or unwitting of his participation in the interview, to that extent he does not know what is happening" (Sullivan, 1954, p. 19). In other words, according to Sullivan, the therapist is, on the one hand, necessarily personally involved in what goes on in the session and, on the other hand, must become aware of it, for therapy to really take place.

As readers know, contemporary psychoanalysis has greatly expanded the space of the analyst's struggle with the process of becoming aware of what he is experiencing in the therapeutic relationship—as opposed to just making hypotheses on what is going on in the patient. From this point of view, Sullivan was both radical and conservative: without participation on the part of the analyst, no therapy takes place; and also, in order for therapy to take place, the analyst must be aware of all that happens in the relationship (and not just in the patient)—a view at variance with that of those contemporary analysts who see therapeutic change also occurring outside of the awareness of it.[6] Indeed, Sullivan was also conservative, that is, close

---

[6] A systematic comparison between Freud and Sullivan was articulated by Merton Gill in his famous paper "The interpersonal paradigm and the degree of the therapist's involvement" (1983). Although he had introduced the concept of the interpersonal field, Sullivan thought—as Freud also did—in terms of the asymmetrical nature of the therapeutic relationship. From this point of view, the principle of co-construction of contemporary intersubjective analysts was merely hinted at, but not fully developed in his work.

to Freud, in his application of the concept of participant observation to our relationship to the cultural and social factors that shape our personal identity. Following Freud, Sullivan had the kind of interdisciplinary orientation that contemporary psychoanalysis has lost. It is to this aspect of his work that we now turn.

SULLIVAN'S INTERDISCIPLINARY ORIENTATION

Chapter 6 of my book on Sullivan deals with "Sullivan as a social scientist." In it, I not only show how his interpersonal point of view is rooted in the works of William James and George Herbert Mead and in the research projects of Chicago sociologists like William Thomas and Robert Park, but also show how Sullivan himself "got his pants dirty doing field work" (to use an expression of Robert Park). Such work is documented in the anthology *The fusion of psychiatry and social science* that Helen Swick Perry edited in 1964 (Sullivan, 1964).

Here is for example what we can read in his "Discussion of the case of Warren Wall. A psychiatric gloss on a sociological study" (Sullivan, 1940/1964), that is, the report he wrote about a series of interviews he conducted with a black young man using his method of participant observation, in the context of a major research project on the condition of black people coordinated by the sociologist Franklin Frazier:

> The tragedy of the Negro in America seems to be chiefly a matter of culturally determined attitudes in the whites, by the manifestations of which the Negro is generally distorted into a pattern of interracial behavior which permits the continuance of the attitudes without much change. This is a vicious circle, the interruption of which is an undertaking of great difficulty. (Sullivan, 1964, p. 106)

And here is Sullivan's "prescription":

> It is evident that, if we are to develop a real approximation to national solidarity, we must find and cultivate a humanistic rather than a paternalistic, and exploiting, or an indifferent attitude to these numerous citizens of our commonwealth. As a psychiatrist, I have to speak particularly against using them as scapegoats for our unacceptable impulses; the fact that they are dark-skinned and poorly adapted to our historic puritanism is really too naïve a basis for projecting most of our privately condemned faults upon them. They deserve to be observed as they are, and the blot of an American interracial problem may then gradually be dissipated. (Sullivan, 1964, p. 107)

Of course, these words also show us how Sullivan had gone beyond Freud's concept of the ego and had envisioned and conceptualized a self whose development depends not only on interpersonal, but also on social and cultural factors. Such a point of view has proved to be particularly useful in the globalized world in which we live, in which so many factors end up shaping our personal identity. On the other hand, even more than Freud, Sullivan connected his interdisciplinary orientation with a visible social commitment—in line with the critical attitude of Freud toward social issues, for example the repression of sexuality in the society of his time.

CONCLUDING REMARKS

As I have tried to show in this chapter, not only did Sullivan create the clinical, developmental, technical, and interdisciplinary premises that lie behind the present intersubjective perspective in psychoanalysis, but also the overall articulation of his work can still represent the best theoretical framework for it. If we go back to Jonathan Dunn's definition of the intersubjective perspective, we can see how Sullivan himself pioneered a new concept of countertransference (thorough his concepts of participation and participant observation) and of ego function (through his concept of interpersonal self). Last but not least, his point of view contributed—almost 50 years ago, in Amsterdam, 1962—to the foundation of the International Federation of Psychoanalytic Societies, (IFPS), and keeping Sullivan's point of view alive also helps us to keep the IFPS alive and well.

Let us go back to Sullivan and see what we can still learn from him. I have been dealing with his life and work for more than twenty years, and I still have the feeling that I keep profiting from his creative experience and insights. I hope that some of you can do the same.

REFERENCES

Baranger, M., & Baranger, W. (1961/2008). The analytic situation as a dynamic field. *International Journal of Psychoanalysis* 89:795–826.

Benedetti, G. (1961). Prefazione all'edizione italiana [Preface to the Italian edition]. In H.S. Sullivan, *La moderna concezione della psichiatria* [Conceptions of modern psychiatry] (pp. vii–xxvii). Milan: Feltrinelli, 1961.

Brown, J.L. (2010). Klein, Bion and intersubjectivity: Becoming, transforming, and dreaming. *Psychoanalytic Dialogues* 20:669–682.

Conci, M. (1993). Prefazione all'edizione italiana [Preface to the Italian edition]. In H.S. Sullivan, *Scritti sulla schizofrenia* [Papers on schizophrenia] (pp. v–ix). Milan: Feltrinelli.

———— (2009). Bion and Sullivan: An enlightening comparison. *International Forum of Psychoanalysis* 18:90–99.

———— (2010). *Sullivan Revisited – Life and Work. Harry Stack Sullivan's Relevance for Contemporary Psychiatry, Psychotherapy and Psychoanalysis*. Trento: Tangram.

Dunn, J. (1995). Intersubjectivity in psychoanalysis: A critical review. *International Journal of Psychoanalysis* 76:723–738.

Gill, M.N. (1983). The interpersonal paradigm and the degree of the therapist's involvement. *Contemporary Psychoanalysis* 19:200–237.

Greenberg, J.R., & Mitchell, S.A. (1983). *Object relations in psychoanalytic theory*. Cambridge, MA: Harvard University Press.

Heimann, P. (1950). On counter-transference. *International Journal of Psychoanalysis* 31:81–84.

Hinshelwood, R.D. (2010). On being objective about the subjective. Clinical aspects of intersubjectivity in contemporary psychoanalysis. Paper presented at the XVIth IFPS Forum, October 23, 2010, Athens, Greece.

Lewin, K. (1935). *A Dynamic Theory of Personality*. New York: McGraw-Hill.

Rioch, J. (1969). Letter to the editor. *W.A. White Newsletter* Spring, pp. 147–156.

Stern, D.N. (1985). *The Interpersonal World of the Infant*. New York: Basic Books.

Sullivan, H.S. (1927). The onset of schizophrenia. In H.S. Sullivan, *Schizophrenia as a Human Process* (pp. 104–136). New York: Norton, 1962.

———— (1928). Schizophrenic individuals as a source of data for comparative investigation in personality. In H.S. Sullivan, *Schizophrenia as a Human Process* (pp. 218–236). New York: Norton, 1962.

———— (1940). *Conceptions of Modern Psychiatry*. New York: Norton.

———— (1940/1964). Discussion of the case of Warren Wall. A psychiatric gloss on a sociological study. In H.S. Sullivan, *The Fusion of Psychiatry and Social Science* (pp. 100–107). New York: Norton.

———— (1953). *Interpersonal Theory of Psychiatry* (H. Swick Perry and M. Ladd Gawel Eds.). New York: Norton.

———— (1954). *The Psychiatric Interview* (H. Swick Perry and M. Ladd Gawel Eds.). New York: Norton.

———— (1962). *Schizophrenia as a Human Process* (H. Swick Perry Ed.). New York: Norton.

———— (1964). *The Fusion of Psychiatry and Social Science* (H. Swick Perry Ed.). New York: Norton.

Swick Perry, H. (1982). *Psychiatrist of America. The Life of Harry Stack Sullivan*. Cambridge, MA: Belknap Press of Harvard University Press.

CHAPTER 6

S.A. MITCHELL (1946–2000) IN ITALY

This is the only chapter of this book that I am now (at the beginning of January, 2018) writing specifically for it, after having transformed eleven of my articles into eleven of its twelve chapters. In this chapter, I will deal with my first encounters with Stephen Mitchell, with our further contact and our collaboration, with the reception of his work in Italy, and with a personal revisitation of his legacy.

Back in 2004, I had delivered a paper on Mitchell's trips to Italy (1988, 1991, and 1996) at the Milan Associazione di Studi Psicoanalitici (ASP) (Conci, 2012a). In addition, at the meeting of the International Association of Relational Psychotherapy and Psychoanalysis (IARPP) organized in Rome in June 2005 by Gianni Nebbiosi and Emanuel Berman, I had given a PowerPoint presentation on the same topic, accompanied by a series of pictures (Conci, 2005). And at the XIVth Forum of the International Federation of Psychoanalytic Societies (IFPS) organized in Rome in May 2006 by the Società Italiana di Psicoanalisi della Relazione (SIPRe), I had given a paper accompanied by a series of pictures on the topic "Sullivan and Mitchell in Italy – The reception of their work and the revisitation of their legacies" (Conci, 2006).

Neither these contributions nor my specific role in the reception of Mitchell's work in Italy are mentioned—except for in a rather marginal way—in the book and in the series of articles that came out in recent years, although most of their authors know me well and I know them—sometimes having known them for many years. I am referring here to the book *La svolta relazionale. Itinerari italiani*, edited by Vittorio Lingiardi, Gherardo Amadei (1951–2016), Giorgio Caviglia, and Francesco De Bei, and to the series of articles on the "Relational Turn" in Italy that was published in Issue 5/2014 of *Psychoanalytic Dialogues* (see Lingiardi & Federici, 2014; Caviglia & Lingiardi, 2014; Nebbiosi & Federici, 2014). One reason behind this omission may be that, as far as I know, none of the above-mentioned authors—with the exception of Gianni Nebbiosi—ever personally met Stephen Mitchell. They all joined the Relational Movement after Mitchell's death at the end of 2000 or in connection with the very first meeting of the IARPP held in New York in January 2002. In other words, the need to establish the historical truth concerning Stephen Mitchell's relationship to Italy between 1986 and 2000 is one of the motivations behind my writing this chapter.

When I wrote my book on Sullivan, I tried to mention all the authors I could find who had dealt with him and his work, and I consequently find it surprising that the colleagues mentioned above, most of whom are university professors, forgot to adequately mention the important role I played in the original reception of Mitchell's work in Italy. I personally connect the word "university" with the concept of a place where all the information concerning a certain topic is gathered, elaborated, and communicated to an interested audience, and not as a place in which the available information goes through a process of deformation. Is this omission the result of a degradation of the intellectual standards of university life? Is this a by-product of the power politics connected to the life of psychoanalysis as an institution?

Before trying to provide an answer to these, for me, important questions, let me try to tell you how I came to know Stephen Mitchell and how our collaboration developed, back in the late 1980s and early 1990s.

1. MEETING STEPHEN AND GETTING TO KNOW HIM

S.A. Mitchell's and J.R. Greenberg's ground-breaking book *Object relations in psychoanalytic theory* (Greenberg and Mitchell, 1983) was published in Italian in 1986, three years after its original publication through Harvard University Press. Its publication took place thanks to the initiative of Giuseppe Fara and Cristina Esposito of the Department of Psychology at the University of Padua—the former a psychoanalyst of the Società Psicoanalitica Italiana (SPI), and the latter a collaborator of his, a young psychologist in analytic training. The book was published by the very well-established Bolognese publisher Il Mulino (a politically center-left publisher of good intellectual standing), and the translation was provided by Carola Mattioli.

In order to understand how significant such an event was in terms of the overall reception of Mitchell's work and of relational psychoanalysis in general, it is important to point out that the book has not yet been translated into German, French, or Spanish. No wonder that the reception of relational psychoanalysis has been either barely successful (Germany), nonexistent (France), or adequate but rather delayed (Spain). In contrast with these countries, relational psychoanalysis has been very well received in Italy, and all Stephen Mitchell's books have been translated into Italian. As we saw in Chapter 4, something similar happened with the work of H.S. Sullivan: of his seven books published in the USA between 1940 and 1972, five were also published in Italian (between 1961 and 1993), only two in German, and only one in French. Most of Sullivan's books had been translated into Spanish in the 1950s and 1960s in Buenos Aires, but I have not been able to establish which of them are still in print.

I do not know of any review in Italian of the book by Greenberg and Mitchell. However, I can say that this has to do with the fact that it was widely circulated and much read by several generations of psychology students (not only in Padua, but also in Rome), but much less so or not at all in the psychoanalytic institutes of the Italian branch of the International Psychoanalytical Association (IPA), that is, the SPI. In fact, Greenberg and Mitchell were not members of the American Psychoanalytic Association (APsaA) or the IPA, and their books never appeared on the reading lists of the SPI's training institutes. But, outside their formal training, many younger members of the SPI had read the book, or had used it as psychology students, before starting their analytic training, and it gradually became quite successful in many quarters. I think this was not only because it was brilliantly written and thought-provoking, but also even more because it was a pioneering contribution to the then wholly new field of "comparative psychoanalysis."

This is why I also read the book so eagerly—this was in June 1987—and why it was so easy to perceive its unique character and importance. At the time, I had not yet started my analytic training in Milan—this happened only in September 1988—but I had had much experience with self-teaching (a crucial term in the Afterword at the end of this book). This of course included psychoanalysis, which I was becoming familiar with through the personal analysis I had started in my hometown of Trento in September 1983 (which I also deal with in the Afterword). Apart from indicating that Greenberg and Mitchell were members of the W.A. White Institute, the book did not provide any information about who and how old the authors were, but this was enough for me to have the clear feeling that the book could only have been written in a "capital of psychoanalysis" like New York City. By "New York City," I of course imply the cosmopolitan and open atmosphere that I had experienced there as a high school exchange student in 1972–1973 (again, see the Afterword). At the same time, I was already well enough acquainted with the analytic literature and its geography that I was able to understand how well the authors had assimilated the various schools of thought they presented in the book's various chapters, that is, not just through the literature, but also through a real exchange with a series of analysts representing the various analytic orientations they dealt with.

Such a combination of scholarship, clinical experience, and scientific exchange and dialogue was still almost nonexistent in the "analytic culture" I had come into contact with in Italy, given the fact that only a very few analysts had trained in or were familiar with the main European training centers (Vienna, Berlin, Paris, and London). In fact, only the founder of Italian psychoanalysis, Edoardo Weiss (1889–1970), had trained in Vienna before World War I. In the early 1930s in Rome he had been able to train medical doctor Nicola Perrotti (1897–1970) and lawyer Emilio Servadio (1904–1995), who became the main teachers of psychoanalysis in Italy after World War II. The same role was played in Milan by the Venetian psychology professor Cesare Musatti (1897–1989), himself without any training analysis, and in Palermo by the Baltic Princess Alexandra von Wolff-Stomersee (1894–1982), who moved to Palermo after her training in Berlin, having married Giuseppe Tomasi di Lampedusa, the author of the famous novel *The leopard*.

As I have also discussed in Chapter 4, whereas analysts in Milan in the 1960s knew psychoanalysis more from the literature than from a real familiarity with its foreign pioneers (see the testimony of Adam Limentani, 1989), only at the end of the 1970s did the SPI come up to the level of the international analytic standards (see Arnaldo Novelletto's testimony, 1992). This is also why (as I show in my Afterword) I felt the need to look for analytic training outside the SPI, and why I looked for and ended up training with analysts who had themselves trained abroad (Simona Taccani, Johannes Cremerius, Gaetano Benedetti, etc.), whose portraits the reader can (again) find in the Afterword. But, going back to the 1983 book by Greenberg and Mitchell, you will now be able to understand even better how, for me, as an Italian reader, the book had a particular freshness and played such an important role. Last but not least, the fact that Greenberg and Mitchell were members of the White Institute further confirmed the good image I had developed of the interpersonal tradition through the contact I had already had not only with Sullivan's books, but also with the cosmopolitan and eclectic (a positively connotated word for me) psychiatric point of view I had found in *The American handbook of psychiatry* (1959) edited by the Italian-American psychiatrist and psychoanalyst Silvano Arieti (1914–1981) (see again both Chapter 4 and the Afterword).

What I have presented above is the background against which my first meeting with Stephen Mitchell took place, in Florence, on Saturday April 9, 1988. I wrote about this in the summer of 2017, for what now forms the Afterword, but I will risk repeating myself here. However, given that the reader can just turn to the Afterword and read the story, I will try to put together here a new—slightly modified—version of our unique first meeting. At the distance of almost thirty years, I can, for example, start by saying that one of the most important ingredients of the very good chemistry that easily established itself between us was the fact that Stephen Mitchell never specifically asked me where I was doing my analytic training and what point of it I had reached; he simply, and very easily, trusted me just on the basis of how well I consecutively translated the workshop he was giving. As the reader who has already looked up the Afterword knows, the story runs as follows: that weekend I had come to Florence from Trento for a family therapy workshop, and in the course of Friday evening I had learned that Jay Greenberg and Stephen Mitchell were in town, and that they would give a workshop the following day. Out of the curiosity I described above, I did not hesitate the following morning to go to the Florence Istituto di Psicoterapia Analitica, which had invited both Greenberg and Mitchell, and ended up sitting, by chance, in Mitchell's workshop. After a few minutes, I realized that the translator had many problems in understanding psychoanalysis, and was not really able to convey to my Italian colleagues what Mitchell was trying to say. As a consequence, I jumped in as a translator and, after a short time, I heard Mitchell saying: "Since you, as a group, started laughing at my jokes, I can gather that we now have a good translator."

As I also report in the Afterword, I was at the time holding a workshop on Sullivan at the University of Venice, and this represented, as shown during the course of the dinner to which I was invited by the Florence Institute, our second common wavelength—the first being represented by what I can call not only a common intellectual way of going about life and a very good cultural background, but also a series of common values, on both the ethical and the political level. From Mitchell came, that same evening, the main stimulus to work toward the book on Sullivan that I eventually published in Italian in the year 2000. And how did our relationship further develop? Having learned from Mitchell about his new book, due to come out in the fall of that same year— *Relational concepts in psychoanalysis. An integration* (1988a)—the book through which he conceptually founded relational psychoanalysis, I decided to spend my Christmas vacation (with my partner Claudia) in New York City, so that I could buy the book, read it, and discuss it with Mitchell. Of course, I was doing this with the hope that my linguistic and intellectual competence would allow me to make an important contribution to the delicate operation of "intellectual transfer" that the Italian reception of his work would require.

Here is the first of the seventeen letters written to me by Stephen that I found in my personal archive in my Trento office. The letter is typewritten and undated, but I received it on August 22, 1988. It reads as follows:

Dear Marco,

I picked up your letter on my way out of town for my vacation at our house in Massachusetts. I am very happy to hear that you will be coming to New York. I would like very much to get together. Give me a call when you arrive, and we will arrange something. My number in New York is 212 — —

I don't think I have any reprints of the Sullivan and teaching article, but I will make a copy for you. I have another paper on Interpersonal Psychoanalysis and Object Relations Theory which I presented some years ago, which might also be of interest. I will give them both to you when I see you.

I mentioned Loewald as someone who doesn't refer directly to Sullivan, but has absorbed his influence very strikingly. More recently Sullivan is actually being cited directly. There was a recent article by Arnold Cooper in *Psychoanalytic Quarterly* comparing Sullivan and Loewald on the therapeutic action of psychoanalysis; there was the recent article 'One psychoanalysis or many?' in the *International* (69, 1988, p.1) by Wallerstein; as well as the use of Sullivan by Stern in *The interpersonal world of the infant.* Stolorow, a key self psychologist, who speaks of 'intersubjectivity', borrows a lot of Sullivan and is beginning to credit him somewhat, and Merton Gill has been very influenced by Sullivan and credits him directly. I could probably think of more. Congratulations on your Venice seminar. As far as I can tell, it looks very interesting.

We will be returning to the City probably on either Sunday, Sept. 4, or the next day. I hope we can arrange to meet.

Best regards,
Steve

Of course, this first letter is very interesting in terms of not only my relationship with Stephen, and the main theme I am exploring in this chapter, but also, for example, the evolution of his relationship with the work of Hans Loewald (1906–1993) and with so-called "mainstream psychoanalysis" in general—given that he mentions the names of both Arnold Cooper (1923–2011) and Robert Wallerstein (1921–2014). Indeed, this also represents for me a good first point to which I can refer in terms of revisiting Mitchell's work and legacy. Here is my first formulation of this: he was convinced that H.S. Sullivan (1892–1949), who, as he writes in his letter, "more recently . . . is actually being cited directly," had made an important, but totally neglected contribution to psychoanalysis, and that it was important for mainstream psychoanalysis to revisit and reintegrate his legacy. In fact, this had been also one of the aims, or one of the by-products, of the 1983 book Mitchell had written with Jay Greenberg. As an aside, I can say that, among the other things that I learned from Stephen in this initial phase of our relationship, was the way in which the book had been written—Stephen had written the Sullivan chapter, and Jay the ego-psychological one. What for me could only be a feeling was for him of course a deep conviction, acquired through his training at the White Institute and through his own clinical work. At the same time, this was the line that I followed not only in the preparation of my book *Sullivan revisited – Life and work*, but also in the way in which I ended up experiencing his work, and—of course—also his legacy, that is, in the light of Sullivan's work and legacy. As I have amply shown in my book (Conci, 2012b), such a legacy was at the same time clinical, theoretical, interdisciplinary, and political.

But let us go back to my identity as a candidate in training (at the Milan Institute founded by Benedetti and Cremerius, as you can read in the Afterword) confronted with such a challenging and important book as *Relational concepts in psychoanalysis. An integration,* and with the responsibility of explaining to my Italian colleagues who the author was, how well the book was written, what the book was all about, how brilliant were many of its new ideas, and how important it was for one of our publishers to provide—as soon as possible—an Italian edition. After reading the book in New York City at the end of 1988, I remember reading it another two times before starting to write my review, which ended up occupying seven pages of Issue No. 1/1990 of the journal *Psicoterapia e Scienze Umane.* In the Afterword, the reader can find all the necessary information about this journal, and about its founder, Pier Francesco Galli. Reading this review again now, in order to discuss it, I must admit that I am still impressed by the great diligence, the great admiration for Mitchell, and the great love for the scientific dimension of our profession with which I wrote it—and which I believed I shared with him. As an aside, I can say that these aspects still represent for me the basic aspects that a good-enough analytic training should transmit to our candidates—diligence in listening to the patient, admiration for colleagues who know more than we do, and love for psychoanalysis as an intellectual discipline.

Last but not least, such a work of intellectual transfer also required a specific philological sensibility, in terms of how to translate into Italian the new terms and concepts that Mitchell himself was introducing into the analytic discourse—the hardest of all being, as I now recall, the term "developmental tilt." From this point of view, psychoanalysis should be taught as a discipline with a series of terms and concepts introduced not only by Freud, but also by all post-Freudian authors, at a certain time (a certain year), in a certain journal article or book chapter, and in a certain context—which is unfortunately seldom the case.

An eloquent example is represented for me—and for Stephen Mitchell as well, I believe—by the word "interpersonal," as introduced into the psychiatric, psychotherapeutic, and psychoanalytic discourse by H.S. Sullivan in 1926 in the article "The onset of schizophrenia," published in the *American Journal of Psychiatry* and included by Helen Swick Perry in the Sullivan anthology *Schizophrenia as a human process* (see Sullivan, 1962). But unfortunately we do not yet have for all of post-Freudian psychoanalysis such a comprehensive dictionary as the one produced by Laplanche and Pontalis (1967, the original French edition; see Laplanche and Pontalis, 1973) for Freudian psychoanalysis. A praiseworthy exception in this regard is represented by Salman Akhtar's *Comprehensive dictionary of psychoanalysis* (2009), which, although it does not contain the item "developmental tilt," at least contains the items "interpersonal psychoanalysis" and "relational psychoanalysis." Furthermore, Akhtar even states—in line, according to me, with Mitchell's legacy—that Sullivan's views were "valuable and most probably contain the roots of the 'relational' and 'intersubjective' approaches in vogue today" (Akhtar, 2009, p. 151).

But let me now briefly turn to the content of my

review (Conci, 1990), which I started with the words
*"Stephen Mitchell è un giovane e brillante analista di
New York"*—"Stephen Mitchell is a young and brilliant
analyst from New York." In the first part of the review, I
briefly introduced Mitchell to the readers of *Psicoterapia
e Scienze Umane* in terms of his training, and defined his
new book as "the ideal continuation" of his 1983 book
with Greenberg. The long second part of the review
centered around a very detailed and clear presentation
of how the author developed his new discourse in the
book's ten chapters, through whose elaboration and exact
formulation I of course learned very much. Indeed, I
often used this part of the review in the following years
when teaching Mitchell's work. Last but not least, I
was able to conclude the review with the following final
considerations, which still seem to me very illuminating—
and which I am still proud to have written:

> I personally wish this book by Mitchell all the good luck it
> deserves. I also hope that it will soon be translated and that
> it will be talked about in the years to come. Since Sullivan's
> (1892–1949) time the interpersonal point of view has not been
> formulated in such a bright and coherent way. On the clinical
> level, Mitchell's approach seems to me to really echo not only
> the extraordinary sensibility and delicacy, but also the unique
> conceptual sophistication, with which Sullivan approached
> his patients. At the same time, it is clear how the ability of
> the author to promote a fruitful dialogue with a whole series
> of analytic schools not only has a great didactic value, but
> it can also aim at reducing the obstacles interposed to the
> development of psychoanalysis as a scientific discipline. And
> all this is really not at all a small achievement. (Conci, 1990,
> p. 130; my translation)

But let me give you an overview of what I learned from
Relational concepts in psychoanalysis. An integration,
both in terms of psychoanalysis as a scientific discipline and
in terms of how different authors had illuminated specific
aspects of human experience—in addition to using this as
a way of again bringing readers in touch with the basic
contents of the book. At the time, as a young candidate,
I was fascinated by the way in which Mitchell in the first
chapter, "The relational matrix," unites a whole series of
what he calls "relational authors" around a new coherent
relational model, after distinguishing their contributions
as "relational by design" (Bowlby), "relational by intent"
(Fairbairn), and "relational by implication" (Winnicott and
Kohut). The second chapter, "'Drive' and the relational
matrix," centers around the epistemological dilemma we
inherited from Freud in terms of what the author defines
as the clinical centrality of relational aspects, and the
theoretical centrality of the concept of "drive" (in German,

Trieb) and of the metapsychology Freud created around it. What the author calls the "integrated relational model" is his way of overcoming such a dilemma, at variance with the two strategies that he called "loose constructionism" (Loewald and Brenner) and "model mixing" (Hartmann, Kernberg, Pine, the first Kohut, Gedo, and Sandler), which he considers unable to adequately meet such a challenge. In other words, both ways of revisiting psychoanalysis, in terms of both the history of psychoanalytic ideas and its epistemological dimension, fascinated me and gave me much food for thought.

At the time, of course, I also found very convincing Mitchell's concepts of "the metaphor of the beast" and "the metaphor of the baby," around which he constructs the next two parts of his book. In other words, on the one hand, sex and the body can be of central importance— he maintains—even without drive theory. On the other hand, only if we overcome the confinement of patients' relational needs to the time of their infancy, that is, what he calls "the developmental tilt," can we create a new relational theory in which both needs and conflicts play an equal part throughout our whole life.

What I particularly have in mind here, in terms of my daily work with my patients, is Mitchell's critical revisitation of Kohut's and Kernberg's ways of therapeutically dealing with our patients' growing narcissistic problems, and his proposal of looking for a relationally based middle way of dealing with them, that is, on the one hand the defensive and, on the other hand, the creative aspects of narcissism. As many readers know, here the author presents the narcissistic patient as a dancer who knows only one dance, and whose repertoire the analyst can only enlarge if he at first accepts that he needs to dance with the patient the only dance the patient knows. In such cases, according to Mitchell:

> The most constructive form of analytic participation derives from the discovery of a path between the contrasting dangers of complicity and challenge, a path that reflects a willingness to play, an acceptance of the importance of narcissistic integration as a special and favored mode of relation, yet also a questioning of why this must be the only way . . . How did it come about that the analysand learned no other steps? Why does the analysand believe that this is the only desirable dance there is? Most analysands need to feel that their dance style is appreciated in order to be open to expanding their repertoire. (Mitchell, 1988a, pp. 207, 212)

Similarly crucial for my daily clinical work as a candidate was Mitchell's concept of the therapeutic action of psychoanalysis, around which centers the fifth part of his book, with the title "Continuity and change." In the foreground of his perspective is how the analytic experience can help us give up "conflictual attachments" and "identifications with archaic objects" (Mitchell, 1988a, p. 278). And how do we best go about doing this? Mitchell's theory of technique:

> portrays the analyst as discovering himself *within* the structures and strictures of the repetitive configurations of the analysand's relational matrix. The struggle to find his way out, the collaborative effort of analyst and analysand to observe and understand these configurations and to discover other channels through which to engage each other, is the crucible of analytic change. (Mitchell, 1988a, p. 292, original emphasis)

This allows Mitchell to also reformulate the concept of interpretation in terms of a "complex relational event." In his words:

> In the relational-conflict model, both the informational content and the affective tone are regarded as crucial, but their effects are understood somewhat differently – in terms of their role in *positioning* the analyst relative to the analysand. An interpretation is a *complex relational event*, not primarily because it alters something inside the analysand, not because it releases a stalled developmental process, but because it says something very important about where the analyst stands vis-à-vis the analysand, about what sort of relatedness is possible between the two of them. (Mitchell, 1988a, pp. 294–295; original emphasis)

In Italy, at the time of my training, there was no psychoanalyst who could so brilliantly deal with the series of unresolved issues of psychoanalytic theory and technique as Mitchell. Eugenio Gaddini (1916–1985) and Franco Fornari (1921–1985) had been the only Italian analysts whose names were known abroad, but neither participated so actively in the main analytic controversies. Their main priority at the time was the introduction into our country of the work of Klein, Winnicott, and Bion. On the other hand, as I make clear in my Afterword, my attachment to and fascination with the cosmopolitan and open atmosphere of New York City of course played a crucial role in the development of my relationship with Stephen Mitchell. Only many years later did my Italian colleague and friend Stefano Bolognini (see Chapter 11) creatively deal with the crucial concept of contemporary psychoanalysis that is the concept of empathy (Bolognini, 2004), thus providing our contemporary analytic discourse with an important Italian contribution. In addition, he even ended up showing a similar clinical sensibility to the one characterizing Mitchell's 1988 book, whose common denominator is "the multiplicity of voices" he heard when working with his patients. I am referring here to Bolognini's 2011 book *Secret passages. The theory and technique of interpsychic relations*, in which he tells us about the crucial role played in his clinical work by a whole series of analytic authors, each of whom illuminates a specific aspect of human experience. Bolognini does not often cite Mitchell, but I know that he read and values his work.

But let me now come to the typewritten letter that Stephen Mitchell sent to me on January 26, 1990, after receiving my review of his book:

> Dear Marco,
>   Congratulations on your wedding.
>   Thanks for the review. It looks great; I wish I could read it.
>   My publisher says that Il Mulino turned down my book and that Boringhieri has an option on it until March 1. That seems different from the information you heard, which I can't explain. I would very much like to have Boringhieri handle it and would appreciate anything you could do to facilitate that.
>   I would love to come to Italy again. Chrzanowski mentioned to me that the Milan Institute was planning to invite me. Let me know what you think would work best.
>   My family and I are fine. The latest new project is that I am going to be the Editor of a new journal called DIALOGUES: RELATIONAL PERSPECTIVES IN PSYCHOANALYSIS. Perhaps we could publish some contributions from Italy!
>   Thanks again for the review and the picture. Let me know what is happening in terms of the translation and a possible visit.
>   Best regards,
>   Steve

First, as you can see, Stephen was very grateful to me for my review, whose main points I had synthesized for him in a previous letter. Second, as it turned out, Il Mulino turned down producing an Italian edition of *Relational concepts in psychoanalysis. An integration*, and the book was eventually published in 1993 by Bollati Boringheri, from Turin, the Italian publisher of Freud's *Opere complete*, that is, his collected works. Third, as is described both in Chapter 10 and in my Afterword, Gerard Charzanowski (1913–2000), from the White Institute, was a very good friend of Gaetano Benedetti, whose merit in this context consists in having supported the process of admission of the Milan ASP into the IFPS—which had been co-founded by the White Institute in 1962. This took place at the October 1989 Forum of the IFPS held in Rio de Janeiro, at which I was present (see the Afterword).

Indeed, the desire of the ASP to invite Mitchell to Milan played a decisive role in allowing me to find for him other Italian invitations around which Stephen and I could organize his second trip to Italy, which took place in April 1991. As far as *Psychoanalytic Dialogues* is concerned, I clearly remember Stephen bringing me then a copy of Issue No. 1. This made me the very first Italian to see the journal, and probably the first Italian subscriber to *Psychoanalytic Dialogues – A Journal of Relational Perspectives*. Last but not least, Stephen's dream of sooner or later publishing a contribution from Italy stimulated me to start working on a paper on the history of psychoanalysis in Italy, a long-term project whose first fruit was the paper I presented at the IFPS Forum held in Florence in May 1994 (see Conci, 1994b).

2. OUR FURTHER COLLABORATION

Stephen's next letter was dated March 13, 1990, and came, typewritten, from his office on 251 West, 71st Street:

> Dear Marco,
>
> I am so pleased that Boringhieri will be doing the book with a preface by you.
>
> No real reviews have actually appeared here yet (it takes a long time). I know one will be coming out next month – I will send them to you as they appear.
>
> I could not come for more than a week, which I would like to do next April . . . How does that sound to you? I would like to receive between 3,000 and 4,000 Dollars, for the week, plus airfare and some of the expenses. Let me know if that sounds reasonable (that is a pretty low fee compared to what I have been receiving in this country).
>
> I spoke to Morris Eagle the same day you called, and he said there would be no problem with your coming to Stockbridge. He said he would send you a note inviting you, which I assume you have received. It is very likely that I will be attending the Rapaport study group also, so I will see you there.
>
> Keep me informed of your own travel plans, and let me know about possibilities for next April.
>
> Best regards,
> Steve

At this point, we knew that I would have the honor of writing the Introduction to the Italian edition of Stephen's 1988 book, which Bollati Boringhieri was to publish in March 1993. In the folder in which I keep the many papers that Stephen sent me between 1988 and 2000, I found three reviews that he sent me at the end of December 1990, which had been published during that year (in the journals *Psychoanalytic Books*, *International Journal of Psychoanalysis*, and *Psychoanalytic Quarterly*); I deal with these in more detail later in this section when I turn to my Introduction to the Italian edition of Mitchell's 1988 book. It also seemed, in my opinion, that Stephen was ready to lower his usual North American fee, not only to be able to promote his own work in Italy, but also so he could have the chance to test, outside the USA, how his new analytic discourse would be received. Not only professional ambition, but also scientific curiosity and the desire to create new dialogues were, in my experience, very important motivations for him.

The plans for Stephen's second trip to Italy, in April 1991, were now becoming more concrete, and in addition I was arranging to travel to Stockbridge in the USA in June 1990 for the Rapaport–Klein Study Group. In fact, as the Afterword describes, Pier Francesco Galli, the founder and editor of *Psicoterapia e Scienze Umane*, had been invited to give a paper (Galli, 1990), and I wanted to be there as part of the small Italian group that was to accompany him. One of the reasons behind the invitation to speak was the fact that Galli had edited the Italian edition of the *Collected papers* of Hungarian clinical psychologist and psychoanalyst David Rapaport (1911–1960), which had been originally edited by Merton Gill (1914–1994) in 1967 (see Rapaport, 1967). As an aside, I can add that the influential 1976 book by George Klein (1917–1971), *Psychoanalytic theory: An exploration of essentials*, was also translated into Italian, but only in 1993 (see Klein, 1993). As I mention in my Afterword, this invitation to Stockbridge was followed by a memorable International Conference in Bologna, in May 1991, organized by Galli and his journal, in which not only Merton Gill and Robert Holt (who turned 100 years old on December 27, 2017), but also Helmut Thomä (1921–2013) and Johannes Cremerius (1918–2002) participated.

As an aside, the possibility of learning from such important representatives of North American psychoanalysis was one of the reasons why I translated not only the paper that Robert Holt gave in Bologna (which came out in the *Psychoanalytic Review* only in 2013), but also—together with Maria Luisa Mantovani—Gill's important article "The interpersonal paradigm and the degree of the therapist's involvement." This is the text of a paper he had originally given at the White Institute in 1980 and which came out in *Contemporary Psychoanalysis* in 1983 (Gill, 1983). Both translations were published in *Psicoterapia e Scienze Umane* (Holt's paper in 1992, and Gill's in 1995), and this also documents the importance of the connection that the journal maintained with the Rapaport–Klein Study Group, which both authors had contributed to founding. Such a connection was later actively pursued by Paolo Migone, the co-editor-in-chief of *Psicoterapia e Scienze Umane*, who is now the co-chair of the Rapaport–Klein Study Group.

In Stephen's next letter to me, dated September 30, 1990, he expressed his satisfaction with my arrangements for the following year's planned trip:

> Dear Marco,
>
> The arrangements sound very good – Rome that first Saturday (April 13), Milan on Friday April 19, and Bologna on Saturday April 20. Most likely Margaret will come with me and we will stay in Rome until Wednesday or Thursday. She will fly back then and I will finish up in Milan and Bologna.
>
> I am sorry the money is tighter than you thought originally. I definitely think that you should be paid for your services, so I will certainly accept somewhat less than the total amount.
>
> Keep me informed about how things are proceeding.
>
> Best regards,
> Steve

As this shows, Stephen was looking forward to his second trip to Italy, whose final schedule was Rome on Saturday 13, Florence the following Wednesday, Milan on Thursday, and Bologna on Saturday April 20. He was, however, also very concerned that the work I was doing for him should be financially recompensed—even at his own expense.

Stephen's kind concern also shows in his next letter, written on December 10 the same year, three weeks before the birth of our daughter Anna:

> Dear Marco,
> Here is the paper you have been asking for. I am sorry I forgot to send it sooner.
>
> I will arrange to have the publisher send you information about the new journal. We have gotten a lot of good material and there is a great deal of subscriber interest. The first issue will appear in a few weeks, and I am very excited about it.
>
> I am glad things are set for the trip to Italy. I am very much looking forward to it. I will make the reservations now. I'll be in touch in a while about details.
>
> Your family should be bigger now? Let me know how things have been going. Looking forward to April.
>
> Best regards,
> Steve

As Stephen refers in his letter to the very first issue of *Psychoanalytic Dialogues*, I find it important to mention the by now famous first section of his "Editorial philosophy" for the journal:

> There is a great irony at the heart of contemporary psychoanalysis. The skilled *psychoanalyst as clinician* is, perhaps, the most careful and systematic listener, the most precise and respectful speaker, the most highly trained and refined communicator, that Western culture has produced. A sustained and dedicated effort to discover and articulate

the personal meanings, the inner logic of the patient's communications, is the most fundamental dimension of the craft of psychoanalysis in all its variations. *Yet, psychoanalysts have enormous difficulty listening and speaking meaningfully to each other.* (Mitchell, 1991a, p. 1; emphasis added)

As the reader can imagine, these words—and the attempt to remedy the lack of dialogue among analytic schools and institutions that Mitchell saw as one of the main functions of the new journal—are very important to me. They have inspired not only my scientific and editorial work, but also the preparation of this volume.

From an editorial point of view, *Psychoanalytic Dialogues* introduced the three following innovations for producing an analytic journal: an editorial board consisting of analysts of different persuasions; their sharing of a specific interest in furthering analytic dialogue among different schools, with particular emphasis on the relational aspects of clinical work; and, last but not least, the production of journal issues centered around specific monographic themes, as opposed to just publishing a series of articles without a clear connection, as had previously been the case. These innovations also represented an important source of inspiration for Jan Stensson, the founding editor of the IFPS journal, the *International Forum of Psychoanalysis* (Stensson, 1992); I myself have continued working in the same direction since I became the co-editor-in-chief of the journal in the summer of 2007—for example, by presenting each issue through an editorial introduction and by the production of monographic issues. This convergence between the two journals materialized in a workshop that took place in New York City in January 1996 (see below).

I have dealt with Stephen's second trip to Italy as a psychoanalyst since the time I first met him (although he may of course have traveled to Italy before that) not only in the unpublished congress papers in English that I hinted at above, at the beginning of this chapter, but also in the paper published in Italian in 2012 (Conci, 2012a), and even in my Introduction to *Gli orientamenti relazionali in psicoanalisi. Per un modello integrato* (see below, and Conci, 1993). In fact, giving papers in Rome, Florence, Milan, and Bologna in April 1991 created such a liking of Stephen as a person and such an interest in his work that the publisher Bollati Boringhieri did not further hesitate in producing the Italian edition of his 1988 book. But let us now look at this second trip in detail.

I am still proud to have been able to organize in Rome, on Saturday April 13, 1991, as the first event of this important trip, a day-long scientific conference at the Institute of Psychology and Psychiatry of the Catholic University, where I had done my residency in psychiatry between 1982 and 1986 (see the Afterword for the scientific and organizational details). I am also proud of having been able to involve in it not only the director of the institute, Professor Leonardo Ancona (see the Afterword), but also some of the most influential Roman psychoanalysts of the time, and—last but not least—the Rome publisher Il Pensiero Scientifico. Professor Ancona himself chaired the morning session, in which Stephen Mitchell presented the paper "Contemporary perspectives on self: Toward an integration," that is, the paper he was about to publish in the second issue of his new journal (Mitchell, 1991b). I had put at the participants' disposal a photocopy of the translation into Italian that I had personally done, which appeared both in the conference volume, with the title *Le matrici relazionali del Sé* [The relational matrixes of the self], and in the journal *Psicoterapia e Scienze Umane*.

The second paper that morning was presented by the SPI colleague Sergio Bordi (1929–2006), who was very familiar with and very sympathetic to the recent new developments in North American psychoanalysis (see, for example, Bordi, 1990), and who was also esteemed and listened to inside the Society. From this point of view, the convergence of views that he showed with Stephen in his paper "Sé soggettivo e organizzazione del Sé nel ciclo vitale" (1991; see the References for the translation of the title) was very important for the reception of Mitchell's work in the SPI. As an aside, after Bordi's death a very interesting anthology of his innovative papers was edited by Paola Capozzi (Bordi, 2009).

The third paper of the morning was my own paper, "La psicoanalisi interpersonale. Da H.S. Sullivan a S.A. Mitchell," (Conci, 1992a), in which I presented and summarized the reception that interpersonal psychoanalysis had had in Italy since the early 1960s. I concluded by expressing the wish that, through Mitchell's contribution, interpersonal psychoanalysis could eventually be taken more seriously, going beyond associating it simply with the valuable clinical work done by Frieda Fromm-Reichmann (1889–1957) with the sickest patients. In fact, in the encyclopedic handbook of psychoanalysis edited by the Venetian colleague Antonio Alberto Semi in 1988, there was no trace of interpersonal psychoanalysis, since it represented an orientation developed outside the IPA, and no Italian SPI colleague was apparently familiar with it.

Besides Sergio Bordi, a further exception to this rule was represented by the first speaker of the afternoon, Massimo Ammaniti, who presented the innovative paper "Il Sé infantile in una prospettiva intergenerazionale." Ammaniti, a child psychiatrist, SPI and IPA psychoanalyst, and university professor at the Department of Psychology of the University of Rome, was introduced by the chairman of the afternoon session, Nino Dazzi, one of the most famous and influential Italian psychologists. The author of a very good introduction to the life and work of William James (Dazzi, 1981), Dazzi was not only familiar with neo-Freudian psychoanalysis, but in the following years also kept in touch with the further development of Mitchell's work; in 2014—together with Francesco De Bei—Dazzi was the author of a paper on Bowlby and Mitchell, which also came out in the above-mentioned issue of *Psychoanalytic Dialogues* (De Bei and Dazzi, 2014).

I am sorry that Ammaniti's text was not published in *Le matrici relazionali del Sé*, and that I do not have a copy of it (as is the case with Bordi's paper), because it belongs to the phase of his research dominated by the work of Daniel Stern (1934–2012); he had interviewed Stern in 1988 for the Italian *Rivista di Psicoanalisi* (Ammaniti and Rossi, 1988), and he introduced his line of research into Italy. It is no wonder that he was so open and ready to meet and work with such a new star of North American psychoanalysis as Stephen Mitchell—the only historical trace left of this event being Ammaniti's one-page introduction to the conference volume (Ammaniti, 1992). As many readers will know, Ammaniti was later able to continue his research on intersubjectivity by working on its neuropsychological bases together with the first-rate researcher and neurophysiologist Vittorio Gallese (Ammaniti and Gallese, 2014).

The last paper of the conference was given by Leonardo Ancona (see the Afterword for further details of his background and orientation), a pioneer of group psychotherapy in Italy, together with his collaborators Raffaele Menarini (the first author of the published paper) and Corrado Pontalti (see the Afterword); the paper was entitled "La costruzione del Sé dal vertice dei campi mentali familiari-gruppali-terapeutici." Starting from a dream described by Mitchell in *Relational concepts in psychoanalysis. An integration*, the authors present in their book chapter Mitchell's contribution to their own way of using psychoanalysis with families and groups, with particular regard for the transgenerational aspects.

Even if the highly successful Rome Conference was the most important and the only public event of Stephen's second trip to Italy, the following events were also very satisfactory experiences for him—and for myself. Having returned to Trento the day after the Rome conference, to work with my patients, I rejoined Stephen in Milan on the afternoon of Thursday April 17. He had stopped over in Florence on the invitation of the Istituto di Psicoterapia Analitica, which had previously met him in April 1988, and Stephen was happy to accept their new invitation. Along with members and candidates of the institute, chaired by Virginia Giliberti Tincolini, Stephen discussed his paper "Comparative theories of aggression," which he had sent me in the summer of 1990, after having presented it at the Toronto Psychoanalytic Society on April 20, 1990. The paper was eventually published in the *Psychoanalytic Quarterly* in 1993, under the title "Aggression and the endangered self" (Mitchell, 1993a). The candidates of the Institute who heard Mitchell's paper included my good friend Carlo Bonomi (see the Afterword), the chair of the next Ferenczi Conference, to be held in Florence in May 2018, and Annamaria Loiacono, the chair of the next IFPS Forum, to take place also in Florence, but in October 2018. I know that both of Mitchell's visits to their Florence institute (1988 and 1991) represented for them an important introduction to international psychoanalysis and stimulated them to collaborate on the organization of the IXth IFPS Forum, which took place in Florence in May 1994 (see the Afterword, and Conci, 1994e).

As we saw in the letter of January 26, 1990, the IFPS also represented the institutional link uniting Mitchell's White Institute and the Milan ASP, in whose training institute I was undergoing my own training (see the Afterword for the specific details). Given the training institute's open and democratic organization (see Chapter 10 and the Afterword), I was able to help Ciro Elia and Lilia D'Alfonso, as representatives of the ASP's executive council, to organize a Scientific Afternoon with Mitchell, for both the ASP's members and the candidates of the Scuola di Psicoterapia Psicoanalitica (SPP), the two groups together numbering about a hundred people. Stephen gave the paper he had presented the previous Saturday in Rome, followed by a very lively discussion, with myself as a consecutive translator. Fortunately, I was by then so in tune with Stephen that I mostly knew how he would react to a certain question or what the lines of his answer would be—which I then learned as being the secret of a good consecutive translation.

This also allowed me to better understand the gaps or deficits in knowledge of the interpersonal tradition from which my colleagues suffered; consequently, I proposed to Ciro Elia, the editor of the ASP journal, that it would be beneficial to translate into Italian, for example, Mitchell's very instructive and brilliant 1988 paper "The intrapsychic and the interpersonal: Different theories, different domains, or historical artifacts?" (Mitchell, 1988b). In the same issue, Pier Giorgio Battaggia, a member of the ASP, published the paper "La prospettiva relazionale nella psicoanalisi. Il contributo di Stephen A. Mitchell" (Battaggia, 1992), in which he discussed Mitchell's contribution in relation to the contemporary critique of Freudian metapsychology and libido theory formulated in several quarters. As an aside, this same issue also contained the Italian version of the paper I had given in Stockholm in August 1991 and for which I had won the IFPS Candidates Award (see the Afterword), which formed the original version of Chapter 1 of this book.

Particularly significant from various points of view was the fourth and last event of Mitchell's 1991 trip to Italy. When I informed Pier Francesco Galli that I was arranging for Stephen Mitchell to come to Italy to present his work, Galli wanted to invite Stephen to Bologna to present a paper and discuss a clinical case—which indeed happened, on Saturday April 20, 1991. The context was the workshops that Galli's journal organized one Saturday a month in a hotel in Bologna, from September to June. Behind Galli's interest lay not only their common connection to the Rapaport–Klein Study Group (see above), but even more so Galli's commitment—as both editor of *Psicoterapia e Scienze Umane*, and editor of the two main Italian analytic book series, the first with Feltrinelli and the second with Bollati Boringhieri—to promote the reception of the interpersonal tradition in Italy. It had not been by chance that the first volume of Feltrinelli's "*Biblioteca di Psicologia Clinica e Psichiatria*" had been Sullivan's *Conceptions of modern psychiatry*, with a very good preface by Gaetano Benedetti (Benedetti, 1961); three more books by Sullivan followed in 1962, 1965, and 1967 (for more specific details, see Chapter 4).

In Bologna, Mitchell's paper "Contemporary perspectives on self: Toward an integration" was followed by a very stimulating discussion—which I translated consecutively. Stephen's dialectical and integrative supervisory line on the presentation of a clinical case by Maria Luisa Mantovani (Bologna) not only gave her and the group of about fifty colleagues present great food for thought, but also represented for her the beginning of a long series of visits to the White Institute and a series of long-standing relationships with several of its members. As far as I am concerned, at the Bologna meeting I not only found further confirmation that it made sense to keep working on my book on Sullivan (see Conci, 2012b, and Chapter 4), but also had the chance to think of the need to translate those papers of the interpersonal tradition that had not yet been translated into Italian and to collate them in an anthology. I am referring here to papers such as Janet Rioch's 1943 paper "The transference phenomenon in psychoanalytic therapy" and Harold Searles' 1977 paper "The analyst's participant observation as influenced by the patient's transference." Both of these appeared in the anthology *La tradizione interpersonale in psichiatria psicoterapia e psicoanalisi* that I published in 1997 with Sergio Dazzi and Maria Luisa Mantovani.

A special mention of the project of this anthology was also contained in my 1993 Introduction to the Italian edition of Mitchell's 1988 book—positioned after the explanation of how I had met Stephen and who he was, and after having hinted at his second Italian trip of 1991. As to the rest of this Introduction, I can say the following: If in my 1990 review of the book I had compared Mitchell to Sullivan, in the meantime I had run across the paper by Mary Julian White "Sullivan and treatment," in which she explained his originality in terms of what she called Sullivan's "fine disregard." This allowed me now, in the Introduction to *Orientamenti relazionali in psicoanalisi. Per un modello integrato*, to apply the same kind of "fine disregard" to Mitchell's new ways of mixing a whole series of cards of Freudian and post-Freudian psychoanalysis. Here are White's words:

> On the master's wall at Rugby is an inscription which reads, 'This stone commemorates the exploit of William Webb Ellis who, with a fine disregard of the rules of football as played at his time, first took the ball in his arms and ran with it, thus originating the distinctive feature of the Rugby game. AD 1823.' It was Sullivan's 'fine disregard' of the rules of classical psychoanalysis that led to his signal contribution, his capacity to see his way through to one operational statement that covered so vast an area. His insistence on viewing psychopathology as arising out of and living on in the fields of interpersonal relations was an enormously useful step. (White, 1952, p. 117)

In other words, Mitchell's "fine disregard" was the way in which—at this stage of my relationship with him and to his work—I for example explained his definition of the concept of "interpretation" in terms of a "complex relational event" (see above, and Mitchell, 1988a, pp.

294–295). This was at variance with the dichotomous view then prevailing of the therapeutic action of psychoanalysis, conceptualized as being based on either the "right interpretation" or a "good relationship" with the patient.

Before moving to a short presentation of my way of organizing the 1993 Introduction, let me briefly talk about the title of the Italian edition of the book. The correct translation should of course have been a literal translation of "Relational concepts in psychoanalysis. An integration," but for commercial reasons the title became the Italian translation of "The relational orientations in psychoanalysis. For an integrated model" (*Gli orientamenti relazionali in psicoanalisi. Per un modello integrato*). Although I had been able to have Bollati Boringhieri produce the book in Italian, and although I wrote its Introduction, I was not consulted about the translation of the title, which ended up making Mitchell's contribution smaller than it really was. In other words, through the book Stephen creates a new "relational orientation" or "relational psychoanalysis" by integrating a whole series of relational concepts into a new orientation—as opposed to speaking of pre-existing relational orientations that he might have synthesized into a new one.

I finished the Introduction by mentioning the three main critiques on the book that I had encountered, and by trying to place it in the then-existing Italian analytic landscape, with particular regard to the theoretical orientation of the SPI. I associated the first type of critique with the above-mentioned review published by Jule Miller in the *International Journal of Psychoanalysis*, according to whom not only is the book "sophisticated and thought-provoking" (Miller, 1990, p. 731), but also "the selections Mitchell makes to facilitate his integration probably would be considered unacceptable by some, perhaps many, adherents of the schools being integrated" (p. 728). In addition, she writes that "although Mitchell wishes to give an adequate role to conflict in his relational-conflict position, his treatment of conflict is not, in my opinion, congruent with conflict as it is understood in traditional analysis" (p. 730). This allows the author to state that Mitchell's "relational-conflict integration seems to consist primarily of a sophisticated version of interpersonal psychoanalysis" (p. 731). At the same time, these critiques do not prevent her from recommending the book as "a work of superior scholarship, written from a sophisticated epistemological stance" (p. 730).

Basing himself on Lawrence Friedman's revisitation of Freud's work in his important 1988 book *The anatomy of psychotherapy*, Robert Hatcher (1990) criticized Mitchell for equating Freud's legacy with his libido theory, thus ignoring his structural theory and the multidimensional character of his legacy. This critique allowed Mitchell to formulate the following response:

> I do not feel it necessary to disclaim Freud's impact on my thinking through smuggling and disguise. Rather, what I am trying to do is point out the varied and pervasive ways in which the meta-theory, the conceptual scaffolding which supports Freud's work, has changed in many schools of contemporary psychoanalytic thought. This is an abandonment of the drive model, not of Freud. In fact, I hoped to show in my book that an integration of the different versions of the relational model provide a roomier, more open and hospitable home for Freud's contributions, a chrysalis from which the butterfly Hatcher and I both long for is much more likely to emerge. (Mitchell, 1990, p. 140)

But the harshest critique came from Alan Skolnikoff, particularly regarding the following words:

> In summary, Mitchell would have made an excellent contribution if he had emphasized the evolution of psychoanalytic theory and practice from a purely drive-oriented psychology to a combined object relations and drive psychology. What many readers will find irritating is his insistence on a so-called 'pure relational model' and his wish to discard the term drive and its important contribution. Although Mitchell's emphasis on the importance of relational concepts is thought-provoking, it is not clear why he has to do away with drive concepts or the concept of intrapsychic motivation. (Skolnikoff, 1991, pp. 484–485)

I come now to the last section of my Introduction. Reading Mitchell's book several times also allowed me to see how many important books on which he based his work had not yet been translated into Italian, although Italy was a country where many analytic books, belonging to many different traditions, had already been translated. I made explicit reference to Roy Schafer's *A new language for psychoanalysis* (1976), and to Hans Loewald's *Papers on psychoanalysis* (1980). As we now know, it is impossible to understand Mitchell's work and legacy without knowing Hans Loewald's work and legacy. "Perhaps the greatest joy in my reading of the psychoanalytic literature in recent years has been my immersion in the work of Hans Loewald," wrote Mitchell in a posthumously published self-portrait (Mitchell, 2004, p. 537). Discovering this gap allowed me to critically mention Luciana Nissim Momigliano's (1919–1998) claim that, by the beginning of the 1990s, the SPI had been able to completely fill the gap that had separated it for decades from contemporary analytic debate, a claim that had been reported by Michele Sforza in his report of the Italo-German Meeting held in June 1991 on Lake Como (see Sforza, 1992, p. 258). Furthermore, I specifically insisted on the necessity of eventually dealing with the North American interpersonal tradition, instead of neglecting it without really knowing it.

To my great surprise, Luciana Nissim Momigliano, one of the most influential Italian psychoanalysts of the time, not only read Mitchell's book and my Introduction to it, but even came to the point of contacting me through a common friend, the historian of psychoanalysis Michele Ranchetti (1925–2008), and of inviting me to visit her in her Milan office. A Jewish physician and resistance fighter from Turin, Nissim Momigliano had been deported to Auschwitz and was a good friend of the famous writer Primo Levi. After training in Milan with Cesare Musatti (1897–1989), one of the fathers of Italian psychoanalysis, and with Franco Fornari, one of the pioneers of the introduction of Kleinian psychoanalysis in Italy, Nissim Momigliano greatly contributed to introducing Bion's clinical point of view into Italy. Her most influential paper, "Due persone che parlano in una stanza" (1984), was meant as an investigation into the analytic dialogue taking place in the analytic situation, conceptualized in terms of a "two-way affair"; this paper was first published in English in 1992, in the anthology *Shared experience: The psychoanalytic dialogue* that Nissim Momigliano edited with Andreina Robutti, and to which Antonino Ferro and Franco De Masi each contributed a chapter.

No wonder that Mitchell's relational and dialogical orientation interested Nissim Momigliano and that she wanted to know more about it—as she told me when I met her in her office on June 24, 1993. In fact, we had such a good dialogue that not only did we keep in contact with each other, but I even reviewed one of her books, *Continuity and change in psychoanalysis. Letters from Milan*, for Joseph Reppen's journal *Psychoanalytic Books* (Conci, 1995a). This was my second positive contact with a prominent member of the SPI (see the Afterword for my contact with Glauco Carloni, at the conference held in Trieste in 1989, to celebrate the 100th anniversary of Edoardo Weiss's birth), and it played a crucial role in the gradual development of a closer contact with both the IPA and the SPI. In fact, getting to know Luciana Nissim Momigliano certainly played a role in my decision to attend the IPA Congress held in Amsterdam a month later (see the Afterword). Later on, it also helped me in establishing good contact with a whole series of analysts who had trained and/or worked with her—for example, Anna Ferruta, Antonino Ferro, Franco Borgogno, and Franco De Masi—which led finally (in 2012) to my becoming a member of the SPI (see the Afterword).

But it is now time to go back to Mitchell's letters. I will not present the letters Nos 6 and 7, because of their more private character, but will move directly to Letter No. 8, which I received on May 17, 1993. It is a very short letter, undated, that runs as follows:

Dear Marco,
    Thanks so much for the lovely introduction and for providing me the gloss.
    Things are moving along here at a very hectic pace.
    I look forward to seeing you in June.
    Best regards,
    Steve

In this we can see not only his gratitude for my Introduction and the work it had involved, but also his looking forward to my next visit. I was due in New York City the following month, June, to attend a five-day course of introduction to the interpersonal tradition that was taking place at the White Institute. Agnar Berle from Oslo attended it with me, and I remember being invited with him to the party that Carola Mann was organizing for Gerard Chrzanowski's eightieth birthday. Agnar Berle became the secretary general of the IFPS in 2000 and organized the IFPS Oslo Forum in 2002—and our meeting at the White Institute contributed to the good relationship we have had with each other ever since. I also remember having lunch with Stephen, and his introducing me after lunch to Lewis Aron. Indeed, I even remember Stephen leaving the restaurant with a cup of coffee and taking it into his office. After that I also started allowing myself to be less "libidinally abstinent" with my patients, as I had learned in my personal analysis (see the Afterword for further details).

Stephen's next letter, typewritten and dated January 26, 1994, reads as follows:

Dear Marco,
    This is just a short note in response to your short letter of Dec. 20.
    I had heard from Basic Books that Bollati Boringhieri had bought HOPE AND DREAD IN PSYCHOANALYSIS, which I was extremely pleased to hear.
    I think that the idea of your writing an introduction is a good one, although I would want this one to be less personal in terms of our relationship and more just aimed at placing this new book in context.
    Also, I would want to see a translation of the new

introduction before it is finalized, so that it would be possible
to have some input if so desired.
    Hope things are going well for you in all your activities.
    Things are hectic as usual here, but going well.
    Best wishes,
    Steve

Citing this letter gives me a chance to deal with my
very short Introduction (two pages) to *Speranza e timore
in psicoanalisi* (Conci, 1995b), which I had already
reviewed in *Psicoterapia e Scienze Umane* (Conci, 1994d).
Of course, it was easy to follow Stephen's important
advice as to the character of my Introduction, since I was
no longer a candidate and I could assume that readers
knew who I was. I could also assume that they knew that
I was not a famous analyst, but simply a young analyst
interested in promoting the reception of Mitchell's work
in Italy. I was therefore able to limit myself to underlining
what I considered as being the following two important
developments that characterized the book. In the first
place, I was very impressed by Mitchell's ability to write—
as only Freud and only a few other analysts were able
to do—not only for his colleagues and for the educated
layman, but also for any reader interested in looking
into the psychological problems connected with the
basic human experiences of hope and dread. Second, the
further evolution of his thinking allowed him to articulate
more clearly than before what he saw as the connection
between "the authentic subjectivity" that the patient is
looking and struggling for and the quality of the analyst's
"participation." Indeed, I was myself fascinated by how
Stephen talked in this book in terms of "reconciliation"
as the basic need of the patient, and of "negotiation" as
one of the most important activities of the analyst (Conci,
1995b, p. 10).

Leaving aside the next two items of correspondence
(a fax of May 15, 1994, and a letter that I received on
August 8, 1994), I can come now to Stephen's Letter No.
12, a typewritten letter that I received in the form of a fax
on November 4, 1994:

Dear Marco,
    Thanks for your fax. It would be great if we could get an
early translation of FREUD AND BEYOND. It has gotten a
very good reaction here so far, especially for people who teach
psychoanalysis on an undergraduate and graduate student
level. I think it will become widely used as a text.
    I am just getting the papers together to send them to
you. It is a bit difficult, because some of them are in my
computer in the country . . .
    I got an invitation from a Dr. Rinaldi from Naples to
speak there sometime this year (except for the one week-end
we are going to be in Florence). His institute and Boringhieri

would pay the expenses and honorarium. I was thinking of writing back and suggesting that I come next year, probably in February (of 1997). What do you think? Is Naples a good place for me to speak? . . . Would you be available to speak with me and translate?

Let me know what you think about the papers, and also about the Naples possibility. Hope all goes well with you – looking forward to seeing you in January.

Best regards,
Steve.

This letter contains a series of topics, which I will deal with in the order in which Stephen formulated them. First, due to the success of the two previous books published by Bollati Boringhieri, the Turin publisher was very fast in buying the rights of and translating *Freud and beyond. A history of modern psychoanalytic thought*, the book written by Stephen together with his wife, Margaret Black; the book therefore came out in Italian the year after it had been published in the USA (see Mitchell and Black, 1995). The book was dedicated to Caitlin and Samantha, Stephen and Margaret's two daughters. Stephen's ability to transmit his fascination with and deep comprehension of psychoanalysis to a larger audience than his colleagues reached here a further peak. Indeed, I also often used the book in the following years when teaching psychiatric residents, university students, and analytic candidates.

Stephen's second topic concerns the papers from which we would choose his presentation for Florence, in April 1996. The third subject was the invitation to Naples. I remember speaking on the phone with Luigi Rinaldi, an SPI colleague from Naples, but unfortunately the plan did not materialize, that is, Mitchell was not able to find the time to go to Naples in April, 1996—but only to come to Florence. Of course, this was a sign of the fact that the interest in Mitchell's work was also spreading inside the Italian IPA group—at variance with the allergy that the SPI had previously had toward interpersonal psychoanalysis. In fact, a positive review of the Italian edition of Mitchell's 1988 book was about to appear in the SPI journal, the *Rivista di Psiconalisi* (Rocchi, 1995).

Let me now come to one of the highlights of my relationship with Stephen Mitchell, that is, the small group seminar that Jan Stensson organized with him in New York City on January 5 and 6, 1996, and in which the following two groups of colleagues participated: Ulla-Britt Parment, Tord Nystedt, Christer Sjödin, Jan Stensson, Valerie Tate Angel, and myself, for the editorial board of the *International Forum of Psychoanalysis*; and Margaret Black, Emmanuel Ghent (1925–2003), and

Stephen Mitchell for the editorial board of *Psychoanalytic Dialogues*; plus New York City colleague Barry Magid. As I wrote in my brief report (Conci, 1996), the theme chosen for this unique meeting was "The 'good life' and the vulnerability of the human being. Psychoanalytic perspectives," and the meeting took place on Friday afternoon at the White Institute, and on Saturday for the whole day at Margaret and Stephen Mitchell's home, on the Upper West Side. This was a time of crisis for psychoanalysis in the USA, as had become clear when *Time Magazine*, in November 1993, had led with a cover story entitled "Is Freud dead?" This is why our New York colleagues were very happy to share with us Jonathan Lear's article in *The New Republic* of December 25, 1995, with the title "The shrink is in. A counterblast in the war on Freud," in which Lear spoke of psychoanalysis in the following terms: "Psychoanalysis is the one form of therapy which leaves it to analysands to determine for themselves what their specific goals will be" (Lear, 1995, p. 21).

But the major aim of our meeting was to get to know each other better, to exchange our professional and editorial experiences, and to create a closer collaboration between each other and our journals. With Jan Stensson proposing the metaphor of "going astray in the woods" for our work as analysts and editors, we ended up sharing the insight that the best thing we can do with the patients we treat and with the papers we read for our journals is to give them the time to both grow and acquire meaning inside ourselves. Not surprisingly, a new experience of time was the common denominator of the two cases presented, without any reliance on written notes—by Stephen on Friday and by Jan on Saturday. From this point of view, working with our patients and choosing the papers to publish in our journals make sense only if we establish a climate of free association and exchange, in which we ourselves can expand and grow. But let me quote my concluding remarks:

> Time is indeed such a crucial dimension of both object constancy and personal identity that the seminar came to an end when we realized that we had been able to create an atmosphere in which enough time was there for every participant to express themselves. In other words, we could by then be sure of having done a good thing for ourselves by taking time off—from our profession and families—to come to New York and enjoy the possibility of 'going astray in the woods'. Our professional identity is secured when we can keep alive and transmit to our patients that very sense of time which the societies we live in are losing sight of. (Conci, 1996, p. 71)

No wonder that in his fax of January 15, 1996, Stephen wrote, among other things, "It was really good to see you. Margaret and I both enjoyed the meeting very much." He also added: "I need to know as soon as possible about hotels in Venice and Florence, because I would like to make reservations right away. So, anything you can let me know, would be greatly appreciated." Stephen was referring here to his third trip to Italy, which took place in April 1996. Having decided to come with his wife and daughters, and to visit Venice and Florence, I organized for him only one scientific event, the presentation of the paper "When interpretations fail: A new look at the therapeutic action of psychoanalysis" (Mitchell, 1996), in Florence, on Saturday April 13, 1996. My role consisted in translating the paper into Italian, in finding the place—the Florence Istituto di Neuroscienze—where the event was to take place, and in inviting a large group of colleagues to present their comments on Stephen's paper.

Stephen's next letter, a fax that I received on February 14, 1996, contained also his explanation of a unique term that played a crucial role in his paper:

Dear Marco,

Thanks very much for your letter. Margaret and I are ecstatic about the quick translation being planned, and the cast of characters and setting for my Florence talk seem really exciting. I really appreciate your thumbnail sketches, so I will have a sense of the other people ahead of time.

The article has not been published yet. It will appear as a chapter in an edited volume on THE THERAPEUTIC ACTION OF PSYCHODYNAMIC PSYCHOTHERAPY, edited by L. Lifson, being published by Analytic Press in 1996.

The changes you propose are fine with me . . . .

The business about bootstraps sounds like it will be a problem as far as translation. I don't mean anything about the patient relying on his own resources. When I say there is a bootstrapping problem, I mean that in the classical model interpretations are supposed to be the effective force for change, but the model does not anchor interpretations anyplace firmly enough so they can possibly effect the change. It would be like saying, we are going to lift a large rock with a lever, but then provide no sturdy point of leverage for the lever to use. If the patient experiences what the analyst says in terms of transference, that must include the analyst's interpretations also. But if the analyst's interpretations are experienced as transference, how can they be the point of leverage for changing the transference? This is what is meant by a bootstrapping problem – you try to pull yourself by the little straps on the top of your (cowboy) boots, but your weight is supported by the boots themselves. It would be like trying to lift yourself up off the floor by tugging on your belt. Boy, I am glad I am not a translator!

Thanks for the advice on hotels etc. Let me know if you need anything from me. I am looking forward to seeing you

again soon.
  Best regards,
  Steve.

Almost a hundred colleagues participated in the event, which lasted the whole morning, with Stephen's paper being discussed by Virginia Giliberti Tincolini of the Florence Istituto di Psicoterapia Analitica and by Daniela De Robertis of the Roman SIPRe, both of whom belonged to the IFPS; and by Giordano Fossi (Florence), Antonello Correale, and Giuseppe Martini (both from Rome), all three members of the SPI. I had contacted the latter three with the help of Florentine colleague Adriana Ramaciotti—through whom I had also come into contact with the Istituto di Neuroscienze. Maria Antonietta Schepisi, the future translator of Mitchell's *Influence and autonomy in psychoanalysis* (Mitchell, 1997), was, as a representative of Bollati Boringhieri, also helpful in organizing the event. The Turin publisher published its fourth and last book by Mitchell in 1999, two years after its original publication in the USA.

In his 1997 book *Influence and autonomy in psychoanalysis* we find Mitchell's Florence paper as Chapter 2, with the title "The therapeutic action. A new look." In this a central role is played by the above-mentioned "bootstrapping problem," which we find formulated in the third section of the chapter, "Bootstraps and a missing platform"—whose translation into Italian is *"sollevarsi tirando i lacci delle scarpe."* This was a crucial theoretical problem not only for Mitchell, but also, for example, for Luciana Nissim Momigliano, who formulated it in terms of how patients react to and/or misinterpret our interpretations. She dealt with this on the basis of her Kleininan and Bionian theoretical background, as her supervisee Antonino Ferro kept doing, thus creating a new way of working with our patients (see, for example, Ferro, 2009; and my review of it, Conci, 2009). Indeed, Mitchell himself deals with this in Chapter 4 of the same book, "Interaction in the Kleinian tradition," that is, with how the post-Kleinian tradition reformulated the problem of analytic interpretation in terms of the importance of studying the patient's reactions to our interpretations.

But, as he showed in his Florence paper and in this chapter, only a relationally oriented analyst could go beyond the "bootstrapping problem" connected with the traditional model of the therapeutic action of our interpretations, and show that interpretations can only work if conceptualized in terms of the new relationship that we create with our patients. In other words, it is exactly the new relationship that we create with our patients which functions as "the platform" that allows us to formulate interpretations that they can understand and profit from. Such a formulation could not be articulated by "psychoanalytic theorists"—writes Mitchell—because they have "searched for a direct passageway between analyst and patient," in order "to make unnecessary the arduous task of examining and interpreting their mutual influence on each other in the service of the patient's personal growth and development" (Mitchell, 1997, p. 51).

If Mitchell in his 1988 book had conceptualized the interpretation itself as a "complex relational event," here is how he further formulates the relationship between interpretation and relationship, at the end of the section "Bootstraps and a missing platform," just after the words quoted above:

> I am arguing that it is not useful to assume such a direct channel, but rather to understand the interactions generated between the patient and analyst in terms of the patient's dynamics as manifestations of old patterns. Meaningful analytic change, in this view, comes not from bypassing old object relations, but from expanding them from the inside out (Bromberg, 1991). This entails new understanding and new transformations of the patient's old relational patterns in the transference, as well as new understandings and transformations of the analyst's customary relational patterns in the countertransferences, including the analyst's capacity to think about analytic interaction in new and different ways. Recent developments in self psychology more directly address the bootstrap problem in their exploration of the repetitive dimensions of the transference (Lachmann and Beebe), the 'dread to repeat' (Ornstein), the inevitability and utility of 'empathic failures', and the fundamentally intersubjective nature of the analytic situation (Stolorow).
>
> The point of convergence of these various lines of innovative thinking about therapeutic action, the missing planet of the analytic process, is to be found in the emotional transformation of the relationship with the analyst (Racker, Levenson, Gill, Hoffman, Greenberg, Spezzano). Interpretations fail because the patient experiences them as old and familiar modes of interaction. The reason interpretations work, when they do, is that the patient experiences them as something new and different, something not encountered before. The effective interpretation is the expression of, and sometimes the vehicle for, something deeper and more significant. *The central locus of analytic change is in the analyst's struggle to find a new way to participate, both within his own experience and then with the patient.* (Mitchell, 1997, pp. 51–52; emphasis added)

A further important and even more precise formulation of Mitchell's way of working is what we find in the section "The analytic compass" in Chapter 6, "The analyst's intentions," of his 1997 book *Influence and autonomy in psychoanalysis.* Here are Stephen's words on this:

> What is it that I try to do? I would describe the intention that shapes my methodology as a self-reflective responsiveness of a particular (psychoanalytic) sort. In putting it this way, I am suggesting that my way of working entails not a striving for a particular state of mind, but an engagement in a process.
>
> I find that aspiring to states of mind like 'evenly hovering attention' (Freud), the 'analytic attitude' (Schafer), and 'reverie' (Bion) forclose other possibilities, other kinds of responsiveness to my patients. There are times when it seems useful for my attention to be highly focused, not evenly hovering; there are times when I feel that my patients need a more genuine response from me, not an attitude; there are times when concerted, careful reasoning seems more fruitful than reverie. I find that I am using myself most productively when I struggle to understand the ways in which a patient is presenting himself to me in a particular session and then try to reflect on the kinds of responses I find myself asking. What version of myself is evoked by the patient's presence today? Who am I? What am I like when I am with him? (Mitchell, 1997, p. 193)

A little further on he writes:

> What I find most helpful is not aspiring to a state of non-intention, but remaining as open as possible to a flow of a variety of intentions, all of which become the object of self-reflective scrutiny . . . The analyst, in this view of analytic process, learns to track and engage in, simultaneously, different lines of thought, affective response, self-organization . . . This is why I find different sorts of inspiration from reading very different analytic writers. I have learned a great deal about detailed, focused inquiry from Sullivan, richly imaginative reverie from Ogden, emotional connection from Searles, a respect for the patient's privacy from Winnicott, a playfulness in the work of Adam Philips, a psychoanalytic form of sacredness from Loewald, and there are many more. What has been most useful to me has been the freedom to respond variously at different times and to be able to draw on a wide variety of potential responses in my repertoire when it seems useful. (Mitchell, 1997, pp. 193–194)

In order for the reader to better understand what these particular words of Mitchell mean to me, I suggest looking at Chapter 1, "Freud's objects – Plurality and complexity in the internal world and in the analyst's working self," of Stefano Bolognini's 2011 book *Secret passages. The theory and technique of intrapsychic relations.* In it, the former president of the SPI (2009–2013) and of the IPA (2013–2017) makes, from his own perspective, a very similar point: that our working self (which he distinguishes from the working ego) should have the chance to consult a whole variety of authors and colleagues, not only those of the tradition or the school in which we have been trained. In his own words:

In a paper dedicated to this formative background ("La famiglia interna dell'analista" [The analyst's internal family]; Bolognini, 2005), I pointed out the opportunity to enlarge the familial field of the professional self to a broadened structure including the equivalents of grandparents, uncles and aunts, cousins and analytic siblings because the totality of these figures, of these potential interlocutors, can constitute a considerable richness in furthering the aim of *internal consultation* during the clinical work. (Bolognini, 2011, p. 12)

Let me now come to the very last letter I received from Stephen, a typewritten letter that arrived on September 2, 1998:

Dear Marco,

I am writing to you on my vacation – I thought it would be a good time to keep in touch.

It sounds like the changes you made in your life are to the good. I hope things are working out with your Viennese girlfriend and your new analysis.

I was interested in your experience in Germany. I am going to speak at a conference in Lindau (Bodensee) in September. It is a conference put together by various German psychoanalytic institutes. I've had no contact at all with German analysts, so I am curious to see what it will be like.

Life has been hectic as usual here. My girls are growing up at an incredible speed. They are 12 and 15. We've been spending a lot of time playing tennis on the vacation – they are both pretty athletic – and it is a lot of fun for me.

Margaret and I are both doing well – and very busy. Our books seems to have been pretty well received. My newest book INFLUENCE AND AUTONOMY IN PA also seems to be finding sympathetic readers. Have you seen it? If my memory serves, I think I had a copy sent to you. If not, let me know and I will.

I am going to step down as editor of PD; it will be taken over by Lew Aron and Jody Davies. I am trying to find more time to write. Lew and I are editing a volume of key papers in relational psychoanalysis. My main project is a non-technical book on subjects like: romance, guilt, self-pity, etc. It is a real departure and challenge, and I am looking forward to having the time to really devote to it.

One year from October I am going to a conference in Lisbon on Fairbairn. So, I don't know if I will be coming back to Italy soon, although Margaret might be coming to Rome for a conference co-sponsored by NIP (she is on the board there).

Hope this letter finds you well and happy.

Warmest regards,
Steve

My first comment about this letter relates to what we have already seen as being Stephen's concern for his friends and his participation in their life, what made him a very good person to be in touch with, to do things with, and to have as a friend. Here we can also picture him as the lovely father sharing a series of sports with his daughters during their summer vacations. As far as Lindau on lake Constance is concerned, I make reference to it in my Afterword as the site of the Lindau Psychotherapy Weeks; to this I can add that Lindau hosts every two years the annual conference of the Deutsche Gesellschaft für Psychoanalyse, Psychotherapie, Psychosomatik und Tiefenpsychologie (DGPT), and this is the conference that Mitchell was invited to attend in September 1998.

Unfortunately, I was not also there with him, but I know very well the colleague who had had the idea of inviting Stephen to present one of the plenary papers, and who later wrote a very good Introduction to the German edition of Stephen's 2000 book *Relationality. From attachment to intersubjectivity*. This was Michael Buchholz, a member and training analyst of my German society, the Deutsche Psychoanalytische Gesellschaft (DPG) who lives in Göttingen and teaches at the International Psychoanalytic University (IPU) in Berlin. I know him well because he has been an associate editor of the *International Forum of Psychoanalysis* since 2008.

But, before dealing with this topic, let me finish my series of comments on this last letter of Stephen's. In it we can also see the very dynamic person he was, stepping down from his important role of editor of *Psychoanalytic Dialogues* to have more time for his writing—which was one of the things he loved most. As far as the conference in Lisbon is concerned, this was undoubtedly the conference organized by David Scharff and Francisco Pereira, at which he gave the paper "Fairbairn and the problem of agency" (Mitchell, 2002b). Last but not least, even though this was the final letter I received from Stephen, this was not our last contact. I saw him for the last time at the XIth IFPS Forum, organized in Brooklyn, New York, in May 2000. But before moving on to this, let me say a word about the reception of Mitchell's work in Germany.

Only three of Mitchell's books have been translated into German—*Relationality* (2000) in 2003, *Can love last?* (2002a) in 2004, and *Influence and autonomy in psychoanalysis* (1997) in 2005—and none of his articles has been translated. The second problem in the much more limited reception of his work in Germany, compared to Italy, is that given the delay and the low number of translations, German (and German-speaking) colleagues do not have any idea of the whole evolution and development of Mitchell's work, starting from his book with Greenberg (1983). As I wrote at the beginning of this chapter, the reception of Sullivan's work has also been very limited, only two books by him—*The psychiatric interview* (1954) in 1976 and *The interpersonal theory of psychiatry* (1953) in 1980—having been translated into German.

One of the main problems behind such a poor reception is the fact that most German colleagues in touch with the international dimension of psychoanalysis look much more to London than to New York in terms of analytic models, literature, and guidance. If Sullivan and Mitchell are little read, little known, and/or a taboo in London, this is also the case in Berlin. I have dealt with these and other aspects of the German analytic landscape in several monographic issues of the *International Forum of Psychoanalysis* that I have edited (see Conci, 2013, 2015)—as well as in Chapter 12 of this anthology. Last but not least, as you can see from the story underlying this chapter, the personal contact established through papers and supervisions is a crucial ingredient of the reception of a person's work abroad, and only a very limited number of colleagues had the chance to get to know and talk with Stephen in Germany—practically only those colleagues who met him in Lindau in September 1998. Had he lived longer, he would have certainly received more invitations to go to Germany, which would have much improved the chances that his work would have been well received in the German-speaking world.

In fact, in Germany there were indeed colleagues eager to get to know Stephen better and learn from him, as we can gather from the following words with which Michael Buchholz—in his Preface to the German edition of *Relationality*—presented the impression that Stephen had made upon him and his colleagues in Lindau:

> All those who could hear him speak got the impression of a man who was not only very friendly and open, but who could combine a unique intellectual clarity with a great clinical competence. Even more important was our experience that the clinical work of the so-called 'relational psychoanalysis' does not at all consist in the simplistic communication of the participation of the analyst, or in a continuous exchange of feelings, and that it in no way implies for the analyst not to have a point of view, or to continually communicate his fantasies, or to ignore the patient's past. On the contrary, we had the chance to convince ourselves that relational psychoanalysis is characterized by a useful anti-authoritarian aspect which frees the analyst from the necessity of always knowing what is going on, and which creates an analytic climate of salutary relatedness. (Buchholz, 2003, p. 7; my translation)

As we can gather from the Acknowledgements in *Relationality. From attachment to intersubjectivity*, the paper that Stephen gave in Lindau, on September 25,

1998, was an earlier version of Chapter 4 of the 2002 book, that is, "Attachment theory and relationality," which he also published in 1999 in *Psychoanalytic Dialogues*.

In the report of the XIth IFPS Forum in the *International Forum of Psychoanalysis* are the following words concerning Mitchell's paper:

> A similar anthropological stance is also what Stephen Mitchell stands for, as he argues in his paper "Varieties of relationality in changing cultural contexts", in which he presented the relational view-point he has been promoting since 1988 as a way leading to the self-awareness human beings cannot do without, no matter how society keeps changing their ways of living and relating to each other. (Conci, 2000, p. 265)

Stephen had spoken immediately after Marianne Horney Eckardt (born 1913), whose paper I had found very much in tune with Stephen's in terms of her proposing and articulating "a patient-oriented therapy free from constraints of theoretical and technical constructs" (Conci, 2000, p. 265). The first speaker of the panel—the second Saturday morning panel, chaired by Margit Winckler and José Del Pilar (both from the USA), with the title "Treatment dilemmas in a technological world. What happens to intimacy and relatedness?"—was the Brazilian colleague Horus Brazil, giving the paper "An ethic for the psychoanalyst in the post-modern age." While writing now about this panel, I have a thought that in my professional photo albums I might even have a picture of myself with Stephen and Marianne Horney Eckart, before the panel started. But my nicest memory of this last meeting with Stephen has of course to do with the fact that I was able to give him a copy of *Sullivan rivisitato*, my book on Sullivan that had just come out at the end of April 2000, after 12 years of work on this fascinating and complex topic.

I no longer remember when and how I learned about Stephen Mitchell's sudden and premature death on December 21, 2000, but it aroused in me "intense shock and pain," as Emanuel Berman wrote in his obituary in the *International Journal of Psychoanalysis* (Berman, 2001, p. 1267). Leaving aside a couple of potential quotations—concerning Mitchell's relationship to Sullivan's work and legacy and his relationship to the "analytic establishment"—which I will refer to in the last section of this chapter, I will limit myself here to quoting the words of Berman that so well capture how I experienced Stephen as a person and colleague and what he still means to me:

> Steve was known as a warm, communicative, informal and

accessible person, who could be quite determined and even stubborn about his beliefs, but never aloof, pompous or condescending. He was a generous mentor, earning the love and loyalty of many younger colleagues whom he encouraged and trusted. Having been a real team person, his projects are not at risk with his death . . . . Mitchell attached the highest importance to studying the work of Freud and other psychoanalytic pioneers, while maintaining his own critical independence. In concluding his statement of editorial philosophy, he expressed the hope that 'Freud's contemporary heirs . . . will help to continue to make psychoanalytic contributions, rather than venerable museum pieces, a generative center in the ongoing rush of modern thought' (Mitchell, 1991, p.6). He was very successful in creating such a generative climate. Using Loewald's powerful image, I believe Steve Mitchell will keep serving future generations of analysts as a lively ancestor, never turning into a hunting ghost but rather encouraging their continuous search for their own fresh voice. (Berman, 2001, p. 1271)

3. THE FURTHER RECEPTION OF MITCHELL'S WORK IN ITALY

I will divide this section into two parts. In the first, I will deal with the Italian editions of Mitchell's last two books, and in the second, I will look at the reception of his legacy in Italy, mostly in terms of the articles and books published about him after his death.

Starting to work in Munich as a guest professor in November 1997 gradually changed my life, to the point that I not only lost the regular contact I had had with Stephen Mitchell since 1988, but also missed the possibility to participate in the events leading to the foundation of the IARPP in 2001, and in its first international conference, held in New York City in January 2002. In the Afterword I discuss the reasons behind such a big step in my life and the ways in which life changed as a consequence. There I deal and develop a whole series of personal themes that played a central role in my professional development, for example that having been a high school exchange student in a New York suburb in the early 1970s was certainly an important ingredient in the relationship I developed with Stephen—and in its transferential aspects. But here what I would like to point out is that, in the late 1990s, not only was I busy with a new phase of my life, but even Bollati Boringhieri was undergoing such a crisis that it missed the possibility of publishing Stephen Mitchell's two last books.

Also due to the interest developed in Mitchell's work and in the IARPP by Vittorio Lingiardi (a psychiatrist and Jungian analyst from Milan who later became one of the most influential university professors of psychology in Italy), *Relationality* (2000; Italian edition, 2002) and *Can love last?* (2002a; Italian edition, 2003) were both published by the Milan publisher Raffaello Cortina, with whom Vittorio collaborated, and were translated by a very competent close collaborator of his, Francesco Gazzillo (who later became a well-known author in the field of empirical research in psychotherapy). This made Italy the only country in which all seven books written by Stephen Mitchell have been translated. Only the anthology on *Relational psychoanalysis. The emergence of a tradition*, which Stephen edited in 1999 with Lewis Aron, has not yet been translated into Italian—neither this anthology nor the following ones. In 2004 Raffaello Cortina also published Lewis Aron's *A meeting of minds: Mutuality in psychoanalysis* (see Aron, 1996), translated by the Rome colleagues Gianni Nebbiosi and Susanna Federici, a married couple of very competent colleagues who became the most important Italian members of the IARPP in the following years. Both belong to its Board of Directors, and Susanna Federici-Nebbiosi became the sixth president of the IARPP, after Lew Aron, Stuart Pizer, Hazel Hipp, Jeremy Safran, and Spyros Orfanos— and before Chana Ullman and Steven Kuchuck.

In 2011, Vittorio Lingiardi, Gherardo Amadei, Giorgio Caviglia, and Francesco De Bei edited *La svolta relazionale. Itinerari italiani*, in which there is no trace of Stephen as a person, or of all the events I have described in detail in this chapter. However, it contains a very well-researched documentation of the many ways in which Mitchell's work influenced the Italian psychoanalytic and psychotherapeutic landscape, particularly after his death. Some of the book's chapters were later published in *Psychoanalytic Dialogues* in 2014 in the form of contributions to a panel, introduced by Vittorio Lingiardi and Susanna Federici. I will first deal with this panel and later make a brief reference to some of the chapters that were left out of the panel or remained unknown to the readers of *Psychoanalytic Dialogues*.

But before doing this, I have to congratulate Francesco De Bei for having put together in 2016 an anthology of twelve papers by Stephen Mitchell, which he himself translated from English (Mitchell, 2016). I had already translated three of these in the 1990s (see the References at the end of this chapter), but there is no mention of this in the book—nor of any contact that Stephen might ever have had with Italy. Another merit of the De Bei volume is that he was able to involve Lewis

Aron in writing an Introduction to the anthology (De Bei and Aron, 2016), in which both illustrate the character and relevance of Mitchell's theoretical and clinical contributions and legacy. At variance with the attitude showed by the SPI in the 1990s, the book was promptly and positively reviewed by Giovanni Meterangelis (2017) in the *Rivista di Psicoanalisi*. Last but not least, I know from Cesare Albasi (an associate professor of psychology at the University of Turin) that he is preparing the Italian edition of the handbook on relational psychoanalysis recently edited by Roy Barsness, *Core competences in relational psychoanalysis*. Cesare was one of the very first students of psychology to write, in the mid-1990s, a *tesi di laurea in psicologia* on Stephen Mitchell's work, for which he contacted me for advice; relational psychoanalysis has continued to inform his scientific production ever since (see, for example, Albasi, 2006).

Here is what Lingiardi and Federici write about the book *La svolta relazionale. Itinerari italiani* in their "Introduction to the panel" in *Psychoanalytic Dialogues*:

> Virtually all of the contributions independently started with the sentence: 'The official entry of relational psychoanalysis in Italy can be traced back to 1986, with the translation of the book written by Greenberg and Mitchell in 1983 entitled *Object relations in psychoanalytic theory*' (as you can imagine, this created an editing problem but also gave us a starting perspective!). However, for a variety of reasons that are clearly illustrated by the volume, and will be addressed in the articles we present to you, relational psychoanalysis took hold only some ten/fifteen years later. As of 2000, many professionals and academics followed with interest the founding of IARPP, enrolling in the association and participating actively in its conferences (New York, 2002 and 2012; Toronto, 2003; Los Angeles, 2004; Rome, 2005; Boston, 2006; Athens, 2007; Tel Aviv, 2009; San Francisco, 2010; Madrid, 2011; Santiago, 2013), thereby laying the foundations for dialogue not just with colleagues from other countries but also among Italian colleagues. (Lingiardi and Federici, 2014, p. 559)

If these words alone are sufficient to justify the importance for me of having written this chapter, which can now fill a large hole in the history of the reception of Mitchell's work in Italy, they at the same time allow me to formulate a series of questions. But before doing this, let me also say that—at variance with the above-reported claim by Lingiardi and Federici—neither in the book nor in the articles in *Psychoanalytic Dialogues* can the reader find any mention of what went on between 1986 and 2000. In fact, the time between 1986 and 2000 represents the very important "incubation time," during which Stephen Mitchell went to Italy three times (1988, 1991, and 1996) and five of his books were translated (Italian editions: Greenberg and Mitchell, 1986; Mitchell, 1993 [1988]; Mitchell, 1995 [1993]; Mitchell and Black, 1996 [1995]; Mitchell, 1999 [1997]), apparently being read and digested by a large audience. And now I come to my questions: since Vittorio Lingiardi (whom I have personally known since the early 1990s) and Susanna Federici (I must have met her in 2004) themselves knew about the role I played in what I am calling the "incubation time 1986–2000," why did they not adequately mention my contribution? And why did the editors of the book *La svolta relazionale. Itinerari italiani* not invite me to contribute a chapter on such an important "incubation time," which I had dealt with not only in my 1993 Introduction to his 1988 book (see above), but also in the papers I mentioned at the beginning of this chapter?

If I had felt hurt by these omissions in both the 2011 book and the 2014 journal articles in *Psychoanalytic Dialogues*, this is now not the main reason why I am raising the problem. I am emphasizing this mainly in order to introduce what I would call "the political dimension of psychoanalysis," which I find necessary for dealing with Mitchell's legacy, as I will try to do in the next section. At the same time, only a consideration of such a political dimension can, for example, allow me to make the following hypothesis: the four editors (and, at the same time, authors) of the 2011 book are (or, better, were, since Gherardo Amadei unfortunately died in 2016, at the age of sixty-five) university professors, a role that I formally gave up in the spring of 2000 (see the Afterword). This is probably the reason why they forgot to contact me—I was no longer around. But now, in order to further substantiate such a hypothesis, let me deal with a specific event that Gianni Nebbiosi and Susanna Federici write about in their own article in *Dialogues*, with the title "The relational model: International relations and dissemination in Italy: A historical account."

First, let me introduce you to their article. Although they mention me by first and last name in connection with my 1993 Introduction to the Italian edition of Mitchell's 1988 book (Nebbiosi and Federici, 2014, p. 591), and they claim to follow Lewis Aron's 1996 principle (see Aron, 1996, p. 3) of concentrating their report upon their own participation in the dissemination of the Relational Model, they sound to me too reductionistic when they write that what they will do in the article will be to:

> attempt to describe how the relational model spread in Italy primarily from the microcosm of the Institute that we founded

– Istituto di Specializzazione in Psicologia Psicoanalitica del
Sé e Psicoanalisi Relazionale – and in which we tried to create
a context within which we could discover the contemporary
theories and meet the psychoanalysts who gave life to the
relational movement. (Nebbiosi and Federici, 2014, p.
591)

Both were present at the 1996 Florence conference
mentioned above, with Mitchell (their names are in
the list of participants that I still have a copy of), and I
met them in the spring of 2004 (at a self-psychological
and relational conference in Germany), where I had the
chance to further inform them about what I called "the
incubation phase" described in this chapter. In other
words, they knew about it and they could have spent
some more words on it—rather than let everything begin
only with their own contribution to the whole story of the
reception of Mitchell's work in Italy.

I value Gianni Nebbiosi and Susanna Federici as
colleagues, I admire their work, and it is true that—
through the foundation of their Rome institute and the
very many international meetings they have promoted—
they have played a crucial role in promoting the study and
dissemination of the Relational Model in Italy. As they
wrote in detail in their article, they found and kept going
for years what I also think to have been the best way to
import a new brand of psychoanalysis into our country,
that is, the creation around themselves of a whole group
of colleagues interested in the topic and in the specific
kind of training they could offer. This allowed them to
become esteemed and important partners of the whole,
very successful, international process of personal and
professional exchange promoted by the IARPP.

Having been introduced to self psychology by
the Italian SPI analyst Franco Paparo, and as Gianni
Nebbiosi had already collaborated for years with a group
in Rome that had introduced Bion's work into Italy,
they were ready—due to both their professional and
linguistic competence—to join the international analytic
community and soon become esteemed members of
it. The first contact took place in October 1995, in San
Francisco, at the XVIIth International Conference of
Self Psychology, where, as they write, their "research
found . . . a point of reference that has remained constant
to date" (Nebbiosi and Federici, 2014, p. 593). A month
later—as we can read in their article—they organized
in Rome their first international meeting, with Robert
Stolorow as a keynote speaker, and since then they have
never stopped working for the dissemination of self

psychology and relational psychoanalysis in Italy. In 1998 they invited Lewis Aron to Rome and then translated into Italian his 1996 book—just one of a whole series of books they have personally translated. In 1999, they founded their Rome institute, the Istituto di Specializzazione in Psicologia Psicoanalitica del Sé e Psicoanalisi Relazionale (ISIPSé), which was recognized by the Italian Ministry for University and Research as a school of psychotherapy in 2005. In June of the same year, the IARPP's IVth International Conference took place in Rome, with Gianni Nebbiosi and Emanuel Berman as co-chairs and with more than 600 participants. In 2012—to cut the story short—Susanna Federici, as already mentioned above, was elected president of the IARPP. I not only think that Gianni and Susanna deserve to have gone such a long way both in Italy and internationally, but I even totally agree with the concluding remarks of their article, centered around the crucial role of a personal contact with the foreign colleagues who inspire us, in order to really grasp and assimilate their contributions. This was always my way of dealing with this aspect of training, and it is also theirs!

But let me now come to the specific event I was hinting at above:

> In the spring of 2000 Nebbiosi went to the Division 39 conference in San Francisco in order to meet Mitchell, whom he had invited to come to Italy the following year. They had a long meeting and took an immediate liking to each other: two months later Mitchell invited Nebbiosi to sit on the founding Board of the International Association of Relational Psychoanalysis and Psychotherapy, IARPP. Unfortunately Mitchell died unexpectedly in December of that year . . . In spite of this terrible loss, the IARPP was founded and the first conference was held in January 2002 in New York City, registering the extraordinary turnout of some twelve hundred participants. Lewis Aron was its first president and Gianni Nebbiosi the vice president. (Nebbiosi and Federici, 2014, p. 597)

What can we now deduce from this story? In my view, we can understand it only if we—again—introduce the political dimension of psychoanalysis, and of the Relational Turn, in the form of the IARPP. From this point of view, the problem is similar to the one formulated above, that is, "Should I contact Marco or not?"—which Stephen Mitchell must have asked himself thinking of me, who had collaborated with him since 1988. My own answer is that Stephen was right in picking Gianni and not me, since Gianni had a whole group behind him and was in the position to invite many North American colleagues to Rome to teach and supervise, whereas I was not at all in such a position. On the other hand, even if I am ready to agree with Stephen on such a choice, I insist at the same time on the necessity of claiming that—if this is true—we are no longer talking of psychoanalysis, but of "psychoanalytic politics." In other words, we are not talking about relational psychoanalysis (on which I was at the time one of the best Italian experts), but about its institutionalization in the form of the IARPP—an aspect that in fact interested me less and for which I was not as well equipped as I was for the scientific aspect. Last but not least, I repeat the fact that I have been introducing this new vertex of the discussion because I believe that, not only in the case of Sullivan, but also in the case of Mitchell, there is no way of evaluating their legacy if not by taking into account both aspects of it—the scientific and the political aspects.

After reading a previous draft of this chapter, a colleague of the White Institute who also knew Mitchell well and who had also had the chance to experience his generosity, told me that, according to her, Mitchell must, at the time, certainly have told Gianni Nebbiosi to invite me to collaborate with him at his Institute. I do not know whether this was in fact the case, but such an invitation never occurred. On the other hand, I am myself sure of the fact that, had Stephen lived longer, he would have certainly helped me to find a North American publisher for my book on Sullivan, having himself not only encouraged me to write it, but also assisted me across the whole work.

Returning now to the content of the articles in *Psychoanalytic Dialogues*, I can say that the same strategy (if this is the right word!) of omission and a similar surprising lack of adequate information is also present in the article by Giorgio Caviglia and Vittorio Lingiardi, "The fortunes of the relational model in Italy: Notes on publishing, teaching and training." I am referring here to what they say about the journal *Psicoterapia e Scienze Umane* and about the Milan ASP, both of which I have already amply talked about above. Discussing the topic of what it meant that the journal founded by Pier Francesco Galli in 1967 "contributed so much to the spread of relational thought in Italy" (Caviglia and Lingiardi, 2014, p. 582), they come to the conclusion that "they did so not because they adhered to the relational movement, but because of their commitment to being open to the dialogue between different models and standpoints, and for a love of research and cultural dissemination" (p. 582). If I, on the one hand, fully agree with this conclusion, I must on the other hand say that the authors seem to lack a real understanding of how the journal worked and still works today, to the point of producing a version of the facts totally at variance with the one I have already given.

Let me give you another couple of examples, very similar to the ones I described above. In the fall of 1990, Stephen Mitchell and Paul Stepansky of Analytic Press sent me the book *Self psychology: Comparisons and contrasts*, edited in 1989 by Detrick and Detrick, asking me if I could propose to Pier Francesco Galli that I translate Philip Bromberg's chapter "Interpersonal psychoanalysis and self psychology: A clinical comparison" (Bromberg, 1989) for his journal. The editor of *Psicoterapia e Scienze Umane* said yes, and I translated Bromberg's very interesting chapter, which came out in the journal in 1993. I took a similar approach for my reviews of books such as Jay Greenberg's *Oedipus and beyond* (see Conci, 1994a) and Skolnick's and Warshaw's *Relational perspectives in psychoanalysis* (see Conci 1994c), that is, I proposed reviewing the books, my proposal was accepted, I wrote the review, and the review was published in the journal. In other words, one of the well-known ingredients of the success of *Psicoterapia e Scienze Umane* was the fact that Pier Francesco Galli was able to attract a whole series of—allow me the word—"brilliant" young colleagues who would feel free to make him the editorial proposals that suited themselves best. So most of the relational articles and reviews published at the time in the journal resulted from my proposals, as opposed to their being the result of some higher editorial policy—the same being true of Mitchell's invitation to Bologna in 1991 (see above).

At the same time, however, I never really had the feeling that, by doing this, either I or the journal was doing anything else than promoting not relational psychoanalysis per se, but simply a closer contact with the international analytic debate. Again, I have known the editors of *La svolta relazionale. Itinerari italiani* for many years: why did they not ask me directly? Indeed, I have learned very much from Pier Francesco Galli as an editor, that is, I have with my collaborators of the *International Forum of Psychoanalysis* the same attitude of promoting a free climate of exchange and collaboration with the journal that I had experienced with him.

A similar lack of precision concerns their report on the Milan ASP, which Caviglia and Lingiardi refer to in the same article, together with the ISIPSé (see above) and the Rome SIPRe, as being the main three Italian psychotherapy training institutes in which relational psychoanalysis was able to take hold. If it is true that one of the main emphases of the training I did there myself between 1988 and 1993 (see Chapter 10 and the Afterword) is represented by "the centrality of the therapeutic relation and the necessity of having an anti-ideological and anti-authoritarian approach in psychoanalytic institutions and practice" (Caviglia and Lingiardi, 2014, p. 585), I must admit that both the SPP (that is, the school) and the ASP (that is, the association) gave much less room to interpersonal and relational psychoanalysis than I had expected after being able to have Mitchell come to Milan to discuss his work in April 1991 (see above). As far as I am concerned, I would very much have liked to teach interpersonal and relational psychoanalysis at the Milan SPP, but I was never invited to do this. In fact, a so-called "anti-authoritarian approach" can also imply a selection of the teaching staff not made according to openly declared and democratically shared standards.

At this point, as an aside, I would like to say the following. When I realized that my desire to become a member of the teaching staff of the Milan SPP did not coincide with the orientation and choices of the institute's board, I thought that it might have been good to create my own institute —as Gianni Nebbiosi and Susanna Federici did in Rome. But, as you can read in the Afterword, a whole series of factors contributed to my going in a variety of other directions, and I do not at all regret the alternative choices I took. Let me identify here at least some of the factors involved. On the one hand, for example, being native of Trento, I was not well enough rooted in any big Italian big town, where a new institute would be most likely to survive and flourish, nor did I have the financial resources of my own to invest in such a project. On the other hand, my priority was not to teach, but to keep learning, learning and writing—and to possibly complete my own training inside an IPA society. This is why I ended up moving to Munich, and creating for myself a new way of life that would allow me not to have to give up my Italian identity and background. Being Italian but being fluent in English and German eventually allowed me to become the co-editor-in-chief of the *International Forum of Psychoanalysis* (in Bilbao, in June 2007), a role in which I always felt and still feel very much fulfilled, both personally and professionally.

If what I have written so far on the reception and dissemination of relational psychoanalysis in Italy does not go in the direction of the type of open and constructive analytic dialogue among colleagues that Mitchell hoped to contribute to through his journal (see above), let me give you an idea of the contents of two of the remaining chapters of the book *La svolta relazionale. Itinerari italiani*—a book for whose variety of topics the editors must be congratulated. These are the chapter written by Giuseppe Moccia and Giovanni Meterangelis on "Relational psychoanalysis and Freudian psychoanalysis" (see Moccia and Meterangelis, 2011), and the chapter by Vittorio Lingiardi and Francesco De Bei on "The relational turn in psychotherapy research" (see Lingiardi and De Bei, 2011). Among the book chapters not included in the above-mentioned panel in *Psychoanalytic Dialogues* are also the chapter by Massimo Giannoni on "Relational psychoanalysis and Jungian psychology," and the chapter by Giovanni Liotti (1945–2018) on "The relational paradigm in the cognitive approach," which, for reasons of space, I must also omit summarizing.

Let me try to briefly summarize what the two SPI colleagues Moccia and Meterangelis write about the impact of relational psychoanalysis on the analytic debate going on in the SPI between the late 1980s and the late 2000s. The premise they start from is the opinion shared by many Italian analysts as to the creative coexistence in Freud's work of both drive and relational aspects. But what made Italian SPI analysts receptive to Mitchell's relational turn was not only the early reception of Bion's work promoted by Francesco Corrao (1922–1994)—an analysand of the already mentioned Baltic Baroness Tomasi di Lampedusa—as early as 1962, but also the commitment of many Italian analysts to analytically working with the sickest patients, that is, those with whom the relational aspect is often more important than the purely interpretative one.

Also contributing to such an Italian openness to the relational aspects of clinical work was the clinical work done by many young analysts in the new psychiatric centers promoted by the "Basaglia Law," that is, the Psychiatric Reform Law of 1978. A further facilitating role was played by the early rediscovery of Ferenczi's legacy in the mid-1970s, by the possibility to discuss clinical materials with such important foreign analysts as Bion (1897–1979) himself (see his *Italian seminars*; Bion, 2005) and Herbert Rosenfeld (1910–1986), and by the exposure to the whole field of infant research I mentioned above, when I dealt with the Rome Day Conference with Mitchell of April 1991. In other words, although the study of Mitchell's work and of relational psychoanalysis at large was never included in formal analytic training, any

Italian SPI colleagues could read his books and profit from them. But here are the two authors' tentative conclusions:

> However, the influence of relational psychoanalysis in its various forms and declinations did contribute to enrich the landscape of Italian psychoanalysis, giving to it a character of multiplicity of perspectives very different from the unitarian character of, for example, French psychoanalysis. We could even say that such 'relational contaminations' of the body of Italian psychoanalysis greatly stimulated the development of a research process on the 'relational origins' of our very analytic foundations, thus further facilitating the dialogue among our different models. (Moccia and Meterangelis, 2011, p. 194; my translation)

Indeed, I know many Italian SPI colleagues who have read Stephen Mitchell's books, and benefited from them, who value his contributions to contemporary psychoanalysis, who have dealt with similar problems (as Ferro and Bolognini have done; see above), or who have developed what one could call their own "relational perspective." These include, to name but a few: Antonino Ferro (SPI president, 2013–2017; Pavia) and Giuseppe Civitarese (former editor, 2013–2017, of the *Rivista di psicoanalisi*; also from Pavia); Stefano Bolognini (Bologna); Franco Borgogno (Turin); Anna Ferruta and Franco De Masi (Milan); and Claudio Neri, Domenico Chianese (SPI president, 2001–2005), Vincenzo Bonaminio and Anna Nicolò (the current SPI president), all from Rome. As I reported above, Massimo Ammaniti, Antonello Correale, Giuseppe Martini, and Giordano Fossi originally participated in helping me promote Mitchell's work—the former in Rome, in April 1991, and the other ones in Florence, in April 1996. In fact, the first time I met each one of the colleagues listed above, I had the feeling that they already knew who I was, that is, the "relatively 'younger' colleague who had helped Stephen Mitchell promote his work in Italy." In other words, they seemed all to be aware of the role I had played in what I have above called "the incubation time in the reception of Mitchell's work in Italy." Last but not least, it would of course make sense to do a small amount of research into which colleagues I have just mentioned explicitly make reference to Mitchell in their publications, and which ones limit themselves to giving him credit in private—in the personal conversations I had with them.

Last but not least, the above-mentioned chapter by Lingiardi and De Bei allows us to become aware of the very creative implications of Stephen Mitchell's relational psychoanalysis for contemporary empirical research in psychotherapy. Although this topic was not of particular interest for Mitchell (and the authors start their chapter mentioning the "Grünbaum syndrome" he had described in his 1997 book), the topic of the analytic relationship has become more and more central in the field. In the authors' words:

> Today, a large part of research in psychotherapy, and not only the psychodynamically oriented research, centers more and more around the study of the therapeutic relationship and of the personality traits of therapist and patient. But, more than this: the field itself has been deeply influenced by the relational approach, and this to the point that its philosophy of inquiry and the data gathered in the last years are characterized by . . . many affinities with contemporary relational thought: Countertransference, therapeutic empathy, self-disclosure, patient-therapist attachment, ruptures and reparations of the relationship, etc., are all central aspects of the field aspects of contemporary psychotherapy research. (Lingiardi and De Bei, 2011, pp. 101–102; my translation)

4. MITCHELL REVISITED: A CLOSE LOOK FROM AFAR

For this last section, I ended up choosing a similar title to that of Chapter 4 because of the deep affinity I always felt between Stephen Mitchell and Harry Stack Sullivan, not only in terms of the main aspects of their work and legacy, but also in terms of some aspects of their personality and professional profile. In fact, I had dedicated to the topic of their affinity the very last section of my book *Sullivan revisited – Life and work*, under the title "A turning point: Relational psychoanalysis" (Conci, 2012b, pp. 447–450). In this, I characterized Sullivan's work and legacy in terms of his impressive clinical competence, his interdisciplinary orientation, his epistemological sensibility, and—last but not least—his desire to go beyond Freud, and to create a "post-Freudian psychoanalysis," that is, what I would today also call his "political agenda." I also claimed not only that Mitchell shared these four qualities, but also that his work and legacy could best be summarized in this way.

As far as Sullivan's clinical competence as well as the priority he gave to the clinical dimension is concerned, just think of books such as *The psychiatric interview* and *Clinical studies in psychiatry*; for his interdisciplinary orientation, think of books such as *The interpersonal theory of psychiatry* and *The fusion of psychiatry and social science*; and for his epistemological sensibility, think in the first place of *Schizophrenia as a human process*, that is, of schizophrenia as "the epistemological challenge" it rightly represented for him, as it did for most of the great researchers in the field of schizophrenia. Last but not least, as far as the fourth characteristic of Sullivan's work and legacy is concerned, it materialized in the foundation of a whole series of private institutions, such as the Washington School of Psychiatry (1936), the journal *Psychiatry* (1938), and the New York William Alanson White Institute, which he founded in 1943 together with Erich Fromm, Frieda Fromm-Reichmann, Clara Thompson, and Janet and David Rioch.

And what about Stephen Mitchell? I always experienced him—and not only through his books—as a very good clinician. His books and his work are based upon a whole series of interdisciplinary data, are full of his passion for philosophy, and are intellectually very well connected to the postmodern intellectual climate. The same is true for the epistemological contents of his work, with particular regard to his use of Thomas Kuhn's theory of scientific revolutions to support his own version of post-Freudian psychoanalysis. Last but not least are his own institutions: the Relational Track at New York University Postdoctoral Program (1988; see Aron, 1996, for the best story about it), the journal *Psychoanalytic Dialogues* (1991), and the IARPP (2001).

The perception of these affinities between Mitchell and Sullivan has of course to do not only with the passion for Sullivan's work that I always felt we shared, and with the way in which I experienced Mitchell as a person, senior colleague, and mentor, but also with the many years I spent studying and writing about Sullivan and his work. As far as their personal and professional traits are concerned, both unfortunately died at a very early age (Sullivan at fifty-seven and Mitchell at fifty-four), and this not only—I believe—because of a similar cardiovascular constitution (leading to a stroke in Sullivan's case, and sudden heart failure in Mitchell's case, as the causes of their deaths), but also because of their uncommon generosity and their courage to go out of their way, to work with colleagues on a whole series of projects. As we have already seen, Emanuel Berman called Mitchell "a real team person" whose "projects are not at risk with his death" (Berman, 2001, p. 1271), and the same was of course true of Sullivan. I do not know of any author in our field for whom most of their books came out after their death—six out of seven in the case of Sullivan. Here is what Jay Greenberg wrote in this regard about Stephen in his 2001 obituary: "Nobody in our field has participated in the creation and growth of so many training facilities, nationally and internationally, as Steve did" (Greenberg,

2001, p. 190). In other words, both Sullivan and Mitchell greatly loved both teaching and supervising, as well as transmitting to their colleagues and candidates their great passion for our field.

As I reported above, this is also the reason why I spent so much time studying their work. In fact, I also agree with Berman when—in his obituary of Mitchell—he writes that Greenberg and Mitchell "served Sullivan's contribution by their inclusive approach—dialectically transcending both orthodoxy and heterodoxy—much better than it was served by the counter-exclusion practiced by 'pure' Sullivanians" (Berman, 2001, p. 1268). Both Greenberg and Mitchell were as charismatic and independent-minded as Sullivan himself was, to an extent that was unknown in the circle of the "pure" Sullivanians. Last but not least, I am starting this last section re-proposing my point of view of 2000, of the affinity between Mitchell and Sullivan, because I do not know any colleague who ever entertained it—besides, albeit only partially, Berman himself. Or, to put it perhaps better: I do not know of any colleague who has valued or disagreed with such a perspective of mine.

Of course, Stephen Mitchell was for me a friend and a mentor, and it is not easy for me to look at him as just an "analytic author," as basically do, for example, both Arnold Richards and Morris Eagle in their critiques of his work, which I will deal with below. In fact, I do not even particularly like to look at our colleagues just as "analytic authors," and this is in fact a concept that this whole book is centered around. Both Stefano Bolognini and Horst Kächele, for example, are not just analytic authors, but in the first place real *Gesprächspartner* (German), that is, *interlocutori* (Italian) or "interlocutors" (English) (see Chapters 11 and 12, and my Afterword, for the development of my basic dialogical attitude), whose personal profiles and biographies are also very important to me. In fact, this reminds me that not only have I never written a book review on a book I did not like or consider worthwhile reading, but also I have often sent my provisional review to the author of the book I was reviewing, asking him if I had understood him correctly! If Stephen Mitchell might have had a formative—dialogical—influence on such of my attitudes, he certainly played a key role in terms of my whole professional development, in terms of the following aspect of his legacy, and the way in which Emanuel Berman talks about it:

> Steve himself was not an IPA member, because neither the White Institute nor the NUY Postdoctoral Program joined

the IPA . . . He turned down a personal invitation to join the American Psychoanalytic Association, saying he could not join an organization which would not accept his students. Paradoxically, Mitchell's prominence contributed to the erosion of boundaries between 'establishment' and 'anti-establishment' in American psychoanalysis. Owen Renik, the editor of the *Psychoanalytic Quarterly* since 1992, who has developed his own version of relational psychoanalysis, welcomed Mitchell in his journal. Arnold Richards, the editor of *JAPA* since 1994, while critical of Mitchell's positions (which in fact aroused intense polemics), has advocated an open dialogue with relational views, and encourages participation by relational authors. The editors of the *International Journal of Psychoanalysis* invited Mitchell to join its North American Editorial Board (1997–1999). This was, to the best of my knowledge, the first time a non-IPA member filled such a position, and a clear indication that the boundaries of meaningful psychoanalytic discourse no longer coincide with organizational boundaries. (Berman, 2001, pp. 1269–1270)

Berman formulates this aspect of Mitchell's legacy so well in this quotation that I will take his formulation one step further, in the following way: for me the most important aspect of Mitchell's legacy consists in his crucial contribution to the creation of a new psychoanalytic landscape, that is, a situation in which "the boundaries of meaningful psychoanalytic discourse no longer coincide with organizational boundaries" (Berman, 2001, p. 1270). It was because of this new situation that I was able to think it might be possible for me to find a way of joining the IPA, which I had the chance to do through the DPG, after having graduated from a non-IPA institute (see also the Afterword). Of course, from this point of view, my priority was not to become a "relational analyst," but "an analyst *tout court*"; to put it better, my opinion and experience is that we theoretically need—given the way in which analytic training is still organized today—both a non-IPA and an IPA training, that is, both a training centered around working analytically with any patient ready to do it, and a training centered only around those patients for whom there is a clear indication for an intensive analytic treatment on the couch. This is also how I ended up thinking that we need to create a new dialogical dimension, in which Freud, Sullivan, Mitchell, and Bion—for example—can talk, through us, with each other.

But the positive consequences of such a legacy go of course beyond my own professional development, and also concern—as Berman himself claimed—the whole world of psychoanalytic journals. The *International Forum of Psychoanalysis* is also a typical product of such a new climate: from its very beginning, Christopher Bollas was our consulting editor; for many years, Henry Zvi Lothane and André Haynal have collaborated with us as corresponding editors; and since 2007 Franco Borgogno has been an associate editor, directly associated with the production of every single issue. In fact, he is also a very active member of the editorial board of the *International Journal of Psychoanalysis*—with which I have also collaborated as a referee since 2013. In other words, I believe we can say that through both his independent-minded way of dealing with analytic institutions, that is, on the one hand, his own institute, the White Institute, and the New York University Postdoctoral Program, and, on the other hand, the APsaA and the IPA, and through his foundation of new—open and more permeable—institutions such as *Psychoanalytic Dialogues* and the IARPP, Stephen Mitchell became one of the pioneers of the creation of a new interinstitutional space, and this is for me—as I have already said—his most important legacy.

But let me now go back to a more precise characterization of what I have called the "political agenda" that I believe Mitchell inherited from Sullivan. Let me try to characterize it better, and to see where it actually came from. Here is, for example, what Mitchell wrote in one of his most-cited articles, "The analyst's knowledge and authority" (1998), in the section entitled "Knowledge claims: Excessive and legitimate":

> First, there are the cultist features of traditional psychoanalytic institutions and literature. Analysts have often claimed for themselves an esoteric knowledge of mysterious realms expressed in a thick jargon that is inaccessible to the uninitiated. Because they felt they had singular, proprietary rights over access to the unconscious, some traditional psychoanalytic authors claimed a unique knowledge of the underpinnings of all human experience . . . Second, there has been a strong authoritarian current to the political management of psychoanalysis, at times almost Stalinist in proportions. From Freud's 'Secret Committee', to the banishment of dissidents, to the kind of control Melanie Klein maintained over the minds and the publications of his followers (see Grosskurth, 1986), to the medicalization of psychoanalysis in the United States and the sometimes medieval practices of both the American Psychoanalytic Association and the International Psychoanalytical Association, the reigning political powers within psychoanalysis have hardly allowed psychoanalytic theorizing to flourish in an atmosphere of freedom and open exchange. But like the Bolsheviks, the guardians of psychoanalysis often seemed not to grasp that the greater danger is not the wrong ideas but rigidly held ideas. This has become much clearer to us today, and part of the vitality of post-classical psychoanalysis comes from its

> emancipation from the constraints of Freudian orthodoxy . . .
> In recent years there has been a broad-scale democratization
> of psychoanalytic institutes that has been constructive and
> liberating. And there have been attempts to democratize the
> analytic relationship. (Mitchell, 1998, pp. 5–6)

Leaving aside for now the technical implications of such a "democratization," which I will look at later in this section, let me provide a couple of other quotations aimed at better understanding Mitchell's political background and orientation.

Very useful from this point of view are the following two testimonies from Jay Greenberg. The first is the fourth section of the already-mentioned obituary that he published in *Contemporary Psychoanalysis*, dealing with Stephen's family background and its influence on his choice of his "analytic heroes":

> Many of Steve's stories about growing up were focused on
> political and social debate in his family, and he was most
> drawn to those colorful characters in the family who despised
> prevailing orthodoxies. It is not surprising, then, that from
> the beginning of his professional career he devoted himself
> to taking on psychoanalytic conventions that he found
> stultifying. He was a radical, but a radical with deep respect
> for the contributions of others. Steve had his intellectual
> heroes; within psychoanalysis there were (among others)
> Sullivan, Klein, Fairbairn, and eventually Loewald. These
> thinkers, and the others whom Mitchell admired, were
> outsiders; each followed his own inner voice. But each was
> anchored in a tradition that gave depth and texture to his
> break with the past. That was the kind of mind that Steve
> loved, and that was the kind of mind that he had. (Greenberg,
> 2001, p. 190)

And here is how Jay described—in the third section of his Foreword to the 2003 Memorial Issue—the kind of conversations that he and Stephen used to have at the time of their training while sitting in their favorite Chinese restaurant; these concerned how they used to experience and deal with the fact that the medical monopoly over psychoanalysis promoted by the APsaA forbade them to identify themselves as "real psychoanalysts":

> In retrospect, I realize that the conversations Steve and
> I were having were unusual for the time. For one thing,
> in keeping with what we had learned in the course of our
> training, when we talked about 'psychoanalysis' we spoke
> in the same breath of Freud and the ego psychologists and
> Sullivan and Fairbairn. For another, we assumed that *we*
> were psychoanalysts, despite being psychologists and despite
> not having been trained in an institute of the American
> Psychoanalytic Association. Of course, we were aware – with
> a mixture of self-doubt and pride that I remember mostly as
> a wordless experience – that our claims to professional status
> would not be accepted by the most orthodox analysts. But
> those analysts seemed so distant to us that what they thought

did not seem to matter much. For the most part, we were untouched by our exclusion. (Greenberg, 2003, p. 353)

But in Greenberg's 2003 Foreword we can also find what he defines as the "continuity in Steve Mitchell's personal psychoanalytic journey from its origins in the book that he and I coauthored to his eventual role as the leader of an emergent theoretical tradition," that is:

> Steve insisted, in what became a central tenet of the relational approach, that analysts must think about and openly talk about what actually goes on in psychoanalytic sessions, to the extent that what goes on can be reported by an analyst making a good-faith effort to do so. This has lead to major changes in the nature of our discourse, because it has fundamentally changed the data from which we develop our theories. This stands in contrast to traditional ways of reporting, which tend to focus on the specific events that the analyst considers salient . . . The broader demands of relational thinking require that analysts include accounts of their own experience in clinical reports . . . Beyond this, the model stresses that we must consider the ways in which analysands' associations are responsive to the behavior and attitude of the analyst . . . These new emphases lead to fuller versions of what actually happens in psychoanalytic sessions. This makes it possible, over time and as trusting conversations among colleagues from different backgrounds develop, to talk about how theory influences our work . . . . Thus, the relational perspective forms a matrix that can help to organize a range of different approaches, facilitating discussions among theorists who might not otherwise be talking to each other. This is true regardless of how any individual theorist might feel about the particular conceptual nuances that characterize relational psychoanalysis itself. Steve's insistence on the centrality of the relational field in the psychoanalytic process – a vision that is increasingly accepted by analysts of all theoretical persuasions – provides a sense of shared experience that makes it possible to talk. All analysts have the relational field in common, even if we operate very differently within it. (Greenberg, 2003, pp. 357–358)

In other words, this is Greenberg's version of how Mitchell was able to create the interinstitutional space I talked about above, putting it in connection with not only his family background and his aspiration to "equal conditions for all," but also his marginalization as an analytic candidate and his understandable aspiration to be measured on the basis of the quality of his clinical work, and not on the basis of the institution in which he was training. From this point of view, what we can call Mitchell's "relational injection" into contemporary psychoanalysis simply means: "Let us find a game we can all play together! Only by doing this, does our profession make sense (and can we have fun doing it); and, at the same time, psychoanalysis can significantly evolve as a discipline!"

From this point of view, it is no sheer coincidence that Mitchell's 1996 visit to Florence coincided with two events. First was the presence of a series of discussants belonging to both the SPI and to two of the three Italian IFPS member societies (the Istituto di Psicoterapia Analitica, Florence, and SIPRe, Rome). Second, as I hinted in the Afterword, it became the meeting place of a whole series of colleagues who, on the afternoon of the same day (Saturday April 13, 1996), gathered together on the initiative of Marco Bacciagaluppi (Milan) to agree on the foundation of a new interinstitutional organization, the Organizzazione degli Psicoanalisti Italiani—Federazione e Registro (OPIFER). The formal foundation took place the following November (Bacciagaluppi, 1998).

OPIFER's aim was, and still is, to create a network of exchange and collaboration among all the Italian psychotherapy institutes working outside the SPI, with particular regard to the possibility of organizing clinical conferences at which its members' clinical work could be discussed. Since 1996 OPIFER has been organizing regular Italian-North American meetings with the American Academy of Psychoanalysis and Dynamic Psychiatry and with the German E. Fromm Society. Sergio Dazzi (Parma), with whom I edited the anthology on the interpersonal tradition is himself one of the past presidents of this organization, as are Marco Bacciagaluppi, Sergio Caruso (Florence), and Pietro Andujar (Milan). One of the first important events organized by OPIFER and by the American Academy was the conference "A psychiatrist between two cultures – Silvano Arieti, 1914–1981 – The sense of psychosis," held in Arieti's native town of Pisa in October 1998 (see Bruschi, 1999).

A similar connection between Stephen Mitchell's political convictions and his development of relational psychoanalysis can be found in both Margaret Black's Foreword to his 2002 book *Can love last? The fate of romance over time*, and in the interview conducted with him by Peter Rudnytsky and published in 2000. Here are Margaret Black's words:

> Inheriting from his family of origin a healthy disdain for authoritarian structures, it quickly became clear that Steve's thinking could not be constrained by rigidly held principles within psychoanalysis, no matter how distressing or disruptive his challenges were to the profession. Early in his own career, shortly after he had completed his training, he was among the first authors within the psychoanalytic tradition to openly and effectively challenge the then firmly held belief that homosexuality was fundamentally pathological (1978, 1981), an effort that eventually resulted in its removal

from the official psychiatric nomenclature of pathology.

Stephen rather romped through the extensive literature in psychoanalysis which was, at the time, sharply segregated into competing theoretical traditions and heavily dominated by the classical Freudian approach, an approach that declared alternative positions to be 'nonanalytic' and therefore marginal. In an effort to encourage more creative thinking in the field, he launched his own journal called *Psychoanalytic Dialogues*, employing what was at the time a revolutionary format of publishing the nonclassical marginalized voices within psychoanalysis as well as organizing respectful discussions among analysts of differing theoretical persuasions so that clinical approaches and theoretical formulations could be more thoughtfully and comparatively considered. He organized conferences, inviting representatives of diverse academic disciplines to consider a common problem in human experience. (Black, 2002, p. 13)

The interview conducted by Peter Rudnytsky, bearing the significant title "Between philosophy and politics," contains a very interesting report on Mitchell's work with Division 39, helping a whole series of psychologists across the USA to create their own autonomous institutes outside the APsaA, an experience that had "an enormous impact" on him (Rudnytsky and Mitchell, 2000, p. 110). But it also contains the following exchange:

PLR: I share your admiration for Fairbairn. What I'm noticing in this conversation is that I'm pressing you to choose between things. What you're often doing, it seems to me, is trying to have it both ways and say there isn't a necessary contradiction between alternative views. Maybe I'm splitting and you are integrating. SAM: That's kind of ironic because Arnold Richards, in his long review of *Relational Concepts*, accused me of being a dichotomizer. So I'm glad to hear that I am a synthesizer. (Rudnytsky and Mitchell, 2000, p. 130)

What Stephen Mitchell is referring to here is the long, very articulate, and critical book review essay on his 1988 book that Janet Bachant and Arnold Richards published in *Psychoanalytic Dialogues* in 1993, which was immediately followed—in the same issue No. 3/1993— by a similarly long and detailed reply by Mitchell. I will not go into the details of that here so as not to exhaust readers' patience, but since I have my own opinion about this important exchange, an opinion directly connected to what I have been saying so far, let me try to explain it by quoting the final considerations that Bachant and Richards, on the one hand, and Mitchell, on the other, came to at the end of their long "statement of the art of psychoanalysis." Bachant and Richards say that:

With his concept of the radical shift in paradigms, Mitchell has gone out on a theoretical limb, and it remains to be seen whether history will judge him a prophet or the vanguard of a new movement. His theory is daring – daring enough to challenge in a very specific way the longstanding Freudian model and well worth grappling with it. (Bachant and Richards, 1993; 2015, p. 208)

Mitchell's final considerations are three times as long:

> Over the past several years I have done a considerable amount of teaching in cities throughout the United States where there has generally been one psychoanalytic institute representing the traditional kind of approach to the history of psychoanalytic ideas proposed by Bachant and Richards. The impact of these institutions on the development of creative thought had been, in my judgment, utterly devastating. (For expressions of similar opinions by authors trained at these institutions, see Kernberg, 1986, Goldberg, 1990, Margolis, 1992). One of the more amazing pedagogical principles, so reminiscent of church practice, has been that no contemporary writers (like Kohut and nondrive, object relations theorists) should be read until quite a few years of mind preparation through the study of Freud and the classical tradition. The reading of my book provided by Bachant and Richards strikes me as an example of overly prepared minds. Rather than trying to suspend their own frame of reference to see what the world looks like from another point of view, they march through what they acknowledge might be something different with their checklist of familiar items. Critiques like this are best evidence that a fresh start at psychoanalytic theorizing is needed, respectful of tradition but without the obligatory forced continuity. (Mitchell, 1993b, p. 479)

Hoping I have been able to at least partially recreate the climate of this historically very relevant exchange, I must, before presenting my considerations on it, remind readers of the fact that Bachant and Richards' definition of Mitchell as a "dichotomizer" has to do with their revisitation of the contemporary positions vis-à-vis analytic metatheory in the five major parties described in the quote below. In Bachant and Richards' words:

> First is the group led by Robert Wallerstein and including Joseph Sandler, who espouse a position of common ground for almost all psychoanalytic theoretical approaches. Second are those who advocate a multi-model approach. This group is best exemplified by Fred Pine, who believes that common ground can be achieved only by an approach that includes and integrates the 'four psychologies' of drive, ego, object, and self. Third are those who reject the drive-object relations polarity – a position most articulately elucidated by Leo Rangell in his concept of 'total composite theory'. This group believes that psychoanalysis has from its inception closely tied together drive, defense, and object-relational concepts. Fourth are the antimetapsychologists, those who strive to minimize theory about theory in psychoanalysis. They are represented by the interpersonalists Levenson and Zucker and by Schafer, Klein, and Holt. The fifth group is the 'dichotomizers', those who separate all theory into two mutually exclusive positions. This group is typified by self psychology with its bipolar self and its division into tragic versus guilty man. Also among the dichotomizers is Mitchell,

who divides the field into two competing perspectives of drive
theory and object relations theory. (Bachant and Richards,
1993, pp. 204–205)

I can now come to my personal considerations. The
verb "dichotomize," as the Italian word "*dicotomizzare*"
(both coming from the original Greek verb "to cut in
two parts"), come very close to the verb "*dissociare*," "to
dissociate," and both denote poor mental functioning.
If Vittorio Lingiardi and the editors and authors of the
above-mentioned book *La svolta relazionale. Itinerari
italiani* reconstruct the history of the reception of
relational psychoanalysis in Italy only from their point of
view of "relational analysts," and do not value my role
as pioneer of such a reception, it is not because of their
poor mental functioning, but because of a specific political
strategy. They all knew me so well that they could not have
simply forgotten me. But before proceeding with this line
of thought, let me explicitly formulate my position here:
although I participated in the IARPP conferences of Los
Angeles (2004), Rome (2005), and Athens (2007), although
I keep reading *Psychoanalytic Dialogues*, and although
I keep being a member of IARPP, I am not a "relational
analyst." I am "just a psychoanalyst," or "a psychoanalyst
tout court." Having said this, I come back to what I call
"political strategy": by this I am referring to the well-
known phenomenon that, for example, the history of
Rome was rewritten as many times as a whole series of
Roman families came to rule what not only Italians know
as *la città eterna* (the eternal city). Of course, being a
strategy of exclusion and not of inclusion, it is not a good
intellectual operation, but it belongs to life, as much as
power and politics do.

By the same token, I can now say that I have always
valued Stephen Mitchell so highly, from an intellectual
point of view, and that I could never believe he really
thought that drive concept and relational concepts
could not coexist in the same intellectual edifice, and
adequately illuminate our clinical work. Why couldn't
what he declared as being epistemologically untenable
not be clinically useful? A neo-Sullivanian author as
Gaetano Benedetti (1920–2013) never dismissed Freudian
metapsychology; and my colleague and friend Stefano
Bolognini also finds such a dialectical combination of
drive and object relations concepts in Freud's work
clinically useful and productive (Bolognini, 2011). And I do
personally agree with my old friend Henry Zvi Lothane's
(1997) claim that Freud was as much "interpersonal" in
his clinical work as he was "monadic" in his libido theory.

Not to mention the fact that Mitchell himself liked Hans Loewald's work so much, informed as it is by his capacity to integrate the drive and the object poles (Loewald, 1980; Whitebook, 2004). In other words, I always thought that Mitchell must have had other reasons for intentionally promoting such a split, that is, what I would prefer to call "political reasons." And here, as we have seen up to now, we can distinguish at least two kinds of political reason, a personal and a professional one.

In relation to the personal reason, I can say the following: if I had been a bright young intellectual as Stephen was, coming from a Jewish family, having studied philosophy at Yale University and psychology at New York University, training to become a psychoanalyst, and understanding that, being only a psychologist, I could never have the chance to reach, in my chosen field, the prominence I thought I would to be able to deserve, I would have also tried to do something to change the situation. I too would have tried to, let us say, mix up the cards with which the game of psychoanalysis was being played. I myself—not having the good luck to live in a capital of psychoanalysis like New York City—have spent the last 35 years seeing patients during the day and studying at night, so that I might feel part of and give my contribution to contemporary debate in my field. From this point of view, I can well understand his personal struggle—and sympathize with him.

As we can gather from several of the quotations above, Mitchell developed an antagonistic attitude to the APsaA, as the association (or the lobby) responsible for having introduced—of all countries in the world, exclusively into the USA—what was then called "the medical monopoly of psychoanalysis," and he gave a very important contribution on the elimination of such a monopoly. This was one of the main topics of his interview with Peter Rudnytsky (Rudnytsky and Mitchell, 2000; see above). As an aside, for a detailed presentation of the problem I recommend the reader to take a look at Robert Wallerstein's 1998 book *Lay analysis: Life inside a controversy.*

At the same time, for reasons not so easy for me to understand, Stephen must have ended up seeing Freud himself, who was personally against the North American medical monopoly of psychoanalysis, as a, let us say, problematic presence. My idea in this regard is the following: the APsaA must have never clearly said that Freud, their worshipped hero, was in fact against the medical monopoly of psychoanalysis, since this would have made of the APsaA an anti-Freudian society. If this is true, my idea goes on as follows: Freud must have been so misused by the APsaA for its own business purposes, that—in my imagination—it had become impossible to look at him as the uniting principle that would have eventually allowed psychologists and medical doctors to play together the game of psychoanalysis. So misused by the American up to then, Freud could not represent such a unifying principle; only what Jay Greenberg (in the above quotation) called "the relational matrix" could do this. Only around this concept could psychoanalysis have been transformed into the new game, which, at that point, psychologists and medical doctors would eventually have been able to play together. And this would be the professional political reason—a sublimated form of the personal one, if you like—that I would attribute to Stephen Mitchell.

As you can imagine, my objection to the view of Arnold Richards (the publisher of this book of mine) would be not to have seen or explicitly talked about what we could call Mitchell's unifying tendency or aspiration behind what he calls his "dichotomizing attitude," that is, not to have explicitly dealt with Mitchell's "political agenda." In terms of Stephen Mitchell, I could object that he had not talked as openly about what he considered to be his own "revolution," as I have been trying to do now.

Now that I have come so far, I am ready to bring Morris Eagle into the picture. I met him through Paolo Migone, the co-editor-in-chief of *Psicoterapia e Scienze Umane* about 30 years ago, and even translated a couple of his papers into Italian. From my contact with Paolo, I know that he is alive and well—living in California and keeping intellectually busy. In this context, I am specifically referring to the important paper he published with David Wolitzky and Jerome Wakefield in 2001, as a response to the Mitchell's 1998 key paper "The analyst's knowledge and authority"; this was entitled "The analyst's knowledge and authority: A critique of the 'new view' in psychoanalysis" (Eagle, Wolitzky, and Wakefield, 2001).

Adopting the point of view developed in the paper by these three prominent authors, here is the way in which I feel I could respond to the above-reported concluding considerations that Mitchell set at the end of his response to Bachant and Richard's critical book review essay. It would go something like this: If the institutes representing the traditional kind of approach to the history of psychoanalytic ideas made such bad use of Freud and the classical tradition as to prevent any favorable reception of the contemporary analytic debate, this of course depends on the fact that, due to the medical monopoly of psychoanalysis, the intellectual climate of the APsaA used to be more clinically than theoretically oriented. MDs, at variance with psychologists, are usually more clinicians than intellectuals. From this point of view, it is not by chance that David Rapaport, the major architect of ego psychology, was himself a psychologist. But now that such a monopoly has been broken, psychologists, with a more theoretical approach, have eventually been able to present Freud as a lively ancestor and not as a haunting ghost. In studying more closely the history of psychoanalysis, one might even discover how much Freud was against the medical monopoly of psychoanalysis and how little consideration he had of North American psychoanalysis, also because of this reason! Unfortunately, Mitchell must at the time have been so disappointed in the use made of Freud by analysts of the APsaA that he could not look at things from this point of view—but had to try to "get rid of Freud," as he indeed did.

At this point, an important aspect to be considered is the following: although Mitchell kept repeating how important Freud was for him, I do not believe that a systematic study of his work is an integral part of the training of any contemporary institute of relational psychoanalysis. And here, of course, we have to admit that Bachant and Richards were right in implying that relational psychoanalysis risked bringing about a further fragmentation and impoverishment of psychoanalysis itself, as a unified and multidimensional body of knowledge. From this point of view, Mitchell's position is actually comparable to that of the intellectual leaders of the Italian student movements of the 1960s: given their negative attitude towards the "bourgeois intellectual tradition," a tradition with which they were very familiar, they ended up contributing to many of their followers' prejudices and a priori dismissal of it.

If this were the case, we would have to consider the following contradiction: the institutionalization of relational psychoanalysis, with its one-sided emphasis on the clinical dimension of our work and identity, would represent a form of perversion of the original intellectual richness of the comparative psychoanalytic perspective proposed by Greenberg and Mitchell in 1983. Or, to put it another way, we would have to formulate the following crucial question: is relational psychoanalysis to be taken only as an extension of Freud's work, as I myself originally experienced it, while following its gradual formulation by Mitchell? Or does it represent a complete and exhaustive point of view that goes beyond Freud's own work or is even alternative to it? From the recent history of psychiatry, we know that the IIIrd (and successive) editions of the *Diagnostic and statistical manual,* formulated as it was with the aim of unifying psychiatric diagnosis around the world, ended up being used by the younger generations as if it were a real handbook of psychiatry (which it was not at all meant to be). This is how a potential enrichment of psychiatry turned out to be an intellectual debacle.

From this point of view, I can even say that Paul Stepansky was—as Mitchell—also rather contradictory. His publishing house profited greatly from the creation of "relational psychoanalysis" as an autonomous branch of psychoanalysis, this representing at the same time the kind of development, away from the central body of psychoanalysis, that he later criticized and even deplored in his important book *Psychoanalysis at the margins* (2009).

But let me now go back to the above-mentioned article by Eagle, Wolitzky, and Wakefield. In their opinion, Mitchell (as well as Owen Renik and other postmodern authors), in their attempt to democratize not only the analytic world, but also the analytic relationship, should not necessarily have given up what they call the "humble realism" necessary for us to work with our patients. In the authors' words:

> Adopting a position of humble realism obviates the temptation to dichotomize between the therapeutic process goals of uncovering and discovering, on the one hand, and of developing new meaning systems and alternative perspectives on the other. One recognizes that the two go hand in hand. If we are not concerned with whether our meaning systems, perspectives, interpretations, and narratives correspond in some way to what is going on in the patent's mind, we are left with an endeavor not essentially different from any form of suggestion, persuasion or conversion . . . We would certainly have to give up any pretensions that psychoanalysis has much to do with such things as how the mind functions and how personality develops. (Eagle et al, 2001, pp. 486–487)

Due to his sudden death, Stephen Mitchell was, of course, not able to write a response to this important critique.

To the reader who has had the patience to stay with me until this point, I can say that I am now eventually ready to end this chapter, and I will conclude with the following quotation from Stephen Mitchell's posthumous paper "My psychoanalytic journey" (2004):

> For previous generations of clinicians, technique referred
> primarily to behavior. What should the analyst do? What
> should the analyst refrain from doing? This cannot possibly
> work for us. We have come to realize that the meaning of
> whatever the analyst does or does not do is contextual and
> co-constructed. The analyst cannot decide on the meaning of
> the 'frame' unilaterally. For some patients, silence is a form of
> holding; for others, it is a form of torture. For some patients,
> interpretation conveys deep recognition and self-expansion;
> for others, it is a form of violent exposure. For some patients,
> the analyst's self-disclosure might offer a unique and precious
> form of authenticity and honesty; for others, it is a form of
> charismatic seduction and narcissistic exploitation. For some
> patients questions represent a precious willingness to join and
> know them; for others, questions are a surreptitious invasion.
> It is no longer compelling to decide that these events are what
> we want them to be and that when patients experience them
> otherwise they are distorting. Interpersonal situations are
> ambiguous and can be interpreted in many different ways,
> depending on our past and our dynamics. (Mitchell, 2004, pp.
> 540–541)

Mitchell's "relational revolution" went a long way in "democratizing" the analytic world, representing "the relational matrix" of our clinical work, and our clinical work per se, a ground on which more and more analysts have started to really meet and deal with each other, in a way that was unthinkable until only a few years ago (see, for example, Tuckett et al, 2008). But what the above words really mean in terms of the relationship between the internal world and external reality is still not so clear to me. Do they mean, as I think they do, that the internal world of our patients and the relationship we develop with them have an equal weight in determining the development of our treatment? Or do they mean that the relational dimension has more weight than our patients' internal world? Unfortunately, Stephen can no longer share our preoccupations with our work and tell us what he thinks.

REFERENCES

Akhtar, S. (2009). *Comprehensive Dictionary of Psychoanalysis*. London: Karnac.

Albasi, C. (2006). *Attaccamenti traumatici. I modelli operativi interni dissociati* [Traumatic attachments. The dissociated internal operational models]. Turin: UTET.

Ammaniti, M. (1991). Il Sé infantile in una prospettiva intergenerazionale [The infantile self from an intergenerational perspective]. Paper presented at the conference *Le matrici relazionali del Sé*, April 13, 1991, Rome.

———— (1992). Presentazione [Introduction]. In S.A. Mitchell, R. Menarini, L. Ancona, C. Pontalti, and M. Conci, *Le matrici relazionali del Sé* [The relational matrixes of the self] (p. 1). Rome: Il Pensiero Scientifico.

Ammaniti, M,. & Gallese, V. (2014). *The Birth of Intersubjectiviy. Psychodynamics, Neurobiology and the Self*. New York: Norton.

Ammaniti, M., & Rossi, P.L. (1988). Interview with Daniel Stern. *Rivista di Psicoanalisi* 34:204–214

Arieti, S. (Ed.) (1959). *The American Handbook of Psychiatry. Two Volumes*. New York: Basic Books.

Aron, L. (1996). *A Meeting of Minds: Mutuality in Psychoanalysis*. Hillsdale, NJ: Analytic Press.

Bacciagaluppi, M. (1998). Introduction. *Journal of the American Academy of Psychoanalysis and Dynamic Psychiatry* 26:1–3.

Bachant, J.L., & Richards, A.D. (1993). Book review essay: "Relational concepts in psychoanalysis. An integration", by Stephen A. Mitchell. *Psychoanalytic Dialogues* 3:431–460. Included in A.D. Richards, *Psychoanalysis: Critical Conversations. Selected Papers by Arnold D. Richards. Volume 1* (A.A. Lynch, Ed.) (pp. 181–210). New York: International Psychoanalytic Books.

Barsness, R.E. (Ed.) (2017). *Core Competencies of Relational Psychoanalysis. A Guide to Practice, Study and Research*. London: Routledge.

Battaggia, P.G. (1992). La prospettiva relazionale nella psicoanalisi. Il contributo di S.A. Mitchell. *Quaderni dell'Associazione di Studi Psicoanalitici*, No. 5, 27–38.

Benedetti, G. (1961). Prefazione all'edizione italiana [Preface to the Italian edition]. In H.S. Sullivan, *La moderna concezione della psichiatria* (pp. vii–xxvii). Milan: Feltrinelli.

Berman, E. (2001). Obituary: Stephen A. Mitchell (1946–2000). *International Journal of Psychoanalysis* 82:1267–1272.

Bion, W.R. (2005). *The Italian Seminars*. London: Karnac. (Original Italian edition, 1985).

Black, M. (2002). Foreword. In S.A. Mitchell, *Can Love Last? The Fate of Romance over Time* (pp. 11–17). New York: Norton.

Bolognini, S. (2004). *Psychoanalytic Empathy*. London: Free Associations Books. (Original Italian edition, 2000).

———— (2005). La famiglia interna dell'analista [The analyst's internal family]. Paper presented at the SPI, June 18, 2005, Milan.

————(2011). *Secret Passages. The Theory and Technique of Interpsychic Relations*. London: Routledge. (Original Italian edition, 2008).

Bordi, S. (1990). Modelli a confronto in psicoanalisi [Comparing psychoanalytic models]. *Prospettive Psicoanalitiche nel Lavoro Istituzionale* 8:71–87.

―――― (1991). Sé soggettivo e organizzazione del Sé nel ciclo vitale [Subjective self and organization of the self in the life cycle]. Paper presented at the conference *Le matrici relazionali del Sé*, April 13, 1991, Rome.

―――― (2009). *Scritti* [Papers] (P. Capozzi, Ed.). Milan: Cortina.

Bromberg, P.M. (1989). Interpersonal psychoanalysis and self psychology: A clinical comparison. In D.W. Detrick and S.P. Detrick (Eds.), *Self Psychology: Comparisons and Contrasts* (pp. 275–291). Hillsdale, NJ: Analytic Press. (Italian version: Psicoanalisi interpersonale e psicologia del Sé: un confronto clinico. M. Conci, Translator. *Psicoterapia e Scienze Umane*, 1993, 27(4):5–23).

Bruschi, R. (1999). Introduction. *Journal of the American Academy of Psychoanalysis and Dynamic Psychiatry* 27:531–539.

Buchholz, M.B. (2003). Vorwort [Preface]. In S.A. Mitchell, *Bindung und Beziehung. Auf dem Weg zu einer relationalen Psychoanalyse* (pp. 7–15). Giessen: Psychosozial-Verlag.

Caviglia, G., & Lingiardi, V. (2014). The fortunes of the relational model in Italy: Notes on publishing, teaching and training. *Psychoanalytic Dialogues* 24:578–589.

Conci, M. (1990). Review of the book by S.A. Mitchell "Relational concepts in psychoanalysis. An integration", Harvard University Press 1988. *Psicoterapia e Scienze Umane* 24(1):124–130.

―――― (1992a). La psicoanalisi interpersonale. Da H.S. Sullivan a S.S. Mitchell [Interpersonal psychoanalysis. From H.S. Sullivan to S.A. Mitchell]. In S.A. Mitchell, R. Menarini, L. Ancona, C. Pontalti, and M. Conci, *Le matrici relazionali del Sé* [The relational matrixes of the self] (pp. 59–72). Rome: Il Pensiero Scientifico, 1992.

―――― (1992b). Temi maschili e femminili nelle lettere del giovane Freud ad Eduard Silberstein [Male and female themes in the young Freud's letters to Eduard Silberstein]. *Quaderni dell'Associazione di Studi Psicoanalitici* 2:54–68.

―――― (1993). Presentazione [Introduction]. In S.A. Mitchell, *Gli orientamenti relazionali in psicoanalisi. Per un modello integrato* (pp. ix–xv). Turin: Bollati Boringhieri.

―――― (1994a). Review of the book by J.R. Greenberg "Oedipus and beyond", Harvard University Press 1991. *Psicoterapia e Scienze Umane* 28(1):130–133.

―――― (1994b). Psychoanalysis in Italy: A reappraisal. *International Forum of Psychoanalysis* 3:117–126.

―――― (1994c). Review of the book by N.J. Skolnick and S.C. Warshaw "Relational perspectives in psychoanalysis", Analytic Press 1992. *Psicoterapia e Scienze Umane* 28(3):143–146.

―――― (1994d). Review of the book by S.A. Mitchell "Hope and dread in psychoanalysis", Basic Books 1993. *Psicoterapia e Scienze Umane* 28(4):130–133.

―――― (1994e). Report on the IX I.F.P.S. Forum, Florence May 12–15, 1994. *International Forum of Psychoanalysis* 3:261–262.

―――― (1995a). Review of the book by L. Nissim Momigliano "Continuity and change in psychoanalysis. Letters from Milan", Karnac Books 1992. *Psychoanalytic Books* 6:199–204.

―――― (1995b). Presentazione [Preface]. In S.A. Mitchell, *Speranza e timore in psicoanalisi* (pp. 9–10). Turin: Bollati Boringhieri.

―――― (1996). The "good life" and the vulnerability of the human being. Psychoanalytic perspectives. A small group seminar in New York City. *International Forum of Psychoanalysis* 5:70–71.

———— (2000). Report on the XI IFPS Forum, New York: Marriott Hotel, Brooklyn, May 4–7, 2000. *International Forum of Psychoanalysis* 9:263–266.

———— (2005). S.A. Mitchell's trips to Italy: 1988, 1991 and 1996. Unpublished paper given at IARPP Conference, June 2005, Rome.

———— (2006). Sullivan and Mitchell in Italy – The reception of their work and the re-visitation of their legacies. Unpublished paper given at the IFPS Forum, May 2006, Rome.

———— (2009). Review of the book by A. Ferro "Mind works. Technique and creativity in psychoanalysis", Routledge 2009. *International Forum of Psychoanalysis* 18:124–127.

———— (2012a). Le radici della svolta relazionale in psicoanalisi. Da Sullivan a Mitchell attraverso l'A.S.P., ossia il punto di vista di Benedetti e Cremerius [The roots of the relational turn in psychoanalysis. From Sullivan to Mitchell, going through the A.S.P., that is, the point of view of Benedetti and Cremerius]. *Setting* No. 33–34:105–139.

———— (2012b). *Sullivan Revisited – Life and Work. Harry Stack Sullivan's Relevance for Contemporary Psychiatry, Psychotherapy and Psychoanalysis* (2nd ed.) Trento: Tangram. (Original Italian edition, 2000).

———— (2013). Editorial – German themes in psychoanalysis. Part one. *International Forum of Psychoanalysis* 22:195–198.

———— (2015). Editorial – German themes in psychoanalysis. Part two. *International Forum of Psychoanalysis* 24:57–59.

Conci, M., Dazzi, S., & Mantovani, M.L. (Eds.) (1997). *La tradizione interpersonale in psichiatria psicoterapia e psicoanalisi* [The interpersonal tradition in psychiatry psychotherapy and psychoanalysis]. Rome: Erre Emme.

Dazzi, N. (1981). *William James: Antologia di scritti psicologici* [William James: Anthology of psychological papers]. Bologna: Il Mulino.

De Bei, F., & Aron, L. (2016). Introduzione [Introduction]. In S.A. Mitchell, *Teoria e clinica psicoanalitica. Scritti scelti* [Psychoanalytic theory and technique. Selected papers] (pp. vii–xxi). Milan: Cortina.

De Bei, F., & Dazzi, N. (2014). Attachment and relational psychoanalysis: Bowlby according to Mitchell. *Psychoanalytic Dialogues* 24:562–577.

Eagle, M.N., Wolitzky, D.L., & Wakefield, J.C. (2001). The analyst's knowledge and authority: A critique of the "new view" in psychoanalysis. *Journal of the American Psychoanalytic Association* 49:457–488.

Ferro, A. (2009). *Mind Works. Technique and Creativity in Psychoanalysis*. London: Routledge. (Original Italian edition, 2006).

Friedman, L. (1988). *The Anatomy of Psychotherapy*. Hillsdale, NJ: Analytic Press.

Galli, P.F. (1990). Psychoanalysis, the story of a crisis. Paper given at the Rapaport–Klein Study Group, June 10, 1990, Stockbridge, MA.

Gill, M.N. (1983). The interpersonal paradigm and the degree of the therapist's involvement. *Contemporary Psychoanalysis* 20:200–237. (Italian edition, 1995).

Greenberg, J.R. (2001). Stephen A. Mitchell: 1946–2000. *Contemporary Psychoanalysis* 37:189–191.

———— (2003). Foreword. *Contemporary Psychoanalysis* 39:353–359.

Greenberg, J.R., & Mitchell, S.A. (1983). *Object Relations in*

Psychoanalytic Theory. Cambridge, MA: Harvard University Press. (Italian edition: *Le relazioni oggettuali nella teoria psicoanalitica*. Bologna: Il Mulino, 1986).

Hatcher, R.L. (1990). Review of the book by S.A. Mitchell "Relational concepts in psychoanalysis. An integration". With a reply by S.A. Mitchell and a reply to it by R.L. Hatcher. *Psychoanalytic Books* 1:127–142.

Holt, R.R. (2013). Freud's occupational choice and the unconscious: Reverberations of Goethe's "On nature". *Psychoanalytic Review* 100:239–266. (Italian translation, 1992).

Klein, G.S. (1993). *Teoria psicoanalitica. I fondamenti*. Milan: Cortina. (Original English edition, 1976).

Laplanche, J., & Pontalis, J.-B. (1973). *The Language of Psychoanalysis*. New York: Norton. (Original French edition, 1967).

Lear, J. (1995). The shrink is in. A counterblast in the war on Freud. *New Republic,* December 25, 1995.

Limentani, A. (1989). Psychoanalysis in Italy: A personal appraisal. In G.E. Viola and F. Rovigatti (Eds.), *L'Italia nella psicoanalisi–Italy in psychoanalysis* (pp. 25–28). Rome: Istituto dell'Enciclopedia Italiana.

Lingiardi, V., & De Bei, F. (2011). La svolta relazionale nella ricerca in psicoterapia [The relational turn in the field of psychotherapy research]. In V. Lingiardi, G. Amadei, G. Caviglia, and F. De Bei (Eds.), *La svolta relazionale. Itinerari italiani* [The relational turn. Italian journeys] (pp. 99–122). Milan: Cortina.

Lingiardi, V., & Federici, S. (2014). The relational turn in Italy: Its history and evolution – Introduction to panel. *Psychoanalytic Dialogues* 24:558–561.

Lingiardi, V., Amadei, G., Caviglia, G., and De Bei, F. (Eds.) (2011). *La svolta relazionale. Itinerari italiani* [The relational turn. Italian journeys]. Milan: Cortina.

Loewald, H. (1980). *Papers on Psychoanalysis*. New Haven, CT: Yale University Press.

Lothane, Z. (1997). Freud and the interpersonal. *International Forum of Psychoanalysis* 6:175–184.

Menarini, R., Ancona, L, & Pontalti, C. (1992). La costruzione del sé dal vertice dei campi mentali familiari-gruppali-terapeutici [The construction of the self from the vertex of the mental therapeutic fields of family and group]. In S.A. Mitchell, R. Menarini, L. Ancona, C. Pontalti, and M. Conci, *Le matrici relazionali del Sé* [The relational matrixes of the self] (pp. 37–58). Rome: Il Pensiero Scientifico.

Meterangelis, G. (2017). Review of the book by S.A. Mitchell edited by F. De Bei "Teoria e clinica psicoanalitica. Scritti scelti", Cortina 2016. *Rivista di Psicoanalisi* 53:705–712.

Miller, J.P., Jr. (1990). Review of the book by S.A. Mitchell "Relational concepts in psychoanalysis. An integration". *International Journal of Psychoanalysis* 71:727–731.

Mitchell, S.A. (1988a). *Relational Concepts in Psychoanalysis. An Integration*. Cambridge, MA: Harvard University Press. (Italian edition: *Gli orientamenti relazionali in psicoanalisi. Per un modello integrato*. S. Rivolta, Translator. Turin: Bollati Boringhieri, 1993).

——— (1988b). The intrapsychic and the interpersonal: Different theories, different domains or historical artifacts? *Psychoanalytic Inquiry* 8:472–496. (Italian edition: L'intrapsichico e l'interpersonale: differenti teorie, ambiti differenti o artefatti storici? M. Conci, Translator. *Quaderni dell'Associazione di Studi Psicoanalitici* 2:7–26).

———— (1990). A reply. *Psychoanalytic Books* 1:136–140.

———— (1991a). Editorial philosophy. *Psychoanalytic Dialogues* 1:1–7.

———— (1991b). Contemporary perspectives on self: Toward an integration. *Psychoanalytic Dialogues* 1:121–147. (Italian translation: *Prospettive contemporanee sul Sé: verso un'integrazione.* M. Conci, Translator. *Psicoterapia e Scienze Umane* 25(3):30–30, 1991. Included in S.A. Mitchell, R. Menarini, L. Ancona, C. Pontalti, M. Conci, *Le matrici relazionali del Sé* [The relational matrixes of the self] (pp. 3–36). Rome: Il Pensiero Scientifico, 1992).

———— (1993a). Aggression and the endangered self. *Psychoanalytic Quarterly* 62:351–382.

———— (1993b). Reply to Bachant and Richards. *Psychoanalytic Dialogues* 3:461–480.

———— (1993c). *Hope and Dread in Psychoanalysis.* New York: Basic Books. (Italian edition: *Speranza e timore in psicoanalisi.* E. Izard, Translator. Turin: Bollati Boringhieri, 1994).

———— (1996). When interpretations fail: A new look at the therapeutic action of psychoanalysis. In E.L. Lifson (Ed.), *Understanding Therapeutic Action: Psychodynamic Concepts of Cure* (pp. 165–186). Hillsdale, NJ: Analytic Press.

———— (1997). *Influence and Autonomy in Psychoanalysis.* Hillsdale, NJ: Analytic Press. (Italian edition: *Influenza e autonomia in psicoanalisi.* M.A. Schepisi, Translator. Turin: Bollati Boringhieri, 1999. German edition: *Psychoanalyse als Dialog. Einfluss und Autonomie in der analytischen Beziehung.* T. Kierdorf and H. Höhr, Translators. Giessen: Psychosozial, 2005).

———— (1998). The analyst's knowledge and authority. *Psychoanalytic Quarterly* 67:1–31.

———— (1999). Attachment theory and the psychoanalytic tradition: Reflections on human relationality. *Psychoanalytic Dialogues* 9:85–107.

———— (2000). *Relationality: From Attachment to Intersubjectivity.* Hillsdale, NJ: Analytic Press. (Italian edition: *Il modello relazionale. Dall'attaccamento all'intersoggettivit.* F. Gazzillo, Translator. Milan: Cortina. German edition: *Bindung und Beziehung. Auf dem Weg zu einer relationalen Psychoanalyse.* M. Altmeyer and M. Altmeyer, Translators. Giessen: Psychosozial-Verlag, 2003).

———— (2002a). *Can Love Last? The Fate of Romance over Time.* New York: Estate of S.A. Mitchell. (Italian edition: *L'amore può durare? Il destino dell'amore romantico.* F. Gazzillo, Translator. Milan: Cortina, 2003. German edition: *Kann denn Liebe ewig sein? Psychoanalytische Erkundungen über Liebe, Begehren und Beständigkeit.* T. Kierdorf and H. Höhr, Translators. Giessen: Psychosozial-Verlag, 2004).

———— (2002b). Fairbairn and the problem of agency. In F. Pereira and D. Scharff (Eds.), *Fairbairn and Relational Theory* (pp. 212–230). London: Karnac.

———— (2004). My psychoanalytic journey. *Psychoanalytic Inquiry* 24:531–541.

———— (2016). *Teoria e clinica psicoanalitica. Scritti scelti* [Psychoanalytic theory and technique. Selected papers] (F. De Bei, Ed. and Translator). Milan: Cortina.

Mitchell, S.A., & Aron, L. (Eds.) (1999). *Relational Psychoanalysis. The Emergence of a Tradition*. Hillsdale, NJ: Analytic Press.

Mitchell, S.A., & Black, M.J. (1995). *Freud and Beyond. A History of Modern Psychoanalytic Thought*. New York: Basic Books. (Italian edition: *L'esperienza della psicoanalisi. Storia del pensiero psicoanalitico moderno*. S. Rivolta, Translator. Turin: Bollati Boringhieri, 1996).

Moccia, G., & Meterangelis, G. (2011). Psicoanalisi relazionale e psicoanalisi freudiana [Relational psychoanalysis and Freudian psychoanalysis]. In V. Lingiardi, G. Amadei, G. Caviglia, and F. De Bei, *La svolta relazionale. Itinerari italiani* [The relational turn. Italian journeys] (pp. 183–197). Milan: Cortina.

Nebbiosi, G., & Federici, S. (2014). The relational model: International relations and dissemination in Italy: A historical account. *Psychoanalytic Dialogues* 24:590–600.

Nissim Momigliano, L. (1984). " . . . Due persone che parlano in una stanza..."(Una ricerca sul dialogo analitico). *Rivista di psicoanalisi* 30:1–17. (English version: Two people talking in a room: An investigation on the analytic dialogue. In L. Nissim Momigliano and A. Robutti, Eds., *Shared Experience: The Psychoanalytic Dialogue*, pp. 5–20. London: Karnac, 1992).

Novelletto, A. (1992). Italy. In P. Kutter (Ed.), *Psychoanalysis International* (Vol. 1, pp. 195–212). Stuttgart: Frommann-Holzboog.

Rapaport, D. (1967). *The Collected Papers of David Rapaport (1942–1960)* (M.N. Gill, Ed.) New York: Basic Books.

Rioch, J. (1943). The transference phenomenon in psychoanalytic therapy. *Psychiatry* 6:147–156.

Rocchi, C. (1995). Review of the book by S.A. Mitchell, "Relational concepts in psychoanalysis. An integration", Harvard University Press 1988. *Rivista di Psicoanalisi* 41:516–522.

Rudnytsky, P.L, & Mitchell, S.A. (2000). Between philosophy and politics. In P.L. Rudnytsky, *Psychoanalytic Conversations. Interviews with Clinicians, Commentators and Critics* (pp. 101–136). Hillsdale, NJ: Analytic Press.

Schafer, R. (1976). *A New Language for Psychoanalysis*. New Haven, CT: Yale University Press.

Searles, H.F. (1977). The analyst's participant observation as influenced by the patient's transference. *Contemporary Psychoanalysis* 13:347–350.

Semi, A.A. (Ed.). (1988) *Trattato di psicoanalisi. Volume primo: teoria e tecnica* [Handbook of psychoanalysis. Vol. 1: Theory and technique]. Milan: Cortina.

Sforza, M. (1992). Italo-German Meeting. Villa Vigoni, Menaggio (Como), June 1991. *Rivista di Psicoanalisi* 31:234–258.

Skolnikoff, A.Z. (1991). Review of the book by S.A. Mitchell "Relational concepts in psychoanalysis. An integration". *Psychoanalytic Quarterly* 60:481–485.

Stensson, J. (1992). Editorial. *International Forum of Psychoanalysis* 1:1–2.

Stepansky, P.E. (2009). *Psychoanalysis at the Margins*. New York: Other Press.

Sullivan, H.S. (1953). *The Interpersonal Theory of Psychiatry* (H. Swick Perry and M. Ladd Gawel, Eds.). New York: Norton.

——— (1954). *The Psychiatric Interview* (H. Swick Perry and M. Ladd

Gawel, Eds.). New York: Norton.

———— (1962). *Schizophrenia as a Human Process* (H. Swick Perry, Ed.). New York: Norton.

Tuckett, D., Basile, R., Birksted-Breen, D., Böhm, T., Denis, P., Ferro, A., Hinz, H., Jemstedt, A., Mariotti, P., and Schubert, J. (2008). *Psychoanalysis Comparable and Incomparable. The Evolution of a Method to Describe and Compare Psychoanalytic Approaches.* London: Routledge.

Wallerstein, R.S. (1998). *Lay Analysis: Life Inside the Controversy.* Hillsdale, NJ: Analytic Press.

White, M. (1952). Sullivan and treatment. In P. Mullahy (Ed.), *The Contributions of Harry Stack Sullivan: A Symposium* (pp. 117–150). New York: Hermitage House.

Whitebook, J. (2004). Hans Loewald: A conservative. *International Journal of Psychoanalysis* 85:97–115.

LIST OF THE LETTERS
BY S.A. MITCHELL TO THE AUTHOR

1. August 22, 1988 (received by me)

2. January 26, 1990 (written by him)

3. March 13, 1990 (written)

4. September 30, 1990 (written)

5. December 10, 1990 (written)

6. May 22, 1992 (received)

7. February 9, 1993 (written)

8. May 17, 1993 (received)

9. January 26, 1994 (written)

10. May 15, 1994 (fax)

11. August 8, 1994 (received)

12. November 4, 1994 (fax)

13. December 25, 1995 (fax)

14. January 15, 1996 (fax)

15. February 14, 1996 (fax)

16. April 1996 (fax)

17. September 2, 1998 (received)

INTRODUCTION TO PART THREE—THE MULTIPLE ROOTS OF W.R. BION'S WORK AND OF THE ANALYTIC FIELD CONCEPT

In the General Introduction, I presented this Part of my book starting with my first introduction to Bion's work, which I had had the good luck of experiencing through the 1975 Italian edition of the *Introducción a las ideas de Bion*, published in 1972 in Buenos Aires by León Grinberg, Dario Sor, and Elizabeth Tabak de Bianchedi (see Grinberg, Sor, & Tabak de Bianchedi, 1977). In their Preface, the authors wrote of how finding the thread of Bion's work allowed them to discover the "surprising coherence" connecting its various parts, and how this helped them to eventually write and publish their own book, the first introduction to his work. Discovering the coherence of my own work while writing the above-mentioned General Introduction and the Introductions to Parts One and Two has also helped me to go on with my work on this anthology.

As a consequence, the reader should not be surprised to hear that I will now continue with Bion, in the first part of this Introduction, by trying to further reconstruct the ways in which I was able, over the course of many years and through a series of contacts and meetings with a wide range of colleagues, to increasingly understand Bion's highly complex and sophisticated work, and eventually start writing about him. By doing this, that is, by presenting the multiple roots of his work and the multiple aspects of his legacy, I also intend to revisit the concept of "comparative psychoanalysis." Such a revisitation will also represent a good premise for my way of dealing with the multiple roots of the analytic field concept—the penultimate section in this chapter. As in the previous two Introductions, the final section will deal with the individual chapters of this Part of the book.

Let me start with Elizabeth Tabak de Bianchedi (1933–2015), the third co-author of the above-mentioned book, and the Viennese-born wife of the Italian-Argentinian child psychiatrist Marcelo Bianchedi. I had the good luck of meeting them both in July 1997, when they visited Collalbo-Klobenstein, the alpine village near Bolzano with the hotel where Freud celebrated his twenty-fifth wedding anniversary in September 1911, and where Francesco Marchioro and I organized many psychoanalytic congresses and meetings—the reader can find more details on these in the Afterword. A few days earlier the Bianchedis had been attending the Bion Centennial Conference organized in Turin by Franco Borgogno, Parthenope Bion Talamo (1945–1998), and Silvio Merciai, and they were having a vacation in Europe.

Having been in contact with the Bianchedis through an analytic institute in Buenos Aires known as the AEPA, we were able to meet in Collalbo-Klobenstein, at the Hotel Post, and to organize for Elisabeth to give a small group of us an introduction to the life and work of Bion. Her starting point was the topic "The various sides of lies," which she had dealt with in Turin (as I found confirmed in the report on the conference written by Michaele Bezoari for the *Rivista di Psicoanalisi* in 1997). As Elizabeth wrote in her 2005 paper "Whose Bion? Who is Bion," her usual introduction to Bion, which she also gave to us then, consisted in first speaking of Freud and Melanie Klein, as the best way of contextualizing Bion's contributions. Additionally, as she also confirmed in her 2005 paper , she clearly transmitted to us her opinion that "the late Bion" was for her as valuable as "the early Bion." Here is what she wrote in this regard in 2005:

> Although I agree with Edna that, from the last chapters of *Transformations* (1965) onwards, his writings become more 'pro- and e-vocative', I believe that his style, now more ambiguous and less positivistic, generates strong possibilities of evolution in those who can stand it . . . . The important ideas of transformations in O ('becoming', being what one is) as complementary to the transformations in K (knowing about what one is) continue to be strongly present in *Attention and interpretation* (1970) and in all his later writings. And the psychoanalytic process is seen as a growing spiral of transformations in K and transformations in O. (Tabak de Bianchedi, 2005, pp. 1530–1531)

In this quotation, Elizabeth Tabak de Bianchedi was of course referring to Edna O'Shaughnessy and her paper "Whose Bion?," which opened the same issue, 6/2005, of the *International Journal of Psychoanalysis*. In this we find a very useful summary of the variety of positions in contemporary psychoanalysis concerning the relationship between "the early Bion" and "the late Bion," including O'Shaughnessy's own opinion:

> After these main writings [of the 1940s, 1950s and 1960s], however, in my view, Bion's thinking becomes less disciplined, and his language then begins to suffer the defects of its qualities. By 'less disciplined', I mean mixing and blurring categories of discourse, embracing contradictions, and sliding between ideas rather than linking them. These features are apparent, indeed intentional, in *A memoir of the future* (1975, 1977, 1979); they are part of the spirit in which Bion offers his autobiographical trilogy. They are present, too, in his later psychoanalytic papers and in the seminar records.

(O'Shaughnessy, 2005, p. 1524)

After giving the example of the multiple meaning and dimensions assigned by Bion to the sign "O," here is how Edna O'Shaughnessy further articulates her position:

> Thus, my reading of Bion's opus is that the arresting qualities of language in his main writings free the reader's thinking, but that, as his late thinking becomes less boundaried, the defects of these very qualities make the texts too open, too provocative and evocative, and weakened by riddling meanings. Some, for example, Bléandonu (1994), take something of a similar view. Others read Bion's opus oppositely and see his later writings not as less disciplined and proliferating of meanings, but as freely transcending caesuras in a way that brings the author's thinking to a culmination, especially about clinical practice. For such a reading, see, for example, Grotstein, 1981. And, between these extremes, there are various shades of opinion. (O'Shaughnessy, 2005, p. 1525)

Given its importance, Chris Mawson published Edna O'Shaughnessy's 2005 paper in the anthology *Bion today* that he edited in 2011.

Fortunately, I have had the good luck of getting to know James Grotstein (1925–2015) personally, meeting him through my friend Henry Zvi Lothane and attending with both them (and Grotstein's wife) an international conference on Freud's Case of President Schreber held at Cerisy-la-Salle, Normandy, in August 1993. My friend Henry Zvi had just published his important book *In defense of Schreber. Soul murder and psychiatry* (1992), which Grotstein reviewed in the *Psychoanalytic Review* (Grotstein, 1993), and which I reviewed in the journal *Psicoterapia e Scienze Umane* (Conci, 1993). As all four of us had traveled to Normandy together, having picked up the Grotsteins at Paris airport, and had been able to spend more time together during that unforgettable week, I really had the chance to get to know Jim well enough to become very interested in his work. Apart from the fact that he talked so enthusiastically about Bion that it was impossible not to be affected by his attitude, he was also ready to openly talk about his experience as an analysand of Bion. This is, for example, how I heard directly from him what he had written in the 1981 paper on Bion quoted above by O'Shaughnessy:

> During another moment in analysis, he gave me a series of interpretations which, unusually, caused me to say, 'I think I follow you'. His replay to that was an ironic, 'Yes, I was afraid of that!'. It was only then that I began to realize that Bion did not want to be followed or understood, let alone idealized. He wanted me and everyone who was in his presence to be responsive to his/her own emanations – and responses. (Grotstein, 1981, p. 507)

Of course, such a level of exchange was also made possible by the peculiar nature of the place, that is by the "genius loci" of the Centre Culturel International de Cerisy-la-Salle, a prestigious venue for intellectual and scholarly encounters that had been founded in 1952 by Anne Heurgon-Desjardins. It has since hosted the famous *"Colloques de Cerisy,"* a series of seminars that constitute an important point of reference in the recent history of French and international intellectual life. Indeed, a whole series of the "big names" of psychiatry and psychoanalysis participated in the "Schreber Colloque" that summer, including Belgian colleagues Jacques Schotte (1928–2007) and Antoine Vergote (1921–2013) of the Catholic University of Leuven, and German colleagues Uwe Henrik Peters and Wolfgang Blankenburg (1928–2002).

But going back to James Grotstein's 1981 paper, after revisiting it in connection with the preparation of this Introduction, I can say that it is still highly worthwhile to keep reading it. Here is what we can for example read in the section with the title "Publication," in terms of Grotstein's unique understanding of Bion's legacy:

> Melanie Klein did not seem to understand that her instinctual theory was radically different from Freud's. It was not based on neuronal discharge but was, rather, based on the infant's need to contact a breast; it was a communicative theory, not a discharge theory. To Klein's *object relations communication theory* Bion added the *publication theory.* In Bion's terms this meant that the infant is communicating *and* also trying to get in contact with himself so as to be 'known' or 'self-conscious' in the literal sense of the term. This 'publication' conjoins with communication (to objects) to seek correlation via feedback. Bion is constantly mindful that man is inherently a dependent creature who has only 180 degrees vision, not 360 degrees. A *second opinion* is therefore necessary for the human condition . . . . His theory of 'publication' has foreshadowed the attempts of Kohut to establish a differentiation between the agenda of the narcissistic self and the object-relations self and thus anticipated the concept of 'mirroring'. (Grotstein, 1981, p. 522, original emphasis)

As the reader can imagine, such an anthropological perspective represents not only the key I used in my revisitation of Freud's correspondence, and of his "discovery" of psychoanalysis, but also the point of view on the human condition which I imagined Bion and Sullivan to have had in common; this is, the view that motivated me to write Chapter 8 of this anthology of papers, , "Bion and Sullivan: An enlightening comparison."

No less interesting and relevant for our contemporary debate is what we can read in the last section of the 1981 paper by Grotstein, under the title "Was Bion a Kleinian?"

We find here first a confirmation of the words of Lee Rather that I mentioned in my General Introduction, in terms of Bion's undogmatic attitude and his favoring "selective integration over orthodoxy" (Rather, 2015, p.53). In addition we also encounter a more specific grounding of this statement in terms of both Grotstein's personal experience of Bion and his very thoughtful way of positioning his contribution and legacy in the context of contemporary psychoanalysis. Here is the more personal part:

> When I was briefly in supervision with him before entering analysis, I asked him that very question. His answer was, 'Heavens, no! I am no more Kleinian than Melanie was. She always thought herself as Freudian, but Anna (Freud) saw to it that she would be labeled "Kleinian".' Behind this anecdote about Klein's not being Kleinian lies, I believe, Bion's profound dislike for the confusion of personalities and theories. 'Once Kleinian or once Freudian, is no longer psychoanalysis', I believe he would state. He was analyzed by both John Rickman, a classical analyst, and by Melanie Klein. I believe he 'digested' their legacy and became a *psychoanalyst*. When he suggests the abnegation of memory and desire, I believe him to mean one should desaturate ideas of dogma so that the analytic container can be opened for new possibilities rather than to be saturated with Klein or Freud or Jung or the like. The psychoanalytic object must be discovered and rediscovered from different vertices. Yet it would never be safe to say that he is *not* a Kleinian if that term be insisted upon. He had learned to play the instrument of phantasy with the notes of splitting, projective identification, manic defenses, and the like so that they emerge as a rare art form with beautiful arpeggios that would have made Klein proud. Technically, therefore, Bion was more 'Kleinian' than not. (Grotstein, 1981, p. 534, original emphasis)

The reader will not be surprised to hear that one of the associations I have to these words is my "second opinion"—to use a word borrowed from a previous quotation of Grotstein as an interpreter of Bion—concerning H.S. Sullivan's identity as a psychoanalyst. In other words, if Anna Freud was right to speak of Klein as "a Kleinian," and not as "a Freudian," I have the right to look at Sullivan as a psychoanalyst, although he did not do this himself—and I may even be right, as Anna Freud had turned out to be.

From this point of view, I was even able to make use of this concept of "the second opinion," as some kind of a common denominator of my own professional life. As the reader will learn in my Afterword, my professional life has gone through very many changes—from assistant psychiatrist at an Italian department of psychiatry, to assistant professor of psychiatry at an Italian university, to guest professor at a German university, to a *kassenärztlicher Psychoanalytiker* in Munich, to co-editor-in-chief of an English-speaking analytic journal. And these changes—to name but a few—have often taken place not just as a consequence of my desire to change and move on in life, but because of "the second opinion" I received from the colleagues with whom I worked. In other words, it was often more clear to them than to me how much I differed from them, and this sometimes more—sometimes more than my desire to change—often forced me to leave behind what I was doing and look for something new. By this, I also mean that I was somehow forced to discover my own major traits and value—not through my own eyes, but through the eyes of all the colleagues I met on my way.

In fact, this way of looking at things is relevant even for my personal life, inasmuch as my father always refused to see in me only the psychoanalyst I wanted to become, but viewed me as also one of the heirs—together with my two brothers—of his construction firm (see the Afterword); this "second opinion" of his also deeply shaped my life. Indeed, it is only recently that I have been able to eventually integrate this into my own identity. Of course, if Edna O'Shaughnessy would read these lines, she would think that I—like "the late Bion"—am also not boundaried enough in my thinking, to which I would respond by saying that psychoanalysis is for me not only a profession, but also a way of dealing with myself and of trying to keep growing as a person. In fact, it took me many years to digest and respond to many of the "second opinions" I have received in my life and to eventually experience them more as compliments and stimuli than as attempts to harm and damage me. There are of course also the "second opinions" that we receive from real friends, which are not only easy to take, but even very stimulating. This was for example the case with Stefano Bolognini's Preface to this book, in terms of the internal coherence that he was able to find in it—even before I was through with the process of writing the five Introductions that accompany it.

But let us now go back to Grotstein, and examine the second, more scientific part of his way of positioning Bion's legacy in the context of contemporary psychoanalysis:

> Yet it must be stated in fairness to Bion that he was far more than just 'Kleinian' . . . . Paradoxically, some of Bion's metapsychological innovations were not agreeable to Klein herself. Bion states that Mrs. Klein, despite her detractors, was firmly rooted in the work of Freud and Abraham and had a difficult time in comprehending Bion's notions of inherent preconceptions. The paradox is that Bion's conception

of inherent preconceptions was the very paradigm that was necessary to make Klein's concept of early mental life credible . . . . Thus, it may not be incorrect to state that Bion was not only meta-Freudian but was also meta-Kleinian.

Bion reflected yet another psychoanalytic orientation, however, which would have gladdened the hearts of followers of Fairbairn, Winnicott, Balint, and Kohut. Unlike most so-called Kleinians and Freudians, Bion emphasized the importance of the self, of the need for the self to have an empathic relationship by the self for itself, and believed that there must also be an object whose empathic containment of the self is of vital importance for the infants' welfare. Bion was therefore the first Kleinian to give metapsychological enfranchisement to the independent importance of an unemphatic (non-containing) external reality. (Grotstein, 1981, pp. 535–536)

According to me, these words of Grotstein show us how well Bion's work and legacy interact with and integrate not only Freud's and Klein's perspectives, but also the perspective on the interaction between internal world and external reality developed by Faibairn, Winnicott, Balint, and Kohut. And this is exactly what makes of Bion's legacy some kind of a "lingua franca," that is, a common currency, of contemporary psychoanalysis. In other words, it explains why he is so widely read and studied today (see also Miller, 2016), and why his theories have played such an important role in generating psychoanalytic field theory (see Silverman, 2017a, p.703). At the same time, Grotstein's words also represent a very good example of the kind of new "comparative psychoanalysis" that I am trying to propose in this book, that is, a comparative psychoanalysis not limited to a comparison of the different clinical approaches proposed by all the authors mentioned above, but one that also includes all the biographical, professional, and contextual variables involved in the production of any analytic point of view.

Last but not least, Jim Grotstein knew Bion so well that we owe to him the best possible explanation of why Bion dedicated the last years of his life to writing a series of highly original, very personal, and dramatic autobiographical books: the three volumes of *A memoir of the future* (1975, 1977, 1979)—*The long week-end* (1982), *All my sins remembered* (1985a), and *The other side of genius* (1985b). In fact, Grotstein condensed the answer into the formula "Making the best of a bad deal," which represents the title of a paper he published in *Contemporary Psychoanalysis* in 1987, as a response to Harald Boris's 1986 paper "Bion re-visited." In Grotstein's words:

One inescapably gets the impression that Bion had a strong need to write his autobiography, not only because of the

need to create a new language (as Williams suggests) or to
complete his analysis (as Boris suggests), but also to beg
mercy of all of those who have idealized him to the position
of messiah or guru with all the attendant expectations and
consequently painful isolation . . . . I was deeply moved by
how he must have felt being sent, prematurely, away from
his balmy, yet troubled Indian home to England – never to
return. How awful it must have been for this teenager to be
trapped in a tank in the middle of one of the most savage
wars in human history, to have lost most of his friends that
he had made. Further, there is the repeated statement of his
belief that he 'died' in a tank on the Amiens-Roye Road in
World War 1. One gets the impression that Bion never fully
survived the war . . . . May not his autobiographies have
been written in part to share this awful experience with
us so that we can vicariously join him in "remembering all
his sins," and have an emphatic peak of the "other side of
genius" – and of the hero – so as to come to his rescue? . . .

All of us who admired, extolled, and loved Bion were
so busy in acknowledging the hero, the messiah, the one
who transcended his experiences, that we knew nothing (and
perhaps cared nothing, I am sorry to say) about Bion the sufferer
who did not transcend his experience. This is what I believe he
needed to convey to us. To these possible explanations for the
writing of his autobiography, let me add a third, one which I
alluded earlier in this contribution when I quoted Dr. Bennett
Simon to the effect that Bion, like Beckett, had withdrawn
behind his shell because there was no one around with a
sufficient holding capacity for him and to contain his agony.
Maybe he wants us . . . not to forget the lost human being
buried deep within the fortress known as "Awesome Bion."

Thus, the explanation for my title of this contribution,
"Making the Best of a Bad Deal." (Grotstein, 1987, pp. 72, 73,
74)

From my point of view, it is clear that the importance
Bion attributed to the biographical aspect as the
background out of which his work emerged further confirms
the specific type of historical research and perspective
that I develop in this book. More specifically, it is at the
same time a confirmation of the importance of having
looked for and transcribed his letters to John Rickman
(1891–1951), which allow us to see how most of the traits
of personality and orientation that make Bion so dear and
important to us were there already before he started his
analysis with Melanie Klein, at the end of the World War
II. On the other hand, Grotstein's reconstruction helps us
also still better understand how Melanie Klein gave him
not only a whole series of conceptual instruments, but
even more the type of emotional containment that he so
badly needed, and which eventually allowed him to be
able to live in the present. And, as Harald Boris wrote in
1986, this is what also became the inspiring concept of his
way of working, that is, "the analyst's capacity to live in
the absolute present" (Boris, 1986, p. 175). "Patients do

not," writes Boris further. "They are in the past or in the future, for time like space is a medium in which contact with self and other can be evaded or equivocated." Last but not least, the relevance of the biographical and autobiographical aspects of Bion's work confirmed to me that it was a good idea to spend so much time and energy writing the Afterword I have attached to this book.

This was also made possible through the treatment and relationship I had with "Dr. L." Through this I on the one hand found the emotional containment I needed for the elaboration of my past, and, on the other hand, lived the experience of emotional transformation in the direction of O that Bion talks about. This experience was, in other words, one of expansion and growth which touched also the scientific and professional level of my identity, that is, the so-called K-dimension. It was not by chance that the transcription of Bion's letters to Rickman was part of the work we did together. In fact, the project of this anthology was also a result of the new sense of self I was able to find through this crucial experience.

Apart from the inspiration I gained from the above-described contacts with Elizabeth Tabak de Bianchedi and James Grotstein, I should say that the introduction to Bion's work I had had as a resident in psychiatry at the Catholic University of Rome through Leonardo Ancona (1920–2008) and his colleagues had already been so beneficial as to stimulate me to start reading Bion's books. I remember reading *Experiences in groups* (1961), *Learning from experience* (1962), *Elements of psychoanalysis* (1963), and *Second thoughts* (1967), the second having been translated into Italian in 1972 by Antonello Armando, Parthenope Bion Talamo, and Sergio Bordi—whom I have already mentioned in Chapter 6.

But Salomon Resnik (1920–2017) was the first older colleague I came in contact with who had actually known Bion and worked with him in supervision, and from whom I also had the chance to learn what our work was all about. Indeed, he had also played an important role in familiarizing Leonardo Ancona and his colleagues with the work of Bion in the mid-1970s (Resnik, Antonetti, and Ficacci, 1982). I am referring here to his group supervisions that I attended in Venice in the mid-1980s, and to the therapeutic group with schizophrenic and borderline patients that he regularly held at the Villa Santa Giuliana Hospital (Verona) in the early 1990s, around which centers his 2005 book *Glacial times. A journey through the world of madness*. One message I connect with the

Venice groups is the concept that we also have to help our patients really become patients, that is, people capable of suffering and of being patient, if we want to achieve the good "team work" that therapy is about. As far as the group therapy sessions Salomon Resnik held in Verona (with the director of the hospital, Giorgio Ferlini [1934–2017], as his co-therapist) are concerned, it was incredible how well he was able to speak with the patients—so well that one could get the impression that he really knew how to speak their language and understood what was going on inside them.

An Argentinian Jew, Salomon Resnik trained in Buenos Aires as a psychiatrist and psychoanalyst, working in close contact with Enrique Pichon Rivière (1907–1977). He moved to Europe in 1957, going first to Paris and then, at the end of 1958, to London. There he worked in several psychiatric hospitals (for example, the Cassel Hospital, directed by Thomas Main), and went through a long analysis with Herbert Rosenfeld (1910–1986), while working for several years in supervision with Bion himself. In 1971 Resnik moved to Paris, at the same time regularly working in Italy, particularly in Venice, which became his second home; he lived primarily in Paris until his death at age 96. His most important books are *The theatre of the dream* (1987), *The delusional person* (2011a), and *An archeology of the mind* (2011b).

I ended up knowing Salomon Resnik's work well enough to review his book *Biographie de l'inconscient* in the *International Journal of Psychoanalysis* (Conci, 2008b). The book centers around Resnik's clinically and interdisciplinarily sophisticated approach to the unconscious dimension of a person's life, and also contains a chapter based on a seminar that Bion gave in Resnik's office in Paris. The opening theme of this is the multiplicity of vertices and perspectives from which we can look at the first session with a patient, including the sensuous and the artistic. "What is the shadow which the patient projects on your mind?" and "What kind of an artist are you?" are the crucial questions that Bion discusses with the group. To Bion, Resnik dedicated also one of his last papers, "Flying thoughts in search of a nest: A tribute to W.R. Bion" (2016), included by Howard Levine and Giuseppe Civitarese in their anthology *The W.R. Bion tradition*, in which Resnik addressed those patients who have a sense of being "full of emptiness," about whom we discover that their thoughts are deprived of feelings. Last but not least, to Antonello Correale (2017) we owe a very well-written obituary of Resnik, centered around what Correale himself had learned from him.

Another older colleague whom I was in contact with for many years and who played an important role in the Italian reception of Bion's work, with particular regard to the application of Bionian psychoanalysis to groups and institutions, was Luigi Pagliarani (1922–2001). A training analysand of Franco Fornari (1921–1985), with whom he also worked in the 1960s in a group centered around the use of psychoanalysis to prevent the threat of nuclear war, Pagliarani is today considered to be the founder of Italian psychosocioanalysis. At the end of the 1960s, Pagliarani introduced into Italy the work of Elliott Jacques (1917–2003) (Pagliarani, 1969), that is, the work around which Jacques centered his 1970 book *Work, creativity and social justice*, and he never got tired of promoting Bion's work and legacy (see, for example, Pagliarani, 1990). In 2008 (Conci, 2008a), I wrote a paper on what I had learned from him, and on his legacy, based on a workshop he had given in Collalbo-Klobenstien in the September 1998, which I also mention in the Afterword.

At this point, before specifically dealing with my paper "Bion and Sullivan: An enlightening comparison," I will briefly deal with the topic of the reception of Bion's work in Italy, thus completing the picture of it which I present in Chapter 9. In Chapter 9, I speak of Francesco Corrao (1922–1994) as the first Italian analyst who met Bion, at the International Psychoanalytic Association Geneva Congress of 1955, and who spent the rest of his life promoting his work in our country. This is how Bion's books came to be promptly translated into Italian (see the References, for the year of their Italian translation) and discussed in the then rather small Italian Psychoanalytic Society (SPI). This produced such an interest in his work that, with the help of Bion's daughter Parthenope Bion Talamo (1945–1998), Corrao and the SPI were able to invite Bion to hold a series of seminars in Rome in July 1977. This was such a crucial event in the life of the Society and of many of its members that Claudio Neri dedicated to it his contribution to the above-mentioned anthology edited by Levine and Civitarese, with the title "A long meeting with Bion" (Neri, 2016). Only in 2005 did Bion's *Italian seminars*—originally published in Italian in 1985 with Francesca Bion as editor—also come out in English. From Claudio Neri we learn that he himself not only wrote the invitation letter to Bion, but also acted "as his guide and chauffeur" (Neri, 2016, p. 26) during his stay in Rome. But here is how Neri was able to transmit to us the climate of these seminars:

> Bion always stood while conducting his seminars; his
> presentation was rich in biblical metaphors and quotations
> from poets. During the seminars certain ideas that have
> remained the cornerstone of my activity ever since crystallized
> in my mind. The first is that Bion should be read in literal
> terms. He says and writes exactly what he thinks. He says and
> writes what he thinks as directly and clearly as he can express.
> Bion also does his best to see that the emotions connected
> with the content of a communication are incorporated in
> that communication . . . . Bion had two outstanding qualities:
> first, he made his pronouncements (however terrible) without
> a trace of arrogance; and, second, he never did so in order
> to show off or to put others down. Bion felt himself to be a
> psychoanalyst and teacher in the service of the truth. He was
> simply telling the truth, whether we like it or not. In the battle
> of truth you have to take sides . . . . If you can't hold out,
> you should preferably get in training until you succeed. (Neri,
> 2016, pp. 26–27)

Through these words I feel I can not only participate in
the exciting experience of listening to Bion (who gave then
altogether nine seminars), but also feel our responsibility
as psychoanalysts to allow our sense of truth to guide our
work; and I know how difficult such a task often is—due
to the resistances that we encounter in both ourselves and
our patients.

To the creative consequences of the openness of the
SPI to Bion's work and legacy belongs in the first place a
monographic issue of the *Rivista di Psiconalisisi* edited
in 1981 by Parthenope Bion Talamo and Claudio Neri,
in which they were able to publish almost twenty papers
written by the most prominent Italian analysts of the
time, and of which they were even able to produce an
English edition; in this way, they succeeded for the first
time in bringing the international community into contact
with the Italian analytic discourse. I remember reading
this at the time of my psychiatry residency, and recall that
I particularly liked the papers by Eugenio Gaddini (1916–
1985), Leonardo Ancona, Luciana Nissim Momigliano
(1919–1998), and Giovanni Hautmann (1927–2017). In
fact, it was only after rereading Eugenio Gaddini's paper,
"Paths through the creativity of Bion" (1981), which I did
while preparing this Introduction, that I realized that he
was the first author I had encountered who emphasized
the importance of John Rickman in Bion's development
of his professional and personal identity; this was perhaps
a source of inspiration for Chapter 7 in this anthology,
which I had evidently forgotten about before. In his paper
"The 'field-relationship' between S. Freud and W.R.
Bion" (1981), Leonardo Ancona shows how well Bion's
work illuminates and deepens Freud's work, a point
of view which might also have contributed to my own

tendency to look for and work in an integrative direction.

In the PEP-disk or PEP-web, the reader can of course also find the paper by Luciana Nissim Momgliano on "Memory and desire" (Nissim Momigliano, 1981), in which we find important traces of the beginning of her confrontation with the clinical dimension of Bion's work, that is, the dimension that she would transmit in the following years to an important series of supervisees, among them Antonino Ferro. Also on PEP-disk is the paper by Giovanni Hautmann, one of the most influential Italian analysts of his generation and himself president of the SPI between 1986 and 1990; his 1981 contribution "My debt towards Bion: From psychoanalysis as a theory to psychoanalysis as a mental function" reflects very well, from the very beginning, the creative confrontation with Bion's thought and legacy that accompanied all his professional life. Here is opening of Hautmann's paper:

> At the end of his 1977 Rome seminar, Bion likened the fate of his contribution to the fall of a leaf from a tree — one cannot say which side it is going to land on. However, we know that Bion cared more that his writings and seminars should produce psychoanalytical thought rather than 'faithful' interpreters of his own thought. The style of his thought, while hardly allowing a detailed exegesis of the text, on the other hand, stimulates further thought . . . . It seems to me that he has not, as he himself writes, so much added new chapters to psycho-analysis as a theory as collocated it among the functions of the mind: container or probe, as he alternately considers it, psycho-analysis through Bion seems a specific form of thought, a way of entering into a mental relationship with another person and with the self. In fact, it was during my meditations over the past years on what happens in the consulting room . . . that I realized that I was using psycho-analysis as a specific function of thought and that this was, for me, Bion's message. (Hautmann, 1981, pp. 573–574)

In fact, *Il mio debito con Bion* is also the title of the collection of his papers that Giovanni Hauptmann published in 1999. In his concept of the nature of Bion's legacy, we can of course also see an important anticipation of the point of view later developed by Antonino Ferro.

Bion's visit to Rome exerted a particularly lasting influence on the further scientific development of Claudio Neri, as we can see from the amount of time and energy he devoted to producing the 1994 anthology *Letture bioninane*, a volume of 484 pages containing the contributions on Bion's legacy put together by thirty-eight Italian and foreign colleagues (see Neri, Correale, & Fadda, eds., 1994). Among these was also Gianni Nebbiosi, whose role in the reception of S.A. Mitchell's work in Italy I dealt with in Chapter 6, and who at the time was working closely with Francesco Corrao, Claudio Neri, and Parthenope Bion Talamo. The anthology *Letture bioniane* represents the first of a series of books published on Claudio Neri's initiative, which also includes many books on Bion, such as *Bion and group psychotherapy* edited by Malcolm Pines (1985), Gérard Bléandonu's (1994) biography of Bion, and Rafael López Corvo's (2002) *The dictionary of the work of W.R. Bion.* Only in October 2015 did I have the good luck to get to know Claudio Neri better by visiting him Rome, after we had exchanged several emails in the summer concerning the papers we would present in Boston, at the workshop at which I presented the original version of Chapter 9.

As far as Parthenope Bion Talamo is concerned, she followed the career move of her musician-husband from Rome to Turin, where in 1992 she created with Franco Borgogno and Silvio Arrigo Merciai a "Bion study group"; in July 1997, this group organized in Turin the Bion Centennial Conference already mentioned (see Bezoari's 1997 report). What I also know about Bion's daughter Parthenope is that she had left London for Italy, studying philosophy in Florence, where she graduated in 1974 with a *tesi di laurea* on the relationship between psychoanalysis and mathematics, in the light of the works of her own father and of Ignacio Matte Blanco (1908–1995). I know this because Marcelo Bianchedi translated her thesis into Spanish in 1999, as *Metapsicología y metamatemática en algunas teorías psicoanalíticas recienets*, and I was given a copy of this as a gift by colleague Jaime Lutenberg in Buenos Aires in October 2008.

In their Preface to this small book (Bianchedi and Bianchedi, 1999), Elisabeth and Marcelo Bianchedi write that they originally met her at the International Psychoanalytical Association (IPA) Congress held in Rome in July 1989, and easily became very good friends, visiting each other as often as possible. They also remind the reader of Parthenope's great conflict around being on the one hand Bion's daughter, and on the other hand a psychoanalyst in her own right. She was able to solve this in a highly creative way, as can be seen in her 1987 paper "Why we can't call ourselves Bionians: Notes on the life and work of W.R. Bion." This represents Chapter 1 of the anthology of her papers put together by Anna Baruzzi in Italian in 2011 and edited in English by Chris Mawson in 2015 under the title *Maps for psychoanalytic exploration.* In this we read:

> To conclude, I would like to say that it is probably this quality

of mental freedom that made Bion such a disconcerting person, and an academic who could not, by his very nature, 'found a school' – we cannot call ourselves Bionians, because that would primarily mean being ourselves, being mentally free of our voyages of discovery – always, however, on the basis of personal iron discipline because freedom and anarchy are synonymous. (Bion Talamo, 2015, p. 7)

And here is how Claudio Neri introduces the book to the reader in his Preface:

One of the numerous threads in this collection may be indicated in a single sentence: Parthenope seeks her father, and after many efforts and vicissitudes, she finds him along with the psychoanalyst. The pages in which Parthenope manages to connect the father of the earliest childhood with the 'mythical psychoanalyst Bion' are very beautiful . . . (Neri, 2015, p. ix)

Of course, given my good knowledge of Bion's life, I experience these words of Claudio Neri also in connection with the tragedy (which not all readers may know about) caused by Parthenope's own birth, that is, the death of her mother, Bion's first wife Betty, after having delivered her. This tragic event created an attachment problem between father and daughter that lasted several years— and probably cast a shadow over their whole life. Here is what we can for example read in Bion's autobiographical work *All my sins remembered: Another part of life*: "I learned to stifle the wish, constantly awakened, that my infant's mother could see her and that we three together would go and have tea on Saturdays afternoons. The facts were otherwise" (Bion, 1985a, p. 74).

Last but not least, as the reader can see in my Afterword, I too had what we can also call an attachment problem with my father, and I know how painful this can be. But, at this point, I can only invite the reader to later read the Afterword and see how I was able to solve this. On the other hand, only after writing this personal note, did I realized that I have not reminded the readers of the tragic end to Parthenope Bion Talamo's own life. In mid-July 1998, at not yet fifty-three years, she, together with her younger daughter Patrizia, died in a car accident on their way to their vacation home.

Going back to the specific topic of this Introduction, that is, the multiple roots of Bion's work and the multiple aspects of his legacy, I can say that Parthenope Bion Talamo's process of elaboration of her relationship with her own father was also a fundamental inspiration for and ingredient of two things: the above-mentioned "Bion study group" that Parthenope Bion Talamo founded with Franco Borgogno and Silvio Arrigo Merciai in 1992, and their organization in Turin of the 1997 Bion Centennial Conference—of which she was president. This is what we can read in the obituary of Parthenope written by Borgogno and Merciai (1998), and what we can learn through their Turin Conference paper "Searching for Bion: *Cogitations*, a new *Clinical diary à la* Ferenczi" (Borgogno and Merciai, 2000), centered as it is around their complete work of reading and meeting with Bion, his work, and his legacy.

Through this work we can, for example, learn about the complex itinerary through which the authors ended up choosing Bion's posthumous book *Cogitations* (Bion, 1992), which was being translated into Italian by Bion Talamo and Merciai, and which came out in 1996 with a Preface by Gianni Nebbiosi; and we can read how they were at first disappointed by it, only gradually discovering its affinity with Sándor Ferenczi's *Clinical diary* (Ferenczi, 1932). Indeed, they discovered the book to be centered around a major split between theory and clinical attitude that Bion solved only very gradually, starting at the end of the 1960s, with his move from London to Los Angeles. This is a Bion who starts citing Ferenczi and whom the authors call "the Bion of the 'turning point'," and whom they see represented at best in his clinical seminars. In the authors' words:

> In short, the Bion that emerges from the *seminars* is similar to that of the final *cogitations*, more vigilant and able to listen to his own voice, less moralistic, given to fewer scholasticisms and preconceptions – but above all neither omnipotent nor omniscient. What we see now is a wish to work with those who turn to him and a readiness to learn from their contributions, along with a greater sense of discipline and a full awareness that he does not know already – a Bion who responsibly accepts feelings, such as when he says: 'Countertransference is a technical term, but as often happens the technical term gets worn away and turns into a kind of worn-out coin which has lost its value . . . . You will hear analysts say, 'I don't like that patient, but I can make use of my countertransference'. He cannot use his countertransference. He may be able to make use of the fact that he dislikes the patient, but that is not countertransference' (Bion, 1990, p.122). (Borgogno & Merciai, 2000; 2018, p. 143)

And, furthermore:

> Now that he has abandoned the asepsis of the great schools of logico-mathematical thought and verified the lack of conceptual and linguistic instruments capable of describing the life of the mind, now that he is less constrained by the duties that come with belonging to a psychoanalytic society (Bion had given up his membership of the British Society and turned down the offer to join the American Society) and perhaps helped by groups that were friendlier and more emotionally in touch, Bion's legacy can be summed up in two quotations:

"When two personalities meet, an emotional storm is created. If they make sufficient contact to be aware of each other, or even sufficient to be unaware of each other, an emotional state is produced by the conjunction of these two individuals, and the resulting disturbance is hardly likely to be regarded as necessarily an improvement on the state of affairs had they never met at all. But since they have met, and since this emotional storm has occurred, the two parties to this storm may decide to 'make the best of a bad job'" (Bion, 1994, p.321).

And: "The bad job happens to me. I cannot get thoroughly analyzed – I don't think there is such a thing. It has to stop some day; after that I have to make the best I can of who I am" (Bion, 1980, p.37). (Borgogno and Merciai, 2000; 2018, p. 143)

I have given so much room to Franco Borgogno's (and Silvio Arrigo Merciai's) very interesting elaboration of his (their) understanding of Bion's work and legacy not only because Franco Borgogno was also one of the Italian colleagues through whom I approached and understood more and more of Bion, but also because we ended up working together and becoming good friends. In 2008, Franco joined the editorial board of the *International Forum of Psychoanalysis*, and in 2009 we edited together a monographic issue of the journal containing a selection of the papers that had been presented at the Bion Conference held in Rome in January 2008 (see below). In addition, in 2013 I reviewed his book *The girl who committed hara-kiri and other clinical and historical essays*—trying to place the book in the context of his overall professional evolution and rich scientific output (Conci, 2013).

I tried to do the same in my 2009 review of Antonino Ferro's book *Mind works. Technique and creativity in psychoanalysis*, having started reading his books in the mid-1990s, and having approached him personally at the 2006 National Congress of the SPI held in Siena, with Anna Ferruta as the scientific secretary and Fernando Riolo as SPI president. In October 2007 I was able to invite Antonino Ferro to Munich, to give a paper and hold two group supervisions at the Munich Akademie für Psychoanalyse und Psychotherapie; he promptly reciprocated by inviting me to Pavia in November, to present to a group of his colleagues (among them Giuseppe Civitarese and Giovanni Foresti) my work on Harry Stack Sullivan and Stephen A. Mitchell.

I would not have been able to write my 2009 review had I not known him as closely as I did. In addition I would not have been able to write anything on Bion, as I was able to do in the summer of 2007, when I started working on Bion and Sullivan, without having first understood enough of Ferro's own way of working with or on Bion. In fact, as the reader may have gleaned by now, I am hardly capable of writing anything without a, for me, satisfactory knowledge of the entire literature produced on the topic on which I am writing. For this reason, I was able to write the 2009 review only after having read all the books that Ferro had published before *Tecnica e creatività* (2006), the original Italian edition of *Mind works*. In addition, *Mind works*, being his fifth book in ten years (1999–2009) to have been translated into English, the whole Italian analytic community was closely following his work, thanks to which Italian psychoanalysis as a whole eventually became internationally known and even significant. Indeed, Ferro's first book, *The bipersonal field: Experiences in child analysis* (1992) had also been the first one to be translated into English, in 1999 (see Ferro, 1999).

Last but not least, given such international prominence, it was not hard for me to collaborate in organizing the invitation Ferro received from the New York William Alanson White Institute to present a paper and supervise a case there, on Saturday January 16, 2010. This is also part of the background behind the invitation we both received from Montana Katz to present a paper on the analytic field concept at the workshop she organized in Cambridge (MA) in July 2015, out of which originated the paper that the reader can find as Chapter 9 of this anthology. The book containing the papers given at this workshop—*Advances in contemporary psychoanalytic field theory – Concept and future development* (2016)—was edited by Montana Katz together with Roosevelt Cassorla and Giuseppe Civitarese, whom I had also originally met at the above-mentioned congress in Siena, and whose scientific production I have been following with increasing interest ever since.

To give the reader a feeling of the way in which Ferro was referring himself to, and making use of, the work and legacy of Bion at the time of *Mind works. Creativity and technique in psychoanalysis*, I will quote directly from my 2009 review. Here is what I wrote about the chapter "Digressions and interpretation" of Ferro's book, in which Bion is repeatedly to be found at the center of Ferro's discourse. In this chapter, Ferro:

> presents Bion's recommendation of being in the session without memory and without desire as his 'vaccine' against the 'epistemic arrogance' of the analyst who 'continues to defend himself like a terrified child clinging to the theoretical skirts of his metapsychological mummy' (p.49). On the contrary, according to the author, we need 'a technique sophisticated enough to hide any 'trace of interpretative

technique' in the way one talks to the patient', and, instead of espousing recipes of one kind or another, we need 'a 'special' analytic recipe for each individual patient' (p.53). (Conci, 2009, p. 125)

It is no wonder that, in her review of the original Italian edition of Ferro's 2002 book *Fattori di malattia, fattori di guarigione*, Anna Ferruta's very good knowledge of his work allowed her to anticipate the theme of *Mind works* with the following words: "Ferro's writing [and I would add here, clinical] skills . . . are like those of a great musician who can allow himself virtuosities while never for a moment forgetting, or lessening, the technical clarity of his performance" (Ferruta, 2003, p. 460). Ferruta ended her review by citing some words by Ferro (taken from the book she was reviewing) that express very well the synthesis between technique and creativity that he specifically formulated in *Mind works*: "The art of a psychoanalyst lies precisely in regulating the 'breathing' of the analytic field . . . the analyst is positioned as a breathing center that must constantly modulate—according to necessity—the breaths of the field" (cf. Ferruta, 2003, p. 462)

But the most important thing, as far as my own relationship with the multiple roots of Bion's work and the multiple aspects of his legacy is concerned, is represented by the fact that, in the summer of 2007, I had been able to dedicate myself to eventually writing about him; I started this from the author I knew best, that is, Harry Stack Sullivan, and by writing the paper "Bion and Sullivan: An enlightening comparison," that is, Chapter 8 of this anthology. Of course, before actually doing this, further specific preparation was required. This first included reading for a second or third time most of Bion's books, as well as Donald Meltzer's (1922–2004) unique summary of Bion's work (Meltzer, 1978). In addition, I needed to bring myself up to date with works in the secondary literature with which I was not yet familiar, for example *The clinical thinking of Wilfred Bion* (1996) by Joan and Neville Symington, which had been translated into Italian in 1998 by Susanna Federici and Gianni Nebbiosi. In fact, it is no wonder that Gianni Nebbiosi—himself already familiar with Stephen Mitchell's work—centered his Preface to the Italian edition (Nebbiosi, 1998) around the way in which the Symingtons emphasize the prominent role attributed by Bion to our relational and emotional life, at the same time minimizing Bion's Freudian and Kleinian background. Another perspective on Bion's work is the one offered by Paulo Cesar Sandler, which I encountered through his 2006 paper "The origins of Bion's work."

But the book that I found most helpful was of course James Grotstein's *A beam of intense darkness. Wilfred Bion's legacy to psychoanalysis*, which I remember having bought at the IPA Berlin Congress at the end of July 2007. The most touching of Grotstein's thirty-one chapters was for me Chapter 27, "Become," in which we can read the following:

> I believe that what Bion means by 'becoming' in the clinical situation is that the analyst, while in a state of reverie, is receptive to his patient's emotional communications by being in exquisitely sensitive contact with *his own inner self* – that is, *his own* unconscious reservoir of counterpart emotions, experiences, phantasies, and so on, which match up with those of the patient. Thus the analyst's unconscious *resonates* with that of the patient. This act constitutes 'becoming' or what I would call, following Plato, the 'flux' or the 'rhythm of becoming'. This act is aided by our inherent possession of 'mirror neurons' (Gallese, 2001; Gallese and Godman, 1998), the neuronal basis for the quality of empathic observation . . . . From a more practical perspective, the concept of 'become' can be applied to infant development and the clinical situation as follows: as the infant evolves from the paranoid-schizoid to the depressive position, one of his tasks is to accept – that is, to 'become', to own – his experience of neediness, including his drives. The same is true for the clinical situation in which the analyst seeks to help the analysand 'own', that is, 'become' their emotions by feeling them." (Grotstein, 2007, p. 307, original emphasis)

Such a point of view about the type of contact to be established with the patient also reminded me of Sullivan's legacy, but I also remember getting from Grotstein's book what I experienced as specific confirmations of the soundness of the comparison between Bion and Sullivan that had been growing in my mind, and which I now only needed to formulate in words. The first example that comes to mind is a variation of an exchange between Grotstein and Bion already mentioned above, which appears in Chapter 2, "What kind of an analyst was Bion?":

> Another unforgettable interpretation occurred after I had responded to a particularly effective interpretation by commenting, 'That was a beautiful interpretation'; 'Yes, a beautiful interpretation, you say. The snag is that my 'beautiful interpretation' was made possible only by virtue of your 'beautiful associations'. You were so keen on listening to me that you neglected listening to yourself speaking to me'. I concluded from that interchange . . . that it was his way of helping me, as a patient, to refocus on how I experience *my* interactions with him . . . . As a derivative of this idea, Bion seemed to suggest that the analysand as well as the analyst should listen to themselves listening to each other. Bion was clearly a direct descendent of Socrates. (Grotstein, 2007, pp. 29–30, original emphasis)

And here is what Sullivan, *mutatis mutandis*, wrote in

the 1937 article "A note on the implications of psychiatry: The study of interpersonal relations, for investigations in the social sciences": "The crying need is for observers who are growing observant of their observing" (Sullivan, 1964, p. 27). Indeed, we should never forget that what we also offer our patients is the possibility—by listening to them without interfering in what they say—of hearing themselves talking. Such an attitude is in itself something specifically analytical, that is, something that potentially produces a new experience for the patient, and that we cannot (so easily) find in our daily life and social interactions.

Two other experiences belonged to my preliminary work for Chapter 8 of this book. The first was of feeling supported in my comparative approach to Bion and Sullivan by Thomas Ogden's 2007 paper on "Reading Harold Searles"; the second, was the experience of letting myself be affected by the way in which Ogden deals with Bion's legacy. This included, for example, how Ogden talks about his work in the 2004 paper "An introduction to the reading of Bion," in which he distinguishes the "early" from the "late" Bion in terms of two markedly different conceptions of psychoanalysis and two correspondingly different writing styles. In Ogden's words:

> If reading early Bion is an experience of movement toward convergence of disparate meanings, the experience of reading late Bion is an experience of movement toward an infinite expansion of meaning . . . . If reading early Bion is an experience of learning from experience, reading late Bion is an experience of disencumbering oneself of the deliberate use of all that one has learned from experience in order to be receptive to all that one does not know . . . . The two stand as different 'vertices' (Bion, 1970, p.73) from which to view the analytic experience. They give stereoscopic depth to one another as opposed to conversing with one another. (Ogden, 2004, p. 293)

This paper also came out as Chapter 6 in Ogden's 2005 book *This art of psychoanalysis*, and I have read every single book of his since then, as soon as each came out. Fortunately, Stephen Mitchell had in the early 1990s already directed my attention to Ogden's first books, for example *The primitive edge of experience* (1989). Sandra Buechler and I recommend its Chapter 7, "The initial analytic meeting," to the colleagues attending the Discussion Group on "Using concepts from Freud, Sullivan, and Ogden to initiate treatment" that we have been holding every year since 2015 at the American Psychoanalytic Association congress in New York City. Another wonderful book is *Rediscovering psychoanalysis* (2009), containing, among others, the very important chapter on "Bion's four principles of mental functioning," which was discussed by Giuseppe Civitarese (2010) as soon as it came out.

Of course, I am very curious about how the readers will react to my Chapter 8, "Bion and Sullivan: An enlightening comparison." Franco Borgogno and I published this in Issue 2/2009 of the *International Forum of Psychoanalysis*, in which we also published six more papers deriving from the International Bion Conference held in Rome in January 2008. After the Bion Conferences held in Buenos Aires (1999), Los Angeles (2002), and Sao Paulo (2004), an Italian committee chaired by Giorgio Corrente organized one in Rome, attracting about 500 participants and hosting a whole series of good papers in Italian, English, and Spanish. Here is the way in which Franco and I introduced the readers to my paper in our Editorial:

> As the fifth paper of this selection, we publish Marco Conci's contribution "Bion and Sullivan: An enlightening comparison", which was inspired by the comparative methodology developed by Jay Greenberg and Stephen Mitchell in their by now classical work *Object relations in psychoanalytic theory*, and by the dialogical approach realized both by Mitchell himself through the journal *Psychoanalytic Dialogues* and by the 'new wave' of Italian psychoanalysis, inaugurated by Antonino Ferro and Stefano Bolognini (and also by one of us, F.B.). Indeed, the paper was originally conceived for the seminar that the author gave in Pavia on November 11, 2007, upon the invitation of Ferro himself and his group (Giovanni Foresti, Giuseppe Civitarese, etc.). In it, the author – who had once revisited Freud's self-analysis in the light of Sullivan's interpersonal theory (cf. Conci, 1998) – shows the many similarities and affinities between Bion and Sullivan, which enable him to conceive them in terms of "secret imaginary twins" (the Bionian term that Didier Anzieu [1989] used in his revisitation of Samuel Beckett's relationship to Bion). As running somewhat parallel to one another can, for example, be conceived two such seminal books as Sullivan's *Interpersonal theory of psychiatry* (1953) and Bion's *Learning from experience* (1962). Or, in other words, from the point of view of Leo Rangell's "unitary theory", Bion's concept of *reverie* and alpha-function and Sullivan's interpersonal "theorems" (of tenderness and of anxiety) can be seen as reciprocally integrating each other – and/or as answers to similar basic questions with which both authors struggled. As a matter of fact, since the author – when he wrote his paper – did not know the integrative direction in which the work of his North American colleagues Levine and Brown was moving, their convergence can well be considered a result of the *Zeitgeist* in which we are living. (Conci & Borgogno, 2009, p. 68, original emphasis)

By such a convergence in the direction of a comparative and/or integrative psychoanalysis, I was not referring just to the papers that Levine and Brown had presented in Rome, which were mainly clinical papers, but more specifically to the general direction of their research work. Here is, for example, how Lawrence Brown concluded the paper "Bion's ego psychology: Implications for an intersubjective view of psychic structure" (Brown, 2009b), on which he was working at the time of the Rome Conference, and which became Chapter 4 of his 2011 important book *Intersubjective process and the unconscious. An integration of Freudian, Kleinian and Bionian perspectives* (Brown, 2011a):

> In postulating alfa function, Bion introduced an intersubjective dimension to our understanding of how the ego makes meaning of emotional events, because alfa function represents the internalization of the mother-infant couple's creation of meaning together through a process best described by Tronick (2005) and Tronick et al. (1998) as the *dyadic expansion of consciousness*. This leads to a deeper understanding of the unconscious exchange between analyst and patient in what Freud (1912) described as the analyst's use of his unconscious as an instrument of the analysis. Thus, there is a constant, unconscious, interactional process between the linked alfa functions of the analysand and the analyst, by which meaning is constantly being created and expanded. When treatment is going well, this results in the mutual growth of the container/contained ($\female$ / $\male$).
>
> 'Bion's ego psychology' has been compared to various other branches of ego psychology, and it is important to take into account all perspectives in psychoanalytic work. The analyst's attention to what is on the workable surface of the clinical hour is greatly enhanced by his gaining access, through attention to his reveries, to the parallel undercurrent of unconscious work in which the analytic couple are simultaneously engaged. Thus, there is considerable clinical utility to expanding the notion of the workable surface to include the mental functioning of the analyst. (Brown, 2009b, p. 52)

In fact, the version of his Rome paper that we published in the monographic issue, with the title "From 'disciplined subjectivity' to 'taming wild thoughts': Bion's elaboration of the analyzing instrument" (Brown, 2009a), centered around a fascinating clinical case (taken from his work with four-year-old Billy). In this came to fruition what he calls "a procreative model of the analyst and the analyst and analysand thinking together," implying "the appearance of something new, a cognitive offspring that owes its existence to the interpenetration of unconscious communication, that is, in many respects, sexual in nature" (Brown, 2009a, p. 83). A similar convergence is what I experienced with Howard Levine, in relation to the integrative direction of his many analytic publications, which I then started reading with great interest, and some of which Franco Borgogno and I mentioned in our

Editorial. Similarly original, if not of a heroic character, is the clinical work around which centered Levine's paper "Reflections on catastrophic change" (Levine, 2009).

A similar high quality also characterizes the papers by Fernando Riolo, Jaime Lutenberg, Rudi Vermote, and Paola Camassa that were included in the same issue. I also remember as highly gratifying the experience of collaborating with them, and with Franco Borgogno, in the production of the monographic issue—in whose Editorial we introduced the reader to both the authors and their papers. This certainly contributed to motivating me to look for a topic and produce an abstract that could be accepted as the basis of a paper to be presented at the following Bion International Conference, to be held in Boston in July 2009, with Howard Levine and Lawrence Brown as co-chairs of the organizing committee. That is how I came to write the paper "Bion and his first analyst, John Rickman (1891–1951): A revisitation of their relationship in the light of Rickman's personality and scientific production and of Bion's letters to him (1939–1951)," included in this anthology as Chapter 7. The first paragraphs of this read as follows:

> At the previous Bion Conference, held in Rome at the end of January 2008, I had given a paper with the title "Bion and Sullivan: An enlightening comparison." Franco Borgogno and I included it in the special issue of the *International Forum of Psychoanalysis* dedicated to this event that we edited together, in which we also included six more papers given in Rome. In my paper, I showed how many things Bion and H.S. Sullivan (1892–1949) had in common, although Bion neither met him nor ever quoted his work in his books.
>
> But Rickman and Sullivan did meet with each other, at least once, in Paris in 1948—as we shall see below. Did not only Rickman and Sullivan, but also Rickman and Bion, have more things in common than we ever dared to imagine? What do we know about Rickman, besides his having been Bion's first training analyst and having worked with him at Northfield Hospital? We know that out of this experience came the first chapter of Bion's *Experiences in groups*, which he wrote together with Rickman. And what else do we know? After reconstructing a picture of Rickman's life and work, I will reconsider Bion's relationship to Rickman in the light of the twenty-seven letters that Bion wrote to him between January 29, 1939 and June 17, 1951, which I found in the Archives of the British Psychoanalytical Society. (Conci, 2011b, p. 68, original emphasis)

Together with this good piece of historical research, I was also able to publish—in Issue 2/2011 of the *International Forum of Psychoanalysis*—a series of commentaries written by colleagues Howard Levine, Lawrence Brown, David Scharff, Robert Caper, Antonino Ferro, Giovanni Foresti, Giuseppe Civitarese, Heinz

Weiss, and Rudi Vermote. In order to introduce the reader to both my paper and the commentaries, I wrote a long Editorial, and I will deal with this next. I will specifically deal with the paper itself and with the commentaries later in this Introduction.

In the Editorial—which had the title "Wilfred Bion's identity as a psychoanalyst in the light of his letters (1939–1951) to his first analyst, John Rickman, and of their multidimensional relationship. Our trainings (and our lives), our letters, and the history, transmission and practice of psychoanalysis"—I reminded the reader of how the history of psychoanalysis represents one of the major interests of our journal. I also covered, as a synthesis, the whole territory I have covered in the Introduction to Part One of this book, in order to connect Bion's letters to Rickman to the whole body of Freud's letters. In fact:

> Through what once used to be our letters and are now our e-mails and/or Skype conversations, we can construct the experience of that peculiar transitional space in which the analytically oriented self-analysis that Freud recommended in 1910 takes place. I thus hope that more and more colleagues will appreciate not only the historical relevance of Freud's (and Bion's) letters, but also their relevance for both our clinical work and our analytic identity. As psychoanalysts, we not only need patients to work with, but also – besides a theory to inspire us – colleagues to talk to. (Conci, 2011a, pp. 66–67)

A further confirmation that my work on Bion's letters to Rickman was a positive idea was the publication—in Issue 1/2012 of the journal *Psychoanalysis and History*, edited by John Forrester (1949–2015)—of Dimitris Vonofakos and Bob Hinshelwood's complete transcription of these letters, followed by a commentary by Michael Roper. I will deal with both of these, together with my paper on it, below, in the third section, and then with my paper and its nine commentaries, later in this Introduction. In 2013, Vonofakos and Hinshelwood also contributed the chapter "Letters to John Rickman—Transition 1939–1951" to the anthology *Bion's sources. The shaping of his paradigms*, edited by Nuno Torres and Robert Hinshelwood himself.

In the same year, Howard Levine and Lawrence Brown were able to eventually publish a selection of the main papers given in Boston (Levine & Brown, eds., 2013). This started with a first section of historical papers, including the original paper by the Israeli colleague Dorit Szykierski (2013) on the relationship between Bion's traumatic experience on the French front in World War I and his later metapsychology, centered as it is around the concept of containment. This was a paper that ran parallel to my attempt to revisit the roots of Bion's creativity in his relationship with Rickman, not only as analyst, but also as colleague and friend. Of the sixteen chapters of the book, which the editors divided into six parts, I will now quote some of the first paragraphs of Howard Levine's final thoughts, given the excellent way in which he was able to summarize the concept of Bion's legacy that emerged from the Boston Conference. Here are his words:

> I think that Bion's work speaks to so many different analysts, in part because he placed such great store on the uniqueness and value of individual, subjective experience and believed that bearing the truth of personal experience, no matter how idiosyncratic or painful, was essential for the growth of the psyche. We hear echoes of this belief in the titles that he chose for his books – *Learning from experience, Attention and interpretation* – and in his explanations to audiences that he would tell them something about how *he* did analysis in the hope that it might help them to understand something about how *they* did analysis.
>
> Bion tried to lead readers and listeners away from the expectation that he would reveal some new and pre-existing universal truth. Instead, he preferred to encourage them to risk giving up the comfort of holding on to what was already known and familiar and attempted to help prepare their minds to encounter some unexpected and not yet known aspect of emerging experience. While his writings certainly added specific 'facts' to our understanding of human psychology, he also taught us to be wary, perhaps even distrustful, of the defensive use to which 'facts' and 'knowledge' (in the static sense) could be put. He cautioned that clinging to the familiarity of the known can obscure what was disturbing, unfamiliar, urgent and central at any given moment. So, too, he warned of the tendencies within the group to reject truth and oppose new knowledge, if it threatened to destabilize the comfortable investments and assumptions of the status quo.
>
> Rather than seeking to create 'Bionians' – acolytes, disciples and adherents – Bion sought to kindle a creative spark in others that would lead to new and unexpected discoveries. This attitude towards students and colleagues was consistent with his understanding and practice of psychoanalysis and his view of the unconscious. He described the former as a probe that expands the very field it seeks to explore and viewed the latter as an ever expanding and infinite domain. He believed that the frontiers of what must be explored and what remained to be understood would be limitless and inexhaustible. Thus, he emphasized process over content, *Transformations* (another choice of a book title) over 'facts' and urged us to pay as much if not more attention to the links and relations between things than on the things themselves. (Levine, 2013, pp. 313–314, original emphasis)

In fact, this is also the perspective with which I have put together in this anthology a series of my contributions to psychoanalysis published between 1992 and 2016. It is my way of reconstructing my personal approach to psychoanalysis, which I propose not as a model in itself, but only as a model of the process of personal research that I consider to be the essence of psychoanalysis itself. From this point of view, I could even speak of this anthology as actually documenting my own way of assimilating Bion's legacy. Another important event of 2013 was the publication of Bion's *Wilfred Bion – Los Angeles seminars and supervision*, edited by Joseph Aguayo and Barnet Malin.

But in 2014 we were at last able to witness the publication of *The complete works of W.R. Bion*, a total of sixteen volumes, edited by Chris Mawson with Francesca Bion as editorial consultant—which Joseph Aguayo reviewed in detail in the *International Journal of Psychoanalysis* in 2017. Fortunately, I was able to have this *magnum opus* at my disposal during the preparation of this Introduction—and I am also able quote from it. The same is true for the two important anthologies on Bion's work and legacy: *Teaching Bion. Modes and approaches*, edited by Meg Harris Williams in 2015, and *The W.R. Bion tradition. Lines of development, evolution of theory and practice over the decades*, by Howard Levine and Giuseppe Civitarese in 2016. They have both further enriched our approach to Bion and shown how much we can still learn from him. As an aside, Bob Hinshelwood's very good chapter in the former anthology, under the title "Teaching Bion's teaching," repeatedly deals with Bion's relationship with Rickman, which Hinshelwood defines as "a mentoring relationship which transformed Bion into an original thinker and gifted writer" (Hinshelwood, 2015, p. 118).

Before finally getting to deal with my revisitation of the field of "comparative psychoanalysis," which is what I have been trying to do over the course of this Introduction, I will say a few words on the reception of Bion's work in Germany and on a recent book on his legacy. I am referring here to Wolfgang Mertens' book *Psychoanalytische Schulen im Gespräch über die Konzepte Wilfred R. Bions* (see the References for the translation of the title), in which the author presents Bion's main concepts in detail and compares them with those of a whole series of contemporary analytic schools, expressing this in the form of a dialogue running through all the seventeen chapters of the book. Given the later reception of Bion's work in Germany as compared to Italy, Mertens' book is an important contribution to the promotion of his work and legacy.

Except for *Experiences in groups*, whose German version came out in 1971, Bion's other books started to be published in German only in the 1990s, mostly thanks to the Freiburg colleague Erika Krejci (1936–2013), who personally translated *Learning from experience* (published 1990), *Elements of psychoanalysis* (published 1990) *and Transformations* (published 1997) (see Hegener, 2016). As if the German colleagues had taken Edna O'Shaughnessy's opinion on "the late Bion" seriously, neither his 1992 book *Cogitations* nor any of his autobiographical writings have been translated into German (see Angeloch, 2017), with the result of privileging "the early Bion" over "the late Bion," and his metapsychology and a part of his clinical work over the overall roots of his work. In fact, the book on Bion's life and work published in 2007 by theologian Wolfgang Wiedemann—who revisited Bion's legacy in terms of the creation of a new relationship between psychoanalysis and religion—still remains the main source in this regard, apart from, of course, the 2008 German edition of Gérard Bléandonu's biography of Bion (original French edition, 1990).

Although Wolfgang Mertens tried to remedy this one-sided reception in his book, more work is still necessary in order to fill this gap; on the other hand, the author succeeds in playing with Bion's ideas, as he probably would have liked us to do (see also Billow, 1999), and in showing how much they influenced contemporary psychoanalysis. In fact, he wrote the book to try to meet the challenge formulated by former IPA president (2009–2013) Charles Hanly (Hanly, 2011) to elaborate a useful clinical comparison of the theories we use in contemporary psychoanalysis. Among the pioneers of the reception of Bion's work in Germany, of course, the names of Hermann Beland, Jutta Gutwinski-Jeggle, and Ross Lazar (2014) also deserve to be mentioned.

1. "COMPARATIVE PSYCHOANALYSIS" REVISITED

What is "comparative psychoanalysis"? To cut a long story short, I am ready to state that "comparative psychoanalysis" is, according to me, exactly the type of approach to an author like Bion which I have developed up to now in this Introduction in order to introduce him to the reader. In other words, it is the kind of approach that I would suggest that all my colleagues should develop as the best possible approach to the history of psychoanalytic ideas. This puts it in contrast to "comparative psychoanalysis" being defined as a specialized branch of psychoanalysis that centers one-sidedly around the comparison of a series of clinical models.

What we need as intellectually sophisticated clinicians is, first, not just a comparison of clinical models, but a knowledge of our favorite authors in terms of the biographical, cultural, and historical roots of their ideas and of their clinical legacy. Second, we need sufficient familiarity with more than one author in order to be able to let a series of authors interact among each other in our minds when we work with our patients. This is indeed what this whole anthology of my papers is all about, that is, the kind of internal coherence connecting them all. On the other hand, since—as the reader has seen—I am not used to concentrating on just my point of view, but prefer to present it in terms of the overall context of ideas out of which I developed it, I will say a few words— write a few pages—on what I know about the concept of "comparative psychoanalysis."

Although the very good dictionary of psychoanalysis published by Salman Akhtar in 2009 does not contain the item "comparative psychoanalysis," the term entered the field almost forty years ago through a series of books and authors. In the classical work of "comparative psychoanalysis," Jay Greenberg and Stephen Mitchell's *Object relations in psychoanalytic theory* (1983), the authors attribute the origin of the term to Roy Schafer, with particular regard to a paper of his published in *Contemporary Psychoanalysis* in 1979 with the title "On becoming a psychoanalyst of one persuasion or another." They view "comparative psychoanalysis" as "a conceptual framework within which the confusion among competing theories can be clarified" (Greenberg and Mitchell, 1983, p. 2), attributing to it the following function:

> A comparative psychoanalysis will aid the theorist and the student of theory by illuminating significant areas of convergence and divergence obscured by the isolation of various psychoanalytic schools from each other and by the internal complexities of each. It will aid the practitioner by drawing out the implications of different theoretical perspectives for a wide range of clinical issues, thus offering a structure for the integration of theory and practice. It is to this goal that our volume is dedicated. (Greenberg, Mitchell, p. 2)

The authors conclude their research by dividing the analytic landscape into two opposing and competing poles, that is, the drive model and the relational model, whose persistence they saw as inevitable, as they stated at the end of the volume:

It seems more likely that both the drive model and the
relational model will persist, undergoing continual revision
and transformation, and that the rich interplay between
these two visions of human experience will generate creative
dialogue. We hope that our efforts will contribute to make
more meaningful dialogue possible. (Greenberg and Mitchell,
1983, p. 408)

This kind of "comparative psychoanalysis," aimed
at a better collegial and clinical dialogue, the results of
Greenberg's and Mitchell's research work and of their
following scientific and political initiatives, played a
role in the professional evolution of a whole series of
colleagues, equally interested in the potential benefits of
such a direction of "conceptual research." Among them
was Arnold Richards, who in 2003 came to the following
assessment of Greenberg's and Mitchell's work and
legacy:

Credit must be given to Greenberg and Mitchell for
their articulation of the intellectual synthesis that lay the
groundwork for a new political alliance, as well as to the
founders of the relational track at NUY for using that
synthesis to shape curriculum. A dozen years later, however,
it is possible to see that their success came at a price. The
energy of the dissidents was fueled at least in part by a sense
of their status as victims, and the fundamental premise of
a dichotomy between drive and relational theories fails to
withstand scrutiny. Melanie Klein, for instance, was classified
by Greenberg and Mitchell (1983) as an object relations
theorist, though she endorsed the concept of the death
instinct. Some in the relational camp, however, including
Jessica Benjamin (1999), have questioned the binary
opposition, between drives, seen as nonrelational, and the
need for relationships, seen as lacking instinctual energy. In
his later work, Greenberg (1991) made room for a concept of
drives within a relational matrix when he proposed safety
and effectance as primary motivations of human behavior.
(Richards, 2003; 2015, p. 55)

But in the following words, with which Arnold
Richards concludes this paper, he expresses the pluralistic
and comparative perspective that I also share and that
also lies at the roots of this book:

Although I call myself a contemporary Freudian, my loyalty,
as I said at the outset, is not to Freud as a human being,
who for all his greatness had his share of frailties, but to
psychoanalysis as a method of thinking, working, and living.
This method, though it originated with Freud, has been
enriched by Klein, Winnicott, Sullivan, Hartmann, Kohut,
and all the other figures who form the tradition to which we
are heir and to which we have the opportunity to contribute
in our turn. In Winnicott's profound words (1971), 'in any
cultural field it is not possible to be original except on the
basis of tradition' (p.99). Psychoanalysis is a coat of many
colors. Let us cease fighting over our inheritance and resolve
instead to share it and to wear it with both humility and pride

as we enter the twenty-first century. (Richards, 2003; 2015,
p. 59)

Robert Wallerstein (1912–2014) had a similar
orientation, in terms of his appreciation of pluralism
and of the need for a serious comparative work aimed at
distinguishing between the theoretical dimension of our
"many psychoanalyses" (to paraphrase the title of his first
presidential address to the IPA, given in Montreal in 1987;
see Wallerstein, 1988) and the clinical framework within
which we can place our so-called "common ground" (to cite
the title of his second presidential address, given in Rome
in 1989; Wallerstein, 1990). Here is how he formulated his
point of view in a very lively and interesting interview
with Luca Di Donna conducted in 2010:

> Later, when I was president of the International
> Psychoanalytical Association, I gave my presidential address
> in Montreal in 1987. At that time, a controversy was stirring
> the American that we no longer had the hegemony of one
> point of view. We had Kohut, we had the Kleinians, and some
> people were paying attention to Lacan. I proposed that we
> should examine the topic of psychoanalytic pluralism from
> a serious perspective. We fight about our state of pluralism:
> some people say that it shouldn't exist, and others that we
> had to live with it as the vitalizing state of affairs in our field.
> My position was that, because of our theoretical pluralism,
> we don't pay sufficient attention to what we have in common.
> I said that in the face of our different metapsychologies—
> Freudian ego psychological, Kleinian, Bionian, Lacanian,
> Kohutian, interpersonal—we need focus on what we
> have in common that holds us together as psychoanalysts.
>
> By the time of the IPA's Rome Congress in 1989, there
> were enough references in the literature to this controversy
> and this address so that the question of "common ground"
> became the focus of the meeting. I wrote a paper (1990),
> my second presidential address, to the 1989 IPA Congress
> in Rome, supporting more strongly the idea that the
> psychoanalytic common ground was in our shared clinical
> theory and clinical practice. The theories of transference and
> countertransference, resistance and defense, anxiety, and
> compromise formation are all seen clinically; you see resistances
> and you experience transference and countertransference
> reactions. That's where our common ground is.
>
> Where we don't have common ground, but instead have
> our diversity, is in how we explain these clinical phenomena
> theoretically. We explain them in terms of whole-object
> relationships and part-object relationships, or the depressive
> position and the paranoid-schizoid position, or in terms of the
> interrelations of the ego, the superego, and the id, or we explain
> them in terms of changing internal object relationships. We
> have different explanatory systems for the same phenomena,
> and the proponents of each system treat the phenomena to a
> large extent in very similar ways, although they explain what
> they're doing in different theoretical languages. (Di Donna,
> 2010, pp. 650–651)

As Robert Wallerstein tells Luca Di Donna, an

important role in the formulation of such a position was also played by the important collaboration that he had had the chance to develop with Otto Kernberg, whose work has also a unique comparative and integrative character. I am referring here to the integration of the Kleinian orientation of Kernberg's Chilean training with the ego-psychological perspective of Edith Jacobson (1897–1982) and with the object relations school that he also contributed to importing into the USA. Of course, his personal familiarity with Spanish, English, German, and French, his incredibly rich network of contacts around the world, and his unique intellectual openness and curiosity, make of him a privileged observer of the international psychoanalytic landscape, and, at the same time, a master in the field of "comparative psychoanalysis." This is also what we can gather from the following final observations taken from Kernberg's very interesting 2011 article "Divergent contemporary trends in psychoanalytic theory":

> Both the neo-Bionian and the relational approaches have contributed new technical advances: in the case of the neo-Bionian approach, the development of the analysis of the psychoanalytic field, countertransference analysis, the importance of unsaturated and evocative forms of interpretation; in the case of relational analysis, a careful exploration of the contributions of the analyst to transference and countertransference, the questioning of an artificial, 'anonymous', rigid stance and its negative effects. Both of them, interestingly enough, have as common sources the contributions of Baranger and Baranger, Ogden, to some extent Winnicott, and an underlying object relations theory approach that, in fact, emerges as a major development in psychoanalytic theory shared by practically all contemporary psychoanalytic approaches.
> My major critique of both the approaches under consideration is their neglect of the complexity of the original and contemporary Freudian approach to psychoanalytic theory and technique, a complexity that includes, at a theoretical level, the totality of the relations involving drive and affect theory; early object relations; the functions of attachment, eroticism, and aggression in determining early normal and pathological structures; the importance of development of character formation; and the interactional aspects of unconscious determinants and actual life experience as contributors to the final clinical picture and the therapeutic approach.
> At a clinical level, neo-Bionian approaches neglect a sharp focus on external reality and on structural diagnosis, on characterological structure and its influence on the development of transference reactions. However, neo-Bionian analysts do continue and expand the analysis of the influence of primitive unconscious fantasy, defenses, and object relations on the developments in transference and countertransference. The relational approach, in contrast, neglects the deepest aspects of unconscious life, and, while focusing on transference and countertransference, neglects the unconscious historical

aspects of the patient's character pathology, the unconscious conflictual significance of acting out of that pathology, and external reality. It seems that both these orientations would neglect one important aspect or other of Freudian theory and technique, the exploration of the deepest aspects of the unconscious by relational analysis, and the full exploration of present reality and character structure by both of them.

From a broader perspective, the sharply diverging differences between these two approaches constitute an interesting subject for empirical research. Psychoanalysis as a profession and as a science is at an early stage of such a major scientific enterprise, although, hopefully, this will be a way in which fundamental theoretical and technical differences can be explored in the future. For the time being, we will have to expect that the experience of an entire generation of psychoanalysts will provide evidence regarding the effectiveness or, lack thereof, of the techniques inspired by these approaches, and provide the knowledge for authentic progress. This is a slower but, ideally, effective way to clarify and resolve differences. (Kernberg, 2011, pp. 660–661)

Two other important North American authors who worked greatly for the promotion of a pluralistic, comparative, and integrative psychoanalysis are Leo Rangell (1913–2011) and Arnold Cooper (1923–2011), whose orientations I mention in one of the footnotes to Chapter 8, representing it also a form of exercise in this same kind of "comparative psychoanalysis." Given its importance, at this point of my discourse, I will now reproduce the footnote here:

One of the most recent and interesting products of this new climate of opinion is represented by the papers given by Leo Rangell, "Reconciliation: the continuing role of theory," and Arnold Cooper, "American psychoanalysis today: plurality of orthodoxies," at the annual meeting of the American Academy of Psychoanalysis and Dynamic Psychiatry, held in San Diego, California, in May 2007, which appeared in print in Issue 2/2008 of the *Journal of the Academy* (Cooper, 2008; Rangell, 2008) with an introduction by Marianne Horney Eckardt (2008), and which I can highly recommend to readers—to whom I can offer here only a small selection of some of the most significant statements made by the speakers. For example, Marianne Horney Eckardt's statement that "the theme of rapprochement has been with us since our very beginning" (since the Academy's foundation in 1956), as a "thought collective," "in our commitment to the importance of fostering communication with each other" (2008, p. 215). Or the following statement by Leo Rangell: "There is no justification in eliminating the interpersonal from Freudian mainstream theory. Interpersonal relations live and constitute its very essence. And the cultural dimension, embraced by Karen Horney, is similarly intrinsic to the total, traditional Freudian ideational tree; the external world is in fact the fourth structural system" (Rangell, 2008, pp. 224–225). And, last but not least, the following considerations made by Arnold Cooper: "Harry Stack Sullivan, today acknowledged as a founder not only of the interpersonal point of view, but as a precursor of the relational and intersubjective viewpoints that are prominent in contemporary psychoanalysis was, at best, quietly ignored and effectively ousted from the mainstream of American psychoanalysis" (2008, p. 238).

The reader who wants to get to know the work and legacy of Rangell and Cooper is recommended to take a look at *My life in theory* (Rangell, 2004) by the former, and *The quite revolution in American psychoanalysis* (Cooper, 2005) by the latter, as well as the interview with Rangell by Beth Kalish-Weiss that we published in 2009 in the *International Forum of Psychoanalysis*. In fact, the best way of understanding and profiting from Rangell's so-called "composite theory" is to become familiar with his long and creative professional life. By his approach, he intends to provide a unitary theory of psychoanalysis centered around an amalgamated view that provides coherence in place of fragmentation.

A further and more recent stage in the evolution of "comparative psychoanalysis" is represented by the work that Steven Ellman put into his 2010 book *When theories touch. A historical and theoretical integration of psychoanalytic thought.* This emphasizes the historical, subjective, and political factors shaping a wide range of analytic theories, out of which Ellman tries to extract and formulate a new theoretical and clinical synthesis. What impressed me is how he can both appreciate the strengths of the single theories, and present them in terms of their roots and context—as I also try to do. Not to mention the fact that—as I also do—Ellman greatly values not only Freud's work and legacy, but also the points of view developed by Sullivan, and Greenberg and Mitchell. But let us now see how, in the Preface of the book, Ellman presents his work:

> I am primarily a psychoanalyst who is, in part, responding to the currents present in contemporary psychoanalysis. One of the currents . . . . Greenberg and Mitchell (1983), and later Mitchell (1995), ... argue that there is basic incompatibility between what they term drive/structural and the relational/ structural model . . . . At different junctures of the present volume, I argue that the way in which Greenberg and Mitchell have stated their position seems as if they are making a logically necessary case. It is my view that there is nothing that is logically necessary about their argument. Rather, they are stating one alternative point of view, and I hope to show that we have moved to a place where different perspectives can be profitably blended, both clinically and theoretically. This, of course, will not abolish some differences between positions, but, rather, try to show the power of a position that attempts to synthesize several points of view. One aspect of this synthesis is a biological perspective that attempts to integrate developmental and clinical phenomena . . . . I am

clearly stating that I will be proposing a multiple factor model
that blends aspects of a number of theories. (Ellman, 2010,
p. xxii)

In other words, Ellman in his book on the one hand
supports my concept of "comparative psychoanalysis," in
terms of learning so much about a whole series of authors
as to be able to establish a meaningful dialogue among
them in our mind, while working with our patients. On
the other hand, he goes beyond such a level of comparison
and tries to make a selection and a new synthesis, whose
main aspects and specificity certainly deserve to be
carefully looked into. I find highly intriguing, for example,
the following acute observation by Ellman:

> The main theme clinically is that in every theoretical
> perspective there is an attempt to facilitate a patient's
> expression of their psychological difficulties, and in each
> of these perspectives there is, at the same time, a way of
> safeguarding the analyst from the full expression of the
> patient's (and analysand's) psychological world. (Ellman,
> 2010, p. xxiii)

In my mind, this intuition represents an important key
to the relationship between the personality structure of
our major analytic authors and the theoretical and clinical
approaches they developed. This kind of an inquiry was
also at the center of the book *Faces in a cloud*, published in
1993 by George Atwood and Robert Stolorow. From this
point of view, I of course fully support Steven Ellman's
attempt to propose his own integration and synthesis
of analytic theories, and I see it as the further step that
my concept of "comparative psychoanalysis" can allow.
But such a step of course presupposes the possibility of
realizing (conceptual and empirical) research projects
that go beyond the working conditions of the individual
analyst.

Of course, two further important models of conceptual
research, and conceptual and empirical research together,
in the field of "comparative psychoanalysis" are the 1990
book by Fred Pine, *Drive, ego, object and self. A synthesis
for clinical work*, and the important 2008 book by David
Tuckett and his team of collaborators on *Psychoanalysis
comparable and incomparable. The evolution of a method
to describe and compare psychoanalytic approaches*.
Behind the unique project presented in this book there is,
of course, the line of research pioneered by Joseph Sandler
(1927–1998) and presented in his 1983 paper "Reflections
on some relations between psychoanalytic concepts and
psychoanalytic practice." This has been carried on by
Jorge Canestri and by Werner Bohleber, the former for
example as editor of the book *Putting theory to work*.

How are theories actually used in practice?, and the latter
as the first author of two original papers centered around
a comparative inquiry into the concepts of enactment and
unconscious phantasy (see Bohleber et al, 2013, 2015).

Although I would be happy to tell the reader more
about all these important projects, books, and articles, I
want at the same time to avoid making this Introduction
longer than it has already become, and will therefore
limit myself to mentioning my experience with the
Comparative Clinical Methods Groups. These groups—
of which the above-mentioned 2008 book by Tuckett et
al is the result—took place for many years at the yearly
conferences of the European Psychoanalytic Federation
(EPF), and I participated in them for six consecutive
years (Vienna, 2008; Brussels, 2009; London, 2010;
Copenhagen, 2011; Paris, 2012; Bale, 2013). I learned not
only to use and profit from this sophisticated comparative
method, but also—I dare to say—became in the meantime
"a European psychoanalyst." This new identity was the
result of the exchanges among a whole series of European
colleagues that took place during and outside meetings,
during the conferences themselves, and concerned
our training, our ways of working, and our ways of
formulating what we do with our patients. As we will see
in Part Four, by "international psychoanalysis" I mean not
only a special branch of psychoanalysis dealing with the
development of psychoanalysis in the various countries
and regions of the world, but, in the first place, our own
individual development of an "international identity."

I will therefore limit myself to ending this section
by returning to the historical dimension of "comparative
psychoanalysis" that I have in mind. I will do this through
the paper that Nellie Thompson and Helene Keable
presented in March 2018 in Berlin at the 31st Symposium
on the History of Psychoanalysis (see the Afterword)
with the title *"The Psychoanalytic Study of the Child*: A
narrative of postwar psychoanalysis"—which they had
published in *American Imago* in 2016. Their sophisticated
historical reconstruction allowed them not only to point
out, but also even to document the similarities between
Heinz Hartmann's (1894–1970) concept of the "average
expectable environment" and Donald Winnicott's (1896–
1971) concept of the "good-enough mother." Here is what
Thompson and Keable wrote in this regard:

> For the last several decades, ideas linked to Hartmann have
> often been reduced to a caricature. A revealing example is
> Hartmann's idea of the 'average expectable environment',
> his concept of the earliest mother-infant relationship. Yet, it

> can be argued that D.W. Winnicott's 'good enough mother' simply supplied a more felicitous description of Hartmann's rendition of this relationship. In this regard, it is instructive to note Winnicott's receptive response to the work of Hartmann, Kris and Loewenstein, which he expressed in a letter to Anna Freud: 'I feel we are all trying to express the same things" (Winnicott, 1954, March 18). In a chapter written specifically in honor of Hartmann, 'A clinical study of the effect of the failure of the average expectable environment on a child's mental functioning' (1965), Winnicott described a diagnostic interview with a six-year-old boy, illustrating it with drawings by the child and by Winnicott, which was also a 'piece of deep therapy'. According to Winnicott, the aim of the treatment was to 'unhitch' a developmental catch, so that the environmental influences could resume their function of facilitating the process of maturation in the child (p.81). Thus he demonstrated the effect on a child of a specific instance of failure in the area of what Hartmann had called the 'average expectable environment.' (Thompson and Keable, 2016, pp. 364–365)

As the reader will see, my own comparative approach concerning Bion and Sullivan is of course based much more—if not exclusively—on the similarity of the questions they tried to formulate and answer than on the answers themselves. This also allows me to say that the kind of "comparative psychoanalysis" I have in mind is, in the first place, based on the further cultivation of our historical research. In fact, as we will see, only the progress recently made in this field has allowed us to come to an eventually clear concept of the various roots and various regional formulations of "analytic field concept."

Last but not least, I want to conclude this section by mentioning the debate on psychoanalytic pluralism that appeared in the June 2018 issue of the German journal *Psyche – Zeitschrift für Psychoanalyse und ihre Anwendungen*. This journal, founded in 1947 by Alexander Mitscherlich (1908–1982) (together with Heinz Kunz and Felix Schottlaender), is the only psychoanalytic journal in the world to come out once a month, and it has played and still plays a very important role in the German analytic landscape. In 2013, I asked Werner Bohleber (who was its editor for many years until the fall of 2017) to present it to the readers of the *International Forum of Psychoanalysis* (Bohleber, 2013), in the context of the first of the three monographic issues I dedicated to German psychoanalysis in the journal between 2013 and 2018.

The debate centers around the question "*Ist der Pluralismus wirklich das letzte Wort in der Psychoanalyse?*," that is, "Is pluralism really the last word in psychoanalysis?," and the answers given to this question by Udo Hock, Elfriede Löchel, Wolfgang Mertens, and Ralf Zwiebel (Hock et al, 2018). The debate—which took place in Frankfurt on October 28, 2017, in the context of a farewell conference for Werner Bohleber as editor of *Psyche*—is so interesting that it would be worthwhile, for example, *Psychoanalytic Quarterly* summarizing it for English-speaking readers in its journal section. Of course, for reasons of space, I have to limit myself to the following short synthesis.

Udo Hock (a Berlin colleague very familiar with French psychoanalysis) speaks of pluralism as a crucial alternative to analytic authoritarianism and dogmatism, and, at the same time, as the necessary background or phase of elaboration of psychoanalysis of all of those colleagues who look for their own analytic voice. Interestingly enough, Ralf Zwiebel (a training analyst of the German Association living in Kassel, who has written several good books on analytic technique, psychoanalysis and Buddhism, and psychoanalysis and film) formulates a very similar opinion, which he condenses into the very well-sounding German formula *"die Integrierung der Vielstimmigkeit durch die Entwickliung der eigenen Stimme"*—"the integration of the many voices through the development of our own voice"—as the meaning of pluralism for our own identity. Also very rich and well articulated is the contribution of Elfriede Löchel (a Bremen training analyst of the German Association who also teaches at the Berlin International Psychoanalytic University), who starts out from the premise that pluralism was from the very beginning the essence of psychoanalysis. Last but not least, Wolfgang Mertens (a training analyst of the Munich Akademie für Psychoanalyse und Psychotherapie and an emeritus professor of psychoanalysis at the Munich University LMU) centers his contribution on the necessity to document and test the pluralism of analytic schools and perspectives through as much empirical research as possible.

Of course, I consider the point of view emerging from this recent German debate as a confirmation of my own concept of "comparative psychoanalysis." Only after having personally looked into all the variables (subjective, cultural, social, and historical) connected to the legacies of our major authors, that is, only after having explored the multiple roots of their work, can we find our own analytic voice. We cannot delegate such an operation to a specialized field of "comparative psychoanalysis" that is intended as a marginal field in which only a small group of clinicians and researchers limit themselves to comparing various clinical and therapeutic concepts. This is even more true for concepts such as "the analytic field concept."

2. THE MULTIPLE ROOTS OF THE ANALYTIC FIELD CONCEPT

We can today speak of the "multiple roots of the analytic field concept," as I do in Chapter 9—with the title "Analytic field theory—a dialogical approach, a pluralistic perspective, and the attempt at a new definition"— basically or only thanks to the historical research work that has been undertaken over the last several years.

In fact, this kind of research eventually brought us into contact with the pioneering work carried out in South America, starting already in the 1960s, by Willy (1922–1994) and Madeleine (1920–2017) Baranger, a French couple that emigrated to Buenos Aires after World War II and, after training as psychoanalysts in the 1950s in Buenos Aires, played a pioneering role in the formulation of this original concept. As I also emphasize in Chapter 9, the Barangers' 1962 paper "The analytic situation as a dynamic field" was translated into English and published, in the *International Journal of Psychoanalysis*, only in 2008 (Baranger and Baranger, 2008), that is, forty-six years after its original publication in Spanish. Having been included in 1990 in the book *La situazione psicoanalitica come campo bipersonale* (Baranger and Baranger, 1990), edited by Stefania Manfredi (1929–2015) and Antonino Ferro, this very important text is only now (June 2018) about to be published in German—it should come out in the fall of 2018 in the journal *Psyche*.

But, as the reader can imagine, to best understand the Barangers' text, their text alone is not enough—we must also have a clear idea of the context in which the Barangers trained and operated. While writing the original version of Chapter 9, I became familiar with Robert Oelsner's 2013 anthology *Transference and countertransference today*, in which he included a 1952 paper by Heinrich Racker (1910–1961) that was at that point not yet available in English. I wrote the original version of Chapter 9, which was published in the fall of 2016 as a book chapter of the book *Advances in contemporary psychoanalytic field theory*, edited by Montana Katz, Roosevelt Cassorla, and Giuseppe Civitarese; Nydia Lisman-Pieczanski and Alberto Pieczanski subsequently edited the anthology *The pioneers of psychoanalysis in South America. An essential guide*, which included chapters on and texts from all the colleagues with whom the Barangers were working at the time. I later found even more fascinating the anthology *The linked self in psychoanalysis. The pioneering work of Enrique Pichon Rivière*, edited in 2017 by Roberto Losso,

L.S. De Setton, and David Scharff, which the editors presented in July 2017 at the IPA Buenos Aires Congress. Of course, I would love to deal with these important texts here, but I do not want to make this already long Introduction even longer than it already is.

Similar work, on the research of original texts and the illumination of their background and context, is what I myself did with Freud, Sullivan, and Bion as pioneers of the analytic field concept. I am, in terms of Freud, thinking of the way in which the young Freud created through his letters the original field of self-refection, upon which he later erected psychoanalysis—this he did in his letters to Emil Fluss, Eduard Silberstein, and Martha Bernays. I am referring also to the way in which I was able to show how Sullivan was able to create around the schizophrenic patient a new field of inquiry and therapy, and how this revolutionary step represented the basis of his later interpersonal theory of psychiatry, that is, of his specific contribution to psychoanalysis. And I am also referring to how I was able, through the publication and revisitation of Wilfred Bion's letters to John Rickman, to illuminate the creative phase of Bion's professional life and scientific evolution in which the concept of "analytic field" originally fertilized his mind and first entered into his work. As the reader will see in Chapter 9, the central role played by the analytic field concept is worthwhile investigating in the work of both the Italian-Swiss Gaetano Benedetti (1920–2013) and the German Hermann Argelander (1920–2004).

But what I want to emphasize in this section is not only the crucial role played by the work of historical research, and by my own historical work, in terms of the illumination and presentation of a whole series of analytic field concepts, but also a challenge that each one of us should meet. This is the challenge of trying to embrace with our study and research the whole landscape of analytic field concepts that have been developed around the world—as opposed to just having a series of regional representatives talk about their own concepts. As the reader can see, I am again speaking here of what I call "comparative psychoanalysis" and "international psychoanalysis," defined not in terms of special branches of psychoanalysis, but in terms of the kind of personal work of elaboration that should take place in our own minds. From this point of view, the historical approach is again the best key for realizing such a synthesis.

Before coming to the final section of this Introduction, let me say a few words about the work of the Barangers, in particular Madeleine (Madé) Baranger, who died on June 19 2017, at age ninety-seven. Rereading the Barangers' above-mentioned paper of 1962, I was struck by how openly they formulated and repeatedly emphasized their dialogical conception of psychoanalysis—to which I totally subscribe and around which this anthology of mine centers. Furthermore, I believe that the Barangers—following Racker and Pichon Rivière—originally meant to correct and integrate Freud's perspective on the analyst and the patient at work in a very similar way to the one held by Sullivan. Right from the beginning of their classical paper, they in fact speak of the need to formulate "a very different and much broader concept of the analytic situation, in which the analyst intervenes—in spite of the necessary 'neutrality' and 'passivity'—as a fully participant member" (Baranger and Baranger, 2008, p. 796). As we have known for many years, Freud was too much afraid that psychoanalysis would be held to be a form of suggestion to dare openly speak of the interactive and mutual aspects of the analytic relationship—not going beyond talking about the patient's free associations and the analyst's "free floating attention" as two parallel processes, as he did for example in "Recommendations to physicians practicing psychoanalysis" (1912).

In fact, what emerged from the interview that Gabriela Bruno conducted with Madeleine Baranger in the year 2000 was the courage, the independence of mind, and the enormous passion for psychoanalysis shared by this extraordinary couple of colleagues, not to mention the relative "freedom of discussion" from which they were able to profit in the marginal location of Montevideo between 1954 and 1965 (Bruno, 2000). At this time— working very hard for many years—they founded the Uruguayan Psychoanalytic Society and created the basis for its brilliant future. This is also the portrait of Madé that emerges from the following words of her last training analysand, the Italian-Argentinian psychologist Chiara Bille, who has been so kind as to allow me to include them in this book:

> Madé had an anti-dogmatic and revolutionary character; she was a *"lutteuse éternelle."* During the first year of my analysis, there was a situation in which I for the first time did not say a word, and spent three consecutive sessions in total silence, as if I were paralyzed, turning acrobatically on the couch for twenty minutes and then falling deeply asleep. I remember the embracing warmth of her office and the sunlight penetrating into it and warming up my face. After I lay down for the fourth session, Madé did not sit down on her chair on my right-hand side, but walked up and down in her office till she addressed me with a menacing voice saying:

'I warn you! If you do not talk today, our work is over!'
So it was that our work immediately changed into
a vivacious and very meaningful dialogue. It was hard
work with Madé! There was no way out of it, and she
was always able to catch my thoughts. She claimed
that it was possible to do a good analysis even with two
sessions, and that candidates should in the first place do a
good job of self-analysis. She always created new fields
of inquiry, and each session was a surprise, a revolution.

With her incredible intuition and ability to listen to
me, Madé was able to understand whether I, as a candidate,
was granted the freedom to choose my own seminars, if my
teachers stimulated me to develop my own thoughts, and
if I could freely express them. In her opinion, candidates
should be able to have their own ideas. To the end of our
work together, she never got tired of telling me "Do not
allow anybody to colonize your mind, try to approach
with curiosity and interest a variety of authors and texts,
and only then try to formulate your own point of view.
The passion for psychoanalysis is the heart of our work!"

Madé taught me to try to be as free and as coherent with
myself as possible. (Bille, 2018)

3. THE INDIVIDUAL CHAPTERS

Here is the abstract of Chapter 7, "Bion and his first
analyst, John Rickman (1891–1951): A revisitation of their
relationship in the light of Rickman's personality and
scientific production and of Bion's letters to him (1939–
1951)," as it was published in the *International Forum of
Psychoanalysis* (Volume 20, No. 2, p. 63; Conci, 2011b):

> The author throws a new light on a neglected aspect of W.R.
> Bion's life and work, i.e. his relationship to his first analyst,
> John Rickman, by making reference not only to the latter's
> career and scientific work, but also to the 27 letters which
> Bion wrote to him in the years 1939–1951 that he found in
> the Archives of the British Psychoanalytical Society. As
> the letters show, in the close collaboration they developed
> during the Second World War as army psychiatrists, we can
> find not only the origins of the new concept of 'therapeutic
> community' and of Bion's later book *Experiences in groups*,
> but also see how crucial their unique relationship was to the
> realization of such important goals.

As I have already mentioned, Dimitris Vonofakos
and Bob Hinshelwood published in 2012 a word-by-word
transcription of the whole text of these letters, which I
will now briefly deal with. Besides being complete, their
transcription also contains some information on the
colleagues mentioned by Bion that I did not have at my
disposal—or I was not able to find.

Here is a short list of the further differences between
my work and theirs, and of the corrective and integrative
feedback I was able to get from this. In the first place,

as Hinshelwood himself communicated to me by mail on September 2, 2010 (see Conci, 2011a), he and Vonofakos came to the conclusion of dating the letter of January 1939 to January 1940, since Bion speaks in it of his desire to continue his analysis with Rickman, with the consequence of my Letter No. 1 becoming their Letter No. 4. A minor difference is that Vonofakos and Hinshelwood also include in their list, which numbers twenty-nine letters in total, the only two letters that Rickman wrote to Bion. As these were rather short and of little significance, I just mentioned them, without putting them into my list, which leaves a total of twenty-seven letters written by Bion to Rickman.

Last but not least, comparing the transcription of the letters I made with the decisive help of Ross Lazar (whose mother tongue was American English) to the transcription made by our two colleagues, I discovered the following three mistakes of family names, which I decided to correct in the version of my 2011 paper published in this book as Chapter 7. The corrections are as follows:

- In my Letter No. 1, I mention a Dr. Carrol, who turns out to be Dr. Carroll, in Vonofakos' and Hinshelwood's version. From their footnote to their Letter No. 1 we also learn who he was: Dennis Carroll was one of the Tavistock psychiatrists drafted into the Royal Army Medical Corps (RAMC), who later worked at Northfield and after World War II became the director of the Portman Clinic.

- In my Letter No. 4, I mention a Dr. Rayner, who was in fact Dr. Baynes (1882–1943), a leading British Jungian analyst.

- In my letter No. 23, I repeatedly mention a Dr. Materly, who should have been Dr. Alan Maberly (1903–1969). Vonofakos and Hinshelwood wrote about him that he had been analyzed by Wilhelm Stekel in Vienna and was also a Tavistock psychiatrist.

But let me now come to how the two British authors approached the letters and to how they assess and value them. For example, at variance with my approach to the letters, they classified them into various phases: a first so-called analytic phase, a second student phase, a third collegial phase, and a fourth phase that they call "the path to independence." And here is how they formulate the importance of this collection of letters, thus confirming my instinct to look into them and dedicate to them a whole issue of the *International Forum of Psychoanalysis*, with nine prominent colleagues formulating their comments about the letters:

In her study of another collection of Bion's letters (1951–72), those to his fiancée and wife, Francesca, Sayers (2002) argues that it was their love affair which altered his perceptions of himself and the world. The evidence of these letters to Rickman is that the metamorphosis from Bion the troubled to Bion the creative was a slower process; it took place during the evolution from being an analysand to being Rickman's colleague and perhaps assisted by the impact of his analysis with Melanie Klein (1945--52). Indeed, one might wonder if the capacity for his obvious passion for Francesca was a *result* of the early transformation due to Rickman.

These letters are an intriguing source of speculation about the formative years of Bion's career from which he emerged as one of the most influential psychoanalysts to the present day. While these letters have not been compared with other correspondence of Bion's at the same time, there is strong evidence of Rickman's immense presence presiding over Bion as he made his remarkable turnaround, throwing off the effects of his experiences in World War I. (Vonofakos and Hinshelwood, 2012, p. 64, original emphasis)

Of a similar tone are the concluding remarks that accompany the above-mentioned book chapter published by these authors in 2013. On the other hand, in the same 2012 issue of *Psychoanalysis and History*, the historian Michael Roper was able to confirm the crucial importance of Bion's relationship to Rickman in the following words:

If the analysis with Rickman was as significant for Bion as Vonofakos and Hinshelwood perceive, that in itself opens a further set of questions, about his subsequent analysis with Klein between 1945 and 1952 . . . . There are, however, some suggestive links to be made between these phases of his work, which the letters help to illuminate. In Rickman's 1938 essay on air raids, he describes the element of recrudescence in the panic of the adult as 'nameless horror' (Rickman, 2003, p. 187; p. 196). The terms 'nameless terror', 'reasonless dread', and 'unreasoning terror' had been used by commentators in World War I to describe the reactions of traumatized soldiers, including by W. H. R. Rivers in his work on shell-shocked soldiers. However, they were not, as far as I am aware, in wide currency (Roper, 2009, pp. 262–6). Recent work on Bion seeks to locate his use of the term 'nameless dread' to describe the impact on the child of a mother who cannot contain its distress, in relation to his wartime experiences (Jacobus, 2005; Sandler, 1993; Souter, 2009). These letters, in shedding light on the importance of Rickman for Bion, show yet another route of his thinking, suggesting an implicit connection, via the relationship with Rickman, between Bion's group phase and his clinical breakthroughs in the 1950s. (Roper, 2012, pp. 107–108)

I can now come to a short summary or further collection of quotations taken from the nine commentaries that I was able to publish in the *International Forum of Psychoanalysis*. I will start with Howard Levine's two-page commentary "On Bion's analysis with Rickman," from which I would like to extract the following quotation:

Taken together, I think that we can surmise that Rickman

possessed essential capacities that Bion would later
conceptualize as central to the process of container/contained
and which must have been of the utmost importance to the
young Bion's attempts to discover the words he needed to
describe and begin to partially recover from the traumatic
war experiences from which he then still suffered. The
warmth and appreciation that Bion expressed for Rickman
in the letters Conci has quoted no doubt followed from
the relief he must have felt that the analysis afforded him.
This, in contrast, to the wry and acerbic comment that he
was supposed to have once made about his second analysis:
that Klein seemed more interested in proving Klein than in
analyzing Bion! (Levine, 2011, p. 88)

In the following paper, "Rickman, Bion, and the
clinical applications of field theory," Lawrence Brown
follows the thread of the field concept, from the work of
Kurt Lewin (1890–1947), to its use in the work done by Bion
and Rickman at the Northfield Hospital, to its eventual
adoption as a central component of inpatient treatment at
the Menninger Clinic—where Brown worked in the mid-
1970s as a postdoctoral fellow in clinical psychology. In
this paper we learn that Rickman was about to be invited
to move to Topeka (Kansas) to work at the Menninger
Clinic, but that this did not happen, partly or mostly
because of what Brown calls "the suspicions that his
Kleinian leanings aroused in American analysts" (Brown,
2011b, p. 91), thus transforming a promising contact
between North American and British psychoanalysis into
"a sad chapter in the history of psychoanalysis" (p. 91).

In the third paper, "The facilitation of genius:
Rickman's mentoring of Bion," David Scharff
(Washington DC) concentrates on Bion's growth through
Rickman's mentoring role using the following words:

It is a record of personal and intellectual growth of one of the
geniuses of our times. For me, it gave a window into the way
intellect develops in the arms of a mentoring relationship and
then, as it must, grows beyond the confines of that beginning.
And the most inspiring part of it is the generosity of Rickman's
support, the way he promoted Bion's individual contribution.
They both knew that it began in their partnership, which was
itself embedded in the wider group of which they were a part.
Over the years of this record, Bion grew into a thinker who
made the beginnings of a fully unique contribution, one that
has inspired the generations that followed these two giants.
(Scharff, 2011, p. 95)

In the fourth paper, "Grace under fire," Robert Caper
(Los Angeles) compares the way in which Bion gave his
first paper in Los Angeles to the way in which—in Letter
No. 23—he described having interacted with the Tavistock
group at the first staff group meeting, formulating the
opinion that both were "demonstrations of what Bion

later referred to as faith, which indicated not a belief in anything supernatural, but rather belief in psychoanalysis or in one's own inner resources" (Caper, 2011, p. 98).

In the fifth paper, "Some perhaps transgressive comments," Antonino Ferro presents a series of threads contained in Bion's letters and ends up following one of the threads offered by James Grotstein in 2007 in terms of "Bion's critique of Klein for not having understood that he had died on August 8, 1918, on the road between Amiens and Roye" (Grotstein, 2007, p. 119). At the same time, Ferro does not miss the opportunity to hint at the fact that Bion's emphasis on the "serious work [that] needs to be done along analytic and field theory lines" (see Letter No. 12) is the only mention of the concept of "field theory" in his entire published work.

In the sixth paper, "Rediscovering Bion's and Rickman's leaderless group projects," Giovanni Foresti sheds light on their collaboration at Northfield Hospital, and emphasizes the unique possibility offered by Bion's letters to Rickman to much better appreciate the man behind the psychoanalyst and catch the social and historical matrix out of which he originally developed. In the seventh paper, "Towards an ethics of responsibility," Giuseppe Civitarese explores a variety of threads of these letters, for example what he calls Bion's "tankishness" in terms of the analyst needing "to remain alive and attentive to what is going on around him at any given moment like the soldier engaged in the battle" (Civitarese, 2011, p. 108). I found the following final considerations particularly touching:

> But speaking of the 'common factor', I would say that if there is one element that may characterize the happy encounter between Bion and Rickman, it is the struggle against the common enemy of arrogant stupidity, of bigotry, of certainty, and of mental narrowness. From the letters and the opportune synthesis of Rickman's scientific work, it is difficult to doubt the decisive influence these ideas exerted on Bion. As mentioned in the 13th letter, the baton that one passes to the other is the unconditional aspiration to nurture people of free spirit ('liberal minded people'). (Civitarese, 2011, p. 112)

The final two papers were written by the German colleague Heinz Weiss and the Belgian colleague Rudi Vermote. In his paper "Linking Rickman's work with Bion's thinking," Heinz Weiss analyzes what they have in common, for example what he calls "their emphasis on 'dynamic receptiveness' (or 'receptive tolerance' in Rickman's words), which comes close to Bion's description of the role of 'maternal reverie' in taking up and digesting the infant's projections (Bion, 1962)" (Weiss, 2011, p. 114).

As far as Rudi Vermote's paper "Getting to know the 'early' Bion" is concerned, I will limit myself to quoting his final considerations, since they reflect so well the very positive attitude towards Bion's letters and towards my work shown by all nine authors I invited to contribute to this issue of the *International Forum of Psychoanalysis*. Vermote states:

> Learning to know Rickman better and the letters of Bion to Rickman offers fresh points of view of the context in which Bion worked and was creative. Conci is right in stating that the connection between a psychoanalyst's life and his work is indeed an interesting field of study. After opening the link between Bion and Sullivan, he now opens up the world of Bion and Rickman. These multiple vertices may help to gain a multidimensional view of Bion and the origin of his ideas. (Vermote, 2011, p. 117)

Of course, presenting all nine commentaries as I just have allows me also to show the multiple aspects of Bion's legacy, much as I have spent the greater part of this Introduction showing the multiple roots of his work.

I can thus come now to Chapter 8 in this anthology, "Bion and Sullivan: An enlightening comparison," limiting myself to presenting to the reader the abstract that accompanied its original 2009 publication:

> The author compares the life and work of two pioneers and major sources of inspiration to the contemporary psychoanalytic debate: W.R. Bion (1897–1979) and H.S. Sullivan (1892–1949). Both their life and their work show similarities that allow the author to illuminate and constructively compare the one with the other. The author proposes his work as a useful exercise in the field of "comparative psychoanalysis," an important key for the reconstruction of the history of our field and for a more scientifically coherent articulation of its theories.

As far as Chapter 9, "Analytic field theory—A dialogical approach, a pluralistic perspective, and the attempt at a new definition," is concerned, I have of course already talked enough about it in the previous pages. I do not at this point have anything more to add except that a very positive review of the book in which it was included, *Advances in contemporary analytic field theory. Concept and future development*, was published by Martin Silverman (2017b) in Issue 4/2017 of *Psychoanalytic Quarterly*.

REFERENCES

Aguayo, J. (2017). Review of "The complete works of W.R. Bion", C. Mawson editor, F. Bion consulting editor, Karnac 2014. *International Journal of Psychoanalysis* 98:221–243.

Aguayo, J., & Malin, B. (Eds.) (2013). *Wilfred Bion – Los Angeles Seminars and Supervision*. London: Karnac.

Akhtar, S. (2009). *Comprehensive Dictionary of Psychoanalysis*. London: Karnac.

Ancona, L. (1981). The "field-relationship" between S. Freud and W.R. Bion. *Rivista di Psicoanalisi* 27(3–4):523–532.

Angeloch, D. (2017). "Sub-thalamic fear" – Über Wilfred Bions "War memoirs 1917–1919" ["Sub-thalamic fear" – On Wilfred Bion's "War memories 1917–1919"]. *Psyche* 71:586–616.

Atwood, G.E., & Stolorow, R.D. (1993). *Faces in a Cloud. Intersubjectivity in Personality Theory*. Northvale, NJ: Aronson.

Baranger, M., & Baranger, W. (2008). The analytic situation as a dynamic field. *International Journal of Psychoanalysis* 89:795–826. (Original Spanish publication, 1961–1962).

Baranger, W., & Baranger, M. (1990). *La situazione psicoanalitica come campo bipersonale* [The psychoanalytic situation as bipersonal field] (S. Manfredi and A. Ferro, Eds.). Milan: Cortina.

Bezoari, M. (1997). "W.R. Bion: Past and future": International Centennial Conference on the Work of W.R. Bion. Torino, 16–19 luglio 1997. *Rivista di Psicoanalisi* 43:715–726.

Bianchedi, E., & Bianchedi, M. (1999). Prefacio – Evocando a Parthenope [Preface – Remembering Parthenope]. In P. Bion Talamo, *Metapsicología y metamatemática en algunas teorías psicoanalíticas recientes* [Metapsychology and metamathematics in some recent psychoanalytic theories] (M. Bianchedi, Translator) (pp. 9–16). Buenos Aires: Polemos.

Bille, C. (2018). Madé Baranger as I remember her: A personal testimony. Personal communication.

Billow, R.M. (1999). LHK: The basis of emotion in Bion's theory. *Contemporary Psychoanalysis* 35:475–489.

Bion, W.R. (1961). *Experiences in Groups*. London: Tavistock. (Italian edition, 1971).

———— (1962). *Learning from Experience*. London: Heinemann. (Italian edition, 1972).

———— (1963). *Elements of Psychoanalysis*. London: Heinemann. (Italian edition, 1973).

———— (1967). *Second Thoughts. Selected Papers of Psychoanalysis*. London: Heinemann. (Italian edition, 1970).

———— (1975). *A Memoir of the Future*. Book I, *The Dream*. Rio de Janeiro: Imago Editoria.

———— (1977). *A Memoir of the Future*. Book II, *The Past Presented*. Rio de Janeiro: Imago Editoria.

———— (1979). *A Memoir of the Future*. Book III, *The Dawn of Oblivion*. Perthshire: Clunie Press.

———— (1980). *Bion in New York and Sao Paulo* (F. Bion, Ed.). Strathclyde: Clunie Press.

———— (1982). *The Long Week-end: A Part of Life*. Abingdon, Oxfordshire: Fleetwood Press.

———— (1985a). *All my Sins Remembered: Another Part of Life*. Abingdon, Oxfordshire: Fleetwood Press. (See also, for the quote: C. Mawson, Ed.; F. Bion, Consulting Ed., *The Complete works of W.R. Bion*, Vol. II, pp. 1–76. London: Karnac, 2014).

———— (1985b). *The Other Side of Genius: Family Letters*. Abingdon, Oxfordshire: Fleetwood Press.

———— (1990). *Brazilian Lectures*. London: Karnac.

———— (1992). *Cogitations*. London: Estate of W.R. Bion. (Italian edition, 1996).

———— (1994). Making the best of a bad job. In *Clinical Seminars and Other Works*. London: Karnac.

———— (2005). *Italian Seminars* (F. Bion, Ed.). London: Karnac. (Original Italian edition, 1985).

Bion Talamo, P. (1999). *Metapsicología y metamatemática en algunas teorías psicoanalíticas recientes* [Metapsychology and metamathematics in some recent psychoanalytic theories] (M. Bianchedi, Translator). Buenos Aires: Polemos.

———— (2015). *Maps for Psychoanalytic Exploration* (A. Baruzzi and C. Mawson, Eds.). London: Karnac. (Original Italian edition, 2011).

Bion Talamo, P., & Neri, C. (Eds.) (1981). *Monographic Issue of the Rivista di Psicoanalisi dedicated to Wilfred R. Bion*. Rome: Il Pensiero Scientifico.

Bion Talamo, P., Borgogno, F., & Merciai, S.A. (Eds.) (2000). *W.R. Bion: Between Past and Future*. London: Karnac. (Original Italian edition, 1998).

Bléandonu, G. (1994). *Wilfred Bion – His Life and Works, 1897–1979*. London: Free Association Books. (Original French edition, 1990. Italian edition, 1993. German edition, 2008).

Bohleber, W. (2013). The journal *Psyche – Zeitschrift für Psychoanalyse und ihre Anwendungen*: a historical overview. *International Forum of Psychoanalysis* 22:199–202.

Bohleber, W., Fonagy, P., Jiménez, J.P., Scarfone, D., Varvin, S., & Zysman, S. (2013). Towards a better use of psychoanalytic concepts: A model illustrated using the concept of enactment. *International Journal of Psychoanalysis* 94:501–530.

Bohleber, W., Jiménez, J.P., Scarfone, D., Varvin, S., & Zysman, S. (2015). Unconscious phantasy and its conceptualization: An attempt at conceptual integration. *International Journal of Psychoanalysis* 96:705–730.

Borgogno, F., & Merciai, S.A. (1998). Parthenope Bion Talamo: Un ricordo [In memory of Parthenope Bion Talamo]. *Rivista di Psicoanalisi* 44:641–647.

———— (2000). Searching for Bion: *Cogitations*, a new *Clinical diary à la* Ferenczi. In P. Bion Talamo, F. Borgogno, and S.A. Merciai (Eds.), *W.R. Bion: Between Past and Future* (pp. 56–78). London: Karnac. (See also *International Forum of Psychoanalysis* 2018; 27:135–145).

Boris, H.N. (1986). Bion re-visited. *Contemporary Psychoanalysis* 22:159–184.

Brown, L.J. (2009a). From "disciplined subjectivity" to "taming wild thoughts": Bion's elaboration of the analyzing instrument. *International Forum of Psychoanalysis* 18:82–85.

———— (2009b). Bion's ego psychology: Implications for an intersubjective view of psychic structure. *Psychoanalytic Quarterly* 78:27–55.

———— (2011a). *Intersubjective Processes and the Unconscious. An Integration of Freudian, Kleinian and Bionian Perspectives*. London: Routledge.

———— (2011b). Rickman, Bion, and the clinical applications of field theory. *International Forum of Psychoanalysis* 20:89–92.

Bruno, G. (2000). *Entrevista a Madeleine Baranger* (Interview with Madeleine Baranger). Retrieved July 10, 2018 from https://

querencia.psico.edu.uy/revista-nro5/gabriela-bruno.htm.

Canestri, J. (Ed.) (2012). *Putting Theory to Work. How Are Theories Actually Used in Practice?* London: Karnac.

Caper, R. (2011). Grace under fire. *International Forum of Psychoanalysis* 20:97–99.

Civitarese, G. (2010). La parentesi di Ogden, ovvero della continuità dell'esperienza cosciente e inconscia [Ogden's interlude: The continuity of conscious and unconscious experience]. *Rivista di Psicoanalisi* 56:771–780.

——— (2011). Towards an ethics of responsibility. *International Forum of Psychoanalysis* 20:108–112.

Conci, M. (1993). Review of the book by Z. Lothane "In defense of Schreber. Soul murder and psychiatry", Analytic Press 1992. *Psicoterapia e Scienze Umane* 27(4):142–144.

——— (2008a). Un seminario con Pagliarani: Collalbo 1998 [A workshop with Pagliarani: Collalbo 1998]. *L'Educazione Sentimentale* No. 10:24–41.

——— (2008b). Review of the book by S. Resnik "Biographie de l'inconscient", Dunod 2006. *International Journal of Psychoanalysis* 89:894–899.

——— (2009). Review of the book by A. Ferro "Mind works. Technique and creativity in psychoanalysis", Routledge 2009. *International Forum of Psychoanalysis* 18:124–127.

——— (2011a). Editorial – Wilfred Bion's identity as a psychoanalyst in the light of his letters (1939–1951) to his first analyst, John Rickman, and of their multidimensional relationship. Our trainings (and our lives), our letters, and the history, transmission and practice of psychoanalysis. *International Forum of Psychoanalysis* 20:63–67.

——— (2011b). Bion and his first analyst, John Rickman (1891–1951): A revisitation of their relationship in the light of Rickman's personality and scientific production and of Bion's letters to him. *International Forum of Psychoanalysis* 20:68–86.

——— (2013). Review of the book by F. Borgogno "The girl who committed hara-kiri and other clinical and historical essays", Karnac 2012. *International Forum of Psychoanalysis* 22:188–194.

Conci, M., & Borgogno, F. (2009). Editorial – Bion, Rangell and Haynal: A pioneer and two protagonists of contemporary psychoanalysis. A selection of papers of the Bion 2008 Conference and two interviews. *International Forum of Psychoanalysis* 18:65–70.

Cooper, A.M. (2005). *The Quiet Revolution in American Psychoanalysis – Selected Paper by A.M. Cooper* (E.L. Auchincloss, Ed.). London: Routledge.

Correale, A. (2017). Obituary for Salomon Resnik. *International Journal of Psychoanalysis* 98:1817–1822.

Di Donna, L. (2010). The life and work of Robert S. Wallerstein: A conversation. *American Imago* 67:617–658.

Ellman, S.J. (2010). *When Theories Touch. A Historical and Theoretical Integration of Psychoanalytic Thought.* London: Karnac.

Ferenczi, S. (1932). *Clinical Diary* (J. Dupont, Ed.). Cambridge, MA: Harvard University Press, 1988. (Original French edition, 1985).

Ferro, A. (1999). *The Bipersonal Field: Experiences in Child Analysis.* London: Routledge. (Original Italian edition, 1992).

——— (2011). Some perhaps transgressive comments. *International Forum of Psychoanalysis* 20:100–102.

Ferruta, A. (2003). Review of the book by A. Ferro "Fattori di malattia, fattori di guarigione", Cortina, 2000. *International Journal of Psychoanalysis* 84:459–462.

Foresti, G. (2011). Rediscovering Bion's and Rickman's leaderless group projects. *International Forum of Psychoanalysis* 20:103–107.

Freud, S. (1912). Recommendations to physicians practicing psychoanalysis. *Standard Edition* 12, pp. 109–120.

Gaddini, E. (1981). Paths through the creativity of Bion. *Rivista di Psicoanalisi* 27(3–4):384–398.

Greenberg, J.R., & Mitchell, S.A. (1983). *Object Relations in Psychoanalytic Theory*. Cambridge, MA: Harvard University Press.

Grinberg, L., Sor, D., & Tabak de Bianchedi, E. (1977). *Introduction to the Work of Bion*. Northvale, NJ: Aronson. (Original Spanish edition, 1972. Italian edition, 1975).

Grotstein, J.S. (1981). Wilfred R. Bion: The man, the psychoanalyst, the mystic. A perspective on his life and work. *Contemporary Psychoanalysis* 17:501–536.

——— (1987). Making the best of a bad deal – On Harold Boris' "Bion revisited". *Contemporary Psychoanalysis* 23:60–76.

——— (1993). Review of the book by Z. Lothane "In defense of Schreber. Soul murder and psychiatry", Analytic Press 1992. *Psychoanalytic Review* 80:633–639.

——— (2007). *A Beam of Intense Darkness. Wilfred Bion's Legacy to Psychoanalysis*. London: Karnac.

Hanly, C. (2011). Narcissism, hypochondria and the problem of alternative theories. *International Journal of Psychoanalysis* 92:593–608.

Harris Williams, M. (Ed.) (2015). *Teaching Bion. Modes and Approaches*. London: Karnac.

Hautmann, G. (1981). My debt towards Bion: From psychoanalysis as a theory to psychoanalysis as a mental function. *Rivista di Psicoanalisi* 27(3–4):573–586.

——— (1999). *Il mio debito con Bion* [My debt towards Bion]. Rome: Borla.

Hegener, W. (2016). Wilfred Bion (1897–1979) – Der Mut zur Unsicherheit und zum Nichtverstehen [Wilfred Bion (1897–1979). The courage to bear insecurity and not understanding]. In M. Conci and W. Mertens (Eds.), *Psychoanalyse im 20. Jahrhundert. Freuds Nachfolger und ihr Beitrag zur modern Psychoanalyse* [Psychoanalysis in the 20th century. Freud's followers and their contribution to modern psychoanalysis] (pp. 100–119). Stuttgart: Kohlhammer.

Hinshelwood, R.D. (2015). Teaching Bion's teaching. In M. Harris Williams (Ed.), *Teaching Bion. Modes and Approaches* (pp. 109–120). London: Karnac.

Hock, U., Löchel, E., Mertens, W., & Zwiebel, R. (2018). *Ist der Pluralismus wirklich das letzte Wort in der Psychoanalyse?* [Is pluralism really the last word in psychoanalysis?]. *Psyche* 72:485–509.

Jacques, E. (1970). *Work, Creativity, and Social Justice*. London: Heinemann.

Katz, S.M., Cassorla, R., & Civitarese, G. (Eds.) (2016). *Advances in Contemporary Field Theory – Concept and Future Development*. London: Routledge.

Kernberg, O.F. (2011). Divergent contemporary trends in psychoanalytic theory. *Psychoanalytic Review* 98:633–664.

Lazar, R.A. (2014). Container–contained. In W. Mertens (Ed.), *Handbuch psychoanaytischer Grundbegriffe* [Handbook of basic psychoanalytic concepts] (pp. 148–153). Stuttgart: Kohlhammer.

Levine, H.B. (2009). Reflections on catastrophic change. *International Forum of Psychoanalysis* 18:77–81.

———— (2011). On Bion's analysis with Rickman. *International Forum of Psychoanalysis* 20:87–88.

———— (2013). Looking back, looking ahead. In H.B. Levine and L.J. Brown (Eds.), *Growth and Turbulence in the in the Container/ Contained: Bion's Continuing Legacy* (pp. 313–318). London: Routledge.

Levine, H.B., & Brown, L.J. (Eds.) (2013). *Growth and Turbulence in the Container/Contained: Bion's Continuing Legacy.* London: Routledge.

Levine, H.B., & Civitarese, G. (Eds.) (2016). *The W.R. Bion Tradition. Lines of Development, Evolution of Theory and Practice over the Decades.* London: Karnac.

Lisman-Pieczanski, N., & Pieczanski, A. (Eds.) (2015). *The Pioneers of Psychoanalysis in South America. An Essential Guide.* London: Routledge.

López Corvo, R.E. (2002). *The Dictionary of the Work of W.R. Bion.* London: Karnac. (Italian edition, 2006).

Losso, R., De Setton, L.S., & Scharff, D.E. (Eds.) (2017). *The Pioneering Work of Enrique Pichon Rivière.* London: Karnac.

Mawson, C. (Ed.) (2011). *Bion Today.* London: Routledge.

Mawson, C. (Ed.), Bion, F. (Consulting Ed.) (2014). *The Complete Works of W.R. Bion. Sixteen Volumes.* London: Karnac.

Meltzer, D. (1978). *The Kleinian Development.* Part 3. *The Clinical Significance of the Work of Bion.* Perthshire: Clunie Press.

Mertens, W. (2018). *Psychoanalytische Schulen im Gespräch über die Konzepte Wilfred R. Bions* [Psychoanalytic schools and their dialogue concerning Bion's concepts]. Giessen: Psychosozial-Verlag.

Miller, I. (2016). *Defining Psychoanalysis. Achieving a Vernacular Expression.* London: Routledge.

Nebbiosi, G. (1996). Prefazione all'edizione italiana [Preface to the Italian edition]. In W.R. Bion, *Cogitations – Pensieri* (pp. 11–19). Rome: Armando.

———— (1998). Prefazione all'edizione italiana [Preface to the Italian edition]. In J. Symington and N. Symington, *Il pensiero clinico di Bion* (pp. ix–xiii). Milan: Cortina.

Neri, C. (2015). Preface. In P. Bion Talamo, *Maps for Psychoanalytic Exploration* (A. Baruzzi and C. Mawson, Eds.) (pp. ix–xv). London: Karnac.

———— (2016). A long meeting with Bion. In H.B. Levine and G. Civitarese (Eds.), *The W.R. Bion Tradition. Lines of Development, Evolution of Theory and Practice over the Decades* (pp. 23–28). London: Karnac.

Neri, C., Correale, A., & Fadda, P. (Eds.) (1994). *Letture bioniane* [Bionian readings]. Rome: Borla.

Nissim Momigliano, L. (1981). Memory and desire. *Rivista di Psicoanalisi* 27(3–4):546–557.

Oelsner, R. (Ed.) (2013). *Transference and Countertransference Today*. London: Routledge.

Ogden, T.H. (1989). *The Primitive Edge of Experience*. Northvale, NJ: Aronson.

——— (2004). An introduction to the reading of Bion. *International Journal of Psychoanalysis* 85:285–300.

——— (2005). *This Art of Psychoanalysis. Dreaming, Undreamt Dreams and Interrupted Cries*. London: Routledge.

——— (2007). Reading Harold Searles. *International Journal of Psychoanalysis* 88:353–359.

——— (2009). *Rediscovering Psychoanalysis. Thinking and Dreaming, Learning and Forgetting*. London: Routledge.

O'Shaughnessy, E. (2005). Whose Bion? *International Journal of Psychoanalysis* 86:1523–1528. (See also C. Mawson, Ed., *Bion Today*, pp. 33–39. London: Routledge).

Pagliarani, L. (1969). La co-gestione dell'ansia. Aspetti e problemi della comunità terapeutica secondo un'ottica socioanalitica [The co-elaboration of anxiety. Aspects and problems of the therapeutic community according to a socioanalytic perspective]. *Psicoterapia e Scienze Umane* No. 12:8–22.

——— (1990). L'ultimo Bion: psico-socio-analista [The last Bion: psycho-socio-analyst]. In E. Cassani and G. Varchetta (Eds.), *Psicosocioanalisi e crisi delle istituzioni* [Psychosocioanalysis and istitutional crisis] (pp. 27–46). Milan: Guerini e Associati.

Pine, F. (1990). *Drive, Ego, Object and Self. A Synthesis for Clinical Work*. New York: Basic Books.

Pines, M. (Ed.) (1985). *Bion and Group Psychotherapy*. London: Routledge. (Italian edition, 1988).

Rangell, L. (2004). *My Life in Theory*. New York: Other Press.

Rangell, L., & Kalish-Weiss, B. (2009). Interview of Dr. Leo Rangell by Dr. Kalish-Weiss, Los Angeles, California, July, 2008. *International Forum of Psychoanalysis* 18:107–116.

Rather, L. (2015). Building a "Bion container". In M. Harris Williams (Ed.), *Teaching Bion. Modes and Approaches* (pp. 49–56). London: Karnac.

Resnik, S. (1987). *The Theatre of the Dream*. London: Routledge. (Original Italian edition, 1982).

——— (2005). *Glacial Times: A Journey Through the World of Madness*. London: Routledge. (Original French edition, 1999).

——— (2011a). *The Delusional Person*. London: Karnac. (Original Italian edition, 1976).

——— (2011b). *An Archeology of the Mind*. Scurelle, Trento: Silvy.

——— (2016). Flying thoughts in search of a nest: A tribute to W.R. Bion. In H.B. Levine and G. Civitarese (Eds.), *The W.R. Bion Tradition. Lines of Development, Evolution of Theory and Practice over the Decades* (pp. 259–269). London: Karnac.

Resnik, S., Antonetti, A., & Ficacci, M.A. (1982). *Semeiologia dell'incontro. Studi di psicopatologia clinica* [Semiology of the encounter. Studies in clinical psychopathology]. Rome: Il Pensiero Scientifico.

Richards, A.D. (2003). Psychoanalytic discourse at the turn of our century: A plea for a measure of humility. *Journal of the American Psychoanalytic Association, 51*, 73–89. (See also A.D. Richards, *Psychoanalysis: Critical Conversations. Selected Papers.*

Volume 1, A.A. Lynch Ed., pp. 45–60. New York: International Psychoanalytic Books, 2015).

Roper, M. (2012). The "spear head of an advance": Bion's wartime letters to Rickman. *Psychoanalysis and History* 14:95–109.

Sandler, J. (1983). Reflections on some relations between psychoanalytic concepts and psychoanalytic practice. *International Journal of Psychoanalysis* 64:35–45.

Sandler, P.C. (2006). The origins of Bion's work. *International Journal of Psychoanalysis* 87:179–201.

Schafer, R (1979). On becoming a psychoanalyst of one persuasion or another. *Contemporary Psychoanalysis* 15:345–368.

Scharff, D. (2011). The facilitation of genius: Rickman's mentoring of Bion. *International Forum of Psychoanalysis* 20:93–96.

Silverman, M.A. (2017a). On the birth and development of psychoanalytic field theory. Part 1. *Psychoanalytic Quarterly* 86:699–727.

———— (2017b). On the birth and development of psychoanalytic field theory. Part 2. *Psychoanalytic Quarterly* 86:919–932.

Sullivan, H.S. (1937). A note on the implications of psychiatry. The study of interpersonal relations, for investigations in the social sciences. In H.S. Sullivan, *The Fusion of Psychiatry and Social Science* (H. Swick Perry, Ed.) (pp. 15–29). New York: Norton.

Symington, J., & Symington N. (1996). *The Clinical Thinking of Wilfred Bion*. London: Routledge. (Italian edition, 1998).

Szykierski, D. (2013). The traumatic roots of containment: The evolution of Bion's metapsychology. In H.B. Levine and L.J. Brown (Eds.), *Growth and Turbulence in the Container/Contained: Bion's Continuing Legacy* (pp. 25–52). London: Routledge.

Tabak de Bianchedi, E. (2005). Whose Bion? Who is Bion? *International Journal of Psychoanalysis* 86:159–1534.

Thompson, N., & Keable, H. (2016). *The Psychoanalytic Study of the Child*: A narrative of postwar psychoanalysis. *American Imago* 73:342–382.

Tuckett, D., Basile, R., Birksted-Breen, D., Böhm, T., Denis, P., Ferro, et al. (2008). *Psychoanalysis Comparable and Incomparable. The Evolution of a Method To Describe and Compare Psychoanalytic Approaches*. London: Routledge.

Vermote, R. (2011). Getting to know the "early" Bion. *International Forum of Psychoanalysis* 20:116–118.

Vonofakos, D., & Hinshelwood, B. (2012). Wilfred Bion's letters to John Rickman (1939–1951). *Psychoanalysis and History* 14:53–94.

Vonofakos, D., & Hinshelwood, R.D. (2013). Letters to John Rickman: Transition 1939–1951. In N. Torres and R.D. Hinshelwood, *Bion's Sources. The Shaping of his Paradigms* (pp. 88–103). London: Routledge.

Wallerstein, R.S. (1988). One psychoanalysis or many. *International Journal of Psychoanalysis* 69:5–21.

———— (1990). Psychoanalysis: The common ground. *International Journal of Psychoanalysis* 71:3–20.

Weiss, H. (2011). Linking Rickman's work with Bion's thinking. *International Forum of Psychoanalysis* 20:113–115.

Wiedemann, W. (2007). *Wilfred Bion – Biografie, Theorie und klinische Praxis des "Mystikers der Psychoanalyse"* [Wilfred Bion – Biography, theory and clinical work of the "mystic of psychoanalysis"]. Giessen: Psychosozial-Verlag.

CHAPTER 7

BION AND HIS FIRST ANALYST, JOHN
RICKMAN (1891–1951): A REVISITATION OF
THEIR RELATIONSHIP IN THE LIGHT OF
RICKMAN'S PERSONALITY AND SCIENTIFIC
PRODUCTION AND OF BION'S LETTERS TO
HIM (1939–1951)[1]

At the previous Bion Conference, held in Rome at the
end of January 2008, I had given a paper with the title
"Bion and Sullivan: An enlightening comparison." Franco
Borgogno and I included it in the special issue of the
International Forum of Psychoanalysis dedicated to this
event that we edited together, in which we also included
six more papers given in Rome. In my paper, I showed
how many things Bion and H.S. Sullivan (1892–1949)
had in common, although Bion neither met him nor ever
quoted his work in his books.

But Rickman and Sullivan did meet with each other,
at least once, in Paris in 1948—as we shall see below. Did
not only Rickman and Sullivan, but also Rickman and
Bion, have more things in common than we ever dared
to imagine? What do we know about Rickman, besides
his having been Bion's first training analyst, and having
worked with him at Northfield Hospital? We know that
out of this experience came the first chapter of Bion's
Experiences in groups which he wrote together with
Rickman. And what else do we know? After reconstructing
a picture of Rickman's life and work, I will reconsider
Bion's relationship to him in the light of the twenty-seven
letters that Bion wrote to him between January 29, 1939
and June 17, 1951, which I found in the Archives of the
British Psychoanalytical Society.

As Gérard Bléandonu wrote in his biography of
Bion, the latter met Rickman in 1937 and was analyzed
by him until September 1939 (Bléandonu, 1994, p. 47).
As World War II broke out, they became colleagues as
army psychiatrists, and their analytic relationship had
to come to an end. "All things considered, Rickman had
worked well with Bion, and his work," wrote Bléandonu,
"enabled Bion to make use of a long analysis with Klein"
(1994, p. 47). Furthermore, "Rickman lived long enough
to witness the positive outcome of his work, and the

[1] The original version of this article was published in Volume 20 (2011)
of the *International Forum of Psychoanalysis*, pp. 68–86. It represents
the revised version of a paper given in Boston in July 2009, in the
context of the international conference "Bion in Boston."

second analysis, as he died only a few weeks after Bion's second marriage" (1994, p. 47). This is more or less all we learn about Rickman from Bion's biographer—who does not take into consideration either his scientific production or his life and personality.

In 1957, Clifford Scott had compiled a collection of papers by Rickman that came out with the title *Selected contributions to psycho-analysis* and a foreword by Sylvia Payne. It was reissued in 2003 by Karnac, with a Preface by Pearl King. Looking at it, anyone can easily see how many themes of Rickman's scientific production were also of great interest to Bion and/or were so central in his own scientific work—for example, Rickman's interest in the psychoanalytic theory and exploration of psychoses; his commitment to the utilization of psychoanalysis in the field of psychiatry; his attempt to introduce psychoanalysis into medical education; his concern for the epistemological status of psychoanalysis; and his interest in establishing connections with a whole series of other disciplines.

In her preface, Pearl King underlined not only Rickman's "extensive range of interests and his inter-disciplinary contacts" (King, 2003a, p. 8), but also his unique experience as editor of scientific journals, with particular regard for the *British Journal of Medical Psychology*. As such, "he was insistent," wrote Pearl King, "that writers . . . should realize that as the observer they were also part of the 'picture'" (2003a, p. 7); in other words, this is how he also espoused H.S. Sullivan's principle of "participant observation."

A possible (and similarly unintentional) connection to the work of Sullivan is also present in Sylvia Payne's description of Rickman's main interests: ". . . the first was his interest in the psychodynamics of groups, and the second was the emphasis he placed on the need to study the technique of communication between a speaker or teacher and his audience" (Payne, 2003, p. 14). In other words, here must be some of the reasons why Hadley Cantril invited both of them, Rickman and Sullivan to be two of the eight speakers of the conference "Tensions that cause wars," which he organized in Paris in the summer of 1948.

But the major source of information we have about Rickman's life, work, and personality is Pearl King's Introduction (King, 2003b), entitled "The rediscovery of John Rickman and his work," to the anthology of his writings that she edited in 2003 under the title *No ordinary psychoanalyst. The exceptional contributions of*

John Rickman, an anthology accompanied by a Foreword by Riccardo Steiner, and to which we will turn below. But here is how Pearl King, a former analysand of his, started to answer the question "Who was John Rickman?":

> The Dr. John Rickman whom I knew, and have since got to know better, was a psychoanalyst who combined an extraordinarily thorough knowledge of psychoanalysis with an intense interest in social processes, and he was able to throw light on some of the problems of social psychology by extending psychoanalytic concepts to cover and understand group and community problems. The setting in which his heuristic capacities flourished best was during an informal discussion group or an impromptu conversation between colleagues coming from different disciplines in the social sciences. The creative enjoyment that John Rickman brought to such discussions was not only because of what he contributed, but also because he enabled the participants to re-experience what they had said or thought, often opening up their understanding in a way that they had not previously experienced. They were then enabled to re-evaluate themselves. Many of the letters to John that I read while editing his papers bore evidence of the impact that his way of working with colleagues had on them. I then realised how important it was for these people to have been 'listened to' by John. (King, 2003b, p. 1)

As we shall see going through Bion's twenty-seven letters to Rickman in detail, this must have been also Bion's experience of Rickman. Here is how Riccardo Steiner, in his Foreword, not only celebrated Pearl King's editorial work, but also emphasized the necessity to keep rediscovering Rickman's legacy:

> The outstanding enthusiasm, loyalty and affectionate scholarship of Pearl King have managed to rescue his work now from an undeserved oblivion. I am sure his work will from now on be better understood and appreciated as it deserves, as will the influence it had on so many aspects of our thinking and its stimulus for further research to clarify the many links that bind our present to our past in psychoanalysis. (Steiner, 2003, p. xiii)

A step in this direction had already been made by the English psychiatrist Tom Harrison, who after "some fifteen years of research and writing" (Harrison, 2000, p. 11), published the very useful and illuminating book *Bion, Rickman, Foulkes and the Northfield experiments*, with a Foreword by Bob Hinshelwood. Hinshelwood not only speaks of Northfield as "perhaps the first and prototype reflective institution" (Hinshelwood, 2000, p. 8), but also underlines both the crucial role which Harrison himself attributes to Rickman and the peculiar quality of the relationship which he maintained with Bion.

But here is Hinshelwood's voice: after having characterized the so-called Northfield Experiments in terms of "the clash of desperate originality with the forces of conservatism" (Hinshelwood, 2000, p. 7), here is how he speaks of the protagonists of such a clash:

> One gets a sense of Bion's irascible impatience with authority, Rickman's Quaker inner stillness, Foulkes' rather frantic ambitiousness, Main's overbearing but eloquent anxiousness, all combining as a community of real people . . . . The greatest of these was John Rickman . . . . He was a close background figure for Bion in all his troubled experiences in army psychiatry. There seems to be a guru quality about Rickman, a prodding inspiration rather than an administrator or an academic writer. That quality of direct inspiration of others leaves a quiet record, and Tom Harrison clearly wants to rescue his hero, and rehabilitate him to the centre of his psychiatric pantheon. All of us readers will have our particular heroes but I for one am persuaded to take Rickman a lot more seriously than I had hitherto. (Hinshelwood, 2000, p. 8)

In Hinshelwood's words, I find further confirmation of the point of view I originally wished to develop in this paper. Indeed, Pearl King reviewed the book, and in her review she did not omit to mention one of the main conclusions reached by the author: that the persisting relevance of the so-called Northfield Experiments has to do with viewing "therapy and rehabilitation" in psychiatry as "a continuous process" (King, 2002, p. 97).

As an aside, the important role played by the Northfield Experiments in the development of the larger therapeutic community movement was underlined also by David Millard, in the chapter on "Maxwell Jones and the therapeutic community" that he published in the important two-volume work *150 years of British psychiatry*, edited in 1996 by Hugh Freeman and German Berrios. Last but not least, another important anthology in which Bion's relationship to Rickman is taken up by several central witnesses of their work and collaboration at Northfield is the book edited in 1985 by Malcolm Pines (and reissued in 2000), under the title *Bion and group psychotherapy*, which features contributions by Eric Trist, John Sutherland, Harold Bridger, and Patrick de Maré.

At this point, before presenting a short sketch of Rickman's life and work, let me tell you about his meeting with Sullivan in Paris in the summer of 1948, which I had originally learned about through Helen Swick Perry's biography of Sullivan (1982). Here is her voice:

> In the last summer of his life (1948), Sullivan set forth with both trepidation and high hopes to participate in three international meetings in Europe . . . . He went first to Paris, where he had been summoned to participate in the UNESCO Tensions Project with seven other specialists from various

parts of the world. They had been brought together for a two-week period to compose a common short statement on the causes of nationalistic aggression and the conditions necessary for international understanding. Afterwards each participant was to write a more extended statement of his own views; and all these papers, together with the Common Statement, were brought together a year later in a book, *Tensions that cause wars*, edited by Hadley Cantril . . . . John Rickman, a psychiatrist and editor of the *British Journal of Medical Psychology*, proposed at the beginning of the first session that the group spend three hours in a general introductory period with 'each man indicating briefly the story of his life, the influences he thought had determined his point of view and his interests, together with an implicit evaluation of his own qualifications for being a member of this particular group'. They all felt that this procedure had saved much valuable time. Indeed it fitted the requirements of participant observation . . . . Sullivan was very proud of the Common Statement issued by this group, and he had it published in *Psychiatry* as soon as he returned from Europe. It has some of the historical perspective of our own Declaration of Independence and some of the economic perspective of the Communist manifesto. It remains cogent and relevant today. (Swick Perry, 1982, p. 408)

The other six outstanding social scientists, who—together with Sullivan and Rickman—participated in the project were the sociologist Gordon Allport of Harvard University, the sociologist Gilberto Freyre of the University of Bahia (Brazil), the sociologist Georges Gurvitch of the Sorbonne, Max Horkheimer as director of the New York Institute for Social Research, the Norwegian philosopher Arne Naess, and the Hungarian sociologist Alexander Szalai. And here is, for example, the last point of the Common Statement, which Sullivan and Rickman must have particularly contributed to:

In this task of acquiring self-knowledge and social insight [leading to the treatment and prevention of international tensions], the social sciences – the sciences of Man – have a vital part to play. One hopeful sign today is the degree to which the boundaries between these sciences are breaking down in the face of the common challenge confronting them. The social scientist can help make clear to people of all nations that the freedom and welfare of one are ultimately bound up with the freedom and welfare of all, that the world need not continue to be a place where men must either kill or be killed. Effort on behalf of one's own group can become compatible with effort on behalf of humanity. (Cantril, ed., 1950, pp. 20–21)

And—last but not least—let me provide the words with which Rickman commented on Sullivan's untimely death (in Paris, on January 14, 1949, almost a month before turning 57), that Hadley Cantril put at the beginning of Sullivan's contribution to his anthology, the paper "Tensions interpersonal and international: A psychiatrist's view":

> One cannot read his contribution without a feeling of sadness
> at the death of a colleague who was so friendly and forward
> looking. In particular his early acceptance of field theory – a
> theory incommoding one's complacency – puts him among the
> pioneers. At the UNESCO discussions he quietly introduced
> this and other views on the problems before us with his native
> generosity of spirit and humor. (Cantril, 1950, p. 81)

Rickman himself (who was a year older than Sullivan)
would unfortunately die about two and a half years later,
on July 1, 1951, aged sixty. But it is now time to turn to his
life and personality.

RICKMAN'S LIFE AND PERSONALITY

Let me start with the portrait of Rickman that Sylvia
Payne put together in 1957:

> Dr. Rickman was a Quaker and came of Quaker stoke. He
> was educated at a Quaker public school and afterwards at
> King's College, Cambridge, where he took a Natural Science
> Tripos and the first part of his Medical Degree. He completed
> his medical training at St. Thomas' Hospital, London,
> graduating in 1916. On qualification he volunteered for the
> Friends' War Victims Relief Unit in Russia, and later wrote
> a number of articles on his experiences when practising
> medicine amongst the Russian peasants . . . . While working
> in Russia he met his future wife, Lydia Cooper Lewis of
> Philadelphia, who was working as a social worker for the
> American Friends' Service Committee. They were married
> in 1918 . . . by Russian civil ceremony . . . . A daughter was
> born to them in 1921. John Rickman did pioneer work in
> Russia of a kind which he was to repeat on more than one
> occasion during his lifetime. In the hospital in which he was
> working he organized the training of Russian peasants girls as
> nurses. His object was to teach the people something which
> might be carried on when the unit left the country. On his
> return from Russia, John Rickman specialized in psychiatry.
> He held a resident post at Fulbourn Asylum, Cambridge,
> and there also he pioneered by holding lectures and seminars
> for nurses. His interest had been aroused in psychoanalysis
> by Dr. W.H.R. Rivers, who was in Cambridge at that time
> and on his advice in 1920 Dr. Rickman went to Vienna to
> see Freud and worked with him there. On leaving Vienna he
> continued his study of psycho-analysis and of psychiatry by
> joining the group of men in London . . . under the leadership
> of Ernest Jones, and by becoming assistant . . . in the
> psychiatric out-patient department of St. Thomas' Hospital.
> In 1926 he wrote his M.D. thesis on a psychological factor in
> the aetiology of prolapse of the uterus. At different phases in
> his career he worked with Freud, Ernest Jones, Ferenczi and
> Melanie Klein, and thus had had the privilege of contact with
> some of the most original research workers in the study of the
> unconscious mind. (Payne, 1957, pp. 9–10)

From this point of view, he was—in other words—
one of the first analysts to go through more than one

analytic experience, and this probably contributed not only to his openness, but also to Bion's own undogmatic attitude, and/or to his later critical distance from Kleinian orthodoxy.

But let us now see what details of Rickman's career as a psychoanalyst Sylvia Payne drew to our attention: in the first place, his role in the foundation of the International Psycho-Analytical Press and the promotion of Freud's work in the English-speaking world; and second, his role in founding, together with Ernest Jones, the London Psychoanalytical Society, in which he continued to play a very active role all along, including his election to president of the British Psychoanalytic Society for the term 1947–1949. Particularly important too was of course the work he did for the *British Journal of Medical Psychology*, between 1925 and 1934 as Assistant Editor, and between 1934 and 1949 as Editor-in-Chief. In addition, the work he did as army psychiatrist, in the Emergency Medical Service, at Wharncliffe Hospital, at Northfield Hospital, and at the War Office Selection Board (WOSB), was also of fundamental importance, as we will see when dealing with Bion's letters to Rickman. After the war, besides again becoming very active in the British Psychoanalytical Society, he played a major role in the reorganization and/or establishment of institutions such as the Cassel Hospital, the Tavistock Clinic, and the Tavistock Institute of Human Relations.

Here is the picture of Rickman's presence and character that Sylvia Payne transmitted to us:

> Dr. Rickman, a tall powerfully built man with traditional quite courtesy of the Englishman, by his presence might appear formidable to those who had not the chance to approach him. Experience showed that he was invariably interested in other people's problems, and would take infinite pains to help colleagues as well as patients in difficult situations. In fact a survey of the work which he did in adult life gives evidence of humility and diffidence about his own intellectual accomplishments in the earlier years, and his readiness to urge a colleague to aspire to a position which he himself had an equal right to acquire. Other evidence of this character trait becomes apparent when the work he accomplished as an editor is considered . . . . Many psycho-analysts, academic psychologists and psychotherapists can testify to the trouble he took in putting their papers into shape for publication, giving valuable advice on form and arrangement, and sponsoring new ideas, some of which are now basic. (Payne, 2003, pp. 10, 11, 12)

In relation to this, a whole series of pictures and documents is contained in the CD-ROM edited by Ken Robinson in connection with an exhibition on Rickman's life and work which took place in 2003 (Robinson, 2003).

But let us now see what Pearl King wrote as regards Rickman's editorial activity in her Introduction of 2003:

> After having completed the research work I had done in the archives and elsewhere in order to 'rediscover' John Rickman for myself, I also had to face one of my discoveries: he was probably one of the most experienced editors ever to help psychologically minded writers. His insistence that writers should not only concentrate on the item or event that they were reporting, but that they should describe the context in which it functioned and its relationship to other sources of relevant knowledge, must have been of help to those whose papers he edited, as well as of help to those who read those papers. (King, 2003, p. 66)

Before taking a look at Rickman's scientific production, let me show you how Pearl King attempted to utilize a similar approach in her reconstruction of his life and contributions. The titles of the sections in which she articulated her reconstruction are as follows:

- Family background
- Education
- J.R. in Russia
- J.R.'s return to Cambridge after his work in Russia
- Life in Vienna
- The establishment of the Institute of Psychoanalysis in London
- The establishment of the London Clinic of Psychoanalysis
- J.R.'s publishing activities in the British Society
- J.R. as an active member of the British Society
- Rickman's decision to work with Ferenczi in Budapest
- Rickman's return to London and his work for the Society
- The Board takes responsibility for the Public Lectures Programme of the Institute
- Rickman's political concerns over threats to psychoanalysis
- The Board of the Institute considers its role should hostilities develop
- Contact with other professional groups
- J.R. and his work during the war
- Participation of psychiatrists in the Emergency Medical Services
- Organization of the psychiatric services of the Armed Forces
- Work while at Haymeads EMS Hospital and the Haymeads Memorandum
- The Wharncliffe Experiment
- Joint Services and EMS Psychiatrists' Conferences
- Contributions to Army Command Psychiatrists to the

development of officer selection procedures
- The development of special military hospitals for psychoneurotics
- J.R. and Wilfred Bion at Northfield Military Hospital
- Major J.R., the psychiatrist at No.6 WOSB
- Negotiations with American psychoanalysts
- Other contacts with American colleagues
- Rickman becomes an active member of the British Society again
- The end of hostilities in Europe
- The demobilisation of psychiatrists and psychologists
- Rickman's visit to Berlin on 14–15 October 1946
- Applications from war-time colleagues to be trained as psychoanalysts
- Rickman's contribution to the Training Programme at the Institute
- Rickman's participation in the UNESCO 'Tensions Project'
- The first Congress of the IPA, held in Zurich, since the beginning of the hostilities took place
- J.R.'s visit to Cairo and Damascus
- J.R. retires as Editor of the British Journal of Medical Psychology.

RICKMAN'S SCIENTIFIC CONTRIBUTION

Let Pearl King now guide us also in the revisitation of Rickman's scientific contribution, which she divided into the following four parts, putting his papers in the chronological order in which they were written:

- Observations on psychoanalytic theory and technique
- The interpersonal and the intra-psychic dynamics of the interview situation
- Disruptive forces in group relations
- On the nature of religious and moral beliefs.

These papers are actually so well written and in many ways still relevant today that it really makes sense to give you a brief synthesis of all of them—a task through which I was myself able to learn a great deal. But before taking up the first one, let us listen again to Pearl King's voice, to some of her most eloquent words about the papers:

> Most of the papers included in this book seem to have been written as if to be read to an audience, although in several cases there is no evidence that they were in fact ever read at a meeting. In these cases, it seems that Rickman is writing to share his ideas with the reader, so that in reading his papers the reader may feel that he is in direct contact with Rickman and his thinking, not seeing him as an 'ex-cathedra statement of fact', but as something that he or she could think about or consider. I have attempted to preserve this atmosphere of the

meeting of ideas, which was so integral to John Rickman's mode of communication. (King, 2003b, pp. 2–3)

Indeed, a similar problem—how to preserve the dialogic nature of his lectures—also had to be faced by Helen Swick Perry as the chair of the committee that edited Sullivan's posthumous work, with particular regard to the lectures he had held during the War at Chestnut Lodge, and out of which came the books *The interpersonal theory of psychiatry*, *The psychiatric interview*, and *Clinical studies in psychiatry*.

That Rickman had his audience in mind when writing his papers is, for example, very clear in the case of the very first paper of the anthology compiled by Pearl King, "Developments in psychoanalysis, 1896–1947." In this text, Rickman shows a highly impressive capacity to operate a synthesis such as to convey to his audience— apparently candidates of the Tavistock Institute of Human Relations—the fundamentals of psychoanalysis in a very few pages while, at the same time, maintaining its high level of sophistication. At the very beginning, he already speaks of "the *transference situation*" as the "special 'instrument'" of psychoanalysis (Rickman, 2003, p. 72). And here is the very clear way in which he presents the tension that we all have to keep struggling with in our daily work with our patients: "Though no other aspect of psychology has thrown so much light on man's development . . . yet psychoanalysis is all based on experience of the present" (Rickman, 2003, p. 73).

After having talked about the origins of psychoanalysis, dreams, and transference, he presents the four periods into which its development can be divided, according to their dominant theme, that is, sexuality, ego, superego and object relations. And here is the very clear way in which he was able to assimilate Melanie Klein's point of view, and in which—and we are already at the end of the paper—he connects psychoanalysis with the human sciences:

> Man combines with his fellows in his restitutive work, as he also sometimes combines with them in his destructiveness. From this recognition of the need in ourselves and in others to restore and create, from the unconscious feeling of sharing of the guilt for destructive impulse, rises a community of feeling for the restitutive and constructive urges. In these feelings we find some of the roots of religion, art and science. (Rickman, 2003, p. 84)

The next paper, "Experimental psychology and psychoanalysis," written by Rickman between 1937 and 1939, is also very clear and instructive. Without going into details of the way in which this paper is constructed, let me tell you how skilfully the author presents psychoanalysis as a research method. Here are his words, still very much relevant today, albeit seventy years later:

> Psychoanalysis is a method of research and therapy which operates in an *a-historical present*, that is to say, the data by which it verifies its hypothesis and brings conviction that it is on the right track are events observable "here-and-now" in the analytic situation. The analyst by *self-effacement* and skilful *interpretation* enables the patient to *produce spontaneously*, and so disclose, the structure and functional relations of the personal and social events he has experienced, or avoided experiencing, most importantly the latter, in the past. *By reliving them in the new setting an increased understanding and mastery of the old and troublesome situations is achieved*, so that they do not worry the patient and more energy *is freed for constructive uses*. (Rickman, 2003, pp. 95–6, original emphasis)

And here is the image that Rickman proposes at the end of the paper, after having indicated the best direction for the progress of the two disciplines:

> I now want to say one word about the present and the future relations of psychology and psychoanalysis. It seems to me that the important thing is for each to develop its own research technique to the fullest extent possible. It would have been disastrous for psychoanalysis if it had all along been thought essential for a second observer to be present, because phantasy is always more inhibited *vis-à-vis* two people . . . . So long as water continues to be drawn from the well of knowledge, it does not seem to me to matter if it is drawn from one bucket or two. (Rickman, 2003, pp. 96–97)

What would have Rickman thought of the merits, limits and relevance of audiotaping sessions? I am sure he would have been able to help us to look at the problem in the most constructive way possible.

And this is actually the kind of attitude behind the next paper, "Scientific method and psychoanalysis," written (to be read to the British Psychoanalytical Society) in 1945. For example, in the paragraph on "The establishment of hypotheses from grouped data," Rickman speaks very clearly of the necessary "tentative character of theory," of the "risks of premature and narrow generalization," and of "dogmatism" as "one of our patent and serious failings" (Rickman, 2003, pp. 102–103). And in the following paragraph, "Problems of verification in analysis," we read of the need for a "closer collaboration" between clinical work and extraclinical research, and we hear the advise to "follow the example of Darwin, who paid less attention to his supporters than he did to the objections raised by his opponents" (Rickman, 2003, pp. 103, 104, 105). The fourth and last paragraph, "The scientific attitude," contains the following:

> The receptive tolerance that we extend to our patients is
> precisely the attitude which, alone, is genuinely favourable
> to free and constructive discussion. In fact, we seem to leave
> behind in the consulting room the attitude which is so urgently
> required in theoretical research . . . This is why pooling and
> collective research is so imperative . . . . Our concern is with
> ideas expressed, not only with sponsors . . . . Everyone and
> anyone should ideally feel free to say exactly what they think
> about any idea, no matter whose idea it is. (Rickman, 2003,
> pp. 106–107)

Here are Rickman's concluding words, after having
stressed the necessity of making further progress in both
"the subjective way of analysis of the analyst, and the
objective way of pooling, interchange and comparison of
results":

> Discussion will be constructive insofar as it is true, and no
> method of furthering useful discussion will succeed unless
> we can manage to create an atmosphere of tolerance and
> objectivity in which intellectual honesty is encouraged.
> (Rickman, 2003, p. 108)

It is no wonder for me that H.S. Sullivan had himself
long tackled with these problems and that, for example,
he had in 1927 already alerted his colleagues about
the risk of premature generalization of psychoanalytic
hypotheses. Indeed, the anthology *Schizophrenia as a
human process* (edited by Helen Swick Perry in 1962 and
in which the reader can find the same admonition given
above by Rickman; Sullivan, 1962) contains not only the
clinical thread of how to approach schizophrenic patients,
but also the important and original epistemological thread
regarding the development of a scientifically rigorous
psychoanalysis.

The fourth and last paper of this section of papers
compiled and edited by Pearl King is perhaps the one
paper which Rickman is still famous for, "Number and
the human sciences," from 1951. Here is how the paper
begins:

> Suppose one of those oft-spoken-of-but-seldom met travellers
> from Mars had visited us to satisfy his native curiosity about
> psychology: he would find a state of affairs that might at
> first seem somewhat puzzling. In the write-up of his field-
> work he would report on one-person psychology, two-person
> psychology, three-person psychology, possibly a four-person
> psychology, and a multi-person psychology; what would
> strike him most would of course be the interrelation of those
> aspects of the subject. (Rickman, 2003, p. 109)

And here is the way in which Rickman underlies the
importance of Bion's pioneer work on small groups:

> Two features of psychoanalytic work are outstanding in

importance for the human sciences. The first is its a-historical character . . . the second is the fact that the problems of the subject under investigation have priority over the intellectual curiosity of the observer . . . In the researches in multi-person psychology the same two features are found in the work of Dr. W.R. Bion . . . It is as yet too soon to appraise his work, and it may be many years before it will be applicable to anthropology, but it must be mentioned because the psychodynamic unit that is investigated consists of about eight persons. (Rickman, 2003, pp. 113–114)

We can come now to the second section of the anthology *No ordinary psychoanalysts*, "The interpersonal and the intra-psychic dynamics of the interview situation," and to its first paper, from 1936–1938, "First aid in psychotherapy," a very unusual theme for a psychoanalyst, but not for a colleague like John Rickman, with his wish to extend the realm of application of psychoanalysis and with his concern for human welfare. The still relevant conclusive considerations that he proposes to us after the presentation of a clinical case are as follows:

First of all, *every crisis is due to loss of satisfaction in object-relationships* and dread of never getting satisfaction again. The cause is never obvious. If it were obvious the patient would be sad on account of his loss or in pain or grief but not ill. The distinction between fear and anxiety is that fear is experienced at the possible loss of an object of satisfaction of which the person is conscious, and anxiety when the loss of an *unconscious* love object becomes imminent. The precipitating factor may be conspicuous enough, the specific factor is only to be got through search. This leads to the second point: *the patient's story is like the manifest content of a dream* – it may or may not in itself tell us something. The cause of the breakdown is, like the *latent content*, unconscious. (Rickman, 2003, p. 129; original emphasis)

Very interesting and also more specifically connected to one of the themes of my paper (Bion's and Rickman's collaboration during the War) is the following paper of this section, "The psychiatric interview in the social setting of the War Office Selection Board," written in 1943. Not only is the use of the group situation as an instrument of selection of the soldiers very interesting, but so also is the presentation of the interview situation as a learning experience for both participants—as Sullivan himself formulated it in *The psychiatric interview*. And here is what we learn about the diagnostic dimension of the interview:

In the field of battle the soldier is called upon to exert the utmost ruthlessness to the enemy and the utmost consideration to those on his own side . . . . Clinical investigations show that of those who are much given to the unwitting *negative attitude* to their friends, a proportion adopts an appeasing attitude to the enemy. They may be witty and amusing in company but they are not reliable in action. It seems to me

that the duty specially falls upon the psychiatrist to spot these
sources of danger. (Rickman, 2003, p. 138; original emphasis)

In other words: only if "compassionate" with his
colleagues can the soldier be "ruthless" with his enemies.

An interesting variation on this theme of Rickman's
work for the WOSB is offered by the following paper,
"The influence of the 'social field' on behaviour in the
interview situation," also from 1943. Here is what we can
read in the section entitled "Ego-development viewed as
the growth of an 'internal society'":

If we employ the concepts of Kurt Lewin (Lewin, 1941),
we can distinguish two kinds of approach to the problems
of clinical psychology and to the problems of the W.O.S.B.
In the one approach the question is 'What *type* of man is
this', while in the other, it is 'What *forces* are at work here?'
The former tends to a static, the latter to a dynamic, view of
clinical medicine. If we follow the latter view, in the light of
recent developments in psychopathology, we may come to the
notion that an individual can be regarded as a *field of forces*
. . . In a word, personality is a composite structure growing
round a central, ever developing, ego nucleus . . . . There is
an internal *society*, which through the mediation of what we
commonly call 'the ego', is in constant and ever changing
inter-play with the *external society*. (Rickman, 2003, pp. 141–
142, original emphasis)

And here is the application of this new point of view
to the work of the WOSB:

Our technique for studying the effect of intra-group tensions .
. . upon the individual . . . is in its infancy. When the time comes
it should be more possible to describe the manifestations of
the candidate's personality relative to the field of social forces
in which they appear. Perhaps the WOSBs have afforded a
favourable occasion for such observations, for candidates
were seen in the social setting of their subgroup . . . no less did
the candidates observe us . . . The aquarium in which we all
swam had at most glass partitions . . . The three-day scheme
to select officers has been described as 'Exercise Goldfish',
but this bowl has no sides: all are observers, all are observed.
(Rickman, 2003, p. 147)

As last paper of this section Pearl King selected
"The technique of interviewing in anthropology and
psychoanalysis," which Rickman read before the Royal
Anthropological Society in 1949. As the skill of conducting
a good interview a common feature of the work in the two
fields, Rickman states how, in his experience, "the principal
instrument of this kind of research" is represented by "the
receptiveness to small changes of direction in human
relationships *within the physician himself*" (Rickman,
2003, p. 152, original emphasis). This in fact also applies
to the group as new field study, which Rickman presents
with the following words:

> The study of group-tension deals with the moment-to-moment oscillations between group-cohesive and group-disruptive forces . . . The pioneer in this field of research, in my view, is Dr. W.R. Bion, whose first exposition on group tensions was published in *The Lancet* in 1943, and whose later contributions were published in *Human Relations* (1948). No one should even begin to undertake this kind of work who desires above all things to conduct a peaceful life. In the group interview of the kind I have in mind, it is often found that one of the first things the group does is roundly to attack the person they have called in to help them. (Rickman, 2003, p. 155)

We are now ready to consider the first paper of the six papers of the next section, "Disruptive forces in group relations," which goes by the title "Does it take all kinds to make a world? Uniformity and diversity in communities," and is based on two lectures that Rickman delivered in March 1938, and which he summarized in the following way:

> I would like in conclusion to make one point as clear as I can. I have been drawing parallels between the child's behaviour in the nursery and the man's behaviour in the big wide world, but I have even gone further than drawing parallels. I have implied that political squabbling is largely due to unresolved nursery conflicts, and that our view of the society in which we live is derived from our early attitude to parents, brothers and sisters . . . . I have placed politics in the centre of this discussion, because it is so much a field of action and aggression, in the group. (Rickman, 2003, p. 182)

The next paper, Chapter 10 of the anthology *No ordinary psychoanalyst*, "Panic and anxiety reactions in groups during air raids," was published on June 4, 1938, in *The Lancet*, the prestigious medical journal for which Rickman wrote important editorials and articles, especially during the war. Here is how he himself summarized his line of thought:

> In conclusion and to repeat: panic in the adult is not a new experience; it is a recrudescence of an earlier state which is screened from us. This gives some of the nameless horror to panic, but it also gives a key to reducing its incidence. Unable to attack its specific causes, we can endeavour to reduce the contributory causes and can follow the ways taken to overcome the periods of panic when our minds were immature: by formation of groups, by manipulative activities, by turning slowly from blind and magical beliefs to a more reasoned interest in the world around us, but above all by acquiring the capacity to recognise and control our own egoism and impulses of hate. On this last depends the success of group-formation and group activities which always exercise a large influence in checking the outbreak of panic. (Rickman, 2003, p. 196)

Whereas Chapter 11, "On the development of professional and unprofessional attitudes," was compiled by Pearl King from two overlapping papers of 1934 and 1938 and deals with the profiles of shaman, priest, and scientist, and with the nature of "quackery," Chapter 12, "Intra-group tension in therapy: Their study as a task of the group," is the text that Rickman and Bion produced on the basis of their collaboration at Northfield Hospital in 1942/1943, which originally came out in *The Lancet* on November 27, 1943 (Bion and Rickman, 1943), and which I will talk about in detail in the next paragraph, dealing with Bion's letters to Rickman.

Also compiled from notes with which Rickman addressed the conference "Present-day problems of peace and war," held in London on September 20–22, 1946, is Chapter 13, "Disruptive forces in group relations: War as a makeshift therapy." Pearl King was able to do her work well, since she had herself attended the conference, at which she had also for the first time heard Rickman (her future training analyst) give a talk. Here is, for example, how Rickman talked in this circumstance about the work of Bion:

> The work of W.R. Bion seems to indicate that the thing a group most dreads is its impotence *vis-à-vis* an enemy, and its worst enemy is its own unfaced group-disruptiveness. He found that when the study of intra-group tension was made the task of the group, that group became more at peace with itself, its capacity for constructiveness rose and, also, its ability to work with other groups in friendly, rivalry increased. (Rickman, 2003, pp. 237–238)

In this paper Rickman speaks of the analyst as "a participant in the field of social forces," in a manner similar to Sullivan's, from whom he of course differed on the basis of his different training and personal biography.

As the sixth and last paper of this section, King chose to publish the text that Rickman contributed to the UNESCO Conference I dealt with in the introductory paragraph, "Some psychodynamic factors behind tensions that cause wars," originally published in the volume *Tensions that cause wars*, edited by Hadley Cantril in 1950. It is a very well written and interesting text, which reasons of space do not allow me to report here about in detail. One of the most impressive traits of this work is how experience-near it is, as, for example, Rickman's concluding words about the aim of an investigation on social tensions show:

> Its aim should not be a summary of social dynamics but the beginning of a new phase of human collaboration, where the goal is more stable social and personal equilibrium. What shape society would then take is yet beyond our ken. It has to emerge from the work of liberation from anxiety and

unmanageable guilt. (Rickman, 2003, p. 265)

We come now very briefly to the fourth section, "On the nature of religious and moral beliefs," which contains the following papers: "A study of Quaker beliefs," "The need for a belief in God," "Man without God?," and "The development of moral function." They all show how Rickman's integratory capacity included not only pedagogy, but also religion—at variance with Freud and in tune with contemporary psychoanalysis.

Let us now briefly turn to the papers selected in 1957 by Clifford Scott and included in the volume *Selected contributions to psycho-analysis*, before we eventually take up Bion's letters to Rickman. Of the twenty-three papers contained in it, I will limit myself to mentioning the ones whose character further deepens the knowledge of Rickman's work. Let us start with the two papers he dedicated to Freud: "Sigmund Freud: A personal impression" (1939) and "Sigmund Freud, 1856–1939: An appreciation" (1941). The former begins: "In Professor Freud two characteristics were present in the highest degree: his friendly simplicity towards one as a human being and the prodigious power of his mind" (Rickman, 1957/2003, p. 59). And here is the way in which he recalled their first meeting in the paper of 1941:

> Just after the last war an eager young pupil went to him for a personal analysis . . . and asked him for the name of his publishers in order to get and study his writings in chronological order. He replied: 'Don't bother. Learn to read in the Book of Nature – your own analysis here – then you can turn whatever other pages you like and you will profit more from them'. (Rickman, 1957/2003, p. 102)

In a second group, of strictly psychoanalytical papers, we could include the following: "Discussion on lay-analysis" (1928), "On the criteria for the termination of an analysis" (1950), "Reflections on the function and organization of a psycho-analytical society" (1951), and "A survey: The development of the psycho-analytical theory of the psychoses (1894–1926)" (1926–1927). As far as Rickman's paper of 1951 is concerned, it is very stimulating and relevant to consider, for example, the way in which he describes the psychoanalytic society as a context in which to cultivate the possibility of "[giving] free play to the process of thinking while speaking" (Rickman, 1957/2003, p. 203).

In a third group of papers, I would include all the papers by Rickman which remind me of similar titles, interests, and ideas proposed by H.S. Sullivan in those very same years (or some years before), for example:

"The general practitioner and psychoanalysis" (1939), "Psychology in medical education" (1947), "The role and future of psycho-therapy within psychiatry" (1950), "The development of psychological medicine" (1950), and "Methodology and research in psycho-pathology" (1951). Of course, some of Rickman's (and Sullivan's) major interests also corresponded to some of Bion's major interests—as we will also see now, once we turn to the letters which Bion wrote to Rickman between 1939 and 1951.

BION'S LETTERS TO RICKMAN

Wilfred Bion's *first letter* to John Rickman belonging to the collection deposited in the Archives of the British Psychoanalytical Society was written in his Harley Street office on January 29, 1939:

> Dear Dr. Rickman, I am writing to ask you if you think there would be any objection to my trying to get a little further with my analysis by transferring to someone else for the time being? I hate the idea of it, and I do not even know if it is practicable financially; but I should feel happier if I had a talk, say with Glover, about the business, if you think something might be gained and nothing lost by doing so.

After having told Rickman that he had already spoken about it with Dr. Carroll, who had seen the change as "practicable," Bion continued as follows: "although no one could say, except yourself, if there were any immediate contra-indications. For my part I have a nasty feeling that I should put up a really remarkable series of resistances, but I suppose one can learn much even from that."

The third and last section of the letter deals with a Wednesday Meeting in which Jung's concept of "collective unconscious" seems to have been one of the themes, about which Bion speaks very disparagingly.

We have to wait for the *second letter*, written by Bion from the Public Health Department in London, until September 9, 1939, a few days after the outbreak of the war. After thanking Rickman for a letter which we unfortunately do not know about, he wrote:

> I've now landed as a group psychiatrist and I am trying to find out just what that means. It *ought* to mean something really important, but it feels at present as if "passive defence" had eaten its way into the mentality of the service and become a complete lack of initiative.

Below, in the fifth section of the letter, he writes: "I'm trying to get all our people in this group to organize an exchange of any ideas or practices that have proved, or might prove, efficacious in dealing with casualties." Bion then closes the letter, "I will not take up more of your time. I hope it will before very long . . . to something about the analysis, but obviously it has to wait at present."

This theme occurs again in the following, *third letter*, of November 7, 1939:

> Dear Dr. Rickman, I am writing to ask you if there is any chance of continuing with my analysis sometime fairly soon. I hesitated to write earlier as the war situation seems as obscure as ever and furthermore I'm left in a miserable financial state – two paying patients.

Such a desire seems also to have to do with the fact that Bion in the following paragraph, writes that he was:

> particularly glad to find that I seemed to be able to draw on quite early bits of my own analysis which I thought I had forgotten. In fact . . . I seemed to have wanted a stage where my contact with patients was profitable for them and was helping me and them to open my own mind too.

And a few lines below: "I have also been able to feel I know enough now to know how much I am still missing."

The *fourth letter*, written by Bion on March 15, 1940, in his Harley Street office, and the longest so far, starts with a critical appraisal of the two papers, by Glover and by Mannheim, and of the Jungian point of view developed by Baynes. Only in the fifth and last section of this letter do we come directly in touch with Bion's state of mind, six months after the beginning of the war:

> I look like being swept into the army. I have been offered a consultant job and as my practice will not come back – I have only seen one new patient after the war and have never had more than two – I can see no other cause. I can't pretend to feel pleased about this but it may after all present a very useful opportunity to get work done of which I ought to know more than I know at present. The serious blow is to have to postpone further the continuation of analysis and training.

In the *fifth letter*, written by Bion to Rickman towards the end of the year, on December 18, 1940, from the Military Hospital of Moston Hall, Chester, we can see the first hint of their future collaboration. As in the previous letter, Bion starts it with "Dear Rickman", and not with "Dear Dr. Rickman," as in the first three letters, and here is what we can read:

> I shall be very glad to come over to Wharncliffe and think I can manage it all right. It will be a relief to hear talk which is backed up by some psychological knowledge for once. This job I have is terrific.

And here is how Bion's growing involvement with his job and his identity as an army psychiatrist find expression in the next section:

> I have been thinking a lot, ever since my first weeks
> in the army, about the single interview technique but
> I have not made much headway; that and the training
> of progressive expression will be very interesting.
> Their collaboration then started to take shape:
> I write a memorandum on a scheme for . . . hospital training.
> . . . It has not had a single comment made . . . If I can dig up
> my copy I'll bring it along . . . Also a few scraps on the single
> interview.

Before taking up the *sixth letter*, of January 4, 1941, in which Bion thanked Rickman

"for making me so very comfortable at Wharncliffe last week-end," let us go back to Pearl King's reconstruction of Rickman's career and see what Wharncliffe was all about: "After one year at Haymeads Hospital, John Rickman was transferred to Wharncliffe Emergency Hospital, Sheffield, where Ronald Hargreaves was the Commandant Psychiatrist," wrote Pearl King at the very beginning of the section entitled "The Wharncliffe Experiment" (King, 2003b, p. 34).

As far as Haymeads Emergency Hospital (located at Bishop's Stortford, not far from Cambridge), an institution of the Emergency Medical Services, is concerned, Rickman had joined it on September 1, 1939, that is, on the day Poland was invaded (cf. King, 2003b, p. 32). At both places—as we learn from Pearl King—he worked as a civilian psychiatrist (cf. King, 2003b). When Rickman was posted to Wharncliffe EMS Hospital, on August 23, 1940, he must have taken with him the plans for an "Occupational Therapy Centre," which were already contained in "The Haymeads Memorandum" of September 6, 1939 (as Pearl King tells us; King, 2003b, p. 34).

According to Pearl King, such an approach to the rehabilitation of the soldiers owed much to the influence of Kurt Lewin's "field concept" (which he had got to know in 1939) and to Rickman's attempt at an integration of it with (Melanie Klein's) object relations theory (cf. King, 2003b, p. 33): "It was a combination of these concepts from different disciplines that was necessary if the psychiatric services were going to be able to keep up with problems of group relations and the health functioning of a large social system like the Army," wrote Pearl King in this regard (King, 2003b, p. 33).

Let us now come to "the Wharncliffe experiment." This consisted of the association of paramilitary training facilities (as opposed to traditional occupational therapy like weaving and painting) with psychological care for the soldier, which Rickman was eventually able to implement with the assistance of a regular soldier, Sergeant Bryant, who ran the Rehabilitation and Training Centre. "The fame of Rickman's work at Wharncliffe spread," Pearl King wrote, "and many people came to see it" (King, 2003b, p. 35). Among them was Wilfred Bion, to whose letter, of January 4, 1941 we can now return.

The letter remarks: "I enjoyed seeing you again very much indeed and it was most refreshing to get somewhere where at least a sane attempt was being made to get work done." And here is how the letter—the first one which I report almost in its entirety, as Pearl King herself did in 2003—continued:

> I dug out my memorandum when I got back here and was pleased to find that it did seem to suggest something like the scheme you are in fact carrying out. Not the least value of a para-military training course seems to me to be that a patient is given a world to adjust to that is nothing like so severe as that isolated and unsupportive world which is presented to him by the bed-ridden existence, aimless and disunited, which he has to face in the special institutions I have seen so far. But I am still doing a lot of thinking about this. I think you have given me some ammunition with which to ginger up this psychiatric service here . . . . I hope I shall have a chance of coming over again. In the meantime, I trust you will have any success and happiness.

About a month later, on February 7, 1941, Bion wrote for the third time from Moston Hall, this being his *seventh letter* to Rickman. It contains a further echo of their recent meeting and a hint at his wish for a more intensive collaboration with him:

> I have been working on another memo to the same effect which I shall send you. But I find it unsatisfactory churning these things out without having an opportunity to put the ideas to the test of experiment. It's mostly reminiscence of training in the last war. I hope I shall be at the next meeting you have at Wharncliffe; please get me invited!

We find an even more personal tone in Bion's *eighth letter*, written at the Old George Hotel in York, probably during a short vacation, on July 27, 1941. For the first time in this correspondence, Bion addresses Rickman as "My dear Rickman" and then writes, "It was very kind of you to take so much trouble with my report; it was most helpful and I should have written to thank you much earlier." A couple of lines later, we learn about Bion's growing involvement in his job: "The difficulty is that each day brings in some new point almost and I find it difficult to be content to send in an incomplete report and leave the fresh points for a later screed." And here is the new note on which this short letter ends: "Betty and I were very glad to see you again," to which the following comment—reflecting a new combination of professional and personal motives—is attached: "Our attempts to have you as my guest in a private party seem fated to end up as adjourned meetings of the 'Conference' instead, but we shall persevere!"

In the following, the *ninth letter*, written by Bion from the 42nd Division on September 24, 1941 we learn of the copy of a report he includes in it, and on which they had apparently been working together. This short letter ends on a similar personal note as the previous one: "Betty joins me in sending our very best wishes and we hope we shall meet again soon."

The longest letter so far is the following one, the *tenth letter*, written by Bion from London on December 14, 1941. The letter not only shows how the exchange between Bion and Rickman had reached a new depth, but also introduces a new cultural and political dimension. Here is Bion's new line of thought:

> I think I mentioned to you that one of my strongest impressions during this second time of the army has been the feeling of amazement . . . that the psychiatrists had failed very seriously in their education of the public. Fundamentally the responsibility for this must rest with people who hold an official place, supported by public funds, as the Maudsley people do. If the general public fear . . . as they appear to do, psychiatrists, psychiatric treatments and psychiatric tests, the blame for that can only belong to those who never make an attempt to tackle these latent anxieties. Maudsley-minded look askance at the psychiatrists who do tackle those fears—but do nothing themselves. In fact . . . any criticism of our work that comes from those who have done no work at all, may react as a very dangerous boomerang. And should be made so react if we know our business.

Bion then further develops this line of thought:

> Unfortunately the fate of genuine psychiatry and psychotherapy seems to me to be wrapped up very closely with the fate of practically every free mental or cultural activity. If we 'win' this war, then the position of the 'Maudsley-minded' will not, I think, be very important. But if the Fascist-Nazi-outfit wins, then the Maudsley wins and it will be good-bye to any real hope of human advance for many a long years. It is a pity that we can win the war and still lose the essential battle in our field. But I can't say I feel very pessimistic about this at the moment.

The Maudsley Hospital, opened for clinical work and teaching in 1923, was a "formidable counterweight," as Trevor Turner wrote (1996, p. 146), to the "claims" of psychoanalysis, that is, one of the British institutions that most contributed to the many resistances encountered by

Freud's new discipline.

From this letter, we also learn of a further meeting at Wharncliffe, which Bion writes about as follows: "Thank you very much indeed for sparing so much of your time when I dropped in at the Wharncliffe the other day. It was very kind of you and it was most helpful."

We now come to the longest letter of the whole correspondence, the *eleventh letter*, written by Bion from Edinburgh on July 12, 1942. Let me tell you about it in detail, from the very beginning:

> Dear Rickman, I am writing this to tell you something of the work I have been on the last six months and to suggest that you should think of coming in to it. My first point about selection, as it has worked out in practice, has been the emergence of the psychiatrists as the peg on which the whole organization hangs. This does not mean that our judgement on any particular case has been a deciding factor, but rather that the presence of the psychiatrist in the unit has exerted a quite unmistakable influence in inducing a sane and fairly balanced approach to the problems of the unit as a whole. We first taught our lay colleagues, by refusing to be certain when they were *not* certain, that in the selection of the potential officers there really *was* a problem. Thus we paved the way for an absence of dogmatism in our approach to the solution. Our influence in this direction has I think been as invaluable as it is difficult to measure. But some hundreds of officers strange to this work have now seen it and have been unmistakably struck by its importance.

As you can see, we can here find for the first time the love for truth that we usually associate with Bion as a psychoanalyst. Bion next writes about how his love for truth and his unusual competence could have further, important consequences for the whole organization:

> Then . . . we have been responsible for instigating reforms which I am sure are of quite fundamental importance. But before I come to that, I must say a little about the influence we have had in checking quite dangerous pessimism and doing something to change it into profitable activity. In this respect I felt myself to have played a big part; because when I first met the A.G. [Adjutant General] he was saying that officer material was bound to deteriorate and indeed this has been published in an official document circulated through all the boards and elsewhere. I tackled this point at once and pointed out that it was quite fallacious. I said that . . . officers should not deteriorate in an army at war and on the contrary the army, if all were well, should sprout officers. I said that if it was not doing so it was because the climate was wrong and that as soon as a new atmosphere was allowed one could expect the new shoots to come on instead of being frozen off. My gardening metaphor has had to do much service since I first produced it but I flattered myself that I was the first person to put this view and that I almost instantaneously reversed the direction of thought about office production. And the results since then have helped to show my statement

was not a piece of dialectics.

And here is what Bion tells us about the success of his point of view on the selection of officers and about the problems, the challenges, and the changes produced by its implementation:

> The next statement I made was that as soon as our selection methods came into operation the number of candidates would go up by leaps and bounds. This too they disbelieved but after being unable to produce more than 20 candidates a week for the first weeks, they are now sending us up 120 a week . . . But the thing about which I am keenest is to come to the touch tomorrow. I have been saying that no candidate should be allowed to come forward unless he has been voted for by his platoon or company. Tomorrow the army commander here is going to look at the detailed instructions which Trist has drawn up for implementing his idea. The men vote for some of their fellows to go up to the W.O.S.B. for testing. The officers also vote; and when the votes correspond the man is sent up. Every officer I have mentioned this to, including many hard baked regulars, have been thrilled by the idea. I am quite convinced myself that, once it is established, everyone will wonder how it ever came about that a man could have been sent up under any other title. I pointed out to the A.G. that if this privilege of election were granted as a sort of regimental privilege to the best regiments a great increase of keenness was to be expected. Furthermore officers and men would be compelled to think seriously about the problems of leadership and this fact by itself would lead to a growth of leadership. Finally the responsibility for the quality of officers would now no longer rest on a few shoulders at the top of the military hierarchy but would be broadly based in the body of the army itself. There have been many difficulties in pushing this to the present point and I have learned the power of the mediocre mind as a really obstructive force. But I am hoping that now, though we can be further delayed, we cannot be stopped.

Last but not least, Bion describes how he went about the political dimension of the reform he had proposed, which became famous with the name of "Regimental Nomination Scheme":

> But in all this there has been much to make me think . . . . In other words, in this country the filter of examinations, selections, etc., is so defective [writes Bion, after having shown its great limitations] that there is nothing to choose between the filtrate and the original liquor. Now this discovery is I think of first note importance – and rather the discovery of the reason why there is nothing to choose between governors and governed.

Before telling you how this letter ends, here is the way in which Eric Trist described this chapter of Bion's work in his paper of 1985, "Working with Bion in the 1940s: The group decade," a chapter originated by the problem of having too low a number of officers in the army:

> At a conference presided over by the Adjutant-General (the late Sir Ronald Adam) . . . improving candidate supply was

identified as the next priority. Bion proposed that, in addition to the usual nominees sent forward by the CO, a regiment that had shown itself to be a good unit should be given the privilege of sending to a Board candidates voted on by every soldier in the name of the regiment. The AG said he liked the idea . . . This was the beginning of what came to be known as the Regimental Nomination experiment. It fell on me, in liaison with Bion, to work out a suitable procedure, based on sociometric concepts . . . . Each man entered a secret ballot . . . The votes were assessed on six criteria . . . While quality was maintained, the supply rate was increased 1,500 per cent. Bion's suggestion had led to the discovery of a method of overcoming the in-group mentality and of inducing co-operation in the larger enterprise of the army. (Trist, 1985, pp. 12–13)

Bion eventually ended his eleventh letter to Rickman thus:

I have already written far too much, but I was most anxious to give you some idea of why I consider this work to be of the utmost importance . . . . But the point I am really anxious about is to engage your interest in the matter and beg you seriously to consider applying to come into it. Your help would be quite invaluable.

Pearl King, having summarized its content, also presents this as "a remarkable letter," both "for the picture it gives of the work that he and his colleagues had been doing with officers at the top of the Army Command and his final plea to beg Rickman seriously to consider 'applying to come into it' and join the RAMC" (King, 2003b, pp. 39–40).

No wonder that these very words come directly before the most important chapter of the collaboration between Bion and Rickman, that is, their collaboration at Northfield Hospital. But before going into it, let me first present to you in its entirety Bion's *twelfth letter* to Rickman, which he wrote to him from London on March 1, 1943, shortly after the end of such an important chapter of their life.

Dear Dr. Rickman, I am writing you this note to thank you very much for the very pleasant evening you gave Betty and myself and to tell you how much we both enjoyed it; I hope we shall some day be able to return your hospitality in our home. It is very disappointing to think that for the time being I shall have to be working without Major Rickman, but, short as our collaboration at Northfield was, I felt I learned an enormous amount and that there will yet be an opportunity of putting it into practice. I wish you had been able to see the enormous admiration that was felt for him by the staff, students and course at Northfield. His departure came to them as a blow so severe that the news remained awkward from the time they heard the news until the moment the students' course saw him off on Friday morning; for me it was pleasant to see that even in these days his worth could strike such deep

roots. Betty joins me in sending our love and very best wishes.
Yours very sincerely, Wilfred Bion.

Let us now see how Pearl King talked about "John Rickman and Wilfred Bion at Northfield Military Hospital":

> After Rickman had been at Northfield for five or six months, Bion asked for a transfer there so that he could join him and they could both start working on the ideas that they had put together in the Wharncliffe Memorandum. Towards the end of 1942, Bion was appointed in charge of the Training Wing in Northfield Hospital, with Rickman, who was already concerned with the training of psychiatrists, to work with him. This wing housed between 100 and 200 patients, which could be seen as a rather large group. Bion used his experience with leaderless groups in the WOBS to inform the way he related to the patients in the Training Wing, which he ran as large leaderless groups, during which he confronted the patients with their responsibility for the intra-group tensions in the group. Although they were patients they had to be helped to remember that they were soldiers as well . . . . Because of the nature of army life into which men were in the process of being rehabilitated, the therapeutic task was clearly identified as developing 'group membership skills', which would enable men to adapt to any community afterwards. Instead of taking up the problems of individuals, Bion's therapeutic focus was on what actions or experiences the group were having or understanding, not on the individual person's reaction or emotional state. After some weeks, Bion could report that a sea change had occurred in the spirit of the wing. There was co-operation between men and their officers following the discussions in the leaderless groups, with the men taking increasing responsibility for helping to influence the situation that they were in. They were beginning to regain their dignity and self-worth as soldiers contributing to the defeat of the Axis-powers. The experiment however ended suddenly. Rickman's daughter Lucy told me that after only six weeks, both Bion and Rickman were given 48 hours' notice to leave Northfield Military Hospital and to report to other postings. (King, 2003b, pp. 40–41)

A few lines below, after having reported how some of their colleagues were "shocked" and others were "rather relieved" by the end of the experiment, Pearl King also gives us the following information:

> Bion was posted to No.7 WOSB, Winchester and John Rickman was posted to No.6 WOSB at Brockham Park in Surrey . . . During the year, Bion and Rickman put together their report of these events and it was published in *The Lancet* in November 1943, under the title 'Intra-group tensions in therapy – Their study as the task of the group.' (King, 2003b, p. 42)

And, as many readers probably know, this was to become chapter 1 of Bion's first book of 1961, *Experiences in groups and other papers.*

Now, before taking a look at this paper, let me report

to you what David Millard wrote in the above-mentioned chapter on Maxwell Jones about both the reasons for the abrupt conclusion of the so-called First Northfield Experiment and its legacy:

> Harrison and Clarke briefly review the reasons which have been advanced for this [abrupt conclusion]: the intolerance of the military establishment of the disarray surrounding the early weeks of a self-managing unit . . . the implicit conflict between the military need to prepare men for return to service and the assumption of most of them that health entailed a return to civilian life; Bion's strict handling of a particular incident of financial dishonesty involving officers. But the important lesson, taken over into the second Northfield Experiment, concerned failing to involve the wider environment (in this case, the whole hospital community and its administration), which came to be seen as a necessity if an unconventional therapeutic regime was to become established and survive. The leading protagonists of the second Northfield Experiment were Foulkes, Bridger, and Main. . . . The second Northfield Experiment occupied about 18 months and its work was described in a single issue of the *Bulletin of the Menninger Clinic* in 1946 . . . where Main first used publicly the term 'therapeutic community.' (Millard, 1996, p. 558)

Before taking up Bion's letters to Rickman again, let us now take a closer look at their paper of 1943. Let us for example start from how Bion saw himself and his role; in the second section of the paper, "Discipline for the neurotic," he speaks of it in terms of:

> two main factors: (1) the presence of the enemy, who provides a common danger and a common aim; and (2) the presence of an officer who, being experienced, knows some of his own failings, respects the integrity of his men, and is not afraid of either their goodwill or their hostility. (Rickman, 2003, p. 221)

The following section, "The experiment," centered around the five main characteristics of the way in which life in the group was to be organized, and around its most important aspect: the 12.10 meeting, as the major site of therapeutic exchange and cooperation. As we can read in the following section, "Some results," "the 12.10 parades had developed very fast into business-like, lively and constructive meetings" (Rickman, 2003, p. 227). Some of Bion's main comments are as follows:

> It is not possible to draw many conclusions from an experiment lasting, in all, six weeks . . . . It was evident, that the 12.10 meetings were increasingly concerned with the expression, on the part of the men, of their ability to make contact with reality and to regulate their relationships with others, and with their tasks, efficiently . . . . The whole concept of the 'occupation' of the training wing as a study of, and a training in, the management of interpersonal relationships within a group seemed to be amply justified as a therapeutic approach. (Rickman, 2003, p. 228)

What I find even more interesting, with particular regard for the topic of this paper, that is, Bion's relationship to Rickman, is how important it was for Rickman—in the discussion about the paper that took place on December 15, 1945, at the Royal Society of Medicine—to show the originality of Bion's contribution. In Rickman's words:

> I am going to stress the difference between Bion's work and other people's because, perhaps out of modesty, he may not let it be sufficiently apparent that a pioneer is different from those who have not broken new ground. . . . There are in fact two kinds of group therapy . . . These methods have their usefulness . . . but they are not at all like Bion's, which is the alternative method. *He does not steer the discourse when handling groups.* This must be taken literally . . . . The second point which comes near, as I see it, to the main characteristic of a Bion group is that the attention of everyone present is led from time to time to *what is happening at the moment in the group.* . . . By Bion's application of the essentials of Freud's technique of research to groups a new phase of development in group psychology is beginning. (Rickman, 2003, p. 233–234)

Last but not least, here is the common conclusion they reached in their *Lancet* paper of 1943, based on Kurt Lewin's work and confirming the direction of research inaugurated by H.S. Sullivan several years before:

> Psychology and psychopathology have focused attention on the individual often to the exclusion of the social field of which he is a part. There is a useful future in the study of the interplay of individual and social psychology (viewed as equally important interacting elements), and wartime makes this study an urgent issue. (Rickman, 2003, p. 231)

I can now come to Bion's *thirteenth letter* to Rickman, written from No. 7 WOSB, Winchester, less than a week after the previous one, on March 7, 1943. Here are the main parts of it:

> Dear Rickman, I've been trying to struggle with the memo, in spare time but not very successfully. Partly I think because the Northfield affair has required a good deal of readjustment of ideas and this has not been easy . . . . The more I look at it the more it seems to me that some very serious work needs to be done along analytical and field theory lines to elucidate . . . the present system . . . But I haven't got very far with it myself. . . . If I am left alone, I should get a chance of recuperating and doing some very hard thinking . . . . I am certain a great deal depends on how people who think with us tackle on problems for the next year or so, and whether there is any backbone in the liberal minded people in the country at large. I'll send you some notes as soon as I get a bit further with them.

Indeed, part of the work of elaboration of the Northfield experience allowed both men to produce the above-mentioned paper for the prestigious medical journal *The Lancet*, as we can also gather from the following two very short letters, the first ones of the whole collection to have been typewritten, on August 23, and November 12, 1943, respectively. "Herewith my revised version," writes Bion in his *fourteenth letter*. It was a sore temptation to revise the whole thing, but I think this would be a mistake." And in the following, *fifteenth letter*: "I have sent the proofs to the Lancet . . . Maine said he was going to suggest a meeting with yourself and myself on Saturday night, but I am not clear about what."

Let us now come to the first of the four letters of 1944, our *sixteenth letter*, a very brief letter, dated January 1, 1944, whose main sentence reads as follows: "Would it be possible for you and Mrs. Rickman to dine with Betty and myself on Saturday evening – we could talk about the paper there if it suited you."

In the following, *seventeenth letter*, of January 13, 1944, Bion informs Rickman that he has received the reprints of the *Lancet* paper and encloses a check to cover them. In the second section we learn how "the Prisoner of war business . . . fell through," and in the third section, Bion writes, in this connection, that he "begin[s] to see the supreme merits of not seeing too much." In the fourth and last section of this letter, Bion writes:

> Work of the Appeal Board is not very exciting as it is difficult to get past the point that most of the people we have seen have had their chance and have failed to take it . . . . But we salvage a certain number who have undoubtedly been sent to the wrong arm.

The next letter, the *eighteenth*, of August 27, 1944, is rather short and laconic, with a main sentence that reads as follows: "I think I partially know what the interesting developments are. If only I could believe in them or their sponsors!"

The following, *nineteenth letter*, written by Bion to Rickman on December 7, 1944, from Sanderstead is longer and more interesting. Bion turned again to Rickman, who was undergoing a period of convalescence after the heart problems he had had in the summer of 1944:

> I don't believe there is much more that can be done in the army . . . . But I do think it is time that we look a forward looking view and the real developments are going to be in civil practice . . . . When I saw Sutherland about a month ago, we both thought that you would have an immense amount to take back to the Institute, when at last time comes for you to be free to do it . . . . Army psychiatry is I think now setting down . . . in the operative word . . . . The whole principle of proper testing and selection is under fire at the highest levels and I doubt whether anything but the taxpayer can save it and so ensure that the officering of the army doesn't become

again the prerogative of the wealthy unemployable I
am very glad that you mean to devote time to reading and
writing.

And here is the way in which Bion viewed their
relationship:

> I do not know why you say that you owe anything to my
> performances; it is quite clear to me that the indebtedness is
> all the other way around and I, in common with all others who
> have had the good fortune to have your criticism and help,
> have felt that anything I have done springs from a stimulating
> and productive line of thought suggested by yourself. If you
> tried to dispute this I could easily muster an overwhelming
> number of votes against you!

The first letter of 1945, the *twentieth letter*, written by
Bion on January 13, 1945, again from Sanderstead, Surrey,
is typewritten and a page and a half long; it contains the
following philosophical considerations—which remind us
of Bion as the analyst whom we all know.

> As I see it, there are two main threads in society which
> are tolerably clearly defined. It seems to me that it is the
> nature of the human animal to combine two contradictory
> characteristics. He is, for want of a better word, extremely
> ambitious and he is also physically very poorly endowed.
> The latter characteristic forces him into close associations
> which the former make him unable to tolerate. He reacts
> very sensitively to anything, such as being taken prisoner,
> that reminds him of his fundamental insecurity. Combination
> with others removes his feebleness – a man by himself could
> not make a railway engine, but if he forms groups he can. But
> once he has formed his combination, he does not want any
> inquiry into its nature as that re-awakens his anxiety about
> his helplessness as an individual. The second thread seems to
> me to be the way in which society lends itself to the progress of
> the very ambitious solitary. He cannot admit his dependence
> and cannot tolerate equality; as a result, he goes into politics
> where he hopes to achieve predominance for himself. The
> aggressive solitary thruster pushes himself to the top. Having
> reached that eminence, he cannot rest till he has asserted his
> authority over similar types in other nations or communities.
> As a result, communities are always controlled by those
> sections of the populace which are the most cantankerous
> and quarrelsome. This kind of man, Authorities in other
> words, are not going to welcome inquiry into group tension
> either. As with the individual patient, I think society itself will
> in the end be driven into an investigation of its tensions by
> its distresses. How many wars on the present scale will be
> required to bring men to this pitch, I cannot imagine. But I
> fear that every possible obstacle will be put in the way of any
> procedure that is likely to bring home to men a discovery of
> the impotence and insignificance of society itself.

But Bion's major interest at the time was, however,
the nature of groups and the ways of working with them,
as we can learn from his *twenty-first letter*, written in
London on November 27, 1945, the first of a new series

centered around the definition of this problem. Here is what he writes to Rickman:

> Just out of hand it comes to me that the essentials are: 1 – a psych. who really can make clinical observations (this seems to me to be practically synonymous with "psycho-analytically trained", but I don't want to provoke a reaction to what will sound to some to be bigotry); 2 – interpretations must be directed to the *common factor* in the behavior of the group at any moment; 3 – the individual must be allowed to get hanged in the sense that interpretations are primarily directed to that aspect of his associations which are significantly shared by the group, and not to the aspect which is relevant to his relationship to a given individual; 4 – the group always consists of x people + y empty chairs.

And here is how Bion relates himself to these ideas:

> I can think of several more but I would rather discuss them with you and Sutherland before putting them out. The problem is to give a few simple indications which will launch the psych. into a situation from which he can only extricate himself and the group by developing a progressively better technique.

And, last but not least, here is Bion's invitation to a new collaboration: "I am starting a fresh group – if any turn up – on Friday night at 6.30. If you are free, you may care to come + we could have a huddle later."

The next short typewritten note of November 29, 1945, enclosing another check—apparently for the common reprints—is comparatively very insignificant, but then we come to Bion's *twenty-third letter* to Rickman, written from his Harley Street office on January 2, 1946, and dealing with the progresses he was making in the field of group work. Here is what we learn:

> We had our first staff group meeting yesterday and I must say I thought the Tavy came out of it very well. I think about 30 people showed up; this included psychiatrists, technical lay staff . . . and lay staff (clerks) – also Maberly + Leonard Brome who do not quite fit into any of the latter categories. I opened the discussion by saying I wanted to know how many people would like to form a guinea pig group + what hours we could appoint for meetings + what fees we should pay the Clinic. I then stopped. Everyone seemed a bit sheepish + then a few people started talking to ease the tension. Leonard Brome said 'Could you give any indications about how groups behave?'. To which I replied. Just like this. Another awkward pause followed. And then further questions to all of which I responded with non-committal grunts. The group hunted round a bit and then Dr. Stein took the floor to explain, since I wouldn't, what he thought Dr. Bion wanted. The group fell on this with gratitude + Dr. Stein took over the group. Then they petered out again. Then the topic of Dr. Bion cropped up, but without much assistance from Dr. Bion. A certain amount of heat began to be generated at this point and I then intervened to point out that they were angry with me because

it was becoming clear that when I had said 'group therapy'
I meant 'group' therapy and not therapy by Dr. Bion. I said
that when I hadn't taken the lead they had first fallen back on
themselves and had then squeezed Dr. Stein into the job since
I wouldn't. After this, things followed pretty conventional
lines with Maberly's hostility and anxiety becoming more
and more marked every minute. I may be wrong but I am
pretty sure Maberly was present as a spy from the enemies'
camp. That is to say he spoke with the assurance of one who
felt he had allies within + outside the group. Dicks took what
I thought a very good and illuminating part. I believe he had
great private relief when I gave my interpretation that group
therapy meant therapy by the group and not by Dr. Bion, nor
was he the only one. At the end I pointed out that there were
two opposite anxieties, that they were all going to be treated
as patients, and another anxiety – that they were *not* being.
Dicks at the end said that, speaking for himself, he felt that
the group had been therapeutic to him and that he thought,
judging by the atmosphere, that it had been so to all of them.
Anyhow, for better or worse, it is launched.

Bion ends this important letter with some practical
considerations:

> Now the important thing is that many people want to join the
> group + I am all for allowing this to develop spontaneously.
> The same happens with patients groups . . . Some patients
> have said they have friends they want to bring along. I raised
> it with the committee + mentioned that you had been and
> that Adrian Stephan wanted to come. I said we might throw
> it open to all genuinely interested. They agreed to this so I
> hope that we can get some tie-up with the psycho-an. that will
> enable them to come + enable us to get more stable recruits.
> Or perhaps I shouldn't say 'tie-up', but just a quite informal
> spontaneous interchange we could do with some sound
> critical advice + cooperation.

Less than four weeks later, on January 28, 1946, Bion
wrote to Richman his *twenty-fourth letter*, in which we
hear not only of his progresses in the field of group work,
but also of his position of candidate at the Institute and
of the beginning of his training analysis with Melanie
Klein. The letter starts with Bion's preoccupation for
Rickman's health and ends with the wish to see him
again, before his departure for Brighton. Given the fact
that this letter contains most of the essential ingredients
of their correspondence, let me report it to you almost in
its entirety:

> My dear Rickman,
>   How very nice to hear from you again. You speak easily
> of what must have been a very unpleasant time indeed, but
> I gather now that there is easy chance of really being able to
> have a happy and fit New Year.
>   I am interested in what you say of the ? I suspect that
> group therapy may one day have a good deal to say about
> the factors making for health, or continued dependence, in a
> hospital for physical ailments.
>   I think I am still learning a good deal + to this extent

there must be a lot in the gr. th. technique. I am *certain* we *must* have a study group. This business needs studying. I find that one important thing with patients – dreadfully important + I kick myself for not having seen it before – is the need to let them make their own experiments + approaches however hard and sterile they may appear to be. *This* time they need to feel in a family in which their ? curiosity and intelligence is *not* turned off.

But I really must *not* go on about this. No letters are any use; they just become ineffective papers. In the Tavey Staff ? one of the interesting things is the way in which the group girds at my contributions but then rapidly finds all other contributions sterile, and comes back to them.

I hope to start at the Institute on the 5th with the 1st year course; I'm just hoping to get the hang of it with Melanie a bit but at first she seemed to take the transference less thoroughly than you did. But maybe this is in part because it is a different stage. Anyway I believe I should profit. The time element is the problem. I seem to do a hideous amount of work but for very little pay.

. . . Excuse haste . . . . I hope to see you before you set off to Brighton.

Yours ever,
Wilfred Bion

A new ingredient of this letter is of course the apparently not so easy transition his first to his second training analyst, who "at first . . . seemed to take the transference less thoroughly than you did."

A wholly new theme forms the center of Bion's last three letters to Rickman—his fiancée and future wife Francesca. "Needless to say, I should like very much to introduce Francesca to you and look forward to the time when we may meet," writes Bion to Rickman in his *twenty-fifth letter* to him of April 19, 1951, after what is apparently an intermission of more than five years. "At the moment," Bion goes on, "we are trying to do everything at once – chiefly home hunting."

In the second section of this very short letter, Bion expresses his thankfulness to Rickman:

> Your second letter also was very welcome. Not only for the news it brings, but because it comes from you. With whom I started my first steps on the path to this goal. There must be a great many who have you to thank for that, and I hope it makes you as pleased to know it, as I think it should.

The next, *twenty-sixth letter*, of May 15, 1951, is even warmer and more familiar: "Dear Rickman, just a line to let you know that Francesca and I mean to marry on June 9th + that you should have an invitation to a reception at Browns Hotel at 3.00PM on that day." Curiously enough, the theme of the second section is the problem of how to find a woman to substitute a certain Mrs Ransom, who had been taking care of Bion's daughter Parthenope and of the household up to then—and who would probably not have got along well with Francesca.

> Do you by any chance know of anyone who could be recruited to look after the child and do her share of chores on housework + board and lodging and 2 Pounds a week? If by any chance you hear of one, I would be very grateful if you let us know.

Bion's *twenty-seventh* and last letter to Rickman was written from his London office at 99, Harley Street eight days after the marriage, on June 17, 1951, and about two weeks before Rickman's unexpected early death. It is a very short and affectionate letter, which I reproduce here in its entirety:

> My dear Rickman,
>   Just a line to thank you again for the really lovely bowl. It has now received its plinth and looks extremely beautiful; it will look even better when we can get the table sufficiently polished to be worthy of it.
>   We are getting into shape here and hope very soon we shall have you here to declare the building open. It won't be complete Ritz-like luxury but it will be better than Russia.
>   With love from us both
>   Francesca and Wilfred Bion

FINAL CONSIDERATIONS

Not only does Bion's biographer Gérard Bléandonu dedicate—as we have seen in the introduction—very little room in his biography to John Rickman and his role in Bion's life and work, but also the source book *Bion's legacy*, that is, the *Bibliography of primary and secondary sources of the life, work and ideas of WR Bion* (Karnac, 2008) is of little help. It lists only one contribution on this theme, Malcolm Pines' very short paper "The influence of Rickman and Klein on Bion" (Pine, 1986). As far as Bion's autobiographical book *The long weekend: 1897–1919* is concerned, it does not go beyond World War I.

The connection between a psychoanalyst's life and his work is a very interesting and relatively new field of study. Many authors have, of course, dealt with the case of Freud. The rich correspondence that he left us represented and still represents a very important way of approaching the problem. I myself started working in this field through my work on Freud's letters to his friend from this youth, Eduard Silberstein (see the Introduction I wrote in 1991 to their Italian edition and the paper on this theme I published in the first volume of this journal in 1992; Conci, 1992).

In my experience, such a theme is so rich, stimulating, and many-sided that, instead of articulating my own point of view on the relationship between Bion and Rickman in the light of the latter's scientific contribution and the former's letters to him, I decided to put my work at the disposal of any Bion expert interested in going through and reacting to it. This is indeed also what I did in Boston in July 2009, when I gave the original version of this paper at the conference "Bion in Boston;" that is, I renounced formulating my final considerations and asked the colleagues who had come to listen to me for their reactions. This allowed us to have a very rich discussion. Such a discussion, and/or the variety of contributions which characterized it, is what I hope my paper will be able to stimulate in colleagues interested in reacting to it.

Before closing, here are some of the dimensions of Bion's relationship to Rickman which I would like colleagues interested in this topic to comment on: how Rickman's scientific contribution influenced Bion's scientific production; how important his relationship to Rickman was in the establishment of his identity as a psychoanalyst; and how crucial Bion's life experience and character were to the nature of his psychoanalytic orientation and legacy.

ACKNOWLEDGMENTS

I thank Andrea Sabbadini for putting me in contact with Ken Robinson, and Ken Robinson for opening up for me the Archives of the British Society. I am also very grateful to Ross Lazar (Munich) for his help in deciphering Bion's handwriting and in reassessing the role and significance of his relationship to Rickman. Last but not least, Riccardo Steiner's support of my work was also a great help.

REFERENCES

Bion, W.R. (1961). *Experiences in Groups and Other Papers*. London: Tavistock.

——— (1982). *The Long Weekend: 1879–1919*. Abingdon: Fleetwood Press.

Bion, W.R., & Rickman, J. (1943). Intra-group tension in therapy – their study as a task of the group. *Lancet*, November 27, 1943.

Bléandonu, G. (1994). *Wilfred Bion. His Life and Works 1897–1979*. London: Free Association Books. (Original French edition, 1990).

Cantril, H. (Ed.). (1950) *Tensions that Cause Wars. Common Statements and Individual Papers by a Group of Social Scientists Brought Together by UNESCO*. Urbana, IL: University of Illinois Press.

Conci, M. (1991). Presentazione all'edizione italiana [Introduction to the Italian edition]. In S. Freud, *"Querido amigo ..." Lettere della giovinezza ad Eduard Silberstein 1971–1881* (pp. vii–xxiv). Turin: Bollati Boringhieri.

——— (1992). Male and female themes in the young Freud's letters to Eduard Silberstein. *International Forum of Psychoanalysis* 1:37–43.

——— (2009). Bion and Sullivan: An enlightening comparison. *International Forum of Psychoanalysis* 18:90–99.

Harrison, T. (2000). *Bion, Rickman, Foulkes and the Northfield Experiments. Advancing on a Different Front* (pp. 7–10). London: Jessica Kingsley.

Hinshelwood, B. (2000). Foreword. In T. Harrison (Ed.), *Bion, Rickman, Foulkes and the Northfield Experiments. Advancing on a Different Front* (pp. 7–10). London: Jessica Kingsley.

Karnac, H. (2008). *Bion's legacy. Bibliography of Primary and Secondary Sources of the Life, Work and Ideas of Wilfred Ruprecht Bion.* London: Karnac.

King, P. (2002). Review of the book by T. Harrison "Bion, Rickman, Foulkes and the Northfield experiments. Advancing on a different front". *Psychoanalytic Psychotherapy* 16:90–97.

——— (2003a). Preface. In J. Rickman, *Selected Contributions to Psycho-analysis* (Compiled by C. Scott) (pp. 7–8). London: Hogarth Press/Karnac.

——— (2003b). The rediscovery of John Rickman and his work. In J. Rickman, *No Ordinary Psychoanalyst. The Exceptional Contributions of John Rickman* (P. King, Ed.) (pp. 1–68). London: Karnac.

Millard, D.W. (1996). Maxwell Jones and the therapeutic community. In H. Freeman, and G. Berrios (Eds.), *150 Years of British Psychiatry.* Vol. II. *The Aftermath* (pp. 581–604). London: Athlone.

Payne, S. (2003). Foreword. In J. Rickman, *Selected Contributions to Psycho-analysis* (Compiled by C. Scott) (pp. 9–16). London: Hogarth Press/Karnac. (Original work published 1957).

Pines, M. (1986). The influence of Rickman and Klein on Bion. *Tavistock Gazette* 20:3–6.

——— (Ed.). (2000) *Bion and Group Psychotherapy.* London: Routledge/Jessica Kingsley. (Original work published 1986).

Rickman, J. (2003). *Selected Contributions to Psycho-analysis* (Compiled by C. Scott). London: Hogarth Press/Karnac. (Original work published 1957).

——— (2003). *No Ordinary Psychoanalyst. The Exceptional Contributions of John Rickman* (P. King, Ed). London: Karnac.

Robinson, K. (Ed.). (2003) CD and DVD on John Rickman.

Steiner, R. (2003). Foreword. In J. Rickman, *No Ordinary Psychoanalyst. The Exceptional Contributions of John Rickman* (P. King, Ed.) (pp. xi–xiii). London: Karnac.

Sullivan, H.S. (1962). *Schizophrenia as a Human Process* (H. Swick Perry, Ed.). New York: Norton.

Swick Perry, H. (1982). *Psychiatrist of America. The Life of Harry Stack Sullivan.* Cambridge, MA: Belknap Press of Harvard University Press.

Trist, E. (1985). Working with Bion in the 1940s: The group decade. In M. Pines (Ed.), *Bion and Group Psychotherapy* (pp. 1–46). London: Jessica Kingsley.

Turner, T. (1996). James Crichton-Browne and the anti-psychoanalysts. In H. Freeman and G.E. Berrios (Eds.), *150 Years of British Psychiatry.* Vol. II: *The Aftermath* (pp. 144–155). London: Athlone.

CHAPTER 8

BION AND SULLIVAN: AN ENLIGHTENING COMPARISON[1]

INTRODUCTION

"An emotional experience outside of a relationship is unconceivable": this is the message contained in Bion's *Learning from experience* (1962), that is, what we can take today as standing for the intersubjective essence of the whole book. In spite of the fact that the primacy of the relationship is unanimously considered as one of the main features of his work, it is noteworthy how discordant the viewpoints are when one attempts to integrate this perspective within the complex scenery of psychoanalytic theories. Although the fascinating revisitation of Bion's work recently proposed by James Grotstein (2007) centers around the primacy of the relationship, I am aware of the fact that—among others—the editors of the anthology *Working with Bion* still conceived of his work in terms of an oscillation between relational and drive models: this is what Parthenope Bion Talamo, Franco Borgogno, and Arrigo Merciai wrote in their Introduction to it of 1998.

Having written a book (Conci, 2000) dedicated to the life and work of H.S. Sullivan (1892–1949), and having had the chance to deepen my knowledge of Bion's work during nearly ten years of personal analysis and supervision with a former student of Donald Meltzer practicing in Munich, I have come to recognize the profound affinity between these two authors, not only in terms of the characteristics of their work, but also in terms of some of their personal vicissitudes. In my experience, Sullivan and Bion throw a very interesting and peculiar light upon each other.

The most recent confirmation of such an intuition of mine came from my revisitation of the overall work of the Italian psychoanalyst Gino Pagliarani (1922–2001), around which centers the contribution I prepared for the monographic issue of the journal *L'educazione sentimentale* dedicated to him (Conci, 2008) and edited by Carla Weber. As a matter of fact, Pagliarani himself does not put together the two authors—but he helped me do it. To be more specific, this kind of help came from a paper Pagliarani published in 1998, in which he revisited

---

[1] The original version of this article was in Volume 18 (2009) of the *International Forum of Psychoanalysis*, pp. 90–99. It represents a revised version of the paper given at the International Bion Conference held in January 2008 in Rome.

in detail Bion's 1948 paper "Psychiatry in a time of crisis" (later included in *Cogitations*; Bion, 1992), a paper which Gérard Bléandonu also had not forgotten to take into consideration, in his intellectual biography of Bion (Bléandonu, 1990). In this paper of 1948, in which he deals with the large gap between the technological development at our disposal and our psychological elaboration of it, Bion comes to a diagnosis and proposes a therapy (in terms of a bigger commitment toward a better mental hygiene of mankind), which not only had Pagliarani felt was in line with the kind of work he himself had developed during his entire life, but which I myself also felt as being very much in tune with Sullivan's point of view.

Such an issue, a better mental hygiene for mankind, was one of the major themes of the journal *Psychiatry*, which Sullivan founded in 1938, and which in the course of World War II also hosted a whole series of papers on the issue of the contribution of psychiatry to the war effort, an issue which Sullivan in the USA was as much committed to as Bion in the UK. As a matter of fact, both of them also ended up concretely dealing with the problem of the psychiatric selection of soldiers and officers, for which solution Sullivan proposed, put into practice, and promoted among his colleagues a particular type of interview, which I also described in my book on him (Conci, 2000, Chapter 6). As Bléandonu tells us in the fifth chapter of his book, Bion worked to the same aim, together with John Sutherland, at the so-called "Leaderless group project," whose result was the development of a particular type of group interview. Looking at how officers behaved in a leaderless group, it was possible to establish their "relational competence," which Bion—given his own experience as a tank-crew member in World War I— saw as the crucial prerequisite of their efficiency on the battle-field. To use a Bionian concept, we could speak of Sullivan and Bion—as regards both the issues which they dealt with in this phase of their careers, and the language they used—in terms of "imaginary twins."

In this paper, I will therefore compare their contributions, the problems they faced, and the solutions they found—while keeping in mind the considerable differences between them. As a matter of fact, in a recent article entitled "Reading Harold Searles," Thomas Ogden (2007) adopted this very same strategy—that is, of comparison, illumination, and integration—between Searles and Bion.

Whereas the preoccupation of showing its uniqueness

has been up to now one of the major goals of all the authors who have tried to revisit Bion's work in its complex articulation, I find it right and useful to try to compare it with the work of other significant authors, in a way similar to what Bacal and Newmann (1990) have done for Kohut's work (1990). As far as the topic "Bion and intersubjectivity" is concerned, James Grotstein, on the one hand, speaks of Bion as "one of the founders of intersubjectivity" (2007, p. 4) and, on the other hand, avoids comparing him with other authors who played a similar role and limits himself to revisiting his work within the context of Freud and Klein. In his revisitation of Bion's work, Paul Sandler moves in a very different direction: after having recognized the central role played by the concepts of "relationship" and of "link," he underscores the fact that this does not mean that Bion can be considered as "a member of the school of object relations, or a forerunner of the intersubjectivists or 'enactists'" (Sandler, 2005, p. 641). At the same time, I do agree with Sandler when—a few lines later—he underlines the existence of "seminal differences between Bion's work and the 'relationist' school . . . that became popular in the nineties" (Sandler, 2005, p. 641).

It is for this reason that I find the interpretation schema proposed by Gianni Nebbiosi (1998) in his Preface to the Italian edition of *The clinical thinking of Wilfred Bion* not only fascinating, but also problematic: he characterizes the book by Joan and Neville Symington in terms of their detailed examination of how "Bion's thinking is rooted in a relational theory." In other words, whereas the Symingtons are successful in showing "the theoretical disjunction between Bion and Freud–Klein," one cannot find in their text any (nonreductive) comparison between Bion and authors of Bion's generation who might have dealt from an intersubjective perspective with the same problems as Bion. A significant exception in this regard is represented by the 1998 paper of Borgogno and Merciai, in which our Turin colleagues revisit Bion's professional and personal evolution in the light of the issue that a pioneer like Sándor Ferenczi (1873–1933) dealt with in his *Clinical diary*, which came out sixty years after his death.

The necessity of building bridges of communication among different psychoanalytic points of view and the large amount of work that has to be done in this direction clearly emerged at the recent International Psychoanalytical Association (IPA) congress in Berlin. Take for example the way in which Helmut Thomä—in the panel of July 25, 2007 chaired by Daniel Widlöcher and under the title "Developments and controversies in psychoanalysis: Past, present and future"—was critical of Bion, whom he defined as a mystic, whose metaphors he could not see as clinically meaningful (Thomä, 2007). As a discussant of the same panel, Antonino Ferro had just said the opposite, but no exchange and dialogue on this topic could really take place between them. In other words, notwithstanding the exceptional stature of the other two participants in the panel (Madeleine Baranger and Martin Bergman), their singular stories stood much more in the foreground than did a comparison of their psychoanalytic points of view. By this I mean to say that what Roy Schafer had already in 1979 called "comparative psychoanalysis," that is, the field to which this contribution of mine on Sullivan and Bion belongs, is not yet practiced as much as it deserves to be.

Not to mention the fact that Helmut Thomä—a former collaborator of Alexander Mitscherlich (1908–1982), and a protagonist of postwar German psychoanalysis—is not only the co-author of a very well done *Handbook of psychoanalytic therapy*, which has already been translated into eleven languages, and one of whose major sources of inspirations is represented by Michael Balint (1896–1970)—of whom Thomä was an analysand in London in the 1960s. Thomä is also one of the pioneers of the German "intersubjective turn in psychoanalysis," which is also the subtitle of the book he edited together with Martin Altmayer in 2005. In other words, in the German psychoanalytic landscape (of which Helmut Thomä represents one the best expressions), Balint and Bion, as well as Bion and the intersubjective point of view, are still perceived as mutually exclusive and/or unconnected with each other, a phenomenon I would place in relation to the lack of a systematic dialogue among different psychoanalytic points of view, which also characterized the above-mentioned panel.

Given the fact that a comparison between Bion and Sullivan represents an even more complex operation than a comparison between Bion and Balint, let me state from the very beginning that, as far as my own understanding of Sullivan's heritage is concerned, I believe that he would have totally agreed with the following statement from Bion's posthumous book *Cogitations*: "It follows that a psychoanalysis is a joint activity of analyst and analysand to determine the truth; that being so, the two are engaged – no matter how imperfectly – in what is in intention a scientific activity" (Bion, 1992, p. 114). Sullivan used, for example, to speak of "consensual validation," that is, of the consensual validation of the language that each one of us uses, and this in terms both of a crucial phase of our psychological development and of the central feature of psychoanalytic treatment. Now, I believe that Bion would have also agreed with this.

Let us therefore now deal with some of the affinities between Sullivan and Bion, starting with the "twin works," which I will deal with in the following section.

INTERPERSONAL THEORY OF PSYCHIATRY (SULLIVAN, 1953) AND LEARNING FROM EXPERIENCE (BION, 1962)

As I made clear in my Preface to the Italian edition of his book *Schizophrenia as a human process* (Conci, 1993), this collection of papers from the 1920s represents the basis upon which Sullivan later (15–25 years later) developed his interpersonal theory, which came out posthumously in 1953.[2] In these papers, he laid the foundations of his approach to the psychoanalytic psychotherapy of schizophrenia and redefined this disease as a disruption of that very same psychological process, bound to a specific interpersonal context, which enables each one of us to

---

[2] Of the seven volumes comprising Sullivan's work, only one, *Conceptions of modern psychiatry*, was published during his lifetime, in 1940, whereas the remaining six came out upon the initiative of the editorial committee that came into existence after his death (in 1949, aged fifty-seven, at a time at which he enjoyed a high reputation, and was chaired by his future biographer, Helen Swick Perry. Of the six posthumously published books, two are anthologies of papers published by him in journals, that is *Schizophrenia as a human process* (1962) and *The fusion of psychiatry and social science* (1964); and three are volumes based on the selection of material from the series of courses and seminars he held at Chestnut Lodge in the 1940s, that is, *Interpersonal theory of psychiatry* (1953), *The psychiatric interview* (1954), and *Clinical studies in psychiatry* (1956). The last one to come out (1972) was *Personal psychopathology*, the only book he had personally written for publication at the beginning of the 1930s and whose publication he had renounced because of the originality of the ideas he had developed and the consequent need and desire to keep reflecting upon them, given also the fact of his then being still one of the most prominent members of the American Psychoanalytic Association. As a matter of fact, the book contains the very first articulation of what would later become Sullivan's interpersonal theory of psychiatry. But here are the central words of my Preface to the Italian edition of *Schizophrenia as a human process* (Conci, 1993, p. viii): "These papers on schizophrenia, which come eventually out in Italian in the hundredth anniversary of Sullivan's death, represent not only the context of origin and of original elaboration of all his later work, but also – in my opinion – the most faithful mirror of the multiple valences which characterise his line of thought. In other words, I see this anthology as the first book by Sullivan which anyone should read."

become real human beings.[3] In other words, and also as regards this aspect of their work, that is, their search for the "key" to schizophrenia, we can conceive of Sullivan and Bion as "imaginary twins." As far as Bion is concerned, I am not primarily thinking in terms of the strictly psychoanalytic work contained in his anthology *Second thoughts*, but more in terms of the developments of the above-cited "Leaderless Group Project" that Bion worked on at Northfield Hospital, UK. It was in the same hospital that pioneers of English psychoanalytic psychiatry such as S.H. Foulkes and T.F. Main, working in Bion's footsteps, created in November 1944 the so-called "Northfield Experiment II," which would inaugurate a new era in psychiatry, that is, the era of the so-called "therapeutic community"—in other words, an analytically oriented therapeutic community, similar to the one Sullivan had tried to create in the 1920s at Sheppard and Enoch Pratt Hospital, near Washington, DC.

And this is exactly the theme of his subsequent interpersonal theory: that as the human being encounters one after another specific interpersonal situation in the course of development, and ways of dealing with and overcoming them, "a very capable animal," wrote Sullivan, "becomes a person – something very different from an animal" (Sullivan, 1953, p. 5). In other words, forty years before Daniel Stern could provide him with all the necessary empirical evidence, Sullivan succeeded in reconstructing *the interpersonal world of the infant*

---

[3] As good examples of such a peculiar orientation, the reader can look at the following quotations taken from Sullivan's published work. Here is, in the first place, the clinical context in which Sullivan for the first time makes use of the term "interpersonal": "We have not seen maladjustment which was without a foundation of erroneous attitudes which parents or their equivalents had thrust upon the child. We have found all sorts of maladjustments in the history of patients who suffered the grave psychosis, but regardless of vicious influences subsequently encountered, the sufferer had acquired the tendency to such an illness while in the home situation. Interpersonal factors seem to be the effective elements in the psychiatry of schizophrenia" (cf. the paper "The onset of schizophrenia," written in, 1927 and published in *Schizophrenia as a human process*, 1962, p. 104). And here is how Sullivan took up again this very same point four years later, in the paper "The modified psychoanalytic treatment of schizophrenia": "In brief, schizophrenia is meaningful only in an *interpersonal context*" (1964, p. 276). It is in this paper that we can also find the following conclusion, which he reached through the pioneering work he conducted between December 1922 and June 1930 at the Sheppard and Enoch Pratt Hospital, near Washington, DC: "The only tools that have shown results that justify any enthusiasm in regard to the treatment of schizophrenia are the *psychoanalytic* procedures and the *socio-psychiatric* program which the writer has evolved from them" (1962, p. 283).

and the six developmental phases from the neonatal period to the dilemmas of adolescence. What made such an achievement possible was his long clinical experience with the sickest patients, his interdisciplinary orientation, his epistemological sensibility and, last but not least, his rare gift for abstraction and speculation. In other words, such an achievement was made possible by the very same tools and multidimensional perspective that, some years later, Bion utilized to find his personal answer to the same fundamental question that Sullivan had set for himself, by writing *Learning from experience* (Bion, 1962)—for example, an answer such as the concept of "alfa function" as the key to and/or the threshold from the inanimate world to the dimension of human experience, that is, that very same experience that we can assimilate, communicate, and utilize for our growth, and thus the function that protects us from psychosis.[4]

And now let me give you some other example of how the answers found by Sullivan and by Bion can illuminate—and integrate with—each other. The formulation by Bion that I quoted at the beginning of this paper is paralleled by the methodological principle that Sullivan calls "participant observation," which he defined as follows: "The actions or operations from which psychiatric information is derived are events in interpersonal fields which include the psychiatrist" (1953, pp. 13–14). But the comparison between the two authors becomes even more striking and fascinating when we consider the first interpersonal situation that Sullivan takes up in his interpersonal theory of psychiatry: that is, the baby feeding at the mother's breast, the channel through which (and here Sullivan and Bion perfectly agree with one another) the mother's capacity for *rêverie* manifests itself, that is, her maternal love. In Chapter 12 of *Learning from experience*, Bion defines the concept of *rêverie* not only as "a factor of the mother's alpha function," (1962, p. 36), but also as "the psychological source of supply of the infant's needs for love and understanding." In this way Klein's concept of projective identification, upon which Bion bases his model, may easily be integrated with the

---

[4] This last aspect can be further underscored by saying that the huge intellectual stature of both Sullivan and Bion brought them (as had been the case, for example, with Ludwig Binswanger, 1881–1966) to experience schizophrenia as the "epistemologic challenge" that it actually represents—such a big challenge as to give a new direction to the work of anyone seriously dealing with it. Should we consequently consider them, also from this point of view, "imaginary twins"? As far as Binswanger was concerned, dealing with schizophrenia brought him to start cultivating and applying to psychiatry the existential point of view (with particular regard for Heidegger's work).

observational data proposed to us by Sullivan and which he encapsulates in the "theorem of tenderness" and the "theorem of anxiety."

Let us now take a look at how Bion described this model—and for the first time connected it in his writings with the concept of *rêverie*—in his important contribution at the IPA congress held in Edinburgh in July 1961, "A theory of thinking," later published in the anthology *Second thoughts*:

> Normal development follows if the relationship between infant and breast permits the infant to project a feeling, say, that it is dying into the mother and to reintroject it after its sojourn in the breast has made it tolerable to the infant psyche. If the projection is not accepted by the mother the infant feels that its feeling that it is dying is stripped of such meaning as it has. It therefore reintrojects, not a fear of dying made tolerable, but a nameless dread. (Bion, 1967, p. 116)

And here are Sullivan's theorems: according to the "theorem of tenderness," "The observed activity of the infant arising from the tension of needs induces tension in the mothering one, which tension is experienced as tenderness and as an impulsion to activities toward the relief of the infant's needs" (1953, p. 39). And the "theorem of anxiety": "The tension of anxiety, when present in the mothering one, induces anxiety in the infant" (Sullivan, 1953, p. 41). As a matter of fact, Sullivan speaks of such a theorem also in terms of the "manifestation of an indefinite – that is, not yet defined – interpersonal process to which I apply the term *empathy*" (Sullivan, 1953, p. 41, original emphasis).

This is the way in which, for both Sullivan and Bion, the capacity for tenderness and empathy, that is, the capacity of human beings to find (and to remain on) the wavelength of their fellow human beings, can be considered as the very foundation of their works—in Sullivan's case, of his interpersonal theory. In it we find the detailed articulation—starting from the first days of life—of his answer to the problem of how that peculiar expansion of experience comes about which characterizes and substantiates human growth: through his contact with "the good breast of the non-anxious mother," the baby can learn to explore himself and find the necessary spatial and temporal orientation. It is through such a development that his experience from prototaxic gradually becomes parataxic, that he develops the dimension of language and learns (and we have already come to school age) to communicate in a syntaxic manner. In other words, it is through such a development that the further expansion of what Bion calls the "K (knowledge) link" will accompany the baby in his personal development, a development in which the central role is played by the dialectical relationship between anxiety and security, that is, the fundamental dialectical movement of all the interpersonal situations in which we are—from one developmental phase to the next—progressively involved.

The fact that the problem of "learning from experience" actually plays a central role in his interpersonal theory clearly emerges from the following quotation, in which Sullivan connects the theoretical and the clinical points of view:

> The resistance of the self-system to change as a result of experience is in large part the reason why, in therapy, we find it profitable to think in terms of complexly organized, rather prolonged, therapeutic operations by which we gradually build up a series of situations which require the self-system to expand – that is to take in experience which had previously, because of selective inattention or otherwise, had no material effect on the patient's susceptibility to anxiety, in particular interpersonal situations. (Sullivan, 1962, p. 192)

The first concrete implication of this point of view which comes to my mind is the—apparently paradoxical— fact that the first problem of our patients is not to come to feel better, but rather to be able to get used to the idea that such a change for the better is possible. Such an achievement requires a whole series of changes taking place at various levels, in the first place at the level of the patients' image of themselves. From this point of view, I find the concreteness of Sullivan's concept of "selective inattention" very important, a concept which he himself introduced (as is the case with the concept of "participant observation") and defined as follows:

> When you consider the opportunities for learning implicit in the various developmental eras of personality, you may well wonder how in the world we can pass through such a great variety of educative experiences . . . without any effects from such educative experiences whatever. . . . To be more specific, how is it, in the realm of the psychiatrist, that our patients will have an experience that can well be described as bumping their heads against a stone wall, and will do it several times a day, with considerable pain . . . but never learn a single thing by it? The explanation, I believe, is to be found in a universal bit of human equipment – selective inattention – which to a great extent enables us to stay as we are, despite remarkable experiences that befall us, simply by keeping the attention on something else – in other words, by *controlling awareness* of the events that impinge upon us. (Sullivan, 1956, p. 38)

Do not you also have the feeling that Sullivan's concreteness brings to our mind the approach that we can find in Bion's clinical seminars?

At this point, the reader will no long be surprised by the fact that the similarity between both the questions that Sullivan and Bion set to themselves and the answers that they come up with brings to my mind a whole series of other aspects they have in common. Here I will limit myself to some of these aspects, taking as a point of reference the above-cited, very good introductory book, *The clinical thinking of Wilfred Bion*, by Joan and Neville Symington. In order to show the peculiarity of Bion's approach, the authors show in the first chapter of their book a whole series of "vertexes" from which his thinking originated and/or developed: Bion and his preference for descriptions as opposed to theories; Bion as trying to focus less on the clinical and symptomatological aspects, but rather on the problems that the patient brought to therapy, with the aim of helping them find their inner truth; Bion and his avoiding the term "mechanism" because of his inanimate character; and, last but not least, his reservations as regards not only the topographical, but also the structural model—introduced by Freud. In every one of these cases, Sullivan's point of view is rather close to Bion's, and, last but not least, Bion's love of the phrase *"Le réponse est la malheur de la question"* is exactly paralleled by Sullivan's statement that the questions were for him much more interesting than the answers.

Of course, Sullivan also agrees with Bion concerning the fact that our psyche functions in the same way as the digestive system, that is, that our relationship with ourselves (and with others) has to be renewed every single day. A good living means a daily psychic work of neutralizing a whole series of anxieties and promoting our self-esteem. Such a psychic work is similar, from Bion's point of view, to the role played by the digestive function and by the blood circulating the necessary nourishment to every single tissue of our body. Not to mention the clinical (and anthropological) attitude which interpersonal theory leads to – that we can live well only inasmuch as we succeed in limiting, handling, and digesting the anxiety that accompanies most of our interpersonal relationships; only by doing this we can adequately communicate and collaborate with our fellow human beings. Speaking clinically, only if the therapist can contain his anxiety and allow and/or help the patient to do the same, can therapy really work, that is, we are in a situation in which reciprocal communication and collaboration can be as easy as possible. This was not only Sullivan's, but also Bion's point of view. Indeed, I will now proceed to dedicate the last two sections of this paper to these two very aspects: the biographical aspect (that is, their own relationship with themselves) and the clinical aspect (that is, their relationship to their patients).

Before doing this, let me say—to the colleagues who know Bion's clinical seminars well but Sullivan's *The psychiatric interview* (1954) less well—that Sullivan's book also centers around those very themes which Bion himself sees as his priorities, that is, first, how to create with the patient a relationship that will stimulate as much as possible his or her capacity for collaboration, and second, how to make reciprocal communication as good as possible. On the other hand, although Bion did not use the concept of "interpersonal field," he well knew what it meant, as we can, for example, gather from the following quotation: "It is not possible to analyse the analysand without being analysed oneself by the patient" (Bion, 2005, p. 79). But here is what Sullivan states in this regard (as I like to inform colleagues who do not know his work and/or remind those who have forgotten his words) in one of the last pages of *The psychiatric interview*:

> What I am driving at is this: When a person comes to an interviewer with a problem, the assumption is that this person has been *restrained from using the totality of his abilities*. The problem of the psychiatrist in treatment is to discover what the *handicaps* to the use of his abilities are . . . . So true is that, that in well over twenty-five years . . . I never found myself called upon to cure "anybody". The patients took care of that, once I had done the necessary brush-cleaning, and so on. It is almost uncanny how things fade out of the picture when their *reason d'être* is revealed. (Sullivan, 1954, pp. 237, 238, 239)

As a matter of fact, Horacio Etchegoyen (IPA President 1993–1997) also did not miss the chance to mention Sullivan's pioneering book *The psychiatric interview* in his fascinating handbook of 1986, in which he speaks of him, "the founder of interpersonal psychoanalysis," as "undoubtedly one of the greatest psychiatrists of our century" (Etchegoyen, 1986, Chapter 4). It had been José Bleger (1922–1972)—whose work played a central role in Etchegoyen's professional development—who was receptive to and contributed to making known in Argentina Sullivan's point of view and his concept of "interpersonal field" (Salomon Resnik, personal communication, 1990).

MENTAL PAIN, PARTICIPANT OBSERVATION, AND CAPACITY FOR AUTONOMY

As Helen Swick Perry showed in her 1982 biography, in the spring of 1909 (at age seventeen and a freshman in college) Sullivan suffered under a dissociative crisis of such gravity as to create a hole of two and a half years in his life, which he only took up again in the fall of 1911, as a medical student in Chicago. Sullivan's biographer did not find any medical documents but came to the conclusion that he was during this time under psychiatric treatment. And this explains why Sullivan, as well as Bion, was not afraid of interacting with the sickest patients, was so motivated to work with them in individual psychotherapy, and was capable of doing this with the sense of hope of the person who, having gone through a deep psychological crisis himself, was able to heal such a deep wound. We can also presume that it was such a personal experience as to have represented for him one of the primary motivations to bring him to show the fallacy of Freud's distinction (originally based on drive theory) between patients considered as capable and as incapable of transference—whom he consequently thought of as untreatable. As we well know, the next step was brought about by Melanie Klein with her concept of projective identification, which can well explain how also the silent patients who apparently live only in their own inner world can allow us to enter into it and reach them there.

This also explains the fact that Sullivan's work and enormous creativity were, as much as Bion's, largely the result of his ongoing work of mastery and integration of the mental pain that accompanied his life, a theme which Bion, at variance with Sullivan, deals with explicitly and repeatedly (as underscored by Antonino Ferro, and Roberto Basile, 2007). This aspect has also been emphasized by Rafael López-Corvo (2002) in his Introduction to his dictionary, in which he reviews the many big tragedies of Bion's life (the early separation from his family and country of origin; the long years of boarding school; World War I; the death of his first wife after delivering his daughter Parthenope) and connects them to his way of living his profession and his psychoanalytic research work. Anyone reading Bion's autobiography, *The long week-end 1879–1919*, can easily understand how "the war left signs of constant disturbances which frequently surfaced in form of terrible memory ghosts" (López-Corvo, 2006, p. 24).

And this is how both Bion and Sullivan, after having learned to observe themselves, began to observe their patients, to participate in their problems, and, last but not least, to integrate both perspectives into their work. Indeed, I do not know of any other psychoanalysts who dedicated so many pages to the clinical and epistemological problems of observing patients. We should also keep in mind that Bion's seminal book *Experiences in groups* (Bion, 1961) was built upon Sullivan's concept of participant observation, which he does not cite, but which allows him to go beyond Freud and his one-sided theoretical approach to the problems of groups. Only by going beyond Freud and his *Group psychology and analysis of the ego* could Bion discover how our internal world also has a group configuration.

Although the issue of the observation of the patients, that is, of how to go about it, would deserve to be specifically dealt with, I limit myself here to the following two quotations. Back in 1927, Sullivan recognized in the careful and empirically grounded observation of the patients "the common field of research and clinical psychiatry" (the title of Chapter 4 of the anthology *Schizophrenia as a human process*; Sullivan, 1962), and here is what Bion stated in the context of his Tavistock Seminars on July 3, 1978: "I don't know of any scientific work that is not based on observation" (Bion, 2005, p. 40).

Although Bion was eight years (1945–1953) in analysis with such a strong personality as Melanie Klein, his originality has always evoked in me the originality of the self-taught person, which is what Sullivan himself, an American psychoanalyst of the first generation, certainly was. Here, for example, is how his supervisee Mary Julian White was able to give us an idea of Sullivan's originality:

> On the master's wall at Rugby is an inscription which reads, "This stone commemorates the exploits of William Webb Ellis who, with a fine disregard of the rules of football as played in his time, first took the ball in his arms and ran with it, thus originating the distinctive feature of the Rugby game. A.D. 1823". It was Sullivan's "fine disregard" of the rules of classical psychoanalysis that led to his signal contribution, his capacity to see his way through to one operational statement that covered so vast an area. His insistence on viewing psychopathology as arising out of and living on in the field of interpersonal relations was an enormously useful step. (White, 1952, pp. 117–118)

If the term "fine disregard" has become one of the favorite terms with which interpersonal psychoanalysts characterize Sullivan's originality and legacy, very similar is the key to Bion's work and legacy which, for example, Joan and Neville Symington proposed in the above-cited book.

Both Bion and Sullivan were self-taught persons capable, having experienced so much mental pain themselves, of developing a good communication with patients. On the other hand, they were also capable of achieving, given their capacity to think independently, a high degree of autonomy. This enabled Sullivan to found his own psychoanalytic institute (the William Alanson White Institute, in 1943), and to make of psychoanalysis a pluralistic discipline more than forty years before Robert Wallerstein did the same through the paper "One psychoanalysis or many?" (at the IPA's Montreal congress, in 1987; Wallerstein, 1988). This high degree of autonomy also enabled Bion to distance himself from Klein's work (and leave London for Los Angeles), and to do it exactly at the point when he could have become her major heir. Could this be also the background to the concept of "becoming"?

WORKING WITH THE PATIENT: BION'S "BECOMING" AND SULLIVAN'S "PARTICIPATING"

One of the great merits of Grotstein's book *A beam of intense darkness* is to show very clearly the clinical usefulness of Bion's concept of "becoming," which he presents as the capacity of the analyst (who can go under the skin of the patient and, at the same time, not leave his or her own body) to affectively empathize with the patient and, at the same time, remain himself, and to function in a manner that his unconscious "*resonates* with that of the patient" (Grotstein, 2007, p. 307). In other words, "the analyst must become the analysand" (Grotstein, 2007, p. 305). Now, from the above-mentioned supervisory experience, I myself learned that the patient changes only when we ourselves experience that which he himself experiences.

And here is what Antonino Ferro recently wrote in this regard, in his attempt to concretely define his principle of "listening to and sharing the manifest meaning of what the patient tells us":

> What the patient tells us must pervade us and soak us through; we must "negotiate" the road through it with him. This then becomes the first step in the process of reception: "I have understood that you, the analyst, have understood what I am telling you". If a patient says that, as a child, after finishing his dinner, he always used to eat a slice of toast with Nutella spread, and reflects that he saw this as a signal to his parents of his need to receive something extra from them, I transfer myself with him into his chosen scene and time, in order to assign "value" to his communication, history and memories, as well as to the meanings that he himself is beginning to produce. (Ferro, 2009, p. 172)

Stefano Bolognini also seems to be moving in a similar direction; he dedicates the ninth chapter of his book on *Psychoanalytic empathy* to the relationship between empathy and sharing, that is, to "sharing as a therapeutic factor," which he defines as follows:

> Sharing constitutes a necessary stage in the psychoanalytic process ("*intender non la può chi non la pruova*" [he who has not experienced it cannot understand it], says Dante) at various levels and in different ways specific to each case with all patients that are living through a disturbance in their contact with themselves. (Bolognini, 2004, p. 102)

And, at the end of the chapter, we can also read this: "the representational creativity of the analyst touches the patient when the latter senses its experiential authenticity, the true proof that the analyst has 'been there' with him" (Bolognini, 2004, p. 106).[5]

As a matter of fact, the way in which the revisitation of Bion's work played a key role in the development and promotion of an intersubjective perspective by a consistent group of Italian psychoanalysts is well documented in a whole series of texts elaborated by Franco Borgogno. This has particular regard for the mental exchange taking place at the interpsychic level, starting with the paper "About 'A memoir of the future' by W.R. Bion," which Borgogno gave in Bologna in 1993 (at the "Multiple seminars" of the Italian Psychoanalytic Society) and which was later republished (as Chapter 6) in his 1999 book *Psychoanalysis as a journey* (the title of the English edition of 2007; Borgogno 1993/1997, 2007). In order to help the patient to understand themselves, for Bion "it is essential that *the analyst should be able to take in and temporarily become the patient, but should not, in any way, take his place when he differentiates himself from the analysand to respond and interpret something to him*" (2007, p. 120). And a little later, Borgogno writes:

> Bion thought that the analyst could *personify*, and thus be *the patient*, but being deeply (albeit temporarily) involved with him on the emotional level and that only later and only in part would he be able to become conscious of something about their interaction through the laborious work of transformation which is "to give birth to the other in oneself." (Borgogno, 2007, p. 121)

---

[5] Of course, as far as Italian psychoanalysis is concerned, a fundamental pioneering role in these developments was played by Luciana Nissim Momigliano (1919–1998), who was not only the editor, together with Andreina Robutti, of the anthology *Shared experience. The psychoanalytic dialogue* (1992), but also the author of the book *Continuity and change in psychoanalysis. Letters from Milan* (1992), which contributed to circulating her name outside of Italy, and which I myself reviewed in Joseph Reppen's journal *Psychoanalytic Books* (Conci, 1995).

What Ferro also calls "the first step in the process of reception" (see above) is, as I understand it, similar to what Sullivan and the interpersonal school of psychoanalysis mean by "participation" and "participant observation," that is, two technical terms of their own coinage and vocabulary. Of course, this is also one of the bridges that I have tried to build with this paper. Fortunately, twenty years after the beginning of the debate over the theme "one psychoanalysis or many?," that is, the debate over a pluralistic psychoanalysis, many are the bridges which have been built inside the psychoanalytic community, thus making possible a level of dialogue and reciprocal fertilization that was unthinkable until only some years ago. Among such bridges, let me recall the great surprise of seeing Jay Greenberg become the coordinator of the North American editorial board of the *International Journal of Psychoanalysis* in the spring of 2007. In 1983, Greenberg had been the co-author—together with the late Stephen Mitchell, with whom he had trained at the White Institute in the 1970s—of the now classical handbook *Object relations in psychoanalytic theory*, he had contributed to the elaboration of the "relational turn in psychoanalysis," and, between 1995 and 2001, he had edited the journal *Contemporary Psychoanalysis*.[6]

---

[6] One of the most recent and interesting products of this new climate of opinion is represented by the papers given by Leo Rangell, "Reconciliation: the continuing role of theory," and Arnold Cooper, "American psychoanalysis today: plurality of orthodoxies," at the annual meeting of the American Academy of Psychoanalysis and Dynamic Psychiatry, held in San Diego, California, in May 2007, which appeared in print in Issue 2/2008 of the *Journal of the Academy* (Cooper, 2008; Rangell, 2008) with an introduction by Marianne Horney Eckardt (2008), and which I can highly recommend to readers—to whom I can offer here only a small selection of some of the most significant statements made by the speakers. For example, Marianne Horney Eckardt's statement that "the theme of rapprochement has been with us since our very beginning" (since the Academy's foundation in 1956), as a "thought collective," "in our commitment to the importance of fostering communication with each other" (2008, p. 215). Or the following statement by Leo Rangell: "There is no justification in eliminating the interpersonal from Freudian mainstream theory. Interpersonal relations live and constitute its very essence. And the cultural dimension, embraced by Karen Horney, is similarly intrinsic to the total, traditional Freudian ideational tree; the external world is in fact the fourth structural system" (Rangell, 2008, pp. 224–225). And, last but not least, the following considerations made by Arnold Cooper: "Harry Stack Sullivan, today acknowledged as a founder not only of the interpersonal point of view, but as a precursor of the relational and intersubjective viewpoints that are prominent in contemporary psychoanalysis was, at best, quietly ignored and effectively ousted from the mainstream of American psychoanalysis" (2008, p. 238).

FINAL CONSIDERATIONS

"Every new reading has constantly opened up to me new horizons and new thoughts" (2007, p. 7), wrote Antonino Ferro concerning his experience of Bion. This is also the experience that I myself very often had with Sullivan, before I had it with Bion.

As a matter of fact, to such a general conclusion I can add also the following question, which grew inside me during the preparation of this paper, starting from the fascinating new book on Bion written by James Grotstein. I am making reference to the intellectual "cannibalism" which he attributes to himself as author of *A beam of intense darkness* and to Bion himself. This is one of the themes of the first section of his book, "Acknowledgements and sources of information," in which, after mentioning the authors and the titles of the main books written about Bion, he justifies the fact of seldom quoting from them in the course of the book by saying he has "'cannibalized', not 'plagiarized'" (Grotstein, 2007, p. xi) them. But here are Grotstein's words (2007, pp. xi–xii):

> Although I may seldom refer to works of the above contributors in the text, I assure them and the readers that I have studied all of their works and absorbed them – that is, in Bion's unique way of putting it, I "dreamed" their works, disassembled them into kaleidoscopic bits, and reassembled them anew as they spontaneously came into my mind. In short, I have "cannibalized", not "plagiarized", the works of my colleagues and have transformed them as they made sense to me anew. (Grotstein, 2007, pp. xi–xii)

And here is the phrase immediately following these words: "Bion once shared with me the fact that he did the same – as did Winnicott" So here is my question: is it conceivable that Bion might have done something similar with Sullivan, that is, assimilated some of his concepts to the point of not even quoting him?

Of course, if I formulate such a question, it is also because I have a hypothesis related to it: in our field, a field of experiential (and not of purely intellectual) nature, what matters the most is not the temporal priority of a concept, in terms of its discovery and/or formulation, but the fact of there being one or more colleagues setting to themselves the same questions and coming to similar (or different) answers. It is through this kind of "consensual validation" (a Sullivanian term), which plagiarism will never allow us to attain, that our discipline can expand and develop as it deserves. There is no doubt about the fact that all the areas which Bion wrote about were things which he personally felt and experienced, although sources external to him (other colleagues, for example) might have also played a role in the process. Of course, such a possibility is also in tune with our nature as "social animals," that is, of human beings involved (when we are lucky!) in continuous nets of reciprocal exchange, the kind of exchange that brings us forward in life and in science, without the need for us to stop going in order to ask ourselves who might have given what to whom.

What counts the most is therefore the choral and collaborative nature of our efforts, not to mention the fact that our clinical work cannot exist without being connected to the history of ideas, that is, the development of our theoretical body, which grows and expands thanks to the comparison of the work done by a whole series of different authors. Also for this reason I find it worthwhile—as I tried to do in this paper—to carefully revisit and reconstruct the history of psychoanalytic ideas. In other words: the more clear their reconstruction, the more constructive will be the work of reciprocal exchange and enrichment.[7]

REFERENCES

Bacal, H.A., & Newman, K.M. (1990). *Theories of Object Relations: Bridges to Self Psychology*. New York: Columbia University Press.

Basile, R. (2007). Prefazione [Preface]. In W.R. Bion, *Seminari Tavistock* (pp. 13–16). Rome: Borla.

Bion, W.R. (1948), Psychiatry in a time of crisis. *British Journal of Medical Psychology* 21(2):81–89.

———— (1961). *Experiences in Groups and Other Papers*. London: Tavistock.

———— (1962). *Learning from Experience*. London: Heinemann Medical Books.

———— (1967). *Second Thoughts. Selected Papers on Psychoanalysis*. New York: Aronson.

———— (1982). *The Long Week-end 1879–1919*. Oxford: Fleetwood Press.

———— (1992). *Cogitations* (F. Bion, Ed.). London: Karnac.

———— (2005). *The Tavistock Seminars* (F. Bion, Ed.). London: Karnac.

Bion Talamo, P., Borgogno, F., & Merciai, S.A. (1998). Introduzione [Introduction]. In Bion Talamo, P., Borgogno, F., & Merciai, S.A. (Eds.), *Lavorare con Bion* (pp. 9–16). Rome: Borla. (English

---

[7] Since I believe that a major contribution to the new, dialogical dimension of contemporary psychoanalysis came from Stephen Mitchell (1946–2000), let me quote the words with which he introduced his "Editorial philosophy" in the first issue of *Psychoanalytic Dialogues*: "There is a great irony at the heart of contemporary psychoanalysis. The skilled *psychoanalyst as a clinician* is, perhaps, the most careful and systematic listener, the most precise and respectful speaker, the most highly trained and refined communicator, that Western culture has produced. . . . Yet, psychoanalysts have enormous difficulty listening and speaking meaningfully to each other" (Mitchell, 1991, p. 1).

edition: *W.R. Bion: Between Past and Future*, pp. 1–9. London, Karnac, 2002).

Bléandonu, G. (1994). *Wilfred R. Bion: His Life and his Work, 1897–1979*. London: Free Association Books. (Original French edition, 1990).

Bolognini, S. (2002). *L'empatia psicoanalitica*. Torino: Bollati Boringhieri. (English edition: *Psychoanalytic empathy*. London: Free Association Books, 2004).

Borgogno, F. (1993). Intorno a "Memoria del futuro" di W.R. Bion [About 'A Memoir of the future' by W.R. Bion]. In F. Borgogno, *Psicoanalisi come percorso* (pp. 116–123). Torino: Bollati Boringhieri, 1999. (English edition: *Psychoanalysis as a Journey*, pp. 117–126. London: Open Gate Press, 2007).

———— (1999). *Psicoanalisi come percorso*. Torino: Bollati Boringhieri. (English edition: *Psychoanalysis as a Journey*. London: Open Gate Press, 2007).

Borgogno, F., & Merciai, S.A. (1998). Incontrare Bion: *Cogitations*, un nuovo *Diario clinico*? [Searching for Bion. *Cogitations*: a new *Clinical diary?*]. In Bion Talamo, P., Borgogno, F., & Merciai, S.A. (Eds.), *Lavorare con Bion* (pp. 43–68). Rome: Borla. (English edition: *W.R. Bion: Between Past and Future*, pp. 56–78. London: Karnac, 2002).

Conci, M. (1993). Prefazione all'edizione italiana [Preface to the Italian edition]. In H.S. Sullivan, *Scritti sulla schizofrenia* (pp. v–ix). Milan: Feltrinelli.

———— (1995). Review of the book by L. Nissim Momigliano "Continuity and change in psychoanalysis. Letters from Milan". *Psychoanalytic Books* 6:199–204.

———— (2000). *Sullivan rivisitato. La sua rilevanza per la psichiatria, la psicoterapia e la psicoanalisi*. Rome: Massari Editore. (English edition: *Sullivan Revisited – Life and Work. Harry Stack Sullivan's Relevance for Contemporary Psychiatry, Psychotherapy and Psychoanalysis*. In preparation).

———— (2007). Un seminario con Pagliarani: Collalbo 1998 [A workshop with Pagliarani: Collalbo 1998]. *L'educazione Sentimentale* No. 10:24–41.

Cooper, A.M. (2008). American psychoanalysis today: A plurality of orthodoxies. *Journal of the American Academy of Psychoanalysis and Dynamic Psychiatry* 36:235–253.

Etchegoyen, H.R. (1986). *Los fundamentos de la tecnica psicoanalitica*. Buenos Aires: Amorrortu. (English edition: *The fundamentals of psychoanalytic technique*. London, Karnac, 1990).

Ferro, A. (2006). *Tecnica e creatività. Il lavoro analitico*. Milan: Cortina. (English edition: *Mind Works. Technique and Creativity in Psychoanalysis*. London, Routledge, 2009).

———— (2007). Introduzione [Introduction]. In W.R. Bion, *Seminari Tavistock* (pp. 7–12). Rome: Borla. (English edition: *The Tavistock Seminars*, F. Bion, Ed. London: Karnac, 2005).

Grotstein, J.S. (2007). *A Beam of Intense Darkness. Wilfred Bion's Legacy to Psychoanalysis*. London: Karnac.

Horney Eckardt, M. (2008). Introduction to "Reconciliation: the continuing role of theory" by Leo Rangell and "American psychoanalysis today: plurality of orthodoxies" by Arnold M. Cooper. *Journal of the American Academy of Psychoanalysis and Dynamic Psychiatry*, 36: 213–215.

López-Corvo, R.E. (2002). *Diccionario de la obra de Wilfred R. Bion*.

Caracas: Rafael López-Corvo. (Italian edition: *Dizionario dell'opera di Wilfred R. Bion*. Rome: Borla, 2006. English edition: *The Dictionary of the Work of W.R. Bion*. London: Karnac, 2005).

Mitchell, S.A. (1991). Editorial philosophy. *Psychoanalytic Dialogues* 1:1–7.

Nebbiosi, G. (1998). Prefazione all'edizione italiana [Preface to the Italian edition]. In J. Symington and N. Symington, *Il pensiero clinico di Bion* (pp. ix–xiii). Milan: Cortina. (English edition: *The Clinical Thinking of Wilfred Bion*. London: Routledge, 1996).

Nissim Momigliano, L. (1992). *Continuity and Change in Psychoanalysis. Letters from Milan*. London: Karnac.

Nissim Mimigliano, L., & Robutti, A. (Eds.) (1992). *L'esperienza condivisa. Saggi sulla relazione psicoanalitica*. Milan: Cortina. (English edition: *Shared Experience: The Psychoanalytic Dialogue*. London: Karnac, 1996).

Ogden, T.H. (2007). Reading Harold Searles. *International Journal of Psychoanalysis* 88:353–369.

Pagliarani, L. (1998). La sfida di Bion, oggi più che ieri. Psicosocioanalisi del potere e dei conflitti [Bion's challenge, today even more than yesterday. Psychosocioanalysis of power and conflict]. *Psicoterapia e scienze umane* 32(2):29–51.

Rangell, L. (2008). Reconciliation: The continuing role of theory. *Journal of the American Academy of Psychoanalysis and Dynamic Psychiatry* 36:217–233.

Sandler, P.C. (2005). *The Language of Bion. A Dictionary of Concepts*. London: Karnac.

Schafer, R. (1979). On becoming an analyst of one persuasion or another. *Contemporary Psychoanalysis* 15(3):345–360.

Stern, D. (1985). *The Interpersonal World of the Infant*. New York: Basic Books.

Sullivan, H.S. (1953). *The Interpersonal Theory of Psychiatry* (H. Swick Perry and M. Ladd Gawel Eds.). New York: Norton.

——— (1954). *The Psychiatric Interview* (H. Swick Perry and M. Ladd Gawel Eds.). New York: Norton.

——— (1956), *Clinical Studies in Psychiatry* (H. Swick Perry Ed.). New York; Norton.

——— (1962). *Schizophrenia as a Human Process* (H. Swick Perry, Ed.). New York: Norton.

Swick Perry, H. (1982). *Psychiatrist of America. The Life of Harry Stack Sullivan*. Cambridge, MA: Harvard University Press.

Symington, J., & Symington, N. (1996). *The Clinical Thinking of Wilfred Bion*. London: Routledge.

Thomä, H. (2007). Intervention in the panel "Developments and controversies in psychoanalysis: Past, present and future." Berlin, XLVth IPA Congress, July 25, Berlin.

Thomä, H., & Altmeyer, M. (Eds.) (2005). *Die vernetzte Seele. Die intersubjektive Wende in der Psychoanalyse* [The interrelated mind. The intersubjective turn in psychoanalysis]. Stuttgart: Klett-Cotta.

Wallerstein, R.S. (1988). One psychoanalysis or many? *International Journal of Psychoanalysis* 69:5–21.

White, M.J. (1952). Sullivan and treatment. In P. Mullahy (Ed.), *The Contributions of Harry Stack Sullivan* (pp. 117–150). New York: Hermitage House.

CHAPTER 9

ANALYTIC FIELD THEORY—A DIALOGICAL APPROACH, A PLURALISTIC PERSPECTIVE, AND THE ATTEMPT AT A NEW DEFINITION[1]

INTRODUCTION

My familiarity with the field concept goes back to the time of my adolescence and still plays a crucial role in my life. Going to the USA as an exchange student in the summer of 1972—and living with a Jewish family in a suburb of New York City–allowed me to eventually understand the social, cultural, and psychological field from which I originally came. I am making reference to a famous and old—but provincial—Italian town of Austrian-Hungarian heritage, in which psychoanalysis was very little known, and in which I was supposed to later enter into my father's firm. Experiencing such a different field, including the attendance of an alternative high school program centered around independent study projects, gave me the courage to understand and to later pursue my own personal and professional goals—and to eventually become a psychiatrist and a psychoanalyst.

From this point of view, the field concept can in the first place allow us to reformulate the way in which Freud connected the knowledge we can gain of ourselves to the dialogue with the Other, the "significant other" represented—at the time of his self-analysis—by Wilhelm Fliess. Here is my reformulation of it: we know ourselves only if we become aware of the field which we come from and/or has shaped us, and such an awareness becomes possible through the dialogue with a significant other— that is, with a "significant field" that we come in touch with.

From such a lucky experience I also learned how important it is for me to look for social fields in which I can function well and be productive. This is what lies behind a whole series of choices I made in my professional and personal life, which culminated in my moving to Munich in 1997, after having trained as a psychoanalyst at the Milan Associazione di Studi Psicoanalitici (ASP)—the institute founded by Gaetano Benedetti (1920–2013) and

---

[1] The original version of this paper was published as a book chapter in *Advances in contemporary psychoanalytic field theory. Concept and future development*, 2016, pp. 113–136, edited by S.M. Katz, R. Cassorla, and G. Civitarese. It represents the revised version of the paper given in Cambridge, MA, in July 2015, at the international workshop on the field concept organized by S.M. Katz.

Johannes Cremerius (1918–2002) in the early 1970s—and after having worked as an assistant professor of psychiatry at an Italian medical school. In 2002 I became a member of the German Psychoanalytic Society (DPG), in 2010 a member of the International Psychoanalytical Association (IPA)—that is, a year after the DPG had been readmitted into it at the 2009 Chicago IPA Congress—and in 2012 a member of the Italian Psychoanalytic Society (SPI). In 2007 I had been elected to the position of co-editor-in-chief of the *International Forum of Psychoanalysis*—the journal of the International Federation of Psychoanalytic Societies (IFPS), to which both the Milan ASP and the DPG belonged.

By giving you all this information, I do not merely mean to introduce myself to the reader, but also to show how my interest in the topic of the analytic field has not just personal but specific professional sources. My training and my scientific evolution have allowed me to come in touch not only with a variety of professional and scientific fields, but also with a whole series of analytic field concepts, which is what my chapter for this book is centered on. In fact, I will try to show how only by considering the variety of analytic field concepts at our disposal (as Donnel Stern started to do in 2013 in *Psychoanalytic Dialogues*) can we come to a new and more adequate definition of it.

I also believe that the position of the participant observer I just described not only represents the kind of pendular movement which we learn from any field we inhabit, but also characterizes the analytic field which Freud himself created and practiced, without wanting to define it as such—at the risk of abandoning his positivistic outlook.

As we will see, the concept of the analytic field was originally formulated by H.S. Sullivan (1892–1949), representing the red thread of his whole work (see Conci, 2102); it was integrated into their Kleinian, Bionian, and interdisciplinary viewpoint by Willy (1922–1994) and Madeleine Baranger (born 1920); and it was later taken by Antonino Ferro as the basis of his revisitation of Bion's legacy—to name just the major articulations of the concept, to which I will add a couple of others. By trying to deal with all of them, we can probably come to a new and more general definition of the concept, and thus take it out of the category of our so-called "regional concepts," to which it presently seems to belong.

But let me now turn to Sullivan's theory.

H.S. SULLIVAN'S FIELD THEORY

In her fascinating biography of Sullivan—the first native North American psychiatrist and psychoanalyst to make an original and lasting contribution to our field—Helen Swick Perry (1982) clearly showed how the dissociative crisis he underwent at age seventeen, in the spring of 1909 at Cornell University, represented a crucial ingredient of the brilliant professional and scientific career which he began in the 1920s in the Washington, DC area—first as a collaborator of William Alanson White (1870–1937) at St. Elisabeth's Hospital and then, between 1922 and 1930, as a chief psychiatrist at the Sheppard Pratt Hospital in Towson, Maryland. This crisis kept him two and a half years out of school—which he resumed in the fall of 1911 at the Chicago College of Medicine and Surgery—but it allowed him personally to experience (and confirm) the crucial difference established by Eugen Bleuler (1857–1939) in 1911 between what he called "schizophrenia" and Emil Kraepelin's concept of "dementia praecox."

As Jay Greenberg and Stephen Mitchell showed in 1983, Sullivan originally made reference to Freud in his struggle against Kraepelin's very pessimistic view; Freud had in fact created around his neurotic patients a field and an approach of human understanding, contact, and communication that allowed them to experience their illness not as a "brain disorder," but as a disturbance arising directly out of their way of conducting their life and/or of reacting to a series of traumatic existential situations. From this point of view, Sullivan was one of the first psychiatrists or psychoanalysts to try to do the same with borderline and schizophrenic patients, combining Freud's dynamic approach with what I would call a "double field theory": the field as the positive environment in which these patients have the right to be treated; and the field as the communicative and constructive qualities of the human relationship which we can develop with them.

In fact, this is the red thread on which centers *Schizophrenia as a human process*, the book edited in 1962 by Helen Swick Perry as an anthology of the papers on the features, nature, and treatment of schizophrenia published by Sullivan between 1924 and 1935. As I wrote in my preface to its Italian edition (Conci, 1993a), this should actually be the first book by Sullivan that everyone should read—or at least everyone who really wants to understand what his *Interpersonal Theory of psychiatry* (1953) and *Psychiatric interview* (1954) are all about. In fact, the word itself—"interpersonal"—which later became the connotative adjective of his own psychiatry and psychoanalysis, was originally formulated by Sullivan in one of these papers, "The onset of schizophrenia," in 1927. Here is the context out of which it emerged:

> We have found all sorts of maladjustments in the history of patients who suffered the great psychosis, but regardless of vicious influences subsequently encountered, the sufferer has acquired the tendency to such an illness while in the home situation. *Interpersonal factors seem the effective elements in the psychiatry of schizophrenia.* (Sullivan, 1964, p. 104, emphasis added)

As I showed in the careful examination of *Schizophrenia as a human process* which I articulated in *Sullivan revisited: Life and work* (2012), Sullivan already knew the concepts of "countertransference" (introduced by Freud in 1910) and "projective identification" (introduced by Melanie Klein in 1946), although he did not use such terms—as was the case for Freud's knowledge of the phenomenon of "participant observation." As far as the first phenomenon is concerned, Sullivan was aware of the fact that the major obstacle to an adequate treatment of the sickest patients is represented by the anxiety they produce in us. As far as the second phenomenon is concerned, he was a good enough therapist to be able to be receptive to and experience the sense of loneliness and mental pain which a silent and regressed schizophrenic patient was able to communicate to him.

But even more important than his pioneering role in the application of Freud's concepts to a group of patients with whom Freud had not directly dealt was what I called Sullivan's "epistemological revolution"— that is, his convincing answer to the question "Where does schizophrenia come from and what can we do about it?" His answer: schizophrenia originates within the interpersonal field which the patient experienced before and during his illness and its therapy centers on creating around him a new and healthy interpersonal field! From my point of view, the dimension of the interpersonal field discovered by Sullivan still represents the foundation of our work, as much as Freud's discovery of the unconscious dimension of our life.

STEPHEN MITCHELL'S RELATIONAL TURN

I find it isomorphic to the topic of field theory to resume the personal thread I hinted at in the introductory section, by telling you that I was lucky enough to meet Stephen Mitchell (1946–2000) in Florence in April 1988, as he and Jay Greenberg had been invited to present their 1983 book *Object relations in psychoanalytic theory*—which was translated into Italian in 1986. When I met Mitchell, I was already fascinated by Sullivan's work, and it was from sharing this fascination with Mitchell that I received the encouragement I needed to write my book on Sullivan. From Mitchell I not only learned how post-Sullivanian interpersonal psychoanalysis had revisited and modified Sullivan's concept of "participant observation," but also how he had just been working on articulating a new psychoanalytic paradigm—the so-called "relational turn"—in his new book *Relational concepts in psychoanalysis. An integration* (1988a). I not only had the honor of introducing him and his work in the Italian edition of 1993 (Conci, 1993b), but also of organizing two further trips of his to Italy (1991 and 1996, with papers presented in Rome, Milan, Bologna, and Florence).

Since I believe that his work and legacy are crucial for the articulation and new definition of the concept of analytic field which I am developing in this chapter, I will share the concepts he formulated in an important paper of 1988, and in Chapter 10 of the above-mentioned book of 1988.

But before doing so, however, let me explain what Mitchell's "relational turn" was all about: it was the way in which he tried to integrate the points of view of Sullivan, Fairbairn, Bowlby, and Kohut, in terms of their complementary character and their common denominator as alternative perspectives to Freud's original concept of psychoanalysis, which he considered unilaterally dominated by the concepts of drive and of intrapsychic fantasy, with the consequence of neglecting external reality and the role of interpersonal relationships. To cut a long story short, the "relational turn" represented Mitchell's way of correcting Sullivan's insufficient emphasis on the internal world by integrating it with compatible ideas, such as the ones mentioned above, and this allowed him to bring Sullivan back into mainstream psychoanalysis, without losing touch with Freud. This turned out to be a very successful scientific and political operation.

That Freud kept representing an important point of reference for him clearly emerges also in the paper "The intra-psychic and the interpersonal: different theories, different domains or theoretical artifacts?" (1988b), which I will now try to summarize through the following words, found by Mitchell to clarify and overcome the sterile

opposition which these two terms so often gave rise to,
and attempt to put them in a dialectical continuity with
each other:

> I have suggested that the terms *intra-psychic* and
> *interpersonal* have been used loosely in the literature as
> banners representing clusters of different kinds of concepts
> and emphases, and I have broken the dichotomy down into
> four contrasts: fantasy vs. perception, psychic reality vs.
> actuality, inner world vs. outer world, and drive theory vs. a
> theory of environmental interaction. We noted that Sullivan
> gave great prominence to both fantasy and psychic reality
> in general, and that, although tentative, he used concepts
> referring to the patient's inner world. Only on Freud's
> concept of drive per se do we find Sullivan uncompromisingly
> opposed, since drives are, by definition, understood to be
> sheltered from the interpersonal field, arising independently
> in the id and encountering the actual world only through the
> mediating activities of the ego. (Mitchell, 1988b, p. 486)

And here are Mitchell's final considerations:

> The distinction between the intra-psychic (taken more
> broadly than drive theory) and the interpersonal ... represents
> complementary views of a common analytic experience whose
> richness and complexity always eludes the efforts we make
> to grasp it through the inevitable limitations of our language
> and our ideas. (Mitchell, 1988b, pp. 494–495)

In other words, all contemporary analytic theories—
included post-Sullivanian psychoanalysis—are in
Mitchell's view post-Kantian theories: that is, theories in
which both reality and fantasy, fantasy and reality, play a
crucial role, but in each one of them to a different extent.

Stephen Mitchell's unique capacity to shuffle anew
the cards of our analytic work also represents a central
ingredient of the revision of the therapeutic action of
psychoanalysis which he developed in the last chapter of
Relational concepts in psychoanalysis. An integration—
"Penelope's loom: psychopathology and the analytic
process"—with particular regard for his proposal on how
to overcome the sterile opposition between the role of the
interpretation and the role of the new relationship that we
establish with the patient—a sterile opposition that played
a central role in our debates for many years. After having
examined the theories of technique of the drive-conflict
and of the developmental-arrest models, and showed how
they differ from the relational-conflict model which he
articulates in the book, in terms of the role which human
interactions play in shaping our psychic life, here is how
he formulates the corresponding model of therapeutic
action:

> The third perspective portrays the analyst as discovering
> himself *within* the structures and strictures of the repetitive

> configurations of the analysand's relational matrix. The
> struggle to find his way out, the collaborative effort of analyst
> and analysand to observe and understand these configurations
> and to discover other channels through which to engage each
> other, is the crucible of analytic change. (Mitchell, 1988a, p.
> 292, original emphasis)

And here is the way in which Mitchell reconceptualized the concept of interpretation as a "complex relational event":

> In the relational-conflict model, both the informational
> content and the affective tone are regarded as crucial, but
> their effects are understood somewhat differently – in terms of
> their role in *positioning* the analyst relative to the analysand.
> An interpretation is a *complex relational event*, not primarily
> because it alters something inside the analysand, not because
> it releases a stalled developmental process, but because it says
> something very important about where the analyst stands
> vis-à-vis the analysand, about what sort of relatedness is
> possible between the two of them. (Mitchell, 1988a, pp. 294–
> 295, original emphasis)

This is how analyst and patient do their work according to Mitchell's field concept of psychoanalysis, based as it is on the revisitation of Sullivan's concept of "interpersonal situation" in terms of a "relational matrix" through which our psychic life gets its basic configuration and through which—through therapy conceived as a new relational matrix—it can also be changed.

FREUD'S IMPLICIT FIELD THEORY

As much as Sullivan did not use the terms "countertransference" and "projective identification," although he was familiar with the clinical phenomena which these terms aim to describe, I believe the same to be true for Freud, as far as the field concept is concerned. I arrived at this conclusion many years ago, when editing the Italian edition of his letters (1871–1881) to Eduard Silberstein—the friend with whom he shared his self-taught study of Spanish. Although still a candidate in training, due to my Austrian-Hungarian heritage I was in fact familiar enough with Freud's language and cultural world, and also with the main collections of his letters, which Johannes Cremerius had encouraged me to explore.

But here is what the eighteen-year-old Freud proposed to his *"querido amigo"* (who had left Vienna to pursue his university studies in Leipzig) on September 4, 1874, in order to keep better in touch with each other:

> The members of the Spanish Academy are among those
> modern men whose days number more than twelve working
> hours and whose nights are robbed of dreams by fatigue . . .

Hence my proposal amounts to stipulating that every Sunday each of us, the two sole luminaries of the A.E., send the other a letter that is nothing short of an entire encyclopedia of the past week and that with total veracity reports all our doings, commissions and omissions, and those of all strangers we encounter, in addition to all outstanding thoughts and observations and at least an adumbration, as it were, of the unavoidable emotions. In that way, each one of us may come to know the surroundings and condition of his friend most precisely, perhaps more precisely than was possible even at the time when we could meet in the same city . . . In our letters we shall transmute the six prosaic and unrelenting working days of the week into the pure gold of poetry and may perhaps find that there is enough of interest within us, and in what remains and changes around us, if only we learn to pay attention. (Boehlich, ed., 1990, pp. 57–58)

Exactly! If we want to learn to pay attention to a whole series of things that we would otherwise repress and/or forget, we must create a communication field around us through which it becomes possible.

Apart from this personal reconstruction of mine, what is generally referred to as "Freud's implicit field theory" is, of course, what he wrote in 1912 in "Recommendations to physicians practicing psycho-analysis" to explain the concept of "free-floating attention":

To put it into a formula: he must turn his own unconscious like a receptive organ towards the transmitting unconscious of the patient. He must adjust himself to the patient as a telephone receiver is adjusted to the transmitting microphone. Just as the receiver converts back into sound-waves the electric oscillations in the telephone line which were set up by sound waves, so the doctor's unconscious is able, from the derivatives of the unconscious which are communicated to him, to reconstruct the unconscious, which has determined the patient's free associations. (Freud, 1912, pp. 115–116)

From this point of view, I am also ready to state that we can easily find an implicit field concept in Freud's work every time he leaves the prescriptive level and embraces the descriptive one (see Greenberg, 1981), as he, for example, does in his book on lay analysis. When we try to describe what happens in our sessions, the field concept becomes suddenly essential. It represents the best way to try to keep track of all the variables of our work, which go well beyond the simple phenomenology of the patient doing the speaking and the analyst doing the interpreting—as Freud himself well knew.

THE BI-PERSONAL FIELD OF WILLY AND MADELEINE BARANGER

After having heard her speak at the Amsterdam (1993) and the Berlin (2007) IPA Congresses, I eventually had the chance to meet Madeleine Baranger at the Athens IFPS Forum in October 2010, at which she presented the paper "The intrapsychic and the intersubjective in contemporary psychoanalysis." Meeting her allowed me to develop the following fantasy concerning the forty-six-year delay (see Churcher, 2008) before a ground-breaking paper like "The analytic situation as a dynamic field" was translated into English: she gave me the feeling of such a good "narcissistic balance" as not to need to become too active in promoting her own work—with the exception of its Italian publication in 1990, due to the initiative of Stefania Manfredi and Antonino Ferro.

> But here is the central part of her Athens paper:
>
> We ourselves proposed the 'field theory' . . . as a new attempt to account for the clinical experience of the interchange. The notion of field is not foreign to the thoughts found in Freud . . . . Our starting point was observation of the analytic situation and its evolution . . . . A growing recognition of countertransference aimed to see analysts not only as observers and investigators of patients, but also as full participants in the process. Following a suggestion by Bion (1961) that the analytic couple constitutes a small group . . . we identified "basic assumptions" in this couple as described for large groups. We understood that they referred to a Kleinian conception described by Susan Isaacs (1952): a basic unconscious fantasy subjacent to the psychoanalytic relation that constantly contributes to structure it. It is not a sum or combination of individual fantasies, but an original set of fantasies created by the field situation itself. Rooted in the unconscious of each member, it includes important areas of their individual histories and personalities. (Baranger, 2012, p. 133)

Meeting Madeleine Baranger encouraged me to increase my understanding of the context out of which such an original perspective had developed and to very carefully read the anthology *The work of confluence* (Baranger and Baranger, 2009). Not only did I find, among the other things, confirmation of the fact that Willy Baranger's training analyst, Enrique Pichon Rivière (1907–1977), knew and appreciated the socio-psychological orientation of H.S. Sullivan (see Tubert-Oklander, 2013, Chapter 6), a fact I had originally learned from Salomon Resnik (see Conci, 2009); I also learned what a crucial role Heinrich Racker (1910–1961) played in the series of developments leading to the Barangers' "field turn" (see de León de Bernardi, 2008). Speaking with Robert Oelsner (in Munich, in the fall of 2013), who recently translated Racker's preliminary communication of 1951 into English, and reading the chapter about Racker I asked him to write for a German anthology on post-Freudian psychoanalysis, I understood how Racker was really the one who had the courage to say, "The king is naked!": that is, "the analytic situation is, essentially, a bipersonal situation" (Baranger and Baranger, 2009, p. 2). As a consequence, "countertransference reactions can provide evidence to the analyst of what is going on in the analysand" (Racker, 2013, p. 18).

And here is how, in one of Racker's papers, I was able to find a "pre-conception" of the Barangers' concept of the analytic field and its way of functioning, with particular regard for the dynamics of the so-called "unconscious phantasy of the couple":

> At the start of a session an analysand wishes to pay his fees. He gives the analyst a thousand peso note and asks for change. The analyst happens to have his money in another room and goes out to fetch it, leaving the thousand pesos upon his desk. During the time between leaving and returning, the fantasy occurs to him that the analysand will take back the money and say that the analyst took it away from him. On his return he finds the thousand pesos where he had left it. When the account has been settled, the analysand lies down and tells the analyst that when he was left alone, he had fantasies of keeping the money, of kissing the note good-bye, and so on. The analyst's fantasy was based upon what he already knew of the patient, who in previous sessions has shown a strong disinclination to pay his fees. The identity of the analyst's fantasy and the patient's fantasy of keeping the money may be explained as springing from a connection between the two unconsciouses, a connection that might be regarded as a "psychological symbiosis" between the two personalities. (Racker, 1957, p. 321)

What I find particularly interesting in this example concerns the structure of the unconscious phantasy, with particular regard for its connection with the past interactions between patient and analyst, a connection which the Barangers originally articulated in 1962 in such a way as to clearly distinguish their concept from the one developed by Susan Isaacs in 1948, that is, more clearly than Madeleine Baranger did in Athens in 2010. In their words, the structure of the unconscious phantasy:

> cannot in any way be considered to be determined by the patient's (or the analyst's) instinctual impulses, although the impulses of both are involved in its structuring. More importantly, neither can it be considered to be the sum of the two internal situations. It is something created *between* the two, within the unit that they form in the moment of the session, something very different from what each of them is separately. (Baranger and Baranger, 2008, p. 806, original emphasis)

In other words, I find this point of view of the Barangers in line and/or compatible with the perspectives developed by both Sullivan and Mitchell—also inasmuch as the expression "created between the two" does not mean to restrict our attention to the present, and to the level of the reciprocal projective identifications, but also includes the whole relational history of the couple.

Not surprisingly, also in line with Mitchell's concept of interpretation is the Barangers' critique of what they—in the same article—call "the natural course of treatment," inasmuch as the treatment "must follow the dynamic laws of the bi-personal situation" (Baranger and Baranger, 2008, p. 813). The same is true for the way in which they conceptualize the therapeutic action of psychoanalysis, that is,:

> The field of the analytic situation is the opportunity, through repetition in a new context, of the original situations that motivated the splitting, to break up this defensive process and to re-integrate the split of sectors of experience into the whole of the patient's life. (Baranger and Baranger, 2008, p. 816)

Very meaningful in this regard is also a less frequently mentioned paper by Willy Baranger, "Contradictions between theory and technique in psychoanalysis" (1969; included within Baranger and Baranger, 2009), in which he expressed his full agreement with Michael Balint's object-relational orientation, and further distanced himself from both Klein and Isaacs. "If we were to think of an analysand's unconscious fantasy as causing the events that occur in the analytic situation," he wrote, "we would be reversing the whole order of how things actually occur" (Baranger and Baranger, 2009, p. 158). And here are the words with which he concluded this important paper:

> Everything that occurs in the analytic situation takes place between two people and is put into words by two people. Any abstraction that tends to make one or the other of these two protagonists disappear will also tend to turn their words into silence. (Baranger and Baranger, 2009, pp. 176–177)

GAETANO BENEDETTI'S CONCEPT OF "TRANSITIONAL SUBJECT"

Born in Catania on July 26, 1920, Gaetano Benedetti died in Basel on December 2, 2013, as you can read in the obituary I wrote with Brian Koehler and Maurizio Peciccia (Conci, Koehler, and Peciccia, 2014). After graduating from medical school in Catania, he chose to specialize in psychiatry, because of his deep sympathy for and empathy with psychiatric patients. Psychiatry was subordinated to neurology at the time in Italy, so Benedetti moved to Zurich, where he had the good fortune of becoming one of the closest collaborators of Eugen Bleuler's son Manfred (1903–1994), who greatly encouraged his pioneering work in the analytic psychotherapy of schizophrenia—work for which he had also been well equipped through his training analysis with Gustav Bally (1893–1966), a Swiss analyst who had trained at the Berlin Institute before the war. Through Bleuler, Benedetti had also the chance to spend a year in the USA (1950/1951), where he came into contact with Frieda Fromm-Reichmann (1889–1958) and Harold Searles. In 1956 he organized in Lausanne —together with Christian Müller (1921–2013)—the first conference of the International Society for the Psychotherapy of Schizophrenia (ISPS), the eighteenth having taken place in Warshaw in 2013. In 1957 he moved to the University of Basel, in this unique Swiss town where he spent the rest of his life, and from where he traveled regularly to Italy to teach and supervise. Around this time he also promoted Sullivan's work (see Benedetti, 1961), founded the above-mentioned Milan ASP (see Conci, 2014) and began his collaboration with Maurizio Peciccia, a research partnership whose chief achievement was the redefinition of schizophrenia in terms of the lack of integration between separate and symbiotic states of the self (Benedetti and Peciccia, 1996).

"Ogden speaks of a 'third' which comes to life between patient and therapist in the course of the analytic process. I believe that Ogden's 'analytic third' corresponds to what I call 'transitional subject'," declared Gaetano Benedetti (2006, p. 83) in an interview with Patrick Faugeras that centered around his life and work, with particular regard for his concept of schizophrenia as a condition of radical loss of self-integration and self-identity. In a coauthored paper (Benedetti and Peciccia) of 1998 in which he also summarized his more than fifty years of work and research, Benedetti mentioned the following steps in the development of his own "therapeutic field":

- from his personal interest in and sympathy with psychotic patients to H.S. Sullivan's concept of "participant observation";

- from the familiarity with his own countertransference and the creation of a stable therapeutic frame to the gradual substitution of the patient's pathological symbiosis with a "therapeutic symbiosis" (Searles);

- from the role of the patient's "self-object" to the creation of the kind of symmetrical situation and/or unconscious communication, measured by the vicissitude of the "transitional subject", through which the patient can acquire the symbolic function he lacks ; and last but not least,

- the development of a new identity through what he called the phase of "progressive psychopathology." (Benedetti and Peciccia, 1998)

As the reader can imagine, I have chosen to present Benedetti's field model, because it allows us—more easily than the Barangers do—to connect Sullivan's participatory stance directly with the crucial level at which the therapeutic action takes place: the dimension of the symmetrical unconscious communication, which allows the analyst to transfer (Benedetti would say "to donate") to the patient his symbolic function, and/or (using the Bionian language of Lawrence Brown, 2011), his alfa function.

THE FIELD CONCEPT IN ITALY

The publication of Antonino Ferro's book *The bipersonal field: Experiences in child analysis* (1999) represented a crucial turning point in the history of Italian psychoanalysis, which eventually started to leave the peripheral position it had occupied until then in the international analytic scene and started acquiring the higher profile it has been progressively enjoying—culminating in the 2013 election of Stefano Bolognini to the IPA presidency. As I showed in the reconstruction I offered in 2008 in the monographic issue "Italian themes in psychoanalysis," behind Ferro's achievement a whole society had worked for many years in the direction of becoming sufficiently familiar with a "foreign discipline" such as psychoanalysis, around which Edoardo Weiss (1889–1970) had been able to create only a very small group of clinicians before the war, and which was not practiced by more than a hundred colleagues at the end of the 1960s.

The first operation consisted in translating, over many years, as many analytic authors as possible. The second, promoted by the publisher Paolo Boringhieri in the early 1960s in conjunction with Cesare Musatti (1897–1989), consisted of the production (between 1966 and 1981) of the Italian edition of Freud's *Standard edition*. But even more important was the third operation: to invite important foreign analysts to Italy, to organize regular supervisions with them, and eventually to start speaking with them, with the possibility of realizing that they could also come to respect us and our work. Here I am thinking not only of Bion's 1977 Italian seminars (Bion, 1983) but also—for example—of the supervisory groups held in Italy by Herbert Rosenfeld (1910–1986) between 1978 and

1985 (edited by Franco de Masi in 1997).

By all this I mean to say that, on the one hand, the scientific field out of which Ferro's work emerged also represents a topic which deserves to be discussed; on the other hand, around him other colleagues also worked on the concept of the analytic field and from them we can also get some useful inputs concerning our topic—and the new definition of the concept which I aim at.

Of the four training analysts working in Italy after the end of the war, only Alessandra Tomasi di Lampedusa (1894–1982) had received an adequate training abroad— at the Berlin Institute. A Baltic baroness, she had married the author of the famous novel *Il gattopardo* (Giuseppe Tomasi di Lampedusa, 1896–1957), with whom she lived in Palermo. Her most important training analysand was Francesco Corrao (1922–1994), who had the good fortune of meeting Bion at the 1955 IPA Congress, held in Geneva, "giving space in his own internal world to the ideas of Bion, from the outset, when they were little known," as Bion's daughter Parthenope (1945–1998) declared in 1993 (Bion Talamo, 2015, p. 103). He not only actively promoted the reception of Bion's work in Italy, but was also a pioneer of analytic group psychotherapy— and, like his training analyst, was himself a president of the SPI between 1969 and 1974. Bion's 1962 *Learning from experience* was translated into Italian in 1972 (it would be another eighteen years before it was translated into German!) and in 1975 Corrao founded the Centro di Ricerche Psicoanalitiche di Gruppo "Il Pollaiolo" in Rome, where he trained a series of colleagues, among them Claudio Neri, whose 1998 book *Gruppo* has been translated into several languages.

Another eloquent example of Corrao's important role in familiarizing the Italian analytic community with the topic of this chapter is represented by *Studi sulla tecnica psicoanalitica*, the Italian edition of Racker's ground-breaking book, which he promoted in 1970. He also wrote a preface to it and persuaded Giuseppe Di Chiara, a future president of the SPI (1993–1997), to translate it into Italian. It is no wonder that Antonino Ferro (himself one of Di Chiara's trainees in Milan) not only became one of the most creative contemporary interpreters of Bion's legacy, but also valued its group and field aspects highly— to the point of co-celebrating "the marriage of Bion and the field concept" at the end of the Bion Conference held in Boston in July 2009 (see Ferro and Sabbadini, 2010, p. 424).

In the meantime, several other colleagues from Ferro's generation had worked very hard in the same direction, as exemplified by the important International Bion Conference organized in Turin in July 1997 by Parthenope Bion Talamo and Franco Borgogno (whose proceedings were published in 2002).

The early and positive reception of Bion's work in Italy was also facilitated by the specific attention to the relational aspect which characterized Italian psychoanalysis from the beginning, as shown in the early interest for a topic like countertransference and/ or in the choice of the topic *La relazione analitica* (The analytic relationship) for its fourth National Congress, held in Taormina (Sicily) in 1980 under the presidency of Eugenio Gaddini (1916–1985). An important contribution to the creation of such a climate had also been made by Franco Fornari (1921–1985), the pioneer—together with Gaddini—of the reception of Klein's work in Italy (see Fornari, 1963). Luciana Nissim Momigliano (1919–1998) moved in the same direction, and her publication of the anthology *Shared experience. The psychoanalytic dialogue* in 1992 (including chapters by Di Chiara, Ferro, and de Masi) represented one of the first signs of the establishment of a specific Italian analytic tradition or of its visibility abroad.

I had the chance to experience Nissim Momigliano's eagerness to start new conversations when—having just promoted the Italian edition of Mitchell's *Relational concepts in psychoanalysis. An integration*—she contacted me, curious to learn from me who Mitchell really was, given the affinity that she felt with his work. At our subsequent meeting in her office in Milan I not only developed an immediate interest in her work, which allowed me to review her second book in English (Conci, 1995), but also set the stage for the work on Sullivan and Bion, which I published many years later (Conci, 2009).

It is no wonder that the 1994 SPI National Congress— whose proceedings were edited in 1997 by Eugenio Gaburri—was specifically dedicated to the theme of the analytic field. Rereading that book when preparing this chapter, I was very impressed by the richness of its ideas. In terms of the new definition of the concept that I aim at, I find particularly useful the following perspective developed in his contribution by Fernando Riolo (one of Corrao's analysands and collaborators, and himself a former president of the SPI between 2005 and 2009), in terms of the relations between the concepts of field and relationship:

> The field is neither the patient nor the analyst, nor the relationship. On the contrary, it is that which does not belong to the relationship . . . either because the field comes after all that which does not yet participate of the symbolic nature of the relationship – like drive, feeling, emotion; or because the field comes before all that which has been expelled from it – like projection, hallucination, action. (Riolo, 1997, p. 67)

This seems to me another way to say what the Barangers do not say so clearly when they say that once a bastion (an unconscious collusion between patient and analyst) has been set in place, the field stops expanding: what Riolo says is that it ceases to exist!

Another useful point of view in terms of my line of thought is the one developed by Di Chiara in his contribution at the same conference:

> The problem is therefore not only how to best follow the evolution of the "bipersonal unconscious phantasy," although this represents an interesting point of reference which may go through a variety of configurations. Even more important is to closely follow the evolution of an even more complex relationship between two people, which takes place at different levels, and which we as analysts have on the one hand to understand as best as we can, but which, on the other, implies for us the necessity of nourishing through the most adequate form of participation. (Di Chiara, 1997, p. 106)

If I understand Di Chiara correctly, he agrees with Benedetti that the unconscious symmetry with which therapeutic action takes place can be established only through the hard-won attainment of the best possible form of participation—in the sense intended by Sullivan.

A LITTLE-KNOWN GERMAN FIELD CONCEPT

In 2013 Werner Bohleber published in the *International Journal of Psychoanalysis* an important paper by Hermann Argelander (1920–2004), "The scenic function of the ego and its role in symptom and character formation," which had originally appeared in German in 1970. The New York analyst Leon Balter was able to identify many similarities between the work of Argelander and the work of Jacob Arlow (1912–2004) once he was able to overcome the impression of having to deal with a similar phenomenon to what Darwin had called "the origin of new species promoted by geographical isolation" (Balter, 2003, p. 355). The concept of "unconscious fantasy" was the principal common denominator that he found in their work, while the other major ingredients of what I define as Argelander's "field concept" are as follows: psychoanalysis is a dialogue which requires the analyst's participation in the emotional life of the patient, and the relationship resulting from such an interaction will allow the patient to express the unconscious conflicts which brought him to ask the analyst for help in terms of concrete unconscious behaviors and/or more or less structured scenes. The motor of such a performance on the side of the patient is what Argelander calls *"die szenische Funktion des Ichs,"* which the analyst can at best understand making use of his *"szenisches Verstehen,"* two crucial German phrases that we may translate as "scenic function of the ego" and "scenic understanding."

Bohleber himself tried to connect Argelander's model with similar past and present developments in psychoanalysis as follows:

> The scene is a dynamic construction shared by analyst and patient, a creation of both parties and not something from the past that is simply found. Scenic understanding is ultimately a modern constructivist concept that was ahead of its time. However, Argelander's thinking always preserved its links to ego psychology. An approach analogous in some respects to this can be discerned in Madeleine and Willy Baranger's view of the analytic situation as a "dynamic field" – these authors too had taken up some ideas of Gestalt psychology – as well as in modern intersubjectivist conceptions of the analytic situation as always being a co-creation of the analyst and the patient. Similarities are also evident between Argelander and, for example, Donnel Stern's hermeneutic conception of the unconscious as "unformulated experience," Stern being another author substantially inspired by the hermeneutics of Gadamer. (Bohleber, 2013, p. 335)

Leaving aside why it took our German colleagues such a long time to inform the international analytic community about such an interesting development in their country (see Conci, 2013), I find it is more worthwhile to ask why they failed to appreciate that Argelander had made such an important contribution to analytic field concepts. Of course, I do not have sufficient room to discuss such an intriguing problem in depth in this chapter, so I will limit myself to presenting the evidence behind my attempt to present and analyze the variety of field concepts at our potential disposal. Who introduced Racker's work in Germany? I found out that it was Argelander, who reviewed the German edition of his ground-breaking book, *Übertragung und Gegenübertragung. Studien zur psychoanalyischen Technik* (1978) in the prestigious journal *Psyche*.

AN ATTEMPT AT A NEW DEFINITION

If I now look back at the various ways in which the analytic field concept has been dealt with by the authors I have considered in this chapter, I can try to characterize it by provisionally establishing the following levels or models:

- Level 1: What I have defined as Freud's "implicit field concept."
- Level 2: Sullivan's concept of "interpersonal situation."
- Level 3: Argelander's concept of "scenic understanding."
- Level 4: Mitchell's concept of "relational matrix."
- Level 5: The example of "bipersonal field" I attributed to Racker; di Chiara's revisitation of the Barangers' concept; Benedetti's concept of "transitional subject."
- Level 6: The Barangers' concept of "bipersonal field."
- Level 7: Riolo's definition of the field in terms of a relationship tending to a condition of symmetry whose complete realization brings the field itself to cease to exist.
- Level 8: Once the symmetrical situation of the so-called "bastion" has been resolved, we can think of the possibility of the field coming into existence again.

If I now were to abstract from these different levels or models a new model of analytic field concept, I would see it as a model which gives an equal role to the two poles of what Sullivan called the analyst's "participant observation," on the one hand, and what the Barangers called the "bipersonal unconscious phantasy," on the other hand—not as originally formulated by Susan Isaacs, but as the product of a specific interaction with a specific history and/or development. In other words, I also consider Sullivan's concept of "participant observation" and Racker's concept of "countertransference" as two different metaphors: that is, ways of expressing the same clinical phenomenon (see Wallerstein, 1988). Both authors think that, in order to understand the patient, the analyst must participate in his problems and, at the same time, be aware of such a participation; this is how, for both of them, such a behavior (Sullivan) and/or such an attitude (Racker) allows us to know the patient better. Both ways of working with our patients have, as a result, the emergence of unconscious fantasies—which also for Sullivan, and even more so for Mitchell, represent an important part of our analytic work.

It is therefore no wonder that Werner Bohleber and his colleagues in the IPA Committee on Conceptual Integration, when describing the second step of their work in their recent paper on unconscious phantasy as a clinical phenomenon, stated:

> Implicit in the phenomenology . . . is a close theoretical relation between the concept of enactment and that of unconscious fantasy. It would be erroneous to think that enactment acts out a fantasy existing prior to the act itself. What the analyst calls unconscious fantasy is rather the verbal articulation of an unsymbolized affective experience. Consequently, the illusion that the fantasy exists prior to the affective shared experience, or prior to the act itself, would belong to the phenomenology of unconscious fantasy. The concept of unconscious fantasy can thus be understood as a metaphor that assists in understanding the patient's psychic material and behavior. (Bohleber et al., 2015, p. 711)

In other words, if I understand them correctly, these colleagues see—as I also do—the external behavioral level and the internal unconscious level in terms of a mutual correlation.

CONCLUDING REMARKS

A review of the various definitions which the analytic field concept has received in the course of the evolution of our analytic discourse apparently allows us to shuffle the cards produced by the latter in an even more significant way than the concept of metaphor, as it was dealt with in the volume edited by Montana Katz in 2012.

In fact, if we want to make of the analytic field concept a general analytic concept, as opposed to a so-called "regional concept," we have to take into consideration the theoretical and historical contexts out of which it has been developed in the various regions of the world.

As I have tried to show, by comparing the different field concepts and by extracting from them what I consider to be their essential ingredients, we can, for example, eventually close the gap between external reality and the way in which the patient and we behave, our analytic attitude and our internal worlds, and/or better see their dialectical and mutual correlation.

Another important implication of the dialogical approach and the pluralistic perspective which I have developed in this chapter is represented by the necessity for us, as analysts, to get to know better the fields in which we ourselves operate—that is, in which our theoretical positions are embedded—and also to bring about a more effective communication among the different analytic communities. It makes little sense to use the field concept in our work with our patients and not to use it in talking with each other—in terms of the fields from which each one of us speaks.

Stephen Mitchell (1991) centered the "editorial philosophy" he had formulated for *Psychoanalytic Dialogues* on the necessity for us, as analysts, to talk more effectively with each other—as effectively as we talk with our patients. Paul Stepansky (2009) argued that we can survive as a discipline only if we move in the direction of a consensually validated working field, as opposed to a disarticulated group of professionals, each minding only his own ideas.

In fact, Freud himself founded psychoanalysis on the basis of his own experience of and familiarity with the Austrian medical tradition, the French psychological tradition, and the British empirical tradition, what makes of psychoanalysis itself the result of a unique kind of "international synthesis" (see Ackerknecht, 1999), the kind of synthesis that I have tried to formulate in this chapter.

REFERENCES

Ackerknecht, E.H. (1999). *Breve storia della psichiatria* (M. Conci, Ed.). Bolsena, VT: Massari. (Original German edition, 1957. English edition, *A Short History of Psychiatry*. New York: Hafner, 1959).

Argelander, H. (1978). Besprechung des Buches von H. Racker "Übertragung und Gegenübertragung. Studien zur psychoanalyischen Technik", 1978. *Psyche* 32:871–875.

——— (2013). The scenic function of the ego and its role in symptom and character formation. *International Journal of Psychoanalysis* 94:337–454. (Original German edition, 1970).

Baranger, M. (2012). The intrapsychic and the intersubjective in contemporary psychoanalysis. *International Forum of Psychoanalysis* 21:30–135.

Baranger, M., & Baranger, W. (2008). The analytic situation as a dynamic field. *International Journal of Psychoanalysis* 89:795–826. (Original Spanish edition, 1962).

——— (2009). *The Work of Confluence. Listening and Interpreting in the Psychoanalytic Field* (L. Glocer Fiorni, Ed.). London: Karnac.

Baranger, W., & Baranger, M. (1990). *La situazione psicoanalitica come campo bipersonale*. Milan: Cortina.

Benedetti, G. (1961). Prefazione [Preface]. In H.S. Sullivan, *La moderna concezione della* psichiatria (pp. vii–xxvii). Milan: Feltrinelli.

Benedetti, G., & Faugeras, P. (2006). L'esperienza delle psicosi. Colloqui di Riehen [The experience of psychosis. The Riehen interviews]. In ASP (Ed.), *La parola come cura. La psicoterapia delle psicosi nell'incontro con Gaetano Benedetti* [Word as cure. The psychotherapy of psychoses in the meeting with Gaetano Benedetti] (pp. 73–99). Milan: Angeli.

Benedetti, G., & Peciccia, M. (1996). The splitting between separate and symbiotic states of the self in the psychodynamic of schizophrenia. *International Forum of Psychoanalysis* 5:23–37.

——— (1998). The ego structure and the self-identity of the schizophrenic human and the task of psychoanalysis. *International Forum of Psychoanalysis* 7:169–174.

Bion, W.R. (1983). *Bion in Rome*. London: Estate of W.R. Bion.

Bion Talamo, P. (2015). *Maps for Psychoanalytic Exploration*. London: Karnac.

Bion Talamo, P., Borgogno, & F. Merciai, S. (Eds.) (2002). *W.R. Bion. Between Past and Future*. London: Karnac.

Boehlich, W. (Ed.) (1990). *The Letters of Sigmund Freud to Eduard Silberstein 1871–1881*. Cambridge, MA: Belknap and Harvard University Press. (Original German edition, 1989).

Bohleber, W. (2013). Introduction to Hermann Argelander's paper "The scenic function of the ego and its role in symptom and character formation". *International Journal of Psychoanalysis* 94:333–336.

Bohleber, W., Jiménez, J.P., Scarfone, D., Varvin, S., & Zysman, S. (2015). Unconscious phantasy and its conceptualization: An attempt at conceptual integration. *International Journal of Psychoanalysis* 96:705–730.

Brown, L.J. (2011). *Intersubjective Processes and the Unconscious*. London: Karnac.

Conci, M. (1991). Presentazione all'edizione italiana [Introduction to the Italian edition]. In S. Freud, *"Querido amigo . . . Lettere della giovinezza ad Eduard Silberstein 1871–1881* (pp. vii–xxvi). Turin: Bollati Boringhieri.

——— (1993a). Prefazione [Preface]. In H.S. Sullivan, *Scritti sulla schizophrenia* (pp. v–ix). Milan: Feltrinelli.

——— (1993b). Presentazione [Introduction]. In S.A. Mitchell, *Gli orientamenti relazionali in psicoanalisi. Per un modello integrato* (pp. ix–xv). Turin: Bollati Boringhieri.

——— (1995). Review of the book by L. Nissim Momigliano "Continuity and change in psychoanalysis. Letters from Milan", Karnac 1992. *Psychoanalytic Books* 6:199–204.

——— (2008). Editorial – Italian themes in psychoanalysis. International dialogue and psychoanalytic identity. *International Forum of Psychoanalysis* 17:65–70.

——— (2009). Bion and Sullivan: An enlightening comparison. *International Forum of Psychoanalysis* 18:90–99.

——— (2012). *Sullivan Revisited – Life and Work* (2nd rev. ed.). Trento: Tangram. (Original Italian edition, 2000. German edition, 2005. Spanish edition, 2012.)

——— (2013). Editorial – Psychoanalysis in Germany. Part One. *International Forum of Psychoanalysis* 22:195–198.

——— (2014). Gaetano Benedetti, Johannes Cremerius, the Milan ASP, and the future of IFPS. *International Forum of Psychoanalysis* 23:85–95.

Conci, M, Koehler, B., & Peciccia, M. (2014). Prof. Dr.med. Gaetano Benedetti (1920–2013), Co-founder ISPS. *Psychosis* 6:1–3.

Churcher, J. (2008). Some notes on the English translation of "The analytic situation as a dynamic field" by W. and M. Baranger. *International Journal of Psychoanalysis* 89:785–793.

de León de Bernardi, B. (2008). Introduction to the paper by M. and W. Baranger "The analytic situation as a dynamic field". *International Journal of Psychoanalysis* 89:773–784.

De Masi, F. (1997). *Herbert Rosenfeld at Work: The Italian Seminars*. London: Karnac.

Di Chiara, G. (1997). La formazione e le evoluzioni del campo analitico [The formation and the evolutions of the analytic field]. In E. Gaburri (Ed.), *Emozione e interpretazione. Psicoanalisi del campo emotivo* [Emotion and interpretation. Psychoanalysis of the analytic field] (pp. 103–112). Turin: Bollati Boringhieri.

Ferro, A. (1999). *The Bipersonal Field: Experiences in Child Analysis.* London: Routledge.

Ferro, A., & Sabbadini, A. (2010). Review of the book by W. and M. Baranger "The work of confluence". *International Journal of Psychoanalysis* 91:415–429.

Fornari, F. (1963). *La vita affettiva originaria del bambino* [The originary affective life of the child]. Milan: Feltrinelli.

Freud, S. (1910). The future prospects of psycho-analytic therapy. *Standard Edition* 11, pp. 139–152.

——— (1912). Recommendations to physicians practicing psycho-analysis. *Standard Edition* 7, pp. 109–120.

Gaburri, E. (Ed.) (1997). *Emozione e interpretazione. Psicoanalisi del campo emotivo* [Emotion and interpretation. Psychoanalysis of the analytic field]. Turin: Bollati Boringhieri.

Greenberg, J.R. (1981). Prescription or description: The therapeutic action of psychoanalysis. *Contemporary Psychoanalysis* 17:239–257.

Greenberg, J.R., & Mitchell, S.A. (1983). *Object Relations in Psychoanalytic Theory.* Cambridge, MA: Harvard University Press.

Katz, M. (Ed.) (2012). *Metaphors and Fields: Common Ground, Common Language and the Future of Psychoanalysis.* London: Routledge.

Klein, M. (1946). Notes on some schizoid mechanisms. *International Journal of Psychoanalysis* 27:99–110.

Mitchell, S.A. (1988a). *Relational Concepts in Psychoanalysis. An Integration.* Cambridge, MA: Harvard University Press.

——— (1988b). The intra-psychic and the interpersonal: Different theories, different domains or theoretical artifacts? *Psychoanalytic Inquiry* 8:472–496.

——— (1991). Editorial philosophy. *Psychoanalytic Dialogues* 1:1–7.

Neri, C. (1998). *Gruppo* [The group]. Rome: Borla.

Nissim Momigliano, L., & Robutti, A. (Eds.) (1992). *Shared Experience. The Psychoanalytic Dialogue.* London: Karnac.

Oelsner, R. (in preparation). Heinrich Racker (1910–961). In M. Conci and W. Mertens (Eds.), *Psychoanalyse im 20. Jahrhundert.* Stuttgart: Kohlhammer.

Ogden, T.H. (1994). The analytic third: Working with intersubjective clinical facts. *International Journal of Psychoanalysis* 75:3–19.

Racker, H. (1957). The meaning and uses of countertransference. *Psychoanalytic Quarterly* 26:303–357.

——— (2013). Observations on countertransference as technical instrument. Preliminary communication. In R. Oelsner (Ed.), *Transference and Countertransference Today* (pp. 18–29). London: Routledge.

Riolo, F. (1997). Il modello di campo in psicoanalisi [The model of the field in psychoanalysis]. In E. Gaburri (Ed.), *Emozione e interpretazione. Psicoanalisi del campo emotivo* [Emotion and interpretation. Psychoanalysis of the analytic field] (pp. 53–68). Turin: Bollati Boringhieri.

Stepansky, P.H. (2009). *Psychoanalysis at the Margins*. New York: Other Press.

Stern, D.B. (2013a). Field theory in psychoanalysis, part 1: Harry Stack Sullivan and Madeleine Baranger. *Psychoanalytic Dialogues* 23:487–501.

——— (2013b). Field theory in psychoanalysis, part 2: Bionian field theory and contemporary interpersonal/relational psychoanalysis. *Psychoanalytic Dialogues* 23:630–645.

Sullivan, H.S. (1964). *Schizophrenia as a Human Process* (H. Swick Perry, Ed.). New York: Norton.

Swick Perry, H. (1982). *Psychiatrist of America. The Life of Harry Stack Sullivan*. Cambridge, MA: Belknap Press of Harvard University Press.

Tubert-Oklander, J. (2013). *Theory of Psychoanalytic Practice. A Relational Process Approach*. London: Karnac.

Wallerstein, R.S. (1988). One psychoanalysis or many? *International Journal of Psychoanalysis* 69:5-21

INTRODUCTION TO PART FOUR—
INTERNATIONAL PSYCHOANALYSIS

In my General Introduction, I presented this last Part of my book by referring to the sociologist Edith Kurzweil (1924–2016) and her pioneering 1989 book *The Freudians. A comparative perspective* from a double point of view, that of content and method—around which this Fourth Part of my anthology, as much as her own book, is centered.

Let me start with content. By presenting in her book the postwar development and main traits of the analytic communities of not only New York, London, and Paris, but also Frankfurt and Vienna, Kurzweil was able to show how different such developments had been; in addition, she tried to define the historical, social, cultural, and professional variables behind them. From this point of view, we can talk of her book in terms of the first book offering us a comparative view of international psychoanalysis that was written by a single author—a single author who had not only reconstructed the history of these communities from a series of (documentary and archival) sources, but also experienced them herself, through the method of "participant observation"—a term introduced into psychoanalysis by Harry Stack Sullivan (1892–1949).

From the second point of view, that is, from the methodological perspective, Edith Kurzweil pioneered the kind of personal experience of, exposure to, and dialogue with international psychoanalysis that should become an essential feature of our own training and identity. As I have already written in the General Introduction, this was and certainly is the case with prominent protagonists of international psychoanalysis such as Stefano Bolognini and Horst Kächele, with the consequence that "international psychoanalysis" was the context within which my interviews with them (see Chapters 11 and 12) took place. The same is true for Gaetano Benedetti (1920–2013) and Johannes Cremerius (1918–2002), with Chapter 10 centering around their work, legacy, and training concepts—all shaped, as they were, by their own experience of what psychoanalysis was like on an international level.

In other words, there are two poles around which this Fourth Part of the book centers. The first is what we know and what literature is at our disposal relating to how psychoanalysis has developed in the various countries of the world. The second, on other hand, is what we can learn about such developments by not only reading about them, but also personally exposing ourselves to or participating in them. After dealing with the first pole in the first part of this Introduction, I will then specifically deal with the Italian and German contexts within which Bolognini and Kächele operate, in terms of not only the necessary historical and professional data concerning them, but also of course my personal experience of them. Only in the third section, talking about the three chapters of this last Part, and dealing mainly with Chapter 10, will I try also to touch upon the problems and challenges of analytic training which Benedetti and Cremerius dealt with by founding the Milan Scuola di Psicoterapia Psicoanalitica. Last but not least, my experience as member of the editorial board and (since the summer of 2007) co-editor-in-chief of the *International Forum of Psychoanalysis* also belongs to this Part of the book, with specific consideration of the several monographic issues I produced with the intention of contributing to the increase in the international exchange and dialogue taking place in the analytic community at large.

Given these premises, I will start discussing the landscape of "international psychoanalysis" by mentioning the very first book that I remember eagerly reading on the subject. In 1982 the German publisher Beltz received permission from the Swiss publisher Kindler to publish and sell single volumes of the psychological encyclopedia in fifteen volumes that it had published in 1976 under the title *Die Psychologie des 20. Jahrhunderts;* this allowed me to buy the four volumes of the encyclopedia dedicated to the topic *Tiefenpsychologie.* It was the fall of 1987, I had already translated a couple of papers by Johannes Cremerius, and I ordered the volumes at the Munich bookstore that he had recommended to me— the then well-known "Bookstore Otto Spatz." I have already talked of Volume 1, *Sigmund Freud – Leben und Werk*, in the Introduction to Part One, as the chapter on "Freuds Briefwechsel," that is, Freud's correspondence, written by Martin Grotjahn (1904–1990) (Grotjahn, 1976), also belonged to the topic of Freud's life and work. Volume 2, with the title *Neue Wege der Psychoanalyse – Psychoanalyse der Gesellschaft – Die psychoanalytische Bewegung*, is the volume I will now introduce.

This volume is centered around the topics "New ways in psychoanalysis" (from the treatment of schizophrenia to psychosomatic medicine), "Psychoanalysis of society" (including a chapter on psychoanalysis and Marxism written by Ernst Federn [1914–2007], the son of Paul Federn), and "The Psychoanalytic Movement." This is the section that opened my eyes to the landscape of international psychoanalysis, since it contained seventeen chapters on it, including a very informative chapter on the history of psychoanalysis in the USA written by Ulrike May (May, 1976), and a, for me, very exciting chapter on the history of psychoanalysis in Italy written by Eugenio Gaddini (1916–1985) (Gaddini, 1976). When I met Ulrike May in Munich in 1996, I learned that her chapter was one of the projects she had worked on while spending a year at the department of the New York University chaired by Robert Holt. As far as Gaddini is concerned, I had once heard him give a paper in Rome on the relationship between body and mind in the first phases of the infant's development, and I also knew his son Andrea (who later also became a psychoanalyst), since he was also a resident in psychiatry at the Catholic University in Rome (see the Afterword). I had never seen any book of this type in Italian, and I was very happy to be familiar enough with German to be able to enjoy reading most of the chapters of that section. The chapter on the history of psychoanalysis in Great Britain had been written by Christopher Dare, and the chapter on the history of psychoanalysis in France by Robert and Ilse Barande. Of course, I was very impressed by seeing how different the history and development of psychoanalysis had been in the countries that were more important to me.

Even more interesting than the development of psychoanalysis was, for me, the problem of its initial reception, that is, of the resistance against its reception in various countries. Let us for example consider Italy, and turn to the above-mentioned book chapter by Gaddini, himself a former president (1978–1982) of the Società Psicoanalitica Italiana (SPI), and the most internationally well-known Italian analyst during the 1960s to 1980s. Gaddini wrote of the following main four sources of resistance against the reception of psychoanalysis: first, the Italian philosophical tradition dominated by the philosophers Benedetto Croce and Giovanni Gentile; second, the Fascist regime (1922–1943), and its anti-Semitism; third, the Catholic Church; and fourth, the positivistically oriented Italian medical doctors (see Gaddini, 1976; 1982, p.651).

As I wrote in the Introduction to the First Part, Edoardo Weiss (1889–1970), the founder of Italian psychoanalysis, was not only the only Italian medical doctor who trained in Vienna, but, having been expelled in 1938, he also never returned to Italy. As a consequence, the promotion of psychoanalysis after World War II remained in the hands of his pupils Emilio Servadio (1904–1995) and Nicola Perrotti (1897–1970), psychology professor Cesare Musatti (1897–1979), and the Berlin-trained Baroness Alessandra Tomasi di Lampedusa (1894–1982), whose tenacious work started bearing fruit only by the end of the 1960s. As I myself wrote in the paper "Die Psychoanalyse in Italien. Anfänge, Entwicklung und gegenwärtige Lage" (Conci, 1996; see the References for the translation of the title), which I published in the German journal for the history of psychoanalysis *Luzifer-Amor* (see also the Afterword), psychoanalysis in Italy started becoming a socially accepted form of therapy only at the end of the 1960s. Around the resistances encountered by psychoanalysis in Italy, and the very gradual and complex process of its reception and acceptance, was centered the book *La psicoanalisi nella cultura italiana* published by the French historian of literature Michel David (1966; with the second, revisited edition in 1990). David also very carefully addressed the very process of assimilation of Freud's new discipline, coming to the following very eloquent conclusion:

> The strangest paradox was that psychoanalysis appeared as a Teutonic product in the first years after World War One, a Jewish product when the Fascist Regime got closer to Hitler's Germany, and an American product when the Americans landed in Italy. (David, 1990, p. 85; my translation).

In other words, it apparently took many decades for the Italian people to understand where psychoanalysis had actually come from, and whether psychoanalysis was the product of German positivism, a "Jewish science," or what we could call one of the ingredients of North American capitalism.

Indeed, other major works deal with the problem of the initial reception of psychoanalysis in individual countries. These include Nathan Hale, Jr.'s (1922–2013) first volume of his *Freud and the Americans*, with the title *The beginnings of psychoanalysis in the United States* (see Hale, 1971), and Elisabeth Roudinesco's first volume of her *Histoire de la psychanalyse en France* (Roudinesco, 1994), which covers the years 1885–1939. I dealt in detail with the former in my book on H.S. Sullivan, also in order to present it to Italian and indeed international readers as a very important source of information on the reception and development of psychoanalysis in the USA. Unfortunately, there are still many colleagues, many psychoanalysts, who hold prejudices against certain societies and cultures, and being well informed is certainly a good way of struggling against all the unnecessary prejudices that often make international dialogue and exchange so difficult and complicated. Of course, I would be happy to dedicate more space to this problem, but I feel the need not to abuse too much of my readers' patience.

I will therefore finish dealing with this specific topic by mentioning two further books centered around the reception of psychoanalysis, the historian Hannah Decker's (1977) *Freud in Germany: Revolution and reaction in science, 1893–1907*, and the sociologist Sherry Turkle's (1978) *Psychoanalytic politics. Jacques Lacan and Freud's French revolution*. From the former, we learn how limited the reception of Freud's work in Germany was around the turn of the twentieth century; the latter describes how Lacan was able to create so much interest around his revisitation of Freud's work by connecting it so well to a series of specific characters of French culture, that is, by producing what the author calls "a French Freud."

If we now move from the important and fascinating problem of the original reception of psychoanalysis in the various countries to the even more important and more crucial problem of the translation of Freud's work into English, we run across a similar trend to that of "the French Freud" created by Lacan. This relates to the vast and highly praiseworthy work of James Strachey (1887–1967) as the creator of the so-called *Standard edition of the complete psychological works of Sigmund Freud*, which came out in twenty-four volumes between 1953 and 1974 (see Strachey and Strachey, eds., 1953–1974). In order to facilitate the reception of Freud's work in the Anglo-Saxon medical world, James Strachey made the choice—which Freud apparently approved of—of using, as "the imaginary model which I have always kept before me," "the writings of some English man of science of wide education born in the middle of the nineteenth century" (Strachey, 1966, p. xix), By doing this he on the one hand attained his goal, but on the other hand created a whole series of problems around which a very rich literature has accumulated in recent decades. And this to the point that a new and alternative translation has been prepared— over long years of work—by South-African colleague Mark Solms, due to come out in 2018.

In the book *Translating Freud*, edited in 1992 by Darius Gray Ornston, Jr., a series of authors tried to present the problems connected to the translation of Freud's works into English, Spanish, and French, reviewing all the relevant literature. For example, among the many criticisms of Strachey's work formulated by Patrick Mahony, I find the following one particularly interesting:

> Read in German, Freud's prose is able not only to describe but to enact and perform; in other words, the difference between description and event is minimized. The English translations take away from that. Freud's here and now was turned into Strachey's there and then, perception was changed into memory, and the exploratory nature of an ongoing investigation was transformed into a post fact hardening and even prescriptive retrospection. (Mahony, 1992, p. 39)

German colleague Helmut Junker begins his contribution to this book by stating that "Strachey's translation often seems easier to understand than the original," that "his clear and didactic flow is quickly understood and sounds more reliable, even more correct, than Freud's own German wording," concluding "when I read Strachey I read 'a tamed Freud' (Junker, 1992, p. 48). No wonder that Alex Holder ends his chapter by stating, "We are beginning to understand why the English Freud sounds so very different from the German Freud" (Holder, 1992, p. 96). Keeping these problems in mind, we can see not only the importance of understanding the criteria according to which Freud's works and language have been translated, but also how important it would be to be familiar with his own mother tongue. As I mentioned in the General Introduction, both Anzieu (1986) and Goldschmidt (2006) have dealt with how much psychoanalysis is rooted in Freud's native language, and—in my view—it is a pity that the study of German has never been included in analytic training.

Behind this book edited by Gray Ornston lie two others: the more famous (1982) book by Bruno Bettelheim (1903–1990) *Freud and man's soul*, with his critique of Strachey's translation of the German word *Seele* as the English work "mind," and Riccardo Steiner's (1987, 1991) important work of historical research on the early origin and gradual development of the concept of the *Standard edition*. Here is the summary of Steiner's very long (seventy-nine pages!) first paper, "A world wide international trade mark of genuineness? Some observations on the history of the English translation of the work of Sigmund Freud, focusing mainly on his technical terms":

> This is the first of a series of papers of mine which I hope will be published in the *Review* on the history of Strachey's

translation of Freud. I have tried to reconstruct the early phases of the translation of Freud's work into English. Starting with the evidence from the documents of the Archives of the British Psycho-Analytical Society, and the correspondence between Jones and Strachey and others at the time of Freud's death, I explore what happened during the first decade of our century at the time of the first discovery and diffusion of psychoanalysis in England and America. I focus particularly on the papers of Brill and Jones, but also others, at the time when Jones went to Canada and helped Brill introduce psychoanalysis to North America. I illustrate their relationship and that with Freud, and the kind of support Freud gave to the first attempts to translate his work into English.

Translations of technical terms were based on a massive use of ancient Greek and Latin radicals. Although there is evidence that Freud also relied on the two ancient languages, there is no doubt that the translation done by Brill and Jones increased very significantly the 'scientificity' of Freud's language at that time. I have tried to place this in its historical context and to stress the tactical reasons for adopting these particular linguistic devices. I also emphasize the conscious and unconscious positive, but also less positive, ideological implications which shaped those early attempts to translate Freud, which Strachey later on had to be confronted with too. (Steiner, 1987, p. 93)

And here is the summary of the (forty-one-page long) second paper, "'To explain the point of view of English readers in English words'":

The paper is closely related to my previous one, entitled 'A world-wide international trade mark of genuineness?' published in this journal in 1987. It deals with the prehistory of Strachey's translation of Freud. Working on Jones's papers, some related literature, some other translations of Freud of those years, and on the unpublished correspondence between Freud and Jones, I hope to have been able to show that in order to understand the specificity, the historical cultural reasons behind the translation of Freud into English done later on by Strachey, one has to consider in detail the period between the return of Jones to England in 1913, the re-foundation of the British Psycho-Analytical Society in 1919 and the foundation of the International Press and of the *International Journal of Psycho-Analysis* in 1919–1920.

All those initiatives are interlinked and Jones's attempts to achieve an hegemonic control of the translation of Freud and his efforts to lay the foundations of the way Freud had to be translated into English, the cultural reasons for his policy based on the use of ancient Greek and Latin radicals to render Freud's technical language, emerge in full. Particularly important were Jones's first attempts to build a Code of technical terms in 1914 and a Glossary in 1918 and his active role as a translator of Freud.

The historical evidence shows that the project to publish a Standard Collected Edition of Freud's work has also to be attributed to Jones at the beginning of the twenties. All these initiatives and organizational achievements are studied with reference to the cultural and, to some extent, even socio-political background of the England of those years. (Steiner, 1991, p. 390)

I have quoted Steiner's work at length partly because it is not easy to summarize it. However, I aim mainly to show how its historical nature and international character seem to represent the best ways to catch the sophisticated and complex operation of the internationalization of psychoanalysis under British leadership that Ernest Jones (1879–1958) was able to realize through the *Standard edition;* indeed, that British leadership still plays an important role in the international analytic community. Last but not least, I also want to emphasize the fact that Riccardo Steiner, an Italian historian from Milan who trained in London with Herbert Rosenfeld (1910–1986), whom I have been in touch with for many years (see the Afterword), represents for me an important model in terms of—as I have already said—both the historical nature and the international character of his research work. This is in addition to the fact that the British (and North American) international dimension established by Jones is also the context in which I am writing this Introduction (and I will publish this book) directly in English—and not my mother tongue, which is no longer the international language it used to be, for example at the time of the Renaissance.

This must be true also for Mark Solms, whose heroic work of revision of the *Standard edition* I believe we can also qualify in these terms. In 2013 Solms had already presented his work with the following words in an article published in the New York *Psychoanalytic Review* (the oldest analytic journal in the English language, as we have seen in the Introduction to Part One):

At the time of writing these brief notes, the *Revised Standard Edition of the Complete Psychological Works of Sigmund Freud (RSE)* is essentially complete and with the printers. I say essentially because there are still a few large tasks remaining that cannot be completed until the proofs are returned. This refers mainly to the indexing, which is being done afresh, but can only be finally completed when the pagination of the volumes is set. The largest of the other remaining tasks is the proofreading itself. This is always a chore, which in this case has to be multiplied by 24.

The job of revising the *Standard Edition* can only be described as 'big'. I had to review every sentence of Strachey's translations of Freud's *Complete psychological works* and check it against the German texts. In some cases the published German texts also had to be checked against the original manuscripts, wherever there was reason to doubt the transcription. (This checking is easier said than done; almost all of the surviving manuscripts are in Washington, DC, which means I could not just take a peek whenever I wanted to. But in this respect, Ilse Grubrich-Simitis, who is more familiar with Freud's manuscripts than anyone, and who is James Strachey's real successor, was extremely helpful to me, as she has had to perform this task for various

German editions of Freud's works over the past few decades.)

To check Strachey's translations properly, I also had to thoroughly familiarize myself with the secondary literature, where many transcription and translation errors have been identified over the years. (Not only in English and German; many errors also came to light in the preparation of *Œuvres complètes de Freud* under the general editorship of Jean Laplanche, for example.) Strachey himself kept a running list of corrections and additions, published in the 24th volume, and these intended revisions of his own were naturally incorporated into the present edition.

Wherever such unequivocal errors had been made (or propagated) by Strachey, my task was simple: I corrected them. If the corrections were substantial or surprising or otherwise interesting, I added brief editorial footnotes to draw attention to them. (Solms, 2013, pp. 201–202)

And furthermore:

The secondary literature includes many comments on the way in which Freud has previously been translated that cannot be described as errors. In many such instances— if not most—there is no simply correct alternative. For example, is it better to translate "*das Ich*" as "the ego" or "the I" or "the me" or "the self"? . . . To my mind the only sensible answer to this question is that there is no correct translation. There are several different ways of going about it, each of which has advantages and disadvantages. What you gain on the roundabouts, you must lose on the swings.

For this reason, I have taken the view that all such controversial (as opposed to erroneous) translations should be annotated and discussed (as opposed to corrected) in the *Revised Standard Edition*. This entailed my compiling two very extensive sets of editorial notes. I say "very extensive" because there are an enormous number of controversial translations in Strachey's *Standard Edition*. . . .

The second set of such editorial endnotes, also collected in the 24th volume, pertain not to general technical terms but rather to specific words or phrases or to sentences or titles of individual works . . . .

I am aware that the decision not to "correct" Strachey's translations in respect of technical terms and other controversial words, phrases, and titles will bring a barrage of criticisms upon my head. Having thoroughly considered the alternatives, however, I am reconciled to my fate. (Solms, 2013, pp. 202, 203, 204)

After making us familiar with the guiding principles of his work, Solms is so open as to clearly inform us about the "political context" in which he worked. He was originally given the task of revising the *Standard edition* in 1991 by the London Institute of Psychoanalysis, the intellectual custodian and legal owner of Strachey's edition, at a time in which Solms was still a candidate in training. Having originally agreed to doing a minor job of revising Strachey's work, he gradually gained in autonomy, and this allowed him to also make major corrections, for example eventually translating the German "*Trieb*" as the

English "drive"—and not "instinct," as Strachey's version
had done. From this 2013 paper we also learn that the
Revised standard edition will contain over forty new texts
by Freud, among them "a suppressed portion of 'The
question of lay analysis', where Freud gave vent to his
embarrassing views about America" (Solms, 2013, p. 207).
Last but not least, the twenty-four volumes of the *Revised
standard edition* will come out together with the four
volumes of Freud's *Neuroscientific works*. In this way
Solms accomplishes the project (which I discussed in the
Introduction to Part One) of giving equal dignity to what
Freud's considered as being his "pre-analytic writings,"
thus excluding them from his *Gesammelte Werke*, which
was published in London between 1940 and 1952 (Freud,
1940–1952).

Around this same aim centers the new German edition
of Freud's works edited by Christfried Tögel with the
collaboration of Urban Zerfass; this addresses the necessity
of uniting in a new *Sigmund-Freud-Gesamtsausgabe*
both Freud's analytic and pre-analytic texts, which
will on completion fill twenty-three volumes. This new
edition is being published by the Giessen publishing
house Psychosozial-Verlag, founded and owned by the
psychoanalyst Hans-Jürgen Wirth, who also published
the German edition of my Sullivan book in 2005. This is
how I, back in 2015 (as the first volume of this new edition
came out; Tögel and Zerfass, 2015), was eventually able
to eventually read the very first publication by Freud,
the paper on the sexual reproduction of eels based on the
research work he had done in the spring of 1876 at the
Marine Biology Institute that the University of Vienna
had created in Trieste. This paper, "Beobachtungen über
Gestaltung und feineren Bau der als Hoden beschriebenen
Lappenorgane des Aals," was originally published by the
Kaiserliche Akademie der Wisssenschften—the Imperial
Academy of Sciences—in 1877. I had unfortunately
not been able to find the paper when I was working as
editor of the Italian edition of the young Freud's letters
to Eduard Silberstein, so was glad to be eventually able
to read it.

A further trait of this new edition is to present all the
texts in their original typographic dress, which makes the
first contact with them very exciting. Of course, this new
edition also follows the chronological order of publication
of all Freud's works and papers, which make up the first
twenty volumes. Volume 21 contains still unpublished
lectures and interviews, Volume 22 a series of Freud's
diaries, and Volume 23 the table of contents of all the

volumes. Up to the time of writing (July 2018), Tögel and Zerfass have been able to publish almost half of the entire new edition, that is, the first eleven volumes.

In a recent review article on the German editions of Freud's works, Michael Schröter (2015) also includes the most recent project initiated in Vienna, coordinated by Christine Dierks of the Vienna Psychoanalytic Society. This focuses on the attempt to produce a historical-critical edition in which both Freud's works and his original letters will appear together and become electronically available. It is an ambitious project that will take years to be completed, but which many of us certainly welcome and connect with the possibility of further research projects into how Freud constructed his work.

A similar wide international view, reaching out to all major editions of Freud's works, characterizes the paper that the Italian historian of psychoanalysis Michele Ranchetti (1925–2008) gave in Bologna in May 1989 at the international conference *"L'opera di Freud a cinquant'anni dalla morte."* This conference centered around Freud's work fifty years after his death, and Ranchetti's paper came out in *Psicoterapia e Scienze Umane* at the end of the same year (Ranchetti, 1989). The paper represents a further confirmation of the research line developed by Riccardo Steiner (who had been a student of Michele Ranchetti in Milan in the early 1960s), and of the fact that the various translations and editions of Freud's works in the various languages can at best be evaluated on the basis of the international perspective that lies at the center of this Part of my book. This is of course also why I am giving so much room to the topic of the various editions of Freud's works—a topic kept alive by both Solms' and Tögel's work.

In the paper itself, Ranchetti spoke about the Italian edition of Freud's work, on which he had collaborated, only after having taken into consideration the whole international landscape concerning this specific chapter of psychoanalysis. This edition, edited by Cesare Musatti and published between 1966 and 1980 by the Turin publisher Paolo Boringhieri (1921–2006) in twelve volumes is—according to Ranchetti—a very good edition. Among other things, we also learn in Ranchetti's paper about his personal visit to the Stracheys at their country home in March 1965, along with Angela Richards and in the company of the publisher Boringhieri, and about their readiness to grant the Italian publisher the right to make use of their critical apparatus. According to the documents that Ranchetti found in the archives of the Turin publishing house, Boringhieri had been able to buy the rights for the Italian publication of Freud's *Gesammelte Werke* in 1959, after Musatti had, in 1956, accepted the role of coordinator of the whole enterprise (Ranchetti, 1989). At variance with the *Standard edition*, the Italian edition was published on the initiative of an intellectually progressive publisher, and the SPI was not directly involved in the project—except through Musatti, who was its president in the 1950s.

A personal friend of Paolo Boringhieri, Michele Ranchetti was one of the major consultants of the whole enterprise. One of his merits consists in having proposed the hiring of Renata Colorni, a German translator who ended up playing a fundamental role in the control of all the translations and in achieving their linguistic uniformity. In a paper on Musatti's part in realizing the project, Rodolfo Reichmann (2006) included an interesting interview with her about her role. Last but not least, in the last years of his life Ranchetti tried to produce a new Italian edition of Freud's works, aimed at giving more room to their contextualization in terms of Freud's relationship with his circle of collaborators, but the project failed because of various editorial errors—whose problematic aspects Antonio Alberto Semi dealt with in 2006 in the Italian *Rivista di Psicoanalisi*.

After my long digression on the translation of Freud's works and on the need to deal with this complex topic from both a historical and an international perspective, I can now come back to the first topic I dealt with, that is, the literature concerning the history and development of psychoanalysis in various countries. The next monographic work on this topic, which I discovered in the 1990s, was the two-volume *Psychoanalysis international. A guide to psychoanalysis throughout the world*, Volume 1: *Europe*, and Volume 2: *America, Asia, Australia, further European countries*; these were edited by the German colleague Peter Kutter (1930–2014) (Kutter, 1992, 1995) and published in English by the German publisher Frommann-Holzboog. Here is what the editor, Peter Kutter, wrote in his "Introduction" to Volume 1:

> The aim of the book is not only to provide an overview of the history of psychoanalysis, but also to report on its current situation in the individual countries, including detailed information regarding societies, institutions and numbers of members, an overview of the important schools and directions, eminent persons and their publications, current trends and information regarding the connections between psychoanalysis and academic institutions,

the publicity of psychoanalysis in the population, etc.

The attentive reader will have no problem in recognizing the individual national characteristics of psychoanalysis in the various countries. They are already evident, for example, in outward appearance of the contributions, for not all the authors followed the suggestions made by the editor . . . . In this way the special features of the conditions in the individual countries become directly evident without the need for long explanations; the connections between psychoanalysis and philosophy in France, for example, Anglo-Saxon pragmatism in Great Britain and the USA, the sociological variant in Germany, its vivacity in Spain, its temperament in Italy, the care with which it is cultivated in Holland as well as in Belgium and the Scandinavian countries. (Kutter, 1992, p. xiii)

In Volume 1, Harald Leupold-Loewenthal (1926–2007), Wolfgang Berner, and Annemarie Laimböck took care of the chapter on psychoanalysis in Austria, Alain de Mijolla dealt with psychoanalysis in France, Peter Kutter himself wrote the chapter on psychoanalysis in Germany, and Pearl King (1918–2015) and Alex Holder compiled the chapter on psychoanalysis in Great Britain. Last but not least, we owe the chapter on psychoanalysis in Italy to Arnaldo Novelletto (1931–2006), and I will now emphasize two aspects of this. First, the delay in adopting a series of international standards was eventually remedied under the presidency of Eugenio Gaddini (1978–1982). Second, quoting a paper by Giuseppe Di Chiara (1985), Novelletto distinguishes the following three specific trends of the scientific life of the Italian Psychoanalytic Society:

a) the deepening of the level of the actual psychological experience of the relationship between the analyst and his subject . . . b) the greater importance given to the person of the analyst, his internal relationships and his participation in the relationship with the patient . . . c) the widely noted necessity of the revision of theoretical models. (Novelletto, 1992, pp. 204–205)

These are the trends that also nourished the training of Stefano Bolognini, as the reader will see in Chapter 11.

In his Foreword to Volume 2, Peter Kutter assigns the following aims to his work:

The first aim of this compendium of *Psychoanalysis international* is a historiographic one . . . . The second aim . . . is to provide a kind of 'map of psychoanalysis' . . . . The third aim of this book . . . is to describe the current situation of psychoanalysis . . . . Finally, the book is intended to serve as a reference book so that the readers can obtain information about the institutes of the IPA. (Kutter, 1995, pp. vii–xi)

In other words, in introducing the second volume the editor admits that he did not consider any analytic developments and groups outside of the International

Psychoanalytical Association (IPA) in either one of the volumes. This is also why the above-mentioned chapter that he had written on Germany centered almost exclusively on the German Psychoanalytic Association (the Deutsche Psychoanalytische Vereinigung, DPV), to the detriment of the German Psychoanalytic Society (the Deutsche Psychoanalytische Gesellschaft, DPG), which did not yet belong to the IPA. We will deal in detail with this complex and very interesting chapter of the history of postwar psychoanalysis in Germany later in this Introduction.

The only exception to Kutter's approach is represented by the chapter written by the Viennese colleague Erika Danneberg (1922–2007) on "Psychoanalysis against the grain (Argentina, Chile, Nicaragua, Cuba)," in which she specifically deals with the work and legacy of Marie Langer (1910–987), one of the founders of both the Argentinian Psychoanalytic Society (1942) and the so-called Platform Group. This latter is an alternative analytic international network that was founded at the IPA Rome Congress of July 1969, at which:

> training candidates organized an alternative congress with not only professional topics: Democratization of the psychoanalytical training institutes and reevaluation of the revolutionary, cultural-critical roots of psychoanalysis. Marie Langer attended it. Platforms were subsequently formed which, according to regional circumstances, were to continue dealing with the controversial topics. (Danneberg, 1995, p. 243)

And here are the words with which Danneberg describes the further evolution of the Platform Group, whose orientation and activities also played an important role in the alternative concept of psychoanalysis developed by the editorial board of the journal *Psicoterapia e Scienze Umane*:

> In Argentina, but also in Italy and in Switzerland, the results were radical: the Zurich Platform – later the Psychoanalytic Seminar – and the Platforma and Documenta in Buenos Aires split from the IPA because of grave differences regarding the admission to psychoanalytic training, the curriculum and the right of co-determination of candidates, as well as relating to the position of psychoanalysis and psychoanalysts in societal-political processes. The movement, which had first become public in Rome, also led to consequences within the IPA. These included, at an organizational level, recognition of the international candidates' organization as well as, in the scientific-theoretical field, renewed and intensified concern with problems of training analysis, lay analysis and countertransference. (Danneberg, 1995, p. 243)

The historian Dagmar Herzog, in her recent book *Cold War Freud. Psychoanalysis in an age of catastrophes*

(2017), eventually reconstructed this significant chapter in the postwar history of international psychoanalysis, presenting some of its protagonists, and analyzing its role in the evolution of psychoanalysis as a whole. Elvio Fachinelli (1928–1989), the Italian training analysand of Cesare Musatti who translated Freud's *The interpretation of dreams* into Italian, the Swiss colleague Berthold Rothschild, and the Italian colleague Marianne Bolko, the latter two members of the editorial board of *Psicoterapia e Scienze Umane*, are some of the protagonists of this chapter, with which I will also deal in more detail later in this Introduction. But here is how Erika Danneberg concluded her chapter in Kutter's second volume, starting from Freud's ban on psychoanalysts becoming involved in politics, the ban that he formulated in the 1930s in the hope of saving psychoanalysis from the risk of liquidation by the Nazi regime:

> The inadmissible mingling of analytical and political abstinence provides an illusionary way of creating an analytical shelter from which the threatening political reality remains excluded. Even Freud succumbed to this illusion with his ban in the thirties. The ban did not save the Psychoanalytical Movement in Europe from its extermination by fascism, but it did do lasting damage to the foundation of psychoanalytical identity . . . . So psychoanalysis of the Left may . . . be . . . a contribution to a new definition of psychoanalytic identity. (Danneberg, 1995, p. 254)

Only in 2011, in connection with the hundredth anniversary of its foundation, did the IPA produce a large volume, totaling forty-nine chapters and 560 pages, that was centered around the development of psychoanalysis in Europe, North America, Latin America, Asia, and Oceania (see Loewenberg and Thompson, eds., 2011a). This included two sections with the titles "International survey" (on the beginning of formal training in the 1920s, and on the process of the formation of new groups) and "IPA leadership" (on the role and accomplishments of the IPA presidents from 1969 until 2009, as presented by the presidents themselves). The hundredth anniversary was celebrated in connection with the 47th IPA Congress held in Mexico City in the summer of 2011, under the presidency of the Canadian colleague Charles Hanly. A second IPA group, the Italian Psychoanalytic Association (AIPsi), was founded in Italy in 1993 (by Jacqueline Amati Mehler and Jorge Canestri among others), and a specific chapter deals with this, alongside the chapter "A brief history of the Italian Psychoanalytic Society" written by Domenico Chianese (SPI president 2001–2005).

As far as Germany is concerned, we are confronted

with two chapters: "The history of psychoanalysis in Germany up to 1950 and its relationship to the IPA," by Ludger Hermanns (Hermanns, 2011), and "The history of psychoanalysis in Germany since 1950," by Werner Bohleber (Bohleber, 2011). In the former paper, we learn about the origins and consequences of the schism that the German analytic community went through after the first postwar IPA Congress, held in Zurich in the summer of 1949, with the failed readmission of the DPG to the IPA, and the 1951 foundation of the DPV. In the latter article, we learn about important episodes such as "The way back to the psychoanalysis of Sigmund Freud," "The return of the repressed: The debate on psychoanalysis during National Socialism," and "The acceptance of the DPG into the IPA"—which took place at the 46th IPA Congress held in Chicago in July 2009.

However, the great event that the editors celebrated in their introductory words, "The geography of the IPA" (Loewenberg and Thompson, 2011b), was of course the first IPA Asian Congress, held in Beijing in October 2010 and representing the expansion of the IPA in Asia and Oceania. This is reflected in the chapters of the fourth section of this anthology dedicated to Australia, China, India, Israel, Japan (two chapters), Korea, Taiwan, and Turkey. Furthermore, in their "Introduction" the editors also touch on the problem of the three training models (the Eitingon model, the French model, and the Uruguayan model) that the IPA ended up recognizing, dedicating particular space to the Uruguayan model. The authors describe this as follows:

> The decentralized Uruguayan model is especially worthy of our interest because of its unique adaptation to the political culture of Uruguay. The Uruguayan Psychoanalytical Association has a collective leadership, as does the polity of the country. Uruguayan psychoanalysis is decentralized, separating the personal analysis of the candidate from institutional considerations through the policy of non-intervention of the analyst in the Association at any point in the training process. Entrance into the Association does not depend on the candidate's analyst. The aspiring student is evaluated for the Association through an interview by a commission which is set up for the purpose. (Loewenberg and Thompson, 2011b, p. 4)

The separation of the personal analysis from the remaining part of the training (courses and supervisions) was also the model instigated by Benedetti and Cremerius at the Milan Institute, which I will talk about in Chapter 10.

In 2009, the Indian-North American colleague

Salman Akhtar had already edited the book *Freud and the Far East. Psychoanalytic perspectives on the people and culture of China, Japan, and Korea* (Akhtar, ed., 2009a). This anthology aimed to present and evaluate the important phenomenon of the expansion of psychoanalysis in these countries, and, at the same time, to set new accents and priorities in terms of the desirability of and need for a more mutual exchange between the Western and Eastern worlds. This is why Akhtar's "Introduction" also touches on the topic of our huge Western ignorance of anything connected to China, Japan, and Korea. In his words:

> Talking of knowledge brings up the painful issue of Western, especially North American, geographical ignorance, and cultural provincialism. The ordinary masses in the United States can be truly appalling in their lack of knowledge and concern about the 'Orient' while driving around the country in their Hondas, Toyotas, Subarus, Hundays, and Suzukis. The educated classes enjoy the movies of Akira Kurosawa, admire the architectural genius of Ieoh Ming Pei, read the fiction of Kazuo Ishiguro and Amy Tan, savor book reviews by Michiko Kakutani, respect the secular pragmatism by Ban Ki Moon, and swoon over the music of Yo-Yo Ma. They have incorporated acupuncture, bonsai, dim sun, feng shui, haiku, karaoke, origami, and sushi in the alphabet of their cosmopolitan lives, though without adequately mentalizing gratitude to the Far Eastern origins of these artifacts and practices. Both groups lead lives that merrily ignore the destruction of Hiroshima and Nagasaki, the Japanese internment camps in the United States during and soon after World War II, the bloodshed during the Korean War, the relentless American bombing of Laos and Cambodia, and its merciless pillage of Vietnam. Disregard for history is coupled with disinterest in the contemporary affairs of the East. Ignorance abounds. (Akhtar, 2009b, p. 3)

I can only agree with Akhtar's desire for this anthology to stimulate the kind of analytic dialogue and exchange through which we can better get to know ourselves; in fact, I understand very well how the exploration of new, and for us unknown and unfamiliar, dimensions of a foreign country and culture can contribute to this goal. In Akhtar's words:

> The book is thus a lexical ambassador with the dual responsibility of bridging the West and East and enhancing psychoanalytic conceptualization in the course of such encounters. By juxtaposing the familiar with the unfamiliar, it seeks to enrich the understanding of both . . . . Shedding light on the periphery eventually illuminates the center. That is where the book leads to: the core of the human heart with all its innocent idiosyncrasies and its inescapable universality. (Akhtar, 2009b, p. 6)

The thoughts of Stefano Bolognini move in a similar direction in his Preface (Bolognini, 2016) to the anthology *Cartografie dell'inconscio. Un nuovo atlante per la psicoanalisi*, edited in 2016 by the Rome colleague Lorena Preta. This book deals with not only the development of psychoanalysis in the Far East, but also the formulation of a series of reflections on the relationship between psychoanalysis and anthropology (see, for example, Lombardozzi, 2016). In fact, Bolognini talks of the international exchanges that are possible today in the light of Sheldon Bach's article "Chimeras: Immunity, interpenetration, and the true self" (2011), that is, in terms of how the inclusion of new, external elements in an organism may have a series of different results depending on the nature of the organism itself and the types of interaction taking place. Bolognini further emphasizes the importance of "the bi-lateral character of the transformative experience in the expansion of psychoanalysis, taking in fact the transplantation place in both directions . . . both in the group of the trainers and of the trainees" (Bolognini, 2016, p. 10). *Cartografie dell'inconscio* is in fact the result of the work of the new IPA Working Party "Geographies of Psychoanalysis" chaired by Lorena Preta herself; this would have not been (conceptually) possible up until a few years ago, that is, as long as the analytic community held to Freud's positivistic idea that all well-trained psychoanalysts work in the same way whatever part of the world they live and work in.

This also explains the reluctance of the analytic community itself to adequately explore the topic of the "immigrant analyst," one of the main vicissitudes that the analytic community faced between the 1930s and the 1950s. León and Rebeca Grinberg started to deal with this issue in 1990, in their classical book *Psychoanalytic perspectives on migration and exile*. But it was Salman Akhtar, in his 1999 book *Immigration and identity. Turmoil, treatment, and transformation*, who eventually helped promote a new climate of opinion in this regard. Given their eloquence, let me now cite the following words of his:

> To be an immigrant and to practice psychotherapy and psychoanalysis largely with native-born patients poses many dilemmas and challenges . . . . In light of this, the lack of literature on this topic is striking. This is even more notable in view of the fact that a large number of early analysts, both in England and in the United States, were immigrants. Perhaps this omission is due to the reluctance of mainstream psychoanalysis to deal with sociological, historical, and cultural factors in adult life in favor of an exclusive focus upon the intrapsychic residues of early childhood. The fact that these European analysts were actually not immigrant but refugees and exiles might have also have contributed to the profession's silence on this

issue. Wanting to forget their traumatic departures, deny
cultural differences with their patients, and become quickly
assimilated at a professional level, these analysts did not want
to draw others' (and their own) attention to their ethnic and
national origins. Hence they wrote little about the dilemmas
of practicing analysis and psychotherapy as 'foreigners'.
    Now the climate is different. Psychoanalysis is
undergoing a major cultural rejuvenation. The increase
in the number of people migrating from one country to
another has resulted in significant shifts in the demographic
makeup of the industrialized nations, especially the United
States and England. Along with an increase in the culturally
diverse patient clientele, there is also an increase in culturally
diverse trainees in psychology, social work, psychiatry and
psychoanalysis. The contemporary theoretical pluralism in
psychoanalysis is yet another factor that makes it possible,
even necessary, to openly discuss technical matters of specific
concern to the foreign-born, that is, the 'immigrant' therapist.
(Akhtar, 1999, pp. 154–155)

It is no wonder that it was only at the 46th Congress
of the IPA held in Chicago at the end of July 2009 that I
dared to propose, and was invited to present, a paper with
the title "Working with Italian patients in Munich – The
case of Penelope" (Conci, 2018b).In the title of this paper
I openly mentioned the concrete place in which I work
(as opposed to placing the "right type of analytic work" in
no particular location), and I emphasized the particular
and concrete conditions in which the work took place. I
also tried to contribute with this paper to the scientific
validation and political implementation of the German
Kassensystem, that is, the German Social Security System
that covers psychoanalytic psychotherapy up to 300
sessions, three times a week, representing a uniquely
favorable situation compared with other areas of the
world. In other words, it is true that we can as analysts
help our migrant patients revisit, in the common mother
tongue, their "old native self" and integrate it into the
"new self" that they are trying to create for themselves in
their host country—in which we ourselves have already
been able to establish ourselves. In fact, this paper (and
my work in Munich) was also my way of confirming the
therapeutic experiences in Rome in the 1980s of Jacqueline
Amati Mehler, Simona Argentieri, and Jorge Canestri,
which they presented in the now classical book *The Babel
of the unconscious. Mother tongue and foreign languages
in the psychoanalytic dimension* (1993)—whose German
edition I, together with my Indonesian-German colleague
Hediaty Utari-Witt, was able to promote (Conci, 2010a).

    Also in relation to this issue—the revisitation and
reevaluation of the topic of the "immigrant analyst"—
the preliminary work of a series of historians played a

major role in facilitating such a change, with particular reference—again—to the work of Riccardo Steiner. I am particularly referring here to his 1989 article "'It is a new kind of diaspora . . .'" (Steiner, 1989a), which he also used as the title of the 2000 anthology, *"It is a new kind of diaspora". Explorations in the sociopolitical and cultural context of psychoanalysis.* This anthology consisted of eight chapters centered around the topics of the expulsion of Jewish analysts from Central Europe and their new lives and careers in the UK and the USA. The words "It is a new kind of diaspora" were taken by the author from an unpublished letter of Anna Freud to Ernest Jones dated March 6, 1934. Here is the summary of the 1989 paper:

> This paper is concerned with the study of the correspondence between Anna Freud and Ernest Jones related to the problems of the emigration of analysts from Berlin and Vienna during the Nazi persecution. The author has also taken into consideration other documents. Besides the human problems, the correspondence enables the reader to get at third hand a picture of the difficulties Jones, his colleagues and Anna Freud had to face. Of particular interest and importance is the possibility to understand the role played by the International Psychoanalytical Association, of which Jones was the President at the time, in rescuing the analysts, and the tactics adopted by Jones especially with regard to Germany – already in the hands of the Nazis. In this connection, two cases are taken into consideration: the expulsion of Reich and the difficulty related to the forced acculturalization of middle-European analysts to their new countries, particularly the United Kingdom and the United States. (Steiner, 1989, p. 72)

Of course, Riccardo Steiner was not the only (historically competent) colleague to deal at the time with this complex problem. In the first place, the paper on which the 2000 anthology is based was originally read at the 1st Congress of the International Association for the History of Psychoanalysis (IAHP), held in Paris in May 1987, and was published in the first issue of the *Revue Internationale d'Histoire de la Psychanalyse*—as the author writes in the "Acknowledgements" accompanying the anthology itself.

Second, in 1988 Edward Timms and Naomi Segal had published the pioneering anthology *Freud in exile. Psychoanalysis and its vicissitudes*, an anthology consisting of four parts and twenty-three very good chapters. Two of the chapters were written by two well-known German colleagues: Uwe Henrik Peters (the psychiatry professor from Cologne whom I met in Cerisy-la-Salle in August 1991; see the Introduction to Part Three) and Frederick Wyatt (1911–1993), a Viennese-Jewish colleague who came back to Germany from the USA in the early 1970s. Here is, for example, how the chapter "The psychoanalytic exodus. Romantic antecedents, and the loss to German intellectual life," written by Uwe Heinrich Peters, begins:

> The two major German-speaking countries, West Germany and Austria, are still facing a situation that is very difficult to describe historically. It is in some respects comparable to the psychological after-effects of the Holocaust on the German population, which caused a type of collective bad conscience and guilt feelings, but without a sense of mourning. There is great admiration for the psychiatrists who emigrated from Germany, and particularly for the psychoanalysts who did so, but here too a lack of mourning for the loss and sometimes even a lack of awareness of it. (Peters, 1988, p. 54)

On the other hand, in his chapter "The severance of psychoanalysis from its cultural matrix," Frederick Wyatt emphasized the loss of the cultural, humanistic (Latin and old Greek) background that psychoanalysis suffered in the USA—as also witnessed by another Viennese analyst, Richard Sterba (1898–1989), in his *Reminiscences of a Viennese psychoanalyst* (1982).

Not only were older and expert analysts working on these topics at the time, but so too were members of my own generation who produced important books; these included the Hungarian-Austrian psychiatrist Paul Harmat and the Viennese psychologist and historian Elke Mühlleitner. I am referring here to Harmat's *Freud, Ferenczi und die ungarische Psychoanalyse*, the first very detailed book (431 pages!) on the history of Hungarian psychoanalysis, including its further development outside of Hungary starting in the 1930s; I reviewed this in *Psicoterapia e Scienze Umane* (Conci, 1990). Also very informative and useful is the dictionary patiently and carefully put together by Mühlleitner with the help of Johannes Reichmayr and a whole international community of colleagues and friends, which has allowed us to come in contact with the life and work of about 150 Viennese pioneers of psychoanalysis (Mühlleitner, 1992). To Elke Mühlleitner we also owe—as I wrote in the Introduction to Part Two—a very good biography of Otto Fenichel (1897–1946), whose life and work in Vienna, Berlin, Prague, and the USA she was able to follow and reconstruct in detail (Mühlleitener, 2009).

To the work produced on the topic of emigration and new beginnings in psychoanalysis by my generation of researchers also belongs the volume *Spaltungen in der Geschichte der Psychoanalyse*, edited by Ludger Hermanns in 1995 and containing the plenary papers given at the 5th Congress of the IAHP, which he organized in Berlin in July 1994. This was a well-attended congress, with a very good mixture of older and younger analysts and historians interested in the history of psychoanalysis, at which I also gave a paper, in a panel chaired by Ulrike May and with Edith Kurzweil as the first speaker. I was the second speaker, and my paper, "Harry Stack Sullivan and the splits in the North American Psychoanalytic Movement" (see the congress program on pp. 287–290 of Hermann's book), came out in German in 1995 in the journal *Luzifer-Amor* (Conci, 1995b).

Given all this work on the history of psychoanalysis, the pluralism that characterizes contemporary psychoanalysis, and the eventual recognition of a series of national traditions outside of the original schools of Vienna, Berlin, Budapest, and London, which had dominated the analytic landscape before World War II, it is no wonder that Dana Birksted-Breen, Sara Flanders, and Alain Gibeault had enough material to be able to produce, in 2010, a huge anthology of 816 pages and forty chapters with the title *Reading French psychoanalysis*. The anthology consists of the following seven sections: 1—"History of psychoanalysis in France" (with two chapters, by Alain de Mijolla and Daniel Widlöcher); 2—"The pioneers and their legacy" (with three chapters, by Jacques Lacan, Sacha Nacht, and Maurice Bouvet); 3—"The setting and the process of psychoanalysis" (with eight chapters, among them chapters by René Diaktine, Bela Grunberger, and Jean Pontalis); 4—"Phantasy and representation" (with eight more chapters, among which are chapters by Serge Lebovici, André Green, and Haydée Faimberg); 5—"The body and the drives" (with eight more chapters, including chapters by Pierre Marty, Didier Anzieu, and René Russilion); 6—"Masculine and feminine sexuality" (with six more chapters, and among them chapters by Janine Chasseguet-Smirgel, Paul Denis, and Joyce McDougall); and 7—"Psychosis" (with five more chapters, among which are contributions by Paul-Claude Racamier and Piera Aulagnier). Noteworthy are also the (fifty-page) long "General Introduction" by Birksted-Breen and Flanders, the introductions written by Gibeault to each of the above-mentioned eight sections, and the twenty-five-page "Glossary"—as well as the fact that many of the articles have been translated here into English for the first time. At the beginning of each chapter, there is also a short sketch of the life and work of the individual author. In order to give the reader a further impression of this important anthology, here are some of the concluding remarks of the "General Introduction":

In this introduction we have wanted to give a general map of French psychoanalysis as seen from our perspective, showing the impact of Lacan on the development of the French psychoanalytic scene and the specific debates within it. The interest in and the influence of the work of Winnicott and Bion in particular have been part of this debate and reaction against Lacan. This has led to developments towards an interest in the more disturbed states, in particular states and pathologies in which there is a deficiency of representation (blank psychosis, cold psychosis, psychosomatic states, 'essential depression'). The study of the analytic work necessary for representation to develop (*'travail de figurabilité'*), the study of specific states within the psychoanalytic situation ('controlled depersonalization'), and the development of specific treatment modes (psychodrama) are the product of this focus. We have argued in favor of the specificity of 'French psychoanalysis', to describe the early influences from within France and, later, from outside France, leading together to these specific contemporary developments. (Birksted-Breen and Flanders, 2010, p. 45)

Last but not least, here are the concluding remarks of the detailed and enthusiastic review of this anthology written by Alfred Margulies:

Not many will read this book as I, a reviewer, did – from cover to cover. But I feel the richer for it . . . . Within this volume one finds a literature that is fresh, alive, and in searching conversation with remarkable writers, with basic texts – especially Freud – and in opposition and interplay with Lacan. Listening in to this exchange and engaging the debate is exhilarating. Reading so many informed, sophisticated, creative, serious and impassioned writers all in the space of one volume etches, illuminates and raises them all, as in a Mozart opera, to one grand voice, each distinct and playing off the others to create something larger, unique and magnificent. This volume is an accomplishment and a gift. Savor it. (Margulies, 2011, p. 1066)

The example of the editors of *Reading French psychoanalysis* was courageously followed by Franco Borgogno, Alberto Luchetti, and Luisa Marino Coe, who worked for several years to produce the anthology *Reading Italian psychoanalysis* (2016), a similar anthology of 738 pages, forty-nine chapters, six sections, and one "Afterword." If the French anthology was made possible by the particular interest in and familiarity with French psychoanalysis of the two British editors, the essential role played by the international context—the topic of this current Introduction—in the production of the Italian anthology is clearly formulated by Borgogno and Luchetti at the very beginning of their "General Introduction." In their words:

The project for this book 'comes from afar': it comes from 160 West 66th Street in New York City, where one of the editors (Franco Borgogno) had been invited by Joseph and Judith Schachter to a party on Saturday January 16th, 2010. On that

occasion many American colleagues expressed their interest
in a collection of the most relevant Italian contributions to
psychoanalysis, saying that Italian psychoanalysis had taken
an original theoretical and technical configuration that could
be sensed from abroad but not fully grasped. It was Arnold
Richards, the owner of International Psychoanalytic Books,
who that very evening invited Borgogno to carry out this task,
an offer that was soon after reiterated by Peter Rudnytsky,
one of the editors of the 'History of psychoanalysis' series at
Karnac Books. With Rudnytsky, Borgogno started to think
about the concrete creation of *Reading Italian psychoanalysis*,
but some months later Karnac – in the person of Oliver
Rathbone – kindly suggested that if we should like to move
the book to the 'New library of psychoanalysis', series at
Routledge (directed by Alessandra Lemma), which had just
published *Reading French psychoanalysis*, they would step
aside. (Borgogno and Luchetti, 2016, p. 1)

At this point, after telling the reader how they ended
up structuring the anthology, Borgogno and Luchetti
try to synthesize the specificity of the profile of Italian
psychoanalysis (intended as a body of contributions
produced by the members of both the SPI and the AIPsi),
in terms of the four following basic traits: isolation and
openness, constant reference to the Freudian tradition,
and, at the same time, a highly pluralistic development.
In fact, we have already dealt with all four of these,
that is: with how small the group of Italian pioneers of
psychoanalysis was before World War II, and how slow
the postwar reception of psychoanalysis was in Italy;
how soon and how many books by authors such as Klein
and Bion, Sullivan and Mitchell, Lacan and Green were
translated into Italian—much earlier and in a more
complete way than they were, for example, in Germany;
what a good edition of Freud's works was produced by
the publisher Paolo Boringhieri; and, last but not least,
how Italy became one of the countries in which the
contemporary pluralistic aspect of psychoanalysis was
able to develop the most—due also to the absence of a
native analytic tradition.

But let me now come to the sections proposed and
chapters selected by the editors, that is, to the way in
which the editors tried to give the reader a sense of the
peculiarity of Italian psychoanalysis. Part 1, "History
of psychoanalysis in Italy," consists of two chapters, the
first written by Giuseppe Di Chiara, and the second by
Anna Ferruta. Part 2, "Metapsychology," is introduced
by Luchetti, and consists of eleven chapters (among them
chapters by Ignacio Matte Blanco, Francesco Corrao,
Jacqueline Amati Mehler, Fernando Riolo, Antonio
Alberto Semi, Giuseppe Civitarese, and Fausto Petrella).
Part 3, "Clinical practice, theory of technique, therapeutic

factors," is introduced by Marino Coe, and includes eleven more chapters (including from authors Glauco Carloni, Stefania Turillazzi Manfredi, Jorge Canestri, Antonino Ferro, Parthenope Bion Talamo, Franco De Masi, and Anna Maria Nicolò). Part 4, "The person of the analyst, countertransference, and the analytic relationship/ field," is introduced by Borgogno and encompasses eight more chapters (among them chapters by Luciana Nissim Momigliano, Stefano Bolognini, Domenico Chianese, Claudio Neri, and Vincenzo Bonaminio). Part 5, "Trauma, psychic pain, mourning and working-through," is introduced by Borgogno, and consists of eight more chapters (including by Edoardo Weiss, Roberto Tagliacozzo, Dina Vallino Macciò, Andreas Giannakoulas, and Tonia Cancrini). Part 6, "Preverbal, precocious, fusional, primitive, states of the mind," is introduced by Borgogno, and includes seven more chapters (among them chapters by Eugenio Gaddini, Franco Fornari, Simona Argentieri, Eugenio Gaburri, Adolfo Pazzagli, Agostino Racalbuto, and Riccardo Lombardi). The volume is closed by a very good "Afterword" written by the London colleague Leslie Caldwell (the editor, together with Helen Taylor Robinson, of the *Collected works of D.W. Winnicott* [2017]) and a bibliography of fifty pages. Here are the final words of the "Afterword – A swift glance at Italian psychoanalysis from abroad":

> An encounter with the very otherness of a national tradition that is not one's own encourages revisiting assumptions, assessing advantages and their limits, having one's own parochialism challenged, and, hopefully, finding an enlarged perspective on shared professional problems, through different perspectives on the uses of psychoanalysis in both clinical work and its extra-clinical application. This volume . . . offers an official national tradition through a wide range of papers revealing its distinctiveness from the inside, through the preoccupations, the emphases, the ways of theorising that, taken together, form a comprehensive account of Italian psychoanalysis. Any collection itself contains implicit interpretative procedures and invites curiosity about its criteria of selection, of what they include and exclude. The body of work made available here is both interesting and demanding and, on the evidence of this volume, Italian psychoanalysis has developed a shared but fluid set of approaches that map contemporary psychoanalysis in a way that is both familiar and thought-provokingly different. (Caldwell, 2016, p. 688)

After having covered so much ground concerning the two poles of, on the one hand, the international context in which the development of psychoanalysis has to be placed, and in which we have to place ourselves today as psychoanalysts, and on the other hand, the cultivation of its history as the best way to emphasize its necessary international nature, I cannot help but mention the one classical book methodologically based on such a dialectic—this represented one of the models I had in mind when I wrote *Sullivan revisited – Life and work*. I am of course referring to Henri Ellenberger's (1905–1993) *magnum opus The discovery of the unconscious* (1970), which was translated into Italian in 1972 and published by Freud's Italian publisher Paolo Boringhieri. In fact, Boringhieri had been advised to do this by one of Ellenberger's best Italian friends, the neurologist and psychiatrist Beppino Disertori (1907–1992), a university professor at the Department of Sociology of the University of Trento (see the Afterword), whose correspondence with Ellenberger I dealt with in a paper I wrote in his honor (Conci, 1995c).

Ellenberger was a multilingual psychiatrist, psychoanalyst, and historian, who was born in Rhodesia to Swiss parents, studied medicine in Paris, moved to German-speaking Switzerland in 1941, where he had a training analysis with Oskar Pfister (1873–1956), and in 1952 became a member of the Swiss Psychoanalytic Society. Ellenberger emigrated to the USA in 1953, where he worked at the Menninger Clinic, and in 1958 he eventually moved to Montreal, where he also became a famous criminologist. This is another reason he is unique in his ability to reconstruct in detail Freud's Vienna, Janet's Paris, and Jung's Zurich, that is, to recreate the historical and cultural context in which these pioneers of dynamic psychiatry all worked. In his book chapter "Henry Ellenberger: The history of psychiatry as the history of the unconscious," Mark Micale talks about Ellenberger's book as "simply indispensable to research in many areas of the history of psychology, psychiatry, and psychoanalysis" (Micale, 1994, p. 112), and about Ellenberger as "the most intelligent and comprehensive chronicler to date of the age of the pure dynamic psychiatries" (p. 127).

I have good reasons to believe that George Makari also shares this point of view, and that Ellenberger's work represented an important model for him too, although I have not found Ellenberger's name cited in the index of either Makari's 2008 book *Revolution in mind. The creation of psychoanalysis*, or his 2015 book *Soul machine. The invention of the modern mind*, in both of which he deals with his subject matter from a clearly international perspective. What we actually see in both Makari's books is an international community of medical doctors, philosophers, and scientists at work on the secrets of the soul—a fascinating adventure for a good writer such as he is to write about. Here is what we can for example read in Makari's "Prologue" to the latter book:

> The MODERN MIND was constructed during the Enlightenment, a defining if now controversial period of Western history. Some have questioned whether such an epoch ever existed and have argued instead for numerous, different national enlightenments. This book moves from the English and Scottish enlightenments to the French and German ones, but as we shall see, these varied intellectual communities were deeply intertwined. While powerfully influences by local differences, their theories of the mind also represent chapters in one interconnected European history . . . . In an effort to integrate these opposed narratives, this history departs from the influential, now much criticized trajectory mapped out by Foucault, while at the same time adopting some of his assumptions . . . .
>   *Soul machine* is a history of critical contests that helped define modern Western culture, not because they came to any decisive conclusion but because they did not. Modernity has answered many questions, but it has never found a way to fully reconcile the complex triumvirate of body, soul, and mind. Instead it has left us hunted, divided, with competing histories, values, and rationales that have been at odds with each other. (Makari, 2015, pp. xv–xvi)

A similar and at the same time unique ability to capture the complexity and still unsolved problems of psychoanalytic historiography is what characterizes the legacy of the historian of science John Forrester (1949–2015), as we can for example see in his book chapter "'A whole climate of opinion': Rewriting the history of psychoanalysis" (1994), in which he takes so seriously the challenge of (re)writing the history of psychoanalysis. Referring to the poet W.A. Auden's lines, here is the way in which he talks about such a challenge:

> If Auden's diagnosis is accurate, writing the history of psychoanalysis is rather like writing the history of twentieth-century cultural weather: its presence is so constant and pervasive that escaping its influence is out of the question. And precisely because of its inescapable character, it cannot be isolated from the myriad striking events that can be more straightforwardly singled out as part of the histories of science, of medicalization, of great ideas, of cultural movements, of modernization, of all the other movements to which it might apparently belong. Freud, it seems, is like electric light – the twentieth century is unthinkable without it, but not many histories of the twentieth century pause to evoke the customary and natural darkness of all previous generations. (Forrester, 1994, p. 174)

It is no wonder that Michel Foucault (1926–1984), the author of *Folie et déraison: Histoire de la folie à l'âge classique* (see Foucault, 1965), has so greatly influenced Forrester's work, as documented by the decision of Matt ffytche and Andreas Mayer to include his paper "Foucault, power-knowledge, and the individual" (Forrester, 2017a) in the issue of *Psychoanalysis and History* that they dedicated to him in 2017 (see also ffytche and Mayer, 2017). John himself was, as the successor of Andrea Sabbadini (1998–2003), the editor of *Psychoanalysis and History* between 2005 and 2014, and as a member of the editorial board I was in contact with him from the very beginning.

Matt ffytche, Forrester's successor as editor of the journal, and Andreas Mayers themselves celebrate him as such, and also include in the issue the reviews of his latest two books: *Thinking in cases*, published in 2016 and reviewed by Bonnie Evans (Evans, 2017), and *Freud in Cambridge*, written with Laura Cameron, published posthumously in 2017 and reviewed by Maud Ellmann (Ellmann, 2017). Also highly recommendable are the papers on Forrester written by Mayer, Darian Leader, and Dany Nobus, which constraints of space do not allow me to deal with. Instead, what I want to do is to go back to Forrester's 2000 paper, "Colleagues, correspondents and the institution—Or: Is a psychoanalysis without institutions possible?," which I started discussing in my Introduction to Part One. There I mentioned Forrester's answer to Jacques Derrida's (1930–2004) question of how an autobiographical writing can give rise, as in the case of Freud, to a worldwide institution, that is, "psychoanalysis is simply the acting-out of Freud's countertransference to his patients, his colleagues, his family and his culture" (Forrester, 2010; 2017b, p. 233). Here are some of the final considerations with which this precious, unfinished essay comes to an end:

> From the analyst's point of view, I am reminded of a dictum of François Perrier: an analyst without a colleague is a madman. I take this dictum in the strong sense: an analyst who does not have a colleague cannot be an analyst; instead he will be legitimately regarded as a madman. This formulation seems tailor-made to make sense of Freud's early development of psychoanalysis, and I have developed the idea by tracing in detail how Freud's writing to Fliess of the drafts of *The interpretation of dreams* functioned as a part of the auto-analytic process. Hence the notion of 'correspondent' in my title: Freud's correspondents are integral parts of the formation of the analytic scene, from Fliess to Jones, Abraham and Ferenczi. (Forrester, 2017b, p. 235)

This point of view applies directly to this anthology of my papers, not only in terms of the contents with which I deal, but even more so in terms of my relating myself to the reader in terms of a correspondent whom I let participate in my research process.

I now come to one of the last points of the research process connected to clarifying what I mean by "international psychoanalysis." I am referring to the further model of historical and sociological research on psychoanalysis that is represented by Dagmar Herzog's book *Cold War Freud. Psychoanalysis in an age of catastrophes* (2017), that is, to the way in which a multilingual and politically committed North American historian, using the method of participant observation, can so successfully combine history, sociology, and politics, using an approach of archival research and personal inquiry, and thus write such a unique and critical book on the history of psychoanalysis. This is how—given her ability to define her historical discourse in not only sociological and political, but also interpersonal terms— we find in the "Introduction" a picture of Marianna Bolko, Elvio Fachinelli, and Berthold Rothschild, co-organizers of the "counter-congress" held in Rome in July 1969, "hanging a poster critical of the IPA congress's program and professional priorities" (Herzog, 2017, p. 6).

But before dealing with that, let me briefly summarize the variety and international breadth of the themes of the book. Part 1, "Leaving the world outside," is positioned in the USA, Chapter 1 dealing with the postwar marginalization of sexuality from analytic discourse, and Chapter 2 with the homophobia accompanying it for many of the postwar years. Part 2, "Nazism's legacies," is located in both the USA and Germany; Chapter 3 deals with both post-Holocaust anti-Semitism and the ascent of the diagnosis of posttraumatic stress disorder; and Chapter 4 with the complicated process involved in returning psychoanalysis to cultural prestige in post-Nazi Germany, with particular regard to the role played in the process by Alexander Mitscherlich (1908–1982). Part 3, "Radical Freud," is situated in both Paris and Zurich, with Chapter 5 centered around a revisitation of the countercultural classic *Anti-Oedipus*, published in 1972 by philosopher Gilles Deleuze (1925–1995) and psychoanalyst Félix Guattari (1930–1992), and Chapter 6, with the title "Ethnopsychoanalysis in the era of decolonization," centered around the multiple legacy of Bolko's and Rothschild's training analyst Paul Parin (1916–2009). This pays particular regard to the ethnopsychoanalytic work he did in West Africa in the 1950s to 1970s with his wife Goldy Parin-Matthèy (1911–1997) and their colleague and friend Fritz Morgenthaler (1919–1984), and to the role they played in the foundation of the Psychoanalytic Seminar Zurich. Here is the way in which Dagmar Herzog introduces them to us at the very beginning of Chapter 6:

> In 1952, a trio of radical psychoanalysts, bound to each other by love, friendship, and shared curiosity, opened a joint practice in Switzerland: Paul Parin, Goldy Parin-Matthèy, and Fritz Morgenthaler . . . . Starting in 1954, the three, together with Fritz's wife Ruth, repeatedly left their practices and their patients in Zurich to embark on several-months-long journey to West Africa, becoming enthralled by the people and, eventually, undertaking anthropological fieldwork. Beginning in 1960, among the Dogon in Mali . . . the Parins and Morgenthaler first experimented with a combination of modified psychoanalytic and ethnographic methods to explore issues of the relationship between selfhood and society; a later trip also brought them to work among the Anyi in Ivory Coast. In these settings the three were developing a hybrid project which came to be called 'ethnopsychoanalysis', a project which they, both on their own initiative and then also in dialogue with their good acquaintance, the Romanian-French-American anthropologist George Devereux (the coiner of the term) are co-credited with him as founding . . . . There are many ways in which we could tell the story of this trio and its significance . . . . Parin, Parin-Matthèy, and Morgenthaler were central figures in a complicated process whose history has not yet been comprehensively written, but which might be described as a mutual rescue operation of psychoanalysis and politics, specifically a kind of independent moral Left politics emerging in Central Europe in the aftermath of Nazism. (Herzog, 2017, pp. 179, 180, 181, 182)

Still unknown in the British and North American analytic communities, Paul Parin was a central figure of postwar European psychoanalysis, and—among other things—André Haynal's training analyst (Haynal, 2017); the same is true for Fritz Morgenthaler, a pioneer of an open-minded approach to homosexuality, and one of the main European correspondents of Heinz Kohut (1913–1981). In other words, one of the aims of this original book is—as the author writes in the "Afterword"—"to redirect the conversation about the history of psychoanalysis and the political Left within the West" (Herzog, 2017, p. 216), inasmuch as the prevalence of what she calls "the American story" came "to occlude from view much work done elsewhere" (p. 216).

I am myself very thankful to Dagmar for having rescued from oblivion the central figure of Italian psychoanalysis Elvio Fachinelli (1928–1989), whom I have already introduced to the reader as the translator (together with his South Tirolean wife Herma Trettl) of Freud's *Interpretation of dreams*, and a training analys and of Cesare Musatti. Fachinelli (see also the Afterword) was born in a little village of the province of Trento by the name of Luserna, situated near Lavarone, where an old Bavarian dialect was still spoken; the reader can find more information in the biographical and scientific profile I wrote on him more than twenty years ago (Conci, 1996–1997). Fachinelli was also a very talented colleague, both in terms of his several contributions to contemporary psychoanalysis (including his last book, *La mente estatica*, 1989) and in terms of his social awareness and political commitment. Furthermore, having gone to elementary school in a suburb of Paris (where his family had migrated from Trento, after the financial crisis of 1929), he had had the chance to become a personal friend of Jacques Lacan (1901–1981), who would (as I learned from his widow in the mid-1990s) have liked him to have become his "Italian ambassador." Here is what Dagmar Herzog writes about Fachinelli in her book:

> Fachinelli, who died prematurely of cancer in 1989, was an extraordinarily creative and generous analyst, an important translator of Freud into Italian but also the first to bring Lacan's work to Italy, an activist on behalf of alternative preschool education, and, like Guattari or the Parins and Morgenthaler, and energetic and joyful utopian and anti-authoritarian. He called . . . 'for letting go of a kind of psychoanalysis which has the answers' (*'una psicoanalisi delle risposte'*) and for moving towards a psychoanalysis which questions (*'una psicoanalisi delle domande'*). (Herzog, 2017, p. 214)

Elvio Fachinelli, already an associate member of the SPI in 1969, stayed with the Society until his premature death, and Rothschild and Bolko did not join the IPA after completing their training at the Psychoanalytic Seminar Zurich—which left the IPA in the mid-1970s. Last but not least, among the positive consequences of the 1969 "counter-congress" inside the IPA was the creation of less hierarchical structures, including more space and rights being given to associate members and candidates.

At this point, I can eventually come to the last point of this Introduction, that is, the ways in which the International Federation of Psychoanalytic Societies (IFPS) and its journal, the *International Forum of Psychoanalysis*, founded in 1992, have contributed to the further development and intensification of international exchange and dialogue. But before I deal with this aspect, let me say a few words about the IFPS.

The IFPS was founded in Amsterdam in 1962 by several societies: the DPG, of which I became a member in 2002, represented by its president Werner Schwidder (1917–1970); the William Alanson White Society, represented by Gerard Chrzanowski (1913–2000); the Mexican Institute founded by Erich Fromm (1900–1980);

and the Austrian *Arbeitskreise*, represented by Igor Caruso (1914–1981). In other words, behind the foundation of the IFPS stood analytic societies and groups that had either lost their membership of the IPA (the DPG), had been denied membership of it (the White Society), or had never applied to it (the groups around Fromm and Caruso). Their common denominator was the need to create and belong to an international network, in order to guarantee their members the possibility of participating in the international analytic debate and exchange necessary for the creation and maintenance of an adequate and credible analytic identity (Chrzanowski, 1975).

During the first fifteen years of its life, the driving force of the IFPS was represented by the DPG, which was able to organize in Berlin in 1977 an international analytic conference with around 1,500 participants (Huppke, 2017), thirty years before the IPA was able to hold in Berlin its own biannual international congress. At the beginning of the 1980s, the DPG started reorienting itself in the direction of the IPA, thus beginning the long and very complex process that ended positively only in July 2009, in Chicago, with its readmission into it. I had the chance to talk at length about this process with Michael Ermann (DPG president 1987–1995) in an interview I published in the third monographic issue on "German themes in psychoanalysis" that I produced for the *International Forum of Psychoanalysis* (see Conci and Ermann, 2018). As a result, the DPG left the IFPS in 2010—even though only fewer than one-fourth of the members of the DPG were then also members of the IPA. But, in the meantime, the IFPS had been able to admit to membership a series of other analytic groups, including the Milan Associazione di Studi Psicoanalitici (ASP), founded by a group of pupils of Gaetano Benedetti (himself also a training analyst of the DPG) and Johannes Cremerius (a training analyst of the DPV) in 1987 (Corsi, 1990). From this point of view, a common denominator of the member societies was for their members to have gone through a training analysis at a frequency of three times a week—as well as their readiness to subscribe to a pluralistic, as opposed to just a Freudian, psychoanalysis.

I originally came in contact with the IFPS by participating in the International Forum held in Rio de Janeiro in October 1989—during which the ASP became a member society of the IFPS and about which I also talk in the Afterword. As I have already written (in the Introduction to Part One as well as in the Afterword), in August 1991 in Stockholm I won the Joseph Barnett

Candidates Award with a paper that was included in the very first issue of the *International Forum of Psychoanalysis*—represented by Chapter 1 of this anthology. At the 1994 IFPS Forum held in Florence, I was invited by the founding editor, Jan Stensson, to join the editorial board and to write a report about the Forum, a service that I have given ever since, every two years, for each of the following IFPS conferences: Athens, 1996; Madrid, 1998; New York, 2000; Oslo, 2002; Belo Horizonte, 2004; Rome, 2006; Santiago de Chile, 2008; Athens, 2010; Mexico City, 2012; Kaunas, 2014, and New York City, 2016.

The *International Forum of Psychoanalysis*, published since 2001 by Taylor and Francis, has since 2004 belonged to the ever-growing number of journals that can be downloaded via PEP-Web. Since June 2007 I have been the co-editor-in-chief of the journal (until September 2014 with Christer Sjödin, Stockholm, and since then with Grigoris Maniadakis, Athens). Since 2010, every one of the about 1,500 members of the Federation has had the right to freely download the journal from the publisher's website. In 2012, the IFPS decided to create a Section of Individual Members, whose first coordinator was Michael Ermann—until then the IFPS had consisted only of a series of member societies. In recent years, there have been more than 14,000 downloads annually, and I still enjoy spending much time and energy playing a major role in the journal's production.

I will describe here a series of five conferences and corresponding issues of the *International Forum of Psychoanalysis* that have centered around our firm determination to promote international exchange and dialogue, that is, to be true to our name. Let me start with the IXth IFPS Forum held in New York (at the Brooklyn Mariott Hotel) on 4–7 May, 2000, and specifically dedicated to the memory and legacy of Erich Fromm (1900–1980). We were able, in a double issue of the journal (Issue 3–4/2000), to publish a selection of the best papers given at the Forum, which I introduced in an Editorial with the title "Erich Fromm, a rediscovered legacy" (Conci, 2000a), and also mentioned in my report on the whole Forum published at the end of the issue itself (Conci, 2000b). I am still impressed by the high quality of the papers we were able to collate in that issue. I do not know of any better collection of papers centered around Fromm's work and legacy, and this is why I want to mention it here.

But here is a list of the papers themselves, which IFPS members and PEP subscribers can download from the journal's webpage. I have not included all of these in the References lest this section of the book become too long. Immediately after my Editorial comes Ernst Falzeder's translation into English of Fromm's very important 1935 paper "The social determinants of psychoanalytic therapy," in which Fromm presented the alternative, patient-centered approach to analytic therapy developed by Sándor Ferenczi. "Dealing with the unconscious in psychotherapeutic practice: Three lectures, 1959" is the following, long, paper published in English for the first time in this issue; it covered three lectures (already published in German, Italian, and Spanish) that had been given by Fromm at the White Institute in May 1959, edited by Rainer Funk (Fromm's literary executor, Tübingen). Also very interesting is the following paper, written by Funk himself (who had originally contacted Fromm in the early 1970s, when Fromm was living in Locarno, Switzerland), on "Erich Fromm's role in the foundation of IFPS: Evidence from the Erich Fromm Archives in Tübingen."

From Carola Mann, an important member of the White analytic community, comes the following paper: "Fromm's impact on interpersonal psychoanalysis: A well kept secret," dealing with the ways in which Fromm is much more present in the oral tradition than in the scientific production of the group in which he worked for many years as a training analyst and supervisor. This paper from New York is followed by two papers, one from Mexico City (Salvador Millán) and one from Bologna (Romano Biancoli), which deal with "The legacy of Fromm in Mexico" and the creation of an Italian "Fromm Institute." The two papers that come next are also very significant. First is Paul Roazen's (1936–2005) "Fromm's *Escape from freedom* and its standing today," the most downloaded paper of the whole issue, which deals with one of the most widely sold of Fromm's books. The article's final considerations read as follows:

> Outside North America Fromm's standing probably never rose as high as it did here, nor has it now fallen so low. But in general I think it remains true that Fromm today ranks as one of the neglected forefathers in the history of psychoanalysis. This current neglect is so even though *Escape from freedom* was initially "reviewed enthusiastically by such prominent public intellectual figures as Margaret Mead, Ashley Montagu, and Dwight Macdonald" . . . . It should not require ill-considered zealotry in behalf of Fromm to accord him the standing that he deserves. Of course there were inadequacies—political, social, as well as psychological—to how Fromm constructed

his point of view. But he did produce a structured way of looking at things, and that perspective once exerted an immensely influential impact. Fromm succeeded in changing the way people thought, and perhaps that helps account for why he was so well-hated. Perhaps a volume of Fromm's surviving letters would help awaken people nowadays to the genuine power of his mind. In any event, Fromm deserves recognition for what he managed to add to the body of work which consists in what psychoanalysis has amounted to. Celebrating his hundredth birthday might be a beginning to reestablishing his rightful position. (Roazen, 2000, p. 240)

The final words of sociologist Neil McLaughlin's paper "Revision from the margins: Fromm's contributions to psychoanalysis" represent a good conclusion to this topic:

Fromm, we have seen, played an important role in creating a dialogue between Marx and Freud, as did Reich earlier in the century. Furthermore, Fromm insisted on combining insights from German Weberian sociology and from the 19th century theorist Bachofen with Freudian thought, just as Harry Stack Sullivan played a crucial role in bringing American pragmatism into psychoanalytic debates. Fromm's multiple ties to Marxists, sociologists and numerous social critics and intellectuals allowed him to bring new ideas into the Freudian fold. In addition, Fromm's connections at the William Alanson White Institute, the Mexican Psychoanalytic Institute and the International Federation of Psychoanalytic Societies allowed him access to younger psychoanalysts interested in opening up the Freudian institutes to new approaches while keeping him relatively isolated from the institutional pressures of mainstream Freudian institutes (McLaughlin, 2000, p. 246)

In May 2008 Michael Ermann organized in Munich the yearly national congress of the DPG around the topic "Psychoanalysis and globalization." The main papers were published as a joint venture between the German journal *Forum der Psychoanalyse*, which Ermann (together with Jürgen Körner und Sven Olaf Hoffmann) had founded in 1985, and the *International Forum of Psychoanalysis*. Here is what Ermann wrote in his Editorial, "Psychoanalysis and globalization," published in Issue 4/2009 of the latter journal:

Psychoanalysis has over the last decades, in the context of globalization of science and scholarship, itself pushed and crossed the boundaries of its traditional frame of reference in Europe, North and South America. It is beginning to establish itself in countries such as Japan, China and the Arab countries. In these places it has encountered ideas of man and made experiences which are fundamentally different to those in the West. As a result globalization presents psychoanalysis with challenges which will not be overcome with traditional approaches. However, if it does rise to the challenges it will prepare the ground for new tasks and areas of study and grow with it. This will have an effect on how psychoanalysis will look in the twentieth century. It will grow in statue and secure its place within global society. (Ermann, 2009, p. 195)

Ermann's Editorial is followed by the paper "Psychic structure and identity in a globalizing world" by the then IPA president, the Brazilian colleague Cláudio Laks Eizirik (2005–2009), whose final comments read as follows:

> In this changing world, psychoanalysis responds to change with change. Not only are our different theoretical schools in full development, but we are also more than ever in a position in which we are able to work analytically in closer emotional contact with our patients, as well as more equipped to analyze patients with severe conditions.
>
> Simultaneously, we face the main challenges of analytic education acknowledging the existence of different methods of analytic education, and developing studies on how to obtain analytic competence. As for our relation with the outside world, we can see that, in each society, country or region, new and stimulating initiatives show that, after a period of a sort of "splendid isolation," psychoanalysis is again, as in Freud's time, in the forefront of the international struggle for the freedom of critical and independent thinking.
>
> At the same time, as I hope I have shown in this paper, psychoanalytic ideas are an important instrument to understand the current state of affairs of our culture, and in what ways it affects psychic structure and identity. As for our institutions, despite unavoidable tensions and crises that are germane to this kind of organization, in my view there is currently more transparency and the opportunity for more open and clear discussions on controversial issues. Our discipline is a work in progress, as we can witness in so many meetings like this one we are having now in Munich.
>
> In this sense we are tuned to our Zeitgeist. (Eizirik, 2009, p. 200)

Eizirik's paper is followed by a series of comments from Michael Ermann, in which he also expresses some preoccupation about the readmission of the DPG into the IPA, in terms of the risk of losing some aspects of its own tradition. Vamik Volkan also presented a paper in Munich, "Large-group identity, international relations and psychoanalysis," in which he showed how "large-group identities" can become the central force that influences international relationships, and how we as psychoanalysts can provide politicians with useful information about this phenomenon as a source of international tensions. Volkan's paper is followed by a series of comments formulated by Alf Gerlach, a German pioneer of the promotion of psychoanalysis in China, which is dealt with in the following paper by Anne-Marie Schlösser, "Oedipus in China: Can we export psychoanalysis?" Here is Schlösser's concise and illuminating answer:

> Can psychoanalysis be exported to China? Yes, it can. Yet it cannot be expected to be taken over—like a counterfeit—as an identical copy. There has to be a differentiation between

teaching about illness and teaching about treatment. Chinese
society will probably take over the theory of neurosis because
the psyche seems to work on ubiquitous principles. Yet it will
reshape the therapeutic techniques derived from this theory
so that they fit into the country's culture. (Schlösser, 2009, p.
224)

In October 2008, the IFPS met in Santiago de
Chile for its XVth Forum, with the title "Identity and
globalization. New challenges for psychoanalysis."
From this was published a selection of the best papers,
in Issue 2/2010 of the journal, which I introduced to
the reader in the Editorial "Global connections and
international contacts—Papers from the XVth Forum of
the International Federation of Psychoanalytic Societies."
Before presenting the papers we had selected for the
issue, I dealt, in the first part of the Editorial, with the
relationship between global connections and international
contacts, framing them as follows:

I believe that we live in a world . . . much more globalized than
really international. And this is also true for psychoanalysis,
and to such an extent that there should be room enough for
both organizations, the IFPS and the IPA, to work to utilize
the possibilities for connection offered by our globalized
world in terms of allowing psychoanalysts to experience the
enrichment of real, person-to-person, international contacts.
And this is not to mention the possibility – thanks too to
the globalized world we live in – of personally bringing
psychoanalysis to countries that are only now starting to
welcome it. Freud himself was a pioneer of the international
contact and dialogue I am talking about here . . . . Freud
himself was born and lived his whole life in a multilingual
world, and psychoanalysis itself was born out of this
experience. (Conci, 2010b, pp. 67–68)

I will now mention the first paper we selected,
which has become one of our most downloaded
papers—"Globalization and loss of identity" by Mexican
sociologist Maria Eugenia Sánchez—whose summary is
also worthwhile reproducing here:

I have tried to present a sociological landscape of the way in
which globalization dynamics and identities are interacting.
To be able to respond to this complex dynamic of identities
that are in constant decomposition and redefinition – in the
context of dramatic macro social transformations that are
taking place – is a great challenge for psychoanalysis. I think
that psychoanalysis, in any of its approaches, has to take
into consideration the new conditions of restriction, violence,
exclusion, and fear that human beings today are facing all
around the world. In addition, it is important to include the
concrete contexts of these subjects, subjects who are living
and processing the global impact in diverse forms. (Sánchez,
2010, p. 76)

This issue also contains one of the finest papers by
my Stockholm colleague Christer Sjödin, from whom I

learned so much in terms of the best way of working for the journal, that is, about what it should mean. Christer himself learned this from Jan Stensson, with whom he shared a Stockholm office for many years, and with whom I myself worked from 1994 to 2004. I believe that they would agree with the following formulation: as it should also be with our clinical work, our editorial work makes sense only if it represents for us—and for the colleagues we work with—an experience of professional and personal growth. Given such a perspective, here are the inspiring final considerations with which Christer concluded his paper:

> Let us hope that we will not enter a situation in which we lose our faith, our capacity to think and to feel because of our fear of a new Flood. To avoid that, we need to create new images, new metaphors, and new stories that will enable us to gain a direct intuitive understanding of the new global world. This time it is not God who is sending a great deluge to destroy disobedient mankind. Instead, we ourselves are responsible for the pollution of our beautiful planet. In such a situation, we need to be clear-minded in order to shoulder the guilt and be able to share our common responsibility for mother Earth. (Sjödin, 2010, p. 82)

In my own paper, "An advantage of globalization: Working with Italian patients abroad in their mother language," I presented the therapeutic work I did in Munich with three Italian patients. I also reformulated what I had stated in the Editorial in terms of how our patients, with our help, can transform the chance offered them by globalization into real psychological growth. Here is how I synthesized my work:

> If globalization has made the world smaller, we can, in the new context created by globalization itself, help our patients transform globalization into a new chance for growth and development, as opposed to a phenomenon that they only passively undergo and only makes them unnecessarily similar to other people. We can work with them in their own language, and help them both to elaborate their past and to integrate themselves better into their host society. With our help, they can thus heal the wounds of their old native self and, at the same time, keep developing the new self that has been made possible by the new environment they live in. In other words, globalization allows us as analysts to help our patients go beyond national boundaries not only materially, but also psychologically. We can thus really help them to become 'citizens of the world'. (Conci, 2010c, p. 108)

At the beginning of August 2013, after attending the IPA Congress held in Prague, during which Stefano Bolognini started his four-year term as president of the IPA, I went by bus from Prague to Příbor (Freiberg, in German) to attend the international symposium organized by Eva Papiasvili and chaired by Harald

Blum, whose title was "Psychological birth and infant development." Valerie Tate Angel, our Regional Editor for North America and a dear colleague whom I have known since the IFPS Stockholm conference of August 1991, not only told Christer Sjödin and me about it, but also proposed that we should give Eva Papiasvili and her New York colleague Linda Mayers the chance to act as guest editors of a monographic issue of the *International Forum of Psychoanalysis* centered around their selection of the papers given in Příbor. Christer and I thought this a good idea, which is why Valerie and I together wrote the Editorial "Evoking Freud's memory: Příbor," which we concluded we the following words:

> The editorial board of the *International Forum of Psychoanalysis* chose wisely in publishing these papers as this issue on Příbor fills in gaps regarding Freud's first three years of life. We encourage the reader to visit the town, which in its own right stands with Freud's other homes in Vienna and London, as a place that will greatly expand one's perception of Freud. (Tate Angel and Conci, 2015, p. 1)

In their "Introductory remarks by the issue editors: A story of beginnings and continuities," Papiasvili and Mayers emphasize the fact that, given its 140 symposium participants, we had all participated in the biggest analytic conference that had ever taken place in Freud's birth place. They also introduce the reader to the very good papers given at the symposium by a series of prominent authors: Stefano Bolognini (with his video opening address), Anni Bergman and Linda Mayers, Václav Buriánek, Martin Mahler, Otto Kernberg, and Harold Blum. The most downloaded papers of this issue have been Kernberg's paper "Neurobiological correlates of object relations theory: The relationship between neurobiological and psychodynamic development" and Blum's paper "Reconstructing Freud's prototype reconstruction."

The last conference I want to talk about took place in Nuremberg, on October 5th, 2014. This conference aimed to honor the memory of Herbert Rosenfeld (1910–1986), who had been born in Nuremberg and had studied medicine in Munich, before emigrating to London. There—as we know—he undertook his training analysis with Melanie Klein (1882–1960), which allowed him to later become one of her most internationally known and appreciated followers. I organized this conference together with Harald Kamm and Martin Ehl of the Nuremberg DPG Institute. With the support of Ingo Focke, the president of the DPG, we were able to invite to Nuremberg not only Rosenfeld's daughter Angela

Rosenfeld, but also the Milan colleague Franco De Masi and the Stuttgart colleague Claudia Frank, given the specific (albeit different) roles each had played in the reception of Rosenfeld's work in Italy and Germany, respectively.

Angela Rosenfeld (a group therapist in Sheffield, UK) was very happy to be invited to Nuremberg for the first time in her life by a local analytic institute, and showed us a series of pictures of her father, while telling us about the major events of his life, and celebrating his analytic legacy with us. This is what her touching paper "My father, Herbert Rosenfeld" is about, and we were able to publish this in the *International Forum of Psychoanalysis* together with twelve of the pictures from her talk. My wife Doris and I were also able to produce a German translation of this paper for the monographic issue of *Luzifer-Amor* dedicated to Herbert Rosenfeld, of which Harald Kamm and I were the guest editors (Conci and Kamm, 2015).

Even more interesting are the peculiarities of the reception of Rosenfeld's work in Germany and Italy, clearly showing the interaction that took place between Rosenfeld and the different contexts and analytic traditions he encountered. Claudia Frank emphasizes how Rosenfeld "transmitted a particularly 'experience-near' approach to the patient, which also acknowledged and took seriously (self) destructive elements in the transference and countertransference" (Frank, 2016, p. 229). Franco De Masi presents his legacy in terms of a new emphasis (new, for Rosenfeld himself, as a Kleinian analyst) on "the importance of the environment," on "the importance of the patient's history," on what De Masi calls "the use and abuse of phantasy," and—last but not least—in relation to the analytic relationship defined in terms of "a developmental process that is built with the contribution of both analyst and patient" (De Masi, 2016, p. 247).

In other words, I believe that we can say that, through the seminars and supervision groups that Rosenfeld held in Germany and Italy in the last years of his life, the German analytic community eventually became familiar with Melanie Klein's work, whereas the Italian analytic community started entering into its post-Kleinian (and later, more Bionian) phase. If I were to express this difference in a short formula, I could say that the different reception made of Rosenfeld in Germany "a classical Kleinian author," and in Italy "a relationally oriented Kleinian author," an apparently justified oxymoron. This is certainly what we can also gather also from the reconstruction of what he himself learned from Rosenfeld, which Franco Borgogno formulated in the article "Narcissism, psychic recognition, and affective validation: a homage to the 'later Rosenfeld,'" which he specifically wrote for the Special Issue 4/2016 of our journal that I am discussing here. In Borgogno's words:

> To conclude, I would repeat that in these pages, I have sought to describe a Rosenfeld who, in his later works, arrived at the same fundamental principles that can be found in Ferenczi's psychoanalytic thought: that is to say, at the emotional and affective validation that is the driving force and the catalyst of growth, as well as enriching the meaning and meaningfulness of the person in the human analytic encounter. For example, shortly before his death, Ferenczi (1932/1988) argued in his *Clinical diary* that what is fundamental in analysis is not a 'suggestion of contents', as unfortunately occurs continuously with regard to everything we say, even if we continue to deny that this is the case, but rather a 'suggestion of courage' so that the other may express his point of view or even access this viewpoint for the first time, thereby being able to gradually attain to and recognize his own subjectivization and subjectivity because somebody has already been so generous as to acknowledge them. (Borgogno, 2016, p. 254)

These "encouraging" words of Franco's now allow me also to say the following: what made the Nuremberg Conference of October 2014 even more interesting for me was the possibility to concretely experience the important "triangulating function" I was able to play as an Italian and, at the same time, a member of the DPG and of the German analytic community. Thanks to Salomon Resnik, Riccardo Steiner, and Andrea Sabbadini, I had known since the 1990s (see also the Afterword) that Herbert Rosenfeld had been born in Nuremberg, and when I came into contact with the Nuremberg DPG Institute and then became a member of it, I thought that my colleagues had undoubtedly already explored such a connection years before. When I discovered that this was not the case, I proposed that I would eventually do this, discovering also that it was apparently easier for me as an Italian to invite Angela Rosenfeld to Germany and for her to accept the invitation than it was for my German colleagues to do so; perhaps this was related to their (justifiable) guilt feelings that Rosenfeld—a German Jew and a member of one of the most prominent and wealthiest Jewish families of Nuremberg—had had to leave Germany against his will. This is for me a good example of how real "international collaboration" can help a national analytic community to overcome its limitations, be they blind spots or (un) justified anxieties.

Indeed, this principle is also the foundation underlying the so-called Nazareth Conferences. These originally brought together only German and Israeli colleagues, but later on also included other national groups, as described in the fascinating book published in 2009 by Shmuel Erlich, his wife Mira Erlich-Ginor and the Berlin colleague Hermann Beland. My colleague and friend Sandra Buechler reviewed it very positively in *Contemporary Psychoanalysis* (Buechler, 2011). Here are some of the introductory words written for their book by the first author:

> This book shows *the unique meaning and importance of the other* to one's own efforts to change. The bottom line of these conferences is a demonstration of how crucial *the actual presence of the other* is in producing the desirable changes in one's identity. This is all the more powerful when this other is not a 'neutral' presence but the one to whom one's identity relates. This cannot be emphasized too strongly. It is one of the major and most poignant contributions and outcomes of the conferences and of this book. (Erlich, 2009, p. 15; original emphasis)

A final word though before we move to the next section of this Introduction, "Psychoanalysis in Italy." There are several things that history and psychoanalysis, with particular regard to "international psychoanalysis," seem to have in common. They share, on the one hand, the concept of the multidetermination of events and fantasies, and, on the other, the necessity to distinguish between them. In addition, they have also in common the important function they can perform in helping us look at ourselves and get to know ourselves better.

1. PSYCHOANALYSIS IN ITALY

Of course, I do not mean to now write at too great a length about "psychoanalysis in Italy," but only to make sure that the reader is familiar enough with the topic to be able to enjoy the interview I conducted with Stefano Bolognini in the summer of 2005, which represents Chapter 11 of this anthology. On the other hand, I have already repeatedly dealt with this topic in the previous introductions and chapters, touching on a series of themes that I will now try to summarize.

Let me first, however, clarify the fact that I speak of "psychoanalysis in Italy," and not of "Italian psychoanalysis," in order to try to include in the topic not only the professional reception of psychoanalysis, but also its reception by Italian culture and society. Second, I do not think that we should limit the discourse to the old concept of the IPA groups as having a monopoly over the definition of psychoanalysis, as if it were a patent of exclusive property, but should also take other groups into consideration, including their contributions to the further development of psychoanalysis—not only as a profession, but also as a discourse, in the wider sense of the term.

But let me now try to summarize the Italian themes I have already touched upon, enriching them with more detail and accompanying them with quotations from the above-mentioned material by Arnaldo Novelletto (1992), Domenico Chianese (2011), Giuseppe Di Chiara (1985, 2016), and Anna Ferruta (2016). My main source of inspiration will not be the very detailed and long (above-mentioned) essay I wrote in German on this subject in 1996 (Conci, 1996), but the Editorial I wrote for the monographic issue of the *International Forum of Psychoanalysis* on "Italian themes in psychoanalysis— International dialogue and psychoanalytic identity," which I edited as Issue 2/2008 (Conci, 2008a) and is still worthwhile reading. In addition, the year 2005 saw the publication of Luca Di Donna's very well-written essay "Psychoanalysis in Italy: Its origins and evolution," which I will also take into account.

We have already seen how Edoardo Weiss was not only the first Italian psychoanalyst, but also the only one, to train in Vienna, having been born a citizen of the Austrian-Hungarian Empire and having studied medicine in Vienna. The only exception, in terms of having trained abroad, in Berlin, is Alessandra von Wolff-Stomersee, who moved to Palermo in 1932 on marrying with her husband Giuseppe Tomasi di Lampedusa, but started working there as a training analyst in 1946. I was able to confirm this from the biographical portrait published in the catalogue of the exhibition *L'Italia nella psicoanalisi – Italy in psychoanalysis*, prepared by Arnaldo Novelletto, Gianni Eugenio Viola, and Franca Rovigatti for the 36th IPA Congress held in Rome in the summer of 1989 (see pp. 133 and 135 in Novelletto, Viola, and Rovigatti, eds., 1989). We also saw the resistances against which the reception of psychoanalysis in Italy had to struggle, and the long time it took for many Italian people to understand where psychoanalysis had come from—as Michel David eloquently wrote in 1966.

These resistances were also partly responsible for the fact that, although the SPI had originally been founded in 1925 in Teramo (Abruzzi) under the presidency of the psychiatrist Marco Levi Bianchini (1875–1961), Weiss felt the need to found it again in Rome in 1932, eventually giving to it the analytic substance that it had lacked of up to then. Two years later, Weiss was able to participate with his Rome pupils and collaborators Emilio Servadio and Nicola Perrotti in the 13th IPA Congress, held in Swiss Lucerne (as also documented by an eloquent picture of them printed on p. 112 of the catalogue I have just mentioned). However, recognition of the SPI as a member society of the IPA came only two years later, at the following congress, held in the Czech Marienbad. The Fascist regime (1922–1943) had stopped the publication of the *Rivista di Psicoanalisi* in 1934, after only two volumes (1932 and 1933) had been produced; in addition, in 1938 Weiss was forced to emigrate and there was no more talk of psychoanalysis in Italy until the end of the war. But whereas Servadio emigrated to India, Perrotti and Musatti went underground.

What we have not yet dealt with is how slow the development of psychoanalysis in Italy was between the First and Second Congresses of the SPI, held in Rome in 1946 and 1950, and the Third, held in Venice in 1976. But in the meantime, Musatti had resurrected the *Rivista di Psicoanalisi* (1955), and a growing number of analytic authors were translated into Italian over many years. Furthermore, the IPA had held its first international congress in Rome in the summer of 1969, and the Italian edition of Freud's works was well under way. At the same time, it is true that in 1950 the SPI had about twenty members and candidates, but in 1976 the congress in Venice was attended by 230 members and candidates—as we can learn from Anna Ferruta's 2016 chapter "Themes and developments of psychoanalysis in Italy." But behind what Novelletto called "the long interval without national congresses," there were "tensions which were growing within the SPI" (Novelletto, 1992, p. 197), which he explained as follows:

> In fact, among the eight analysts, spread between Rome and Milan, who had been trained in the meantime by the IPA to carry out training analyses, dissension arose concerning the arrangement and evaluation of training. The situation went on like this until 1961: at the IPA congress held in Edinburgh, the executive council, under the presidency of W. Gillespie, appointed a commission composed of three Swiss analysts in order to solve the matter: R. de Saussure, F. Morgenthaler and P. Parin. The next year, the commission proposed a series of temporary standards, which later became permanent and let to a new society structure, as was sanctioned in the constitution and the regulations approved by the assembly of the members in 1974 and which is still in force. (Novelletto, 1992, p. 197)

But here is how Giuseppe Di Chiara, in 2016, reconstructs the same critical phase:

> Between 1950 and 1960 a great number of third generation analysts had reached maturity: these were pioneer students, young and middle-aged, who were highly motivated with excellent psychoanalytic competence. They read and studied not only Freud's works, but also papers by French, American, and English psychoanalysts; they were active and productive, while waiting impatiently to be trusted by their pioneer founders with the leadership of the society, mainly with reference to the transmission of psychoanalysis, that was essential if they were to become training and supervising analysts. In Milan, F. Fornari introduced group psychoanalysis and psychoanalysis of institutions, through the work of M. Klein. In Rome, Gaddini engaged in frequent correspondence with Winnicott, whose work he studied and extended. In Bologna, Carloni rediscovered Ferenczi's work and spread his ideas. From Palermo, Corrao became the first promotor of post-Kleinian authors, such as Racker, Meltzer, Rosenfeld, and, especially, W.R. Bion. A significant, widening gap opened between the number of training analysts running the training (and the Society) and those who were associate and full members. Because of this tension, the third SPI congress could not be held and a group of young analysts protested directly to the IPA leadership. (Di Chiara, 2016, pp. 12–13)

I have, of course, already dealt at length with, for example, the Italian reception of Bion's work, and Francesco Corrao's pioneering role in it. But what Di Chiara emphasizes in his chapter is how important Corrao's role also was from an institutional point of view, as the first SPI president of his generation (1969–1974), after the series of pioneers who had preceded him (Nicola Perrotti, 1946–1951; Cesare Musatti, 1951–1955 and 1959–1963; Alessandra Tomasi di Lampedusa, 1955–1959; and Emilio Servadio, 1963–1969), and before Franco Fornari (1974–1978), Eugenio Gaddini (1978–1982), Glauco Carloni (1982–1986), and Giovanni Hautmann (1986–1990). In fact, it was with Corrao as SPI president that the Italian Psychoanalytic Centers (Rome 1 and Rome 2, Milan, Bologna, Florence, Palermo, Naples, Venice, Genoa, Turin, and Padua) were founded. This aimed to counterbalance the power of the three training institutes (Rome 1, Rome 2, and Milan, the Veneto-Emilia Institute being founded only later) and the senior training analysts, and to allow all the members to more freely develop their scientific, cultural and social lives.

Of course, we have also seen how Gaetano Benedetti and his pupil and collaborator Pier Francesco Galli were able to get the open, progressive, and even left-oriented Milan publisher Giangiacomo Feltrinelli (1926–1972) to instigate a new book series devoted to the new field of psychology, psychiatry, and psychoanalysis. The first volume of this was Harry Stack Sullivan's *Conceptions of modern psychiatry*, which came out in 1961 with a still inspiring "Preface" by Gaetano Benedetti (Benedetti, 1961). This was followed not only by three more books by Sullivan during the 1960s, but also by, for example, the two books by Frieda Fromm-Reichmann—*Principles of intensive psychotherapy* (1950) and *Psychoanalysis and psychotherapy* (1959)—which were widely read by most psychiatrists and future analysts interested in doing good work with their patients. In 1969 Galli was also able to have Paolo Boringhieri publish the Italian edition of the Italian-American Silvano Arieti's (1914–1981) analytically oriented *The American handbook of psychiatry* (1959), which became the most widely read psychiatric handbook for several generations of Italian psychiatrists, including mine. It is my feeling that the exposure to the work of these authors influenced not only the interest of a large group of SPI colleagues in analytic psychotherapy with psychotic and borderline patients, but also the general orientation of vast sectors of the SPI in the direction of a specific interest in the analytic relationship, which was explicitly formulated by Eugenio Gaddini in the presidential address he gave at the Fourth SPI Congress, held in Taormina (Catania) in 1980 (Gaddini, 1980).

But before referring to the eloquent way in which Anna Ferruta takes up this theme in her above-mentioned chapter, let me say how Pier Francesco Galli, who had in 1967 founded the journal *Psicoterapia e Scienze Umane*, was able, strengthened by the professional success he was having as a consultant for both Feltrinelli and Boringhieri, to remain coherent to his original inspiration of cultivating psychoanalysis not as an institution, but as a critical discourse. The journal he has edited for many years with his wife Marianna Bolko and with Paolo Migone is still trying to promote this aim, not only through its international editorial board (which also includes Robert Holt, Morris Eagle, and Lawrence Friedman), but also its recent inclusion on PEP-Web, which Paolo Migone (for several years also co-chair of the famous Rapaport–Klein Study Group) was able to bring about. In fact, the relevant role played in the Italian psychoanalytic and psychotherapeutic landscape by this journal was also emphasized by Luca Di Donna in his 2005 article "Psychoanalysis in Italy: Its origins and evolution," in connection with the crucial role played in the Italian psychiatric landscape of the 1960s to1980s by the radical psychiatrist Franco Basaglia (1924–1980):

> With the impetus of Basaglia's work that stimulated both
> psychiatry and the social sciences, many analysts also realized
> that psychoanalytic training and ideology were restrictive and
> conservative. Pier Francesco Galli, an analyst and a critical
> thinker, founded a new magazine in 1967, *Psicoterapia e
> Scienze Umane* which challenged psychoanalytic institutions
> and training. Galli did not want to form a new institution but
> to open a new discourse. In this forum, such significant figures
> as Arieti, Benedetti from Switzerland, and Cremerius from
> Germany challenged institutions and prevailing ideas. Some
> of the best contributions were Cremerius's series of articles
> against training analysis and psychoanalytic technique. He
> believed that the spirit of Freud was completely lost both
> technically and theoretically. The magazine still maintains a
> rigorous intellectual following and has an English website.
> (Di Donna, 2005, pp. 40–41)

In fact, a new way of working in psychiatry was
created by the Italian Psychiatric Reform Law No.
180/1978, which closed the old psychiatric hospitals (the
manicomi) to new admissions, referring them instead to
special wards in the general hospitals. The major priority
of the law was to move the main part of the work, in terms
of financial resources, political support, and therapeutic
work, from the old psychiatric hospitals to a network of
mental health centers in the territory outside them. This
new way of working in psychiatry was an important and
influential experience for many colleagues over several
generations—including many SPI analysts. This is why
it represents not only one of the themes I deal with in my
interview with Stefano Bolognini (see Chapter 11), but
also one of the themes I talk about in the Afterword.

Having worked as a young psychiatrist in the context
of our post-reform psychiatry for several years, I still
believe that the closure of the old hospitals was a good
thing. However, the new way of working in the mental
health centers has turned out to be much more challenging
and complex than originally thought. There are certainly
also patients whom we can adequately cure only in a
hospital setting, which we in Italy lack—and which many
of us naively thought no longer to be necessary. The
significant extent to which this experience has influenced
Italian psychoanalysis allows Luca Di Donna to state
how "Italian psychoanalysis's understanding of psychotic
states may be one of its most articulated contributions,
because it infuses theoretical ideas into the complex areas
of community mental health, institutions, and group
processes" (Di Donna, 2005, p. 48).

Having known Cesare Musatti very well, Anna
Ferruta (whose husband Rodolfo Reichmann was
Musatti's biographer) centers the first section of the

above-mentioned chapter "Themes and developments
of psychoanalysis in Italy" around him and his work
as editor of the Italian edition of Freud's works. She
shows how it represented a common denominator and
point of reference of all Italian psychoanalysts, and how,
at the same time, it offered an easy access to Freud's
work to anyone curious about it—at variance with the
systematic work of censorship exercised for centuries
by the Catholic Church. In her second section, "The
question of language," Ferruta captures very well the
specific Italian phenomenon that I mentioned in Chapter
6 through the words of Adam Limentani (1989); I am
referring to his experience of meeting in Italy colleagues
who were more well read in psychoanalysis than his
London colleagues—due to the lack of an "Italian school
of psychoanalysis." On the one hand, Ferruta speaks of
the multilingual character of Italian psychoanalysis,
having its own pioneer analysts—as I wrote above, citing
Di Chiara—often translated a series of foreign authors.
She also comes to the conclusion that "from being an
obstacle, linguistic isolation has become an advantage: it
has favored receptivity and the wish to learn from others,
with no hesitation and no prejudice" (Ferruta, 2016, pp.
23–24). This is how the original multilingualism of Italian
psychoanalysis "is not only a historical feature, but a
specific theoretical element," allowing Italian analysts
to "accommodate several approaches to the unconscious
with sufficient accuracy and diversification" (p. 24).
Historically speaking, Anna Ferruta speaks of the above-
mentioned 1976 Third National Congress of the SPI, held
in Venice, as "offering a significant panorama of this path
of growth" and representing a kind of "acknowledgement
that Italian psychoanalysis finally belonged with full
rights to the international psychoanalytic community" (p.
25).

Luca Di Donna is even more generous in the
comparison between Italian and North American
psychoanalysis with which he opens the section of his
2005 article, entitled "1980s: The beginning of an Italian
Renaissance." In North American psychoanalysis, he
writes, "the relational point of view swiftly became
predominant . . . replacing the earlier dominance of ego
psychology" (Di Donna, 2005, p. 43), whereas no foreign
influence had ended up prevailing upon the others in
Italy. In his words:

> One psychoanalytic theory with a standard fixed technical
> model never dominated Italy. Instead, Italian psychoanalysis
> always kept in mind the interplay of the individual and

society. Leaning more toward the left, Italian analysts were strongly interested in Marx, philosophy and applied psychoanalysis. And, tangential to psychoanalysis, the work of Orlando, Lavaggetto, and Eco played an important role in Italian culture. These authors applied semiology and narrative in analyzing important psychoanalytic texts, expanding the concept of interpretation in psychoanalysis. A new formation of Italian analysts began challenging some of the classic views, and some of them began to follow the new American theoretical models. (Di Donna, 2005, p. 43)

In fact, the beginning of the "Italian Renaissance" that Di Donna talks about in his article can be well related to the above-mentioned Fourth Congress held in Taormina in 1980, in which the central role played by the concept of the "analytic relationship" in the Italian analytic discourse found a final confirmation in Eugenio Gaddini's presidential address. Anna Ferruta herself sees this concept as "the most significant of the transformations to emerge in the development of Italian psychoanalytic thought," coming to imply "a shift in focus to the work of the analytic couple" (Ferruta, 2016, p. 26), and she dedicates the third section of her chapter to this. Indeed, of all the "multilingual pioneers" mentioned above, Eugenio Gaddini was the only one "who spoke English well and who actively attended international congresses. For this reason . . . Gaddini was for a long time the only Italian author to be quoted abroad"—as Stefano Bolognini states in his answer to my question No. 10 (see Chapter 11). Of the several papers Gaddini published in the *International Journal of Psychoanalysis*, the most famous became his innovative paper of 1969 "On imitation," and in 1992 a selection of his papers came out in English with the title *A psychoanalytic theory of infantile experience: Conceptual and clinical reflections.*

Much less well known abroad at the time was the work of Franco Fornari (1921–1985), a training analysand of Musatti who introduced the work of Melanie Klein into Italy through the 1963 book *La vita affettiva originaria del bambino*, and who published many books in Italian, although only one in English, *The psychoanalysis of war* (1964). I mention him in the Afterword because, teaching at the University of Trento in the 1960s, he helped many sociology students become interested in psychoanalysis, although it was not until the late 1970s that I heard him give a brilliant paper at the University of Florence and discuss it with his Florentine pupil Graziella Magherini. Riccardo Steiner knew him very well, and this is why in the *International Review of Psychoanalysis* we can find the obituary Steiner wrote for him in 1986—and in the *International Journal* in 1989 the obituary Steiner wrote for Fornari's training analyst Cesare Musatti (Steiner, 1989b).

Shifting the analytic focus to the analytic couple at work, the transference itself "develops not only as repetition, but also as new experience at the heart of the relationship, which acquires its emotional specificity as an emotional event, and not only as an insight," writes Anna Ferruta (2016, p. 26). In this way, she introduces Franco Fornari's most important pupil, Luciana Nissim Momigliano (1919–1998). I wrote about her in Chapter 6, mentioning the invitation I received from her in June 1993 to visit her in her Milan office after I had been able to promote the Italian edition of Stephen Mitchell's 1988 book *Relational concepts in psychoanalysis. An integration*—and mentioning the review I wrote of her 1992 anthology *Continuity and change. Letters from Milan* (see Conci, 1995a). Stefano Bolognini remembers her as "a very individual figure, and a very lively person, with an incredible sensibility and capacity for communication" (see his answer to my question No. 12). A Jewish pediatrician, she had also been a resistance fighter, and as such she had been deported to Auschwitz, and had been able to survive the concentration camp, as had her close friend Primo Levi (1919–1987), the author of *Se questo é un uomo* (known in the USA as *Survival in Auschwitz;* see Levi, 1958).

Anna Ferruta describes as "hugely influential" Nissim Momigliano's 1984 paper "Two people talking in a room: An investigation into the analytic dialogue" (Nissim Momigliano, 2016), which represents the opening essay of the 1992 anthology that Nissim Momigliano edited with Andreina Robutti, *Shared experience: The psychoanalytic dialogue*. This important anthology also contains chapters written by Giuseppe Di Chiara, Antonino Ferro, Michele Bezoari, Francesco Barale, and Franco De Masi. In her 1984 paper, the author presents analytic work as "a 'two-way affair', at the centre of which is the double-helical dialogue of the analytic couple formed by the patient as 'best colleague', and by an analyst provided with reverie and respectful listening" (Ferruta, 2016, p. 27). Reviewing the 1992 anthology in *Psychoanalytic Books*, Donna Orange wrote:

> One could rename this book 'Psychoanalysis in a New Key'. It brings a lyrical Italian voice—one new to most American readers—to the understanding of the psychoanalytic process. As in Winnicott, the words are heavily Kleinian, but also as in Winnicott, the melody is new. (Orange, 1994, p. 118)

Before coming to the work of not only Ferro (Pavia)

and Bolognini (Bologna), but also De Masi (Milan), Borgogno (Turin), and the Rome colleague Vincenzo Bonaminio, an important institutional problem needs to be dealt with, that is, the foundation of the AIPsi by a group of former SPI members. Here is what Domenico Chianese (SPI president 2001–2005, after Di Chiara, 1993–1997, and Fausto Petrella, 1997–2001, and before Fernando Riolo, 2005–2009) wrote about this complicated chapter in the recent history of Italian psychoanalysis:

> Towards the end of the 1980s, a long period of crises hit the SPI: within these crises were intertwined moral questions, the personal vicissitudes of some analysts, and political vicissitudes. It was during this period that voices began to circulate about the morally grave behavior of a noted, elderly training analyst of the SPI. The conflict could not be solved within the SPI itself; in 1992, Joseph Sandler, president of the IPA, sent a committee let by Serge Lebovici to visit Italy. After a long inquiry, the training analyst accused of ethically incorrect behavior was expelled by the SPI. Servadio, Giannotti, Amati Mehler, Argentieri, Canestri, and others split away from the SPI and . . . went on to form another society, the AIPsi, which was officially recognized by the IPA. These were confused and dramatic years: a painful and bloody generational change, which was followed by a wide-scale movement of renewal let by Giuseppe Di Chiara . . . . From these crucial years emerged a more open, democratic society. The power of the training analysts was reduced. On a cultural level, there was a development and widening of horizons and an opening of exchanges with European and world-wide psychoanalysis through periodical conventions and other activities. (Chianese, 2011, p. 118)

As Jacqueline Amati Mehler and Giovanna Ambrosio report in their own chapter, the AIPsi was accepted as a provisional society in Amsterdam in 1993 (at the first IPA congress in which I participated; see the Afterword), and as a component society in Barcelona in 1997 (see Amati Mehler and Ambrosio, 2011, p. 122). An interesting fact behind the split is Emilio Servadio's participation in it: he was the closest collaborator of Edoardo Weiss, and the only Italian analyst besides Weiss to have published a paper in a foreign journal in the 1930s; the international exchange and dialogue that he always cultivated represent one of the main traits of the much smaller Association.

As Stefano Bolognini stated in his answer to my question No. 10, relating to Antonino Ferro and the translation of his books into English, with which I dealt in the Introduction to Part Three, "the change was so great as to almost bring about a reversal of the situation," a reversal in terms of the eventual beginning of the still ongoing process of translation of a growing number of Italian analytic papers and books into English and other languages. As we have seen, Ferro's work is rooted in the thinking of the late Bion, blended with the narrative approach of Corrao and the field perspective pioneered by the Barangers. In his IPA Chicago Congress keynote paper, "Transformations in dreaming and characters in the psychoanalytic field" (2009), also published in the anthology *Reading Italian psychoanalysis*, Ferro formulates the transition from a psychoanalysis of contents to a psychoanalysis that develops the apparatus for thinking. This is on the basis of a concept of the unconscious "in constant construction and transformation—as Anna Ferruta writes—an unconscious which must be dreamt (thoughts searching for a thinker) and which constantly and gradually expands itself as its being dreamt" (Ferruta, 2016, p. 30). But here is what Luca Di Donna wrote about him and his work in 2005:

> First and foremost a clinician, Ferro infuses his work with passion. Although rooted in his classical-to-the-extreme psychoanalytic culture, his theoretical ideas radically challenge many aspects of this classical position. His friend Barale has characterized him as 'a radical intersubjectivist'. Writing in a beautiful and clear manner with many allusions to art and literature, Ferro provides a new way of thinking. He is like a great chef with new ingredients and new recipes, who is not afraid to present a new dish. (Di Donna, 2005, p. 48)

Although Antonino Ferro is certainly a particularly gifted and creative person, I believe that it is important to look at his international success in terms of the described parabola that Italian psychoanalysis as a whole went through. Particularly relevant is the personal contact, exchange, and dialogue with a series of foreign colleagues that was established in the 1980s to 1990s, following Gaddini's example, by a series of Italian analysts of the following generation, after they had diligently assimilated most of the lessons of the best foreign pioneers of our field.

This is the hypothesis I have already formulated in the 2008 Editorial "Italian themes in psychoanalysis – International dialogue and psychoanalytic identity," as follows:

> After years spent reading foreign literature, foreign analysts started being invited to Italy, and a process of real discussion and exchange began to develop, an exchange that has gradually become a reciprocal process of mutual influence. This is what we can learn, for example, from Vincenzo Bonaminio's introduction to *The Freudian moment*, in which he presents Christopher Bollas as 'a part of Italian psychoanalysis' and as acknowledging that 'the Italian other is the receptive unconscious to which he speaks', a phenomenon depending on the fact that 'Italian psychoanalysis, though informed by many different schools

of analytic thought, has remained open, with an independent
mind'. In other words, having emancipated themselves from
their 'mother tongue', and having come in live contact with
the representatives of the various analytic traditions present
on the international scene, Italian colleagues were able to
develop a pluralistic psychoanalysis, and to do it right at
the time when, after the disappearance of the last pioneers
(the last being Anna Freud, who died in 1982), international
psychoanalysis eventually evolved in the same direction.
      But here is the crux of the story, in Bonaminio's words: 'I
first met Christopher Bollas in 1977. By invitation of Andreas
Giannakoulas, who, together with Adriano Giannotti
founded a Training Programme in Child and Adolescent
Psychoanalytic Psychotherapy inside the University of Rome
that has been running since 1976, a number of outstanding
psychoanalysts visited the Institute of Child Neuropsychiatry
to contribute their expertise to the clinical training of the
students. Among them, Paula Heimann, Frances Tustin,
Marion Milner, Adam Limentani, and Christopher Bollas
himself have left the most durable traces of their influence
on what has become *our clinical tradition* over the years'.
(Conci, 2008a, p. 67, original emphasis)

Today, following the above-reported orientations
of Ferruta and Di Donna, I could even say that Italian
psychoanalysis was pluralistic from the very beginning,
and thus reformulate my 2008 position as follows: its
original pluralistic and multilingual matrix allowed
Italian psychoanalysis to eventually become visible and
even to play an important role on the international stage,
once international psychoanalysis itself started moving in
the same direction, that is, the multilingual and pluralistic
direction which we Italians had been the pioneers of—for
many years only in terms of the books we read, but later
also in terms of a whole series of personal contacts.

Revisiting and reassessing the interview I conducted
with Stefano Bolognini in the summer of 2005, I can now
(at the end of July, 2018) say that one of its major threads
is the reconstruction of the way in which the close contacts
he established with international psychoanalysis allowed
him to revisit the concept of analytic empathy in such
an original way as to make an important contribution
to international psychoanalytic literature. In fact, in the
following years, by more closely getting to know not only
Antonino Ferro, but also Vincenzo Bonamino, Franco
Borgogno, and Franco De Masi, I was able to see how
all this had also been true in their case. In other words,
we see in all these authors such a good assimilation of a
foreign concept or tradition as to enable them to propose
an extension or reformulation of it; on the other hand,
we can also see such a reformulation as being rooted in
the pluralistic and multilingual background of Italian
psychoanalysis.

We have already seen how this is the case with Ferro's work. In the case of De Masi, I can for example say that I do not know of any other post-Kleinian author who values so greatly the contribution of Heinz Kohut as De Masi does in *The sadomasochistic perversion* (De Masi, 2003). With Borgogno, I can say that I do not know of any other author who has formulated such a new synthesis of the works of Paula Heimann (1899–1982), Bion, and Ferenczi (see, for example Borgogno, 2008). And in the case of Vincenzo Bonaminio, I can refer to the ways in which he assimilated and extended what in the above quotation he calls "our clinical tradition," as we can see in his many articles (see, for example, Bonaminio, 2008), and, last but not least, through the light that he was able to throw on the work of Bolognini, another important ingredient of our interview (see Chapter 11). Fortunately, Vincenzo's scientific direction is also the direction in which Antonino Ferro's successor as president of the SPI (2013–2017), Vincenzo's close colleague and friend Anna Maria Nicolò, has been working for many years (see Nicolò, 2016).

Last but not least, the interplay between Italian and international psychoanalysis is one of the major threads of the first edition of the *Italian Psychoanalytic Annual – Freud after all*, which I reviewed in 2008 in the above-mentioned issue of the *International Forum of Psychoanalysis* (Conci, 2008c). In this monographic issue, we published not only Stefano Bolognini's paper "Reconsidering narcissism from a contemporary, complex psychoanalytic view" (Bolognini, 2008) but also papers by Antonino Ferro and Giovanni Foresti, Giuseppe Civitarese and Giovanni Foresti, and Barbara Piovano.

2. PSYCHOANALYSIS IN GERMANY

As I have written in the Afterword, during the last weekend of May 1986 I participated in Zurich in my first international analytic conference, the conference *Institutionalisierung-Desinstitutionalisierung*, organized by the Psychoanalytic Seminar Zurich, the alternative psychoanalytic institution founded by, among others, Paul Parin at the end of the 1950s. The best English source of information about the Seminar, its later conflicts with, and its 1977 separation from the Swiss Society is the above-mentioned book by Dagmar Herzog *Cold War Freud. Psychoanalysis in an age of catastrophes* (2017). To the German-speaking reader I can recommend the monographic issue that the journal *Luzifer-Amor* produced about this particular and unique alternative analytic institution in 1993. The subsequent so-called International Network Conferences, the English translation of the German *"Internationale Vernetzungstagungen,"* whose history went back to the already mentioned Platform Group (see the chapter by Erika Danneberg in the 1995 anthology edited by Peter Kutter), took place in Milan (June 1988) and in Frankfurt (June 1989). At the 1986 conference, Robert Hinshelwood (whom I still remember meeting there for the first time) gave a paper with the title "Between the devil and the deep blue sea: Relations with the dominant class." This dealt with the "apolitical" tendencies in British psychoanalysis, and this became the source of the title of the conference proceedings, published in 1987 by the Psychoanalytic Seminar Zurich.

But the burning question circulating at these conferences did not concern alternative models of analytic training, but rather the elaboration of the Holocaust, a question that German colleagues were still so taken up by that they preferred to talk about it among themselves. Indeed, this burning question had been liberated from the repression it had been subjected to for more than thirty years only at the beginning of the 1980s, and it had exploded and eventually started being openly talked about only in connection with the IPA Congress held in Hamburg in the summer of 1985. It is in this context that I started becoming curious about and gradually more and more familiar with the complicated and very interesting history of German psychoanalysis, of which I then started becoming a "participant observer" through my migration to Munich in November 1997.

Already in the late 1980s I remember having had the feeling that German colleagues would not have been able to make it alone, that the elaboration of such a heavy burden could be carried through only (or at best) a process of triangulation involving the help of the international analytic community. This is also the feeling conveyed by Janice Haaken in her 1990 account of the above-mentioned 1989 conference, "The Siegfried Bernfeld Conference: Uncovering the psychoanalytic political unconscious," with particular regard to the way in which she reported the reactions to "Psychoanalysis without its past history," the paper given by the Jewish colleague Sammy Speier (1944–2003):

> Reactions to Speier's presentation were charged and surprisingly ambivalent. A Swiss psychoanalyst accused Speier of exaggerating the collaborative role of psychoanalysts, and persisted in his impassioned objections to Speier's arguments long after those on the panel, as well as other conference

participants, called for him to yield the microphone. Many participants felt that this response illustrated the very point that Speier and other presenters were making: that to critically face the truth about one's intellectual 'parents' brings unbearable anxiety and the necessity of defense.

In a more empathic and supportive tone, Emilio Modena, a psychoanalyst from Zurich, countered Speier's despairing conclusions rather than his historical discoveries. He spoke from the 'part-German, part-non-German middle European experience of non-Jews', and argued that there is still a notion of Germans seeing themselves as 'a special people' even in a critical review of history. For the Germans to see themselves as the worst of all peoples is not so distant from seeing themselves as the best of all peoples. He argued against Speier's claim that German fascism was *the* fascism and that the Holocaust was the end of critical psychoanalysis in Germany. Neither is true, he claimed.

Modena seemed to be suggesting that the unremitting, inconsolable grief and depression over the horrors of the Nazi era contain narcissistic defenses that must be recognized. He was expressing some criticism here toward the Germans and their preoccupation with the Nazi past.

Their history does make the Germans absorbed by their own destructive identifications with the past as well as being the inevitable objects of hostility—and sometimes displaced hostility—from other national groups. But it seemed that for many of the German analysts, holding onto the 'bad' was necessary if there was to be any integration of its meaning. The defensive tendency to 'get rid of it' continually worked against assimilation of the disturbing truths of the past. (Haaken, 1990, pp. 297–298)

In other words, only an adequate climate of international exchange can help colleagues involved in the elaboration of such a heavy burden, as with our German colleagues in this particular case, to constructively face their past, here their Nazi past. This is so true that, as we will see below, a crucial contribution to the removal of the repression concerning this heavy burden actually came from abroad, from the pioneering work of historical reconstruction of Jeffrey Cocks (1985), and from the rejection, by the IPA business meeting held in 1977 in Jerusalem, of the DPV's proposal to host the next IPA congress in Berlin. On the other hand, it is also true that, as we will see below, the IPA was for a long time not at all ready to help the German analytic community face and elaborate its Nazi past—and certainly not in 1949 in Zurich. But, as far as I am concerned, the final confirmation of my feeling came through the above-mentioned "Rosenfeld Conference," which I took the initiative of proposing to organize in Nuremberg in October 2014, inviting Rosenfeld's daughter Angela as the main speaker.

In the meantime, I had already edited the first of a

series of three monographic issues of the *International Forum of Psychoanalysis* on the topic "German themes in psychoanalysis." Issue 4/2013 contains the interview that, together with Ingrid Erhardt, I conducted in Munich on February 15, 2013, with Horst Kächele, represented by Chapter 12 of this anthology (Conci et al, 2013). As the reader will see, we also asked Kächele about the Holocaust, and its (ongoing) role in the relationships between the German and the international analytic communities. He told us, among the other things, that " it takes—and not only for German colleagues—a continuous exposure to international contacts to keep an international dialogue developing" (see his answer to our question No. 19). And this is precisely why I edited the three monographic issues. I will talk about them in this section, in order to help the reader better understand and profit from the interview with Horst Kächele.

But before doing this, I will try to summarize the history of psychoanalysis in Germany, taking as my point of reference the two chapters that Ludger Hermanns and Werner Bohleber published in 2011 in the above-mentioned anthology edited by Peter Loewenberg and Nellie Thompson, these chapters being "The history of psychoanalysis in Germany up to 1950 and its relationship to the IPA," and "The history of psychoanalysis in Germany since 1950." Last but not least, since Anne-Marie Sandler (1925–2018) had, at the time of writing, very recently died, I dedicate this section to her. She was the colleague who played the most important role in the "work of triangulation" that brought the DPG (of which I became a member in 2002) back into the IPA at the 2009 IPA Congress held in Chicago.

As I mentioned in the Introduction to Part One, the best historical source concerning the beginnings and first phase of development of psychoanalysis in Germany is represented by *The complete correspondence of Sigmund Freud and Karl Abraham 1907–1925*, edited in 2002 by Ernst Falzeder —whose German edition was put together by Falzeder and Hermanns in 2009. After coming into contact with psychoanalysis in Zurich through Bleuler and Jung, Karl Abraham (1877–1925) moved to Berlin at the end of 1907, where he soon became one of the first "full- time analysts" after Freud. He also began to gather around himself the group of colleagues that, in March 1910, constituted the first local branch of the newly founded IPA. In this initial phase, Karen Horney (1885–1952) was one of his most promising pupils.

The following important chapter of history is of course represented by the foundation of the Berlin Polyclinic and Institute, which took place in February 1920 as a result of a donation from Max Eitingon (1881–1943). Eitingon's crucial role in Berlin and in the IPA, up to the time of his 1934 emigration to Palestine and afterwards, clearly emerges in the regular correspondence he had with Freud—edited, as we have seen, in two volumes by Michael Schröter in 2004. As Ludger Hermanns suggests, this institution realized not only Freud's desire to see analytic training formalized in what later became known as the so-called "Eitingon model" (training analysis, supervisions, and theoretical courses), but also the hope Freud had expressed in Budapest in 1918 (Freud, 1919) of seeing his colleagues devise a form of analytic psychotherapy tailored to the needs of wider social strata. This is how the Berlin Institute and Polyclinic soon became both the most important analytic training center, training the pioneers of several analytic national traditions. Collaborating with Abraham and Eitingon were Hanns Sachs (1881–1947, the first professional training analyst) and Ernst Simmel (1882–1947, a socialist psychiatrist). Franz Alexander (1891–1964) was the first candidate to graduate from the Institute, and Otto Fenichel (1897–1946) and Wilhelm Reich (1897–1957) played a key role in candidates' clinical and theoretical training.

Whereas Abraham had been able to keep his growing group together, after his premature death Melanie Klein—having lost his protection—went to London, and at the beginning of the 1930s, Sándor Rado (1890–1972) and Alexander were invited to go to the USA as directors of the new institutes in Chicago and New York. In the meantime, only in Munich, Frankfurt, and Leipzig had small analytic groups started to operate, but it was only in Frankfurt that an institute had been founded; this was in 1930, with the involvement of Frieda Fromm-Reichmann, Erich Fromm, and Georg Groddeck, and with the support of the Frankfurt Institute of Social Research chaired by Max Horkheimer (1895–1973). After the first IPA congresses had taken place in Nuremberg (1910), Weimar (1911), Munich (1913), Berlin (1922), and Bad Homburg (1925), the last congress to take place in Germany for more than fifty years was held in Wiesbaden in 1932. There Sándor Ferenczi gave his innovative and controversial paper "Confusion of the tongues between the adults and the child – (The language of tenderness and of passion)," which was published in English only in 1949 (Ferenczi, 1949).

A much longer delay characterizes the precise reconstruction of the next phase of the history of psychoanalysis in Germany, that is, the phase coinciding with the Third Reich, 1933–1945. This delay concerns in the first place a reconstruction of the range of events leading to the exclusion of all Jewish members from the DPG (the German Psychoanalytic Society, the GPS, as the Berlin Psychoanalytic Society was called in 1926). The last twenty of these members (after the most famous ones had already left it in 1933–1934) were forced to resign during the membership meeting that took place in Berlin, in the presence of Ernest Jones, on December 1, 1935. Ludger Hermanns defines this as "the nadir of the GPS" (Hermanns, 2011, p. 52), and from him we learn that the GPS remained with fourteen members, the "Aryans" Felix Boehm (1881–1958) and Carl Müller-Braunschweig (1881–1958) having already supplanted the previous Jewish executive board members Eitingon, Simmel, and Fenichel some weeks before. At the same time, it is true that both Boehm and Müller-Braunschweig maintained their leading role over the group during the twelve years of the Third Reich, with the approval of both Freud and Jones, who were in fact "primarily interested in preserving psychoanalysis in Germany, even if Jews could no longer practice it" (Hermanns, 2011,p. 52).

This is how only a few months later, in April 1936, the Berlin Psychoanalytic Institute came to merge with other psychotherapy schools in the so-called "German Institute for Psychological Research and Psychotherapy," under the directorship of Marshal Göring's cousin, the psychiatrist Matthias Heinrich Göring (1879–1945). The leading analysts of the wartime DPG—besides Boehm and Müller-Braunschweig, Harald Schultz-Hencke (1892–1953), and Werner Kemper (1899–1975)—held at the beginning important positions at the so-called "Göring Institute," contributing to the development of what Hermanns calls "the new German study of the mind" (Hermanns, 2011, p. 53). After Freud had been forced to leave Vienna in June 1938, not only the Vienna Psychoanalytic Society, but also the DPG was forced to dissolve. For the next seven years, the DPG psychoanalysts led only "a shadow existence" (Hermanns, 2011, p. 54) as "Working Group A" of the Göring Institute, with Müller-Braunschweig being forbidden to teach and publish, and the majority of them concealing their clinical work and attempting to continue to do psychoanalysis as best they could. The darkest phase in the history of psychoanalysis in Germany came to the an end only with the country's capitulation on May

8, 1945.

But the very long process of elaboration of this dark chapter of German history came to the end only with the 2009 readmission of the DPG into the IPA. In other words, it took many years before the wounds suffered by the German analytic community during the Nazi regime could be opened and treated, and also before the problems connected with the pseudo-solution, the schismatic solution that resulted from the 1949 IPA Zurich Congress, could really be faced. In fact, it took not only many years to exactly understand how the schism in the German analytic community between the DPG (the Society) and the DPV (the Association) had come about, but also an even longer time to understand that such a schism had in no way represented the best possible solution for Germany—at variance with what many colleagues thought for many years. Given these premises, all I can do is try to tell you how I was able to reconstruct the dynamics of the schism, and its major consequences, for myself. But before doing this, let me give you my most important sources of information.

The merit for having pioneered the field of study of the history of psychiatry, psychotherapy, and psychoanalysis during the Third Reich goes to the American historian Geoffrey Cocks, whose 1975 dissertation *Psyche and swastika* was transformed in 1985 into the first edition of his book *Psychotherapy in the Third Reich: The Göring Institute* (Cocks, 1985). From his 1994 book chapter "German psychiatry, psychotherapy and psychoanalysis during the Nazi period: Historiographical reflections," we can gather how important his "triangulating role" was in terms of stimulating German historians, psychiatrists, and psychoanalysts to also start working on this taboo topic of their recent history. In fact, also in 1985, the DPG colleague Regine Lockot published the book *Erinnern und Durcharbeiten*, "Remembering and working-through," the first German reconstruction of the history of the Göring Institute. This came out together with the unique catalogue accompanying the exhibition *"Here life goes on in a most peculiar way . . ."—Psychoanalysis before and after 1933*, prepared by DPV candidates Karen Brecht, Volker Friedrich, Ludger Hermanns, Isidor Kaminer, and Dierk Juelich for the 1985 Hamburg Congress, of which it became one of the major "attractions." But only through her 1994 book *Die Reinigung der Psychoanalyse*, that is, "The purification of psychoanalysis," did Regine Lockot precisely reconstruct the premises, events, and consequences of the 1949 Zurich Congress.

Among the later revisitations of the 1949 schism and of its consequences for the German analytic community, I can mention Michael Ermann's book *Verstrickung und Einsicht. Nachdenken über die Psychoanalyse in Deutschland* (1996). In this, the former president of the DPG (1987–1995) reconstructs the evolution of postwar psychoanalysis in Germany in the light of the changes which he experienced with his society, and which he, at the same time, was able to bring about in it. *Death of a Jewish science. Psychoanalysis in the Third Reich*, by James Goggin and Eileen Brockman Goggin, was in 2001 the first book published in English on this specific topic, prompting me to review it (Conci, 2003) in the monographic issue of the *International Forum of Psychoanalysis* on "Psychoanalysis and the Third Reich" edited by Henry Zvi Lothane in 2003. An important contribution to the clarification of how difficult it was for the IPA to openly deal with the challenges posed by the new political situation in Berlin, Vienna, and Rome in the 1930s came in 2011 from Riccardo Steiner, in a paper in which he presented and commented on the complete correspondence exchanged by Freud and Jones in this regard (Steiner, 2011).

But here is my version of the events in and after the Zurich Congress. Although Carl Müller-Braunschweig and Harald Schultz-Hencke had worked together in the Göring Institute, they had two different concepts of psychoanalysis. Schultz-Hencke was already critical of Freud's libido theory in the 1920s, having gradually moved in a neo-Freudian direction similar to the one developed in the USA by Karen Horney. At the same time, Müller-Braunschweig and Schultz-Hencke of course also had two different personalities and, apparently, two different agendas for the future. Having stayed closer to Freudian orthodoxy, Müller-Braunschweig attacked Schultz-Hencke in front of the IPA international community meeting in Zurich. He did this by openly (and unexpectedly) criticizing the paper he had just presented, with the consequence that, after a rather controversial discussion in the business meeting, the majority of IPA members rejected the readmission of the DPG. into the IPA, stipulating that a future admission would depend on the DPG expelling Schulz-Hencke and reestablishing a proper Freudian training. Given Schulz-Hencke's prominence, the DPG did not comply with this stipulation, and its president, Müller-Braunschweig, left it. In June 1950, with a small group of colleagues, he founded the Deutsche Psychoanalytische Vereinigung (the DPV, referred to in English as the GPA), which was promptly recognized by the IPA at the following congress held in Amsterdam in 1951.

In this way, Müller-Braunschweig was able to have the IPA avoid the problem of dealing with how he and Schultz-Hencke had collaborated with the Nazi regime. In addition, by presenting himself as "the better German," he was able to have the IPA delegate to him the creation of a new member society, without which IPA psychoanalysis could not have again taken root in Germany. This is how the German analytic community came to be split between "the bad DPG" and the "good DPV," with the former pretending to have "saved" psychoanalysis through the Göring Institute, and the latter pretending to be the only representative in Germany of the "pure and genuine psychoanalysis" cultivated and guaranteed by the IPA. This polarized and problematic climate lasted for more than thirty years: only at the beginning of the 1980s did the history of all these events really begin to be written, debated, and elaborated. This was the new climate that also allowed the DPG, in the second half of the 1980s, to start reorienting itself and, after a long and complicated process of "conversion," be readmitted into the IPA.

But let me now go back to the above-mentioned chapter by Ludger Hermanns and show how many questions concerning the Zurich Congress and its consequences are still open, and how many interpretations of them still characterize the debate about it. Here are Hermanns' final considerations in this regard:

> Over the last 25 years, German psychoanalysts have conducted a passionate debate on how the schism . . . should be understood psychologically, politically, and in terms of group dynamics . . . . Was it merely a clever move by the old strategist Carl Müller-Braunschweig, who, after meticulously following the IPA Zurich's requirements, was immediately rewarded at the next congress in Amsterdam by having his newly founded GPA accepted? Did Müller-Braunschweig, as various interpreters have suspected (Beese, 1987; Dührssen, 1994; Lockot, 1995; Ermann, 1996), thereby avoid drawing attention to his opportunistic behavior during the Nazi period by shifting the IPA's focus to one of theoretical controversy and combating the revisionist tendency in Schultz-Hencke that Freud had already remarked on? Had a schism in fact occurred much earlier, with the dissolution of the original GPS and the emergence of a psychotherapeutic movement in the Third Reich? Could the founding of the GPA be seen as an attempt at repairing it (Eickhoff, 1995; Hermanns, 2008)? Was there an 'illusionary' pattern of group identity in the GPA's founding myth? (Hermanns, 2011, p. 57)

An important contribution not only to the clarification of this last question, but also to the reconstruction of how the IPA was eventually able to stimulate a crucial psychological conversion in DPV members, is represented by Hermann Beland's 1988 paper "How they know themselves: Confronting the past – A contribution to the history of the German Psychoanalytic Association," which Norbert Freedman included in the monographic issue on the 1985 IPA Hamburg Congress that he edited in 1988 for the journal *Psychoanalysis and Contemporary Thought*.

From this point of view, it is true that the Hamburg Congress represented the most important turning point in the whole debate, and, at the same time, the beginning of a wholly new phase in the life of the German analytic community. In other words, only at this point in time was the IPA eventually able to exercise the triangulating function that only an international body potentially has at its disposal. The consequence was that the German colleagues of the DPG and the DPV, no longer as rigidly identified with the roles of the "bad" and the "good" German, were able eventually to start to talk with each other. An immediate consequence of the Hamburg Congress was the initiative taken by Michael Ermann and Jürgen Körner (both DPG members) and Sven Olaf Hoffmann (a DPV member) to found a new journal, *Forum der Psychoanalyse*, through which to give shape to such a new dialogue. This is why I invited Michael Ermann to write a paper about this event and about the journal, which came out in Issue 2/2015, my second monographic issue on "German themes in psychoanalysis"; he entitled his contribution: "*Forum der Psychoanalyse*: A journal documenting the 'normalization' of the psychoanalytic field in Germany." Only in 1996 did the two societies come together in the context of a conference in which they eventually tried to work together on "The schism of the analytic community in Germany and its consequences"—a conference that was directed, according to the Tavistock model, by Ross Lazar (see Lazar, 2000). No wonder then that Hermann Beland begins the above-mentioned paper, which still deserves to be very carefully read, with the following premises:

> An important result of the Hamburg Congress was the opening it provided for a public discussion of the state of psychoanalysis in Germany. This created an entirely new situation. Now it could finally be said openly that the German colleagues as a group are implicated in the consequences of the annihilation of the Jews. How do they come to terms with their collective guilt, their unconscious expectation of retribution, their unconscious need for punishment? Is there such a thing as an encapsulated Nazi introject, and will it be released from its capsule in training analyses? Will the Germans

acknowledge those collective superego traditions that led to
their enthusiasm for Hitler and ultimately to the murders?
Will they find a transition from paranoid to depressive guilt?

Along with the distinct gain of the Hamburg
Congress—that of allowing these questions to reach the
public at last—group processes have also become clearer.
Germans as a group are becoming more and more conscious
of their tendency toward paranoid reactions. And, on the
non-German side, the tendency toward oversimplification,
leading to erroneous judgments, is also becoming clearer.
Open dialogue, then, serves clarification. A public
exposure of German conditions—of psychoanalysis in
Germany and of Germans in psychoanalysis—can be
helpful by functioning as interpretation, pointing out the
consequences of collective unconscious defense processes.

This paper is an attempt to interpret several group
processes at work in postwar German psychoanalysis as a
reaction to an unconscious awareness of Nazi crimes. Most of
the material by and large reflects the present state of debate
within the German Psychoanalytic Association (DPV) and
can serve as a source of information about the process of self-
examination. (Beland, 1988, pp. 267–268)

It is again no wonder that Beland entitles the
immediately following first section of this important
paper "Latency," referring to the long delay not only of
German society as a whole, but also of the DPV, to face
the Nazi crimes and to give up the defense against a mass
melancholia that Alexander (1908–1982) and Margarete
Mitscherlich (1917–2012) had diagnosed in their 1967
book *Die Unfähigkeit zu trauern;* this was translated into
English in 1975 as *The inability to mourn: Principles
of collective behavior* (Mitscherlich and Mitscherlich,
1975). On the other hand, as far as the DPV is concerned,
such a lack of awareness of a collective and personal
responsibility, and the corresponding, unconscious sense
of guilt, were—according to Beland—kept at bay by two
specific and peculiar events: the official recognition of the
DPV by the IPA, and the rapid expansion of the DPV.
This is in fact how the life of the DPV was accompanied
for decades by the "overt illusion to belong to the
persecuted," and also how "psychoanalysis allowed us to
escape from the burden of our national past, by means of
its existence" (Beland, 1988, pp. 271–272). As far as the
numbers involved in that rapid expansion are concerned,
in 1985 the DPV had approximately 600 members, 400
candidates, and twelve training institutes, an incredible
expansion that Beland also interprets in terms of a manic
defense mechanism (see Beland, 2011 pp.273–274).

Given this analysis of the myths and strategies of his
society, in the second part of the paper Beland examines
the initial stages of the conversion process we have been
talking about, starting with the IPA membership meeting

of the 1977 Jerusalem Congress, which took the decision to reject the DPV's proposal to hold the 1981 congress in Berlin. This sudden shock was to be elaborated through a series of institutional meetings (Bamberg, 1980; Cologne-Wiesbaden, 1983; Wiesbaden, 1984), whose details I cannot deal with here for lack of space, but which helped the analytic community of the DPV to start "to confront and resolve their collective problem: to become German psychoanalysts as well as psychoanalysts who are Germans with a German past" (Beland, 1988, p. 282).

Also very interesting is how Michael Ermann, in the nine chapters of the above-mentioned book (Ermann, 1996), dealt analytically with the crucial questions emerging from the even more complicated past of his own society, the DPG. In the first chapter, "*Der Selbstverlust der Psychotherapie und Psychoanalyse unter dem Nazionalsozialismus*" (The self-loss of psychotherapy and psychoanalysis under National Socialism; 1991), we learn how the members of the "Aryanized DPG," by compromising with the Nazi regime in order to save psychoanalysis, ended up losing their own analytic values, convictions, and identity. In the second chapter, "*Gründungsmythen und Spaltung in der Nachkriegs-Psychoanalyse*" (The foundation myths and the schism in postwar psychoanalysis; 1989), we learn how the schism was produced by the unconscious guilt feelings of the former members of the Göring Institute, with the consequence that the members of the old DPG would unconsciously identify with the "German persecutors," and the members of the new DPV would unconsciously identity—as we have seen above—with the "Jewish victims." This also brought about the split between "being German" and "being a psychoanalyst," which was solved only after the Hamburg Congress. As an aside, this also allows me to explicitly say why the title of this section is "Psychoanalysis in Germany" and not "German psychoanalysis," since "*eine deutsche Psychoanalyse*," that is, "a German psychoanalysis," a psychoanalysis without its Jewish members, and thus without Freud, is what the Göring Institute was about.

In the third chapter, "*Eine Krise der psychoanalytischen Identität und die Wahrmehmung der Vergangenheit*" (The crisis of the psychoanalytic identity and the perception of the past; 1986), we learn two things, first that the postwar DPG identified so closely and for so long with Schultz-Hencke's neo-analytic approach because of its identity-giving role. Second, starting only with the Freiburg DPG Congress of November 1983, did the false-self identity connected with such a legacy eventually became for the DPG at large a burden to be analyzed.

In the fourth chapter, *"Über Freud, die Vergangenheit der Psychoanalyse und ihre Gegenwart"* (On Freud, the past of psychoanalysis and its present; 1989), we witness an even deeper level of analysis of the postwar schism. This viewed the 1949 schism as the repetition of the schism created by the Göring Institute between a "German" and a "Jewish" psychoanalysis, with the postwar schism having to be seen as a defense mechanism shared by the whole German analytic community, which could (and can) be solved only by dealing with it together, as a community. Furthermore, having expelled its Jewish members, and consequently Freud himself, the German analytic community remained—according to Ermann— "pre-oedipally bound to Freud," with a consequent "paralysis of its creativity"; and he considers this "a reason for the absence of any substantial German contribution to psychoanalysis in the last fifty years" (Ermann, 1996, p. 66).

But with Chapter 5, *"Eine Begegnung in Deutschland"* (A meeting in Germany; 1991), eventually comes the turning point of this whole dramatic and highly instructive story. In this we witness the event of the Israeli colleague Rafael Moses—the first Israeli analyst ever to have been invited to a national congress of the DPG—deliver the paper *"Ein israelischer Psychoanalytiker spricht zur DPG"* (An Israeli analyst speaks to the DPG; 1991), and discuss it with Michel Ermann, as DPG president, at the yearly national congress of the society held in Hannover in 1990. Only at that point does it seem to have become definitely clear how the large wound in the DPG's identity consisted in having lost Freud as a "good internal object," including the consequence for DPG members of using psychoanalysis with their own patients, but not with themselves! In other words, this was one of the main turning points in the life of the DPG, which culminated in its being readmitted into the IPA in 2009.

Before coming back to this long and complex process, I will try to take up again and finish the bibliographic discourse I introduced above, talking about the monographic issue of *Psychoanalysis and Contemporary Thought* edited by Norbert Freedman. The issue closes with the paper by the then IPA president (1985–1989) Robert Wallerstein, "Psychoanalysis in Nazi Germany: Historical and psychoanalytic lessons" (Wallerstein,

1988). In this Wallerstein talks about his own experience of the congress and, at the same time, comments on the papers included in the issue. His final considerations are inspired by John Kafka's paper "On reestablishing contact" (2008), that is, by the considerations of one of the American colleagues who made this crucial topic one of his life tasks (having been born in Linz, Austria, in 1921; see also Kafka, 2016), and for this reason we can be very thankful to him. Here are Wallerstein's comments:

> What then can we all do at this juncture and what is the message of this whole volume? In answer, we can take part along with John Kafka in the painful but vital process of 'reestablishing contact with German psychoanalysts today', of avoiding the temptation in so doing to what he calls 'phony reconciliation' while pondering the haunting question that he closes with—'Would we [if we had been them] have been among the 'resistors?'—and ultimately of joining together with analysts in all countries—in Germany, in Israel, and everywhere else—in furthering the effort to understand, to comprehend, to endure, and thereby make it at least a little less likely that the horror of the Holocaust will ever happen again. As Freud (1927) said in *The Future of an Illusion*, 'The voice of the intellect is a soft one, but it does not rest till it has gained a hearing' (p.53). Can we help it prevail even against the most demonic in man? (Wallerstein, 2008, pp. 369–370)

Continuing this bibliographic excursion, I must mention the monographic issue on "Psychiatry, psychotherapy and psychoanalysis in the Third Reich" edited by Henry Zvi Lothane for the *Psychoanalytic Review* in 2001. In this he included papers by James Goggin and Eileen Brockman Goggin, Geoffrey Cocks, Edith Kurzweil, and Uwe Henrik Peters. The "Introduction" ends with the following words:

> Shouldn't we just forget all this Nazi hunting? It has its pitfalls, for historic interpretation is determined by one's identity, identifications, and, thus, loyalties. However, a historian should strive to be as impartial as Freud wanted a psychoanalyst to be. Shouldn't we then just dismiss the past and mind our daily business? I think not. I believe herein lies an important historical and moral lesson: We should forgive all those that erred but we should not forget. The Socratic ideal of the examined life is just as important for the history of individuals as it is for the history of organizations: Those who ignore their past are doomed to repeat it. Every persecution has its victims and its perpetrators. The latter and their heirs should welcome historical exploration because perpetrators are prone to the same disease as victims: chronic posttraumatic stress disorder.
>
> I wish to express my gratitude to all the contributors to this issue and pay special tribute to Dr. Bernd Nitzschke, who was my chief inspiration and who gave unstintingly of his time, knowledge, and support all along the way. (Lothane, 2001, p. 152)

In 1997, the Düsseldorf colleague Bernd Nitzschke had co-edited, with the Austrian historian of psychoanalysis Karl Fallend, a book centered around a revisitation of the case of Wilhelm Reich (Fallend and Nitzschke, eds., 1997), which centered around their connecting his 1934 formal exclusion from the IPA with how its executive committee reacted to the danger for the DPG of ceasing to exist under the Nazi regime. Given the importance of such a connection, Lothane had himself translated for the *Psychoanalytic Review* Nitzschke's 1999 article "Psychoanalysis during National Socialism—Present day consequences of a historical controversy in the 'case' of Wilhelm Reich," whose main topic he summarized as follows in 2001:

> Faced with the choice of either dissolving the German and Austrian psychoanalytic societies or dancing with the devil, Freud, his daughter Anna, and Jones chose to accommodate the demands of the Nazi regime (mediated in various ways by the German analysts Boehm and Müller-Braunschweig, members of the DPG) in the hope of saving psychoanalysis. Reich branded this situation as a disgrace and was kicked out as an undesirable. As noted by Nitzschke, after the war Anna Freud would concede that self-dissolution would have been the more honorable way, 'conceding that *before* the war she and others stubbornly fought against Wilhelm Reich who had been the lone representative of such a stand' (Nitzschke, 1999, p. 364). (Lothane, 2001, p. 146)

Last but not least, as guest editor of the monographic issue of the *International Forum of Psychoanalysis* entitled "Power politics and psychoanalysis," Issue 2–3/2003, Henry Zvi Lothane contextualized the German issues we have been dealing with from a more general, that is, international perspective. He included in this issue not only the moving paper "Wilhelm Reich and Anna Freud: His expulsion from psychoanalysis" by Lore Reich Rubin (Wilhelm Reich's youngest child, a medical doctor and psychoanalyst, born in Vienna in 1928), but also "Psychoanalysis in Austria after 1933–1934: History and historiography," by Johannes Reichmayr and Elke Mühlleitner, "Psychoanalysis in the Netherlands during World War II" by Harry Stroeken, "Psychoanalysis and psychotherapy in France between 1939 and 1945" by Alain de Mijolla, and "Émigré analysts in Boston, 1930–1940" by Sanford Gifford—as well as my above-mentioned review of the book by James and Eileen Goggin. In order to save some space, I will not put these articles in the References, and will only quote the author's final considerations:

> The "dirty" reality of power and power struggles were an important factor in the confrontations between Freud and others in the confrontations with Reich and Schultz-Hencke

and between the DPG and the DPV. As these contributions show, in these power confrontations there were neither one dimensional villains nor saints, nor a clear boundary between the bad guys and the good guys, between black cynics and lily-white idealists, but rather, the more mundane manifestations of shortsighted opportunism. Rather, we should be aware of the ever-recurrent and ubiquitous conflicts of interest and conflicts of ethics in the human condition: between right and might, power and powerlessness. The protagonists may have lacked full insight into their politics, whereas it is easier for us to understand these in hindsight. And this is the other reason why we should study history and its lessons. (Lothane, 2003, p. 96)

Of course, the main texts through which the German analytic community eventually started dealing with the Nazi past were published by the above-mentioned Frankfurt journal *Psyche – Zeitschrift für Psychoanalyse*, which I will now briefly deal with. With the help of PEP-Web, I was able, for example, to establish the fact that the turning point represented for the DPV by the IPA's 1977 refusal to meet in Berlin in 1981 was represented, for German society as a whole, by another challenge coming from abroad, the American film *"Holocaust – Die Geschichte der Familie Weiss."* The four parts of the film, directed by Marvin Chomsky, were shown on German television in the last week of January 1979 (nine months after its original transmission in the USA), and the film was apparently so effective in lifting the hard-to-overcome German amnesia relating to the facts of the Third Reich that the chief editor of *Psyche*, Helmut Dahmer, celebrated it as " a breach that needs to be expanded" (Dahmer, 1979, p. 1045). But only in the November 1982 issue of the journal can we find the paper by Hans-Martin Lohmann (1944–2014) and Lutz Rosenkötter (1925–2007) "Psychoanalyse im Hitlerdeutschland. Wie war es wirklich?" (see the References for the English translation), whose very first sentence reads as follows: "Almost forty years after the defeat of National Socialism, the history of psychoanalysis in Germany between 1933 and 1945 is still unwritten" (Lohmann and Rosenkötter, 1982, p. 961; my translation).

But an even bigger turning point was represented by the initiative of the journal's editorial board, in the person of chief editor Helmut Dahmer, to publish in the December 1983 issue Carl Müller-Braunschweig's short article "Psychoanalyse und Weltanschauung" (originally published in 1933; see Müller-Braunschweig, 1983). This was accompanied by not only a critical comment of Dahmer's, with the title "Kapitulation vor der 'Weltanschauung'" (Dahmer, 1983), but also an article by his son Hans Müller-Braunschweig (himself a psychoanalyst, 1926–2014), through which he had the chance to place his father's "collaboration with the Nazi regime" into a more general (and less critical) perspective (Müller-Braunschweig, 1983). Indeed, by rereading this today, we can see how, in this short article, Carl Müller-Braunschweig had tried to put psychoanalysis into the service of the Nazi Sate and ideology. In addition—and this is for me even more important—we can see how he had tried to contribute to the creation of a "German psychotherapy." In other words, the revisitation of this crucial episode is very important for the general scope of the long and complex discourse that I have proposed in this Introduction, inasmuch as it shows how only if we are able to maintain a series of international standards (as opposed to giving them up), can we keep the psychoanalytic discourse alive and remain true to it.

Of course, such a publication exploded as a bomb in those sectors of the DPV which had idealized their founder Carl Müller-Braunschweig, and which saw their analytic identity as circumscribed by the clinical work they did with their patients—as opposed to connecting it also to the need for a critical approach to our past, including our errors. In fact, we have here a bomb that does not ever seem to have stopped exploding, if we consider the fact that a journal of "applied psychoanalysis" specifically committed to the discussion of its historical, cultural, and social aspects, the Austrian journal *Werkblatt*, recently published a monographic issue dedicated to this topic, bearing the title "Noch einmal: Psychoanalyse unter Hitler" (see Fallend, 2017).

Last but not least, Hans-Martin Lohmann published in 1984 a first anthology of *Psyche* papers, on *Psychoanalyse und Nationalsozialismus*, in which he also included the epoch-making article by Kurt Eissler (1908–1999) "Die Ermordung von wievielen seiner Kinder muss ein Mensch symptomfrei ertragen können, um eine normale Konstitution zu haben?," an important paper (with a very eloquent and sad title that translates as "The killing of how many of his children must a human being tolerate without symptoms, in order to be of normal constitution?") of which I have not been able to find any English version on PEP-Web. This paper deals with the "little known feud" between American psychiatrists and German tribunals on the recognition of a right to financial compensation for the psychic traumas and wounds suffered by the survivors of Nazi concentration camps.

I bought Lohmann's anthology in Frankfurt during the conference organized by the Bernfeld-Gruppe, in order to start trying to understand what, for example, Sammy Speier was talking about in his above-mentioned paper. I am mentioning this aspect so the reader can even better understand how many years it took me to find out and formulate for myself the main aspects of the topic under discussion, which I have tried to present here at length, since it is still too little known of around the world. Indeed, after doing this work, I was even able— thanks to PEP-Web—to find a text by Speier similar to the one he had presented in Frankfurt in 1989, a text with a title that can be translated as "The psychoanalyst without face, psychoanalysis without history," which he had published in 1987 in the journal *Psyche – Zeitschrift für Psychoanalyse*. The summary of this article reads as follows:

> Auschwitz created a reality beyond imagination and verbalization. This reality requires a new focus on the boundaries of classical—strictly reconstructive— psychoanalysis. When we seek the truth in psychoanalytic treatment, we must consider external reality along with its inner representation. (Speier, 1987, p. 491)

Before coming to the last two topics of this section, that is, the "long march" of the DPG in the direction of the IPA, and the above-mentioned monographic issues on "German themes in psychoanalysis," I will give the reader some more background information on these by turning to the previously mentioned chapter by Werner Bohleber "The history of psychoanalysis in Germany since 1950" (Bohleber, 2011) and dealing with it in detail.

In the first section of this chapter, "The way back to the psychoanalysis of Sigmund Freud," Bohleber covers the 1950s and introduces us not only to Müller-Braunschweig's philosophical revisitation of Freud, but also to the anthropological perspective that he shared with Alexander Mitscherlich and with the Stuttgart analyst Felix Schottlaender (1892–1958), with whom the latter founded the journal *Psyche* in 1947. A crucial role in reestablishing psychoanalysis in West Germany was played in 1956 by the celebration of the 100th anniversary of Freud's birth that Mitscherlich was able to organize in Frankfurt, with Theodor Heuss (president of the Federal Republic) attending the key lecture given by Erik Erikson (1902–1994). The following weeks saw a series of lectures by émigré analysts such as René Spitz (1887– 1974), Michael Balint (1896–1970), Ludwig Binswanger (1881–1966), and Gustav Bally (1893–1966). At the end of the 1950s, the German publisher Gottfried Bermann Fischer became Freud's publisher in Germany—as Paolo Boringhieri had become in Italy—with Ilse Grubrich-Simitis in charge of this important enterprise.

In the second section, "The establishment and revival of psychoanalysis in the Federal Republic," Bohleber covers the 1960s, with particular regard to the establishment of the Frankfurt "Sigmund Freud Institute" in 1960, entirely funded by the State of Hessen. He also particularly considers the foundation of a series of DPV training institutes, starting with Hamburg in 1959, and followed by Giessen (1961), Freiburg (1966), Ulm (1967), Stuttgart-Tübingen (1971), and Munich (1973). In 1967 German health insurance started covering psychoanalytic psychotherapy, and analysts such as Horst-Eberhard Richter (1923–2011) and Johannes Cremerius were able to engage many university students in such a good analytic dialogue that several of them decided to undergo analytic training. Alexander Mitscherlich's 1963 book *Auf dem Weg zur vaterlosen Gesellschaft* (which I read as a university student; see Mitscherlich, 1963) "enjoyed enormous public success"—writes Werner Bohleber— "and, indeed, provided a plausible, comprehensible, and general explanation of the unresolved past in the debate within the Federal Republic" (Bohleber, 2011, pp. 69–70)

In the third section, "A scientific zenith: from natural scientific ego psychology to hermeneutic psychoanalysis," Bohleber deals with what I would call a "golden season" of the DPV. This golden season is basically still unknown to the international analytic community, given the fact that its protagonists, not having yet elaborated the trauma of the Nazi regime, dared hardly or not at all to translate their work into English and personally present it at international conferences. The case I know best (see the Afterword and the next section below, as well as Chapter 10) is that of Johannes Cremerius, as I had been a pupil of his in Milan and a personal friend of him and his wife Annemarie. He was very prolific and influential in Germany and Italy, but completely unknown abroad. The same is true of the above-mentioned Horst-Eberhard Richter, the concept of "scenic understanding" formulated by Hermann Argelander (1920–2004), and the concepts of "destruction of speech" and "forms of interaction" developed by Alfred Lorenzer (1922–2002). Possible exceptions to this disappointing aspect of their professional lives were represented by Wolfgang Loch (1915–1995) and Helmut Thomä (1921–2013). Rightly, Bohleber places all these contributions in the climate created by the best internationally known German professors of the time: the philosopher Hans Georg Gadamer (1900–2002) and the sociologist Jürgen Habermas (born 1929), and their works *Wahrheit und Methode* (Truth and method; 1960) and *Erkenntnis und Interesse* (Knowledge and human interests; 1968). Needless to say, for my own concept of psychoanalysis, it would not have made sense for me to introduce the reader to the works of all these important and neglected colleagues without having first presented— as I do here—the context in which they worked.

In the next two sections of Bohleber's chapter, "The return of the repressed: The debate on psychoanalysis during National Socialism" and "Ruptures in the formation of identity among German psychoanalysts," Bohleber covers the two crucial topics we have dealt with above. He also gives us the following useful explanation of the loss of confidence that abruptly shook the relationship between the younger generation and the first postwar generation of German teachers that I just introduced. As the reader can imagine, this group of analysts was so busy reimporting psychoanalysis from abroad, that is, reconstructing a normal and productive life for themselves and their families in a new democratic Germany, as was the case with all the other members of their generation, that they themselves did not have the time or desire to inquire into the conditions, of removal of the Nazi past, in which their task of reintroducing Freud's work in Germany had taken place. Here are Bohleber's words:

> During the 1980s, investigations by this young generation of analysts into the involvement of German society and their own parents under the National Socialist regime were carried over to the history of psychoanalysis. The repressed National Socialist past and its return in memory now overwhelmed the imagination of the younger generation of psychoanalysts. The experience of disappointment attaching to the silence of their teachers with respect to the way in which psychoanalysis had been compromised under the National Socialist regime also encompassed what their analytic fathers had built up and achieved psychoanalytically. Their scientific achievements then fell victim to a lack of esteem and were largely forgotten. The psychoanalysis they had learned from their fathers was no longer the 'undiminished' and 'undiluted' psychoanalysis of Sigmund Freud, but, rather, a teaching linked to the compromised psychoanalysis that had survived and had thus remained under the spell of National Socialism. (Bohleber, 2011, p. 77)

These words of Bohleber can better illuminate the particular tension, let us call it "the intergenerational tension," that characterized the above-mentioned Frankfurt conference of June 1989. It can also help explain, for example, the delay in the German reception of the work of Melanie Klein, who, at variance with the ego psychologists, was not particularly appreciated by Freud, and was even an antagonist of his daughter Anna. In fact, the same is probably true of the reception of both interpersonal and relational psychoanalysis, given their status as potential alternatives to the work of Freud, and to the image of Freud that our German colleagues needed to keep idealizing for a long time. This is in addition to the fact that, from the DPG's point of view, Schultz-Hencke's neo-Freudian orientation was burdensome enough for them to be willing to become familiar with foreign authors such as Sullivan—not to mention Fromm and Horney who, having had the good idea to emigrate, had not shared the destiny of their people, and thus did not even deserve so much credit. This is how, after dealing with the "Nazareth Conferences," which took place for the first time in 1994, under the auspices of the IPA, the DPV, and the DPG (see Erlich et al, 2009), and which allowed the two groups to eventually examine together their common history and the defense mechanisms connected to it, Werner Bohleber speaks of the great success of the 2007 IPA Congress eventually held in Berlin. He also talks of German psychoanalysis as "no longer obliged to conceal itself," given "its scientific achievements and high-level clinical standards" (Bohleber, 2011, p. 78).

As the reader can imagine, "The acceptance of the DPG into the IPA" represents the eighth and last section of Bohleber's chapter, coming before two sections that I have to renounce dealing with, but whose titles are "The conflict about high-frequency psychoanalysis in the public health care system" and "The establishment of psychoanalysis in the East German states." As we saw above, Rafael Moses was the first IPA analyst to attend one of the yearly national congresses of the DPG (Hannover, 1990) and "speak to the DPG" (see the title of his paper; Moses, 1991) about its relationship to Freudian psychoanalysis and to the IPA. On the other hand, it is true that, already in the second half of the 1980s, there had been an intensification of contact between several DPG members and groups and foreign training analysts (especially in London and Paris), with the organization of regular supervision groups, driven as DPG members were by their determination to overcome their clinical, scientific, and institutional isolation. The work on transference–countertransference in the here-and-now, the essential aspect of contemporary analytic training, had not been part of their training, since Schultz-Hencke's analytic approach neglected this fundamental dimension of our work. The IFPS, whose foundation in 1962 Werner Schwidder, as president of the DPG, had promoted, could not of course replace the IPA, nor was it ever used by the members of the DPG as a way to evade confronting the problem of the German past. The return of the DPG into the international community had to go through the IPA.

Last but not least, it is also true that what those members of the DPG who were the most motivated to go abroad for supervision missed the most was the high-frequency analytic work done, in the first place, in London, as this did not belong to their training, nor had it in fact, since 1993, been part of the therapeutic measures covered by the German Social Security System. In fact, since 1993 the German System has covered only three treatments sessions a week (and no longer four). The desire to do high-frequency analytic work is also what I felt when I moved to Munich in November 1997 (see the Afterword), this representing a still unmet need of my training in Milan (see below). This was one of my main motivations to work in the direction of becoming a member of the DPG (2002), and later (June 2010) of the IPA. But how was this need of the DPG met? The DPG had the great luck to find in Anne-Marie Sandler the London colleague who—after overcoming her own resistances—was able to accompany on this path all the DPG members who were interested in it. She did this, in the first place, through the yearly clinical-technical workshops that she conducted in Germany from 1991 onwards for over twenty-five years (see Wellendorf, 2007; Focke, 2010; Sandler, 2015).

In the personal and professional self-portrait that Anne-Marie Sandler published in German in 2015 (in the tenth volume of the book series *Psychoanalyse in Selbstdarstellungen*, which Ludger Hermanns had started editing in the early 1990s), she writes about how the original contact with the DPG was established. She also describes the resistance she had to overcome in herself, as a Jewish woman, in order to commit herself to such a challenging project and such a demanding task of bringing the DPG—as it turned out to be—back into the IPA. "Conflict and reconciliation" is the title that Anne-Marie Sandler gave to her *Selbstdarstellung*, that is, story with a happy end, which I will now summarize.

At the end of the 1980s, Sandler was a good friend of the DPV president, child analyst Lore Schacht; she told Sandler she had met Michael Ermann, who was ready to support the DPG's desire to come out of its isolation and move in the direction of the IPA, and that she believed that a series of papers given to the members of the DPG by prominent IPA analysts would help to accomplish such a project. Shortly afterward, her husband Joseph Sandler (1927–1998; IPA president, 1989–1993) received an invitation to Munich to a child psychoanalysis conference, and she gave in to his wish that she accompany him, even though at the time she did not particularly love either Germany or Bavaria. Alternatively, perhaps an unconscious desire to eventually overcome her irrational anxiety about dealing with an important part of her own family background and identity was what prompted her to accompany her husband to Munich. In fact, she had grown up as a bilingual Jewish girl in Geneva, and had then developed a very troubled relationship with the German-speaking part of herself. Whatever the truth, Anne-Marie Sandler remembered it as a very difficult trip, during which she did not feel well and spent much of her time in the hotel. But it was there, in Munich in 1990, that she met Michael Ermann, who invited her to the next DPG national congress, to be held in Bad Soden, a suburb of Frankfurt. This is also how the section of her self-portrait with the title "My conflict concerning Germany comes to the surface" ends, and a new section with the title "Bad Soden and its consequences" begins.

But before going into this, it may be important to also add the fact that Sandler's previous section starts with a dinner invitation in her home town of London that she received from Serge Lebovici (1915–2000; IPA president, 1973–1977). During the course of the evening, he told her that he could well understand why she, in Jerusalem, had been against accepting the DPV's too premature an invitation to Berlin; however, he was surprised that, so many years after the end of the war, she was still vehemently rejecting the idea of visiting Germany and speaking German. What more could one ask from life, if not the meeting between Anne-Marie Sandler needing to reconcile herself with German language and culture, and so many members of the DPG needing to learn from her what it means to work analytically at a higher frequency than they were used to? No wonder that the meeting in Bad Soden went so well that Anne-Marie Sandler's life became very closely associated with that of the DPG for years to come. In fact, the story does not end with her becoming—in Stuttgart, in 1997—an honorary member of the DPG; after the following section of her self-portrait dedicated to the illness and death of her husband Joe, it continues with three more sections, with the titles "The long way back home for the DPG," "The deepening of my relationship with the DPG," and "Reintegration: A parallel process."

In the section "The long way back home," we learn about the so-called "Exploratory Committee" set up by Otto Kernberg (IPA president, 1997–2001), after the majority of DPG members had expressed their support for the negotiations with the IPA conducted by the new president Jürgen Körner (1995–2001). Kernberg proposed to Anne-Marie Sandler that she should chair the Committee, and he had Inga Villarreal (Bogota), André Haynal (Geneva), and John Kafka (Washington DC), and later also Sverre Varvin (Oslo), join her in the work. Their task was, with the DPG, to formulate and find the best way to accomplish its readmission into the IPA. This work was carried out along with a group of representatives of the DPG—Jürgen Körner himself, Franz Wellendorf (who became Körner's successor in 2001), Ingo Focke (who became Wellendorf's successor in 2011), Ursula Kreuzer-Haustein (Göttingen), and Bernd Guttmann (Berlin).

The joint work of the two committees came to the following conclusions. First, every request for admission to the IPA from a DPG member should be evaluated through a one-and-a-half-hour interview conducted by three members of the Joint Committee. Second, it was decided to move in the direction of creating a two-track society, that is a society with two categories of members (DPG-IPA members on the one hand, and DPG members on the other), and two types of analytic training (a DPG-IPA training, and a DPG training). As far as the evaluation itself was concerned, it was agreed that the candidate would discuss with the Joint Committee an analytic treatment conducted for at least a year, four times a week—independently from the frequency of his or her own training analysis. To be even more specific, the main part of the evaluation session would consist (and still consists) of the careful discussion of the process notes of two recent consecutive sessions, whereas up until then the Joint Committee had had at its disposal only the short report submitted by the candidate about the first sessions with the patient and the further development of the treatment. A large first group of DPG members having positively concluded the evaluation process, twenty-seven DPG members became IPA members at the 2001 IPA Congress held in Nice, and the DPG was admitted into the IPA as "Provisional Society of the Council"—later "of the Board."

The evaluation process continued in the following

years to involve a growing number of DPG members, who became not only IPA members, but also (through a longer evaluation session) IPA training analysts, until "the crisis before the last hurdle" (as Ingo Focke called it; 2010, p. 1,200) came about. By this, he was referring to the need for the DPG to start offering the second type of training, that is, the DPG-IPA training that had been agreed upon years before, alongside the old DPG training. Only after the realization of such a condition was the IPA ready to readmit the DPG into the IPA as a component society. Many DPG members were, however, more interested in the DPG's membership in the IPA than in themselves becoming IPA members by undergoing the evaluation process—which some members felt as being a superfluous ritual. On the other hand, such a two-track model was something that was also new for the IPA, and it took some time for the DPG to convince them that this was the only reasonable solution. Once this last hurdle had also been solved, and once the DPG had satisfied all the necessary criteria, it was eventually readmitted into the IPA at the business meeting chaired in Chicago by Cláudio Eizirik (IPA president, 2009–2013) on July 31 2009. Today, nine years later at the time of writing, the DPG has 886 DPG members and 204 DPG-IPA members—and gave up its membership of the IFPS in 2010.

In the following section of Sandler's 2015 self-portrait, "The deepening of my relationship with the DPG," we learn about the form of the yearly "Sandler Conferences" of the DPG (on the Friday afternoon, discussing an analytic theme in the light of a classical article; on the Saturday morning and afternoon discussion of a treatment presented by a member and chaired by Mrs. Sandler; and on the Sunday morning, Anne-Marie Sandler presenting a sample of her own clinical work to members); we also hear how there were always more than eighty of the admitted members willing to attend these conferences. On the other hand, we can read the honest admission that she probably would not have committed herself so greatly to the DPG's cause had she not lost her husband Joe back in 1998. In the last section, "Reintegration: A parallel process," we eventually discover how much Anne-Marie Sandler learned through the whole process from her new "German colleagues," whom she was eventually able to experience as single individuals with whom she could constructively work and identify. The final result—which made her very happy—was of course a complete reconciliation with the German language, culture, and society.

As I have already said above, a similar purpose of

familiarization and reconciliation is also what lies behind the three monographic issues on "German themes in psychoanalysis" that I edited in 2013, 2015, and 2018. I will now, as briefly as possible, present these to the reader, having, I hope, supplied all the information necessary to appreciate both my project and its contents. Not surprisingly, I presented this project in the first Editorial I wrote about it (Conci, 2013), referring to Edith Kurzweil's book *The Freudians. A comparative perspective* as one of my sources of inspiration, as I did at the beginning of this Introduction.

After mentioning how successful the 2007 Berlin IPA Congress had been, I introduced the problem of the 1949 German schism at the Zurich Congress, and talked about my first contact with the German analytic community, at the Frankfurt conference organized in 1989 by the Bernfeld-Gruppe. In other words, in this first Editorial I introduced myself as a "participant observer of the German analytic scene," defining the aim of the monographic issue in terms of the "work of triangulation" that I felt was necessary, in order to familiarize the international analytic community with the major German analytic themes. In this context, I also mentioned the important work started by Shmuel Erlich, his wife Mira Erlich-Ginor, and Hermann Beland in 1994 with the Nazareth Conferences as a way to help primarily, but not exclusively, German colleagues to find a positive, dialogical, and constructive relationship with the international analytic community. Only at that point will it be easier for them to be proud of what "German psychoanalysis" has to offer, and capable of making use of the term "German psychoanalysis" without fear of being misunderstood as trying to go back to one of the ideals of the Nazi *Weltanschauung*. From this point of view, the aim of this and the two following monographic issues was, and also is, to present what I could call the particular "achievements of German psychoanalysis," that is, the areas in which our German colleagues have produced contributions that deserve to become more familiar to and be integrated by the international analytic community.

This is why I invited Werner Bohleber (Frankfurt) to give our readers a "historical overview" of the journal *Psyche – Zeitschrift für Psychoanalyse* (Bohleber, 2013), the only analytic journal in the world to come out one time a month, twelve times a year—and to be owned by a publishing house, Klett-Cotta (Stuttgart), rather than an analytic group. Since 1988 a member of the editorial board, Werner Bohleber became the editor of *Psyche* in 1997 and worked as such until the fall of 2017. As a second contribution to our issue, I was happy to publish Harry Stroeken's (Utrecht) article "The fate of German-Jewish psychoanalyst refugees in the Netherlands: An overview" (see Stroeken, 2013), centered around the biography of the six German-Jewish analysts who fled from Germany to the Netherlands in the 1930s: Waterman and Landauer, who died in a concentration camp; Levy-Suhl, who died shortly after the war; and Theodor Reik, Hans Keilson, and Hans Lampl, who lived in the USA and in the Netherlands for the rest of their lives. The history of the Holocaust is of course an integral part of the history of psychoanalysis in Germany.

In the third paper of this first monographic issue, Ulrike May (Berlin) presents a philological revisitation of Freud's Beyond the pleasure principle, showing readers the various stages of Freud's writing process (May, 2013). May's contribution is a unique paper and at the same time a specific product of the tradition of historical research in psychoanalysis developed in Germany in the last thirty years, which I particularly referred to in Part One of this anthology. The contribution after this comes from Hans-Jürgen Wirth (Giessen), another protagonist of the recent history of psychoanalysis in Germany, both because of his work in the field of a socially and politically critical psychoanalysis, as pioneered by his teacher Horst-Eberhard Richter, and as the founder and owner of the major German publishing house, Psychosozial-Verlag, committed exclusively to psychoanalysis and psychotherapy. His paper (Wirth, 2013) deals with the burning topic of the militant and the peaceful use of nuclear energy, which German Chancellor Angela Merkel's turned Germany's back on after Fukushima.

This is the point (of the journal) and the context in which the interview that Ingrid Erhardt and I conducted with Horst Kächele in February 2013, which now forms Chapter 12 of this anthology, was originally published. As Horst Kächele is one of the most internationally well-known German colleagues, I am happy to have had the chance of producing such a long, articulated (and fascinating) interview concerning both his life and his work. The Ulm School of empirical research, together with the three volumes produced by Helmut Thomä and Horst Kächele between 1985 and 2006 with the title *Psychoanalytic practice* (Thomä and Kächele, 1985–2006), represents one of the leading schools (and one of the leading handbooks of psychoanalysis) in the world, although (as Horst states in the interview) he does not like the word "school." Strangely enough, such a tradition is only hinted at and not adequately celebrated in Werner Bohleber's 2011 chapter on "The history of psychoanalysis in Germany since 1950." As an aside, Bohleber's wife, Marianne Leuzinger-Bohleber, is also an internationally well-known researcher in this field, to whom we for example owe the famous catamnestic study on the efficacy of high-frequency analytic therapy that the DPV commissioned to her to do (Leuzinger-Bohleber, Stuhr, Rüger, and Beutel, 2003) as one of its responses to the above-mentioned 1993 decision of the German Social Security System not to cover the cost of four sessions in a week. Horst Kächele's latest book is *Nodal points: Critical voices in contemporary psychotherapy/ psychoanalysis*, written together with the New York colleague Joseph Schachter (Schachter and Kächele, 2017). No wonder that I finished the Editorial expressing the wish for an anthology on "German psychoanalysis" similar to the above-mentioned anthology *Reading French psychoanalysis*. For how long will the term "German psychoanalysis" still be some kind of a taboo?

In my second Editorial (see Conci, 2015), in order to best introduce the papers through which I chose to further familiarize our readers with the specific themes of German psychoanalysis, I briefly dwelled upon the crucial historiographical work of both Geoffrey Cocks and Regine Lockot, whom I had not mentioned in the first Editorial. I then went on to illustrate the turning point in the history of psychoanalysis in Germany represented by the 1985 Hamburg Congress. As we have already seen, one of its consequences was the foundation of the journal *Forum der Psychoanalyse*, which I invited Michael Ermann to talk about in the opening article of the issue (Ermann, 2015). The Hamburg Congress also represented a crucial turning point in the life and professional career of the Israeli colleague Ilany Kogan, who delivered there the paper that she had written with Hillel Klein (who could not come to Hamburg) (Klein and Kogan, 1986). Kogan then rapidly became an important interlocutor of the German analytic community in the dialogue on the Holocaust and its clinical consequences. This problem gradually became more and more central to her own clinical work and scientific production (see, for example, Kogan, 2007), which I contributed to promoting in Germany (Conci, 2011). Her work in this field is what Ilany Kogan deals with in her article "From psychic holes to psychic representations" (Kogan, 2015), the second article of the issue.

A former director of the Institute of Psychoanalysis,

Psychotherapy and Psychosomatic Medicine at the University of Saarbrücken and a training analyst of the DPG, Siegfried Zepf is well known in Germany for having written a three-volume handbook of psychoanalysis (Zepf, 2006), and for his special passion for psychoanalytic theory. He demonstrates this in the following paper of the issue, on "Freud's concept of conversion" (Zepf, 2015). An even more active (and younger) protagonist of the scientific and professional debate on psychoanalysis and psychotherapy that has taken place in Germany over the last thirty years is Michael Buchholz (Göttingen). I have already mentioned Buchholz in Chapter 6 as having been the German colleague who invited Stephen Mitchell to Germany in September 1998, and who introduced the German edition of his book *Relationality* (see Buchholz, 2003). In 2008 I reviewed (Conci, 2008d) the intellectually very fascinating three-volume work whose title can be translated into English as "The unconscious – A project in three volumes," which Buchholz edited with Günter Gödde (Berlin) in 2005–2006. Through his article "Growth: What reconciliation of conflicts could mean. A lesson from the history of psychoanalysis" (Buchholz, 2015), we come into contact with his great passion for and knowledge of psychoanalysis—which he cultivates not only as a DPG training analyst, but also as a professor at the Berlin International Psychoanalytic University (IPU; see below) and an associate editor of the *International Forum of Psychoanalysis*.

No wonder that Michael Buchholz is also a co-author of the following article, "Countertransference as an object of empirical research?," together with Horst Kächele, Ingrid Erhardt, and Carolina Seybert (Kächele et al, 2015); this article centers around all the efforts aimed at devising a methodology to measure countertransference. The last article of this monographic issue is an important posthumous paper by Helmut Thomä, "Remarks on the first century of the International Psychoanalytical Association and a utopian vision of the future" (Thomä, 2015), written by the author directly in English for the *International Journal of Psychoanalysis*, which ended up not publishing it. The editorial board and I were proud to be able to publish this in our journal, especially given the fact that it actually contains Thomä's final legacy to the international analytic community.

In my third Editorial (Conci, 2018a), after having summarized the content of the two previous issues, I touched upon another area of excellence of psychoanalysis in Germany, which deserves to be better known abroad.

So too, of course, do the superlative level reached in Germany by both empirical and historical research in psychoanalysis, and the good tradition of a critical applied psychoanalysis originally introduced by Mitscherlich in Frankfurt. But here I am particularly referring to a Social Security System unique in the world, which still covers analytic psychotherapy of up to three times a week, and up to 300 sessions, which we can consider as being the realization of the above-mentioned hopes formulated by Freud at the 1918 IPA Budapest Congress (Freud, 1919). The international analytic community would be more familiar with this way of working, if we, at our conferences (both IPA and IFPS conferences), gave more room to small clinical working groups in which the participants could present not only the nature, but also the context of their analytic work, as opposed to spending too much time in plenary sessions passively listening to the papers of our best colleagues—that is, the colleagues we can more easily idealize.

On the other hand, all those German colleagues who cultivate the British ideal of an "open-ended psychoanalysis"—as for example Andrea Sabbadini (2014) talks about it—do not find it easy to be proud of this way of working. One of its further limitations is of course the inclusion in the analytic setting of the health insurance covering the treatment. Another possible limitation is represented by the fact the German model of financial coverage of analytic (and cognitive-behavioral) psychotherapy excludes lay analysts from such coverage, representing at the same time for medical doctors and psychologists such a secure source of income that they are—in my experience—less motivated than those abroad to work scientifically, or to write papers and publish books. On the other hand, it is true that, for every patient with whom we want to work analytically three times a week, we have to write a detailed clinical report to be approved by a senior colleague in the role of consultant to the health insurance. Given all these reports, more clinical papers coming from Germany should have been published in our journals, both in Germany and abroad, than actually seems to be the case. If this is true, we encounter again here the problem of the relationship between our German colleagues and the international analytic community, which I have been aiming to help present and clarify so far. This is of course also true for the interview with Horst Kächele, considering for example the fact that, given the way of working I just described, it is much easier to do empirical research in psychoanalysis in Germany than in the rest of the world. Indeed, this is one of the topics that Ingrid Erhardt and I discuss at length with him in the article published as Chapter 12, a discussion that he ends with the words, "For me, it is difficult to grasp the fact that there are still European countries without financial coverage of psychotherapy" (see his answer No. 12).

The analytic sessions covered by the German Social Security System still last—at variance with many countries in the world—for fifty minutes. From this point of view, the duration of our sessions is of more concern to the German Social Security System than to the IPA. In fact, there seems to be no general prescription from the IPA in this regard, and forty-five minutes seems to be the time span used by many colleagues throughout the world. This is also why the second contribution of this issue (coming after the interview I conducted with Michael Ermann; see below), which has the title "The concept of the 50-minute hour: Time forming a frame for the unconscious" (Will, 2018), not only well represents the clinical tradition developed by our German colleagues, but also could only have been written by a German colleague—that is, a German colleague as well up to date with the international literature as my Munich colleague and friend Herbert Will. A similar intention of showing and documenting the specificity of our way of working with analytic patients in Germany is also true of the third article of this third monographic issue, my article "Working with Italian patients in Munich – The case of Penelope" (Conci, 2018b), the modified version of the above-mentioned paper that I had presented at the 2009 IPA Chicago Congress. Unique in the world, the German system allows many foreign patients living and working in Germany to have the experience of going through an analytic therapy, which they would not be able to have in their native countries—or would not be able to pay for out of their own pockets. Some of them, like the Italian patient I deal with in my article, also have the chance to do this in their mother tongue—which also represents, given the difficulty of the German language, no small advantage of the German system.

As we have seen above, the Berlin Psychoanalytic Institute—founded in 1920 by Karl Abraham and financed by Max Eitingon—became the model for all subsequent analytic institutes as they were gradually founded in Vienna and Budapest, in London and Paris, in New York and Chicago. Max Eitingon has also given his name to a model of analytic training, the "Eitingon model" (consisting of training analysis, supervisions, and theoretical courses, with the training analysis taking place during the training itself and with a training analyst of the institute), which for years represented the IPA's only official model, and which still represents the one most used around the world. In her contribution to this monographic issue, Lili Gast (Berlin) presents the Berlin IPU as standing in this Berlin academic tradition, and being the realization of Freud's utopia of having the university teach and promote psychoanalysis (Gast, 2018). A private university, the IPU was established in 2009 through a very generous donation from Christa Rohde-Dachser, and thanks to the passion put into this important project by Jürgen Körner—an emeritus professor of social psychology at the Berlin *Freie Universität* and also past-president of the DPG. Rodhe-Dachser, the daughter of a famous German businessman, is not only a DPG training analyst, but was also the successor of Alexander Mitscherlich at the University of Frankfurt in 1987, where she taught until her retirement in 2003. The author of pioneering books on the borderline syndrome and on the psychoanalysis of femininity (Rohde-Dachser, 1979, 1991), she founded in 1994 the Frankfurt DPG Institute, which she chaired for ten years. The IPU was recognized by the German State in 2014, and in the academic year 2015/2016 it had 583 students and 112 scientific collaborators, fifty-nine of whom had a permanent appointment. The IPU offers several BA and MA programs both in German and in English, and has already become an important research center attended by highly motivated and intelligent students from around the world. These will hopefully grow into a new generation of researchers and analysts capable of promoting psychoanalysis in many different countries.

A very complex and fascinating contribution to the third monographic issue I edited is "Like a phoenix from the ashes – or 'sack cloth and ashes'? The reconstitution of psychoanalytic institutions in Germany since 1945 and its consequences," by Ross Lazar (1945–2017; Lazar, 2018). Ross Lazar died suddenly on July 23, 2017, from the cancer against which he had been struggling for the last couple of years of his life; I am very grateful that I was able to have him translate this article from the original German into his native English before he died, and then to provide the necessary editorial work. I have already spoken about him above, referring to him as the coordinator of the 1996 Conference held in Bavaria (Seeon, Chiemsee) organized directly by the DPV and the DPG, to—for the first time—look into their common past, and into the defenses put up by both bodies against the Nazi past and against their own guilt feelings about it. Last but not least, I speak of him as "Dr. L." in the Afterword.

The three major threads contained in this article are as follows. The first is the history of psychoanalysis in Germany, with particular regard to the events leading to the collaboration of the Aryanized DPG with the Göring Institute, the 1949 IPA Zurich Congress, the schism that took place after it, and the consequences of all these events on postwar psychoanalysis in Germany. The second thread is the tradition of the critique of analytic training and of psychoanalysis as an institution that is represented by the work of not only Paul Parin, Johannes Cremerius, and Otto Kernberg, but also Kenneth Eisold (see, for example, Eisold, 1994), and Douglas Kirsner (2009). Third ingredient is Lazar's own experience as group supervisor and institutional consultant to a whole series of analytic institutions in Germany and Austria. In this article—which can be seen as an important synthesis of Lazar's legacy to younger analytic generations—the author comes to the following conclusions: if we want to succeed in keeping psychoanalysis alive and well, we have to do our best in terms of the reorganization of our training programs, including the transformation of the so-called training analysis into a personal analysis, and the abolition of the training analyst status and its substitution by a group of competent analysts ready to apply themselves to playing such a function.

But who was Ross Lazar? A North American Jew, who grew up in a suburb of New York City, Ross Lazar graduated from Harvard University in the field of education and, at the beginning of the 1970s, went to London to do his analytic training at the Tavistock Institute. Here he worked in particular with Esther Bick (1902–1983) and Donald Meltzer (1922–2004), whose so-called "atelier model" (Meltzer, 1971) played a fundamental role in his supervisory and teaching activity. Lazar's German wife Gisela (they had married in the USA in 1969) was of course with him in London, where their two children were born, the family then moving to Munich (Gisela's home town) at the end of the 1970s. Here Ross Lazar worked for several years at the department of child psychiatry chaired by Jochen Storch, a pioneer of child psychoanalysis in Munich, before moving into full-time private practice in 1982. At the time, the work of both Klein and Bion was very little known in Germany, and Lazar played a crucial role (not only in Bavaria) in introducing their important analytic contributions. This is also true of the methodology of baby observation, and for the Tavistock model of analytic work with groups and institutions.

"Wilhelm Reich in Soviet Russia: Psychoanalysis, Marxism and the Stalinist reaction" is an original historical paper that we received from Galina Hristeva (Stuttgart) and Philip Bennett (USA) and which I put at the end of this third monographic issue (Hristeva and Bennett, 2018). I have known and valued the work of Galina Hristeva in the field of the history of psychoanalysis since I chaired the panel (at the 2011 IPA Congress held in Mexico City) at which she presented the paper that won the IPA Sacerdoti Award—the award financed by Cesare Sacerdoti, the Florentine Jewish publisher better known as the former owner of Karnac Books, London. Thanks to Hristeva's Bulgarian background and her knowledge of Russian, the paper includes, as an Appendix, her translation of the summary of both the lecture "Psychoanalysis as a natural science," held by Reich in Moscow in September 1929, and the five major responses it received, originally published in the journal of the Communist Academy. According to Hristeva and Bennett, in the negative reactions that Reich's paper received are planted the seeds of the negative concept of psychoanalysis originally formulated in the 1935 edition of the *Great Soviet Encyclopedia.* Furthermore, they also express the opinion that the report which Reich wrote of his trip to Russia for the journal *Die Psychoanalytische Bewegung* was so heavily biased in favor of Soviet Russia as to most probably represent the first step along the path leading to his expulsion from the IPA in 1934.

To the field of the history of psychoanalysis, which is so well represented in Germany, also belongs the last contribution in this issue, the review of Issue 2/2015 of the journal *Psychoanalyse – Texte zur Sozialforschung,* dedicated to the seventieth birthday of Bernd Nitzschke, whom the author of the review, Henry Zvi Lothane, defines as "one among Freud's oppositional heirs." Lothane's voice is also particularly valuable because he is one of the last New York Jewish colleagues I know who is fluent in German and can give an important contribution to the kind of international perspective that I have been trying to develop in this Introduction.

Last but not least, I do not want to leave unmentioned the fact that, at the beginning of the Editorial of Issue 1/2018, I also mentioned two recent North American books dealing with the same chapters of the history of psychoanalysis in Germany, whose publication I experience as confirmation of the growing interest in these topics. I am referring here to *Contemporary psychoanalysis and the legacy of the Third Reich. History, memory, tradition* by Emily Kuriloff (2014), and *History flows through us. Germany, the Holocaust, and the importance of empathy* edited by Roger Frie (2018), both books being written by colleagues of the William Alanson White analytic community.

This detail connected to the community of the White Institute and Society allows me to eventually end this long section by mentioning the following not irrelevant fact. The very first article in English "On psychoanalysis in the Third Reich," written by Rose Spiegel, came out in 1975 in the White analytic community's journal *Contemporary Psychoanalysis*. Here is what we can learn about the background of this pioneering article in Gerard Chrzanowski's 1997 obituary of Spiegel:

> After I graduated from training I lost contact with Rose until a good twenty years later. We both were busy, and it took until 1962 for our interests to begin to converge. That was the year of the first meeting of the International Federation of Psychoanalytic Societies, an organization that was being founded jointly by the White Institute, Fromm's Mexican institute, the reconstituted German analytic group, and a Vienna-based institute. Rose attended the first meeting and her indomitable curiosity soon extended to questioning the role of analysis in former Nazi Germany. How did analysts who did not have to leave Germany, but had to disavow Freud, manage to conduct analyses, when they were always under the potential scrutiny of an informer? Were such analyses indeed possible?
>
> Intrigued by these questions and by some wish to understand the effects of a fascist regime on psychoanalytic principles, Rose and I began to develop an outline for a book that would be based on interviews with German and Viennese analysts who had remained in Europe during the Hitler years. At some later point we were joined by Arthur Feiner, who was helpful in contributing—thanks to his wife's Hungarian background—an interview with a Hungarian analyst of the same period. The interviews were largely conducted by me, since I spoke German fluently; however, the interviews themselves, the questions that were asked, arose out of our collaboration and our wide-flung travels, which took us to various European countries where analysts had worked during and under the Nazi regime.
>
> Sadly to say—despite the reams of interview material—the book so far has not materialized . . . . We did publish some of our impressions, but the bulk of the work is still waiting, and it is sad that Rose will not see the results of our joint endeavor. (Chrzanowski, 1997, pp.177–178)

What I aim to say through this connection is that, in the 1960s and 1970s, the IFPS, at variance with the IPA, was apparently a group in which the topic of Rose Spiegel's pioneering article could more openly be dealt with. From this point of view, I can even dare to formulate the hypothesis that Michael Ermann himself profited from the IFPS in terms of the international contacts he was able to make there, and that these contacts helped him eventually face the challenge of reelaborating the German past, and elaborating the strategy that allowed him to bring the DPG back into the IPA. If this is true, this would, again, make a good case for international analytic dialogue and collaboration. If there had been more exchange and dialogue about the topic of psychoanalysis during the Third Reich in the IPA, I doubt that the German DPV colleagues would have felt so surprised and offended to see the IPA, in Jerusalem in 1977, refuse their proposal to meet in Berlin in 1981.

What is certainly true is that Michael Ermann not only succeeded (with the help, of course, of his successors Körner, Wellendorf, Focke, and Grabska) in the operation of bringing the DPG back into the IPA, but was also active in the IFPS for almost thirty-five years—for this long time he was in fact a member of the IFPS executive committee, having resigned from it only in New York in May 2016. This is one of the central topics of the interview I conducted with him by email between October 2013 and February 2017, which was published in my third monographic issue on "German themes in psychoanalysis" (Conci and Ermann, 2018) directly after the Editorial. From this point of view, Michael Ermann represented and still represents for me a very important model and source of inspiration, especially as my own professional life has developed in the same directions. After meeting him at the IFPS Conference held in Stockholm in August 1991, at which I presented the paper included in this anthology as Chapter 1, I had the chance (as I talk about in more detail in the Afterword) to work for two years as a guest professor at the Department of Psychosomatic Medicine and Psychotherapy of the University of Munich, which he chaired; this allowed me, in the spring of 1999, to start working in Munich as a *kassenärztlicher Psychoanalityker*. With Michael Ermann's support, I became in 2002 a DPG member, in June 2007 a co-editor-in-chief of the *International Forum of Psychoanalysis*, and in June 2010 a member of the IPA. Among Michael's legacies to the IFPS are: the IFPS journal, founded by Jan Stennson in 1992, but which Michael himself convincingly supported, the IFPS Archives (originally started by Carlo Bonomi, and now chaired by Klaus Hoffmann), and the IFPS Individual Members Section (approved in Mexico City in 2012). And this was in addition to his regular contribution

to the organization of all the IFPS congresses, starting
with the IFPS Forum held in Zurich in 1985. As I wrote
in my "Short introduction" to the interview:

> I believe we share what I would call 'the common passion
> for international psychoanalysis', that is, for the international
> dialogue and exchange we can develop as individuals and
> colleagues, thus bridging a whole series of linguistic and
> cultural barriers, and this independently of the nature of the
> medium in which it takes place – a fancier one like the IPA,
> or a more simply furnished one like the IFPS. To illustrate
> this with a musical metaphor, it is not only a big symphony
> orchestra that can produce good music, but also a little band
> or choir – and we feel good about and are happy to join both
> groups. (Conci and Ermann, 2018, p. 5)

3. THE INDIVIDUAL CHAPTERS

I am happy to have been able to give so much room to the
topics of "Psychoanalysis in Italy" and "Psychoanalysis in
Germany," that is, to the contexts in which my interviews
with Stefano Bolognini (see Chapter 11) and Horst
Kächele (see Chapter 12) belong, because of the general
lack of information about these topics. The same is true
for what I have called "international psychoanalysis,"
presenting it as the context within which the two topics
just mentioned belong. As we have seen, it is not possible
to understand the evolution and development of either
psychoanalysis in Italy or psychoanalysis in Germany
without having a precise idea of how they interacted
with the international context in which they were, and
indeed are, embedded. Having been able to develop these
themes at the necessary length, I can at this point limit
myself to introducing the reader to Chapter 10, "Gaetano
Benedetti, Johannes Cremerius, the Milan ASP, and the
future of IFPS"—which I had published as a paper in the
International Forum of Psychoanalysis in 2014.

In the meantime, Gaetano Benedetti died, on
December 3, 2013, in Bâle, and I participated in his
funeral, together with a large group of Italian and
Swiss pupils and collaborators. With Brian Koehler and
Maurizio Peciccia, I wrote an obituary for the journal
Psychosis, the journal of the International Society for
the Psychotherapy of Schizophrenia (ISPS), celebrating
his role as pioneer of the psychotherapy of schizophrenia
and, together with Christian Müller (1921–2013), founder
of the ISPS in 1956 (Conci, Koehler, and Peciccia, 2014).
Since his death I have not yet had the chance to go on
with the work of cataloging and reconstructing his
correspondence, upon which I based the article "Gaetano
Benedetti in his correspondence" published in 2008 in the

above-mentioned monographic issue on "Italian themes in psychoanalysis" (Conci, 2008b). However, I mean to do this as soon as possible, partly because his letters, even the simplest ones, are so well written and inspiring, and partly because of the many languages in which the letters are written, that is, the international character of the network that he contributed to creating.

In Chapter 10, however, the reader will find all the information necessary to understand Benedetti's life and work, and his fundamental contribution to the constitution, in the early 1970s, of the group of colleagues who in the early 1980s founded the Milan Scuola di Psicoterapia Psicoanaltica (SPP), and in 1987 (see Corsi, 1990) the Milan ASP. The same is true for the life, work and main contributions of Johannes Cremerius, which I would also like the English-speaking readers of this anthology to eventually become more familiar with. As I have already written, talking about the "golden age" of psychoanalysis in Germany, Cremerius belongs to the generation of German analysts to whom we owe important and original contributions that they themselves had not been able (or did not dare) to present to the English-speaking members of our analytic community. From this point of view, I would certainly like to find the time to help promote the knowledge of Cremerius's work in the English-speaking world, and this is also why I decided to include in this anthology the 2014 article—the revised version of a paper I had given in Mexico City in October 2012, at a panel celebrating the fiftieth anniversary of the foundation of IFPS. This deficit is partially true also for Benedetti, more well-known internationally than Cremerius, but who was also not able to publish more than one book in English – *Psychotherapy of schizophrenia* (Benedetti, 1987).

The second central theme of Chapter 10 is the alternative model of training which Benedetti and Cremerius were able to realize through the SPP, and which I myself was able to profit from, the possibility to do one's personal analysis before starting analytic training per se, and to thus do it outside of the analytic institute at which the training is taking place. As I write in the Afterword, in which I deal at length with my analytic training, I believe that it was a good thing for me to have the possibility to experience this alternative kind of training. It actually corresponded to my personality, as had been the case for the alternative high school program I attended in a suburb of New York in 1972–1973, which I also talk about in detail in the Afterword. In fact, this anthology itself is a very good documentation of the kind of self-taught way that I was able to invent for myself in the field of psychoanalysis. By "self-taught" I refer only to the fact of how important it was for me to personally chose as many of my teachers as possible—as opposed to having them prescribed to me by an institution. In the meantime, this model of training, which Cremerius had drawn from his attendance of the Psychoanalytic Seminar Zurich in the early 1960s, has been approved of by the IPA. About ten years ago, after many years of debate and discussion, the IPA finally recognized the validity of both the French and the Uruguayan models, attributing to them equal dignity and status with the traditional "Eitingon model."

To add to this, more and more colleagues inside the IPA itself have in recent years openly criticized the usual procedure of the "training analysis" or proposed— with very good arguments—that it should be abolished. This includes, for example, Horst Kächele and Helmut Thomä, who in a 2000 letter to the *International Journal of Psychoanalysis* expressed their support for "a radical disentanglement of the professional curriculum from the self-experience," given a situation in which "none of the contemporary models and practices secure the autonomy of the candidates' personal analysis" (Kächele and Thomä, 2000, p. 807). I believe that such a revision of the organization of training could not only guarantee "the autonomy of the candidates' personal analysis," but also have the beneficial consequence of setting many institutional energies free from the hierarchical structure of our institutes, centered as it is around the different status of ordinary members and training and supervising analysts. These free energies could be constructively employed in elaborating the better strategies necessary for keeping psychoanalysis alive in the twenty-first century.

If I were to organize my introduction to Chapter 10 in the same way as I have done for Chapters 11 and 12, I would now start to present at least some of the literature I just hinted at, in terms of the most relevant recent critiques of our training system and of our analytic institutions, including the many discussions concerning the future of psychoanalysis. But, of course—given how much I have already tested the my readers' patience—I will limit myself to just a few names, to then concentrate on what we can still learn from the testimony of Siegfried Bernfeld (1962), and from the critical contribution of Johannes Cremerius. Of course, the first name that comes to mind is that of Otto Kernberg, whose seminal paper "Institutional problems of psychoanalytic education" (1986) I know well, having translated it immediately after its original publication into Italian, to be published in *Psicoterapia e Scienze Umane* in 1987. I will limit myself here to saying that, in the meantime, Kernberg's own contribution to this field of psychoanalysis has grown so much that, in 2016, he was able to put together thirteen of his papers in the anthology *Psychoanalytic education at the crossroads. Reformation, change and the future of psychoanalytic training.* This includes his impressive and alarming paper "Suicide prevention for psychoanalytic institutes and societies" from 2012, and his 2013 contribution on the topic "The twilight of the training analysis system" (Kernberg, 2014).

In 2017, my Munich colleague and friend Peter Zagermann edited the anthology *The future of psychoanalysis. The debate about the training analysis system* (Zagermann, 2017a), including fourteen chapters and accompanied by a "Foreword" by Stefano Bolognini. In this Bolognini speaks of the need for a "quadripartite model" of analytic education, centered around "the capacity to work together, to share constant working through with the colleagues, and to actively participate in institutional life" (Bolognini, 2017, p. xix). As the reader knows, this anthology of mine also centers around such a need and desire to stimulate international exchange and dialogue in the analytic community. In his own contribution, which Ross Lazar also speaks about in his above-mentioned 2018 article, and which bears the title "Theses on the heart of darkness. The unresolved Oedipus complex of psychoanalytic institution formation" (Zagermann, 2017b), Peter Zagermann retraces the creation of the above-mentioned "elite of the training analysts" to the unresolved Oedipus complex of our institutions. According to him, this is the mechanism behind the fact that:

> a new member can be admitted into the circle of the training committee only if he or she has assimilated him- or herself to a degree that it must not be feared any more that he or she uncover the fiction of the superiority of the members of the training committee. (Zagermann, 2017b, p. 326)

Very useful, from the point of view of the political management of this aspect, are the "twenty-five years of debate and transformation at the Israeli Psychoanalytic Society," which Emanuel Berman presents in his contribution to Zagermann's anthology (Berman, 2017). Here are the final considerations with which Peter Zagermann concludes his chapter, that is, the way in which, after revisiting both the French and the Uruguayan models, he expresses his support for Otto Kernberg's

2013 proposal, as he formulated it in his plenary address to the annual conference of the American Psychoanalytic Association (Kernberg, 2014):

> For the train of thought developed in this paper, I consider it especially important to point out that both alternative models – the French and the Uruguayan one – arose explicitly as a reaction to the problem of power concentration in the Eitingon model. Therefore, they relate to it in negation, reflecting its problems, whereby the French model does away with the training analyst function totally, while the Uruguayan concept attempts a kind of a democratic basis alternative . . . . Kernberg's demand (2006, 2013) that, in principle, all graduates of an institute, thus, summarily, all members of a constituent organization, acquire a certification and, thus qualification to conduct training analyses without any further additional nomination within three to five years after graduation – as Kernberg suggests – and that in principle the individual functions are to be kept separate, actually makes a connection between the essential characteristics of the French model on the one hand, with its emphasis on a strictly personal, uninterfered analysis, and the Uruguayan model, on the other.
>   Such a range of access, as far as possible, to the functions of training analyst as well as supervisor would also have the advantage of not needing to introduce further safety measures against uncontrolled power concentration, as, for instance, a fixed-term nomination for training analysts or an institutional separation of the function of training analyst and supervisor. Each certified member would be a training analyst and supervisor in so far as fulfillment of that function was demanded of him or her at a specific moment in time. (Zagermann, 2017b, p. 334)

A paper given by Michael Ermann in Munich at the end of August 1992, in the context of the IFPS scientific conference that he had organized in Munich (see the Afterword), was published in 1993 in the *International Forum of Psychoanalysis* under the title "The training of psychoanalysts and the analyst's sense of responsibility." In this Michael Ermann expressed his agreement with the need repeatedly formulated by Johannes Cremerius that the personal analysis should be taken out of the training process and out of the analytic institute. He justified this as follows:

> Today, the training analysis should be something more and something entirely different from what Freud understood in 1937: it should be more than an introduction to the psychoanalytical method with the aim of ensuring that the analyst has a good understanding of the existence of the unconscious and it should be something entirely different from a way of assessing his personality. The training analysis should, from the point of view of the elaboration of the paranoid position, stabilize the integration of former partial object relationships, and prepare the future analyst to deal with the destructive phenomena which we encounter everywhere, in our clinical work and in society in general. However, this requires that very strict demarcations are

maintained between the analytical space and the environment
and that all regimentation is avoided. (Ermann, 1993, p. 41)

And here is the way in which he tried to account for
the fact that, despite the cogent criticisms from prominent
critics, the fundamental structure of training remains
unchanged:

> My suspicion is that 'analyses in the training situation' (A.
> Freud, 1938) fulfil an unconscious need in us as analysts, and
> that consequently they are not subjected to serious questioning.
>
> The need which they fulfil is that for harmony in our
> working environment which is otherwise characterized by a
> ruthless use of object—love and hate, desire and destruction .
> . . . This need of the training analyst for harmony runs parallel
> to the need for control and maintenance of power on the part
> of the institute, a need in which the training analyst has some
> share by virtue of his position as a member of the institute.
>
> Thus the training analysis carried out in the institute
> provides satisfaction to the training analyst in two ways, thereby
> posing an obstacle to the fulfilment of his analytical function.
>
> To the extent that we continue to conduct training
> analyses in a training situation, against our better judgement,
> we are using the institute's need for control as a vehicle to
> satisfy these hidden needs. There is a risk that such analyses
> will fail to achieve their goal and will promote adaptation
> to an inadequate environment, instead of opening ways to
> developing autonomy and responsibility. (Ermann, 1993, p.
> 42)

I can now come to Siegfried Bernfeld's (1892–1953)
classic paper "On psychoanalytic training," a paper which
he had given to the San Francisco Psychoanalytic Society
in November 1952, and which Rudolf Ekstein (1912–
2005) was able to have the *Psychoanalytic Quarterly*
publish in 1962 (Bernfeld, 1962). In it I found the concept
of "student-centered teaching," which Bernfeld had
experienced with Freud himself, and which he attributes
to him; and I experience this as the concept that guided
my own analytic evolution and development, as well as
the research itinerary around which this anthology of my
papers centers. But here are Bernfeld's recollections of
Freud and of his concept of analytic training:

> The idea of personal analysis is not much younger than
> psychoanalysis itself. Freud was early impressed by the
> difficulty of communicating his findings; obviously they could
> not be demonstrated to others like other work of a clinical
> nature. There was only one way in which Freud's propositions
> could be tested, namely by an analysis of the tester—either
> by his self-analysis or by a personal analysis. From the
> late nineties on, students in Freud's classes occasionally
> submitted their dreams to him. Sometimes a physician or
> a psychologist asked his help in the treatment of neurotic
> symptoms. These early analyses were truly didactic. Freud
> was eager to show neurotic mechanisms and the repressions
> of childhood traumata; he wanted to demonstrate their
> workings and his methods of exploration. I have read letters

he wrote in the twenties in which he discussed prospective didactic analyses with several aspirants. Even then he was ready to give an introduction to psychoanalysis by means of self-observation, so to speak. He considered periods of a few months as sufficient for this, or rather as better than nothing.

Around 1905, Freud began conducting analyses with psychoanalysts of much longer duration and far higher therapeutic aims. He adjusted the duration of the analysis and the amount of straight teaching included in it according to the wishes and the circumstances of the student-patient and according to the nature of the neurotic complaints. Whenever he deemed it advisable, he included didactic material in the personal analysis. With many of his students he discussed psychoanalytic theory, their own patients, the politics of the young group, and the papers they intended to write. In general, he tended to let the analysis grow into a relationship between two colleagues, one of whom happened to know a little more than the other. From the first to the very end, Freud kept his didactic cases absolutely free from interference by rules, administrative directives, or political considerations. His teaching was completely student-centered (to use my pedagogical terminology) or more simply he acted as a psychoanalyst should. He continued this long after the establishment of institutes, to the dismay and embarrassment of 'the authorities', as he sometimes, and a little ironically, referred to them.

For example, in 1922 I discussed with Freud my intention of establishing myself in Vienna as a practicing analyst. I had been told that our Berlin group encouraged psychoanalysts, especially beginners, to have a didactic analysis before starting their practice, and I asked Freud whether he thought this preparation desirable for me. His answer was: 'Nonsense. Go right ahead. You certainly will have difficulties. When you get into trouble, we will see what we can do about it'. Only a week later, he sent me my first didactic case, an English professor who wished to study psychoanalysis and planned to stay in Vienna about one month. Alarmed by the task and the conditions, I went back to Freud; but he only said: 'You know more than he does. Show him as much as you can'.

This, I still believe, would be the ideal training atmosphere, though I quite understand the strong motives and good reasons that led to the formalization of training. Yet I have never been fully convinced that the weaknesses of a school-like organization are outweighed by its advantages. (Bernfeld, 1962, p. 461–463)

This concept of teaching and training has also informed the article "A prescription for ideal training: Let us pay attention to the history of psychoanalysis, its cultural and linguistic roots, the work candidates do with each other, and the need for international dialogue," which I published in *Contemporary Psychoanalysis* in 2009.

Very similar to Bernfeld's relationship to Freud were the relationships I was able to develop with Johannes Cremerius—through my work as a translator into Italian of some of his best papers of critiquing psychoanalysis as an institution—and, many years later, in Munich, with Ross Lazar. Both played an important "mentoring function" for me, a mentoring function similar to the one that Sandra Buechler attributes to her supervisor Ralph Crowley (1905–1984) in the fourth chapter of her recent book *Psychoanalytic reflections: Training and practice* (Buechler, 2017), with the title "A letter to my first supervisor." A good mentor as a teacher sees in us a series of potentialities that we are not yet aware of, and encourages us to keep going and to pursue the realization of what we already have, in a still unformulated form, inside ourselves. In some ways, the clinical work we do with our patients should also have a similar character— as Benedetti himself showed me in more than one supervisory session.

Because of my gratitude to Cremerius for having been the first older colleague to encourage me to keep working on myself and to keep studying psychoanalysis, in order to become the good analyst that he felt I could become, I will—as my last operation of this very long Introduction—introduce the reader to some of his best papers of "institutional critique." I propose to start with his 1982 paper "Die Bedeutung der Dissidenten für die Psychoanalyse," go on with his 1986 paper "Spurensicherung. Die 'Psychoanalytische Bewegung' und das Elend der psychoanalaytischen Institution," and then take up his 1987 paper "Wenn wir Psychoanalytiker die psychoanalytische Ausbildung organisieren, müssen wir sie psychoanalytisch organisieren!," before finishing this short revisitation with the 1990 paper "Training analysis and power: The transformation of a method of training and learning into an instrument of power in institutionalized psychoanalysis"—the English version of his seminal (1989) paper "Lehranalyse und Macht."

In his 1982 paper, which would translate into English as "The significance of the dissident for psychoanalysis" (Cremerius, 1982), Cremerius presents the tendency of the analytic community to let its discourse be overtaken by forms of thought more appropriate to a religious community, such as the canonization of the supposed correct doctrine and the banishment of heterodox views, with subsequent splinter groups and sect formation. For example, the dogmatization of Freud's detached technical approach that took place in Germany in the 1950s (but not only in Germany) has since then diverted the attention of the analytic community from Freud's own "dissident" way of working, that is, from his "personal" approach to his patients, inasmuch as it went beyond the rules he himself had established in his 1912–1915 papers on technique.

This is the way in which analytic discourse tends to develop in terms of the opposite poles of "orthodox" and "dissident," forcing us into an identification with one or the other, as opposed to allowing all of us to find out and come to our own analytic identity and personal style. Such a polarization belongs more to a religious than to a scientific way of dealing with our relationship with knowledge and reality, and we should overcome it.

Also very rich and complex was the first of Cremerius's papers that I translated from German into Italian, the long article "Staying on track – The 'psychoanalytic movement' and the poverty of the psychoanalytic institution" (see Cremerius, 1986). In this Cremerius tried to show how the fate of both lay analysis and training analysis documents the way in which the "Psychoanalytic Movement" has been transformed into institutional structures of power politics. This is how central concepts and positions of psychoanalysis have been sacrificed to a senseless and alienating regimentation. Staying on track, and reconstructing these historical developments, we can not only understand the history of these deformations, but also find ways of possibly revising them. The 1987 paper, with the English title "If we psychoanalysts wish to organize psychoanalytic training, we must organize it psychoanalytically!" (Cremerius, 1987), which I have also translated into Italian, is a long, original, and sophisticated article, centered around the following thesis: if psychoanalytic training is to be reorganized psychoanalytically, an individual responsibility of teachers and students must take the place of rituals and regimentation, and freedom of research and doctrine must replace the guild mentality.

Last but not least, "Training analysis and power: The transformation of a method of training and learning into an instrument of power in institutionalized psychoanalysis" was the English version of the paper "Lehranalyse und Macht" [Training analysis and power], which Cremerius had given in Milan, in June 1988, at the above-mentioned International Network Conference; I have also translated this into Italian, for *Psicoterapia e Scienze Umane*. Here are the author's final considerations:

> What can we do to abolish the anti-analytic liaison between training and power? What can we do so that training analysis can be carried out in the spirit of freedom, as a free encounter between analyst and analysand without coercion and without outside directives?
>   Up to now the attempts of institutionalized psychoanalysis to create a more liberal training system, like the French, the Canadian and the Swiss Psychoanalytic

Associations—that is, a personal analysis instead of a training analysis and no training analyst status—have neither abolished the liaison between training and power nor brought about a change of climate in the institutes.

What is required, in order to get closer to this goal is a radical reform of the training system. A reform which will lead the training institutes out of their ghetto position, will open them up and will make it possible for them to catch up with the standard of late twentieth-century human sciences . . . . To summarize, this means that institutionalized psychoanalysis should accept that psychoanalysis has already entered the stage of 'normal science' (Kuhn, 1962), and finds itself in the same position as philosophy in the universities, where there is no longer a monopoly of *one* philosophy, but a pluralism of philosophical concepts. From these facts psychoanalysis should draw the necessary conclusions. (Cremerius, 1990, pp. 129–130)

As the reader can see from these words, Johannes Cremerius's priority was to change analytic training and our analytic institutes in the direction of making psychoanalysis a "normal science" in the sense meant by the historian of science Thomas Kuhn (1922–1996), the same priority that has kept motivating Otto Kernberg not to give up on his own critique of our institutions and the political action needed. Of course, this is also one of the common denominators of the chapters in this anthology, which all aim to present psychoanalysis as an intellectual discipline that is worth studying and further developing.

But the most important message I have gained from Johannes Cremerius's work and legacy is his concept of the need to meet the challenge of finding the necessary continuity and coherence not only between what we say to our patients and what we do with them, and between our clinical and our scientific work, but also between the way in which we use psychoanalysis to work with and help our patients and the way in which we use it for ourselves, in our own lives. In the above-mentioned book *Psychoanalytic reflections: Training and practice*, my dear colleague and friend Sandra Buechler writes about her own relationship to psychoanalysis in terms of what she calls a "vocation," defined as an attitude involving "falling in love with something, having a conviction about it and making it part of your personal identity" (Buechler, 2017, p. 307). This is why, as a first step in the preparation of this anthology, I wrote the "Afterword" that accompanies it. Through it I have tried to show how psychoanalysis is not only my intellectual passion and the source of inspiration of the work I do with my patients, but also the source of the principles of truth and coherence that I have tried to apply to my own life, and from whose application to my own life I have became the person I am. This is why I hope that readers will sooner or later immerse themselves into it—and also enjoy it just as much.

REFERENCES

Akhtar, S. (1999). *Immigration and Identity. Turmoil, Treatment, and Transformation*. Northvale, NJ: Aronson.

———(2009b). Introduction. In *Freud and the Far East. Psychoanalytic Perspectives on the People and Culture of China, Japan, and Korea* (pp. 1–6). New York: Aronson.

Akhtar, S. (Ed.) (2009a). *Freud and the Far East. Psychoanalytic Perspectives on the People and Culture of China, Japan, and Korea*. New York: Aronson.

Amati Mehler, J., & Ambrosio, G. (2011). The Italian Psychoanalytical Association. In P. Loewenberg and N. Thompson (Eds.), *100 Years of the IPA. The Centenary History of the International Psychoanalytical Association 1910–2010. Evolution and Change* (pp. 121–126). London: Karnac.

Amati Mehler, J., Argentieri, S., & Canestri, J. (1993). *The Babel of the Unconscious. Mother Tongue and Foreign Languages in the Psychoanalytic Dimension*. Madison, CT: International Universities Press. (Original Italian edition, 1990. German edition, 2010).

Anzieu, D. (1986). The place of Germanic language and culture in Freud's discovery of psychoanalysis between 1895 and 1900. *International Journal of Psychoanalysis* 67:219–226.

Arieti, S. (Ed.) (1959). *The American Handbook of Psychiatry. Two Volumes*. New York: Norton.

Bach, S. (2011). Chimeras: Immunity, interpenetration, and the true self. In *Chimeras and Other Writings. The Selected Papers of Sheldon Bach* (pp. 3–21). New York: International Psychoanalytic Books, 2016.

Beland, H. (1988). How they know themselves: Confronting the past – A contribution to the history of the German Psychoanalytic Association. *Psychoanalysis and Contemporary Thought* 11:267–283.

Benedetti, G. (1961). Prefazione all'edizione italiana [Preface to the Italian edition]. In H.S. Sullivan, *La moderna concezione della psichiatria* (pp. vii–xxvii). Milan: Feltrinelli. (Original American edition, 1940).

——— (1987). *Psychotherapy of Schizophrenia*. New York: New York University Press.

Berman, E. (2017). Change from within in a traditional psychoanalytic institute: Twenty-five years of debate and transformation at the Israeli Psychoanalytic Society. In P. Zagermann (Ed.), *The Future of Psychoanalysis. The Debate About the Training Analyst System* (pp. 1–34). London: Routledge.

Bernfeld, S. (1962). On psychoanalytic training. *Psychoanalytic Quarterly* 31:453–482.

Bettelheim, B. (1982). *Freud and Man's Soul*. New York: Knopf.

Birksted-Breen, D., & Flanders, S. (2010). General introduction. In D. Birksted-Breen, S. Flanders, and A. Gibeault (Eds.), *Reading French Psychoanalysis* (pp. 1–51). London: Routledge.

Birksted-Breen, D., Flanders, S., & Gibeault, A. (Eds.) (2010). *Reading French Psychoanalysis*. London: Routledge.

Bohleber, W. (2011). The history of psychoanalysis in Germany since 1950. In P. Loewenberg and N.L. Thompson (Eds.), *100 Years of the IPA. The Centenary History of the International Psychoanalytical Association 1910–2010. Evolution and Change* (pp. 62–86). London: Karnac.

―――― (2013). The journal *Psyche – Zeitschrift für Psychoanalyse und ihre Anwendungen:* A historical overview. *International Forum of Psychoanalysis* 22:199–202.

Bolognini, S. (2008). Reconsidering narcissism from a contemporary, complex psychoanalytic view. *International Forum of Psychoanalysis* 17:104–111.

―――― (2016). Presentazione [Preface]. In L. Preta (Ed.), *Cartografie dell'inconscio. Un nuovo atlante per la psicoanalisi* [Cartographies for the unconscious. A new atlas for psychoanalysis] (pp. 9–11). Milan: Mimesis.

―――― (2017). Foreword. In P. Zagermann (Ed.), *The Future of Psychoanalysis. The Debate About the Training Analyst System* (pp. xvii–xix). London: Routledge.

Bonaminio, V. (2007). Introduction. In C. Bollas, *The Freudian Moment* (pp. xi–xiii). London, Karnac.

―――― (2008). The person of the analyst: Interpreting, not interpreting and countertransference. *Psychoanalytic Quarterly* 77:1115–1146.

Borgogno, F. (2008). The relevance of "role reversal" in today's psychoanalytic work. *International Forum of Psychoanalysis* 17:213–220.

―――― (2016). Narcissism, psychic recognition, and affective validation: A homage to the "later Rosenfeld". *International Forum of Psychoanalysis* 25:249–256.

Borgogno, F., & Luchetti, A. (2016). General introduction. In F. Borgogno, A. Luchetti, and L. Marino Coe (Eds.), *Reading Italian Psychoanalysis* (pp. 1–6). London: Routledge.

Borgogno, F., Luchetti, A., & Marino Coe, L. (Eds.) (2016). *Reading Italian Psychoanalysis*. London: Routledge.

Brecht, K., Friedrich, V., Hermanns, L.M., Kaminer, I.J., & Juelich, D.H. (Eds.) (1993). *"Here Life Goes on in a Most Peculiar Way . . ." – Psychoanalysis Before and after 1933*. Hamburg: Kellner. (Original German edition, 1985).

Buchholz, M.B. (2003). Vorwort [Preface]. In S.A. Mitchell, *Bindung und Beziehung. Auf dem Weg zu einer relationalen Psychoanalyse* (pp.7–15). Giessen: Psychosozial-Verlag. (Original American edition, 2000).

―――― (2015). Growth: What reconciliation of conflicts could mean. A lesson from the history of psychoanalysis. *International Forum of Psychoanalysis* 24:88–97.

Buechler, S. (2011). Review of the book edited by S. Erlich, Ginor-Erlich, M. Beland, "Fed with tears, poisoned with milk - The 'Nazareth' group-relations conferences. Germans and Israelis - The past in the present", Psychosozial-Verlag 2009. *Contemporary Psychoanalysis* 47:150–154.

―――― (2017). *Psychoanalytic Reflections: Training and Practice*. New York: International Psychoanalytic Books.

Caldwell, L. (2016). Afterword – A swift glance at Italian psychoanalysis from abroad. In F. Borgogno, A. Luchetti, and L. Marino Coe (Eds.), *Reading Italian Psychoanalysis* (pp. 679–688). London: Routledge.

Caldwell, L., and Taylor Robinson, H. (Eds.) (2017). *The Collected Works of D.W. Winnicott*. Oxford: Oxford University Press.

Chianese, D. (2011). A brief history of the Italian Psychoanalytical Society. In P. Loewenberg and N. Thompson (Eds.), *100 Years of the IPA. The Centenary History of the International Psychoanalytical Association 1910–2010. Evolution and Change* (pp. 107–120). London: Karnac.

Chrzanowski, G. (1975). On the International Forum. *Contemporary Psychoanalysis* 11:100–103.

——— (1997). Eulogy for Rose Spiegel, MD. *Contemporary Psychoanalysis* 33:177–183.

Cocks, G. (1985). *Psychotherapy in the Third Reich: The Göring Institute*. New York: Oxford University Press.

——— (1994). German psychiatry, psychotherapy and psychoanalysis during the Nazi period: Historiographical reflections. In M.S. Micale and R. Porter (Eds.), *Discovering the History of Psychiatry* (pp. 282–296). New York: Oxford University Press.

Conci, M. (1990). Review of the book by P. Harmat "Freud, Ferenczi und die ungarische Psychoanalyse", Diskord 1988. *Psicoterapia e Scienze Umane* 25(2):131–133.

——— (1995a). Review of the book by L. Nissim Momigliano "Continuity and change in psychoanalysis. Letters from Milan", Karnac 1992. *Psychoanalytic Books* 6:199–204.

——— (1995b). H.S. Sullivan und die Spaltungen in der amerikanischen psychoanalytischen Gemeinschaft der vierziger Jahre [Harry Stack Sullivan and the schisms in the American analytic community of the 1940s]. *Luzifer-Amor* No. 16:32–55.

——— (1995c). Disertori neuropsichiatra alla luce del carteggio con H. Ellenberger [Disertori neuropsychiatrist in the light of his correspondence with H. Ellenberger]. In *Sotto il segno dell'uomo: Beppino Disertori. Atti del convegno, Trento 11.2.1995* [Under the sign of man: Beppino Disertori. Proceedings of the conference, Trento, February 2, 1995] (pp. 47–60). Trento: Comune di Trento.

——— (1996). Die Psychoanalyse in Italien. Anfänge, Entwicklung und gegenwärtige Lage [Psychoanalysis in Italy. Beginnings, development and present situation]. *Luzifer-Amor* No. 18:114–155.

——— (1996–1997). Elvio Fachinelli: A profile. *Journal of European Psychoanalysis* Nos 3–4, 157–162.

——— (2000a). Editorial – Erich Fromm, a rediscovered legacy. *International Forum of Psychoanalysis* 9:141–144.

——— (2000b). Report on the XI IFPS Forum, New York: Marriott Hotel, Brooklyn, May 4–7, 2000. *International Forum of Psychoanalysis* 9:263–266.

——— (2003). Review of the book by J.E. Goggin and E. Brockman Goggin "Death of a Jewish science. Psychoanalysis in the Third Reich", Purdue University Press 2001. *International Forum of Psychoanalysis* 12:173–178.

——— (2008a). Italian themes in psychoanalysis – International dialogue and psychoanalytic identity. *International Forum of Psychoanalysis* 17:65–70.

——— (2008b). Gaetano Benedetti in his correspondence. *International Forum of Psychoanalysis* 17:112–129.

——— (2008c). Review of the "Italian psychoanalytic annual – Freud after all", Borla 2007. *International Forum of Psychoanalysis* 17:130–132.

————(2008d). Review of the books edited by M. Buchholz and G. Gödde "Das Unbewusste – Ein Projekt in drei Bänden", Psychosozial-Verlag 2005–2006. *International Forum of Psychoanalysis* 17:254–256.

———— (2009). A prescription for ideal training: Let us pay attention to the history of psychoanalysis, its cultural and linguistic roots, the work candidates do with each other, and the need for international dialogue. *Contemporary Psychoanalysis* 45:394–405.

———— (2010a). Geleitwort [Introduction]. In J. Amati Mehler, S. Argentieri, and J. Canestri, *Das Babel des Unbewussten. Muttersprache und Fremdsprachen in der psychoanalytischen Dimension* (pp. 13–26). Giessen: Psychosozial-Verlag. (Original Italian edition, 1990).

———— (2010b). Editorial – Global connections and international contacts. Papers from the XVth Forum of the International Federation of Psychoanalytic Societies. *International Forum of Psychoanalysis* 19:67–70.

———— (2010c). An advantage of globalization: Working with Italian patients abroad in their mother language. *International Forum of Psychoanalysis* 19:98–109.

———— (2011). Vorwort [Preface]. In I. Kogan, *Mit der Trauer kämpfen* [The struggle against mourning] (pp. 9–16). Stuttgart: Klett-Cotta.

———— (2013). Editorial – German themes in psychoanalysis. Part One. *International Forum of Psychoanalysis* 22:195–198.

———— (2015). Editorial – German themes in psychoanalysis. Part Two. *International Forum of Psychoanalysis* 24:57–59.

———— (2018a). Editorial – German themes in psychoanalysis. Part Three. *International Forum of Psychoanalysis* 27:1–4.

———— (2018b). Working with Italian patients in Munich – The case of Penelope. *International Forum of Psychoanalysis* 27:24–34.

Conci, M., & Kamm, H. (2015). Tagung zum Gedenken an den Psychoanalytiker Herbert Rosenfeld, Nürnberg 1910 – London 1986 [Conference in memory of the psychoanalyst Herbert Rosenfeld, Nuremberg 1910 – London 1986]. *Luzifer-Amor* No. 56:7–19.

Conci, M., Erhardt, I., & Kächele, H. (2013). Marco Conci and Ingrid Erhardt interview Horst Kächele. *International Forum of Psychoanalysis* 22:228–243.

Conci, M., Koehler, B., & Peciccia, M. (2014). Prof. Dr.med. Gaetano Benedetti (1920–2013), Co-founder ISPS. *Psychosis* 6:1–3.

Corsi, T. (1990). La Scuola e l'Associazione: inizi e sviluppi [The School and the Association: beginnings and developments]. *Quaderni dell'Associazione di Studi Psicoanalitici* No. 1:7–12.

Cremerius, J. (1982). Die Bedeutung der Dissidenten für die Psychoanalyse [The significance of the dissident for psychoanalysis]. *Psyche* 36:481–504.

———— (1986). Spurensicherung. Die "Psychoanalytische Bewegung" und das Elend der psychoanalytischen Institution [Staying on track. The "psychoanalytic movement" and the poverty of the psychoanalytic institution]. *Psyche* 40:1063–1091.

———— (1987). Wenn wir als Psychoanalytiker die psychoanalytische Ausbildung organisieren, müssen wir sie psychoanalytisch organisieren! [If we psychoanalysts wish to organize psychoanalytic training, we must organize it psychoanalytically!]. *Psyche* 41:1067–1096.

———— (1990). Training analysis and power: The transformation of a method of training and learning into an instrument of power in institutionalized psychoanalysis. *Free Associations* No. 20:114–138. (Original German version, 1989).

Dahmer, H. (1979). "Holocaust" und die Amnesie ["Holocaust" and amnesia]. *Psyche* 33:1039–1045.

———— (1983). Kapitulation vor der "Weltanschauung". Zum einem Aufsatz von Carl Müller-Braunschweig aus dem Jahre 1933 [Capitulation to "Weltanschauung". On a 1933 article by Carl Müller-Braunschweig]. *Psyche* 37:116–135.

Danneberg, E. (1995). Psychoanalysis against the grain (Argentina, Chile, Nicaragua, Cuba). In P. Kutter (Ed.), *Psychoanalysis International. A Guide to Psychoanalysis Throughout the World.* Vol. 2, *America, Asia, Australia, Further European Countries* (pp. 241–256). Stuttgart: Frommann-Holzboog.

David, M. (1966, 1990). *La psicoanalisi nella cultura italiana* [Psychoanalysis in Italian culture]. Turin: Bollati Boringhieri.

Decker, H.S. (1977) *Freud in Germany: Revolution and Reaction in Science, 1893–1907*. New York: International Universities Press.

De Masi, F. (2003). *The Sadomasochistic Perversion: The Entity and the Theory*. London: Routledge. (Original Italian edition, 2001).

———— (2016). Herbert Rosenfeld in Italy, 1978–1985. *International Forum of Psychoanalysis* 25:241–248.

Di Chiara, G. (1985). Breve profilo del pensiero psicoanalitico nella Società Psicoanalitica Italiana [A short profile of the analytic thought in the Italian Psychoanalytic Society]. In A.M. Accerboni (Ed.), *La cultura psicoanalitica. Atti del convegno* [Analytic culture. Proceedings of the conference]. Pordenone: Studio Tesi.

———— (2016). Psychoanalysis in Italy. In F. Borgogno, A. Luchetti, and L. Marino Coe (Eds.), *Reading Italian Psychoanalysis* (pp. 10–17). London, Routldege.

Di Donna, L. (2005). Psychoanalysis in Italy: Its origins and evolution. *Fort da* 11:35–59.

Erlich, S., Erlich-Ginor, M., & Beland, H. (2009). *Fed with Tears, Poisoned with Milk - The "Nazareth" Group-Relations-Conferences. Germans and Israelis - The Past in the Present.* Giessen: Psychosozial-Verlag.

Eisold, K. (1994). The intolerance of diversity in psychoanalytic institutions. *International Journal of Psychoanalysis* 75:785–800.

Eissler, K.R. (1963–1964). Die Ermordung von wievielen seiner Kinder muss ein Mensch symptomfrei ertragen können, um eine normale Konstitution zu haben? [The killing of how many of his children must a human being tolerate without symptoms, in order to be of normal constitution?]. *Psyche* 17:241–191.

Eizirik, C.L. (2009). Psychic structure and identity in a globalising world. *International Forum of Psychoanalysis* 18:196–201.

Ellenberger, H.F. (1970). *The Discovery of the Unconscious*. New York: Basic Books. (Italian edition, 1972).

Ellmann, M. (2017). Review of the book by J. Forrester, "Freud in Cambridge", Cambridge University Press 2017. *Psychoanalysis and History* 19:239–248.

Ermann, M. (1993). The training of psychoanalysts and the analyst's sense of responsibility. *International Forum of Psychoanalysis* 2:37–43.

———— (1996). *Verstrickung und Einsicht. Nachdenken über die*

Psychoanalyse in Deutschland [Collusion and insight. Reflections on psychoanalysis in Germany]. Tübingen: Diskord.

——— (2009). Editorial – Psychoanalysis and globalisation. *International Forum of Psychoanalysis* 18:195.

——— (2015). *Forum der Psychoanalyse*: A journal documenting the "normalization" of the psychoanalytic field in Germany. *International Forum of Psychoanalysis* 24:60–62.

Evans, B. (2017). Review of the book by J. Forrester "Thinking in cases", Polity Press 2016. *Psychoanalysis and History* 19:248–256.

Fachinelli, E. (1989). *La mente estatica* [The estatic mind]. Milan: Adelphi.

Fallend, K. (2017). Editorial – Noch einmal: Psychoanalyse unter Hitler [Editorial – Once more: psychoanalysis under Hitler]. *Werkblatt* No. 79:2–3.

Fallend, K., & Nitzschke, B. (Eds.) (1997). *Der "Fall" Wilhelm Reich: Beiträge zum Verhältnis zwischen Psychoanalyse und Politik* [The "case" of Wilhelm Reich: contributions to the relationship between psychoanalysis and politics]. Frankfurt: Suhrkamp.

Falzeder, E. (Ed.) (2002). *The Complete Correspondence of Sigmund Freud and Karl Abraham 1907–1925*. London: Karnac.

Ferenczi, S. (1949). Confusion of the tongues between the adults and the child – (The language of tenderness and of passion). *International Journal of Psychoanalysis* 30:225–230. (Original German publication, 1933).

Ferro, A. (2009). Transformations in dreaming and characters in the psychoanalytic field. *International Journal of Psychoanalysis* 90:209–230.

Ferruta, A. (2016). Themes and developments of psychoanalysis in Italy. In F. Borgogno, A. Luchetti, and L. Marino Coe (Eds.), *Reading Italian Psychoanalysis* (pp. 18–35). London: Routledge.

ffytche, M., & Mayer, A. (2017). Editorial. *Psychoanalysis and History* 19:145–150.

Focke, I. (2010). Der Weg der DPG in die IPV – Wunsch und Ambivalenz [The way of the DPG into the IPA – Desire and ambivalence]. *Psyche* 12:1187–1205.

Fornari, F. (1963). *La vita affettiva originaria del bambino* [The original affective life of the child]. Milan: Feltrinelli.

——— (1964). *The Psychoanalysis of War*. Garden City, NY: Anchor Press.

Forrester, J. (1994). "A whole climate of opinion": Rewriting the history of psychoanalysis. In M.S. Micale and R. Porter (Eds.), *Discovering the History of Psychoanalysis* (pp. 174–190). New York: Oxford University Press.

——— (2017a) Foucault, power-knowledge, and the individual, *Psychoanalysis and History* 19:215–231.

——— (2017b). Colleagues, correspondents and the institution – Or: is psychoanalysis without institutions possible? *Psychoanalysis and History* 19:233–237.

Foucault, M. (1965). *Madness and Civilization*. New York: Pantheon. (Original French edition, 1961).

Frank, C. (2016). Herbert Rosenfeld in Germany: On the seductive/corruptive effect of idealizing destructive elements then and now. *International Forum of Psychoanalysis* 25:229–240.

Freud, S. (1919). Lines of advance in psycho-analytic therapy. *Standard*

Edition 17, pp. 159–168.

——— (1940–1952). *Gesammelte Werke in 18 Bänden* [Complete works in 18 volumes]. London: Imago.

Frie, R. (Ed.) (2018). *History Flows Through Us. Germany, the Holocaust, and the Importance of Empathy*. London: Routledge.

Fromm-Reichmann, F. (1950). *Principles of Intensive Psychotherapy*. Chicago: University of Chicago Press. (Italian edition, 1962).

——— (1959). *Psychoanalysis and Psychotherapy* (D.M. Bullard, Ed.). Washington DC: American Psychiatric Press. (Italian edition, 1964).

Gaddini, E. (1969). On imitation. *International Journal of Psychoanalysis* 50:475–484.

——— (1976). Die Psychoanalyse in Italien [Psychoanalysis in Italy]. In D. Eicke (Ed.), *Tiefenpsychologie. Band 2. Neue Wege der Psychoanalyse – Psychoanalyse der Gesellschaft – Die psychoanalytische Bewegung* [Deep psychology. Vol. 2. New ways in psychoanalysis – Psychoanalysis of society – The analytic movement] (pp. 650–667). Weinheim: Beltz, 1982.

——— (1980). Relazione introduttiva [Introductory paper]. *Rivista di Psicoanalisi* 26:279–287.

Gaddini, E. (1992). *A Psychoanalytic Theory of Infantile Experience: Conceptual and Clinical Reflections*. London: Routledge.

Gast, L. (2018). Freud's utopia revisited: The International Psychoanalytic University Berlin. *International Forum of Psychoanalysis* 27:35–39.

Goldschmidt, G.-A. (2006). *Freud wartet auf das Wort* [Freud waits for the word]. Zurich: Amman.

Gray Ornston, D., Jr. (Ed.) (1992). *Translating Freud*. New Haven, CT: Yale University Press.

Grinberg, L., & Grinberg, R. (1990). *Psychoanalytic Perspectives on Migration and Exile*. New Haven, CT: International Universities Press.

Grotjahn, M. (1976). Freuds Briefwechsel [Freud's correspondence]. In D. Eicke (Ed.), *Psychologie des "20. Jahrhunderts". Tiefenpsychologie. Band 1. Sigmund Freud – Leben und Werk* [Psychology of the 20th century. Deep psychology. Vol. 1. Sigmund Freud – Life and work] (pp. 29–140). Munich: Kindler.

Haaken, J. (1990). The Siegfried Bernfeld Conference: Uncovering the psychoanalytical political unconscious. *American Journal of Psychoanalysis* 50:289–304.

Hale, N.G., Jr. (1971). *Freud and the Americans*. Vol. 1, *The Beginnings of Psychoanalysis in the United States*. New York: Oxford University Press.

Harmat, P. (1988). *Freud, Ferenczi und die ungarische Psychoanalyse* [Freud, Ferenczi and Hungarian psychoanalysis]. Tübingen: Diskord.

Haynal, A.E. (2017). *Encounters with the Irrational. My Story. With an Interview by Judit Mészáros*. New York: International Psychoanalytic Books.

Hermanns, L. (2011). The history of psychoanalysis in Germany up to 1950 and its relationship to the IPA. In P. Loewenberg and N.L. Thompson (Eds.), *100 Years of the IPA. The Centenary History of the International Psychoanalytical Association 1910–2010. Evolution and Change* (pp. 47–61). London: Karnac.

Hermanns, L. (Ed.) (1995). *Spaltungen in der Geschichte der*

Psychoanalyse [Schisms in the history of psychoanalysis]. Tübingen: Diskord.

Herzog, D. (2017). *Cold War Freud. Psychoanalysis in an Age of Catastrophes*. Cambridge: Cambridge University Press.

Hinshelwood, R.D. (1987). Between the devil and the deep blue sea: Relations with the dominant class. In Psychoanalytiches Seminar Zurich (Ed.), *Between the Devil and the Deep Blue Sea* (pp. 184–196). Freiburg: Kore.

Holder, A. (1992). A historical-critical edition. In D. Gray Ornston, Jr. (Ed.), *Translating Freud* (pp. 75–96). New Haven, CT: Yale University Press.

Hristeva, G., & Bennett, P. (2018). Wilhelm Reich in Soviet Russia: Psychoanalysis, Marxism and the Stalinist reaction. *International Forum of Psychoanalysis* 27:54–69.

Huppke, A. (2017). Die Geschichte der IFPS, 1962–1977 [The history of IFPS, 1962–1977]. Paper given in Berlin in March 2017 at the XXXth Symposium on the History of Psychoanalysis.

Junker, H. (1992). Standard translation and complete analysis. In D. Gray Ornston, Jr. (Ed.), *Translating Freud* (pp. 48–62). New Haven, CT: Yale University Press.

Kächele, H., & Thomä, H. (2000). Letter to the editor. On the devaluation of the Eitingon-Freud model of psychoanalytic education. *International Journal of Psychoanalysis* 81:806–807.

Kächele, H., Erhardt, I., Buchholz, M., & Seybert, C. (2015). Countertransference as an object of empirical research? *International Forum of Psychoanalysis* 24:96–108.

Kafka, J.S. (2008). On reestablishing contact. *Psychoanalysis and Contemporary Thought* 11:299–308.

———— (2016). *Psychoanalysis: Unveiling the Past Discovering the New: Selected Papers of John S. Kafka*. New York: International Psychoanalytic Books.

Kernberg, O.F. (1986). Institutional problems of psychoanalytic education. *Journal of the American Psychoanalytic Association* 34:799–834. (Italian translation, 1987).

———— (2012). Suicide prevention for psychoanalytic institutes and societies. *Journal of the American Psychoanalytic Association* 60:707–719.

———— (2014). The twilight of the training analysis system. *Psychoanalytic Review* 101:151–174.

———— (2016). *Psychoanalytic Education at the Crossroads. Reformation, Change and the Future of Psychoanalytic Training*. London: Routledge.

Kirsner, D. (2009). *Unfree Associations: Inside Psychoanalytic Institutes*. New York: Aronson.

Klein, H., & Kogan, I. (1986). Identification and denial in the shadow of Nazism. *International Journal of Psychoanalysis* 67:45–52.

Kogan, I. (2007). *The Struggle Against Mourning*. New York: Aronson.

———— (2015). From psychic holes to psychic representations. *International Forum of Psychoanalysis* 24:63–76.

Kuriloff, E.A. (2014). *Contemporary Psychoanalysis and the Legacy of the Third Reich. History, Memory, Tradition*. London: Routledge.

Kurzweil, E. (1989). *The Freudians. A Comparative Perspective*. New Haven, CT: Yale University Press.

Kutter, P. (1992). Introduction. In P. Kutter (Ed.), *Psychoanalysis*

International. A Guide to Psychoanalysis Throughout the World. Vol. 1, *Europe* (pp. xi–xv). Stuttgart: Frommann-Holzboog.

——— (1995). Foreword. In P. Kutter (Ed.), *Psychoanalysis International. A Guide to Psychoanalysis Throughout the World.* Vol. 2, *America, Asia, Australia, Further European Countries* (pp. vii–xii). Stuttgart: Frommann-Holzboog

Kutter, P. (Ed.) (1992, 1995). *Psychoanalysis International. A Guide to Psychoanalysis Throughout the World.* Vol. 1, *Europe.* Vol. 2, *America, Asia, Australia, Further European Countries.* Stuttgart: Frommann-Holzboog.

Lazar, R.A. (2000). Psychoanalyse, "Group Relations" und Organisation: Konfliktbearbeitung nach dem Tavistock-Arbeitskonferenz-Modell ["Group Relations" and organization: Conflict elaboration according to the Tavistock model]. In M. Lohmer (Ed.), *Psychodynamische Organisationsberatung. Konflikte und Potentiale in Veränderungsprozessen* [Psychodynamic organisation counselling. Conflicts and potentials in the processes of change] (pp. 40–47). Stuttgart: Klett-Cotta.

——— (2018). Like a phoenix from the ashes – or "sack cloth and ashes"? The reconstitution of psychoanalytic institutions in Germany since 1945 and its consequences. *International Forum of Psychoanalysis* 27:40–53.

Leuzinger-Bohleber, M., Stuhr, U., Rüger, B., & Beutel, M. (2003). How to study the "quality" of psychoanalytic treatments" and their long-term effects on patients' well-being: A representative, multi-perspective follow-up study. *International Journal of Psychoanalysis* 84:263–290.

Levi, P. (1958). *Survival in Auschwitz (If This is a Man).* (Original Italian edition, 1947).

Limentani, A. (1989). Psychoanalysis in Italy: A personal appraisal. In G.E. Viola and F. Rovigatti (Eds.), *L'Italia nella psicoanalisi – Italy in psychoanalysis* (pp. 25–28). Rome: Istituto dell'Enciclopedia Italiana.

Lockot, R. (1985). *Erinnern und Durcharbeiten. Zur Geschichte der Psychoanalyse und der Psychotherapie im Nazionalsozialismus.* [Remembering and working-through. The history of psychoanalysis and psychotherapy during the Nazi Regime]. Frankfurt: Fischer.

——— (1994). *Die Reinigung der Psychoanalyse. Die Deutsche Psychoanalytische Gesellschaft im Spiegel von Dokumenten und zeitzeugen (1933–1951)* [The purification of psychoanalysis. The German Psychoanalytic Society in the light of documents and time witnesses (1933–1951)]. Tübingen: Diskord.

Loewenberg, P., & Thompson, N.L. (2011b). The geography of the IPA. In P. Lowenberg and N.L. Thompson (Eds.), *100 Years of the IPA. The Centenary History of the International Psychoanalytical Association 1910–2010. Evolution and Change* (pp. xxv–xxvii). London: Karnac.

——— (2011). Introduction. In P. Loewenberg and N.L. Thompson (Eds.), *100 Years of the IPA. The Centenary History of the International Psychoanalytical Association 1910–2010. Evolution and Change* (pp. 1–5). London: Karnac.

Loewenberg, P., & Thompson, N.L. (Eds.) (2011a). *100 Years of the IPA. The Centenary History of the International Psychoanalytical Association 1910–2010. Evolution and Change.* London: Karnac.

Lohmann, H.-M. (Ed.) (1984). *Psychoanalyse und Nazionalsozialismus. Beiträge zur Bearbeitung eines unbewältigten Themas*

[Psychoanalysis and national socialism. Contributions to the elaboration of an unresolved theme]. Frankfurt: Fischer.

Lohmann, H.-M., & Rosenkötter, L. (1982). Psychoanalyse im Hitlerdeutschland. Wie war es wirklich? [Psychoanalysis in Hitler's Germany. How was it really?]. *Psyche* 36:961–988.

Lombardozzi, A. (2016). Per un'antropologia dell'incontro psicoanalitco tra culture [For an anthropology of the analytic encounter among cultures]. In L. Preta (Ed.), *Cartografie dell'inconscio. Un nuovo atlante per la psicoanalisi* [Cartographies for the unconscious. A new atlas for psychoanalysis] (pp. 81–86). Milan: Mimesis.

Lothane, Z. (2001). Introduction: Psychiatry, psychotherapy, and psychoanalysis in the Third Reich. *Psychoanalytic Review* 88:143–153.

——— (2003). Power politics and psychoanalysis: An introduction. *International Forum of Psychoanalysis* 12:85-97.

——— (2018). Review of Issue 2–2015 of the journal *Psychoanalyse – Texte zur Sozialforschung. International Forum of Psychoanalysis* 27:70–72.

Mahony, P.J. (1992). A psychoanalytic translation of Freud. In D. Gray Ornston, Jr. (Ed.), *Translating Freud* (pp. 24–47). New Haven, CT: Yale University Press.

Makari, G. (2008). *Revolution in Mind. The Creation of Psychoanalysis.* New York: Harper Collins.

——— (2015). *Soul Machine. The Invention of the Modern Mind.* New York: Norton.

Margulies, A. (2011). Review of the book edited by D. Birksted-Breen, S. Flanders, A. Gibeault, "Reading French psychoanalysis", Routledge 2010. *International Journal of Psychoanalysis* 92:1059–1066.

May, U. (1976). Die Psychoanalyse in den USA. In D. Eicke (Ed.), *Tiefenpsychologie. Band 2. Neue Wege der Psychoanalyse – Psychoanalyse der Gesellschaft – Die psychoanalytische Bewegung* [Deep psychology. Vol. 2. New ways in psychoanalysis – Psychoanalysis of society – The analytic movement] (pp. 482–527). Weinheim: Beltz, 1982.

——— (2013). Freud's *Beyond the pleasure principle*: The end of psychoanalysis or its new beginning? *International Forum of Psychoanalysis* 22:208–216.

McLaughlin, N. (2000). Revision from the margins: Fromm's contributions to psychoanalysis. *International Forum of Psychoanalysis* 9:241–247.

Meltzer, D. (1971). Towards an atelier system. In A. Hahn (Ed.), *Sincerity and Other Works* (pp. 285–289). London, Karnac, 1994.

Micale, M.S. (1994). Henry Ellenberger: The history of psychiatry as the history of the unconscious. In M.S. Micale and R. Porter (Eds.), *Discovering the History of Psychiatry* (pp. 112–134). New York: Oxford University Press.

Mitscherlich, A. (1967). *Society Without the Father.* New York: Harcourt, Brace & World. (Original German edition, 1963).

Mitscherlich, A., & Mitscherlich, M. (1975). *The Inability to Mourn: Principles of Collective Behavior.* New York: Random House. (Original German edition, 1967).

Moses, R. (1991). Ein israelischer Psychoanalytiker spricht zur DPG [An Isreaeli analyst speaks to the DPG]. *Forum der Psychoanalyse* 7:62–68.

Mühlleitener, E. (1992). *Biographisches Lexikon der Psychoanalyse. Die Mitglieder der Psychologischen Mittwoch-Gesellschaft und der Wiener Psychoanalytischen Vereinigung 1902–1938* [Biographical dictionary of psychoanalysis. The members of the Psychological Wednesday-Society and of the Vienna Psychoanalytic Association 1902–1938]. Tübingen: Diskord.

———(2009). *Ich – Fenichel. Das Leben eines Psychoanalytikers im 20. Jahrhundert* [I – Fenichel. The life of a psychoanalyst in the 20th century]. Vienna: Paul Zsolnay.

Müller-Braunschweig, C. (1983). Psychoanalyse und Weltanschauung. *Psyche* 37:1136–1139. (Original publication, 1933).

Müller-Braunschweig, H. (1983). Fünfzig Jahre danach [Fifty years later]. *Psyche* 37:1140–1145.

Nicolò, A.M. (2106). Transference in adolescence. In F. Borgogno, A. Luchetti, and L. Marino Coe (Eds.), *Reading Italian Psychoanalysis* (pp. 301–312). London: Routledge.

Nissim Momigliano, L. (2016). Two people talking in a room: An investigation in to the analytic dialogue. In F. Borgogno, A. Luchetti, and L. Marino Coe (Eds.), *Reading Italian Psychoanalysis* (pp. 347–358). London: Routledge. (Original Italian publication, 1984).

Nissim Momigliano, L., & Robutti, A. (Eds.) (1992). *Shared Experience: The Psychoanalytic Dialogue*. London: Karnac.

Nitzschke, B. (1999). Psychoanalysis during national socialism – Present day consequences of a historical controversy in the 'case' of Wilhelm Reich. *Psychoanalytic Review* 86:351–366.

Novelletto, A. (1992). Italy. In P. Kutter (Ed.), *Psychoanalysis International. A Guide to Psychoanalysis Throughout the World*. Vol. 1, *Europe* (pp. 195–212). Stuttgart: Frommann-Holzboog.

Novelletto, A., Viola, G.E., & Rovigatti, F. (1989). *L'Italia nella psicoanalisi – Italy in Psychoanalysis. Catalogue of the Exhibition*. Rome: Istituto dell'Enciclopedia Italiana.

Orange, D. (1994). Review of the book edited by L. Nissim Momigliano and A. Robutti "Shared experience: The analytic dialogue", Karnac 1992. *Psychoanalytic Books* 5:118–121.

Papiasvili, E.D., & Mayers, L.A. (2015). Introductory remarks by the issue editors: A story of beginnings and continuities. *International Forum of Psychoanalysis* 24:2–7.

Peters, U.H. (1988). The psychoanalytic exodus. Romantic antecedents, and the loss to German intellectual life. In E. Timms and N. Segal (Eds.), *Freud in Exile. Psychoanalysis and its Vicissitudes* (pp. 54–64). New Haven, CT: Yale University Press.

Ranchetti, M. (1989). Le "Opere" di Freud [The works of Freud]. *Psicoterapia e Scienze Umane*, 23(4):3–27.

Reichmann, R. (2006). Musatti e le opere di Freud (con un'intervista a Renata Colorni) [Musatti and the works of Freud (with an interview with Renata Colorni)]. *Rivista di Psicoanalisi* 52:129–148.

Roazen, P. (2000). Fromm's *Escape from freedom* and his standing today. *International Forum of Psychoanalysis* 9:239–240.

Rohde-Dachser, C. (1979). *Das Borderline-Syndrome* [The borderline syndrome]. Bern: Huber.

———(1991). *Expedition in den dunklen Kontinent* [Expedition in the dark continent]. Berlin: Springer.

Rosenfeld, A. (2015). My father, Herbert Rosenfeld. *International Forum of Psychoanalysis* 25:220–228.

Roudinesco, E. (1994). *Histoire de la psychanalyse en France. 1: 1885–*

1939 [The history of psychoanalysis in France. 1: 1885–1939]. Paris: Fayard.

Sabbadini, A. (2014). *Boundaries and Bridges. Perspectives on Time and Space in Psychoanalysis*. London: Karnac.

Sánchez, M.E. (2010). Globalization and loss of identity. *International Forum of Psychoanalysis* 19:71–77.

Sandler, A.-M. (2015). Konflikt und Versöhnung [Conflict and reconciliation]. In L.M. Hermanns (Ed.), *Psychoanalyse in Selbstdarstellungen. Band X* [Psychoanalysis in the form of self-portraits. Vol. X] (pp. 221–287). Frankfurt: Brandes & Apsel.

Schachter, J., & Kächele, H. (2017). *Nodal Points: Critical Voices in Contemporary Psychotherapy/Psychoanalysis*. New York: International Psychoanalytic Books.

Schlösser, A.-M. (2009). Oedipus in China: Can we export psychoanalysis? *International Forum of Psychoanalysis* 18:219–224.

Schröter, M. (2015). Über Vergangenheit, Gegenwart und Zukunft der Freud-Editionen in deutscher Sprache [On the past, present and future of Freud's editions in the German language]. *Psyche* 69:551–569.

Schröter, M. (Ed.) (2004). *Sigmund Freud und Max Eitingon. Briefwechsel 1906–1939. Zwei Bände* [Sigmund Freud and Max Eitingon. Correspondence 1906–1939. Two volumes]. Tübingen: Diskord.

Semi, A.A. (2006). E' sufficiente tradurre (bene) Freud? [Is it enough to (well) translate Freud?]. *Rivista di Psicoanalisi* 52:177–188.

Servadio, E. (1935). Psychoanalyse und Telepathie [Psychoanalysis and telepathy]. *Imago* 21:489–497.

Sjödin, C. (2010). Psychoanalytic reflections on global warming and its relation to omnipotence and ethical responsibility. *International Forum of Psychoanalysis* 19:78–83.

Solms, M. (2013). Notes on the Revised Standard Edition. *Psychoanalytic Review* 100:201–210.

Solms, M. (Ed.). *Revised Standard Edition of the Psychological Works of Sigmund Freud, 24 Volumes – Complete Neuroscientific Works of Sigmund Freud, 4 Volumes*. In preparation.

Speier, S. (1987). Der gesichtslose Psychoanalytiker — die ges(ch)ichtslose Psychoanalyse [The psychoanalyst without face – psychoanalysis without history]. *Psyche* 41:481–491.

Spiegel, R. (1975). On psychoanalysis in the Third Reich. *Contemporary Psychoanalysis* 11:472–492.

Steiner, R. (1986). F. Fornari (1921–1985). *International Review of Psychoanalysis* 13:97–99.

——— (1987). A world wide international trade mark of genuineness? Some observations on the history of the English translation of the work of Sigmund Freud, focusing mainly on his technical terms. *International Review of Psycho-Analysis* 14:33–102.

——— (1989a). "It is a new kind of diaspora . . .". *International Review of Psycho-Analysis* 16:35–72.

——— (1989b). C.L. Musatti (1897–1989). *International Journal of Psychoanalysis* 70:725–726.

——— (1991). "To explain the point of view of English readers in English words". *International Review of Psycho-Analysis* 18:351–392.

——— (2000). *"It is a New Kind of Diaspora". Explorations in the Sociopolitical and Cultural Context of Psychoanalysis*. London:

Karnac.

——— (2011). "In all questions, my interest is not in the individual people but in the analytic movement as a whole. It will be hard enough here in Europe in the times to come to keep it going. After all, we are just a handful of people who have that in mind . . .". *International Journal of Psychoanalysis* 92:505–591.

Sterba, R. (1982). *Reminiscences of a Viennese Psychoanalyst*. Detroit: Wayne State University Press.

Strachey, J. (1966). General preface. *Standard Edition* 1, pp. xii–xxvi.

Strachey, J., & Strachey, A. (Eds.) (1953–1974). *The Standard Edition of the Complete Psychological Works of Sigmund Freud. 24 Volumes*. London: Hogarth Press.

Stroeken, H. (2013). The fate of German-Jewish psychoanalyst refugees in the Netherlands: An overview. *International Forum of Psychoanalysis* 22:203–207.

Tate Angel, V., & Conci, M. (2015). Editorial – Evoking Freud's memory: Pﬁbor. *International Forum of Psychoanalysis* 24:1.

Thomä, H. (2015). Remarks on the first century of the International Psychoanalytic Association and a utopian vision of the future. *International Forum of Psychoanalysis* 24:110–132.

Thomä, H., & Kächele, H. (1985–2006). *Psychoanalytic Practice. Three Volumes – Principles, Clinical Studies, Research*. Berlin: Springer.

Timms, E., & Segal, N. (Eds.) (1988). *Freud in Exile. Psychoanalysis and its Vicissitudes*. New Haven, CT: Yale University Press.

Tögel, C. (Ed.) (2015). *Sigmund Freud – Gesamtausgabe – Band 1, 1877– 1885. Unter Mitarbeit von U. Zerfass* [Sigmund Freud – Collected works – Vol. 1, 1877–1885. With the collaboration of U. Zerfass]. Giessen: Psychosozial-Verlag.

Turkle, S. (1978) *Psychoanalytic Politics. Jacques Lacan and Freud's French Revolution*. London: Burnett Books.

Wallerstein, R.S. (1988). Psychoanalysis in Nazi Germany: Historical and psychoanalytic lessons. *Psychoanalysis and Contemporary Thought* 11:351–370.

Wellendorf, F. (2007). Zur Geschichte der DPG nach dem Zweiten Weltkrieg [On the history of the DPG after the Second World War]. *Psyche* 61:404–411.

Will, H. (2018). The concept of the 50–minute hour: Time forming a frame for the unconscious. *International Forum of Psychoanalysis* 27:14–23.

Wirth, H.-J. (2013). From Hiroshima to Chernobyl to Fukushima: What does the "militant" use of nuclear power mean for our mental state, and how about its "peaceful" use? *International Forum of Psychoanalysis* 22:217–227.

Wyatt, F. (1988). The severance of psychoanalysis from its cultural matrix. In E. Timms and N. Segal (Eds.), *Freud in Exile. Psychoanalysis and its Vicissitudes* (pp. 145–155). New Haven, CT: Yale University Press.

Zagermann, P. (2017b). Theses on the heart of darkness. The unresolved Oedipus complex of psychoanalytic institution formation. In P. Zagermann (Ed.), *The Future of Psychoanalysis. The Debate about the Training Analyst System* (pp. 311–337). London: Routledge.

Zagermann, P. (Ed.) (2017a). *The Future of Psychoanalysis. The Debate about the Training Analyst System*. London: Routledge.

Zepf, S. (2006). *Allgemeine psychoanalytische Neurosenlehre, Psychosomatik, und Sozialpsychologie. 4 Bände* [General psychoanalytic theory of neuroses, psychosomatics and social psychology]. Giessen: Psychosozial-Verlag.

——— (2015). Some notes on Freud's concept of conversion. *International Forum of Psychoanalysis* 24:77–87.

CHAPTER 10

GAETANO BENEDETTI, JOHANNES CREMERIUS, THE MILAN ASP, AND THE FUTURE OF IFPS[1]

INTRODUCTION

I have been actively involved in the life of the International Federation of Psychoanalytic Societies (IFPS) since the VIIIth IFPS Forum, which took place in Rio de Janeiro on October 10–14, 1989, when I was a second-year candidate in training at the Milan Scuola di Psicoterapia Psicoanalitica (SPP), and during which the Milan Associazione di Studi Psicoanalitici (ASP) became a member society of the IFPS. I not only traveled to Brazil together with Guido Medri and Ciro Elia, two of the founding members of the SPP, but also participated in the panel on the psychotherapeutic treatment of psychoses, which they gave together with Gaetano Benedetti. The panel was meant to inform IFSP members about the line of work developed by our Milan group, in the context of our training institute, the SPP, and of our association, the ASP. Laura Andreoli and Daniela Maggioni had not been able to come with us to Brazil, and I participated in the panel by reading their paper in English.

The original contact between our group and the IFPS had been established by Benedetti himself, at the Zurich Forum of 1985, through the New York colleague Gerard Chrzanowski (1913–2000), a member of the White Institute and one of the protagonists of the life of our Federation since its foundation in Amsterdam in 1962 (Mann, 2001). Chrzanowski—also a psychiatrist and a psychoanalyst committed to the treatment of the sickest patients—had known Benedetti and his work for many years and held him in high esteem. As we will see below, in 1987 he wrote to Benedetti inviting him and his Milan group to join IFPS.

Whereas Benedetti still lives in Bâle and turned 92 last July, Johannes Cremerius—who was two years his senior—died more than ten years ago, on March 15, 2002. In the section of this paper dedicated to his life and work, I will show both how and why working as a supervisor in Milan was so important to him that he kept doing

---

[1] The original version of this article was published in Volume 23 (2014) of the *International Forum of Psychoanalysis,* pp. 85–95. It represents the revised version of a paper given in Mexico City in October 2012, at the XVIIth IFPS Forum.

regularly (at least once a month) for more than thirty years (1966–1999), and how his work shaped the structure of both the SPP and the ASP.

Although the ASP came formally into existence only in 1987 (Corsi Piacentini, 1990), the SPP had already been formalized as an institute with a precise training curriculum at the beginning of the 1980s. The group of founding members (besides Teresa Corsi, Ciro Elia, and Guido Medri, Piergiorgio Battaggia, Aldo Cantoni, Lilia D'Alfonso, Annamaria Fabbrichesi, and Marina Saviotti also belonged to it) had come together at the beginning of the 1970s, with the purpose of asking Benedetti and Cremerius to continue supervising their clinical work and helping them complete their analytic training after the end of a previous training experience in the context of the Centro Studi di Psicoterapia Clinica. In the letter written to Pier Francesco Galli that I will show below, Benedetti explained why he had decided to accept such a proposal. How happy the members of the group were about Benedetti's acceptance of their invitation also emerges from a set of letters I found in his correspondence (see below).

Pier Francesco Galli (born in 1931 and still living in Bologna) had in fact not only been the first important Italian collaborator of Benedetti, since their first meeting in the context of the psychology department of the Milan Catholic University in the late 1950s (see below). He was also the founder, at the beginning of the 1960s, of the above-mentioned Centro Studi di Psicoterapia Clinica, at a time when the Italian IPA group, that is, the Società Psicoanalitica Italiana (SPI), was still a rather small and internationally isolated group. As I showed in my 1994 paper "Psychoanalysis in Italy: A reappraisal," this allowed Galli and Benedetti to play a very important role both in the translation, publication, and diffusion of English-speaking and German-speaking analytic literature through the famous publishing house Feltrinelli, and in the organization of important international seminars and congresses, like the International Psychotherapy Conference, which they organized in Milan in the summer of 1970 (Galli, 1973).

In other words, as I showed in my 1996 paper "Die Psychoanalyse in Italien: Anfänge, Entwicklung und gegenwärtige Lage," psychoanalysis became popular in Italy only after the 1968 Student Movement, that is, at a time when the SPI was both too small and not yet well enough organized to be able to adequately meet the many requests for training coming from a growing number of psychiatrists and psychologists. As the SPI analyst Arnaldo Novelletto wrote in 1992, Eugenio Gaddini (1916–1985, SPI president 1978–1982) "was the first in Italy to actively do everything possible in order to adapt the psychoanalytic institution in its various aspects (organs and society regulations, congresses, journal, teaching activities) to the standards of the IPA" (Novelletto, 1992, p. 201). Although a regular university curriculum in psychology was created only at the beginning of the 1970s in Padua and Roma, a growing number of philosophy graduates were specializing in psychology in the 1960s, and many of them were interested in analytic training. This helps us to explain why Benedetti and Cremerius were invited by the above-mentioned group of young professionals to work with them to complete their "unorthodox" analytic training—they had undergone a personal analysis with a senior analyst (often a SPI member) and a series of supervisory experiences without having been "analytic candidates" in the proper sense of the word (that is, candidates of an institute of the IPA).

In fact, the IPA itself had at the time such an authoritarian structure that the candidates could only passively participate and not actively intervene in IPA events, and this made it of course less attractive for all the leftist-oriented young people seeking analytic training in Italy. Such a structure had a first visible crisis at the IPA Congress held in Rome in August 1969, during which an alternative psychoanalytic network called "Plataforma Internacional" was founded—and through which the journal founded by Galli in 1967, *Psicoterapia e scienze umane*, gained in readers and influence (Migone, 1990). Among the founders of Plataforma Internacional were Elvio Fachinelli (1928–1989), an associate member of the SPI, Berthold Rothschild (a member of the Zurich Psychoanalytic Seminar), and Marianna Bolko (a later co-editor of *Psicoterapia e scienze umane*), all pioneers of a critical and socially committed psychoanalysis— Fachinelli, one of the most brilliant Italian analysts of the 1970s (Conci, 2011) never applied to become a full member of the SPI. It is no wonder that all these pioneers had good personal contacts with and were sympathetic to the possibility that Benedetti and Cremerius offered the above-mentioned group of young psychiatrists and psychologists to create in Milan what later became an "alternative psychoanalytic institution."

But let me now come to the attempt to summarize the ways in which the professional orientation and the work of Benedetti and Cremerius shaped our group, that is, the SPP and ASP. First is the critical position that both Benedetti and Cremerius had in common vis-à-vis what used to be called "institutionalized psychoanalysis," and their readiness to experiment with new ways of organizing the candidates' training. This had as a consequence the abolition of the so-called "training analysis" and its substitution with a personal analysis, conducted with a trustworthy and reliable analyst outside the training institute itself and which had to take place before the beginning of the training proper.

Second, the interest that both shared in extending the use of psychoanalysis to the treatment of the sickest patients was of course accompanied by the concept of a continuum between psychoanalysis and psychoanalytic psychotherapy, and by an emphasis on the so-called "intrinsic factors" of analytic work.

Third, one of the consequences of this point of view at the institutional level was the admission to the training of candidates who were not only MDs and psychologists—a concept that the SPP had to renounce to after the promulgation of the 1989 Italian Law regulating the field of psychotherapy.

Fourth, in as much as teamwork is essential in the treatment of the sickest patients, and at variance with the IPA training according to the so-called "Eitingon model," group supervision had in our training as much place as did individual supervision (see also D'Alfonso, 2000; and Conci, 2010).

Last but not least, both Benedetti and Cremerius were not only open to a dialogue with other disciplines and to the necessity of the development of a "socially critical psychoanalysis," but were also interested in getting in contact with the growing dimension of empirical research; in other words, these three dimensions were also part of our training.

Since the application of the 1989 Italian Law that eventually regulated the profession of psychologist and created the new profession of "psychotherapist" (which only MDs and psychologists could have access to), the whole field of analytic training has gone through great transformations, basically in the sense of the subordination of psychoanalysis to analytic psychotherapy. By "psychoanalysis" I mean an intellectual discipline with a history, a set of theories, and a variety of applications, and by "analytic psychotherapy" I mean the one-sided emphasis on the therapeutic application of the intellectual corpus of psychoanalysis. Such a change, which depends on a *Zeitgeist* affecting our profession in the whole world, did not spare our group. However, the seeds implanted in it by Benedetti and Cremerius in the 1970s are somehow still alive and they deserve to be spelled out in the light of their own life and work—and with the aim of contributing some stimulating ideas to the future agenda we want to give to our Federation.

GAETANO BENEDETTI

Let me start to introduce Gaetano Benedetti through his *Selbstdarstellung*, that is, the autobiographical portrait that he published in 1994 in a German anthology edited by Ludger Hermanns. The oldest of the three sons of a very good surgeon and of a well-educated mother, Benedetti grew up in Catania, where he was born on June 26, 1920,[2] and where he graduated from medical school at the end of the World War II. Following in his father's footsteps and turning them in the direction of psychiatry, he moved to Zurich in 1947 in order to specialize in psychiatry—a very neglected specialty in Italy at that time—under Eugen Bleuler's (1857–1939) son Manfred (1903–1994; see Scharfetter, 2006). This encounter and the subsequent collaboration changed both his professional and his personal life.

Manfred Bleuler soon discovered that "Benedetti's empathy for his patients was like that of Eugen Bleuler, which at this time still pervaded the atmosphere of the *Klinik*" (Bleuler, 1987, p. xi; Benedetti, 1998)—as he wrote in his foreword to Benedetti's English anthology of his papers, published by New York University Press in 1987. In the preface of this book, entitled *Psychotherapy of schizophrenia*, whose very attractive cover page shows a patient "going her own way toward health in a tunnel of light" (Benedetti, 1987, p. 217), Benedetti placed his own scientific contribution in the tradition of Jung's application of Freud's psychoanalysis to the treatment of schizophrenia (Benedetti, 1987, p. xv). As far as Benedetti's personal life is concerned, at the Burghölzli

---

[2] In my paper "Gaetano Benedetti in his correspondence" (Conci, 2008), I had given Benedetti's birth date as July 7, 1920. Only in connection with the celebration of his ninetieth birthday did I discover that Benedetti was actually born on June 26, but it was only on July 7 that his birth was officially communicated to the town hall of Catania. At this celebration, organized by the ASP in Milan on June 26, 2010, I gave a paper (Conci, 2012b) about his organization, together with Pier Maria Furlan, of the IXth Symposium for the Psychotherapy of Schizophrenia held in Turin in August 1988 (see also below).

he also met his future wife Annette—a very gentle and intelligent nurse—who unfortunately died in February 2004 and with whom he had four children.

After working in close contact with Manfred Bleuler, undergoing his IPA training analysis with the famous Zurich analyst Gustav Bally (1893–1966), and spending about a year in the USA in 1950–1951 (where he came into contact with Silvano Arieti, Frieda Fromm-Reichmann, and Harold Searles), Benedetti became a full professor of psychiatry in Zurich in 1953, and in Rome in 1955. But even more important is the fact that, together with Christian Müller (1921–2013), himself a Swiss psychiatrist and psychoanalyst (and the son of the famous psychiatrist Max Müller), he organized the First International Symposium on the Psychotherapy of Schizophrenia, in Lausanne in 1956. The following year, Benedetti left Zurich for Bâle, where he became Heinrich Meng's (1887–1972) successor as professor of "mental hygiene and psychotherapy" and where he worked in the context of the psychotherapy service of the department of psychiatry until his retirement in 1985.[3]

Even more important than Benedetti's teaching activity in Bâle are the Symposia that regularly followed the first one, that is, Zurich (1959), Lausanne (1964), Turku (1971), Oslo (1975), Lausanne (1978), Heidelberg (1981), Yale (1985), Turin (1988), and Stockholm (1991), in all of which Benedetti was personally involved. Out of the first small congresses held in French and German (Conci, 2012a), Benedetti and Müller ended up creating a large interdisciplinary and international English-speaking movement that is still active today (Alanen, Silver, and González de Chávez, 2006). The International Society for Psychological and Social Approaches to Psychosis (ISPS) now consists of numerous national sections, publishes the journal *Psychosis: Psychological, Social and Integrative Approaches*, and held its 18th Symposium at the end of August 2013 in Warsaw—under the leadership of the British psychiatrist and psychoanalyst Brian Martindale. But the best attended of all these Symposia, with more than 1,300 participants, was the one organized by Benedetti and Pier Maria Furlan in Turin in 1988, around the theme of the necessary integration of all the effective psychological and social approaches to schizophrenia (Benedetti and Furlan, 1993).

---

[3] For more detailed information about Benedetti's relationship with both Bally and Meng, see Conci (2008). In this, I deal also with Benedetti's relationship with Chrzanowski.

Of course, the Turin Symposium was also so successful because Benedetti had been lecturing, supervising, and publishing a part of his work in Italy for more than thirty years, including the creation of the Milan group which I mentioned above, at the beginning of the 1970s. As I showed in my 2006 paper "Seminari a Milano," he had given his very first Italian paper, "The problem of conscience in the hallucinations of schizophrenics," at Milan Catholic University on March 25, 1955, upon the invitation of one of the pioneers of Italian psychology, Padre Agostino Gemelli (1878–1959). It was there that he met important patients and future co-workers such as Mara Palazzoli Selvini (1916–1999), the later pioneer of Italian family therapy, and the above-mentioned Pier Francesco Galli. Coming back to the book series that Galli and Benedetti published with Feltrinelli, let me remind you of the fact that H.S. Sullivan's (1892–1949) *Conceptions of modern psychiatry* (*La moderna concezione della psichiatria*) was the first book of the series; this came out in 1961 with a very good Preface by Benedetti himself (Benedetti, 1961). In fact, it played an important role in the way I approached Sullivan in *Sullivan revisited. Life and work*, which can also be seen as a continuation of Benedetti's own work.[4]

But let me now come to one of the most interesting letters of Benedetti's correspondence, which I received from him as a gift in the summer of 2005 (Conci, 2008)—and which I did not include in it, since I had not yet got hold of it. It is a letter that Benedetti wrote to Galli on June 1, 1971, detailing some of his reasons for choosing to devolve most of his energies to supervising and teaching the Milan group out of which both SPP and ASP would later evolve. Here is what we can read starting from the third section:

> After the various experiences and disappointments I had, I do not wish any more to become a full member of the Society. I always felt limited in my freedom . . . . I prefer to orient myself according to the words of Simone Weil 'The exercise of intelligence requires a total freedom . . . '.
> I well understand that my pupils could find it very helpful, if I were an official representative of the Society. For this very reason in the past I tried more than once to move in this direction, but to no avail.
> As a matter of fact, I ended up concluding that it is

---

[4] This is also the reason why Benedetti accepted my invitation to write a Preface (Benedetti, 2005) to the German edition of my book *Sullivan neu entdecken*. In fact, having personally promoted the Italian edition of Sullivan's *Schizophrenia as a human process* (Conci, 1993), I had myself completed the task of promoting Sullivan's work in Italy, which he had started thirty-two years earlier (Benedetti, 1961).

even better if my pupils come in the position of not expecting anything from me in terms of their personal analysis.

On the other hand, there are institutions which recognize my activity, even without the need for me to apply for it. The German Psychoanalytic Society has given me the position of training analyst through its Freiburg Institute; the American Academy of Psychoanalysis wanted me to join it as a fellow. And this should be enough.

This letter integrates and completes very well what Benedetti had already written in the above-mentioned self-portrait of 1994:

My interest for and work in the field of the psychotherapy of psychoses had as a consequence a certain degree of isolation, both in psychoanalysis and in psychiatry . . . . For example, my request to become a full member of the Swiss Psychoanalytic Society (I was an associate member since my call to Bâle) was rejected "because I – as De Saussure, then president of the Society said – had founded in Milan an institute outside of the I.P.A."

Through meetings with him and with Berna I tried to convince them of my point of view, according to which the psychotherapy of psychoses represents a fundamental task of psychoanalysis, goes beyond narrow scholastic concepts and actually contributes to its universality – but to no avail.

As usual in my life, I decided to keep my autonomy and I became even more motivated to pursue my own work independently. (Benedetti, 1994, p. 44; my translation)[5]

Besides Benedetti's love for his native country, this is the institutional background that allows us to understand why he chose the Milan group as the main center of his teaching activity. His relationship with the Swiss IPA group, as well as his teaching of medical students and psychiatric residents at the department of psychiatry of the University of Bâle, was hardly satisfying—dominated as it was by very traditional psychiatrists as Stähelin and Kielholz.[6]

Only with a group of younger analysts supervised by him in their work with schizophrenic and borderline patients could Benedetti do the research work that interested him the most, which found its first expression in the book *Paziente e analista nella terapia delle psicosi*, published by Benedetti and by his best Milan pupils and collaborators in 1979. These collaborators were Teresa Corsi Piacentini, Lilia D'Alfonso, Ciro Elia, Guido Medri,

---

[5] Indeed, Benedetti (as Fachinelli had also done; see above) always remained an associate member of the IPA, and his name is still (November 2013) present on its roster.

[6] Benedetti's Swiss pupil Carlo Calanchini described the work of supervision of psychiatric residents that Benedetti carried out for many years in Bâle in his 2006 book chapter "Seminari a Basilea." After this experience, Calanchini completed his analytic training within the Milan SPP and is still an ASP member.

and Marina Saviotti—Teresa, Ciro, and Guido actively participated in the life of IFPS between 1989 and 1998. In fact, it was in the context of such research work that Benedetti was able to write in his native tongue what he always considered as being his masterwork: *Alienazione e personazione nella psicoterapia della malattia mentale*, published in 1980. Translated into German in 1983 with the title *Todeslandschaften der Seele* (Landscapes of death of the soul), the book was published in French in 1995— thanks to the dedication and work of Patrick Faugeras— under the title *La mort dans l'âme*, but it is unfortunately not yet available in English. A further book, written together with an even bigger group of ASP members, was *Paziente e terapeuta nell'esperienza psicotica* (1991).[7]

Before taking up the above-mentioned first contacts between our Milan group and the IFPS, let me touch on two aspects of the Spanish and Mexican chapters of Benedetti's international reception and contacts. Before addressing a very significant letter to one of his most important Mexican correspondents, I would like to start with Benedetti's book *Psicoterapia clinica*, which came out in Barcelona in 1983; "*Traducida ya al japonés, noruego y finés, se ha convertido en un clásico sobre el tema*" ("Already translated into Japanese, Norwegian and Finnish, it has become a classic on this theme") we can read on the back cover page of the book, whose subtitle is *Introducción a la psicoterapia de las psicosis*.

In the about fifty folders of letters by and to Benedetti that I have in my office, I found a very moving exchange

---

[7] These contributors were Laura Andreoli, Antonella Cannavò, Lilia D'Alfonso, Ciro Elia, Clelia Leozappa, Daniela Maggioni, Lauretta Ottolenghi, Francesca Pavese, Alberto Sibilla, and Carla Tomassina. Among other things that deserve to be mentioned about this book is the fact that Chapter 4, "Narcisismo: perdita, depressione, psicosi" (Narcissism: loss, depression, psychosis), represents the text of the paper given by Benedetti at the above-mentioned 1989 IFPS Forum of Rio de Janeiro.

But the most important theme I would mention in connection with it is how Benedetti's readiness to interact with his pupils (including his sane narcissism) made of many of us active collaborators in the development of his work. As far as I am concerned, I can mention the Afterword I wrote (Conci, 1997) to his book *La psicoterapia come sfida esistenziale* (originally published in German in 1992), in which I showed how the integrative nature of his therapeutic attitude was also grounded in the kind of person he was—as Patrick Faugeras also showed in 2000. Of course, the best demonstration of Benedetti's capacity to stimulate the creativity of his co-workers is his collaboration with Maurizio Peciccia—as he, for example, described it in 2000. From this came the book *Sogno, inconscio, psicosi* (Benedetti and Peciccia, 1995) and their revisitation of the psychodynamics of schizophrenia published in our journal (Peciccia and Benedetti, 1996).

between him and Jorge Silva García (a Mexican protagonist of the life of our Federation) dating back to October 1985. To Silva García's report on how promptly and generously the Mexican people had all helped each other after the terrible earthquake of September 19, 1985, Benedetti replied expressing his solidarity with him and his people, closing his letter with the following very personal words:

> I find consolation in the thought that every word we say in behalf of others survives death, remains in existence and invisible continues to exist in the Collective Unconscious. This is an extraordinary experience of mine, the experience of the survival of our thoughts and of the imperceptible communication which exists among us all. My psychotherapeutic work with both psychotic and neurotic patients has given me the most convincing proof of this.

And now, here is the letter that Chrzanowski wrote to Benedetti on June 2, 1987, on behalf of the Executive Committee of IFPS, of which he was a member:

> Dear Professor Benedetti, it has been a long time since I had the opportunity to see you. At the last Forum of the IFPS in Zurich I was told that you were heading a group and might be interested in joining the IFPS. Please be advised that we would be very happy if you would send us an application for membership in the International Federation of Psychoanalytic Societies.

And here is Benedetti's answer to Chrzanowski, on behalf of the Milan ASP, on June 23, 1987:

> Dear Dr. Chrzanowski, I am delighted to receive your letter of June 2nd, 1987 and regret for not having been able to keep in touch with you since our last meeting of the Forum of the IFPS in Zurich. This is due to the enormous work preceding my retirement from the University of Basel, having reached the age-limit. Referring to our talk in Zurich, I am sending you our application of our Association of Psychoanalysis in Milan, Italy to the International Federation of Psychoanalytic Societies.

As I discovered only in connection with the preparation of this paper, the next letter—dated November 3, 1987—was written by the New York analyst and IFPS Secretary-General Ann R. Turkel, who communicated to Benedetti that Chrzanowski himself and the Swiss colleague Gion Condrau would make a site visit to Milan that was preliminary to and necessary for the society's admission to membership. It took place at the beginning of 1988 and led to the acceptance of the ASP as a member society of IFPS at the Forum of Rio de Janeiro in October 1989.

JOHANNES CREMERIUS

Johannes Cremerius also contributed a *Selbstdarstellung* to the above-mentioned anthology edited by Ludger Hermanns in 1994 (Cremerius, 1994). One reason why it makes sense to take it into consideration here is that Cremerius's life and work are almost unknown outside the German-speaking and Italian-speaking analytic communities. As Edith Kurzweil showed in her 1989 book *The Freudians. A comparative perspective*, it took many years for German colleagues to elaborate the tragedy of World War II and to feel reintegrated into the analytic mainstream. Hardly any prominent German colleague— with the exception of Alexander Mitscherlich (1908– 1982)—tried (or dared) to have their work translated into English until the end of the 1980s (Conci, Erhardt, and Kächele, 2013).

Behind Cremerius's frequent contacts with the Italian analytic community and the work he regularly (at least once a month) did in Milan between 1966 and 1999 lay the fact that he had attended a year of medical school in Pavia (near Milan) during World War II.[8] He had been born in North-West Germany (near Düsseldorf) on May 16, 1918, and had grown up inside a Protestant family with very high cultural and ethical standards. Although greatly fascinated by literature and philosophy, he chose to study medicine and become a psychiatrist. From his autobiographical chapter, we learn about the crucial importance that the internist Victor von Weiszäcker (1886–1957) and his analytically oriented psychosomatic medicine played—as had been the case with Mitscherlich—in his choice of a psychoanalytic career (Cremerius, 1994, pp. 78–80). This is why he went to Munich in 1948 (with his wife Annemarie), where he became a collaborator of Walter Seitz, himself an internist interested in and open to psychoanalysis, and where he started his first analytic training with Fritz Riemann (1902–1979), a member of the German Psychoanalytic Society.[9]

---

[8] Here is what Cremerius wrote in this regard in his afterword to the Italian edition of his 1994 self-portrait: "When I entered Pavia's Collegio Ghislieri in the fall of 1939, I could not imagine how important and meaningful such a step would have become in my life. Here my love for Italy was born. Italy became my second fatherland" (Cremerius, 2000, p. 116; my translation).

[9] Riemann was at the time the most prominent analyst of the Munich Akademie für Psychotherapie und Psychoanalyse. Cremerius discussed at length in his self-portrait both his analysis and his relationship to him, as well as the historical background behind the Akademie itself, that is, the totally lacking elaboration of the Nazi past from which the

Another important turning point in Cremerius's life was represented by the six months that he was able to spend in the USA visiting analytically oriented psychiatric hospitals (such as Chestnut Lodge and the Menninger Clinic) and analytic institutes (e.g., New York, Boston, and Chicago), through which he developed a solid relationship with the international analytic community. In fact, I still remember him telling us candidates in Milan about his personal meeting with pioneers of the psychoanalytic movement such as Franz Alexander and Karen Horney, Kurt Eissler and Rudolph Loewenstein, Frieda Fromm-Reichmann and Harold Searles, that is, analysts whom no member of the Italian IPA group (with the possible exception of Emilio Servadio and Eugenio Gaddini) had ever met! This motivated Cremerius not only to join the German Psychoanalytic Association,[10] but also in his later move to Zurich (1960), where he underwent a second analysis with Benedetti's training analyst Gustav Bally and came into close contact with Paul Parin (1916–2009) and his group. This second training experience allowed him to feel much more at home in the IPA, of which he had become a member by joining the German Psychoanalytic Association in the 1950s, after finishing his analysis with Fritz Riemann. In 1963, Cremerius accepted the invitation of Horst-Eberhard Richter (1923–2011) to join him at the medical school of the University of Giessen (near Frankfurt) and collaborate with him in teaching medical students and training analytic candidates, including the possibility to go through the necessary *Habilitation* to become a full university professor. In Giessen, he also started working as a training analyst, and from Giessen he started regularly traveling to Italy in the mid-1960s.

In 1970 Cremerius—with his wife and their daughter—moved to Freiburg, where he headed the university department of psychosomatic medicine and psychotherapy until his retirement in 1993. From Freiburg, he was able to come to Milan much more easily, as he regularly did once a month until 1999. In Freiburg, he wrote the papers and books that made him famous in

leading group had come (Cremerius, 1994, pp. 82–83). After long years of work and heated (and constructive) discussions inside the Akademie, its history was eventually revisited in detail in the book edited in 2008 by Thea Bauriedl and Astrid Brundke.

[10]The German Psychoanalytic Association had been founded in 1950 by Karl Müller-Braunschweig (1881–1958), who left the German Psychoanalytic Society after the Society had been left out of the IPA at the 1949 IPA Congress, held in Zurich. The first important book on this very controversial topic was written by Regine Lockot (1985). Michael Ermann (1996) provided an important contribution to its re-elaboration; a recent reconstruction can be found in Bohleber (2012).

both the German- and the Italian-speaking worlds (see below), he actively participated in the elaboration of the tragedy of the Third Reich,[11] and he developed the critique of "institutionalized psychoanalysis," for which he is still famous (see below).

Although Cremerius had a critical mind and a charismatic personality, what he was even more appreciated for by his Milan supervisees was his revisitation of orthodox ego psychology in the light of the work first of Michael Balint (1896–1970), and later of Sándor Ferenczi (1873–1933). Here is how he presented "the analyst's job" in the summary at the beginning of the original German edition of his two-volume book *Vom Handwerk des Analytikers* (Cremerius, 1984), putting the emphasis on the nondogmatic, flexible, and artistic character of such a job:

> The following two volumes describe the daily work of the psychoanalyst with his patients and report the various technical problems posed with regard to the method of treatment . . . . The attempt is made to depict a mode of operation that is both situation and patient centered. The attention will be directed first to all problems of interaction, dynamics of transference and countertransference, that is, the "two-person psychology" (Balint). From this point of view, certain Freudian terms, originating from his objective-objectifying standpoint, need to be redefined . . . . In my opinion, the standard methods deduced from Freud's writings are not workable. I consider it to be a theoretical construction, an ideal treatment under ideal conditions . . . . Does there still exist an agreement about 'standard technique'? It will be demonstrated that today we have a pluralism of opinions; that a liberalization has taken place to which many theories have fallen victim . . . . In this way began the development of psychoanalysis into a 'science' (Kuhn). The author hopes to be able to contribute to the progress of this development, that is, to an opening, to a critical revision, to an unreserved discussion about dogma. (Cremerius 1984, p. 4; my translation)

The two volumes (Cremerius, 1984; for a total of fourteen chapters, as opposed to the one-volume Italian edition, under the title *Il mestiere dell'analista*, in ten chapters) contain very good and still relevant contributions not yet translated into English, for example: "Transference and countertransference in patients with serious super-ego pathology" and "Are there two

---

[11]The very long and painful process of elaborating the involvement of German analysts in the Nazi regime, whose main form was their clinical work within the so-called Göring Institute (Cocks, 1985), eventually took place only in the 1980s. The 1977 refusal of the IPA to hold one of its next congresses in Berlin stimulated a group of analytic candidates to eventually document this history through an exhibition that took place at the 1985 IPA Congress held in Hamburg (Brecht et al., 1993).

psychoanalytic techniques?" (Volume 1), and "Freud at work behind his shoulders – His technique in the mirror of pupils and patients" and "The meaningful role of the dissidents in psychoanalysis – Psychoanalysis beyond orthodoxy and dissidence" (Volume 2).

Such an original attitude also extended to a critical revisitation of the history of psychoanalysis, and of the problems and contradictions of psychoanalysis as an institution. This was the content of such very inspiring papers—which I know well for having translated them from German into Italian—as "Training analysis and power" (Cremerius, 1989) and "Selection system and power politics" (Cremerius, 1990). The main contradiction that he pointed to dealt of course with the many ways in which the institutionalization of psychoanalysis, mainly in the form of the IPA, very often, and/or on many levels, resulted and still results in the very betrayal of psychoanalysis itself. As far as the so-called "training analysis" is concerned, he saw it as a situation leading to unanalyzable transference–countertransference dynamics, with the result that submission to the authority of the training analyst prevails over the free search for self-knowledge for which psychoanalysis should stand.[12]

And here is how Cremerius reconstructed his participation in and contribution to the foundation and nature of our Milan Institute and Society in his Afterword (Cremerius, 2000) to the Italian edition of his *Selbstdarstellung* (Cremerius, 1994):

> In 1966 I was approached by Emanuele Gualandri after a paper I gave in Milan and he asked me if I would like to work more in Italy. He belonged to a group of psychoanalysts who had gathered around P.F. Galli, with the need and the aim to deepen their knowledge of Freudian psychoanalysis. They were eager to do with me technical seminars and group and individual supervisions. I accepted and since then I went to Milan from Frankfurt twice a month, Friday and Saturday. After my move to Freiburg I went

---

[12]In fact, this is also the position that Otto Kernberg developed, starting with his 1986 paper "Institutional problems in psychoanalytic education" (which I also translated for *Psicoterapia e scienze umane*; Kernberg, 1987), and of which he is today—himself a former IPA president, 1997–2001—the most important spokesman. Here is what he wrote in 2006: "As mentioned before, the personal analysis of psychoanalytic candidates should be disconnected completely from the rest of psychoanalytic training, as is already the case in the French system" (Kernberg, 2006, p. 1664).

This is also why Kernberg was invited to give the paper "Training in psychoanalysis and dynamic psychotherapy today: Conflicts and challenges" (Kernberg, 2011) at the celebration of the forty-fifth anniversary of the foundation of *Psicoterapia e scienze umane,* which took place in Bologna on September 20, 2011.

to Milan only once a month, but worked there three days.

At the beginning of the 1970s some members of these seminars started organizing a training institute and asked me to contribute to its structure and to the nature of its curriculum. I was happy to do it and I kept working there till 1999. We had agreed upon organizing the training according to Freudian principles: admission also of "lay people" to the training; no "training analysis", but only a personal analysis with a trustworthy and reliable analyst before the beginning of training; no training analysts; the supervision of clinical work as belonging to the training from the very beginning. (Cremerius, 2000, p. 117, my translation)[13]

Before coming to the next section, specifically devoted to the foundation and life of the ASP, let me propose to you the following words of Cremerius, taken from the only interview in English with him that I know of. As an aside, in the English-speaking world Cremerius was unfortunately known mainly as a pioneer of the revisitation and new articulation of the long-forgotten and repressed work of Sándor Ferenczi (1873–1933). A case in point is Arnold Rachman's mention of Cremerius's 1982 paper on Ferenczi's famous Wiesbaden paper of 1932, which can be found in Rachman's 1997 book on Ferenczi. The interview I just mentioned was conducted by ASP member Marco Francesconi in 1999 and published in English in 2002 in the *Journal of European Psychoanalysis*, and in 2009 in the anthology *In Freud's tracks* edited by Sergio Benvenuto and Anthony Molino (Cremerius, 2009):

> My development mainly followed the Kant, Hegel, Schopenhauer line, then the Enlightenment idea, which is difficult to reconcile with the Christian religion. For me Freud is one of the great Enlightenment thinkers . . . . After

---

[13]An even more detailed description and analysis of Cremerius's contribution to our training curriculum and to the atmosphere of our group can be found in Chapter 9, "Psychoanalytische Psychotherapie in Mailand," of the posthumous volume *Ein Leben als Psychoanalytiker in Deutschland*, edited in 2006 by his close friend Wolfram Mauser. Here are Cremerius's words: "Since we did not want to repeat the hierarchical-authoritarian structure of the training institutes of the IPA, which we saw as a betrayal of the Enlightenment spirit of psychoanalysis, we decided to renounce to symbols of power like the role of 'training analyst.' We therefore limited ourselves to a functional structure composed of teachers and students . . . . This turned out to be very advantageous for the climate of the institute, which was free of the transferential tensions which usually burden analytic institutes for years . . . . This kind of organization of the training is very similar – as I later learned – to the one worked out by the French Psychoanalytic Association (APF) . . . In this way we also hoped to avoid the intellectual regression of the students" (Cremerius, 2006, pp. 275–277). In fact, the so-called "French training model" promoted by the APF was approved by the IPA in 2007 as one of its three official training models (Bohleber, 2011). Furthermore, in the fall of 2011, the Italian Psychoanalytic Society approved a modification of its statutes, according to which full SPI members may also conduct training analyses.

> the war I followed psychoanalysis not so much as a therapy,
> but more as an Enlightenment idea, an "enlightening idea"
> . . . . Every time I struggle for the Enlightenment I am told:
> "But just look: it has been totally defeated!". I reply: "I do
> not give a damn!". Everything suffers its defeats . . . . The
> Enlightenment has to be a risk: otherwise it would become
> a habit. *Habit* is the enemy of our life. (Cremerius, 2009, pp.
> 32, 46)[14]

These words allow me to propose the two following final considerations. First, Cremerius's approach to psychoanalysis is very similar to the one articulated by Morris Eagle in his recent article "Psychoanalysis and the Enlightenment vision: An overview" (Eagle, 2011). Second, if the key to Benedetti's approach to psychoanalysis is the psychotherapy of schizophrenia, the key to Cremerius's approach to it is the philosophy of the Enlightenment, that is, our struggle for the clarity of vision that we need in order to live a (healthy and) worthwhile life.

A BRIEF NOTE ON THE ASP

In 1990 the Associazione di Studi Psicoanalitici produced the first issue of the journal *Quaderni dell'Associazione di Studi Psicoanalitici*. The issue contained a brief article by Teresa Corsi Piacentini entitled "The School and the Association: Beginning and developments" (Corsi Piacentini, 1990), from which we learn the details of the foundation of the School at the beginning of the 1980s and of the foundation of the Association, as a separate body, in 1987. Besides a presentation by Ciro Elia, this issue also included an article by Benedetti and one by Cremerius. The journal came out in this format for six years for a total of 12 issues, and in 1996 a new journal was started, under the title *Setting. Quaderni dell'Associazione di Studi Psicoanaltici*, whose issue No. 30 came out in June 2012.

This issue contains papers by international authors such as Helmut Thomä and Horst Kächele, Salman Akhtar and Sylvain Missonier, as well as some of the papers given at the panel held in Milan on June 26, 2010, to celebrate Benedetti's ninetieth birthday, and, last but

---

[14] Such an Enlightenment vision also inspired Cremerius's view of the future of psychoanalysis, as he formulated it in the German paper "Die Zukunft der Psychoanalyse" (written in 1995), which gave the title to the collection of papers that came out in English in 1999, and in Italian (with Giorgio Meneguz as editor) in the year 2000 (Cremerius, 2000b). In fact, "Ein psychoanalytischer Aufklärer" (An enlightened psychoanalyst) was also the title of the review that Ludger Lütkehaus published in the *Neue Zürcher Zeitung* in 2006 on the portrait of Cremerius that came out of the above-mentioned autobiography edited by Wolfram Mauser.

not least, the announcement of the online version of the *International Forum of Psychoanalysis*. In other words, the journal has tried to implement the approach to psychoanalysis developed by Benedetti and Cremerius, in terms of its openness to international psychoanalysis, to empirical research, and to the dialogue with other disciplines.

The same is true for a whole series of scientific meetings and congresses organized by the ASP in the last twenty-five years, for example the large international congress on "Affects and thought. Psychoanalytic orientations," which took place in Milan in March 1996 (Accerboni et al., eds., 1998). Its main themes were the concept of "unconscious mental representation," the relationship between psychoanalysis and neurosciences, the psychoanalytic process and the psychoanalysis of the feminine development and identity. The group of the international speakers included Arnold Modell, Horst Kächele and his Ulm Group, Janine Chasseguet-Smirgel, and Ethel Spector Person; several colleagues from the Italian Psychoanalytic Society—Sergio Bordi, Antonino Ferro, Stefania Turillazzi Manfredi, and Silvia Amati Sas—also gave papers. Benedetti (1998) spoke of the crisis which psychoanalysis was then (and is still) undergoing in terms of a challenge that is important to meet.

And the same is also true of the Fourth International Congress of the ASP, held on May 16 and 17, 2008, on the subjects of transference, therapeutic stalemate, and therapeutic alliance, and psychoanalysis and religion, with papers given by Jeremy Safran, Vittorio Lingiardi, Salvatore Freni, Gherardo Amadei and Anthony Molino. A good example of a very good smaller event is the workshop with Frank Lachmann, under the title "Empathy as co-construction and co-creation," which I organized in Milan together with Daniela Maggioni on January 13, 2005. And here are the scientific meetings organized in 2012 by our executive committee for the approximately one hundred members and one hundred candidates of ASP and SPP: on February 25 the internationally well-known French analyst César Bottella, on October 27 Cosimo Schinaia (the author of an important book on pedophilia), and on December 1 Giuseppe Civitarese, one of the closest collaborators of Antonino Ferro.

Last but not least, as far the further elaboration of the legacy of Benedetti and Cremerius is concerned, while a book with a series of papers on Cremerius's legacy is in preparation, two books have already appeared dedicated to Benedetti's legacy: in 2006 *La parola come cura* (Associazione di Studi Psicoanalitici, 2010) on the initiative of Daniela Maggioni, and in 2010 *Una vita accanto alla sofferenza mentale. Seminari clinico-teorici (1973–1996)* (Benedetti, 2010), edited by Claudia Bartocci. In my Introduction to the latter volume, I showed the central role that the instrument of group supervision—which both Benedetti and Cremerius used—played in our training, at variance with the IPA training, in which individual supervision plays the major role.

THE ASP AND THE FUTURE OF THE IFPS

What contributions to the future of the IFPS and of psychoanalysis in general can we derive from what I have dealt with so far? On the basis of what I said about the legacies of Benedetti and Cremerius and of the way in which the Milan ASP has been trying to assimilate them, I can now propose the following seven points:

- being really part of an international network and personally participating in international dialogue (as both Benedetti and Cremerius taught us to do);

- personal analysis before the training proper, instead of training analysis during the training;

- group supervision of clinical work as the main instrument of training proper;

- the primacy of the analysis of countertransference, in the work with the sickest patients (Benedetti);

- the primacy of the analysis of the transference in both psychoanalytic and psychotherapeutic work (Cremerius);

- the development of psychoanalysis as a "normal science" (Kuhn) in connection with empirical research (Cremerius); and, last but not least

- psychoanalysis as Enlightenment (Cremerius), that is, as the search for truth, as a social critique, and as an interdisciplinary dialogue.

In other words, going beyond the problem of how much or how little the present *Zeitgeist* is against or in favor of psychoanalysis, our priority should be the best possible training of our students. This is what will assure us a future and the above seven points do go in this direction.

REFERENCES

Accerboni, A.M, Andreoli, L., Barbieri, V., Elia, C., Maggioni, D., & Panero, M. (Eds.) (1998). *Affetti e pensiero. Orientamenti psicoanalitici* [Affects and thought. Psychoanalytic orientations]. Milan: Moretti e Vitali.

Alanen, Y., Silver, A.-L., & González de Chávez, M. (Eds.) (2006). *Fifty Years of Humanistic Treatment of Psychosis, 1956–2006*. Madrid: Paradox.

Associazione di Studi Psicoanalitici (Ed.) (2006). *La parola come cura. La psicoterapia delle psicosi nell'incontro con Gaetano Benedetti* [Word as cure. Psychotherapy of psychoses in the meeting with Gaetano Benedetti]. Milan: Angeli.

Bauriedl, T., & Brundke, A. (eds.) (2008). *Psychoanalyse in München – Eine Spurensuche* [Psychoanalysis in Munich – A historical reconstruction]. Giessen: Psychosozial-Verlag.

Benedetti, G. (1961). Prefazione [Preface]. In H.S. Sullivan, *La moderna concezione della psichiatria* [Conceptions of modern psychiatry] (pp. vii–xxvii). Milan: Feltrinelli.

——— (1980). *Alienazione e personazione nella psicoterapia della malattia mentale* [Alienation and personation in the psychotherapy of mental illness]. Turin: Einaudi. (German edition: *Todeslandschaften der Seele*. Göttingen: Vandenhöck & Ruprecht, 1983. French edition: *La mort dans l'âme. Psychotérapie de la schizophrénie: existence et transfert*. Ramonville Saint-Agne: Erès, 1995).

——— (1983). *Psicoterapia clinica. Introducción a la psicoterapia de las psicosis* [Clinical psychotherapy. Introduction to the psychotherapy of psychoses]. Barcelona: Herder.

——— (1987). Preface. In G. Benedetti, *Psychotherapy of schizophrenia* (pp. xv–xvii). New York: New York University Press.

——— (1991). *Paziente e terapeuta nell'esperienza psicotica* [Patient and therapist in the psychotic experience]. Turin: Bollati Boringheri.

——— (1994). Mein Weg zur Psychoanalyse und zur Psychiatrie [My way to psychoanalysis and psychotherapy]. In L. Hermanns (Ed.), *Psychoanalyse in Selbstdarstellungen. Band 2* [Psychoanalysis in self-portraits. Vol. 2] (pp. 11–72). Tübingen: Diskord.

——— (1997). *La psicoterapia come sfida esistenziale* [Psychotherapy as existential challenge]. Milan: Cortina. (Original German edition, 1992).

——— (1998). Presentazione [Preface]. In A.M. Accerboni, L. Andreoli, V. Barbieri, C. Elia, Maggioni, & M. Panero (Eds.) (1998). *Affetti e pensiero. Orientamenti psicoanalitici* [Affects and thought. Psychoanalytic orientations] (pp. 9–11). Milan: Moretti & Vital.

——— (2005). Geleitwort [Preface]. In M. Conci, *Sullivan neu entdecken* [Sullivan revisited. Life and work] (pp. 13–14). Giessen: Psychosozial-Verlag.

——— (2010). *Una vita accanto alla sofferenza mentale. Seminari clinico-teorici (1973–1996)* [A life beside mental suffering. Clinical-theoretical workshops] (C. Bartocci, Ed.). Milan: Angeli.

Benedetti, G., & Furlan, P.M. (Eds.) (1993). *The Psychotherapy of Schizophrenia. Effective Clinical Approaches – Controversies, Critiques and Recommendations*. Bern: Hochgrefe & Huber.

Benedetti, G., & Peciccia, M. (1995). *Sogno, inconscio, psicosi* [Dream, unconscious, psychosis]. Pescara: Metis.

Benedetti, G., Corsi Piacentini, T., D'Alfonso L., Elia, C., Medri, G., &

Saviotti, M. (1979). *Paziente e analista nella terapia delle psicosi* [Patient and analyst in the therapy of psychoses]. Milan, Feltrinelli.

Bleuler, M. (1987). Foreword: Gaetano Benedetti and his patients. In G. Benedetti, *Psychotherapy of Schizophrenia* (pp. ix–xiii). New York: New York University Press.

Bohleber, W. (2011). 100 Jahre Internationale Psychoanalytische Vereinigung [100 years International Psychoanalytic Association]. *Psyche* 65:730–751.

——— (2012). The history of psychoanalysis in Germany since 1950. In P. Loewenberg and N.L. Thompson (Eds.), *100 Years of the IPA, 1910–2010. Evolution and Change* (pp. 62–86). London: Karnac.

Brecht, K., Friedrich, V., Hermanns, L., Kaminer, I., & Juelich, H. (Eds.) (1993). *"Here Life Goes on in the Most Peculiar Way . . . ". Psychoanalysis Before and After 1933.* Hamburg: Kellner. (Original German edition, 1993).

Calanchini, C. (2006). Seminari a Basilea [Workshops in Bâle]. In Associazione di Studi Psicoanalitici (Ed.) *La parola come cura. La psicoterapia delle psicosi nell'incontro con Gaetano Benedetti* [Word as cure. Psychotherapy of psychoses in the meeting with Gaetano Benedetti] (pp. 226–247). Milan: Angeli.

Cocks, G. (1985). *Psychotherapy in the Third Reich.* Oxford: Oxford University Press.

Conci, M. (1993). Prefazione [Preface]. In H.S. Sullivan, *Scritti sulla schizophrenia* [Schizophrenia as a human process] (pp. vii–xi). Milan: Feltrinelli.

——— (1994). Psychoanalysis in Italy: A reappraisal. *International Forum of Psychoanalysis* 3:117–126.

——— (1996). Die Psychoanalyse in Italien: Anfänge, Entwicklung und gegenwärtige Lage [Psychoanalysis in Italy: Beginnings, development and present situation]. *Luzifer-Amor* No. 18:114–155.

——— (1997). Postfazione [Afterword]. In G. Benedetti, *La psicoterapia come sfida esistenziale* [Psychotherapy as an existential challenge] (pp. 293–313). Milano: Feltrinelli.

——— (2006). Seminari a Milano [Workshops in Milan]. In Associazione di Studi Psicoanalitici (Ed.) *La parola come cura. La psicoterapia delle psicosi nell'incontro con Gaetano Benedetti* [Word as cure. Psychotherapy of psychoses in the meeting with Gaetano Benedetti] (pp. 226–247). Milan: Angeli.

——— (2008). Gaetano Benedetti in his correspondence. *International Forum of Psychoanalysis* 17:112–129.

——— (2010). Introduzione [Introduction]. In G. Benedetti, *Una vita accanto alla sofferenza mentale. Seminari clinico-teorici (1973–1996)* [A life beside mental suffering. Clinical-theoretical workshops] (C. Bartocci, Ed.) (pp. 13–19). Milan: Angeli.

——— (2011). Fachinelli: il dialogo con Freud [Fachinelli: the dialogue with Freud]. In N. Pirillo (Ed.), *Elvio Fachinelli e la domanda della sfinge* [Elvio Fachinelli and the question of the Sphinx] (pp. 41–71). Naples: Liguori Editore.

——— (2012a). Gaetano Benedetti e i Simposi I.S.P.S. Prima parte: 1956–1978 [Gaetano Benedetti and the I.S.P.S. Symposia. Part one: 1956–1978]. Paper given in Perugia on June 8, 2012, in the context of the ISPS Italy Founding Conference.

——— (2012b). Un'importante lettera di Gaetano Benedetti [An important letter by Gaetano Benedetti]. *Setting* No. 30:120–125.

Conci, M., Erhardt, I., & Kächele, H. (2013). Marco Conci and Ingrid

Erhardt interview Horst Kächele. *International Forum of Psychoanalysis* 22:228–243.

Corsi Picentini, T. (1990). La Scuola e l'Associazione: inizi e sviluppi [The School and the Association: Beginnings and developments]. *Quaderni dell'Associazione di Studi Psicoanalitici* No. 1:7–12.

Cremerius, J. (1983). "Sprachverwirrung zwischen dem Erwachsenen und dem Kind. Die Sprache der Zärtlichkeit und der Leidenschaft". 50 Jahre später wieder gelesen und neu reflektiert ["Confusion of tongues between the adult and the child. The language of tenderness and the language of passion". Read and reflected upon anew 50 years later]. *Psyche* 37:988–1015.

———— (1984). *Vom Handwerk des Analytikers, Das Werkzeug der psychoanalytischen Technik. Zwei Bände* [The job of the analyst. The instrument of analytic technique. Two volumes]. Stuttgart: Frommann-Holzboog. (Italian edition, 1985).

———— (1989). Analisi didattica e potere [Training analysis and power]. *Psicoterapia e Scienze Umane* 23(3):3–38.

———— (1990). Sistema di selezione e politica di potere [Selection system and power politics]. *Psicoterapia e Scienze Umane* 24(4):28–44. (Original German publication, 1987).

———— (1994). Psychoanalyse als Beruf oder "Zieh' aus mein Herz und suche Freud" [Psychoanalysis as profession or "Go out of your heart and look for Freud"]. In L. Hermanns (Ed.), *Psychoanalyse in Selbstdarstellungen. Band 2* [Psychoanalysis in self-portraits. Vol. 2] (pp. 73–144). Tübingen: Diskord.

———— (2000a). Postfazione [Afterword]. In S. Kuciukian (Ed.), *Benedetti e Cremerius: il lungo viaggio. Le autobiografie di due maestri della psicoanalisi* [Benedetti and Cremerius: The long journey. The self-portraits of two masters of psychoanalysis], pp.116–118. Milan, Angeli.

———— (2000b). *Il futuro della psicoanalisi. Resoconti e problemi di psicoterapia* [The future of psychoanalysis. Psychotherapeutic themes and problems] (G. Meneguz, Ed.). Rome: Armando. (Original German edition of the essay by the same title, 1995. Original English edition of the same anthology, 1999).

———— (2006). *Ein Leben als Psychoanalytiker in Deutschland* [A life as a psychoanalyst in Germany] (W. Mauser, Ed.). Würzburg: Königshausen & Neumann.

———— (2009). Life and times, values and visions. Interview with Johannes Cremerius. In S. Benvenuto and A. Molino (Eds.), *In Freud's Tracks. Conversations from the "Journal of European Psychoanalysis"* (pp. 27–46). Northvale, NJ: Aronson.

D'Alfonso, L. (2000). Die Farben der Erinnerung [The colors of memory]. In B. Rachel (Ed.), *Die Kunst des Hoffens. Begegnung mit Gaetano Benedetti* [The art of hoping. Meeting Gaetano Benedetti] (pp. 11–27). Göttingen: Vandenhöck & Ruprecht.

Eagle, M.N. (2011). Psychoanalysis and the Enlightenment vision: An overview. *Journal of the American Psychoanalytic Association* 59:1099–1118.

Ermann, M. (1996). *Verstrickung und Einsicht. Nachdenken über die Psychoanalyse in Deutschland* [Collusion and insight. Rethinking German psychoanalysis]. Tübingen: Diskord.

Faugeras, P. (2000). Übersetzen als Dimension der Begegnung [Translating as a dimension of meeting]. In B. Rachel (Ed.), *Die Kunst des Hoffens. Begegnung mit Gaetano Benedetti* [The art of hoping. Meeting Gaetano Benedetti] (pp. 28–46). Göttingen:

Vandenhöck & Ruprecht.

Galli, P.F. (Ed.) (1973). *Psicoterapia e scienze umane. Atti dell'VIII Congresso Internazionale di Psicoterapia* [Psychotherapy and science. Proceedings of the VIII International Psychotherapy Congress]. Milan: Feltrinelli.

Kernberg, O.F. (1986). Institutional problems of psychoanalytic education. *Journal of the American Psychoanalytic Association* 34:799–834. (Italian translation, 1987).

———— (2011). La formazione in psicoanalisi e psicoterapia dinamica: conflitti e sfide [Training in psychoanalysis and psychotherapy: Conflicts and challenges]. *Psicoterapia e Scienze Umane* 45(4):460–471.

Kurzweil, E. (1989). *The Freudians. A Comparative Perspective.* New Haven, CT: Yale University Press.

Lockot, R. (1985). *Erinnern und Durcharbeiten* [Remembering and elaborating]. Frankfurt: Fischer.

Lütkehaus, L. (2006). Ein psychoanalytischer Aufklärer. Autobiographisches von Johannes Cremerius [An enlightened psychoanalyst. An autobiography of Cremerius]. *Neue Zürcher Zeitung*, January 19.

Mann, C. (2001). In memoriam: Gerard Chrzanowski, 1913–2000. *International Forum of Psychoanalysis* 10:94–96.

Migone, P. (1990). I venti anni di "Plataforma Internacional" [Twenty years of "Plataforma Internacional"]. *Il Ruolo Terapeutico* No. 53:41–43.

Novelletto, A. (1992). Italy. In P. Kutter (Ed.), *Psychoanalysis International* (Vol. 1, pp. 195–212). Stuttgrat: Frommann-Holzboog.

Peciccia, M. (2000). Die Entwicklung meines Denkens im Gespräch mit Gaetano Benedetti [The development of my thought in dialogue with Gaetano Benedetti]. In B. Rachel (Ed.), *Die Kunst des Hoffens. Begegnung mit Gaetano Benedetti* [The art of hoping. Meeting Gaetano Benedetti] (pp. 47–86). Göttingen: Vandenhöck & Ruprecht.

Peciccia, M., & Benedetti, G. (1996). The splitting between the separate and the symbiotic states of the self in the psychodynamic of schizophrenia. *International Forum of Psychoanalysis* 5:23–38.

Rachman, A.W. (1997). *Sándor Ferenczi. The Psychotherapist of Tenderness and Passion.* Northvale, NJ: Aronson.

Scharfetter, C. (2006). Manfred Bleuler (1903–1994). In H. Hippius, B. Holdorff, and H. Schliack (Eds.), *Nervenärzte 2. Biographien* [Doctors for mental diseases. Vol. 2. Biographies] (pp. 29–40). Stuttgart, Thieme.

CHAPTER 11

MARCO CONCI INTERVIEWS STEFANO BOLOGNINI[1]

Stefano Bolognini is one of the most active, competent, and well-known Italian psychoanalysts. He is a medical doctor and a psychiatrist. He lives and works in Bologna, where he trained as a psychoanalyst of the Società Psicoanalitica Italiana (SPI), that is, the Italian Psychoanalytical Society, after having studied medicine in Padua, specialized in psychiatry in Verona, and worked as a psychiatrist in Venice. An Associate Member of the SPI since 1985, he became a training analyst in 1988. Between 1997 and 2001, Dr. Bolognini was also Scientific Secretary of the SPI and, as such, promoted important international contacts and significant scientific initiatives, for example the anthology *Il sogno cent'anni dopo* (The dream, a hundred years later), 2000. He has been a member of the European editorial board of the *International Journal of Psychoanalysis*—currently headed by Dr. Antonino Ferro—since 2002, and of the Comité Internationale de Lectoure of the *Revue Française de Psychanalyse* since 2004. Since 2003, Dr. Bolognini has been both President of the Centro Psicoanalitico di Bologna—the Bologna Psychoanalytical Centre—and European Delegate on the International Psychoanalytical Association (IPA) Board.

With his 2002 publication *L'empatia psicoanalitica*, promptly translated into German, English (as *Psychoanalytic empathy*; London, Free Association Books, 2004) and Spanish, with translations into French, Brazilian-Portuguese, and Russian currently being underway, Dr. Bolognini revisited a problematic and important concept in a philologically very accurate way, redefining it in an original, suggestive, and useful manner. He also showed how well he can bring about dialogue and integration, and how rich are both the stimuli and the debate that have for several years characterized Italian psychoanalysis.

We spoke about all this—and much more—over the course of the summer of 2005, conducting very stimulating and articulate research and dialogue after an initial meeting on Sunday July 10 at Lavarone (Trent), one of Freud's favorite Italian vacation sites—where he stayed for longer periods of time in the summer of 1906,

[1] The original version of this interview was published in Volume 15 (2006) of the *International Forum of Psychoanalysis*, pp. 44–57. The interview was translated into English by Marco Conci.

1907, and 1923.

THE INTERVIEW

Q1. M.C.: One of the major elements of fascination of psychoanalysis is the relationship that each of us as a person—with our individual biographies—entertains with our field of work, that is, psychoanalysis as science, as art, and as profession. In 1999, you published a small volume under the title *Come vento, come onda. Dalla finestra dello psicoanalista, i nostri (bi)sogni di gloria* (As wind, as wave. From the window of the psychoanalyst, our needs and dreams of glory), dedicating it to your parents (Alessandro and Giulia) and to your training analyst (Egon Molinari). The general theme of the book is represented by the fantasies, myths, and illusions that we all need "in order to give breath and nourishment to our mental life" (as you wrote on page 14), and the autobiographical and self-analytic key with which you develop it (the heavy theme of our "narcissistic balance") allows the reader to enter into a stimulating and creative relationship not only with him- or herself, but also with you. This is what happened to me when I read the book to get ready for our interview. Now, so that readers can participate in this special atmosphere, I would like to adopt this as the starting point for our interview. I will start with the chapter entitled "The place where we live" by asking you which Italian town you grew up in. In what ways did it contribute to your development as a person? And finally, what is your relationship with it today?

S.B.: I was born in Bologna in 1949, my parents both being natives of the city. After living for the first six years of my life by the sea of Liguria (where my father worked as a chemical engineer), we moved to Mestre (Venice), where I lived—including my medical studies in nearby Padua—until I was thirty-seven. I worked as a psychiatrist in the departments of psychiatry at the hospitals of Venice and Treviso and started working as a psychoanalyst in Mestre. I eventually moved to Bologna in 1986, just because I wanted to live there.

Bologna was my native town. I returned there very often, and I must confess that when I eventually realized the plan of starting a new life there, I experienced the fear of suddenly waking up from a dream: after all my dreams . . . "what would I have really done there?," as Chatwin would say. But none of this happened! In Bologna, I found my home again—my hills and people speaking with my own accent. Everything was really again as it used to be.

And I never regretted the decision, even though I love Veneto very much, having lived there for thirty years.

Professionally, I owe much to the group of colleagues who practice in Venice. I was a member of the Centro Veneto di Psicoanalisi—the Veneto Center of Psychoanalysis—from 1980 (the year of its official foundation) until 1986, and I breathed from the beginning its two souls: the classical, Freudian one and the one connected with the psychoanalytic treatment of the sickest patients. I then moved to the Centro Psicoanalitico di Bologna (where I had actually done most of my training: with Egon Molinari, my training analysis, and with Glauco Carloni, with whom I did my first treatment under supervision). The center had worked much more in the light of the heritage of Ferenczi, Balint, and Winnicott, and from it came the first Italian edition of Ferenczi's collected works (published by Guaraldi, Rimini). It also had a particular connection with the person and the work of the Parisian colleague Bela Grunberger, himself of Hungarian origin. As a matter of fact, the family of Dr. Molinari himself, the founder of the center of which I am now the President, was of Hungarian origin.

I believe that this analytic background might have contributed to my interest in the concept of empathy, which goes back to the beginning of my training.

Q2. M.C.: It would of course be relevant, in order to get to also know your work better, if you could also tell us something about your family of origin, or, alternatively, answer the following question: How did your childhood and adolescence contribute to your choice of psychoanalysis as a profession? As we all know, the most common connection (between personal development and professional choice) is given by the reparative attitudes that we develop in childhood, given a certain birth order and/or family climate. Can you tell us something about your personal experience in this regard?

S.B.: Every analyst, as you know, finds his or her way to our profession in the first place as a patient, beyond any pretence of choosing it out of scientific interest, the challenge of the unknown or other motivations of a philosophical nature—which are usually some sort of a dissimulation of one's needs and problems. We doubtless work as psychoanalysts after having gone through a personal journey centered around reparative needs, toward ourselves, toward our internal objects, or both.

Without entering into too much detail, I can say that the example of my maternal grandfather, who was a medical doctor, did help me, on the conscious and official level, to choose a therapeutic profession. But the truth was that some parts of myself had been really left behind, compared with others, in terms of the process of development and integration of my personal identity, and they badly needed to be recuperated and integrated. The analytic treatment gave me substantial and unforgettable help, which I try to pay back through my daily clinical work.

As far as psychoanalytic institutions are concerned, I can add that the fact of having grown up in a big family, surrounded by a big community of relatives who did got along well with each other, allows me to welcome and enjoy the exchange and cohabitation with my colleagues. At variance with what several analysts say, many of my best friends are themselves colleagues, and I like and enjoy the work I do for my society and for the IPA.

Q3. M.C.: As a matter of fact, in your book *As wind, as wave*, there is also an enjoyable chapter entitled "The teacher-scientist," in which you tell the reader of the passion for his subject that your Ancient Greek teacher (a fan of the question of whether or not Homer had written the *Iliad* and the *Odyssey*) had been able to convey to you. It is in connection with this that I ask you when you started to read Freud. Or, to put it in another way, when was it that psychoanalysis—which, as far as your books are concerned, you know very well and in great depth— conquered you on the intellectual level?

S.B.: As is true for many of us, my first reading of Freud took place in high school. But it was not a "full immersion" : I read Freud's *Traumdeutung*, which impressed me very much, but I did not go any further. During my medical studies my reading of Freud (I remember *The psychopathology of everyday-life*, *Psychology of the masses*, and *The future of an illusion*) began to become more regular.

During my sixth and last year of medical school, I went to meet colleagues working at the Centro Psicoterapico Provinciale di Palazzo Boldù, in Venice, the public center for psychotherapy founded by the psychoanalyst Professor Giorgio Sacerdoti. At the beginning of the 1970s, these were colleagues 'working' with a great intellectual passion and prestige, representing the most advanced psychoanalytic center in the public psychiatric sector of the whole region. This was a very fortunate choice— the right place to start on a psychoanalytic training at the time—and I still do not know how much of this was due to sheer good luck and how much to some kind of a preconscious intuition.

Q4. M.C.: "The lovable and persuasive voice of some kind of psychoanalytic singer who writes his own songs" (which Fausto Petrella attributes to you in his preface to *As wind, as wave*) deals also with your medical studies and the beginning of your professional activity, in the chapter "A mighty vocation." What memories do you have of your medical studies? Or, in other words: How did they contribute to your identity as a psychoanalyst?

S.B.: I will never be a "psychoanalyst-philosopher," and I thus believe that, for example, a certain part of French psychoanalysis (not all of it of course, as very good clinicians also belong to it) will never capture my interest. I am here making reference to that part of it which is too philosophical and speculative, bound too much to the linguistic level and too little to the level of the therapeutic relationship – a dimension in which words per se are more important than the emotional experience. My medical studies trained me in the direction of feeling very responsible for the patient; I aim for an unequivocally therapeutic relationship, using a frame, a method, and a process that often have little in common with the traditional doctor–patient relationship.

Another specific point of reference is given by the familiarity I acquired, in the course of my work as a psychiatrist, with the treatment of the mentally sickest patients. Working as a psychiatrist helps us, on the one hand, not to regard as banal the difficulty of such treatments, and, on the other hand, to be less anxious about them. Through this work, we learn to attribute the right value to any little progress our patients can make and this alone helps greatly! Work with the sickest patients—given the possibility of not experiencing this in a dissociated way, compared with one's analytic training—allows us to accept with satisfaction and serenity the concept of the analytically oriented "management of psychotic patients," that is, the possibility that such an attitude can promote in us the witnessing of slow, but decisive changes in the direction of a less pathologically tainted life. I speak of a not uncommon event, one less rare than we usually believe.

Q5. M.C.: Before we change topic, I would like to make a suggestion and invite you to an exchange of ideas with regards to the title of your book, to which I have been making reference up to now. The very title *Come vento, come onda* (As wind, as wave) makes us of course think about the "meteorological" character, that is, the big, often capricious and unpredictable variability of our "narcissistic vicissitudes"—of the evolution of our self-esteem—and, last but not least, of our relationship to ourselves. As we all know, such a theme plays a central role in contemporary psychoanalysis and was pioneered by authors like Winnicott and Kohut (not to mention Erikson, Kernberg, and many others, among them, as long ago as the 1930s, H. S. Sullivan). How and when did you begin to find such a theme interesting? Or, in other words: Which authors helped you the most to clarify this complex and fascinating dimension of our existence?

S.B.: I would say that the formulation of your question already contains part of my answer in terms of the names of the authors who contributed the most to the study of this specific aspect of psychic life. To them, I would add the name of Ferenczi, for his pioneering capacity to perceive the aspects of possible mortification and humiliation of a human being, including some of the possible iatrogenic developments of an analytic treatment. I could also mention Bela Grunberger, for his precious description of the various phases of the evolution of narcissism, and André Green, with his "life- and death-narcissism." Also influential has been the Italian Davide Lopez, with his concept of *persona*, that is, his original study of the evolution of narcissism in the sufficiently mature and genitally oriented individual.

More generally speaking, I think that psychoanalysis cannot concentrate only upon the narcissistic vicissitudes of the patient, to the neglect of other dimensions, such as drives, conflict, intersubjectivity, memory, etc. Furthermore, I think that a contemporary analyst cannot but work in a complex way, keeping track of the narcissistic dimension (in its pathological and also its physiological aspects) as a cornerstone of the survival, development, and growth of the patient.

Q6. M.C.: A further theme that I would like to hear more from you about is the theme of your psychiatric training and professional activity. Between 1974 and 1980, you worked at the Centro Psicoterapico Provinciale di Palazzo Boldù, a Venetian institution that played a crucial role in Italy in the introduction of a psychotherapeutic and psychoanalytic dimension. What can you tell us about it?

S.B.: Although I have already mentioned this institution,

I agree that we need to talk a little more about it. Public opinion believed for many years, on the basis of highly superficial newspaper campaigns, that the famous Italian battle (parallel to the French one) for the "psychiatric revolution" of the 1960s and 1970s was fought between two kinds of psychiatry: the traditional-pharmacological one, headed mostly by colleagues in the university departments of psychiatry, and the anti-psychiatric one (in some ways connected to the work of Maxwell Jones, that is, to a much more politically oriented version of his concept of "therapeutic community"), bound to the figure of Franco Basaglia (1924–1980) and his collaborators. In fact, there was one more kind of psychiatry been practiced at the time: the psychoanalytic psychiatry of some hospital and out-of-hospital services, and of some university departments of psychiatry. Its aim was of course not the analytic treatment of psychiatric patients, but the creation of a therapeutic setting based on psychoanalytic concepts, with particular regard to the analytically based handling of the sickest patients and to the analytically oriented interaction between therapeutic team and patients.

Giorgio Sacerdoti, Director of the psychiatric services of the Province of Venice and an SPI training analyst, was able to convince the provincial administration of the usefulness of a psychotherapy center and, to go with it, a day hospital for young psychotic patients. He thus created a structure with an important role at not only a therapeutic, but also a cultural level. The scientific meetings organized by this center represented for many years the real starting point of the training of many psychoanalysts and psychotherapists, and contributed greatly to a deep change in the modalities of hospital and out-of-hospital treatment of many hundreds of patients in the whole region.

And this was not an isolated initiative. In other Italian towns, other psychoanalysts created similar centers, functioning in a different way from the two approaches to psychiatry mentioned. Of course, such serious, long and patient daily work was not talked about by the newspapers, but its effects deeply transformed our psychiatry, making it at the same time more scientific and more humane, and are still visible today.

Q7. M.C.: Taking a look at the list of your scientific papers, I noticed that, among the first ten, at least half bore a title connected to the group dimension of our work—from the viewpoint of an analysis of how the group functions, of the interventions in/on the group, and/or of the group supervision. Can we situate in this phase of your work some of the premises that later brought you to dedicate yourself with so much attention to a better definition of the intrapsychic, interpsychic, intersubjective, and interpersonal dimensions? Could you clarify for us—without completely exhausting the topic, which I hope to come back to again later—what you mean by such terms.

S.B.: In my reading, the *interpsychic* level has to do with basic functional levels that can be shared between two human beings (as well as, for example, between a human being and a dog!), in a situation of "operational confluence" of functions, investments, and mental work in general. For example, two craftsmen working around or on the same object often happen to synchronize their minds, in an automatic and imperceptible way, and thus come to a very good level of reciprocal integration. Husband and wife with a long-standing relationship share many mental processes in a situation of functional fusionality, which allows them also a great economy of energy. Also, the dog and its owner can share more than one interpsychic moment, due to their reciprocal synchronization. But this can also happen by chance between two persons unknown to each other: it is not their subjectivity to be at play. In other words, no connection with the whole complexity of the historical/constitutional/relational level is necessary, which makes of each one of us a singular individual.

The interpsychic is basically *presubjective*. Interpsychic moments happen too in our analytic work, when we work together with the patient independently on our different identities of analyst and patient. At this level, the two minds function collaboratively, each parallel to the other.

Different from the interpsychic is the *intersubjective*. Here a potent role is played by the specific factors that differentiate one individual from another and that inevitably concur in rendering a relationship unique and specific. Let me give two concrete examples of this: psychoanalysis and child-rearing, each with specific rules and operational indications. This notwithstanding, the fact of having a particular analyst instead of another, or particular parents instead of other ones, will inevitably produce different patients and children in homogeneous cultural and procedural contexts. Subjectivity does not concern the functioning on parallel levels, but on more interactive and transformative levels.

But "subject" does not mean "person": the *interpersonal* is, according to me, a further dimension in which a role is played not only by the differences between the reciprocal subjectivities, but also by the well-defined borders of the reciprocal entities, which cannot be implicated in intersubjective exchange, even less so in interpsychic cooperation.

As a consequence, we can have, in a single session, moments in which there are two minds that collaborate or simply functionally live together—the *interpsychic*—other moments in which two subjective centers, with all their biography, their internal worlds, atmospheres, relational modalities, wishes, conflicts, fears, etc. interact and thus transform each other—the *intersubjective*—and still other moments in which Dr. X and Patient Y, as well as being defined persons, come into contact with each other, on a level of conscious separateness and confrontation.

In the groups I witnessed, I saw the development of all these functional levels, in a discontinuous and alternate way, and it was natural for me to make use of them in terms of the analytic couple. Today, I still work as a supervisor of psychiatric teams and of the teams in centers for adolescent patients, but I no longer do group therapy.

Q8. M.C.: 1978, the year of your specialization in psychiatry at the department of psychiatry of the University of Verona, reminds me of the "Basaglia Law," the Italian psychiatric reform, which (approved in May 1978 by the national parliament) closed the old psychiatric hospitals to new admissions, prescribed the creation of new psychiatric wards in general hospitals, and thus moved the center of gravity of psychiatric work from the hospital to the community. Such a law is still in force and has, notwithstanding its faults (in the first place, the lack of adequate hospital space for patients with subacute conditions and personality disorders), probably enriched the psychotherapeutic dimension of our psychiatry. An increased attention toward the relationship with the individual patient was certainly my experience as a psychiatrist in the first half of the 1980s. Without the possibility of relying on the old mental hospitals, psychotherapy (and pharmacotherapy) eventually gained much in importance. What was your experience in this regard?

S.B.: I do think that Franco Basaglia played a very important role in deconstructing the old psychiatric practice, centered around segregation of the patients and a closure to innovation. I am less appreciative of his further proposals because of their lack of technical sophistication. Unfortunately, and for a complex series of reasons, Basaglia and his movement on the one hand, and the group of the analytically trained psychiatrists on the other, almost never succeeded in collaborating with each other, hardly ever succeeded in collaborating with each other after having united their forces in the deconstruction phase. Some of the reasons for such an impasse were of a scientific-methodological nature: Basaglia's priority was the "liberation" of mental patients, and this position—which I agree with in theory—unfortunately brought him to concentrate most of his attention and action on the external aspects of our work, and to lose sight of the mental illness existing inside the patient. Basaglia was an idealist revolutionary who lost sight of the complexity of psychiatric work. From this point of view, the analytically trained psychiatrists were more realistic: it was not enough to "liberate" patients, it was necessary also to treat them—a rather onerous, but not impossible task.

Paradoxically, Basaglia's revolution did, in practical terms, make more room for the third psychiatry I described above, that is, analytically informed psychiatry, and this is connected to the fact that when the new law made it mandatory to work with patients outside the old hospitals, the concepts of psychoanalysis became extremely helpful in terms of creating environments and relationships through which patients could be psychologically held and contained. Of course, neither Basaglia and his group nor the analytically informed psychiatrists could have done their work without the help of the new drugs, which allowed easier and more effective treatment for the sickest patients.

The three psychiatries actually needed to collaborate with one another, and this is the problem which we are still faced with: they do not yet collaborate well enough, no matter how much their complementarity is in theoretical terms beyond any doubt.

Q9. M.C.: As regards the relationship between psychiatry and psychoanalysis, with particular regard to the 1970s and 1980s, I think it is important to remind our overseas (and perhaps some of our Italian) colleagues that, in some Italian university department of psychiatry (Genoa with Franco Giberti, Romolo Rossi, and Roberto Speziale-Bagliacca; Pavia with Dario De Martis and Fausto Petrella; Florence with Adolfo Pazzagli; and Rome/ Catholic University with Leonardo Ancona and Sergio De Risio), our university psychiatry did assimilate psychoanalysis and also teach it to medical students and psychiatric residents. In other words, we did have in Italy a phenomenon similar to that happening in the USA in the 1950s and 1960s, one at variance with, for example, that in Germany, where psychoanalysis entered the university system not through psychiatry, but through psychosomatic medicine. As a matter of fact, my impression is that the recent international success of Italian psychoanalysis (about which we will specifically talk later on) partly has to do with the colleagues who, as students, went through such a medical and psychiatric training. What do you think about this?

S.B.: In many Italian universities, psychoanalysis became, from the early 1970s, an important ingredient of the courses offered in psychiatry and psychology. This had to do with the personal—rather than institutional—initiative of many professors, but it was a widespread phenomenon. In the psychiatric hospital services, one could also often see colleagues reading handbooks like the ones by Arieti and Fenichel, or books like that written by Fromm-Reichmann. On the basis of the transference they would activate in their students, the university professors who were also psychoanalysts motivated many of them to look for and undergo a personal analytic experience. This phenomenon is also responsible for the fact that the SPI today represents the fourth biggest IPA society in the world (with about 850 members and 250 candidates).

Q10. M.C.: If it was thanks to Franco Basaglia (who was born in Venice in 1924 and died prematurely, of a brain tumor, in 1980) that Italian psychiatry had become famous in the world, it was actually through the rapidly growing area of community psychiatry that the Italian family therapy movement, founded by Mara Palazzoli Selvini (1916–1999), also became a much requested Italian product—almost as much so as clothes and cars! In those same years, a very bright representative of Italian psychoanalysis, Franco Fornari (1921–1985), was developing a very original and interesting psychoanalytic point of view, which unfortunately did not circulate very much outside Italy. How come? How do you explain this fact?

S.B.: Family therapy diffused widely in Italy, with great theoretical and clinical differences between the various schools. The work of Franco Fornari is little known abroad for a very simple reason: as was the case with almost all the most authoritative Italian psychoanalysts of his generation (Carloni, Corrao, Hautmann, Tagliacozzo, and others), he did not go abroad because he did not speak English—only read it. The only Italian analyst of the same generation who was able to make his work known abroad was Eugenio Gaddini (1916–1985), who spoke English well and who actively attended international congresses. For this reason, besides the intrinsic value of his ideas, Gaddini was for a long time the only Italian author to be quoted abroad.

Italian analysts have exclusively imported psychoanalysis for about thirty years. Such a trend started changing in the 1990s, thanks to Antonino Ferro, and the change was so great as to almost bring about a reversal of the situation in that a growing quantity of Italian contributions are now presented at international congresses and published in the big international journals.

Q11. M.C.: At this point I would like to deal with your analytic training proper. In other words, I would like you to tell us something about Egon Molinari, your training analyst, and/or about your training at the Bologna Psychoanalytic Center. I personally had the chance to briefly get to know Egon Molinari in Trieste in December 1989, at the congress organized by Anna Maria Accerboni to celebrate the hundredth anniversary of the birth of Edoardo Weiss (1889–1970; the first Italian psychoanalyst), where I had presented a paper on the letters of the young Freud to his school-friend E. Silberstein. Molinari was a very nice person, himself a native of Trieste, and I was able to pass on to him the regards of Johannes Cremerius (1918–2002), whom I had the good luck of knowing very well, and who also knew Molinari well. In other words, Molinari was a person whom I would very much have liked to get to know better!

S.B.: Yes, Egon Molinari kept alive and continued the Central European cultural tradition of the first Italian psychoanalysis: born in Trieste with an Hungarian family background, he settled down in Bologna at the beginning of the 1950s, and founded the Bologna Psychoanalytic Center, the third Italian center (after Rome and Milan), both historically and in terms of its institutional relevance. Molinari died three years ago, aged ninety-two, having almost always attended the twice-monthly scientific meetings of our center. He always sat in the first row and intervened in a brilliant and affectionate way even in the last years of his life, when he had responsibly chosen not to carry out any more analyses but only psychotherapies. Together with his first Bolognese pupil, Glauco Carloni (who was also a president of the SPI, as was later the case also with Giovanni Hautmann, from Florence, himself an analysand of Molinari), he edited the Guaraldi edition of Ferenczi's works and contributed to keeping his point of view alive.

Molinari was an orthodox Freudian, but he was actually extremely open, mainly because he was incurably curious. He had the advantage of knowing German—the language of his childhood—so that he could regularly read the German journal *Psyche* and of course Freud's *Gesammelte Werke* in the original language. But he was familiar with English too and also read the most recent authors. He was a very human analyst. He did not talk much during sessions, but he listened with a depth that I could clearly perceive. In crucial moments, I would feel him very close to me, in a very timely and adequate manner, and with a clear awareness of the needs and fragilities (as well as potentialities) of a patient in a state of analytic regression.

Q12. M.C.: Now, before I deal with your scientific production, particularly your long-term work on the concept of "psychoanalytic empathy," allow me to ask you also the following question: Outside your colleagues in the Bologna Psychoanalytic Center, what other Italian colleagues, of the older generation, helped you to define your psychoanalytic identity? The first one who comes to mind is Luciana Nissim Momigliano (1919–1998), who played such an important role in recent developments in Italian psychoanalysis. Indeed, I recall a long and significant meeting I had with her (in June 1993), with particular reference to her reception of and sympathy for the relational point of view developed by Stephen Mitchell (1946–2000), which I had helped to introduce into Italy.

S.B.: I had the good luck also to work with other senior analysts, very different from each other: my two supervisors, Glauco Carloni (a Ferenczian) and Giorgio Sacerdoti (a Freudian), my group analyst Salomon Resnik (post-Kleinian and Bionian), and various teachers, among whom was Franco Fornari, mentioned above, certainly an extraordinarily clear teacher, and Luciana Nissim, a very individual figure and a very lively person, with an incredible sensibility and capacity for communication. I was also particularly impressed with the seminars given by León Grinberg (particularly on the theme of identification), Horacio Etchegoyen, and Betty Joseph.

As a matter of fact, one's training continues through out one's whole life and even today, by regularly participating in international clinical groups (as the so-

called CAPS), I find colleagues capable of inspiring me
and teaching me new clinical and theoretical aspects.
Haydée Faimberg, Joyce McDougall, and Egle Laufer
have provided me with inspiring clinical experiences over
the course of the past year, and through these I have felt
very enriched.

Q13. M.C.: In fact, the achievement of our professional
identity is also made easier by the exchange and dialogue
we can develop with the colleagues of our own generation.
Who were the members of your peer group? What did
you learn from them? And what did you do together with
them?

S.B.: I recently wrote a paper entitled "The family of the
analyst," which actually deals with this complex external
institutional reality that gradually transforms itself in an
internal reality. And the "brothers," the members of one's
peer group, are an integral part of this.

My first (elder) brothers were the analysts of Venetian
psychiatry. From Alberto Semi, I learned how one should
write a "classical" scientific paper (indeed, he remained
my official referee for a critical opinion on the articulation
of a paper); from Luigi Boccanegra, I learned how to work
with nurses; and from Giancarlo Cecchinato, I learned
the style of conducting of a therapeutic community.

Then came the time of the seminars at the Milan
Training Institute (at the time Bologna did not yet have
a training institute, only a scientific center), and there I
developed fundamental friendships that are still very
strong. I shared my training with Antonino Ferro, Franco
Borgogno, Emanuele Bonasia, and many others, and with
them all a kind of *imprinting* remains: we are all brothers of
the same generation and still tend to understand ourselves
as members of that original group. Sadly, Parthenope
Bion, the daughter of the famous British analyst and an
extraordinary young analyst herself, has left us, tragically
perishing in a car accident in 1998.

With Ferro and with the Roman colleague Vincenzo
Bonaminio I share a friendship that has lasted many
years, recently reinforced by the creative adventure of
the *International Journal of Psychoanalysis*, for which,
together with other colleagues, we edit a yearly anthology
published in Italian.

As time went on, so the network of friendships has
become larger and larger, now including some foreign
"brothers and sisters" (Europeans, and North and South
Americans), with whom I am in constant exchange and
with whom I organize panels and situations of scientific

exchange. This was beyond my wildest dreams until about ten years ago as my spoken English was not very good then and the Internet did not yet really exist.

Q14. M.C.: You conclude the introduction to your book *Psychoanalytic empathy* with the words, which Stephen Mitchell, the founder of the journal *Psychoanalytic Dialogues*, would certainly have subscribed to, "In psychoanalytic thought, we always dialogue with someone." Now, is there any other author or colleague you can think of who has played an important role in your analytic training (and identity)? What about Roy Schafer, who is, after Freud, the most-cited author in your book mentioned above?

S.B.: My relationship with North American psychoanalysis started by reading the two volumes of technique by Ralph Greenson, but it intensified as a reaction to the fact that many Italian analysts had a preconceived and distorted attitude toward many North American authors.

Roy Schafer interested me very much right from the beginning, and when Fred Bush recently confided to me that he had experienced him as some kind of an idol during the years of his training, I shook hands with him and said, "Dear friend, I also had the same experience!" Schafer's *The Analytic Attitude* remains one of the cornerstones of my training in the 1980s.

No less exciting was the discovery of the work of Kohut, an extraordinary author in my opinion, who was penalized for the simple reason that he focused too much on his theme. This exposed him, not only in Europe, but also in the USA, to the risk of an "either/or" choice— either with him or against him—as if it were not possible to integrate his observations with those of other analytic authors. If Kohut were still alive, he would perhaps feel sorry for the fact that a colleague, like me, going beyond metapsychological purism, lets him live inside his "analytic family" together with deeply different authors. But I trust my preconscious, which at times makes me think of Winnicott, at times of Klein, and at times of Kohut (and the list could continue!), based on the different moments of a session or on a phase of an analysis.

Since I am a friend of theirs, I read the papers of Owen Renik, Henry Smith, Glen Gabbard, Evelyn Schwaber, Fred Bush, Theodore Jacobs, Charles Spezzano, and many other North American analysts, and I have the feeling of being in touch with many of them during my analytic work. I also read with great pleasure the work of the English authors (of all three groups), in whom I recognize some kind of a qualitative primacy in clinical work, and also some South American authors, who will probably represent a new direction in future psychoanalysis.

Q15. M.C.: At this point, let us at last deal with your book on empathy. In other words, let us discuss the long, complex, and interesting research work on this theme that culminated in 2002 with the publication of *Psychoanalytic empathy* and which I think it worthwhile telling readers about. Looking at the list of your publications, your starting point was a historical revisitation of the concept, "*Nota storica-critica: empatia*," published in collaboration with Luisa Borghi in the *Rivista di Psicoanalisi*, the SPI journal founded by Edoardo Weiss in 1932 and re-established by Cesare Musatti (1897–1989) in 1955 after Mussolini had forbidden it in 1935. What decided you to deal with the problem then? What were your preoccupations? What your ambitions?

S.B.: In 1984, I presented to the Centro Veneto a first paper on this theme, based on a review of the literature. The *Rivista* invited Luisa (who had also dealt with the problem) and me to write something specific on the subject. I did not then imagine that this would be the beginning of such a long research project!

I believe I started dealing with this theme for a whole series of reasons. In the first place, I wanted to understand, also on a "scientific" level, the source of the capacity of attunement, which my own analyst himself had shown—presumably on the basis of his experience of many years of work—in relation to some of my complex psychological states. Second, I thought that if I had had precise rules at my disposal, I could easily and systematically find an attunement with patients (which is what I used to call, making fun of myself, "finding the analytic philosophical stone"). Third, it was clear to me that, in the rare situations in which empathy appears, the analyst finds in a spontaneous and appropriate way the right words, functions creatively, and really cooperates with the patient. At this level should therefore reside the cornerstone of analytic work.

I have purposely exaggerated, in a self-mocking way, the manifest naivety of my premises in order to augment the contrast with the results of my research work: empathy cannot be a method, but only a complex event; likewise, we can study it in order to more easily allow its appearance, but certainly not in order to determine it in an omnipotent way. In addition, psychoanalytic empathy—and this is a very important result of my work—is something very different from natural, everyday empathy.

At this point, before formulating the next question, which will deal more specifically with Bolognini's book, I would like to present a short review of *Psychoanalytic empathy*.

Psychoanalytic empathy (191 pages in the 2004 English edition, published by Free Association Books, London, and translated by Malcolm Garfield, with Anthony Molino as editorial consultant) contains a preface by Donald Campbell and an introduction, under the title "The psychoanalyst's theoretical models, harmony and consistency," by the author. The book consists of two parts and altogether fourteen chapters. The English edition contains neither the opening comments by Antonio Alberto Semi (Venice), nor the closing words by Vincenzo Bonaminio (Rome), which I would like to take up in my next question.

In the six chapters of the first part, "Historical review," the author deals with romantic empathy (from Novalis, 1798, to Titchener, 1909); Freud and empathy; the pioneers (that is, H. Deutsch, 1926, S. Ferenczi, 1928, and R. Fliess, 1942); the rediscovery of empathy in the 1950s (C. Olden, 1958, R. Schafer, 1959, and R. Greenson, 1960, and also H. Kohut and P.-N. Pao); and, last but not least, with an Italian contribution, the contribution of S. Spazàl (who had trained in Chicago and died prematurely in 1990), a pioneer of the comparison among different analytic models and a supporter of the equation "empathy = concordant countertransference," with which Bolognini disagrees. At the end of the first part of the book, Bolognini writes:

> True empathy very rarely comes about only at the level of concordant resonance: human beings are too complex, the vicissitudes of human relations are too complicated . . . the concept of empathy should not be restricted to concordance with what is ego-syntonic for the patient, otherwise it is true that empathy is no longer a psychoanalytic concept. Psychoanalytic empathy, as we shall see, is a more complex function. (Bolognini, 2004, pp. 65–66)

Turning now to the second part, "A contemporary perspective," we already find in the seventh chapter, "The analyst's internal attitude: analysis *with* the ego and analysis *with* the self," the author working on the articulation of a specific metapsychology of empathy. In the following chapter, "Empathy and countertransference: the analyst's affects as a problem and a resource," Bolognini turns his attention from the clinical vignettes of the previous chapter to the detailed presentation of a complex and fascinating clinical case, "Aldo, the heartless executive." Through this, he illustrates his position on countertransference, which he qualifies as intermediate between P. Heimann's globalistic and J. Arlow's and C. Brenner's classical concepts.

In the ninth chapter, "Empathy and sharing: A necessary distinction," the author shows us how the process of sharing (a work with the self), a phenomenon on which we cannot decide beforehand but which happens in an inevitable way, represents only a precursor of an empathic comprehension. As a further proof of the dialectical character of Bolognini's orientation stands the following chapter, "The 'kind-hearted' versus the good analyst: Empathy and hate in countertransference," in which he shows us how Winnicott's hate in the countertransference represents an important precursor of empathy.

In the eleventh chapter, "Empathy and 'empathism'," a re-elaboration of an article of the same title that appeared in the *International Journal of Psychoanalysis* in 1997, Bolognini specifically illustrates—in terms of the case of "Alessandra, a refined young lady"—how true empathy often comes into being by actually resisting the pressure from patients to assume a concordant disposition. It is in the following chapter, "Empathy and the unconscious," that we find the following definition, at the same time metapsychological and operational:

> Empathy is a condition of conscious and preconscious contact characterised by separateness, complexity, and a linked structure, a wide perceptual spectrum, including every colour in the emotional palette; above all, it constitutes a progressive, shared, and deep contact with the complementarity of the object, with the other's defensive ego and split-off-parts, no less than the other's ego-syntonic subjectivity. (Bolognini, 2004, p. 141)

The book ends with Chapters 13, "Empathy and fusion," and 14, "Natural empathy and psychoanalytical empathy," and with the author's conclusions. After underlying the "highly delicate" character of this research theme, Bolognini presents a meaningful clinical case, "Mr. P.'s leave-taking," which allows him to conclude the book with the following words: "And my thoughts turned to our profession, so strange and unpredictable that we can hardly ever decide what is ours to experience next" (Bolognini, 2004, p. 179).

Q16. M.C.: The original Italian edition of your book contains some concluding comments, under the title "Simplicity and complexity," written by Vincenzo Bonaminio (Rome), in which he underlines "the sense of the complexity of mental life," which you so well succeeded in articulating within the book. Such an observation helps me to formulate the following question: If I have correctly understood your point of view, it is actually in your perception of the complexity of mental life that you see the cornerstone, the specific aspect of psychoanalysis. Am I right?

S.B.: Yes, you are right. A century of psychoanalysis has educated us to complexity. What prevents us from recognizing it and fully appreciating it is, most often, a transferential problem in relation to any of the founders of our discipline, when we transferentially experience them as a parental, as totalizing figures, whom we cannot betray and with whom we have to identify wholly—Freud, M. Klein, Winnicott, Bion, Kohut, Lacan, etc.! The transference that these pioneers produce in most analysts tends always to be of this same kind.

In one of my latest papers, "The analyst's internal family," I spoke of the need to extend our family field to our analytic grandparents, uncles and aunts, and cousins, because these internalized figures constitute an enormous richness. Each one of them has described some specific aspect of our mental functioning, and it is up to us to integrate these notions as best as we can into the rest of our knowledge. Such notions are less contradictory than many of us believe, invoking a theoretical rigor that is often an unequivocal sign of rigidity and intolerance.

Complexity is of course not something relaxing: it demands more work and more internal space than does the elementary way of functioning centered around the either/or principle. But we, as analysts, are well trained in the practice of suspending judgment, of considering alternative viewpoints and of alternately identifying with the different characters present on the stage of the internal world of our patients. I believe that we should be well trained for the preparation of a complex mental scenery.

Philosophers are of course better than we are at this, but they deal only with abstract concepts and not with emotional experiences. What I usually say in this regard is that "they go around without any hand-baggage," which is what allows them to tolerate complexity more easily. Indeed, when we as analysts discuss theory, we have to deal with a much greater complexity than that encountered by all those people who do not have to deal with its experiential and personal complexity.

Q17. M.C.: Bonaminio's concluding remarks offer us further important food for thought. "Should I define

Bolognini and his work in the context of the complexity of contemporary psychoanalysis, I would use the term of *postmodern classicism*" (Bonaminio; in Bolognini, 2002, p. 221, original emphasis). Bonaminio justifies the first term with your attention to the reconstructive dimension of analytic work, and the second with your awareness that there is no Truth (with a capital T) that the analyst makes the patient discover. What do you think?

S.B.: I feel thankful toward Vincenzo Bonaminio—whose comments are always so thoughtful and bright—for such a definition, with which I fully agree. I experience myself as working inside classical psychoanalysis, which I treasure very much and of which I "throw away" almost nothing. At the same time, I do have with it a relationship that I experience as familiar, as opposed to sacred or idealizing. This is what, I believe, allows me, to look at all new contributions with interest, without feeling too much guilty or afraid.

I believe that our old masters had the courage to explore the unknown without limiting themselves to the "sacred books," and that this is the first thing that we have to learn from them. At the same time, I do not suffer under any compulsory need to get rid of the "family pictures" and library; I do not feel any intolerance toward my roots, under the condition that I can repeat them and, at the same time, add to them my own creativity and the creativity of my generation. In other words, this is how I understand Bonaminio's definition: as a substantial, and, at the same time, familiar and not idealized appreciation of the classical.

Q18. M.C.: At this point, before specifically dealing with some of the most interesting chapters of your book, allow me to ask you another question of a general nature. As far as your introduction is concerned, I was particularly impressed with the courageous brightness with which you, on the one hand, insist upon the necessary eclectic (meaning other-directed) orientation of psychoanalytic research, and, on the other hand, assume as a necessary point of reference the integrated and coherent nature of the person of the analyst. Stephen Mitchell, whom I came to know well, also had a similar orientation. The same is also true for Gaetano Benedetti, my supervisor in Milan. Such a point of view requires an enormous psychic work. How is it possible at all to do it?

S.B.: The harmony and theoretical-technical integration of the analyst depends of course on his or her personality, personal vicissitudes, and analytic training. In addition, I would not undervalue the importance of the place, of the environment in which each of us lives and works during his or her life after training. An analytic group, an institute, or a society can contribute more than we can think of to analysts' wellbeing, to favor their integrative (or splitting) tendencies, and to refine the atmosphere of their internal world and/or to influence it in an idealizing, persecutory, hyper-scholastic, and imitative direction. Institutions or groups in which some kind of theoretical dictatorship is present risk producing clones (consider, for example, Iraqi citizens bearing moustaches à la Saddam), instead of a community of colleagues capable of original and personal exchanges. Real freedom is of course something else again, something that only we can find for ourselves and that no one can give us.

As far as harmony is concerned, I see it as the result of a relative acceptance of conflicts in a fundamentally loving climate and on the basis of a good basic narcissistic balance. Such a balance, as we know, comes in the first place from our mother and father, and only later on from our analysis.

Q19. M.C.: As far as the various chapters of your book are now specifically concerned, I found Chapter 7, "The analyst's internal attitude: analysis *with* the ego and analysis *with* the self," so fascinating that I ask you to present synthetically here, for the benefit of our readers, the four configurations of the contact between analyst and patient that you describe in it, and that can actually represent some kind of a "psychoanalytic compass."

S.B.: In my opinion, in the contact *patient's ego/analyst's ego*, the two persons exchange thoughts with one another, in a more or less reasonable way, and with conceptualizations that are rather detached from the level of self-experience.

In the contact *analyst's ego/ego-self of the patient*, a rather frequent phenomenon, the analyst "sees" but does not "hear" what the patient is living. He is sometimes able to conceptually frame what is going on, but not to the point of analytically interacting in a creative way, since he moves on the level of abstract words and not of felt experiences. The patient feels frustrated on the analytic level, or, curiously—and with a little resignation—feels he has to be patient enough to wait for the analyst to get to a higher level of integration.

The contact *analyst's ego-self/patient's self* is the one that is typical of the first phase of an analysis, when the analyst (more in contact with himself than the patient) directs his attention to the defensive ego of the patient, which resists a deeper contact.

In the fourth configuration, the contact *ego-self of the analyst/ego-self of the patient*, which is usually the result of the common analytic work, we experience the realization of some fundamental changes: the preconscious channels become larger; the primary and secondary processes alternate with natural and creative fluidity; introjective processes prevail upon projective processes; and projective processes are no longer more ascribed to the patient but are "treated" by the analytic couple at work, which begins to transform the projective contents and the internal world responsible for their containment. This is of course a very schematic description, but I know how helpful it can be.

Q20. M.C.: I found very fascinating the case of "Sara, a case of contagious defeatism," in Chapter 9, in which you deal with the importance of sharing, that is, you show its decisive role as a motor of treatment. This is the case of the defeatist patient, who, having eventually reached a state of relief, calls an end to the session, having succeeded in transmitting her huge negativity to the analyst, whose feeling of surrender and resignation she can now perceive; in this, "the experience of sharing seems to have conceded the possibility of passing from transference to relationship" (Bolognini, 2002, p. 100). In other words, this is a situation in which you could experience in a concrete manner how "the representational creativity of the analyst touches the patient when the latter senses its experiential authenticity, the true proof that the analyst has 'been there' with him" (Bolognini, 2002, p. 106).

As a matter of fact, much of our work, which we find hard to talk about with our colleagues (and even to recognize ourselves), consists in this journey, in this "film" (we could even say) that we make with the patient, a film in which we participate so much that we are often unable to look at it from the outside—and admit it to ourselves and/or talk about it with our colleagues. And this is actually what you deal with in this chapter.

But, it seems—and now I come to my question—that it is not only in this chapter that you deal with this: indeed, it seems to me to be a theme that you repeatedly address. What comes to mind in this connection is, for example, the case of Lorenzo, the patient whom you talked about in New Orleans in 2004, in the article "*Il bar nel deserto. Simmetria e asimmetria nel trattamento di adolescenti difficili*" (The bar in the desert. Symmetry and asymmetry in the treatment of difficult adolescents; *Rivista di Psicoanalisi*, 2005).

S.B.: The clinical case of the "The bar in the desert" has been translated into and published in various languages, since it shows in a rather open way how analytic work is not elegant, aseptic, and linear, as we would like to propose it, as if it should be part of a handbook. As a matter of fact, Sara's case was utilized by Nanni Moretti in his film *La stanza del figlio* (The room of the son) for this very same reason. Reality, true reality, is usually not elegant! The authors of Latin and Italian literature, who so often dealt with the beginning of life in a poetic way, were able to recognize that *"inter faeces et urinas nascimur"* (we get born between faeces and urine) and *"ed è rischio di morte il nascimento"* (the process of birth entails the risk of death;" see the Italian writer Giacomo Leopardi, 1798–1837).

Many years ago, I was able to greatly appreciate Ralph Greenson's description of the treatment of the young Lance, a transsexual child with big introjective needs and big needs of fatherly sharing. Many sessions had taken place in the analyst's swimming pool, and the analyst had not stayed out of it; on the contrary, he had immersed himself in it, and had co-functioned (as we would say today) in a fluid way in a relational medium. I am of course making reference not to the concrete aspect of that—original and interesting—description, but to its symbolic aspect, which I conceptualize in terms of a theory of technique based on a partial experiential sharing, wherever necessary of course.

Q21. M.C.: I come now to another very interesting theme of your book, the theme of fusionality (see Chapter 13), and to the following question (which you formulate on page 156 and which I ask you to give an answer to on the basis of your present and longer experience), that is: "do humans have the possibility to achieve a good level of fusion without this leading to confusion?" What do you think?

S.B.: I think you have touched a very important point. We can produce the best interpretation, but it will be of no use if there is a relational climate that is neither conducive to nor adequate for its transmission.

"Not confusive fusionality" or physiological fusionality is the kind of situation in which a mother feeds, washes, or in the case of animals, licks her child, a situation that is always mediated by body fluids. As time goes on, with symbolic and verbal development, body liquids are substituted by relational equivalents, which create anyway an intimate contact and exchange. A psycho-physical fusionality also accompanies the exchange between two partners in love with each other, and even in the relationship between the dog and his owner there can be an interpsychic situation of a sometimes fusional nature.

In our analytic sessions, we can witness a defensive use of a pathological fusionality on the side of the patient, for example when he or she shows a parasitical symbiosis accompanied by perverse elements. But we more often witness a dramatic conflict between the wish (or need) to recuperate a failed primary psychological fusion, on the one hand, and a desperate need to keep a narcissistic autonomy toward the object, on the other. Healthy and genital individuals can allow themselves moments of pleasure and areas of aware fusionality, consensually agreed upon with their love object, without the fear of losing themselves or being eaten up and destroyed.

Q22. M.C.: This very theme of fusionality—in the way in which you present it in your book, which allows us to start moving in a new direction—represents a central theme of Italian psychoanalysis. You write of a panel of 1985, which you define as having been of "'historic' importance" (Bolognini, 2002, p. 156). Can you tell us briefly about this and thus start dealing with the specific contribution of Italian psychoanalysis, of which your book is such an important expression.

S.B.: The 1985 panel that I mentioned saw colleagues Roberto Tagliacozzo, Giulio Cesare Soavi, Lydia Pallier, and Giancarlo Petacchi collaborate on the articulation of this theme, with excellent results. They explored in an original way both the defensive-resistential aspect and the creative aspect of the fusional dimension.

Fifteen years later, Paolo Fonda published an article of extraordinary theoretical-clinical quality, "*La fusionalità e i rapporti oggettuali*" ("Fusionality and object relations"), which came out in 2000 in the *Rivista di Psicoanalisi*. In it he dealt with the organizational modalities of fusional experience, in which he identified in the "*punti di coincidenza*," in the areas at the borders between two persons, the area of the contact, of the openness, and of the temporary, partial, and physiological suspension of separateness. Fonda underlined the healthy and necessary aspects of these processes.

In a paper of mine from 1997, "*Empatia e patologie*

gravi" ("Empathy and the sickest patients"), in the volume
Quale psicoanalisi per le psicosi? (Which psychoanalysis
for the psychoses?), edited by Correale and Rinaldi, I had
also dealt with these processes and then continued to
explore this area of healthy fusionality in *Psychoanalytic
empathy*.

I believe that also Antonino Ferro, when he refers
to the work of reverie, actually describes a condition in
which specific functional fusionalities take place and
positively operate in the analytic relationship (in the same
way as in the relationship of the mother to the baby), in a
climate of separateness.

Q23. M.C.: Another central concept in the recent process
of the elaboration of new analytic concepts on the part
of Italian psychoanalysis, in which you have been also
very much involved and which eventually contributed
to the creation of what we could call an "Italian School
of Psychoanalysis," is the concept of the "analytic field."
This concept, that is, *"La risposta dell'analista e le
trasformazioni del campo"* ("The analyst's response and
the transformations of the field"), was the theme of the Xth
SPI congress, which took place in Rimini in October 1994,
some of whose major contributions were put together
by Eugenio Gaburri (Milan) in the volume *Emozione e
interpretazione. Psicoanalisi del campo emotivo* (Emotion
and interpretation. Psychoanalysis of the emotional field).
What can you tell us in this regard?

S.B: The field concept is a concept that Francesco Corrao
took from physics and which he applied to the emotional
field and its continuous transformations. It has been
utilized by analysts basically to remove analogies of a
mechanical nature from the image of psychoanalysis.
Such a concept actually allows us to underline the fluidity
and—again—complexity of analytic events. As always
happens, every analyst was then ready to elaborate his
or her own version of the concept: the descriptions of
Corrao, Riolo, Ferro, Bezoari, Gaburri, Chianese, and
other colleagues do not wholly coincide with one another.
We can say, however, that they all contributed to further
enriching the field concept.

My own contribution is very simple and is focused
on the clinical level: the presence of emotional currents
"in the field" makes me avoid too early an attribution of
such currents to internal states of the patient or analyst.
In such cases, it is not so important immediately to
determine whether such currents reflect emotions of the
one or the other: they are there, "in the field." The most

important thing is, first, that they came to life, and second, to see whether they can be further transformed instead of attributing them too quickly to one or other.

Q24. M.C.: The next SPI congress, the XIth, took place in Rome in 1998 (SPI national congresses taking place every four years), and its theme was "*Il sogno cento anni dopo*" ("The dream, a hundred years later"). This was the title of the volume drawn from it that you edited in 2000 (as Scientific Secretary of the SPI, you yourself had organized the congress!) and that carries an introduction in which you explain to readers both the organizational structure and the most recent scientific evolution of the SPI, and define its specificity. I think it would be really worthwhile dealing again with these aspects, for the benefit of our readers.

S.B.: Yes, briefly. The geographical and organizational structure of the SPI partly explains its history and its present scientific creativity. The SPI has two main administrative offices, Rome and Milan, the cities of the pioneers of Italian psychoanalysis, but most of its scientific life takes place in the so-called Centri Psicoanalitici, numbering ten in total. From the north to the south they are Turin, Milan, Padua, Genoa, Bologna, Florence, Rome 1, Rome 2, Naples, and Palermo. At this point, colleagues usually ask me whether this means that there are ten institutes. In fact, these are not institutes, in terms of institutions centered around the training of candidates, but centers, where the scientific activity takes place. I know that, abroad, local centers easily become psychoanalytic institutes and even societies. On the contrary, we in Italy have one IPA society (two of course if we add the small AIPsi—the *Associazione Italiana di Psicoanalisi* – the result of a split that caused a small group of colleagues to leave our society at the beginning of the 1990s), four training institutes (Milan, Bologna/Padua, Rome 1, and Rome 2) and ten scientific centers. Interestingly, each center has its own history and often well-kept original analytic culture—Freudian, Ferenczian, Kleinian, Bionian, etc. This has allowed a wide differentiation inside the SPI and made it impossible for a single mainstream to emerge to the detriment of all other currents, which are still amply represented inside the society.

Today, the SPI represents not only the fourth IPA society in terms of the number of members, but also the one with the highest internal level of differentiation, with highly beneficial effects in terms of scientific debate and richness of publications.

Q25. M.C.: Since issue 4 of 2003, Antonino Ferro has acted as European Editor of the *International Journal of Psychoanalysis*. Of the twenty-five members currently (see issue 4 of 2005) comprising the editorial committee, nine are Italian. What other factors—beyond the ones you mentioned in 2000, in your introduction to the book I mentioned—contributed to such a brilliant result?

S.B.: The number of papers being sent to the journal from Italy keeps growing, and the selection process is also at present often favorable to the members of our society. I believe that the factors making such a success possible are: (1) the increasing participation of Italian analysts in international analytic events and activities, which is made possible by (2) an increasing knowledge of English, and by (3) the very long tradition of translation and reception of the major analytic schools, a process that started in the 1960s (the time when, for example, M. Klein's work was first translated into Italian) and has eventually allowed us to produce a new, original version of psychoanalysis, which we have recently even begun to export abroad. Italian analysts are now invited abroad, and foreign journals publish our papers—both of which were almost unthinkable up to only a few years ago!

As you know, for very many years, no Italian analyst apart from Gaddini and Ignacio Matte Blanco was ever invited abroad. Not to mention the fact that, even today, almost no foreign colleague knows the high-quality work of the above-mentioned Franco Fornari, who together with another three or four colleagues dominated the Italian analytic scene of the 1970s and 1980s. Now the situation has changed, and Italian analytic books are being read not only outside Italy, but also outside Europe.

Q26. M.C.: You have just come back from the XLIVth IPA congress, which took place in Rio de Janeiro at the end of July, and whose main theme was the concept of trauma in psychoanalysis. Could you give us a brief scientific report of the first IPA congress ever held in Brazil?

S.B.: Although André Green, in the pages of *International Journal of Psychoanalysis*, recently—and rather harshly—criticized Wallerstein's concept of the "many psychoanalyses," the Rio Congress in my opinion confirmed the progressive, substantial acceptance of such a concept, that is, of a fertile variety of analytic currents of thought. And, in my opinion, the novelty consists not in the variety per se, but also in its "fertile" nature. My feeling is that most analysts are tired of fighting "religious wars" and find it more and more normal and desirable to exchange ideas and organize panels with colleagues of different backgrounds and orientations. Panels consisting of speakers of homogeneous backgrounds are, because of their parochial character, no longer attractive.

The concept of "trauma" was re-evaluated and revisited from all possible points of view, recuperating it wholly to the psychoanalytic perspective, and without the need for a categorical distinction between internal and external sources of trauma. Furthermore, the clinical dimension prevailed over the theoretical one: analysts want to hear more about sessions with and clinical histories of patients.

Last but not least, the congress also witnessed an important reappearance and return to the foreground of Latin-American psychoanalysis, after a few years of a relative and partial diminution of its appeal.

Q27. M.C.: At this point, both because of my curiosity and because of the need to eventually come up with a short question (something I have not yet managed—out of the great respect and esteem that I have for your work), let me ask you: Which were the authors whose work was most made reference to in Rio?

S.B.: Bion and Winnicott.

Q28. M.C.: A further question, of a similar nature, is the following: What can you tell us about Brazilian psychoanalysis in particular (the Brazilian Dr. Cláudio Eizirik becoming, in Rio, the first Brazilian IPA President) and about South American psychoanalysis more generally?

S.B.: Contemporary Brazilian psychoanalysis is characterized by two aspects: by its freshness, which certainly also has to do with the election of Dr. Eizirik to the IPA Presidency, and by its deep respect for the patient. I went to Brazil twice in 2005 and was able to get a good feeling for how colleagues in San Paolo, Rio, and Recife work. They have a style of work very much in tune with their patients' internal state and very respectful of its specificity. They know analytic theories very well but do not let them disrupt the process created by the analytic couple at work. Theory is a "third" that helps and sustains; it is a vehicle of the work and not its master.

Much enthusiasm, as well as the excellent traditional cultural and scientific background, is what I found in the meeting with the Argentinian Psychoanalytical Society in Buenos Aires, in a country very much affected by a deep economic crisis, but clearly able to find a way out of it. Uruguayan psychoanalysis moved me very much for its richness, also in a country affected by a very deep economic crisis. The working atmosphere there was very warm, and the relationship between candidates and senior analysts very productive. It provided a moving image of a healthy family trying to maintain a productive climate in an incredibly hard social situation. I deeply appreciated and admired these colleagues.

Q29. M.C.: You presented two contributions in Rio, centered around two patients whom you called Wilma and Lia, both victims of a traumatic past. I particularly liked the case of Wilma in your paper "Wilma's wounds." At the point in the paper where you wrote that this therapy "taught me to let myself be transformed little by little in an object more suitable to her unsaturated needs," I was reminded not only of Winnicott, but also of your work about sharing, which I drew the attention of our readers to in an earlier question. To my mind, the case of Lia is not dissimilar—am I right? Can you tell us something more about it?

S.B.: What these two clinical situations (which I presented at different panels, one in English and the other in Spanish) have in common was the massive defense activated by extremely heavy traumatic experiences. The technical problem was not how to "deductively" reconstruct the vicissitudes of the patients and to present them to their conscious ego, but rather the necessity of recuperating their contact with what their self had experienced. For the analyst too this is of course something unpleasant and anxiety-provoking. In other words, none of us likes to relive together with the patient the sensory and emotional aspects of traumas such as a car accident or the violence exerted upon a child, the kinds of experience that the esthetics and lyrical aspects of our profession tend to keep us at a distance from.

Q30. M.C.: At this point, before posing my last question, let me thank you for your patience and for what I feel has been the very good level of our exchange. So to my last question: Does your next book already have a title? And what will its contents be?

S.B.: My next book, which I would like to finish next year, will deal with theoretical themes (the interpsychic, the creative elaboration of dreams, the concept of "positive" in psychoanalysis and of the physiological narcissistic balance), and with clinical themes (fear and panic, the erotization of the transference, the specific clinical consequences of splitting, the drainage of internal relations, and the psychoanalytic consultation). I believe it could bear the title *Passaggi segreti* (Secret passages). I do not like theory without the clinical aspects that go with it, and this integrative orientation will lie even more at the center of the book I am working on.

And, dear Marco, to say that I feel grateful for such a wide, accurate—and hopefully smooth and fluent—interview is the least I can say.

CHAPTER 12

MARCO CONCI AND INGRID ERHARDT
INTERVIEW HORST KÄCHELE[1]

INTRODUCTION BY MARCO CONCI

I had the good luck to meet Horst Kächele for the first time more than twenty years ago, in May 1990, in Venice, in the context of the very first conference held in Italy on psychotherapy research. I was so fascinated by his approach to psychoanalysis that I volunteered to translate into Italian one of his latest articles, "Psychoanalytische Therapieforschung 1930–1990" (Research in psychoanalytic therapy 1930–1990), which had appeared in the June 1993 issue of the Milan journal *Setting* (Kächele, 1993).

Before meeting him, I had already read, in the original German, the two volumes of the *Lehrbuch der psychoanalytischen Therapie* (1985, 1988), the *Textbook of psychoanalytic therapy*, which he and Helmut Thomä had written together. One of the reasons why I could appreciate their work so much had to do with the fact that Johannes Cremerius (1918–2002) and Gaetano Benedetti had already, during my training at the Milan Scuola di Psicoterapia Psicoanalitica, put me in touch with the "German tradition" from which such a textbook came. For example, Cremerius had also been very much influenced by Michael Balint (1896–1970), as Thomä himself had been. It had also been through Cremerius that I had got in touch with the German tradition of analytically oriented psychosomatic medicine—a medical field in which Thomä and Kächele worked—that is, with the legacies of Alexander Mitscherlich (1908–1982) and of his mentor, Viktor von Weiszäcker (1886–1957). Helmut Thomä had worked in Heidelberg under Mitscherlich before coming to Ulm in 1968.

Last but not least, through Gaetano Benedetti, Helmut Thomä was in contact with the Italian group that published the journal *Psicoterapia e scienze umane*, founded by Pier Francesco Galli in 1967. In the context of the journal's network, I met Thomä in Bologna in June 1991 at the International Workshop organized by Galli and centered around papers given by Morris Eagle, Robert Holt, and Frank Sulloway.

Since our very first meeting in Venice, Horst Kächele

[1] The original version of this interview was published in Volume 22 (2013) of the *International Forum of Psychoanalysis*, pp. 228–243.

had been very friendly toward me and soon invited me to attend the yearly "Workshop on Empirical Research in Psychoanalysis" that he and Helmut Thomä regularly organized in Ulm in the spring time. I remember attending these workshops several times during the 1990s and meeting there a whole series of German and foreign colleagues. The atmosphere of these meetings was so pleasant, direct, and personal as to activate my fantasies of what the very first circles of enthusiastic psychoanalysts might have been like. But, for a number of reasons, I never actively worked in the field of empirical psychotherapeutic research, and our ways parted from each other again. However, even though I did not go into Horst's field, I at least came closer to him by emigrating to Germany and becoming a "German psychoanalyst." This allowed me to keep following his work from fairly close quarters and to have the chance to keep appreciating the direction in which he kept moving.

And this is the reason why, as co-editor-in-chief of the *International Forum of Psychoanalysis*, I decided to interview Horst and give him the opportunity to reach out to our international readers. In other words, let me declare from the start the "positive bias" behind this interview, that is, how worthwhile I believe it is to listen to Horst Kächele. Listening to him may even have a crucial importance for the future of psychoanalysis, for how we can change its course for the better by dealing with our profession and with our science in a more constructive and useful way. Horst has in fact spent most of his life as analyst and as researcher dealing with this problem. But since I did not have the chance ever to work in his field— of empirical research—Ingrid Erhardt helped me to conduct this interview. She is a young analyst in training and a researcher in the field in which Horst works.

The interview took place in Munich on February 15, 2013. It was tape-recorded and transcribed by Ingrid Erhardt and by me, prepared for publication by me, and then approved by Horst Kächele—who added to it a whole series of very useful bibliographical references. It centers around forty questions (Q) and answers (A), divided into four groups.

THE INTERVIEW

Q1: You are today an internationally fairly well-known German psychoanalyst, psychotherapy researcher, and professor in our field. How did you come to psychoanalysis as a young medical doctor?

A1: My interest in psychoanalysis started before I became a medical student. At the age of sixteen, I worked for a bookshop in Stuttgart, which enabled me to peep into meetings of clergymen and psychotherapists. One side effect of this student job was an entry ticket into a very exciting personal environment: that of artists, writers, homosexuals, and psychoanalysts. So, by the time of the *Abitur* (the German high school diploma), I had made up my mind that psychoanalysis would be my field. I did not know many details about psychoanalysis, but I knew already a lot about the societal context of psychotherapy. These were the kind of people I wanted to be with.

Since I was a very serious young person, I went to my father, who was an economist, and told him that I wanted to enter this field, that I needed a costly training, and that I wanted to make the application immediately, at the age of eighteen. I applied for an admission interview at the Academy of Psychotherapy in Stuttgart. Professor Bitter, the chair of the institute, accepted me for psychoanalytic training, but when I realized that such a training would tie me down to my home town for quite a while, I cancelled such a premature move.

My decision to study medicine was based more on my familiarity with poets such as Gottfried Benn or writers like Arthur Schnitzler, who had themselves been medical doctors, than on a real familiarity with the field. At the *Gymnasium*, I had been good at mathematics and sports, and I loved to read poetry. I knew little about medicine, but it later turned out to have been a good decision. Marburg was the German university town where I started my medical studies.

In order to acquire some real knowledge about the "facts of life," I applied for a job as a "cleaning woman" in the department of anatomy. But I did not tell my parents about it; my father especially would not have approved of it [Laughs]. But one day, the professor of anatomy came to me and asked me whether my family was so poor that I had to earn my living. So I said to him, "No, I do this just out of curiosity!" He was so impressed that he recommended me for the *Studienstiftung des deutschen Volkes*, a famous German foundation to which only about 1 per cent of the students were admitted. I used the money I received from this to buy second-hand books on psychoanalysis and other related fields, while my father paid for my medical books. My first book was *Medizinische Psychologie* (Medical psychology) by the famous German psychiatrist Ernst Kretschmer, a book published in the 1920s.

Being in this program meant that you belonged to the elite of students, and it made it particularly easy to have direct access to a whole series of professors and researchers. It was a door-opener for my academic career. Another thing I also remember is that, in our elite student group, I once presented Freud's concept of affects from his 1895 *Project of a scientific psychology.*

Q2: Is there any other aspect of your medical studies that might be interesting for us and for our readers?

A2: My doctoral dissertation at the University of Munich, whose title was "Concepts of Psychogenic Death in the Medical Literature." This topic had been suggested to me by Dr. Siegfried Elhardt, a psychoanalyst at the psychosomatic outpatient department of the University of Munich, where I had done an internship. In connection with this, I went to the UK, to the University of Leeds, for seven months, with a grant from the *Studienstiftung*, and there I started looking for the literature.

Having returned to Munich for personal reasons, I entered psychoanalytic therapy with Dr. Antoon Houben (supported by the *Studienstiftung*). As my nearly finished dissertation resided only in my head, I had the first wonderful opportunity of experiencing the power of psychoanalysis as we overcame this working inhibition very quickly.

What I did in the dissertation was conceptual analysis, conceptual research, a term that was not used then. At that time, I was deeply convinced that I would have never done any empirical study. The people I met in connection with my work at the dissertation were well educated and inspiring, but were not researchers. So the background I myself came from was not science; only the people from the *Studienstiftung* were scientists.

However, recommended by one of the editors of the *Zeitschrift für Psychosomatische Medizin und Psychoanalyse*, my doctoral dissertation became my first publication (1970).

Q3: The theme of the psychological problems of those German adults who had been children during World War II has only recently become a topic of discussion in Germany. Michael Ermann, a pioneer in the research work on this topic, has called them the *Kriegskinder*, "the children of the war." You were born in 1944, so you are also a *Kriegskind*. How has this influenced your growth and development?

A3: I would not call myself a "war child" because my parents lived in fairly favorable circumstances. My father had joined the airplane factory Heinkel in 1939, before the war started. He was an economist and had been hired for his competence in administration. He first he worked in Rostock (in the north-eastern part of Germany), where he met his future wife—my mother. Two years later, they moved to Jenbach, a little village on the River Inn in Tyrol (Austria). My father, in a rather quaint way, was even proud to have acted "unpolitically," although he was running a factory that produced machinery for the Heinkel airplanes. The place was staffed with many foreign workers in connection to the war, and my father was especially proud of the way he treated them to keep them working. Later, we had many quarrels about his way of being "unpolitical" in such dark times.

I have three brothers. My eldest brother was born in Innsbruck in 1942, I was born in Kufstein in 1944, and a younger brother was born in March 1945 when the Third Reich collapsed. I think he was a *Kriegskind* as he hardly survived. Five years later, my youngest brother was born.

In March 1945, the French troops marched into the small town of Jenbach and interrogated my father because of his position in the factory. The Austrians then hired him to put the factory back to civilian production. So he was not in trouble because he was not involved in politics. Later, after his death, I hired a historian to check the story of these years. I wanted to know whether the reports of the young family's life during the war could be substantially confirmed. And it turned out that what my parents told us children was fairly correct. My family stayed one more year in Jenbach; then the Austrians suddenly wanted my father, with his wife and three children, to leave the country within a week. So, in 1946, we left overnight with two suitcases. And thus it was that my parents lost everything and moved to Heilbronn (a pleasant town between Stuttgart and Heidelberg), where my grandparents made a decent living by running a bakery.

After one economically difficult year, my father was hired by the American army as a public attorney in the de-Nazification campaign. This not only brought a full salary and a nice four-room flat, but was at the same time concrete proof to us as adolescents that he had not been actively involved in the Nazi system. However, when I once presented my psychoanalytic treatment of the daughter of an SS officer to the Israeli Psychoanalytic Society, I pointed out to the audience that, in principle, I shared with my patient the long-lasting insecurity that, one day, a politically incriminating document might turn up.

Q4: Another question that we feel is important, in order to understand you and your work better, is: who were your models and mentors? Who were the people, in both your youth and university time, who influenced you the most? To put it in another way, or to connect it to an earlier period of your life, we could ask you: Who were your heroes?

A4: My family was not very religious, but as a younger person I was a "tough" Protestant. When I was fourteen or fifteen years old, I was a fervent member of a youth group called "dj.1-11"—a subgroup of the *Wandervogel*, a famous German youth movement. Hitchhiking through Europe and regularly attending a choir for international folk-singing in Stuttgart at the *Institut für Völkerbeziehungen* (Institute for International Relations) provided some kind of alternative culture to my bourgeois family climate. As I mentioned before, meeting in the 1950s highly educated adults with a strong personalized view on postwar Germany, who were not interested in making money but were committed to the cultural rehabilitation of our country, was very formative for me. These were my heroes.

Q5: As psychoanalysts, we are of course also interested to hear something about your mother.

A5: My mother came from an artistically tinged, financially unstable bourgeois family that ran a shop dealing with musical instruments. Based on her childhood recollections, she had had a lot of fun with her four brothers. My father, as a young doctor of economics, met her after his successful application for the directory staff of the Heinkel Airplane Company in Rostock. He was a fairly shy and quiet person, and a friend from student time provided him the opportunity to meet this woman, eight years younger than him. She had worked as an office secretary, and they got married very quickly.

For her, being a housewife and mother was fully satisfying. She was proud of her four sons. I learned cooking from her, and I was the one who would take care of others, in school as well as at home. My father had suffered from chronic tuberculosis since his early adolescence. In 1954, when I was ten years old, he had to undergo major lung surgery, and his life expectancy was not very high. At that time, he consulted a psychotherapist who recommended that he give up his demanding and stressful job at Heinkel and change to a smaller company, which he did. Due to a very disciplined lifestyle, he was able to work until sixty-five and survived for more than forty years after his operation. My mother was a very strong and powerful person. She did also beat us up, although we laughed about it and we were not traumatized by it.

What is interesting for my personal development is that my eldest brother was somehow not accepted by my father. Time and again my father brought up the story that he must have been exchanged in the hospital after his birth. So people often assumed that I was the eldest son, even though I was the second. In my training analysis with Dr. Roskamp, I had an initial dream that I was a Red Cross officer in Siberia who was looking for someone. This image is clearly taken directly from the first scene of the famous movie *Doctor Zhivago*. After three years, my training analyst said that he did not understand the dream and suggested that I should ask my mother about it. I did this, and my mother cried and told me her secret, which turned out to be the first time that she had spoken about it with one of her sons. She had had a relationship with an artist before she met my father and she had had a child with this man. She had given this boy away in order to save her marriage to my father. So my father did not accept his own first-born because he obviously did not initially feel safe with the young, vital woman my mother was—because of what he thought she might have experienced before meeting him.

Q6: How come you went to Ulm for your residency and psychoanalytic training?

A6: Doctoral students at the psychosomatic outpatient department in Munich were encouraged to attend the *Lindauer Psychotherapiewochen* (Lindau Psychotherapy Weeks), a very good psychotherapy training conference lasting a week that took (and still takes) place in Lindau, on Lake Constance. This was a truly formative experience. Similar to the experience of being a member of the *Studienstiftung*, the chance to meet influential representatives of the psychotherapy world at an early academic age was crucial. Many lecturers pointed out that the medical school, which had been newly established (1968) in Ulm, had not only a very good natural science orientation, but had also an explicit program for the development of psychosomatics and psychotherapy. Professor Thure von Uexküll (1908–2004), the head of the psychosomatic department, had invited Professor Helmut Thomä from Heidelberg to co-chair the new department.

I knew Professor Thomä as the author of an important book on anorexia nervosa that had been published in 1962; while working on my doctoral dissertation, I had read his book, I had liked his style of writing a lot, and I had expressed by letter my naïve wish to work with him, which he dryly rebuffed: "Wait and see!" Yet I knew that he and my first analyst, Dr. Houben, had worked together in Heidelberg on the topic of validation in psychoanalysis.

Q7: You worked with Helmut Thomä for more than forty years. Can you tell us something about your working relationship and what connects you to him?

A7: The leading psychoanalysts at that time in Germany— Mitscherlich, Heigl, Görres, and Thomä—had in 1964 published a memorandum about psychoanalysis, arguing that the Nazis had destroyed it. As a consequence, the *Deutsche Forschungsgemeinschaft* (DFG; the German Research Foundation) decided to establish a research program for rebuilding psychoanalysis. This program included scholarships for training analysis and grants for research.

As my wife and I had to plan our medical residency, we went to Ulm (from October 1969 to September 1970). During my residency in surgery—together with Dr. Köhle from the department of psychosomatic medicine— we initiated a Balint group for nurses (Köhle, Kächele, Franz, Urban, and Geist, 1973). During the second part of the residency, which was in internal medicine, I had ample opportunities to probe my skills in interviewing hematological patients. During this year, I also applied for psychoanalytic training at the Ulm Psychoanalytic Institute. Maybe due to his impression of me in my application interview, or maybe because of my intensive involvement in the then still small psychosomatic group, Professor Thomä offered me a position as research assistant, covered by a grant that he had received from the DFG.

I started my research job in October 1970. As my task was to analyze tape-recorded treatments by psychoanalysts from Ulm, I made the decision to do my training analysis in Stuttgart with Dr. Roskamp, and I started working with him in February 1971. As an aside, this was also a very good idea.

Focusing on your question about how our working relationship developed, it seems to me that we both shared a theoretical curiosity and a pleasure in working on unsolved issues. Helmut Thomä was a well-established, leading German psychoanalyst, at that time even president of the *Deutsche Psychoanalytische Vereinigung* (DPV; the German Psychoanalytic Association), whereas I was a true beginner, twenty-three years younger. I never had to act as an Oedipal rival; I was more in the role of a grandson with a grandfather who enjoyed his grandchild's progress. Dr. Thomä's enjoyment over the small steps in developing our research agenda, his generosity in providing me with a research team, his inclination to continue his own clinical and theoretical interests, and his not interfering with the daily research process were absolutely crucial for my development. I also could observe and see how he handled his real Oedipal entourage, colleagues like the later professors Henseler, Ohlmeier, Radebold, and so on, which was an amazing experience. One of the important pieces of advice I received from a female colleague was: "Do not make your self-esteem depend on Thomä's opinion of you." Indeed, he could be very critical to others, because, I would say now, he was so self-critical.

On the other hand, when we were writing together, it was amazing how relaxed he was in handling my criticisms of his clumsy style and how mercilessly he would criticize my own productions. It was like a good fight on the tennis court. This is how working and writing together has been the title of a small paper we once published in the *IPA Newsletter* (Kächele and Thomä, 1993).

Q8: Another crucial point for us is the following: treading in Helmut Thomä's footsteps, you had the chance to unite the career of the psychoanalytic clinician with the career of the psychoanalytic researcher. From this point of view, you really realized Freud's concept of the psychoanalyst as a professional capable of treating patients and, at the same time, of doing research starting from his own clinical work.

A8: The difference between Thomä's and my career is that he was a clinical researcher. He wrote many masterful case reports covering a diversity of clinical issues, but he never did any formal empirical research himself. In contrast, his colleague Professor Adolf-Ernst Meyer from Hamburg was the first psychoanalyst in Germany to be a top leader in empirical research in psychotherapy and psychosomatics. This is why I would not use the expression that "I followed in Thomä's footsteps." Instead, I added the extra-clinical dimension to our work.[2] We both valued and shared theoretical discussions and debates, and I identified with his deep commitment to working with difficult patients. Right from the start, we agreed that I would do things that he did not do, did not want, or could not do. So together we were such a good and powerful team. But of course, I learned from him as a very experienced clinician, as he was twenty-five years ahead of me in terms of clinical experience.

Q9: What about coming now back to your statement that—at the time of your medical dissertation—you were sure you were not interested in empirical research? What made you change your mind?

A9: In my first year in Ulm, I sifted the empirical research literature and made suggestions where to go with the research. I became very excited about what kind of interesting research avenues had fairly recently been started. For example, the Society for Psychotherapy Research, which would have become my home base for research topics, had been established in 1967. This job gave me the unique chance to read and study the research literature on my own. There was not much available at that time in terms of research on psychoanalytic treatment. Still, I was surprised about what I could discover just by reading. The few analysts truly interested in empirical research wrote impressive stuff; for example, in 1952 Kubie presented a research agenda of the problems and techniques of psychoanalytic validation and progress that is still relevant today (Kubie, 1952).

I looked for colleagues who would help me to implement a research program. Very early in my job, I wrote letters to Hans Strupp, Lester Luborsky, and Hartvig Dahl asking for advice. Meeting the right people helped me to get involved, and to become attached to them and to the theory research agenda. To study the masters first, before finding one's own track, is as important in art as it is in science. These personal relationships promoted my change from conceptual to empirical research. Today, I can certainly appreciate detailed conceptual work, yet research should go back and forth between concepts and data. I built the bridge between clinical and empirical research, and Thomä built the bridge between clinical and conceptual work, in our forty-year-long research enterprise. And of course, Helmut Thomä set a role model

---

[2] Here I follow M. Leuzinger-Bohleber's usage of contrasting clinical and extra-clinical research.

for hard and ambitious work.

Q10: As far as we know, the systematic tape-recording of analytic sessions was initiated at that time._

A10: Yes. It is very interesting that Hartvig Dahl in New York, Merton Gill in Chicago and Adolf-Ernst Meyer in Hamburg started at the same time as Helmut Thomä in Ulm with tape-recordings in psychoanalysis. You may call this phase "From the reconstructed to the observed world of psychoanalysis." To tape-record my first psychotherapy and psychoanalytic training cases from the very start would have been impossible in any other psychoanalytic institution in Germany. Still, the whole psychoanalytic field moved "from narration to observation." This was also the title of my presidential talk in front of the Society for Psychotherapy Research in 1990 (Kächele, 1991).

Q11: Whom would you consider to have been your mentor in your early career?

A11: My mentor in research in Germany was Professor Adolf-Ernst Meyer, chair of the department of psychosomatic medicine in Hamburg. In met him in 1972 at a psychoanalytic conference in Baden-Baden. He became my role model as a researcher–clinician. He studied psychology while he was acting as chair—can you imagine that? He felt the need to perform detailed data analytic work himself. He conveyed to me the idea that the crude albeit tedious work of typing data onto punched cards was a necessary step in learning how-to-do-research. He was often one of my peer reviewers in the service of the DFG; he was quite outspoken, not sparing critique when it was indicated. From him, I learned that it is possible and feasible to remain friends and still be critical about each other's work.

My clinical mentor was certainly Helmut Thomä; we had regular supervisions for a long time, and we even played tennis on a weekly basis. But for forty years, we did not use the personal *du* for "you": we continued to use the formal *Sie*. It was only when our laudator for the Mary Sigourney Award, Fred Pine, realized that we had been on this formal level for all these years that he insisted that we change and eventually use the informal *du*.

Q12: Let us now come to the first of our *second set of questions*. Its formulation will require a longer set of premises. Not all our readers know that German psychoanalysts have the unique—almost incredible—

good luck of working not only with affluent private patients, but also with patients who in any other country in the world would not be able to pay themselves for our work. Since 1967, the German *Krankenkassen*, the state-supervised insurance companies, have covered the cost of psychoanalytic and of psychodynamic therapy. In 1987, psychoanalysts recommended also including cognitive-behavioral therapy in the scheme. Analytic psychotherapy is covered for up to 300 sessions, two or three times a week, and once-weekly psychodynamic and cognitive-behavioral therapy up to eighty to a hundred sessions. In addition, because some German colleagues seem to have mixed feelings about this system, it is important for me to ask you your opinion about it. I believe that our readers would be very interested in your point of view on this. In other words, what are in your opinion the advantages, and the disadvantages of such a system of financial coverage?

A12: Well, only a few—maybe prominent—German colleagues have disagreed with third-party payment by the German health system. To ask for *advantages and disadvantages* gives a wrong impression; maybe you should ask for main effects and side effects. Only a training analyst or someone who has a very good reputation in a big city can nowadays in Germany afford to make a living without treating insured patients. There are hardly any real private patients in Germany.

The background of the present system is the German insurance system, which goes back to Chancellor Bismarck in the 1880s. It was a political move that everybody had to be insured. This was not due to a moral position but instead a strategy of the German state to counteract the expansion of the Social Democratic Party. So the only issue after World War II was why had it taken so long to include psychoanalysis and psychotherapy in the existing system. It took so long because—as everywhere in the world—psychotherapy has, for whatever reasons, difficulties acquiring a good reputation. Another aspect, in my view, has been a tendency of psychoanalysts to convey to the public the impression that everybody needed at least 500 sessions and should attend therapy four times a week. If they had said that the majority of patients could be seen once a week in about thirty to fifty sessions, that would have facilitated the inclusion of psychotherapy in the system.

The founding of the Central Institute for Psychogenic Illnesses (an institute that was financially sponsored by a local insurance society) in Berlin after the war was the first step in the recognition of neurosis as illness by a German public institution (Dräger, 1971). This institution published the first large-scale empirical study on outcome in psychoanalytic therapy in 1962, reporting impressive data on the outcome of medium-intensity analytic psychotherapy (Dührssen, 1962). In Germany, this whole insurance issue is tied to an invisible division of psychoanalysts into a more pragmatic group (Schultz-Hencke, Dührssen, Heigl-Evers, Rudolf) and—as I would call it—a "more IPA-oriented group." Although A. Mitscherlich actively endorsed the realization of the inclusion of analytic psychotherapy into the insurance system, the leaders of his society, the DPV, were quite reluctant to do this. Much more active in this direction were the colleagues of the *Deutsche Psychoanalytische Gesellschaft* (DPG; the German Psychoanalytic Society) and those working at the universities. DPG colleagues had more jobs at the universities, and they knew that psychoanalysis is easier to establish as a science if you promote psychoanalytic psychotherapy.

The findings of the Dührssen study helped greatly in incorporating psychoanalytic therapy into the insurance system. As the insurance system has certain operating principles, psychoanalysts had to find a way to fit into the system. One needed ideas about etiology, psychopathology, differential indication, and so on. To medicalize psychoanalysis meant to bring it into the frame of a normal medical intervention, which implies research on process and outcome, quality assessment, and so on. This German development actually fulfilled and still fulfills Freud's 1918 prediction—the formulation of the necessity to bind together the gold of psychoanalysis with the copper of psychotherapy, if we are to be able to reach out to and to offer our form of therapy to society at large.[3] For me, it is difficult to grasp the fact that there are still European countries without financial coverage of psychotherapy (Kächele and Pirmoradi, 2009).

Q13: Do we understand you correctly if we say that the advantage of the system is the possibility for all insured

---

[3] Here are the concluding remarks of the paper "Lines of advance in psycho-analytic therapy," which Freud gave at the Fourth Congress of the IPA held in Budapest in September 1918: "It is very probable, too, that the large-scale application of our therapy will compel us to alloy the pure gold of analysis freely with the copper of direct suggestion; and hypnotic influence, too, might find a place in it again, as it has in the treatment of war neuroses. But, whatever form this psychotherapy for the people might take, whatever the elements out of which it is compounded, its most effective and most important ingredients will assuredly remain those borrowed from strict and untendentious psycho-analysis" (Freud, 1919, p. 168).

people to have access to it, whereas its disadvantage can be the medicalization of psychotherapy?

A13: I do not think that these two arguments are on the same level of discourse. Critics from other countries too often turn the term "medicalization" into something negative, without knowing the details. We have a fairly well functioning peer review system, and patients from all walks of life have access to psychotherapy. The university departments of psychosomatic medicine and clinical psychology have successfully implemented research. So, in my view, medicalization really means moving psychoanalysis into a normal science and making it available to everyone, and not only to the unhappy "happy few."

I really wonder about this issue: if psychoanalysis were only available for the affluent section of the population, how could one ever substantiate the claim of psychoanalytic theory to be relevant for all people? I do understand that the term "medicalization" sometimes, for example, conveys the fact that doctors tend to medicalize manifestations of distress by only prescribing tablets and so on, and that people are made the object of a medical intervention. Yet I never heard that someone successfully prescribed psychotherapy or even psychoanalysis. And there is no evidence that self-payment improves the outcome of psychoanalysis.

Q14: Another important point we would like to discuss with you is this: from our point of view, we see a connection between the "focal concept of therapy" that you and Thomä developed, as opposed to therapy in terms of a "process without a preconceived termination," and the German insurance system, which was the frame of your work. What do you think about this? A further question could be: In what ways did this aspect come together with the way in which your definition was based on Balint and on your empirical research?

A14: In general, it is obvious that the cultural psychoanalytic experiences that any therapist has impacts on his or her thinking. Likewise, Dr. Thomä's one-year Fulbright fellowship at Yale Psychiatric Institute in 1955–1956, and his one-year-long training analysis with Dr. Balint, shaped his clinical and scientific thinking. Another source of inspiration for us was the work of Thomas French from the Chicago Institute (French, 1954). In his model of psychoanalysis, the focus is conceptualized as a region of interchange between day residues and unconscious elements that condenses the inputs and the data coming from both realms. A treatment process has to maximize the connections between the here-and-now and past experiences—only then will it work. Our focal conception of psychoanalytic therapy is a mixture between the two authors. From Balint stems the notion of focal therapy which counteracted the idea that severely disturbed patients always need very long treatments; what they need is a step-by-step working process. Although the number of steps is not predictable, each step may count. The Chicago focus concept stresses the current transference and its stepwise working-through.

The German insurance frame that you mentioned in your question might well also be of some pragmatic importance. If psychoanalytic treatments have to be planned in chunks of eighty sessions, this will of course have an impact on one's clinical thinking. The French expression "*une tranche d´analyse*" also points to a similar stepwise procedural thinking. So the focal concept might be understood as a modest concept that helps to modify and to adapt one's psychoanalytic treatment to the real world.

The third influence came from studying the analytic process by scrutinizing it with tape-recordings. At any moment, a therapist makes selections and choices concerning both the patient's free associations and the data coming from one's own process of evenly hovering attention. We can reflect on only a few topics at the same time. And at the same time, we constantly have to make a selection about which aspect to focus on. It is inevitable that we will focalize.

Q15: The useful handling of free associations was a critique point that had already been made by Harry Stack Sullivan in the 1940s. In particular, he criticized those colleagues who would let patients free-associate without an end and without interacting with their free associations.

A15: "Free association" is one of the fairytale concepts of psychoanalysis—much beloved yet little studied. It is here, in the domain of what analysts really do, where our work and the work of all recording analysts need more clarity. The acknowledgment that psychoanalysis as a therapeutic and scientific enterprise deserves basic groundwork, for example by discourse-analytic studies, is still fairly rare (Peräkylä, 2008).

Q16: Let us now come to our next question, through which we will introduce a new theme. In 1989, the analytically trained sociologist Edith Kurzweil published a book with the title *The Freudians. A comparative perspective* (Kurzweil, 1989), whose very first sentence was: "Every country produces the psychoanalysis it needs, although it does this unconsciously." In her book, she then tried to present the cultural, social, and national influences to which psychoanalysis was exposed in a whole series of countries—including Germany—whose analytic communities she had visited, according to the methodology of "participant observation." In other words, she was one of the first people to clearly say something that not all our colleagues yet see or agree with—that psychoanalysis is not the same everywhere. What do you think about all this? How do you see German psychoanalysis from this point of view?

A16: Yes, I know Edith Kurzweil's work, and I agree with her. It is easy to realize how psychoanalysis is embedded in a country. To my mind comes also Morris Eagle, who recently connected Western psychoanalysis with the important cultural phenomenon of the Enlightenment (Eagle, 2011b).

As far as postwar German psychoanalysis is concerned, one important input was certainly provided by the Frankfurt School and its "critical social theory." People in the late 1960s heavily embraced psychoanalytic theory, especially its dimension of cultural and social critique. Another important favorable factor in the German reception of psychoanalysis after World War II was the field of anthropological medicine, as articulated by Viktor von Weizsäcker, Mitscherlich's mentor at the University of Heidelberg. At its roots still lay the traces of Romantic medicine, as had been elaborated in the writings of Dr. Carus from Dresden. Starting from Romantic medicine, a pervasive anthropological point of view was developed within German internal medicine, which influenced also Alexander Mitscherlich.

This tradition was also endorsed by Professor von Uexküll, who cultivated a friendly attitude towards psychoanalysis that influenced the appointments of the first generation of chairs of psychotherapy, psychosomatic medicine, and psychoanalysis. He was responsible for the reform in the organization of our medical studies, which in 1970 brought about the inclusion of medical psychology, medical sociology, and psychosomatic medicine.

From this point of view, it is not by chance that, in Germany, psychoanalysis and psychosomatic medicine fertilized each other for two or three decades.

We also should also not forget that the German anti-psychoanalytic psychiatric tradition facilitated the establishment of psychoanalysis and psychosomatic medicine as alternative, collaborative fields.

Q17: To now go back to the general theme of the social and cultural specificity of psychoanalysis, according to the single country in which it takes root and develops, we would like to ask you: Do you see any difference among psychoanalysts coming from different countries and cultures?

A17: First, I am inclined to see more differences between clinicians and researchers, independently from their country of origin. At the same time, yes, there are differences, for example in the way of writing about psychoanalysis. Rather typical, for example, is the way in which French colleagues write. And our Italian colleagues are often very poetic, to a degree that would not be as easily accepted in Germany. In addition, the diversity inside groups is also quite substantial. As an empirically minded researcher, I would say that not only national identity, but also personal character makes a difference.

Q18: We would now like to deal with the fascinating theme of "international psychoanalysis" by formulating a more personal question. We were always impressed by how easily both Thomä and you can address an international audience, by how both of you can address it in English. What lies behind this capacity of yours is, in my view, your having been able to elaborate the Holocaust, and this to a greater extent than many other German colleagues. If this is true, what was your own way of elaborating the Holocaust?

A18: I think it is fair to say that, as I mentioned before, one important achievement of Thomä's was to apply for a Fulbright scholarship at Yale Psychiatric Institute in the mid-1950s, a place dominated by Jewish colleagues. In the early 1980s, I was at the National Institute of Mental Health in Bethesda (Maryland) and I realized how it must have been for him the 1950s. For Thomä, it was crucial to meet as a co-resident at Yale the former Austrian Jewish emigrant, now immigrant, John Kafka. When John Kafka came to Ulm the first time, he was the first Jew I met and developed a personal relationship with.

For Thomä, it was very important that Ulm should be part of the larger scientific psychoanalytic community. This is why our textbook had to come out in English at the same time as in German. This is why in Ulm we always had many foreign visitors. These visits by foreign guests and colleagues shaped our range of critical thinking.

Q19: And what is your feeling about how the elaboration of the Holocaust still plays a role in the relationship between the German and the international analytic communities?

A19: When I started working in the field, there were only a few German voices in the international debate. But this did not depend only on the Holocaust. We are ashamed of having destroyed many other people, not only seven million Jews, but also many millions of Russians. As a German, I truly feel that my personal and professional life is overshadowed by this cruel history. So it might not be a surprise that German voices were low-key in postwar international psychoanalytic circles.

Checking for papers by German authors in the *International Journal of Psychoanalysis*, it is only recently that we find an increase in their number. Thomä and Wolfgang Loch were for years the only German voices that international colleagues would hear. Since neither Hermann Argelander nor Alfred Lorenzer went abroad, their important work is very little known outside of Germany.

From this point of view, it was of course also very important to have had the international analytic community come to Berlin for the IPA Congress in July 2007. And indeed, it takes—and not only for German colleagues—a continuous exposure to international contacts to keep an international dialogue developing.

If I were to speak about the general issue of international dialogue from an empirical point of view, I would ask the following question: how many people, for example from the USA or Brazil, are ready to expose themselves to the international scene? This would be the empirical way in which I would address the problem. From this point of view, we have to do with a general problem that goes beyond our specific German case.

Q20: And how would you characterize German psychoanalysis? How would you present it to our readers? How pluralistic is it? What is specific about it?

A20: There are different aspects of this very complex problem. Although Otto Kernberg speaks fluent German and often visits us, he seems to know only three kinds of psychoanalysis: English, French, and North American.

This is what you can read in the several papers he has written on international psychoanalysis. Our journal *Psyche* (Frankfurt) has 7,000 subscribers and comes out once a month, but only a few colleagues outside the German-speaking world know about it. But the same could be said about Brazilian psychoanalysis: what do you know about Brazilian psychoanalysis?

What is new is that there are in Germany are many, as I call them, "Indians," meaning Freudians, Kleinians, Bionians, and so on. In other words, in each group you find people going in a new direction. Take Ogden, for example: so many analysts are now interested in his work. These diverse interests testify to the enormous capacity for renewal, but also speak to the process of Babelization (Jimenéz, 2008). By this, I mean that there is no debate, no efforts at a comparative evaluation. This is also the conclusion to which Paul Stepansky came in his book *Psychoanalysis at the margins* (2009). Psychoanalysis as a cultural field loses its identity, so that anything goes. Without debate and a comparative approach, we do not create any science. Psychoanalysis thus becomes a *façon de parler*—a lot of theoretical sketches without empirical confirmation!

To now mention a really specific aspect of German psychoanalysis, meaning a specific German contribution to the field of psychoanalysis, I can think of the concept of "scenic understanding," as Hermann Argelander defined it in the early 1970s. This is also a concept that is very little known outside Germany—in terms of the way it was conceptualized in our country.

Q21: Your answer in terms of the way in which psychoanalysis is nowadays diluted in a whole series of different points of view reminds me of Robert Wallerstein's famous concept of "common ground," which he repeatedly dealt with, starting with the paper he gave in Montreal in 1987 under the title "One psychoanalysis or many?" (Wallerstein, 1988).

A21: I appreciate Robert Wallerstein's attempt to keep psychoanalysts together, but what we actually need is a series of clearer concepts. As long as we do not have clear definitions, there cannot be a psychoanalysis as science. From this point of view, common ground is what I would call "common underground," a kind of a vague agreement on some basic assumptions. We should work more on protocols and create more of a shared culture. What we need is a set theory, based on a mutually agreed upon definition of concepts. When I can start out from a transcript, I can speak about psychoanalysis much better. See, for example, how good a contact any psychoanalyst can keep with his patient. This is how we can also better understand how a therapist listens and how another one does.

Q22: We would now like to come to the first of a *third series of questions* directly concerning your research work. You differentiate between six phases in psychoanalytic research (1—clinical case studies, 2—descriptive studies, 3—experimental studies, 4—clinical controlled studies, 5—naturalistic studies, and 6—patient-focused studies). Besides the many research fields you have been working in, you are an important ambassador for (psychoanalytic) process research. What paradigm will be in the focus of future research, and what should be focused on to further develop psychoanalytic theory and contribute to the establishment of psychoanalysis in the scientific community?

A22: The most important task still consists in furthering analysts' interest in research findings, in furthering their ability to critically evaluate the results of research and to implement it in their own practice. If the field continues to develop as a loose collection of tribal partisans, organized psychoanalysis will sooner or later disappear. The challenge for today and the near future resides in the impact of multimedia developments on our field. Telephone analysis is no longer a taboo. But what about Skype analysis? Sooner or later, psychoanalysis will increasingly have to take place in virtual environments.

Are psychoanalysts in the position to respond to the needs of a multimedia-oriented society? The majority of analysts limit themselves to just espousing a critical attitude towards these "brave new worlds." This will not be enough. Taking up the field of communication research, especially conversational analysis, we might be in a position to better understand what analytic dialogue can achieve in the context of the new media (Kächele and Buchholz, 2013).

"Shuttle analysis" has been discovered as a means to provide adequate personal experience in far-off regions of the world; it could be an incentive to rethink the evidence for the still strict position on the required formal training analysis, although much evidence has been accumulating that training analysis does not create more satisfaction than privately organized analytic experiences (Schachter, Gorman, Pfäfflin, and Kächele, 2013).

As in any other profession, normal MDs do not do

research; still, the participation of analysts in office networks could improve the quality of transfer from real word to research agenda. We need university-based work and research. The IPA-sponsored Open Door Review (Fonagy, Kächel, Krause, Jones, Perron, and Lopez, 1999) has been a good step in assembling what we have and what we do not have at hand. In the early 1950s, there was only the Menninger study; we now have about thirty to forty research projects and/or centers. As an aside, very few studies focus on high-frequency treatments. In terms of research policy, this makes sense: first establish that once-a-week therapy has enough evidence, then compare twice-weekly with once-weekly therapy, then twice-weekly three times weekly, and so on.

A recent nationwide study conducted in Germany confirms what we all know: only 0.5 per cent of treatments take place four times a week; three-times-a week therapy covers 1.5 per cent of all treatments, twice-a-week 8 per cent. This means that 90 per cent of the treatments run once a week, with half of the therapy behavioral and half of it psychodynamic (Albani, Blaser, Geyer, Schmutzer, and Brähler, 2010).

Single-case research is a very important learning device. But the famous Freud cases are good old friends to whom we should say goodbye so that we can create our own new specimen cases, well-documented cases that are publicly available to all "students of psychoanalysis."

Q23: Let us now come to the Ulmer Textbank. It was the largest archive of therapy documents in the world. There were several thousand treatment documents and several hundred sessions in audio and transcripts. Can you describe how the Textbank was developed?

A23: At first, Dr. Thomä recorded one analytic case, then another. When I also started to tape-record my training cases, I realized that soon we would run into simple storage problems. In the early 1970s, computers became a research tool across all social science fields due to their capacity to store and analyze data. Donald Spence was, to my knowledge, the first psychoanalyst to teach a PI-1 software program at the Pisa summer school for computational linguistics in 1973, which I attended. Soon afterwards, I learned about an exciting computer-based content-analytic study on a tape-recorded analysis by the New York colleague Hartvig Dahl (Dahl, 1974).

Realizing that this trend had developed across many social science fields, I finally hired Erhard Mergenthaler as a student of computer science. In Germany, we clearly were the first to promote this kind of research. When asked what a textbank is, the most simple answer is that it works like a blood bank. Some people—the donors—provide the materials, and others—the recipients—receive them. The project was funded with a large grant from the DFG (Mergenthaler, 1985). The main issue is and will be how to assure anonymity.

Q24: In the analytic community and in analytic training, the traditional case study or vignette is still the gold standard for describing and evaluating the analytic process and progress, and serves as the most important means to demonstrate analytic technique and concepts. How did the empirical single case study develop out of Freud's "analytic novels"?

A24: Take, for example, Freud's discussion of the Schreber case. Here, Freud had a published document at his disposal. In the 1950s, Elisabeth Zetzel discovered that Freud had forgotten to destroy the notes he had taken about the first nine sessions of the Ratman case (Zetzel, 1966). This made people curious about how Freud really worked and was an important stimulus in the direction of collecting more data on the way we all work. Of course, by destroying all his material, Freud wanted to make it more difficult for people to challenge his work.

Q25: And now a question concerning the future. What questions—according to you—should our work of research in psychoanalysis deal with in the future in order for psychoanalysis to meet its scientific challenges, and in order for our profession to gain in credibility?

A25: First, I would point to the role of clinical contributions as true gold mines if they were to be available via databanks. With Mattias Desmet from the University of Ghent, we have now established the Single Case Archive as such a tool (Desmet et al., 2013).

Another important topic that has moved into the center of attention is the therapists' contribution. Instead of competing the therapies against each other, as in a horse race, some researchers like Lester Luborsky (Luborsky, McLellan, Woody, O'Brien, and Auerbach, 1985) and Rolf Sandell (Sandell, Carlson, Schubert, Grant, Lazar, and Broberg, 2006) study the amount of variation between therapists and the impact of training analysis on therapeutic proficiency. These findings are impressive. It seems that we spend too much effort on dissecting treatments instead of identifying relevant parameters like patients' and therapists' contributions.

The most recent field of research I have started is what we can call "the culture of errors." The problem in our field is that we have very little understanding about how treatments fail. One out of three treatments does not go well. In the USA, 30–40 per cent of patients leave treatment for reasons that we do not yet know. The data on training analysis show of course only 20 per cent premature terminations (Schachter, Gorman, Kächele, and Pfäfflin, 2013).

There are big and there are small sins, but we do not know yet exactly what they are.

Q26: This reminds us of the theme of rupture and repair studied, for example, by Jeremy Safran (Safran, Muran, Samstag, and Stevens, 2002). What do you think about this?

A26: Ruptures are indeed inevitable and we should know more about them and how to repair them.

Q27: The topic of side effects is an important topic not only in pharmacology, but also in other branches of medicine. What about our field?

A27: Yes, we should create something similar—a list of side effects of psychotherapy. We also have to talk about "informed consent": no patient signs any informed consent papers in Germany. This is a new topic in our field. As far as side effects are concerned, one of the first second-hand books I bought in Marburg as a medical student was about medical side effects. In other words, I always thought that it is a feature of the maturity of a field to be able to disclose its side effects and dissect its failures.

Q28: But how can we do research in this field?

A28: You cannot of course expect colleagues to denounce themselves. We can only go about the problem indirectly. A typical example of indirect measure is sexual sins: if you ask, "Have you ever molested a patient sexually?," only 2 per of analysts answer yes. If you ask, "Have you ever treated a patient who has been sexually molested?," you get a positive answer of about 12 per cent. On these topics, you only get indirect measures and/or anonymous reports.

Q29: But let us now come to the problem of analytic training. What advice would you give to candidates who are interested not only in analytic training, but also in empirical research in psychoanalysis? Considering how hard it is to work in both fields at the same time, should candidates not rather chose only one of the two paths? And what conditions do you see as being necessary in order for them to be able to pursue both paths and to combine them?

A29: It is not realistic to expect people who do clinical work also to do research in a systematic way. In German psychosomatic hospitals, a certain amount of research is still possible, but you need a frame, somebody to go to for advice. I did much work to try to support empirical research in South America, in Russia, and so on. You need to create specific networks; this is the basic preliminary condition for people to have the chance to start, and to keep, working in the field of empirical research in psychotherapy.

Q30: And what could analytic institutes do to make more space for empirical research?

A30: Candidates should know about research. Hartvig Dahl was for 20 years the director of research at the New York Institute, but only a very few people were really interested in his work. Candidates should be informed and should be up to date with the research being done in the field. There is a growing body of very interesting data, for example some papers, that candidates should also know about. For example, there are papers which every candidate should know about. The first one I can think of is the paper by Leichsenring and Rabung (2011) detailing the evidence for longer treatments. From an ethical point—in terms of resource allocation—as well as from a scientific point of view, the burning question today is: who needs more than forty sessions or more than a year of treatment? Another important thing to do would be to attend a course on the state of the art of psychodynamic research, the significance of which has recently been very shown by Levy, Ablon, and Kächele (2012).

I have little interest in the private practice of psychoanalysis as some kind of a lifestyle enrichment. My real concern is the above-mentioned message of Freud's Budapest paper. This is still also the common ground of German psychoanalysis, that is, identifying those people who really need analytic treatment. When I read a paper about a discovery made by an analyst in the tenth year of analysis, I do not find it interesting. On the basis of my long-term clinical experience with patients treated by bone marrow transplantation, I learned to appreciate the medical perspective that provides evidence for treatments that can be life-saving.

Q31: How should we change psychoanalytic training so that young analysts can combine the analytic tradition with today's scientific challenges? They could potentially learn to do this well enough that they could personally contribute more than colleagues do today to the scientific and professional status of psychoanalysis. What do you think?

A31: Some years ago Helmut Thomä and I (Thomä and Kächele, 1999) wrote a memorandum on the issue that we should take the training analysis out of the training system. The atmosphere created by the training analysis damages a relaxed learning process. I strongly feel it to be more in line with a proper psychoanalytic spirit to make the personal experience of psychoanalysis part of the candidate's personal responsibility, and I would give more space to the clinical work done under adequate supervision.

Q32: When did you start having this opinion about training analysis?

A32: I can recall a substantial paper about this topic by Helmut Thomä in the *Annual of Psychoanalysis* in 1993. I personally had the chance to analyze the data on the length of the 300 training analyses that took place in the DPV over three decades. It was astonishing how the number of sessions kept increasing year by year. However, there are no empirical data connecting the length of the training analysis with its quality and effects (Von Rad and Kächele, 1999).

Q33: And what is your feeling, your point of view, of the survival of our profession?

A33: Let me cite Peter Fonagy's interview with Eliott Jurist in the *Psychoanalytic Psychology* journal (Jurist, 2010). He said that IPA psychoanalysis will be dead in forty years, with psychoanalysis absorbed into other fields. For example, good concepts such as transference, counter-transference, and defense will probably be absorbed into other approaches. There is the clear feeling of a decay. Enthusiasm is diminishing. It is a cultural phenomenon. How can psychoanalysis adapt to a changing world? What are the Chinese peoples doing with psychoanalysis?

Q34: We come now to the first of the *fourth and last group of our questions*, a series of questions of a more general character. One of the problems that we would very much like to discuss with you is, of course, the scientific status of psychoanalysis. Many people—many colleagues among them—not only criticize psychoanalysis as a science, but also even deny to it a scientific status. One of the mostly formulated critical observations is that our psychoanalytic work and/or the psychoanalytic relationship are so complex that no empirical research, quantitative nor qualitative, can rightly account for it.

A34: I would like to start answering this question through a quotation of John Bowlby's that I like very much. I take this from a paper he presented in front of the Canadian Psychoanalytic Society in 1979 (Bowlby, 1979). Here are his words: "The task of the clinician is to increase complexity, the task of the researcher is the opposite, he has to simplify."

The object of research is *not the whole* of psychoanalysis. This is not a sensible question. A researcher has to find out certain aspects over which he has some kind of control. A ghost is very difficult to make the object of science. Ghosts are usually the object of narrations; you can tell stories about ghosts. For me, research is not the same as science. The science of psychoanalysis encompasses more than empirical research. Psychoanalysis is a field with a peculiar scientific discourse. There are scientific aspects of psychoanalytic therapies in which only a weakly contoured methodology will be able to grasp certain phenomena, for example those of countertransference (see the article on "Countertransference as object of empirical research ?" by Kächele, Erhardt, Seybert, and Buchholz).

There are theoretical concepts such as the notions of the unconscious, the preconscious, regression, and so on, that are partially operational and partially not. Psychoanalysis is a field with a mixed scientific discourse. Ricoeur distinguished in 1970 a "how it works" discourse and a "why it works" discourse. George Klein (1970) made the same distinction. In his clinical work, an analyst wants to understand the motivational issue of "why"; he does not care for "how motivation works." A research analyst, however, studies the "how question;" he or she may use, for example, the methodology of conversational research and raise the issue "how does an analyst frame his ideas so that the patient is able to assimilate them?" (Peräkylä, 2004). How dreams are generated is a question a clinician cannot answer. The same is true for the nature of the relationship between helping alliance and transference, which has been studied for decades in the field of psychotherapy research. The clinician, together with the patient, creates understanding, makes sense, creates sense—he limits himself to assuming that this is helpful in the long run.

There are experimental studies on defense; there are experimental studies on dreams, like the one the research group in Frankfurt has been conducting, in which they experimentally tested Freud's theory of the preconscious (Leuschner, Hau, and Fischmann, 2000). Or take the theory of microworlds developed by the Swiss psychoanalyst and professor of clinical psychology Ulrich Moser (2008). Psychoanalytic science is a rich field with many different aspects. In my view, it is basically no different from other fields in which a profession is anchored in a basic science, but the science aspect only partially maps out what is needed for its practical application (Buchholz, 1999).

From this point of view, one of my favorite topics is the use of the voice in psychoanalysis. No one has ever systematically studied this topic and the variety of vocalizations in psychoanalysis. Why have analysts been so blind to the use of their own main instruments for more than a hundred years? Another theme could be the following: how feminine must a man be in order to be a good analyst? These are all scientific issues, and research consists in finding ways to investigate them empirically.

Q35: To put the problem in different terms: even with a growing interest in research work done in the field of the effectiveness of psychoanalysis, there are still colleagues, that is, psychoanalysts, who openly criticize and question the significance of such research work, with particular regard for the empirical. What would you say to these colleagues? How do you deal with them?

A35: Of course, people are free to be as blind as they want to be. Our colleagues are only practitioners; this is fine, this not the point. The problem is how the government deals with the problem, whether or not the government finances research. For example, the Swedish government recently decided that there is no longer any money for psychodynamic research.

Q36: Psychoanalytic therapy was recently dismissed from the service catalogue of the Dutch public health service. In Germany too, the number of the psychoanalysts who are full university professors has been greatly diminishing over the past few years. On the other hand, the cognitive-behavioral point of view has kept gaining followers and academic space. Is this a sign of the "impending death of psychoanalysis" which Robert Bornstein (2001) talked about in 2001?

A36: The problem is that cognitive-behavioral therapy is no longer cognitive-behavioral therapy. Leading representatives of this approach are borrowing and integrating core concepts of psychoanalysis into their own theoretical body. Take for example schema therapy: the basic concept is clearly psychodynamic—the difference resides in more active treatment strategies. Names may disappear, but good concepts will not. The names are changing, but less so the concepts.

On the other hand, it is true that traditional psychoanalysis was usually much more interested in investigating motivation for feeling and thinking than in searching for what induces change (Luborsky and Schimek, 1964). And this is the price we now have to pay for this.

Q37: Do you mean that you favor a patient-focused approach as opposed to a technique centered approach?

A37: Yes, I do. From an empirical point of view, an important question we should try to answer is the following: which are the patients who would need more than fifty sessions? Psychoanalysis is not for everyone. This is also the direction taken by Kernberg in terms of his work with personality disorders. For me, the work of Fonagy and his group is also an application and implementation of key psychoanalytic concepts. Psychoanalysis needs to be developed in different directions and dimensions. "This is no longer psychoanalysis!," people said of Kernberg's work in the 1970s, and some still say it now.

Q38: One important problem in our field is that there are not enough candidates. Young MDs and young psychologists do not chose psychoanalysis, but seem to look for more established therapy trainings.

A38: It is true that they are not attracted to psychoanalysis as they used to be. It is too rigid. From this point of view, psychoanalysis is going to dry out for biological reasons, for the lack of young people training in it. We need to create an environment that makes psychoanalysis more attractive for young people, to come in and join us.

From this point of view, the whole debate around the

scientific status of psychoanalysis is not the real problem. The deadly gun is the age issue. If young people do not join us, psychoanalysis will be running out of business. It would not be the first field of science that is running out of business.

Q39: But this is fortunately not the only face or aspect concerning the present status of psychoanalysis in the world. Psychoanalysis is now being discovered and/or talked about in the countries of Eastern European, and also in countries where people had never previously heard of it. We know that you have been traveling widely, that you had the chance to see your handbook translated into more than fifteen languages. We would be curious to know how you can explain this opposite phenomenon, that is, such a growing interest in psychoanalysis in other parts of the world, especially those which do not have a psychoanalytic tradition.

A39: Well, you have to differentiate. Eastern Europe has always been part of Europe. It was under political repression, and the population have been recuperating their old European identity. The same happened in Russia. Educated European people have no problem reconnecting with their European thinking. This is a world of its own, although this might be less true for countries like Armenia, Georgia, Kazakhstan, and all the other former Soviet Union countries. In these, the interest in psychoanalysis covering both therapeutics and cultural aspects fits into a move toward Westernization. The really interesting new fields are the Asian countries like India, Japan, and China, and the Arabic and Islamic countries.

India was the first of these regions to discover psychoanalysis, but these far-off activities were hardly perceived by the West. And Freud, who had corresponded with the first Indian psychoanalyst, did not appreciate his deviant ideas.

With regard to China, it is interesting to remember that there was already an interest in psychoanalysis in the 1920s in the field of literature, the arts, and poetry. There is informative documentation about this early period; at that time, the first translations of Freud into Chinese had already been made. Now that the upper middle class, with its higher education level, has discovered psychoanalysis as a lifestyle, I am pretty sure that they will explore and maybe utilize psychoanalysis as a therapy. This is also true also for other parts of the world; everywhere where there is a higher educated class, they are open for psychoanalysis.

A different issue is represented by the Islamic countries. In an Islamic country, it is hard to imagine that a man analyzes a woman. But why not women working with women? Again, educated people are interested in psychoanalysis there too. Last year, our textbook came out in the Persian language. We had an introductory seminar in Isfahan with a group of fifty women and men, mainly psychologists and social workers. In Teheran, there is already a psychoanalytic institute. It all comes down to the question of how much education there is, and of how Westernized such an education is.

You also have to keep in mind that what psychoanalysis stands for in the world is not primarily the specific treatment it offers, but the message that Freud stands for—a cultural message, a cultural symbol.

Q40: Another way for us to deal with the same topic is the following: we know that you travel around the world not only to present the growing number of translations of your handbook, but also to teach and to do research. For example, we know that you train researchers in South America and future analysts in Eastern Europe. What are your goals from this point of view? How do you see your role in this development?

A40: When I am invited, I bring to people the Ulm Triadic Model, which consists of theory, research, and practice. This is a unique mixture and people seem to like it. Even if you only talk about theory or practice, you talk differently with a research background. I think that it produces a more reflective and modest way of dealing with psychoanalysis. This is a modesty that comes from research and from the need to better understand patients' points of view.

The Ulm message wants to activate critical thinking. Our textbook is a critical book of psychoanalysis. In German, you cannot call it a "critical theory" because that would make people think of the Frankfurt School. But it is critical in a way. It is a "nonbelieving" textbook; I would say we are "nonbelieving psychoanalysts."

There is a British statement that "Theories—like soldiers—never die, they just fade away." This may happen to a fair number of psychoanalytic terms. Concepts arise, peak, and disappear—depending on the backbone in terms of scientific underpinning. There is an interesting book by Morris Eagle on contemporary psychoanalysis, which I can recommend. It is called *From classical to contemporary psychoanalysis. A critique and integration* (Eagle, 2011a). This is rich in critique and full of integrative ideas. It talks about what is useful in present-day psychoanalysis and what is no longer viable. It is a way of looking at the state of the art of psychoanalysis which—in my mind—is a useful way that points to a creative future.

REFERENCES

Albani, C., Blaser, G., Geyer, M., Schmutzer, G., & Brähler, E. (2010). Ambulante Psychotherapie in Deutschland aus Sicht der Patienten. Teil 1: Versorgungssituation [Outpatient psychotherapy in Germany from the patients' point of view. Part 1: The therapy network]. *Psychotherapeut* 55(6):503–514.

Bornstein, R.F. (2001). The impending death of psychoanalysis. *Psychoanalytic Psychology* 18:3–20.

Bowlby, J. (1979). Psychoanalysis as art and science. *International Review of Psychoanalysis* 6:3–14.

Buchholz, M.B. (1999). *Psychotherapie als Profession* [Psychotherapy as profession]. Giessen: Psychosozial-Verlag.

Dahl, H. (1974). The measurement of meaning in psychoanalysis by computer analysis of verbal context. *Journal of the American Psychoanalytic Association* 22:37–57.

Desmet, M., Meganck, R., Seybert, C., Willemsen, J., Geerardyn, F., Declercq, F., Inslegers, R., Trenson, E., Vanheule, S., Schindler, I., Kirsner, L., & Kächele, H. (2013). Psychoanalytic single case studies published in ISI-ranked journals: A review of basic characteristics of patient, therapist, therapy and research method. *Psychotherapy & Psychosomatics* 82:120–121.

Dräger, K. (1971). Bemerkungen zu den Zeitumständen und zum Schicksal der Psychoanalyse und der Psychotherapie in Deutschland zwischen 1933 und 1949 [Observations on the time conditions and on the destiny of psychoanalysis and psychotherapy in Germany between 1933 and 1949]. *Psyche* 25:255–268.

Dührssen, A. (1962). *Katamnestische Ergebnisse bei 1004 Patienten nach analytischer Psychotherapie* [Catamnestic results of 1004 patients after analytic psychotherapy]. *Zeitschrift für psychosomatische Medizin und Psychoanalyse* 8:94–113.

Eagle, M.N. (2011a). *From Classical to Contemporary Psychoanalysis. A Critique and Integration*. New York: Routledge.

——— (2011b). Psychoanalysis and the Enlightenment vision: An overview. *Journal of the American Psychoanalytic Association* 59:1099–1118.

Fonagy, P., Kächele, H., Krause, R., Jones, E. E., Perron, R., & Lopez, D. (Eds.) (1999). *An Open Door Review of the Outcome of Psychoanalysis*. London: Research Committee of the International Psychoanalytic Association.

French, T.M. (1954). *The Integration of Behavior*. Vol. II. *The Integrative Process in Dreams*. Chicago: University of Chicago Press.

Freud, S. (1919). Lines of advance in psycho-analytic therapy. *Standard Edition* 17, pp. 157–168.

Jiménez, J.P. (2008). Theoretical plurality and pluralism in psychoanalytic practice. *International Journal of Psychoanalysis* 89:579–599.

Jurist, E.L. (2010). Eliott Jurist interviews Peter Fonagy. *Psychoanalytic Psychology* 27(1):2–7.

Kächele, H. (1991). Narration and observation in psychotherapy research. Reporting on a 20 year long journey from qualitative case reports to quantitative studies on the psychoanalytic process. *Psychotherapy Research* 2(1):1–15.

———— (1993). La ricerca sulla terapia psicoanalitica, 1930–1990 [Research on psychoanalytic therapy 1930–1980]. *Quaderni Associazione di Studi Psicoanalitici* 2(7):9–35.

Kächele, H., & Buchholz, M.B. (in print). Eine Notfall-SMS-Intervention bei chronischer Suizidalität – Wie die Konversationsanalyse klinische Beobachtung bereichert [A life-saving SMS intervention in a patient with a chronic suicide tendency. How conversation analysis enriches clinical obervation]. *Zeitschrift für Psychotraumatologie, Psychotherapiewissenschaft, Psychologische Medizin.*.

Kächele, H., Erhardt, I., Seybert, C., & Buchholz, M.B. (in print). Countertransference as object of empirical research? *International Forum of Psychoanalysis*.

Kächele, H., & Pirmoradi, S (2009). Psychotherapy in European public mental health services. *International Journal of Psychotherapy* 13:40–48.

Kächele, H., & Thomä, H. (1993). On working and writing together. *IPA Newsletter*, Summer, pp. 23–25.

Klein, G.S. (1970). Two theories or one? *Bulletin of the Menninger Clinic* 37(2):102–132.

Köhle, K, Kächele, H., Franz, H., Urban, H., & Geist, W. (1973). The training of a nursing staff in psychosomatic medicine in a medical clinic. *Psychosomatics* 14:336–340.

Kubie, L.S. (1952). Problems and techniques of psychoanalytic validation and progress. In E. Pumpian-Mindlin (Ed.), *Psychoanalysis as Science. The Hixon Lectures on the Scientific Status of Psychoanalysis* (pp. 46–124). New York: Basic Books.

Kurzweil, E. (1989). *The Freudians. A Comparative Perspective.* New Haven, CT: Yale University Press.

Leichsenring, F., & Rabung, S. (2011). Long-term psychodynamic psychotherapy in complex mental disorders: Update of a review. *British Journal of Psychiatry*, 199:15–22.

Leuschner, W., Hau, S., & Fischmann, T. (2000). *Die akustische Beeinflussung von Träumen* [The acoustic conditionment of dreams]. Tübingen: Edition diskord.

Levy, R.A., Ablon, J.S., & Kächele, H. (Eds.) (2012). *Psychodynamic Psychotherapy Research: Practice Based Evidence and Evidence Based Practice.* New York: Humana/Springer.

Luborsky, L., & Schimek, J. (1964). Psychoanalytic theories of therapeutic and developmental change – implications for assessment. In P. Worchel and D. Byrne (Eds.), *Personality Change* (pp. 73–79). New York: Wiley.

Luborsky, L., McLellan, A.T., Woody, G.B., O'Brien, C.P., & Auerbach, A.H. (1985). Therapists' success and its determinants. *Archives of General Psychiatry* 42(6):602–611.

Mergenthaler, E. (1985). *Textbank Systems. Computer Science Applied in the Field of Psychoanalysis.* Berlin: Springer.

Moser, U. (2008). *Traum, Wahn und Mikrowelten* [Dream, delusion and microworlds]. Frankfurt: Brandes & Apsel.

Peräkylä, A. (2004). Making links in psychoanalytic interpretations: A conversational analytic perspective. *Psychotherapy Research*

14(3):289–307.

——— (2008). Conversation analysis in psychoanalysis: Interpretation, affect, and intersubjectivity. In A. Peräkylä, C. Antaki, S. Vehvilnaninen, and I. Leudar (Eds.), *Conversation Analysis and Psychotherapy* (pp. 100–119). Cambridge: Cambridge University Press.

Safran, J.D., Muran, J.C., Samstag, L.W., & Stevens, C. (2002). Repairing alliance ruptures. In J.C. Norcross (Ed.), *Psychotherapy Relationships that Work* (pp. 235–254). New York: Oxford, University Press.

Sandell, R., Carlsson, J., Schubert, J., Grant, J., Lazar, A., & Broberg, J. (2006). Therapists´ therapies: The relation between training therapy and patient change in long-term psychotherapy and psychoanalysis. *Psychotherapy Research* 16(3):306–316.

Schachter, J., Gorman, B.S., Kächele, H., & Pfäfflin, F. (2013). Comparison of vignette-based ratings of satisfaction with psychoanalytic treatment by training analysts and by non-training analysts. *Psychoanalytic Psychology* 30(1):37–56.

Stepansky, P.E (2009). *Psychoanalysis at the Margins*. New York: Other Press.

Thomä, H. (1993). Training analysis and psychoanalytic education: Proposals for reform. *Annual of Psychoanalysis* 21:3–75.

Thomä, H., & Kächele, H. (1999). Memorandum on a reform of psychoanalytic education. *International Psychoanalysis News* 8:33–35.

von Rad, M., & Kächele, H. (1999). Editorial: Lehrtherapie [Editorial: Training analysis]. *Psychotherapie, Psychosomatik, Medizinische Psychologie* 49:73–74.

Wallerstein, R. (1988). One psychoanalysis or many? *International Journal of Psychoanalysis* 69:5–21.

Zetzel, E.R. (1966). Additional notes upon a case of obsessional neurosis: Freud 1909. *International Journal of Psychoanalysis* 47:123–129.

AFTERWORD—WHY AND HOW I BECAME A PSYCHOANALYST

I was born in Trento, Italy, in the spring of 1955. Trento—together with Bolzano and Trieste—had become Italian only at the end of World War I, in November 1918. Two local heroes had played a very significant role in the historical events through which our region (Trentino-Alto Adige, or Trentino-Südtirol in German) had been annexed to Italy and through which, after World War II, it was given a specific statute of administrative autonomy within Italy. I am referring here to Cesare Battisti (1875–1916) and Alcide De Gasperi (1881–1854). My father held both in high esteem and he passed this on to me—together with other virtues and inclinations, which will emerge in the course of this Afterword.

Both Battisti and De Gasperi had represented our region in Vienna, in the Austro-Hungarian Parliament, before World War I. Both were bilingual, and both had studied in both Austria and Italy. Cesare Battisti was hanged in Trento, at Buonconsiglio Castle, after having being condemned to death as a traitor for having joined the Italian army. His personal sacrifice contributed greatly to promoting a big wave of sympathy for the Italian cause in our territory and throughout the rest of Italy. De Gasperi, on the basis of his skill in entertaining multilateral international relationships, was able not only to have the Allies—at the Paris Talks—recognize the value of our struggle against Nazi Germany in the last year and a half of the war, but also to allow Italy to rapidly move in the direction of the financial wellbeing that started to characterize our country in the 1960s. My father, Fabio Conci (1920–2003), a civil engineer who founded his own firm before the end of the war, felt very thankful to De Gasperi and very much in tune with his view of the world.

In fact, his own father, my grandfather Pio Conci (1871–1943), had come from a similar background, that is, he had also studied jurisprudence in Austria (Vienna and Graz), and had become a judge of the Hapsburg Empire. At variance with his wife Ida Zontini (1880–1966), he came from a Trento family *di sentimenti italiani*—of Italian feelings—and had consequently been deported to an Austrian *Lager* during World War I. My grandmother's brothers had served the Hapsburgs as their firm had been engaged in the construction of a series of fortresses on the Southern border of the Empire, separating Trentino from the Italian region of Lombardy. I still have a picture showing several members of the Imperial Family visiting my grandmother's family, a family *di sentimenti austriaci*, at the turn of the century at the hotel the family had been able to build with the money coming from Vienna, in the small village of Lardaro, not far from Lake Garda. Indeed, this successful business allowed my father's cousin to later buy the famous Hotel Du Lac Du Parc at Riva del Garda, where Freud himself spent several days of vacation with his sister-in-law Minna Bernays in September 1900, after a few days visiting our whole region.

Here is how Freud described this vacation in a very detailed letter written to Wilhelm Fliess from Vienna on September 14, 1900:

Dear Wilhelm,
      Astonished that you stayed away longer than we did. I have been in Vienna since September 10. I am very glad you had such a good time. It was extremely nice for me, too. I shall compress my report about the six weeks. After we [Fliess and Freud] parted, we [Martha and Freud] drove to Trafoi. It was a cold, bad journey until we got there. But then Trafoi richly rewarded us; the *Gasthaus zur schönen Aussicht* was comfortable and [the food was] ample. We repeatedly took the beautiful Stilfser road. Then we traveled—all our intermediate trips took place during thunderstorms and under other aggravating circumstances—to Sulden, where two of the most glorious days came our way just when we had despaired of the weather. The Schaubach hut to which we walked on "slippery ice" was imposing. Today I no longer know why I did not carry out my intention of thanking you from there for having recommended it. We then went via Merano for a stopover to the Mendola, where we met Lustgarten and other Viennese friends. It was sweltering, and [we were] lazy there. For a change we took a day's carriage ride through the Non Valley (Cles), a treasure trove of antiquities. Martha then left for home via Bolzano and absolutely insisted that I follow Lustgarten to Venice to act as his guide. I did so, but there to my surprise I met my brother-in-law Heinrich and Rosa, who after a day and a half in Venice took me along with them to Berghof on Lake Ossiach. I was right in the swing of tramping around and was amenable to everything. In Berghof I found my sister Anna with the American children, who look just like my own, and a day later Uncle Alexander arrived unexpectedly. Finally—we have now reached August 26—came the relief. I mean Minna, with whom I drove through the Puster Valley to Trentino, making several short stops along the way. Only when I was completely in the South did I begin to feel really comfortable; under ice and snow something was missing, though at the time I could not have defined it. The sun was very amiable in Trentino, in no way as intolerable as in Vienna. From Trentino we made an excursion to the extraordinarily beautiful Castel Toblino. That is where the choice *vino santo* grows, which is pressed only at Christmas. There I also saw my beloved olive tree again. Minna wanted a taste of a high-altitude sojourn; therefore we went over a spectacular mountain road to Lavarone (1,200 meters), a high plateau on the side of the

Valsugana, where we found the most magnificent forest of
conifers and undreamed-of solitude. The nights began to be
cool, however, so I headed directly for Lake Garda, as you
must have known from the card from Torbole. We finally
stopped for five days at Riva, divinely accommodated and
fed, luxuriating without regrets, and untroubled—unless the
meeting of the Society of Professors at the Hotel du Lac is
to be regarded as a "trouble." Present: Sigm. Mayer (from
Prague), whose assistant I was to have been, Tschermak, Jodl,
Felsenreich from Vienna, Dimmer from Graz, Hildebrand
from Innsbruck. We kept away. Two long boat trips took us
one time to Salo and the other to Sirmione, where I climbed
around in the ruins of what is purported to be Catullus' villa.
(Masson, ed., 1985, p. 400)

As you can see, Freud not only loved touring our
region (from Trafoi and the Stilfser Pass to Meran, the
Mendola Pass, and the Non Valley; from the Puster
Valley to Trento; and then on to Castel Toblino, Lavarone,
Torbole, and Riva on Lake Garda), but even compared
the "amiable sun" of Trentino with the "intolerable sun" of
Vienna, that is, he experienced Trento and Vienna—as I
also do—as two places belonging to the same geographical
and experiential dimension with which he was familiar.
Of course, we can also see how he apparently enjoyed
Minna's company more than Martha's, but this is—in the
context of this Afterword—another matter.

Similarly, my mother's father Domenico Bolech
(1886–1950) felt more at home in the old Austro-
Hungarian Empire—for which he had served as a soldier
in World War I—than in the new Italian State. Such an
attitude, shared by many Italian-speaking inhabitants
of Trentino, also depended on the fact that Mussolini
came to power four years after the end of the war (1922),
rapidly abolishing the kind of parliamentary democracy
that Vienna had also been able to guarantee to its non-
German-speaking citizens. But in my grandfather's case
the following background also played a role: his family
(Bolech) had moved to Trentino during the seventeenth
century, apparently from Poland, from a Jewish-Polish
community. This sense of identity had been gradually
lost in the family, but it certainly still survived in terms
of, for example, the autonomy of mind or the sense of
initiative that characterized him, himself a successful
businessman—and partly my own mother. The youngest
of nine children, my mother (born in 1929 and still alive
and well) studied pharmacy in Bologna, where she
graduated in the summer of 1953, two months before
marrying my father.

But before telling you about our family life, let me
introduce you to one of my mother's brothers, the uncle

whom I felt the closest to: Pierino Bolech (1923–1984). In line with his mother's religious faith and his father's political orientation, he went to Innsbruck to become a Catholic priest, ending up serving as a *Kamilliter* at one of Vienna's largest hospitals, the Lainz Hospital. There he was not only a pioneer in the application of *Tiefenpsychologie* (depth psychology) to the selection of priests, but also became a pioneer of the Vatican's *Ostpolitik* (whose center was in Vienna) and a personal friend of the Polish cardinal Woytila—who as Pope John Paul II promoted him to being the Vatican's liaison officer to the World Health Organization. Visiting my uncle in Lainz in the second half of June 1972 contributed to changing my life—as you will see below.

The bilingual cultural and linguistic background I have described so far in terms of my parents' family dynamics of course belongs to the history of our town (Trento) and our province (Trentino), which I will now briefly deal with. Trento was conquered by the Romans in the late first century BC, after several clashes with the Rhaetian tribes, and after having been a Celtic village. The Romans gave it the name Tridentum, in honor of the god of the waters Neptune, represented by the Adige river, around which the village had been developed, and it became an important stop on the Roman road that led from Verona to Innsbruck. After the fall of the Western Roman Empire, Trento was conquered by a series of Gothic tribes, finally becoming part of the Holy Roman Empire.

In 1027, Emperor Conrad II created the Prince-Bishops of Trento, who wielded both temporal and religious powers, thus having to deal with both the Emperors and the Popes, maintaining both powers until the arrival in Trento of Napoleon Bonaparte in 1796. In the sixteenth century, given its strategic geographical position, Trento became notable for the Council of Trent (1545–1563) which gave rise to the Counter-Reformation. The prince-bishops at this time were Bernardo Clesio and Cristoforo Madruzzo, both able European politicians and Renaissance humanists, who greatly expanded and embellished the city—including their own palace, Buonconsiglio Castle. On Napoleon's defeat in 1814, Trento was again annexed by the Hapsburg Empire. Church government was finally extinguished, and Trento was henceforth governed by the secular administration of Tyrol. In the following decades, Trento experienced a modernization of administration and economy, with the first railroad in the Adige valley opening in 1859 to connect Trento with Innsbruck and Verona. And this is exactly the mode of transportation by which Freud himself—in a little more than one day—was so easily able to travel from Vienna to Bolzano and Trento.

Let me now tell you about my family life—a not very easy undertaking! Being the oldest of three brothers (Paolo being born 1957, and Lorenzo in 1958) was of course a mixed blessing. In the first place, my parents concentrated their attention more upon me than upon my brothers, so I was not only greatly stimulated by them, but also had to deal with a whole series of expectations of me that they developed. This is why I had to struggle very hard to find my own identity. For example, my father very much wanted me to work with him in his construction firm, and found it very hard to accept the fact that I did not want to do this. In fact, even in my adolescence I had known that I could not work with him, but I did not dare tell him. I also dared not tell him that I had other interests and professional goals, and that I did not think we would really get along with each other if we worked together. I saw how much room his authoritarian aspects occupied in the way he went about working in his firm, and I did not think I would be able to deal with this problematic aspect of his character—the firm would have remained "his firm" and would have never become "our firm."

But this is of course only one aspect of the problem. As the first-born, I had also always been at the center of my mother's attention. She not only made of me her "favorite son," tried to keep me close to her, and stimulated me intellectually, but also made of me an "Oedipal son." This included her trying to educate me in such a way as not to become "so self-centered and authoritarian" as my father was, or as she perceived him to be; I should have to develop in directions other than the one that would have allowed me to work with him in the construction firm. Had she not married my father, she would have liked to study medicine—and since she could not do it herself, the option was open for me to do it, to do it for her. As you will see, my choice of medicine (psychiatry and psychoanalysis) was even more complicated than this, but these were the ways in which my parents, with their personalities, expectations, and conflicts, played a major role in it.

Fortunately, my childhood and elementary school years were not so full of conflicts. I remember being taken care of as a child by several nannies who helped my mother and lived with us. I remember spending many hours playing with my brothers, for example at soccer, at which I became quite good. My brother Paolo and I also played classical guitar, familiarizing ourselves with several musical repertoires. I remember my father teaching us how to ski and going skiing with the whole family as often as possible; indeed, I also remember having, with both my brothers, trained for and participated in many ski races between the ages of six and fourteen. In the summer, we of course went hiking, with the whole family, in the Dolomites, which my father knew quite well and loved very much; we also had a house in the mountains, where we as children used to spend the whole summer with our mother, and with a whole series of friends.

At the same time, I remember that I enjoyed going to school, at least until I was fourteen. In our *scuola elementare* I had the same teacher for all five years; her name was Adriana Lorenzoni, a nice-looking and very competent teacher, who also liked to write plays and produce them with her whole class, and was intellectually very stimulating. The same was true of my mother, who had taught me how to read and write in the summer before starting elementary school. A similar role was played in the next three grades—at the Catholic private school that I attended with my brothers—by the priest who taught the subjects then known as *materie letterarie* (Italian, Latin, history, geography, and German). The priest's name was Giovanni Rossi, and he had much esteem for me because I was the best pupil in the class in all the three grades, from October 1966 to June 1969, a situation that led to my having almost no friends at all—an unhappy condition that he, unfortunately, could not understand.

Also contributing to my good performance in school was the fact that, since the summer of 1967, I had been regularly spending the month of August studying German at a Bavarian summer school located on the beautiful Starnbergersee—here I could spend the afternoon free from school with a whole series of foreign friends, doing all sorts of sports. This aspect of my education actually deserves special attention. Already in our childhood, our parents talked French to each other every time they did not want us to understand them—which, of course, we ended up doing; studying French together had actually been one of the first projects my father had got my mother involved in after getting married. My father loved foreign languages (he could understand and speak German, French, and English), and transmitted this passion to me and to my brothers. In addition, besides being a very successful engineer, he had been able to unite his passion for alpine sports and his competence as a manager in a brilliant career as a member of the executive council of the Italian Ski Federation—of which he was the president between 1964 and 1970—and of the International Ski Federation (FIS).

Starting with the 1948 Winter Olympics held in St. Moritz (Switzerland), my father participated—in his role as a member of the Italian and then the FIS council—in all subsequent Winter Olympics, until the Nagano (Japan) Games of 1998. He not only contributed to the FIS assigning the 1970 Ski World Championships to Gardena Valley (Bolzano), but also played a major role in increasing the popularity in Italy of alpine skiing (which only a few thousand Italians practiced in the 1950s). It became the second most popular sport after soccer— thanks also to the excellent performances of skiers such as Gustav Thöni and Alberto Tomba. In other words, mine was not only a father I could be proud of, but also a father to whom, from this point of view, I still feel very well connected. This is actually the way in which I experience all the international psychoanalytic meetings I participate in, where several languages are spoken and I can understand them all, and at which I feel my internal father accompanying me—and being proud of me, even though I did not work with him in his firm.

My father was in addition actually also a very lucky person. Assisting at the various Ski World Cup events in the best European ski resorts, he could keep up to date with their tourist development approaches and apply what he saw to his work in the Dolomites, where he ended up constructing a chain of apartment houses that still belongs to our family—and that I and my brothers still take care of. By "tourist development" I mean of course the local industry that was started in my area in the 1880s to host the Viennese class of citizens to which Freud belonged, and to which my father had dedicated his *tesi di laurea* at the University of Bologna in 1944, where he had studied during the war, being excluded from service because of phlebitis. From this point of view, he was very lucky: he was all his life able to do the things he liked the best, and he was very successful in them.

However, as I mentioned above, things were never quite that easy in our family. Now that I think about it again, I can even say that at the end of the 1960s the *Zeitgeist* itself changed dramatically—even in Trento. As I said before, at the end of our *scuola media*, the equivalent of junior high school, I realized that being the best pupil of my class had brought me into a situation in which I had almost no friends, a condition in which I felt lonely and unhappy, a condition that—and here comes the first conflict—not only my professor, but also my mother, did not understand at all. In fact, the feeling I got from here was that her pride as a mother was more important than my wellbeing. If this was the interpersonal change that had arisen between us, my way of perceiving her had also changed, due to a changed social and cultural climate. If it had been acceptable for her not to work in the 1950s, when we were children, this status was now no longer good for her (or for us children). Not having a working life, a life of her own outside of the family, she started transforming our house into a kind of a museum for the contemporary art she kept collecting. Take our rooms for example: we could not hang any posters we liked on the walls since our rooms were not "our rooms" but belonged to her—to the showrooms she was busy creating.

As you probably can imagine, as a result of the new *Zeitgeist* brought about also in Trento by the 1968 student movements, I started reading Karl Marx, from whom I learned that the structure of our life determines our ideas and how we behave. But before telling you about this general political aspect, let me tell you that, although I tried for several years to convince my mother of the need to find a personal working relationship with the outside world, I was not able to have any influence as my father was against the idea. It was "politically correct" for his wife not to be working, as it had been in the 1950s, but, more than this, his wife of course had to be all the time at his disposal, and had to accompany him on all his trips— being his own boss, he could come and go as he wished! This also meant that there was in our family a lack of social rules, a lack of discipline and collaboration around a family project—which was also one of the reasons why, as we shall see below, I eventually decided to study medicine. After writing these words, I of course realize how emotional I still am about these unsolved conflicts, but I think that they played a major role in my critical attitude toward my family and my attempt to find my own way in life.

But let me now go back to my familiarity with Marx's ideas, the ideological motor of the 1968 student movements I encountered in Trento. Here is the story. Bruno Kessler (1924–1991), the most creative Trentino politician since the end of the war, created in Trento at the beginning of the 1960s the first Italian *facoltà di sociologia*, that is, sociology department. If his intention had been to introduce sociology to Italy as a way of bringing Italian public administrators up to date with contemporary social science, this new course of studies in fact ended up attracting the most politically active young people in the whole country. Most of them contributed to strongly challenging the conservative political climate of the Catholic provincial town that Trento had been up to then—but some ended up creating the so-called Red Brigades.

At a public concert of the school of Cesare Lutzemberger (1918–2008), in May 1968, I had happened to play a classical guitar composition with Margherita Cagol (1945–1975), one of Lutzemberger's best pupils and also later the wife of Renato Curcio (b. 1941), the founder of the Red Brigades—as we all of course learned only several years later. Margherita and Renato had both studied sociology in Trento, falling in love with each other while dreaming of a new utopian classless society of their own. As some readers probably remember, in the spring of 1978 the Red Brigades kidnapped and eventually killed one of the best Italian politicians of the time, Aldo Moro (1916–1978). This climate of violence that permeated the whole country had begun on December 12th, 1969, in Milan, with a bomb exploding at a bank close to the Piazza Duomo. This event and its surrounding political debates also stood at the center of my first platonic relationship with a girl, Marta, from Milan.

I met Marta in the summer of 1971, while attending my fifth German summer course (for the fourth I had gone to Salzburg, in the previous July) in an alpine village close to Innsbruck, Mayrhofen. It was through her that I eventually learned that I came from a "bourgeois family," and that I could better understand what it was all about both if I kept studying Marx, and if I took an interest in psychology—as she also was doing. She recommended to me not only Camilla Cederna's (1911–1997) *Pinelli. Una finestra sulla strage*—in which the famous Milan journalist accused the Milan police department of having caused the death of the anarchist Giuseppe Pinelli (1928–1969), mistakenly held responsible for the bombs of December 12, 1969—but also an introduction to psychology.

It had also been a merit of the sociologists at the University of Trento to devote enough space, for the first time in Italy, to psychology and psychoanalysis, which had started to become of popular interest in Italy only at the end of the 1960s. Two famous Milanese psychoanalysts, Franco Fornari (1921–1985) and Elvio Fachinelli (1928–

1989), had taught in Trento, holding there one of the first courses on psychoanalysis at an Italian university. Only in 1971 did psychology become an autonomous course of studies in Italy, in Padua and Rome. Last but not least, the anti-hierarchical climate that characterized the University of Trento's sociology department had also been a basic ingredient of the alternative way of working in psychiatry that Franco Basaglia (1924–1980) had begun to achieve at the beginning of the 1960s at the Psychiatric Hospital of Gorizia—as documented in the recent book by the English historian John Foot (2015). Although it would take some more years for psychiatry to become my professional goal, the disappointment I had experienced with my parents and with the Italian school system had moved me in the direction of relying more on myself, and of going after my own intellectual interests.

Of course, this was the solution I found after several years of what we used to call "a deep existential crisis," which characterized the beginning of my adolescence. In this regard, I remember holding every day a diary session, in which I would speak with myself and try to understand what we then called *il senso della vita*, whether life made any sense, and how we should best make it meaningful for ourselves. And I remember reading J.-P. Sartre's *La nausea*, and identifying with the sense of nausea and of alienation from the banality of bourgeois everyday life experienced by its protagonist, Antoine Roquentin. I remember too asking myself how I would be able to love myself enough if I myself had received so little love from my parents. From this point of view, I believe that I was already able to have a feeling for the psychological distinction between what I felt as being my parents' "conditional love" and the so-called "unconditional love" that we all as human beings should have the right to receive. My mother would love me only if I kept being the best student in school, and my father only if I had told him that I would later work with him in his firm. Fortunately, I was able to understand that these attitude of theirs did not make sense, that their capacity for love was limited, and that it was not worth forcing myself to match their expectations in order to receive such a poisoned form of love from them. From this point of view, I also believe that my capacity to look at their limitations saved my life and created the basis of my later choice to become a psychoanalyst.

I also know that not all my school friends were as lucky as to be able to think the way I did. Several of them kept meeting the expectations of their parents and their professors, limiting themselves to being the best students of our class far beyond the time I had stopped doing it, and ending up either getting psychiatrically sick or not being able to finish their university studies. For one of them, Cristina, I had even developed a deep sympathy that she never reciprocated, and that I later interpreted as connected to my wish to help her emerge out of a dilemma similar to the one I had been able to solve for myself. Of course, in my later psychiatric and psychoanalytic work I also met many patients who had become sick because they had believed more in their parents and their teachers than in themselves. On the other hand, all three analysts whom I worked from 1983 confirmed to me that it had been a very good thing for me to have such a healthy intuition about how to relate to my parents and to myself.

As far as my parents are concerned, it is only recently that I have been able to think of them in terms of the new German concept of *Kriegskinder*, "children of the war"—a concept developed by my colleague and friend Michael Ermann among others, which has not yet reached Italy. As children and adolescents going through the war, they must have suffered because of the lack of people around them helping them contain their anxieties, and answering their questions, and this diminished their own capacity for empathy and forced them to rely only on themselves and their capacity for performance. Of course, this meant working for years in analysis on all the feelings that I had not been able to experience, and on the anxieties to which I had felt exposed with nobody to help me face them.

But let me now return to how my life further developed. In October 1969 I started attending the Italian *liceo classico*, our Classical senior high school, a five-year school program from which I graduated in July 1974—after spending a year, August 1972 to July 1973, in the USA as an exchange student. The school's basic subjects were quite similar to the ones Freud himself had studied at his own *Gymnasium*, in the Viennese neighborhood of Leopoldstadt: Latin and Greek, Italian and German, history and philosophy, mathematics, physics, natural sciences, and art history—and of course gymnastics and the Catholic religion.

But what alienated me and many other students was not only the scarce attention given to our psychological problems, but even more the way in which school was taught, that is, very isolated from all that was happening around us. The teaching of Latin and Greek was for example founded on the assumption that nothing new had

happened in the world since the time of the Romans—
except for a series of technological developments. On the
other hand, we read a series of classics, such as Dante
Alighieri's *Divine comedy*, Sophocles' *Antigone*, and
Lucretius' *De rerum naturae*, that made us familiar
with a whole series of human experiences, passions, and
questions. But, at this point, I spent most of my free
time reading and studying on my own, in order to better
understand myself and the world. Not only did I venture
into the study of new foreign languages like Spanish,
Russian, and Esperanto, but I also read much literature,
history, and philosophy on my own. I can still remember
a whole series of novels by Hesse and Dostoevsky, various
books on the French Revolution and on the rise of Fascism
in Italy, and a series of works by philosophers such as
Plato, Kant, Heidegger, and Sartre.

In the fall of 1971 I participated in the selection
process by which I was to end up spending a year in the
USA organized by American Field Service (AFS). My
parents were of course in favor of this experience, and I
prepared myself by reading a whole series of books. I can
still remember books like Fromm's *Escape from freedom*,
Goodman's *Growing up absurd. Problems of youth in the
organized system*, and Silbermann's *Crisis in black and
white*, which had by then all been translated into Italian.
In January 1972, at the Esperanto class, I had also met
a girl, Marcella, whom I started going out with and
with whom I could share my thoughts and fantasies—
as well as the books I read. She was also a very sensible
person, whom life kept confronting with a whole series of
problems that she was not able to master—and this must
have contributed to her early death of pulmonary cancer,
at fifty-nine, in the summer of 2013. (A couple of years
ago, her sister Lucy gave me all the cards I had written
to her from Vienna in June 1972, and from the USA in
the following months.) I received a good introduction to
the climate of psychological liberty that I could eventually
enjoy in the USA when I visited my uncle Pierino in
Vienna in June 1972. He too thought that if I did not feel
inclined to pursue my father's profession and to work
with him, I had the right to feel free to dedicate myself to
something else—for example, to becoming an MD and a
psychiatrist.

As you can imagine, I was very happy to leave my
family, my school, and my town for a whole year, and I had
the feeling that this experience could positively change
my life—which is indeed what happened. In fact, I am
still a member of AFS-Italy (called "Intercultura"), with

which I actively collaborated as a returnee, and through which my daughter Anna herself spent a year in Germany (2007–2008). Of course, I was also very proud to belong to the group of about 120 Italian students (being the only one from Trentino) who flew to the USA in August 1972 to spend a year there, living with a family and attending the senior year of high school. I will never forget, for example, the week we all spent together in San Gimignano (Siena) for the last phase of our preparation, including the famous lecture on the recent history of our country that Roberto Ruffino, the secretary-general of AFS-Italy, gave to the group—in which he reminded us how many problems our young Italian democracy still had. It was, for example, only two years before, in 1970, that divorce had become legally possible.

Although I already knew some English (mainly because of a summer course in Sussex, in August 1970, after the month I had spent in Salzburg), it of course took several months before I was able to understand the American accent and before I was able to feel at home with the language. At the time, an international call cost so much that I had only a few chances to talk with my family, even apart from the fact that I was totally immersed in the new culture and society. And this was not always so easy! But, in my case, it was so important and worthwhile that I was able to fully elaborate the whole experience, to integrate it so well into the rest of my life as to make of my contacts with the US a permanent part of it. This is the background not only of the research project behind my book *Sullivan revisited – Life and work* (see Conci, 2010, 2012), but even of this anthology. The anthology is a collection of papers that I wrote directly in English, between 1991 and 2016, a competence I had the chance to acquire back in 1972/1973, as a senior at Mamaroneck High School, New York State.

But even more important than the school was of course the family I lived with, a Jewish family in Larchmont, NY—half an hour by train from New York City's Grand Central Station, on the New York to New Haven railway line. By living with them I was able to much better understood a whole series of traits in my own family, and have the chance to get to know myself still better. For example, the society I came from was much more hierarchical and conservative, and I had never experienced any parties or family gatherings at which old and young people would get together and talk with each other. I remember my "American father" asking me questions about my ideas and feelings with a curiosity that my own father had never had, or had never been able to show me. I also ended up re-experiencing with my "American mother" part of the emotional attachment that I had developed with my own mother and of which I had not been enough aware.

And this is not to mention the fact that in Trento I had never met a Jewish person, perhaps as a result of the tragic story of Simon of Trento. Because Simon disappeared in 1475, on the eve of Good Friday, the city's small Jewish community was accused of killing him and draining his blood for Jewish ritual purposes. Eight Jews were tortured and burned at the stake, and their families forced to convert to Christianity. The bishop of Trento, Johannes Hinderbach, had Simonino canonized and published the first book printed in Trento. Only in the 1990s did the city of Trento apologize to the Italian Jewish community for this dark episode and unveil a plaque commemorating the formal apology.

Indeed, it was a very unusual family of progressive Jews who welcomed me into their home in America; they were happy with and capable of a real exchange. It was not by chance that the older sister, Linda, married a Chilean refugee, and her brother, Bennet, married a Danish social worker, thus bringing about a real international family. Last but not least, they made me feel so much a part of their lives that for many years I had the feeling of really being a part of them, of having developed a new Jewish-American identity—and in fact nobody ever took me for an Italian, given both the way I behave and my own accent. What is sure is that the "American identity" I developed made of me a happier person, a person capable of using the word "happy" and of feeling so, as opposed to the way I felt before—to the fact that nobody I knew in Italy at the time would say "*Sono felice*." And if you learn to use the word "happy," you can really end up feeling so!

An important contribution to these good feelings and my deep personal transformation came also of course from the school I attended. At Mamaroneck High School I had the chance to attend a special alternative program known as School Within A School (SWAS), which functioned according to the ideas formulated by Ivan Illich in his highly original book *Deschooling society* (1971). This allowed me to design my own curriculum, with the help of an advisor, and thus to further amplify the self-teaching orientation which I had been developing on my own in Trento—and which I also believe to be of fundamental importance for our work as psychiatrists and psychoanalysts. Designing my own curriculum meant not only free choice of the courses I attended, but even included the possibility of attending courses outside of the school itself. And that is how I ended up attending a "Philosophy of history" course at Manhattanville College, and a "Sociology of psychotherapy" course at the State University of New York at Purchase, for which I also wrote various papers. In fact, this is how I learned to use a typewriter, to write in English, and to understand how much I enjoyed writing altogether—as I am doing now. The authors I dealt with in my papers were Fromm and Marcuse, Heidegger and Sartre, Fritz Perls, and Rollo May. I still have the papers somewhere in my office, and I was very proud of them for a long time.

Also very stimulating were a series of courses taught within SWAS, for example a "Black studies" course, in which we read *From slavery to freedom. A history of African Americans*, or the contemporary art history class, which not only exposed me to the books of Herbert Reed, but also allowed me to visit the MOMA and the Guggenheim. Of course, going as often as possible into the City of New York was also a learning opportunity that I made good use of and that both family and school encouraged, even though not all areas of the City were at that time really safe. I discovered at that point the bookstore I usually still visit every time I am in New York—Strand, on Broadway and 12th Street.

The early 1970s was not an easy time for the USA. In the fall of 1972 Richard Nixon won the presidential campaign against a weak Democratic candidate, George McGovern, but his behavior during the campaign—the Watergate scandal—forced him to resign in August 1974, after many months of conflict with Congress and heated discussions in various sectors of society. Among other things, I remember the Christmas 1972 Vietnam bombings he ordered. But of course there were at the time still other problems that I experienced in my daily life or to which I was exposed. The relationship between boys and girls was, for example, rather complicated at that time in the New York City suburbs: it was not longer clear which should be initiating a date. And, as an Italian, I of course suffered under the lack of the spontaneous socialization chances offered by our bars and restaurants, especially in the suburbs. In fact, one of the books of the year was Philip Slater's *The pursuit of loneliness. American culture at the breaking point* (1970). What I of course had had to get used to was not only the different culture, but also the peculiar technological developments, which we had not experienced in Italy. And here come again to mind some of the books I read on my own so that I could better relate to American society and culture, for example David Riesman's *The lonely crowd* (Riesman, Glazer, and Denney, 1950), Wright Mills' *White collar: The American middle classes* (1951), and Marshall McLuhan's *Understanding media. The extensions of man* (1964).

One thing I am still sure about is that I had already then understood—at variance with Freud and with many Europeans, not only those of Freud's own generation—that the USA has its own culture, a unique culture that deserves to be carefully studied. Such a study may even help us Europeans to correct some of the limitations of our own culture. A small example: the main thing we learned at school at the time about Italian literature was the critical tradition dealing with it, and we were never asked what we would think or feel about a novel or a poem. This was at the time the first question concerning the product of any art form asked in the American high school I attended. In fact, the best thing to do would be to unite and integrate the two points of view—which is the reason why I believe so greatly in international dialogue and exchange.

Last but not least, I was very lucky also in terms of seeing not only New York City and Westchester County, but also other parts of the USA, including California and Oregon, which I visited in May 1973 as my parents' gift for my eighteenth birthday; there I also met an American girl, Susan, who was fascinated by the European intellectual tradition and with whom I kept in touch for several years. The AFS itself offered us exchange students a two-week bus tour through the north-eastern part of the States, which helped us manage the period of transition of returning to our home countries.

When I returned home, it was of course not at all easy to readjust to my old environment. In fact, it was impossible. The hardest challenge was to avoid repressing the whole experience, relegating it to a part of my identity that had to be kept secret. I was back in my old school, having to attend the last year of *liceo classico*, and I did not know how to face this crucial challenge—and my schoolmates did not help me; they simply would not ask me any questions about what I might have experienced in the year spent abroad. Fortunately, we had a new professor of history, Roberto Bertucci, and he helped me very much in this regard. He listened to me and encouraged me to try to be myself. The result was that I was able to propose a reading group on our identity problems, centered around the discussion of a whole series of novels, which allowed me to share with the students who attended it what I had gone through in the USA. With his help I was also able to again become one of the best students of my class and to pass our *esame di maturità*—the final exams, held in July 1974—with the best grade. The good experience I had had with my "American father" and with other male teachers in the USA had probably allowed me to think that Roberto Bertucci could help me. And so it was, even in terms of my university choice, which I was able to make only a few weeks before starting university—with medical school. I had been so happy in the USA that I had decided to go abroad again for my university studies, this time to Innsbruck in Austria, but the decision as to what to study there came only at the last minute.

I was not at all fond of the basic sciences around which the first years of medical school center. In fact, I had very little interest in medicine as a whole, psychiatry and psychoanalysis being my only goals connected to it. I was also still very afraid to disappoint my father or to lose his esteem and financial support. But Roberto Bertucci was able to discuss the problem with me and to help me come to the conclusion that I would be able to make it, to spend years studying subjects that did not particularly interest me, if the goal was to become a psychiatrist; and that my father would be able to forgive me and would not refuse to support me financially. And so it was. Through a recommendation letter of one of my professors, Renzo Dalponte, to the dean of the medical school, Werner Platzer, I was admitted to study medicine in Innsbruck. The choice of Innsbruck, which I had made before knowing exactly what I would study there (as I had originally thought of sociology or law), turned out to be the best possible choice. As I did not know anybody there, I thought that I could more easily concentrate on the study of anatomy and physics; although I liked it to only a limited extent, I would be able to tolerate doing it, since I was improving my German at the same time, which was far more interesting for me.

On an even deeper level, the study of medicine reflected and maybe even corresponded with—as I have written above—my need to give myself the kind of working discipline and interpersonal and social horizon that I had not so far been able to develop, and which had not been in any way part of my family education. Up to then I had developed—as you have seen—many intellectual interests, but I feared not being able to concentrate on one of them sufficiently to make a living out of it—or be successful at it. My deepest anxiety was in fact ending up reading one book after another, through the night, and then sleeping during the day, no longer talking to anyone, never being able to find the shared rhythm of adult life and work within a social group or community. Indeed, the development of our talents best takes place through a systematic interaction with all those with whom we can collaborate and from whom we can learn. From this point of view, studying medicine meant for me an active struggle against the schizoid and antisocial aspects of my personality—and it worked!

Now, since it worked for me, I have assumed twenty years later that a similar motivation might also have played a crucial role in Freud's choice to study medicine, that is, to overcome the purely defensive and neurotic function of his own investment in intellectual activity. It allowed him to give up his self-centered intellectual pursuits and put his personal resources to the service of the scientific community, also in the hope that joining it would mitigate his loneliness and make of him a mature and socially competent human being. This is what readers have the chance to read in my article "Why did Freud choose medical school?," which forms the second chapter of this anthology.

After choosing Innsbruck but before choosing to study medicine there, my father was able to find a room for me through one of his friends in the FIS—and this is where I spent my first year of medical school: on the hill of Hötting, in a small street called Stamserfeldgasse. Every day, starting in the first week of October, I would get up at 6.30 am, go down the Höttingergasse, cross the river Inn, go through the Innrain, and arrive at the large room where Professor Brandstetter delivered his *Physikvorlesung*. But our main occupation in the first semester was the introductory anatomy course, centered on the study of osteology, during which we all had the chance to develop a very familiar relationship with all the bones of our body, which were put at our disposal during this practical course. Two months later came the first exam, the so-called *Knochenkolloquium* (osteology exam), which—to my surprise—I passed. In the meantime, I had the chance to verify the fact that my German was good enough for my purpose, and that becoming familiar with the bones (and of course also with the corresponding muscles and articulations) of my body had positively contributed to my sense of reality; but, even more importantly, I had the chance to start enjoying the fact that I shared a daily routine with a community of students my own age, and that this would allow us to sooner or later become good doctors. In other words, I was eventually moving in a precise direction, instead of having to invent my life every day, as I felt I had done up to then. This was of course not quite true, but this was my impression—and these were the reasons for my sense of relief.

This also allowed me to spend our winter vacation working in Selva Gardena (Wolkenstein, Grödnertal), helping the lady who managed the weekly rental of the vacation apartments my father had just built there with his firm. As president of the organizing committee of the 1970 Ski World Championships, he had had the chance to buy a very nice piece of land in the center of one of the nicest ski resorts of the Dolomites, where our family has since spent its vacation—and where I still spend my vacations with my wife Doris. If I was free to study what interested me the most, the family firm would have always been there, and I had to at least understand how it worked—that was my father's opinion. In fact, this is still the case, and as the firm has not yet been split into parts belonging to each of us three brothers, we still formally run it together.

Before going back to Innsbruck for the second semester, I joined two American women friends, E. and L., on a trip to France, which I still remember, because it contributed to my further *educazione sentimentale*, including their making me familiar with Simone de Beauvoir's classic *The second sex*. But even more important was the fact that I had the chance to talk with them about what would become the next step of my itinerary of personal research. Now that I had succeeded in the operation of becoming a medical student, including the sense of belonging to a group, I had the feeling that I needed to find a group to which I felt I wanted to belong—and for this reason I had also started to look back to my own country, Italy.

Since 1972 Giovanni Berlinguer (1922–1984) had been the new secretary of the Italian Communist Party, and had been able to create a large progressive political coalition around himself, first having made himself and his party autonomous from Moscow. Furthermore, he supported Franco Basaglia and his movement, Psichiatria Democratica, which had been able to demonstrate that it was possible to close the old psychiatric hospitals and base the whole psychiatric assistance program on a well-organized network of mental health centers in the community. I found this project very interesting and wanted to be part of it. This is why I had started thinking of going back to Italy, and this is what I talked about with E. and L., about my wish to be part of a we-identity once I had found my own professional identity.

Back in Innsbruck, I kept attending the anatomy course, I started attending the biology course, and I studied very hard to pass the *Physikprüfung* (the physics exam), which I did—again with a sense of surprise—in June 1975, thus fulfilling the requirements for admission to the third semester at the University of Padua in the fall. That spring I also remember having the chance, due to my now fluent German, to start reading some Freud, Jung, and Adler in their native language—a very pleasant experience. Before moving to Padua, I had planned to spend a couple of months with my "American family," partly to discuss with them my move back to Italy. In fact, they would have liked me to apply to medical school in the USA, but I did not have a good feeling about this—I did not think I would have been able to give up the complex identity I had so far developed and work in the direction of becoming an "American citizen." Anyhow, one of the things I did that summer was to visit a series of former high school friends at the Ivy League universities they were attending—I remember going to Dartmouth, Brown, Harvard, and Yale. Of course, with my "American family" I also had the chance to enjoy some of the things that make summer in Westchester, for example sailing on Long Island Sound and attending the "Shakespeare in the Park" performances in Central Park.

Back from the USA, and before moving to Padua—where my father had helped me find a new room through his contacts in a construction firm—I remember spending a very nice Saturday with my parents and with members of the Trento Rotary Club to which they belonged—I believe at least one picture of this has survived. We drove from Trento to Padua, where we got on a boat, the *Burchiello*, heading along the Brenta river towards Venice and stopping at the nicest Venetian villas, which gave us a chance to visit them. This boat trip is still regularly offered and I highly recommend it. Describing it may also help the reader in this transition back to Italy, that is, to Padua and its territory. Indeed, I often at the time even listened to Vivaldi's *Quattro stagioni*, trying to picture which Venetian landscapes might have inspired him. Close to me, in the Via del Portello, near to the medical school, lived my cousin Roberto, who was also studying medicine; indeed, a large group of students from Trento were also attending medical school in Padua.

In December 1975 I was able to pass—in Padua—
the chemistry exam, in February 1976 the histology exam,
and then came microbiology, biochemistry, and history of
medicine, which I also passed with good grades. Even if
there was no longer any doubt that I would be able to
complete my medical studies, the problem remained of
where this would be. My first reason for moving to Padua
had been the agreements that existed with Innsbruck and
the certainty of being automatically admitted there to the
second year of medical school—otherwise I would have
moved to Bologna, a less conservative and more vivacious
town, where my parents had also studied.

Indeed, this is what I had meant to do for the third
year, but in the fall of 1976 I ended up moving not to
Bologna, but to Florence. In December 1975, while
visiting my cousin Chiara there, I had met Maria and we
had fallen in love. She belonged to a well-known Trento
family that had for several centuries run a big textile shop.
Her grandparents—because of their *sentimenti italiani*—
had moved to Florence at the beginning of World War
I—her grandfather becoming a pioneer of garden
architecture. Maria was studying architecture and also
working part time to support herself, her family having
lost most of its financial assets. After regularly seeing each
other over the following months, more in Florence than
in Padua, I decided that I would move to Florence, also
considering the possibility of our living there together. My
parents were very skeptical about my move, and feared
that I might have ended up living too far away, Florence
being located south of the Apennines and representing
a totally different social and cultural dimension. It was,
however, precisely this aspect that greatly attracted me,
also considering the fact that anybody born and raised in
Trento, as I was, has to spend some time in a real Italian
center like Florence if he or she is to understand what
Italy is all about—and to feel really Italian.

My hope was also to find and become part of a group
of students with whom I could share my interests and
ideals, as fortunately happened. And this was what I
started trying to do when, at the end of September 1976,
I attended in Arezzo the first national congress of the
Psichiatria Democratica movement, where I heard not
only Franco Basaglia, but also Giovanni Jervis (1933–
2009) discuss the future of psychiatry in Italy. The poster
from the congress still hangs in the waiting room of my
Trento office. In 1975 Jervis had published his *Manuale
critico di psichiatria*, through which I had the chance
of both identifying with him and clearly seeing my

professional future.

Mine and Maria's first home in Florence—an apartment we shared with other students—was located in the very central Via della Colonna, No. 17, near the corner with Borgo Pinti. Close by is the Via Cesare Battisti, connecting the Piazza San Marco with the Piazza dell'Annunziata; Cesare Battisti had not only himself studied in Florence, but also married a woman from Florence, Ernesta Bittanti. I had never had such a close relationship with a girl before, and Maria and I of course tried to spend as much time together as we could— not only talking together, but also cooking and going to movies and exhibitions. Florence was a very lively and interesting town in the mid-1970s, both culturally and politically, not to mention its unique history and beautiful surroundings, such as Fiesole and the Chianti Valley. Maria had a car, a Citroën Dyane, and we tried to find the time to visit Tuscany. In the summer of 1977, I believe, we went camping on the Island of Elba.

Another important desire I was able to realize in Florence that first academic year, 1976/1977, was to attend the clinical psychiatry course, led by Adolfo Pazzagli, for fifth-year students—while I was attending my third year. Only a couple of years before, psychiatry had become autonomous from neurology in our medical schools, and Adolfo Pazzagli, who was also a psychoanalyst, belonged to the small group of Italian psychiatry professors committed to the development of an analytically oriented psychiatry. He later became internationally known for the initiative of organizing in Florence—together with Harold Blum—a series of symposia on psychoanalysis and art. In fact, Pazzagli also offered the students attending his course the possibility of participating in small research and discussions groups, and I had the good luck to participate in a Balint Group, coordinated by two young psychiatrists and analytic candidates—Gianni Varrasi and Folco Di Volo. Coming in touch with the emotions developed by my fellow medical students in their contacts with their first patients further convinced me that this was exactly what I wanted to do—to become not only a psychiatrist, but also a psychoanalyst. In connection with this experience, I read Michael Balint's *The doctor, his patient and the illness* (1955), and also started systematically reading Freud.

Last but not least, the complex Italian political climate of the winter and spring of 1977 had also affected the University of Florence, with a group of students occupying the medical school for several weeks. This allowed me to make my first friends—in the first place Annibale Biggeri, who later became a professor of medical statistics. In this connection I remember reading books critiquing the traditional practice of medicine, like Ivan Illich's *Limits to medicine* (1976) and Thomas Scheff's *Being mentally ill. A sociological theory* (1996).

In the meantime, it had become rather hard to concentrate on my medical studies, confronted as I was with the problem of passing the exam in anatomy—a subject I had already dealt with in both Innsbruck and Padua—which I succeeded in doing only in April 1978. In the meantime I found relief in reading Giovanni Jervis' second book, *Il buon rieducatore* (1977), the title of the autobiographical chapter in a collection of his papers, which brought me even closer to him. At the same time, I not only kept reading Freud's works, but also discovered Harry Stack Sullivan's *The interpersonal theory of psychiatry* (Sullivan, 1953), including his unique pages on pre-adolescence and adolescence. In other words, my reeducation through medical school kept advancing and I was able to feel hopeful about the future, as I had been able to find my own direction in life. At the same time as studying for the anatomy exam, in the academic year 1977/1978 I had been attending physiology and general pathology courses, which eventually brought us students closer to the heart of medicine. In the meantime, I had found two friends, Roberto, with whom I shared exam preparations, and Marco, with whom I could share the books I read and my interest for psychiatry—including the problem of how to deal with it academically.

In the fall of 1978, Maria moved to Milan, finding it more convenient for both her studies and the possibility of finding a better part-time job. Unfortunately, I could not do anything to encourage her to stay in Florence, which I greatly regretted. Our relationship continued for several years but then eventually came to an end—in the winter of 1982. In the meantime I had passed both the physiology and the general pathology exams—in January and April 1979, respectively.

One of the problems that had brought my friend Marco and I together was the fact that, although we both valued Adolfo Pazzagli's approach to psychiatry, we had not been able to connect with him or any of his collaborators—also related to the fact that both coordinators of the Balint Group I had attended had no formal position there. This is why, in the spring of 1979, Marco and I attended the child neuropsychiatry course led by Massimo Papini (1942–2017), a young, sophisticated, and very socially committed Italian protagonist of the struggle for a unified approach to child neurology and psychiatry—a point of view pioneered in Italy by Giovanni Bollea (1913–2011). Papini had just, in 1973, opened a ward for neurologically and psychiatrically sick children at the Florence Medical School, and was apparently looking for younger colleagues to share in his projects and work with him—so he had a very welcoming and encouraging attitude towards us. But since adult psychiatry had been our goal, I remember us contacting Giovanni Jervis—who had become professor of dynamic psychology at the University of Rome—and meeting him for lunch in Trastevere, to discuss this; his advice was to choose the field in which we would have more room for ourselves. This allowed us to approach Massimo Papini after taking the exam with him in June 1979 and agree to collaborate with any project that would be important for them—not for us. Of course, this is a distinction that I learned to adequately appreciate only later in my life—not a project of ours, but a project of theirs!

What we ended up working on, Marco and I together, was the introduction of laboratory techniques necessary for the diagnosis of a series of genetic metabolic disorders, the sphingolipidoses; the most famous of these is Tay-Sachs disease, in which an enzyme deficiency results in a buildup of gangliosides within the nervous cells of the brain and spinal cord. Whereas Marco concentrated on the technical and clinical aspects, I collected all the literature, with specific regard to the fascinating history of the description, diagnosis, and biochemical understanding of this class of diseases—in other words, this became my first research project in the field of the history of medicine. Since this was not what they had in mind, it would have of course been better to, for example, turn to Adolfo Pazzagli and propose to him a specific topic of research or work—with the risk that it might not have interested him. But my relationship to my own (internal) father was too fragile and I was too insecure to dare take such a step.

In the end, since they were not looking for a historian of medicine but for a young colleague with my friend's technical and clinical skills, I ended up not being admitted to residency training there—whereas Marco was. In the two weeks I spent in November 1981 in New York City (which I had not returned to since the summer of 1975), I had made some contacts with the hospital services treating sphingolipidoses, and I had brought back some literature, but this was not appreciated—or maybe was not a priority for them. However, all this happened more than two years later, after we had graduated from medical school, on October 26, 1981—with a *tesi di laurea*, a final thesis, illuminating the complementary aspects of the project we had dealt with individually. In the meantime, working together on this project helped us find the right rhythm and best psychological attitude for our last two years of medical school. Our grades got even better and we ended up graduating with the best grade—110/110 *cum laude*. My parents and Marco's were all there—and a couple of years ago our colleague Cristina gave me a picture she had taken of me discussing my work with the graduation commission.

I was never able to obtain a credible explanation for the unjustified wound I felt had been inflicted on me, considering the fact that the possibility of specializing in child neuropsychiatry had originally been part of the deal with Massimo Papini, back in the summer of 1979. The explanation above came to me while writing this *Selbstdarstellung*—as Freud called his "Autobiographical study" of 1924. But the grain of truth contained in it feels right to me. Now they had come to know me closely and they had no use for my skills, or—as an important variation on the same theme—they thought that it would not be so easy for them to just have me do what they wanted or needed. From this point of view, this is a situation I repeatedly experienced in my life. And this reminds me now of the only words of explanation that I remember having received from them, which went something like: "You are too sophisticated to just become a child neuropsychiatrist!"

In relation to this, and also in connection to the series of similar experiences I have had over the course of my life, I think that there are two—or even three—aspects to consider. On the one hand, the team indeed might not have had any use for me—because of their own limitations or different priorities. On the other hand, because of the fear I had experienced with my father that I might be instrumentalized by him, I was so afraid that this might happen again that I did not even try to negotiate the relationship. On the contrary, I neurotically expected people to behave as "the good father" whom I had not had, simply waiting around for such a miraculous change to happen, without getting involved, just passively waiting for the miracle to happen. Last but not least, I would of course also have liked to be courted, to become the object of an explicit appreciation or a specific request. From this point of view, I feel that I have always had problems in fighting for what I thought (inside myself) I would deserve.

The rejection of my application to specialize in child neuropsychiatry in Florence was a terrible trauma, which took me several years to recover from. In order to understand this better, it is useful to know that I had even given up my formal residence in Trento and become *un cittadino di Firenze* (a citizen of Florence)—I assumed that I would be able to create a new life for myself there. As Professor Papini had said neither "We will admit you next year" nor "You are of no use to us, but I will help you to be accepted as a resident at the University of— let us say—Milan, since you deserve it," this meant that I had to start all over again somewhere else. To add to this my father said a couple of things. On the one hand was, "Although you are a medical doctor, you are still welcome to work in my firm," and, on the other was, "Since you are a doctor, you can now support yourself"—well knowing that I had not chosen medicine to just support myself, but of course to make something special out of it, from a scientific point of view. In other words, if I had thought that I had found my own way in life, this no longer seemed the case. Indeed, I was left with the impression that it was true that in Italy you could not achieve anything without a family behind you, which was not my case in Florence.

Fortunately, my passion for my work helped me slowly find a new direction. The first thing I did was to apply to a school of psychotherapy in Cremona (Lombardy), which I started to attend every Thursday from January 1982— traveling alternatively from the south, that is, Florence, and from the north, that is, Trento. In the meantime I was studying for the State Exam, after which I registered as an MD in Florence. On April 1, I started working as a psychiatrist in training at the Hospital of Prato (Florence), where I had applied for a six-month training job; however, six weeks later I had the good luck to start working as an assistant psychiatrist in a small mental health center in Este, half an hour south of Padua—for one million Lire a month, which would be 2,000 Euros today. A colleague whom I had met at the Cremona School had started working there as a chief psychiatrist and he needed an assistant to work with him, doing all he could to have the hospital give the position to me. Only later did I discover that he was gay and must have been attracted to me physically—but at the time I was too desperate to even notice something like this. This new position of course also meant leaving Florence within a couple of days, something that only a few people would have been ready to do, but, at that point I was ready for the change—while knowing that I would not live there again.

Picture a small mental health center serving a vast agricultural territory, with many patients discharged from the Padua Psychiatric Hospital living at home and needing to be regularly visited, or to be treated with a monthly injection of antipsychotic drug. This was, in fact, a lovely area, immediately south of the spas of Abano and Montegrotto Terme, and I spent the summer being driven around by the nurses and visiting the patients, doing our best to enable them to continue living at home with their families. In other words, I had ended up working in a psychiatric service that daily struggled to apply the 1978 Italian Psychiatric Reform Law, which had blocked all new admissions to the old hospitals (only previous patients having the possibility to be readmitted to those, for a certain time), admissions now being to special small wards created in general hospitals. Being a small psychiatric service, we did not yet have such a ward and thus tried to avoid hospitalizations—for which we relied on the Padua General Hospital.

And this is what contributed to making me a good emergency psychiatrist, capable of differential diagnosis and care for a patient's state with a good probability of helping them give up their role of victim and become the protagonist of their psychological crisis. In other words, I really had the possibility of understanding what William Alanson White (1870–1937) and Franco Basaglia meant when they said that the fewer psychiatric beds we have at our disposal, the more we are forced to use our brains. This is indeed what Sullivan wrote about White in his *Conceptions of modern psychiatry* (1940), which, together with his *The psychiatric interview* (1954) and his *Clinical studies in psychiatry* (1956), soon became my "psychiatric Bible." In fact, the crucial contradiction of the New Italian Psychiatry was that, on the one hand, we had the chance to treat our patients outside of the hospital, but, on the other hand, there was not enough of a psychotherapeutic tradition and competence—not to mention the fact that Basaglia himself and many of his colleagues were prejudiced against psychoanalysis and psychotherapy. This was also the way in which my curiosity and my predisposition to study on my own made me discover the work of Gaetano Benedetti (1920–2013), who had introduced Sullivan's work into Italy—for example through a very good preface to his *La moderna concezione della psichiatria*, published in Italian in 1961.

As a consequence of my job in Este (and Montagnana, where our second, smaller, mental health center was located), I had moved back to Padua, where I was renting a small apartment in the Via Savonarola, arriving home late in the evenings after ten hours of daily work. On the weekends I was often in Trento, thus having the chance to show my parents how happy I was with my job as psychiatrist. In fact, both my passion for my work and my mother's readiness to help me ended up producing the miracle that was so crucial for me at that point—the admission into the residency program in adult psychiatry of the Catholic University in Rome. This became possible not only through my good performance in the admission exams of December 1982, but also because of the help of psychiatrist Corrado Pontalti from Trento, who had completed his medical studies there in 1967 and worked there as an assistant professor, and whom my mother had known for many years.

The Catholic University had been founded in Milan in the 1920s by Father Agostino Gemelli (1878–1959), himself a medical doctor and academic psychologist, and a medical school had been added to it in Rome in the early 1960s—also creating a hospital for the Vatican and the Popes. At variance with the anti-psychoanalytic orientation of his teacher Padre Gemelli, Leonardo Ancona (1920–2006) himself became a psychoanalyst, a pioneer of Italian group analysis, and one of the few Italian professors of psychiatry who taught his students the practice of an analytically oriented psychiatry. This orientation—also followed, as we have seen, by Adolfo Pazzagli in Florence—had been pioneered in Italy by Dario De Martis and Fausto Petrella at the University of Pavia, and by Franco Giberti and Romolo Rossi at the University of Genoa, all of them psychoanalysts members of the Italian Psychoanalytic Society (SPI) and International Psychoanalytical Association (IPA). Ancona's training analyst had been Ignacio Matte Blanco (1908–1995), who had come to Rome in the mid-1960s after having been an important pioneer of psychoanalysis in Chile, and having been trained in London in the 1930s. Not only he, but also Eugenio Gaddini (1916–1985) and Salomon Resnik (1920–2017), taught and contributed to forging the psychodynamic orientation of the Institutes of Psychology and Psychiatry headed by Leonardo Ancona. In other words I was very lucky to come in touch with and train in such a good tradition. But back in 1982, before the European reform of the medical residency programs, being a resident in psychiatry was limited to attending classes and passing the corresponding exams for a total of four years—under the assumption that most of us already had a hospital position somewhere in Italy, as was the case with me. The colleagues who did not have one—we were a class of more than 10 men and women—worked for free at the University Department until they found a hospital position.

Besides Ancona, a very brilliant and open man, I valued the teachings of Corrado Pontalti in the fields of family and group therapy, and of Filippo Ferro in the fields of the history of psychiatry, psychopathology and clinical psychiatry. Indeed, they were both so stimulating that I started collaborating with the Italian journal of family therapy, founded in 1977 by Maurizio Andolfi, and with which I had come directly in touch through Claudio Angelo (see below), and also further cultivated my own interest in the history of psychiatry and psychoanalysis. In fact, the *tesi di specializzazione* that allowed me to specialize in psychiatry (on July 11, 1986), centered around the historical, statistical, and therapeutic aspects of my work in the old Psychiatric Hospital of the Province of Trento, located in Pergine Valsugana, where I worked from June 1984 until October 1986. Before going back to the beginning of 1983, I want to mention the best friend I made in Rome, Luigi Casella, an internist living and working just outside Rome (Grottaferrata), who had developed an interest in psychosomatic medicine through his group analysis with Fabrizio Napolitani (1925–1996)—another important pioneer of Italian group analysis. We saw each other regularly for many years, and he would often host me when I happened to be in Rome—mostly for a congress.

One first important outcome of my new identity as *specializzando in psichiatria* (a psychiatric resident, albeit not residing in Rome) upon my work in Padua was that I started concentrating on a few patients with chronic schizophrenia, seeing them at least once a week and trying to help them come out of the "frozen emotional state" in which they were caught. This experience—which I shared with the psychologist of my team, Annalisa Dell'Oro—resulted in one of my first publications: "Saverio e noi: vicissitudini terapeutiche nell'incontro con un paziente psicotico" (Conci and Dell'Oro, 1985; for a translation, see the References). To be precise, this was my third publication—of a total of 220 at the end of August, 2017. But in July 1983, after about 14 months of work, I had to give up my position because of the mandatory Civil Service to which I had applied, as an alternative to the usual Military Service, and which I had the chance to do at the Trento Child Psychiatry Center—from July 1983 till June 1984.

In fact, I had hoped that the Italian State would forget about me, but this was not the case—many young people, for example my brother Paolo, ended up not serving at all because there were many more applications than the Ministry of Defense was able to process. From this point of view, this was for me a kind of a second defeat, considering the fact that I had to go back to Trento and even live with my parents, until the spring of 1984. On the other hand, I was able to spend most of my Civil Service time doing epidemiological research on the patient population of the Trento Child Psychiatry Center, and I only had to spend a couple of hours a day assisting a young person with an intellectual deficit do simple jobs at a home for the elderly. I had much time left for studying on my own, using also the good library of the above-mentioned old Psychiatric Hospital, where in addition I had the chance to get to know the chief psychiatrist, who appreciated me to the point of giving me a position as assistant psychiatrist, starting in June 1984. Last but not least, in September 1983 I was eventually able to start in Trento my personal psychoanalysis.

After graduating from medical school, I had already sought contact with the most prominent Florentine training analyst, Giovanni Hautmann (1927–2017), whose son Gregorio had been in my medical school class—and who also trained as a psychoanalyst in the SPI, of which his father was president between 1986 and 1990. Giovanni Hautmann kindly received me around ten in the evening in his office for the time necessary to tell me that his waiting list was closed for the next three years, but to give me the addresses of his fellow training analysts belonging to the SPI Milan Institute—to which he formally belonged. Besides him, there were in Florence only a couple more training analysts (certainly, Stefania Manfredi), all very busy given the large number of requests for treatment. In other words, many Italian colleagues of my generation ended up doing at first a personal analysis, preferably with an analyst who was about to become a training analyst, in the hope of making their admission to training easier—or of having the chance to transform the personal analysis into a training analysis without changing analyst. This also contributed to my giving up the idea of applying to the SPI to become an analytic candidate, and allowed me to give priority to a good personal analysis in order to eventually deal with my problems with the necessary professional help; it also allowed me to understand whether I really wanted to become an analyst or whether I was happy enough to work as an analytically oriented psychiatrist, which was in fact my priority at the time. This is how, in July 1982, I had already contacted and seen in Trento, for two preliminary sessions, Simona Taccani, with whom I had agreed to start working in September 1983. The main reason I had decided to contact an analyst in Trento was that I had come to the conclusion that, at this point of my life, my priorities were to work as a psychiatrist and to be able to finance both myself and my analysis, and that Trento was where it was easier to combine the three things.

Simona Taccani was a psychiatrist from Milan, where she had graduated from medical school in 1963, who had done her psychiatric and analytic training in Lausanne at the Hôpital de Cery, the University Hospital of the Medical School of Lausanne (Switzerland); this was headed by Christian Müller (1921–2013), who wrote in detail about his work there in his posthumous book *Erlebte Psychiatrie 1946–1986* (2016). In fact, Simona Taccani was part of a group of Italian psychiatrists, whose most famous representative was Giampaolo Lai (born 1931), who during the 1950s, 1960s, and 1970s, went abroad for their psychiatric and analytic training, considering the fact that the SPI was still small and rather provincial, and that university psychiatry was still dominated by neurology. In 1982 had also appeared the Italian edition (which I had immediately bought and read) of Paul-Claude Racamier's (1924–1996) *Le psychanalyst sans divan*, one of the best documents of French psychoanalytic psychiatry, of whose original French edition of 1972 Simona Taccani had been one of the co-authors. To the colleagues in town—among them my old friend Fabrizio, a psychologist, who knew her as a teacher and supervisor—Simona Taccani was also known for being the niece of Mara Palazzoli Selvini (1916–1999), the Italian pioneer of family therapy, of whose team she had also been a member at the end of the 1960s.

In 1977, together with her husband, an analytically trained psychologist, Simona Taccani had moved to Trento, where they set up not only the first private practice for psychoanalysis and psychotherapy in Trento, but even a small psychotherapy institute called the Centro di Ricerca di Psicoterapia. Although she was not an IPA member, she was competent enough for the kind of help I needed, which I felt when I first met her. I also appreciated the fact that she was not from Trento and that she was a woman, since—as I well remember—at the time I would not have been able to open up to a man, or to trust that a man would listen to me—as my father had failed to do this. In fact, my first good impression was that she was very different from both of my parents, which I thought would allow me to eventually have the chance to find the room I personally needed. She herself certainly had a strong personality, but she was also, at the same time, very reserved, even to the point of appearing shy.

In fact, as an analyst (or, better, as my analyst) I remember Simona Taccani as being, for example, rather abstinent. It was not possible, at least in my experience, to shake hands at the beginning and end of our sessions, as many of us do today—but only on special occasions like Christmas or the summer break. I also remember her as being very silent, even capable of not reacting to a silence of mine for quite a while. But for me—and I also remember this aspect very well—this also meant the possibility of being left alone, and of being forced to go over my thoughts and my emotions, and find a way of formulating them, that is, to have the chance of finding my own voice. And here I remember telling her, during the two preliminary interviews of July 1982, that I already knew many things about myself, but that I did not yet know what to do with them, and that I did not yet have a voice of my own—which made of me a very good analytic patient. In other words, her attitude forced me, or allowed, me to look into myself, and to slowly digest a whole series of experiences. It was a healing experience to just be attentively listened to, which she was very good at doing. Of course when I started working with her in September 1983, I was in the first place acutely suffering from having had to leave Padua and return to Trento, to go through my Civil Service, and I remember her being very good at containing my pain. As we know, the containment we receive produces in ourselves a new capacity to contain, and this must have been the direction she was able to show me. In this process consists in fact "the analytic paradox," according to which the analyst who does not activate herself to assist us helps us more than the apparently helpful analyst—and this allows us to expand and use our own psychological resources.

From this point of view, Simona Taccani was very good at helping me become much more aware of the boundaries, not only between myself and her, but also between me and the rest of the world. Since she was very good at doing her job as an analyst, I necessarily had to become a good and competent patient—sometimes to the point of having the feeling of working too much, and of also doing her work. But from this point of view, I also remember how well she dealt with my narcissistic problems, that is, she would let me talk and talk, until I came to the insight that I was perhaps doing all the talking, in order to prevent her from saying anything that I might be afraid to hear. This is how I learned to be eventually able to ask her direct questions, which she would now and then answer—I do not remember to ever have put her under so much pressure that she left her own normal analytic stance. But, again, from this point of view, I even came to the point of having the feeling that there was nothing I could do—as Winnicott would say—to gain the feeling that I could have an impact upon her.

And this now allows me to also say what follows here: gradually I must have had the feeling that her ego-psychological concentration on my defenses, and on their evolution, left too much out of the picture. From this point of view, I remember her being much more capable of listening to me in terms of Freud's structural model of ego, id and superego, than of being able to follow the concrete details of my experience, with which I did not remember her really interacting by asking questions or making comments. And this was one of the reasons for, or one of the reactive formations for, my growing interest in Sullivan and interpersonal psychoanalysis.

But, aside from these memories of our sessions and of the ways in which I think I benefited from her way of working, I can certainly say that when we terminated our work six years later, in December 1989, many positive things had happened, in both my personal and my professional life. Before turning to those, let me mention the following specific episode of a concrete and constructive interaction that is at variance with what I have said above. In the spring of 1986 I had come back from a two-week trip to New York City with the photocopy of Gertrud Schwing's (1905–1992) 1940 book *Ein Weg zur Seele des Geisteskranken* (see Schwing, 1954), having found it at the New York Psychoanalytic Institute, and—after discussing the various alternatives in our sessions—Simona Taccani and I ended up conceiving the joint venture of realizing together its Italian edition. *La pazzia e l'amore* came out in 1988, I having provided the translation (together with Roberto Schöllberger) and the prologue (Conci, 1988), and she the Italian title, the publisher, and an introduction—plus the translation of a review that Racamier had published of the book in 1955 in *L'Évolution psychiatrique*. In *A way to the soul of the mentally ill,* which had appeared in English in 1954 with a preface by Frieda Fromm-Reichmann, the Swiss nurse Gertrud Schwing described her pioneering experiences of contact with chronic psychotic patients under the supervision of Paul Federn (1871–1950). In the fall of 2016, a second edition of the book was published, and I received two copies from Simona Taccani. Last but not least, some of my problems of course remained unsolved—but I dealt with them in the two further analyses, which I shall talk about later.

Together with the many positive things that I can connect with my personal analysis with Simona Taccani, there are in fact also some problematic aspects and at least one rather dramatic event. As I have already described, in June 1984 I resumed working as a psychiatrist at the old Psychiatric Hospital of Pergine Valsugana, which had been opened in 1882 by the Hapsburg administration to cover the psychiatric needs of both Trentino and Südtirol. Although I was only an assistant psychiatrist, the scarcity of medical doctors meant that I had to take care of two wards with a total of more than 100 patients—all of them patients with chronic conditions whom it had not been possible to discharge. I not only worked long hours, but even tried to collaborate with the colleagues of Cles (the main center of the Non Valley, which Freud had visited in the summer of 1900) on a project to discharge some patients into a halfway house that they had put at my disposal. As part of this project, I drove them in my car back and forth between Pergine and Cles, where they could spend the day with the local psychiatric team— coordinated by colleagues Renzo De Stefani and Carlo Bologna, the only psychiatrists in the whole province still motivated to do this work of deinstitutionalization. How we were able to allow one patient (Mario) to leave the old Psychiatric Hospital and go back to his native community became the topic of a paper I published in 1988 with the psychologist of the Non Valley Mental Health Center, Patrizia Cortelletti.

During my Civil Service, in the fall of 1983, I had also started to attend the family therapy sessions that Claudio Angelo conducted every Thursday evening behind a one-way mirror at the Bolzano Psychiatric Service; I had eventually started catching up again with my German, which I had almost totally forgotten since I had left Innsbruck in July 1975. This also helped me to readjust, to find a new relationship with what the German-speaking people call *die Heimat.* In fact, I went so far in this direction that I fell in love with a

Südtiroler Psychiaterin, a German-speaking colleague from Bolzano, B., with whom I developed a rather intense but conflictual relationship. Of course, I also regularly had to go to Rome to attend the residency classes. But the main reason for the emotional stress that I ended up developing in this situation of overwork had to do with my limited capacity to find my own line, to perceive and defend my own boundaries, and not to enter into fusional or unclearly defined relationships—with my family of origin, with my work, with B., and with a series of other girls with whom I was in contact with through my work. The close relationship with my mother that I had had as a boy had made me vulnerable to any woman wanting something from me, and I could not adequately defend myself—coming to the point of going out with more than one woman at the same time. If Simona Taccani had been able to help me formulate and understand this problem, it was only through the later analytic experience with two male analysts that I could arrive at its solution.

If you now add to this situation of overwork and stress the facts that I was also smoking a pack of cigarettes a day (I had started smoking at age seventeen, and a pack a day had gradually become a routine) and that I had a family predisposition to coronary disease, you might not be surprised to hear that three weeks before turning thirty years old, on Sunday April 28, 1985, I suddenly suffered from an acute ischemic attack. Fortunately, I was in Bolzano, attending a congress at which I had just delivered a paper, when the very painful feeling of having a closet on my chest suddenly exploded—B. drove me right away to the hospital, where we arrived in a few minutes, and in whose emergency room I was immediately assisted by a very competent doctor who was able to deliver me from the heart attack by injecting a new drug, streptokinase. The fact that the cardiologist on call that morning was Walter Pitscheider, the future chief of cardiology at Bolzano San Maurizio Hospital, was another piece of good luck.

Today, more than thirty years since that dramatic experience, I continue to feel well. Since then I have regularly controlled my heart condition, and even came to the point of accepting the advice to undergo, in Trento, in August 2001, preventive open heart surgery to create two arterial bypasses. I have never suffered from angina pectoris, and am still a very good skier, but I suffered for many years under the fear of suddenly having a heart attack—which I kept under control through diet, sport, and regular checkups. Analytically speaking, this dramatic episode helped me understand how much I tended to neglect myself, and I remember Simona Taccani helping me to metabolize this in the direction of transforming the crisis into an important lesson for the rest of my life. Of course, the aim of every analytic process is to come into a much fuller contact with oneself and to be able to perceive and to elaborate all the pain and suffering that we tend to repress, to deny, or to transform into psychosomatic illness.

A very good sign that my work with Simona Taccani was helping me was the fact that I could start conceiving a positive expectation for my father to help me with my professional life—even though he did not agree with my choice of it. And this is what happened at the end of 1985, when he suddenly remembered that he had met in the 1960s, through a very good Munich-based friend of his, someone who was "probably," he said, "a famous German psychoanalyst"—Johannes Cremerius. After protesting that he could have told me about this much earlier, I was able to thank him and to contact my father's friend Rudi Wallner, who had arranged for me to meet his friend Cremerius, with whom they were going to spend the Christmas vacation in Non Valley—in St. Felix, on at the border between Trento and Bolzano.

Johannes Cremerius (1918–2002) was very famous at the time in Italy, since he had been giving lectures, teaching, supervising, and publishing his work in our country since the mid-1960s, mostly in the context of professional networks outside of the SPI, although he himself was a member of both the Deutsche Psychoanalytische Vereinigung (DPV) and the IPA. He collaborated with the journal *Psicoterapia e Scienze Umane* (which I regularly read) and, with Gaetano Benedetti, had founded in Milan an alternative psychoanalytic institute, the Scuola di Psicoterapia Psicoanalitica (SPP), which I had already been considering for my professional future. Our first meeting took place against this backdrop, in the afternoon of January 2, 1986, a cold winter day that we spent talking in the light of his fireplace, me getting to know him—and his wife Annemarie—and he getting to know me. Writing about this now, I can still feel how excited and happy I was at the prospect of a meaningful exchange with such an esteemed older colleague, and at the possibility that this might even change my own professional future. In fact, in the summer of 1985 he had just published in Italian what is probably his most important book, *Il mestiere dell'analista*—which I was then already reading, and had brought with me for him to sign.

In May 2017, in Bergamo, I had the chance to have dinner with Otto Kernberg and to tell him about my relationship with Cremerius—after having spent the afternoon as a consecutive translator of the exchange of ideas he had had there with physiologist Vittorio Gallese, a meeting organized by Carla Weber, the president of the Milan Associazione di Studi Psicoanalitici (ASP). Kernberg told me he had profited greatly from the discussions he had had with Cremerius in the 1980s and 1990s on the institutional and training problems of our field.

Of course, I told Cremerius not only about me, but also about my personal analysis, and asked him to advise me in terms of how to go about analytic training. Even for him this was no easy question, remembering his split allegiances to both the IPA and the Milan SPP—as I can grasp even better today. After giving much thought to the matter, he told me that he would be happy to help me be admitted to the Milan SPP—and I was happy to accept his advice, his approval of my choice, and his recommendation. In the summer/fall of 1986, after graduating from the Catholic University Residency Program, I went through the three preliminary interviews (with Drs Medri, Cantoni, and Elia), and I started my five-year training there in September 1988. Only many years later, talking about this aspect of my life with Stefano Bolognini, was I able to understand that my path toward the IPA might have been shorter if Cremerius had put me in touch with Egon Molinari (1911–2002), with whom he shared the high esteem he had for Sándor Ferenczi's work and legacy. As you will see, I became an IPA member only in 2010 (almost twenty-seven years after having started my personal analysis with Simona Taccani!), and an SPI member in 2012. But Cremerius had probably understood that I—like he himself, as I later discovered—like longer paths better than shorter ones. At the same time, at variance with me, he also knew that I might end up translating into Italian for him a whole series of important papers that he probably had already then in mind to write, and which of course I did not know about.

But this is also something I do not regret, since I learned so much by carefully translating Cremerius's papers, the first of which was "Alla ricerca di tracce perdute. Il 'Movimento psicoanalitico' e la miseria dell'istituzione psicoanalitica" (1987), an important paper on the history of psychoanalysis as an institution. It was by translating his papers that I got the best possible introduction to the history of psychoanalysis, which

became one of my favorite fields of research. Last but not
least, I owe to him my very first contact with the Munich
Akademie für Psychotherapie und Psychoanalyse, the
institute of Cremerius's first training in the 1950s as a
pupil of Fritz Riemann (1902–1979)—which became my
Munich psychoanalytic home when I moved there in the
fall of 1997. My first wife, Claudia, and I had accompanied
him and Annemarie there to give a paper in December
1990, four weeks before the birth of our daughter Anna.
In fact, Cremerius was a further model for me in that he
had had a first training outside of the IPA in the 1950s,
and a second training, in the Swiss IPA, in the early
1960s. In the mid-1960s, he had become a training analyst
and a university professor in Giessen, before moving to
Freiburg in the early 1970s. I want to add these details
because I know that Cremerius and his work are hardly
known in the English-speaking world, probably the
result of some kind of taboo against the German analysts
of his generation—most of whom, with the exception of
Alexander Mitscherlich (1908–1982) and Helmut Thomä
(1921–2013), did not dare to publish anything in English.

   Johannes Cremerius played such an important role in
my life not only in terms of establishing contact with the
Milan SPP, but also by indirectly creating the situation in
which I got to know Pier Francesco Galli (born 1931), the
founder and editor of *Psicoterapia e Scienze Umane*, with
whom I actively collaborated for almost ten years (1986–
1995)—translating papers from German and English,
and writing book reviews and articles. My introduction to
Galli took place at the conference "Institutionalisierung-
Desinstitutionalisierung," which the Psychoanalytic
Seminar Zurich (the alternative psychoanalytic institution
founded by, among others, Paul Parin [1916–2009])
held in Zurich on the last weekend of May of 1986, to
which Cremerius invited me. After our meeting, it was
clear that I would have translated Cremerius's paper,
the one already cited above, for Galli's journal. Indeed,
my own unconscious had been so much activated by the
preparation for this trip to Zurich, which I made together
with my friend Roberto Schöllberger, an analysand of
Norman Elrod (1928–2002), that I had even brought
with me an important article by the New York analyst
Joel Kovel, "The American mental health industry"
(1980). Along with the above-mentioned book by Gertrud
Schwing, I had found this in New York City in April—and
had even called up Kovel for his permission to undertake
a possible translation into Italian. Galli knew the article
and I was very happy to start working for his journal by

translating it—which I did in the summer. At this point, I am sure the reader can imagine—among other things—how important it was for me to be able to show to my (internal) father that my professional choice had been justified, and that I had a particularly good competence in what I was doing—not to mention the possibility of publishing enough papers that I would have the chance to later run for a university position, as indeed happened.

From both these points of view, my collaboration with *Psicoterapia e Scienze Umane* was extremely useful—as were the many patients whom Galli sent me after I had started working in private practice in Trento in October 1988. Our contact was also made easier by the fact that he and his group organized monthly scientific meetings on Saturdays in Bologna, from October to May, in which I regularly participated between the fall of 1988 and the summer of 1994. In these we had the chance to meet and personally get to know a whole series of important analytic authors (not only Paul Parin and Berthold Rothschild from Zurich, but also Merton Gill, Robert Holt, Morris Eagle, and Stephen Mitchell from the USA, and Anne Hurry and Peter Fonagy from London). In this way, I learned how important it is to meet and talk with an author if we are to really understand what his or her work is like.

In addition, the work of translating can be very useful for getting into closer contact with our literature, and becoming scientifically productive ourselves. And, as far as translations are concerned, I made many indeed—a total of seventeen for *Psicoterapia e Scienze Umane*, including the paper by Berthold Rothschild that came out a few months before I wrote this Afterword, and a total of five for Galli's Saturday Meetings. As far as Cremerius's papers are concerned, my translations number seven (four for Galli's journal and three for other journals). With regard to the many book reviews I have published in *Psicoterapia e Scienze Umane*, the first was of Russel Jacoby's *The repression of psychoanalysis. Otto Fenichel and the political Freudians* (Conci, 1987), and the most important was the review I wrote in 1990 of Stephen Mitchell's *Relational concepts in psychoanalysis. An integration* (Mitchell, 1988; see Conci, 1990a). In fact, I now count a total of fourteen book reviews. As far as articles are concerned, the most important are the paper I wrote with Lucio Pinkus on Sullivan's *Schizophrenia as a human process* (Conci and Pinkus, 1989), and my paper on the young Freud's letters to his friend Eduard Silberstein from Trieste (in the spring of 1876) (Conci,

1990b). Last but not least, let me mention not only that Otto Kernberg has often been a guest of *Psicoterapia e Scienze Umane*, but that the journal has also, since the beginning of 2017, been available through PEP-Web and the PEP-disk—a crucial turning point in the fifty years of the journal, founded in 1967, and brought about by the co-editor-in-chief Paolo Migone.

The paper on Sullivan I have just mentioned is also very important from another point of view. It represents the result of the workshop on "H.S. Sullivan: The meeting of psychiatry and social science" that I held at the University of Venice in the spring of 1988, in connection with the dynamic psychology course taught there by Lucio Pinkus; he was the full professor of psychology there who not only invited me to collaborate with him, but also greatly helped me to later get a position as an assistant professor of psychiatry at the Brescia Medical School, starting in September 1991. Lucio was and is a very unusual person: born in 1942 the son of a Berlin medical doctor, who was able to escape Nazi Germany and move to Italy, Lucio had not only studied psychology and trained as a Jungian analyst, but was also a priest, a member of the religious order of the "Servi di Maria." A highly original and anti-conformist individual, he has spent his life trying to reach out to, create a dialogue with, and assist various kinds of people, including for example some former members of the Red Brigades—as one can read in his autobiography of 2012. I had met him in the fall of 1987 through my future wife Claudia, and he played a major role not only in my professional, but also in my personal life—which I will take up again later. I very much enjoyed collaborating with him and held two more workshops in the following two years, centered around the work of psychoanalysts with interdisciplinary interests such as Erik Erikson (spring 1989) and Alexander Mitscherlich (spring 1990).

But, let me now come to what I consider another piece of very good luck—getting to know Stephen Mitchell, in Florence, on April 9, 1988, a Saturday. That weekend I was in Florence with my friend Carlo (the Non Valley psychiatrist) to attend a workshop on family therapy, and I found out that Stephen Mitchell and Jay Greenberg were in Florence to give lectures and workshops, on the invitation of the Istituto di Psicoterapia Analitica. Since I had read their 1983 book, *Object relations in psychoanalytic theory*, which had been translated into Italian in 1986, I was very curious to meet them—and this is what I did, giving up the family therapy workshop to do so.

It happened, while attending Mitchell's workshop, that I discovered that the translation was not good enough, so I jumped in as a translator. After some time of reciprocal attunement, Mitchell declared that he was now satisfied with the translation, since the group was eventually laughing at his jokes—which he apparently had been making the whole time in order to see if the translation was good enough. At the end of our work, the director of the Institute, Virginia Giliberti Tincolini, invited me to join them all for dinner, and this gave me the chance to really get to know Stephen Mitchell. I had the chance not only to tell him how fond I was of Sullivan's work, and that I had relied on Helen Swick Perry's 1982 biography in my Venice workshop, but also to hear him tell me that he completely shared my interest in Sullivan. And this to the point that—in the course of the same evening, seeing that I really knew Sullivan well—he suggested that I should write a book on Sullivan, putting together his life and his work, as nobody had yet done this. As you can by now imagine, I did not react by saying "No, thanks, I have enough things to do," but said, "Wonderful, but with the condition that you help me!" This is how the book project started, but it took a great deal of work and many years to write and publish it—at first in Italian (2000), then in German (2005), and eventually in English (2010, 2012) and Spanish (2012).

But let me now go back to Stephen Mitchell, of whom I remember not only the unique way in which he encouraged colleagues, me included, to write, but also his capacity to keep up with his many friends—again me included. Having heard about his new book, the above-mentioned 1988 book, I went to New York City during the following Christmas vacation, bought it, read it, and discussed it with him—to then write the thorough review already mentioned above. Given the interest in his work that I had contributed to creating in Italy, I organized for him (and his wife Margaret Black) a first trip to Italy in April 1991 and a second (including Margaret and their two daughters) in April 1996. In 1993 I had the chance to write an introduction to the Italian edition of his 1988 book (Conci, 1993b), and in 1995 a shorter one to the Italian edition of his 1993 book *Hope and dread in psychoanalysis* (Conci, 1995a).

Our contact lessened as I left for Munich in the fall of 1997—and I was not in Lindau when he spoke there in 1998. I saw him last at the New York Forum of the International Federation of Psychoanalytic Societies (IFPS) in May 2000, from which I am sure I have a photograph of him and Marianne Horney Eckardt. His premature death was also for me a terrible loss, whose consequences still occupy my mind and heart. But this is what I specifically deal with in Chapter 6 of this book— where I go into the details of the Italian trips I organized for him and also try to come to an overall assessment of his legacy. Although I gave a paper on the role I played in the initial reception of relational psychoanalysis in Italy at the International Association for Relational Psychoanalysis and Psychotherapy Rome Conference of June 2005 (Conci, 2014), my name was hardly mentioned in the paper written about it by Giorgio Caviglia and Vittorio Lingiardi (2014)—only Stephen, Margaret, and I apparently knew about it.

Two months later, at the beginning of June 1988, the group from *Psicoterapia e Scienze Umane* organized in Milan a further conference of the so-called Collegamento Psicoanalitico Internazionale, the international network that had met two years before in Zurich, and at which I had had much work translating the papers of Cremerius, Parin, and Rothschild. The congress was well attended and I got to know a whole series of Swiss, German, and Austrian colleagues—in the archive I have in my office I found the names of Hans Red (Zurich), Detlef Michaelis (Frankfurt), and Johannes Reichmayr (Vienna). In addition, Robert Hinshelwood, whom I had already met in Zurich in 1986, was there, as was Armando Bauleo, the Argentinian pupil of Enrique Pichon Rivière (1907–1977) who worked in Venice. There I also met for the first time Michele Ranchetti (1925–2008), a historian of the Church, also a poet and translator, but, for me in the first instance, a pioneer of the study of the reception of Freud's work in Italy; I later had the chance to collaborate and even establish a good friendship with him. As I had the chance to learn a couple of months before writing this Afterword, also present was Karl Fallend from Salzburg, one of the youngest students of Igor Caruso (1914–1981), who in 1984 had founded the alternative psychoanalytic journal *Werkblatt*. The specific title of the congress was rather sophisticated—"Sono ancora utili gli idioti?" [Are idiots still useful?] – but the main topic was actually the problem of power in psychoanalysis, and the question of whether the analytic training system makes of us only more or less good professionals, or whether it also betrays the true spirit of psychoanalysis in terms of its potential for critical thinking. If the topic was not easy, I do remember a large effort to exchange ideas and get to know each other, to create a real international dialogue.

The journal *Werkblatt* is still in existence, and I assume that the Salzburg group behind it also profited from the Milan meeting.

It was in this context that I also got to know L., a psychologist from Bologna, but originally from Trento, who would remain for several years an important part of my life. In the first two weeks of August we made a trip to Germany, visiting Munich, Freiburg, Heidelberg, and Berlin, and seeing there some of the colleagues we had got to know in Milan. In September we both attended the IXth International Symposium on the Psychotherapy of Schizophrenia organized in Turin by Gaetano Benedetti and Pier Maria Furlan, an unusually successful congress, with around 1,300 participants (see Furlan, 2006). There I presented the paper on Sullivan's *Schizophrenia as a human process*, on which I later based the above-mentioned article published with Lucio Pinkus. The paper stimulated Pier Francesco Galli to himself renew his own love for Sullivan's work and to propose to the publisher Feltrinelli to eventually translate it into Italian. The book came out in 1993 with a preface by me (Conci, 1993a), thus becoming the fifth out of seven books by Sullivan published in our country between 1961 and 1993. L. was also interested in Sullivan and in interpersonal psychoanalysis, and in the early 1990s she started going to New York City to attend courses at the William Alanson White Institute. From this point of view, she became for me a very important intellectual partner. We also worked for several years with Sergio Dazzi from Parma to produce an Italian selection of the most important papers of the interpersonal tradition, *La tradizione interpersonale in pschiatria, psicoterapia e psicoanalisi*, which came out in 1997. Although we did many things together, we were never able to become a couple, and our—complex and troubled—relationship came to the end.

What I have not yet talked about is of course my analytic training in Milan, which I began in September 1988, immediately after the Turin Symposium. The fact that the SPP was an alternative analytic institute meant that Benedetti, Cremerius, and their group of teachers and supervisors had created an institute in which there was, in the first place, no more training analysis as traditionally conceived. The training analysis was replaced by a personal analysis three times a week, which had to be completed (or be about to be completed) before starting the training itself. The training lasted for five years from each mid-September to the end of June, and took place every Thursday afternoon and at least one Saturday morning a month, during which the group and individual supervisions and theoretical courses took place. When I applied, my analysis had come to its termination phase, having lasted about fifteen more months. Now, since Simona Taccani also had an office in Milan, we met about ten times a month, for a total, after six years, of about 600 sessions. Of course, the executive committee of the SPP considered her to be a very competent analyst, and this aspect of course also belonged to the requirements of the personal analysis. Having outlined the general framework of the training, the first thing that comes to mind is that it was so good that, at the point at which I started going to Milan, I also entered full-time private practice in Trento. I had spent part of the summer discussing this topic with my father—eventually succeeding in convincing him that I would be able to make a good living without the monthly salary from the hospital.

What I learned, from this point of view, at the beginning of my training was as follows: if you have a good supervisor, you also find good patients—or, to put it another way, it does not make sense to look for a supervisor only after you have a patient, since what works is the opposite combination. Technically speaking, if you already have a supervisor, you will be able to talk on the phone with the patient who is asking you for an appointment in such a way that he or she will feel good about you. In fact, I immediately started doing regular supervisions with Guido Medri and soon had several patients with whom I worked two and three times a week, face to face and on the couch—the word "couch" being one that I associate with a very specific memory. During my first supervisory session, Guido Medri naturally said that I now had to buy a couch, but did not specify what kind of a couch. Of course, I ended up buying the same couch on which I had lain as a patient, the famous couch designed by Le Corbusier. However, what I find even more pertinent is that I ended up discussing this choice not with the supervisor, but with my colleague Grazia Rodella, who was a member of my class (of twelve candidates), and with whom I shared not only the same supervisor, but even the train ride back from Milan to Desenzano (the train stop on Garda Lake between Brescia and Verona, the place where she lived and worked). By this, I mean that if a fundamental—and at the same time very much neglected—dimension of every analytic training is the elaboration that can only take place in a peer dimension, I had been certainly lucky in Milan.

This regular exchange with Grazia concerned not

only the individual supervisions, but also the group supervision sessions of one and a half hours that we regularly attended for five years—the first three years with Lilia D'Alfonso and the next two with Teresa Corsi (1935–2008; see Omodei Zorini, 2009) as group supervisors. I am of course speaking of the following phenomenon: that a supervisor tends to function like an analyst, meaning that he or she more often hints, suggests, and interprets rather than explains anything, with the consequence that the more important work we do starts only at the end of the supervision and consists in its elaboration. And this work is much easier and more fruitful if we can do it with our peers. A further concrete—and typical—example is that, of course, it was with Grazia that we had to conclude that we had better not adopt the interpretations of our individual supervisors until we had really digested them and made them our own—as our patients can feel the difference between whether we are speaking with our own voice or that of our supervisor! Of course, working three times a month together in the context of a group supervision greatly facilitated the peer exchange that I have just described. From this point of view, I would say that the two dimensions—the group supervision as the central ingredient of the training, and the consequent facilitation of the peer exchange—belonged together, making of our training really a group process, that is, much more so than in the individually based, traditional Eitingon IPA model (see also Conci, 2010a).

In other words, the result of the combination of the abolition of the traditional training analysis and the fundamental role of the group supervision was represented by the much more spontaneous and less ritualized communication climate of the whole institute, and this was exactly the work climate that characterized the supervision groups that Cremerius and Benedetti created with us—Cremerius once a month for all five years, and Benedetti once a month for the last three years of the training. Indeed, the SPP itself had been founded by a group of Benedetti and Cremerius's supervisees at the end of the 1970s, after they themselves had worked with them for a period of about eight years—a topic I have dealt with in various papers (see, for example, Conci, 2016b) and which the reader can find in Part Four of this book, specifically in Chapter 10. Since working with Benedetti and Cremerius had completely changed the professional life of these supervisees, they decided to try to create an institute in which this form of training could be shared with and transmitted to a series of younger generations.

If this operation was certainly successful until the mid-1990s, that is, while Benedetti and Cremerius were actively involved in the process, this original inspiration seems to me to have been increasingly lost—and this is also one of the reasons why it is so important to write this chapter of our history.

What were the supervision groups with Benedetti and Cremerius like? They produced the spontaneous, constructive, and creative climate described above in two wholly different ways. What Cremerius invited the candidate (or, better, analyst in training—AiT) to do was to briefly report the most important data concerning the patient and the treatment, and then to concentrate on two specific sessions in terms of the climate of the sessions, the words exchanged, and the resulting interaction—and if possible do it freely, as opposed to reading a written report. At this point, the participants were invited to discuss the clinical material, while the reporting AiT was asked not to react to their comments. What Cremerius would try to do was, on the one hand, synthesize the work of the group in terms of the transference–countertransference dynamic emerging from the treatment, and, on the other hand, isolate some specific aspect of the treatment and develop a theoretical reflection on it. For example, take the phenomenon of the patient who talks too much, or the patient who talks too little—what dynamic problems lie behind these phenomena, and how can we deal with them? Cremerius's overall priority was to create in the group the same atmosphere of free and constructive association and exchange as in a good analytic session. But not only this, as the biggest challenge for a supervisor is to be able to show how the clinical and the theoretical aspects illuminate one another and belong together, which only a few supervisors can do—and he was one of them.

Here is how Benedetti pursued the same goals (see also Conci, 2006). Because of his hearing problems (he heard well only through his right ear), he asked the candidate to write and send him a complete report of the patient and the treatment. At the beginning of the supervisory session, he would then invite the AiT to summarize their report and share it with the group; Benedetti then invited all of us to formulate our emotions and ideas about the case, as if we all were famous doctors in an important consultation, and he was able to transform any such feedback into a precious contribution. In other words, it was important for him that all of us would talk, and that by doing so all of us would have the opportunity to learn. Last but not least, Benedetti would read aloud the written report he had very diligently prepared about the case, in which—almost by a miracle—he had already formulated almost all of the major aspects of the case dealt with by the group during the supervisory session.

But let me now at this point catch up with my personal life. In the spring of 1986 I had met Claudia, also a medical doctor, a gynecologist, and also from Trento. I met her through a sister of my mother, whom she knew because she had spent a year in Vienna learning how to use the new technique of echography for prenatal diagnosis, and had thus met my favorite uncle, Pierino Bolech, before his premature death in 1984. Claudia came from a middle-class family and was the oldest of five children. In order to study medicine in Bologna, she had had to support herself and, in addition, win out over her parents' resistances as they wished a simpler life for her. From this point of view, she belonged to the generation of Italian women who struggled hard to be able to be, at the same time, successful professionals and good mothers. In fact, she had sacrificed much of her life to the professional aspect, as I also had (and have) done. From this point of view, she could understand me very well, and I her. A further advantage she had over the women whom I was seeing at the time was that she had the courage to dare to get to know my mother before getting to know me. By this apparent paradox, I mean the following: I had so little room in my own family, and such a conflictual relationship with it, that I would not dare introduce a woman I loved to them. If I loved a woman, I would, or felt I should, keep her away from my family. From this point of view, the reader can even be justified in reinterpreting everything so far as a repeated attempt on my side to find an alternative family—one that would accept and appreciate me, and that I would have liked to join.

Historically speaking, this has been the case with many psychoanalysts, who have felt attracted to Freud and psychoanalysis in terms of the "new home" they have been looking for. Since this is not a historical, but a personal report, I will limit myself here to only a few of the many such cases that come to mind. On the one hand, I can think of Sándor Ferenczi and his many letters to Freud in which he relates to him as a father, and to psychoanalysis as their common home—which I know well, as they were the topic of a Discussion Group that I held at the Winter Meeting of the American Psychoanalytic Association in 2016 and 2017. On the other hand, I am reminded of Erich Fromm (1900–1980), who in his important book of 1959 *Sigmumd Freud's mission: An analysis of his personality and influence* pictured the first analysts around Freud in the same way I am doing, as "homeless people in search of a new home." Last but not least, in May 2016—at the yearly congress of the German Psychoanalytic Society held in Stuttgart—I gave a paper by the title "Die analytische Beziehung als Heimat" (Conci, 2016c).

It is not easy to talk about Claudia, my first wife and Anna's mother—but I will now try to. To Claudia I also owe my original contact with Lucio Pinkus—who had proposed to her a research project, her reaction being to introduce him to me; and I am grateful for the sympathy she had for my ambition of a university career. On my side, I shared with her my growing relationship with Annemarie and Johannes Cremerius, who also valued her very much—she also was able to become close to their daughter, Janine. In other words, we had many things in common, but probably not the most important: she was ready to get married, and I was not. At the same time, I can even say that I knew I was not ready yet for such a step, but I believe that I considered it a good thing to do at the time—far from perfect, but anyhow contributing to bringing me forward in life. This is how we got married, on Saturday September 23, 1989, in Arco (near Lake Garda)—with Lucio Pinkus celebrating the marriage, Johannes Cremerius as my best man, and Stephan Szalay, an Austrian gynecology professor, as her best man. As an aside, Freud scholars among the readers might be able to identify the date as the 50th anniversary of Freud's death—a coincidence of which I was always aware.

And then, at the end of December 1990, Anna was born, and we were both happy to have her with us. Had I waited to be in the position of really wanting to have children, several more years would have gone by—and at the time of writing Anna is almost twenty-seven years old, and we have never had such a good relationship as we have had in the last few years. However, as can certainly be understood from earlier in the Afterword, I have always associated my own childhood and youth more with work than with play—and only many years into my adult life was I able to feel so comfortable as to want to have a family. This is why I am still thankful to Claudia for trying. We separated in the fall of 1996, at a time when it still took five years in Italy to get a divorce. But we never lost sight of each other, we always (or almost always) knew where we were and what we were doing, and we were always (or almost always) capable of being "good-enough parents" for Anna.

Of course, I also have a series of happy memories of my relationship with Claudia, and I will now move on to the three important congresses to which she accompanied me. The first coincided with a part of our honeymoon— here we came together with a group of colleagues: Guido Medri and Ciro Elia and their wives from Milan, and Paolo Migone from Parma. This was the VIIIth Forum of the IFPS, which took place in Rio de Janeiro in the second week of October 1989. Since I had chosen the SPP for my training, it was of course important for me that the association the SPP had created in 1979, the ASP, would come to have good international connections, and I was very curious to see this for myself. Here is the story, which I have also dealt with in Part Four of this book.

At the previous Forum held in Zurich in 1985, Gerard Chrzanowski (1913–2000) had again seen Gaetano Benedetti, whom he had known from their time together at the Burghölzli under Manfred Bleuler (1903–1994), and had found out that the ASP might be interested in joining the IFPS—whose foundation Chrzanowski himself had contributed to in 1962, in the name of the New York White Institute. The other three founding societies had been the Deutsche Psychoanalytische Gesellschaft (DPG), Igor Caruso's Austrian Arbeitskreise, and the Mexican Society founded by Erich Fromm (see Chrzanowski, 1993). Since 1985 contacts had intensified and site visits to Milan had taken place, and the IFPS was ready to admit the ASP as a member society at the Rio de Janeiro Forum. Indeed, Benedetti, Medri, and Elia had prepared a workshop through which to introduce the members of the Federation to their work—this was to include a paper written by Laura Andreoli and Daniela Maggioni, but as they were unable to attend, I read it for them. As you can see, what I am speaking about is a little hierarchical organization, in which I from the beginning had the feeling that there was something for me to do. Indeed, in 1994 I became an assistant editor of the IFPS journal, the *International Forum of Psychoanalysis*, and since 2007 I have been its co-editor-in-chief (until 2014 with Christer Sjödin, Stockholm, and since 2014 with Grigoris Maniadakis, Athens), and for me this means that my competence to do the work was in this case more important than my age or other institutional conditions.

Besides this, I of course also want to say that if I consider myself not to have been entirely lucky in my personal life, as far as my professional life is concerned I often—preconsciously—knew exactly what to do and in what direction to move, as if I had the kind of compass that allows the tennis player to always be where the ball lands. In other words, at the time I had the feeling that it could be important to be in Rio de Janeiro, and so it was. If you are there from the beginning, it is easier to keep being there for a long time. As an aside, this is also the secret of the people who, in Italy, are five to ten years older than I am: at their time the world was smaller, and most of them became chiefs of medical departments, full university professors, and/or training analysts, which could not be the case for me—1955 was the birth year in Italy of the highest number of students getting into medical school and there was never enough room for all of us! However, it is true that for Anna and her generation it might all be even harder. What I feel lucky about in terms of my generation is the continuity of the contacts I have had. Take as an example Paolo Migone, who trained as a psychoanalyst in New York City in the early 1980s, whom I have known since 1987, and with whom I am still in contact.

As you can see, Claudia has disappeared again from my memories—but she knows what I am talking about, and she has even known Paolo Migone for a longer time than I have, since her medical school years in Bologna. Anyhow, it might be a relief for the reader to learn that after the Rio de Janeiro Forum we did take some vacation: in Salvador de Bahia, at the Iguaçeu Falls and in Brasilia—coming back from Brazil with the impression of having been in a very interesting, but also rather wild and *unheimlich* place.

The next congress I want to talk about took place that same year, at the beginning of December, in Trieste. It was organized by the SPI and by the historian of psychoanalysis Anna Maria Accerboni (1939–2006), to celebrate the 100th anniversary of the birth of the first Italian psychoanalyst, Edoardo Weiss (1889–1970). But here is what my compass had suggested me to do a month before: on a Thursday evening, Claudia and I took the train from Venice to Vienna, from where we were to go to Budapest with Johannes and Annemarie Cremerius, to attend one of the first international analytic congresses, organized by Livia Nemes—the exact day was Thursday November 9, 1989, the day the Berlin Wall fell. During the Friday morning spent in Vienna, we went to the analytic bookstore I used to know there (behind the *Stephansdom*) and I bought a book in German that had come out a couple of months before, edited by Walter Boehlich, which was translated as *The letters of Sigmund Freud to Eduard Silberstein 1871–1881* (Boehlich, 1990).

As I have already described, knowing Cremerius and translating his papers had brought me very much in contact with the history of psychoanalysis, both the history he had lived (in the early 1950s, he had been to the USA, where he had met Franz Alexander, Kurt Eissler, Rudolph Loewenstein, etc.) and the historical literature he knew. This is how I had by then read all of Freud's letters (to Fliess, with Jung, with Abraham, with Edoardo Weiss, etc.) and how I knew which ones were eventually about to come out—as was the case of the letters to his school-friend Silberstein. The young Freud had studied Spanish with his high school friend Silberstein, and they had founded the so-called "Academia Castellana," as Ernest Jones wrote in the first volume of his Freud biography (Jones, 1953). Now, to cut a long story short, the anthology of Freud's letters to Silberstein edited in German by Boehlich in 1989 contains some very interesting letters that Freud wrote to his friend from Trieste in the spring of 1876, and Anna Maria Accerboni had agreed for a famous Viennese colleague to come and talk about them; however, this colleague fell ill, and Anna Maria Accerboni asked me to prepare, in ten days, a paper on these letters. And this is what I did. The consequence was that Freud's Italian publisher, Bollati Boringhieri (Turin), contacted me to become the Italian editor of the letters, which came out in Italian—with me as their editor—in the spring of 1991. Indeed, this is the background behind the three first chapters of this current book.

Many years have gone by and I do not know any Italian colleague who has ever worked in this area, that is, one who knows enough German to be familiar with the Austrian roots of our field. This is why, for example, Freud's letters to his Freiberg friend Emil Fluss (1856–1927), originally published in German and English at the end of the 1960s, remained untranslated into Italian until I—together with my second wife, Doris—completed the work in 2016 (Conci, 2016e). In connection with this, in Trieste in December 1989 I also got to know Ludger Hermanns from Berlin, through whom I came more directly in touch with the wealth of historical research and work done in Germany. Ludger had collaborated on the preparation of the exhibition on the history of psychoanalysis in Germany shown at the 34th IPA Congress held in Hamburg in 1985 (see Brecht, Friedrich, Hermanns, and Juelich, 1993)—the first IPA congress in Germany since the one held in Wiesbaden in 1932. The possibility of sharing my research work on the history of psychoanalysis with a group of colleagues was one of the reasons why I moved to Munich in 1997; in addition, Ludger is the coordinator of the IPA History of Psychoanalysis Committee, on which I am a consultant—both of us nominated by Stefano Bolognini in the spring of 2016 and confirmed by Virginia Ungar and Sergio Nick after the 50th IPA Congress held in July 2017 in Buenos Aires.

As an aside, and as a confirmation of my "stubbornness," I would like also to report the following event that happened in Trieste in December 1989. Glauco Carloni (SPI president 1982–1986) from Bologna, who was attending the congress together with Egon Molinari (a native of Trieste), approached me after I had given my paper on Freud's letters to Silberstein. Glauco Carloni gave me his office address and invited me to visit him in Bologna. I was of course, at the time, happy enough with all that was happening in my life, so I did not follow this up—but if my priority had been to train in and become a member of the SPI (which became the case only in 2012), this would have probably been a good way to do it. Had I visited him in Bologna, I would have probably been admitted to train in the SPI, and the whole process would have lasted less than the twenty-three years it actually took me to reach that point! Only since 2012 have I been a member of the Centro Psicoanalitico di Bologna, which, having been founded by Egon Molinari and Glauco Carloni, the two pioneers of psychoanalysis in Bologna, carries their names—Centro Psicoanalitico di Bologna "Glauco Carloni-Egon Molinari."

The next congress to which Claudia accompanied me represented for me an important introduction to German and international psychoanalysis. I am referring here to the unique scientific event represented by the "Lindauer Psychotherapiewochen", whose 40th meeting took place in Lindau, a beautiful spot on Lake Constance (bordering Austria, Germany, and Switzerland), between April 16 and 28, 1990. I do not know any similar events in Italy such as these, which bring together for two weeks a total of a thousand or more psychoanalysts and psychotherapists of various orientations, who attend lectures, discussion groups, and workshops held by German- and English-speaking colleagues. This is a *Musterbeispiel*, that is, a paradigmatic case of the excellent organization of which the German people are so capable, not of course in terms of hosting so many people in one place at the same time, but in terms of creating a national accreditation system allowing the individuals attending the "Lindau Psychotherapy Weeks" to collect credits for their own training and continuing education in their own city or state.

This presupposes a level of collaboration still unheard of in Italy and in the international psychoanalytic world. But if this does not change, this means that we will not be capable of realizing one of the essential ingredients of Freud's legacy—the international character of psychoanalysis. And by this I mean the following: that Freud grew up multilingual (Yiddish, German, and Czech); that psychoanalysis represents his synthesis of Viennese neuroanatomy (Brücke and Meynert), French clinical research (Charcot), and the English empirical tradition (Darwin); and that psychoanalysis was able to so easily conquer the world, because it spread so well internationally through the kind of personal contacts of an intellectual elite that made its diffusion faster than through the normal university channels. Now, in Lindau this kind of elite has continued to gather for two weeks a year, and share its work, every year, with about a thousand colleagues from the whole German-speaking world, most of them attending either the first or the second week.

In April 1990 in Lindau, Cremerius introduced me to Otto Kernberg, and I was able to tell him that I had translated into Italian for *Psicoterapia e Scienze Umane* his pioneering—by now very famous—paper "Institutional problems of psychoanalytic education" (1986); of course, I had to meet him several more times before he was able to remember me. In Lindau, I listened to the paper that Michael Ermann gave on the revisitation of the history of psychoanalysis and psychotherapy during the Nazi regime, which he later sent to me (Ermann, 1990). There too I participated in a workshop on the Budapest School given by the Hungarian-German colleague Rudolf Pfitzner, together with Budapest colleague János Harmatta (1917–2004). And there I participated in the afternoon clinical workshop held every day by Cremerius himself—audiotaping it all, with the help of Edith Geuss, the wife of Wolfgang Mertens, both from Munich. I still have the tapes, here in my Trento office.

The next congress that Claudia—then pregnant with Anna—also attended with me was the Third International Meeting of the International Association for the History of Psychoanalysis (IAHP), organized by Alain de Mijolla and Pearl King in London on July 20–22, 1990, under the title "The socio-political involvement of psychoanalysts"— with which I also connect a whole series of, for me, very meaningful and important personal and professional encounters. There I even remember shaking hands with Adam Limentani (1913–1994), a Roman Jew who, after graduating from medical school in Rome, emigrated to London, where he trained as a psychoanalyst and even became president of the IPA (1981–1985). The plenary speakers at the Meeting were Geoffrey Cocks, Riccardo Steiner, Didier Anzieu (1923–1999), and León Grinberg (1921–2007). And here are some of the authors of the short papers in English: Otto Kernberg, Paul Roazen (1936–2005), and Edith Kurzweil (1925–2016). André Haynal gave his short paper in French, and Ernst Federn (1914–2007) his in German. Another paper was given by Enzo Morpurgo (1920–2002), the only Italian analyst (besides Anna Maria Accerboni); he was there with his wife Valeria Egidi, and we easily became friends. They were also good friends of Riccardo Steiner, whom they introduced me to.

But the three people whom I got closer to were Ernst Federn, Edith Kurzweil, and Paul Roazen. I remember speaking with them about their books *Witnessing psychoanalysis* (1990), *The Freudians. A comparative perspective* (1989), and *Encountering Freud. The politics and the histories of psychoanalysis* (Roazen, 1990), which I reviewed for *Psicoterapia e Scienze Umane* (Conci, 1990c, 1992b). As far as Paul Roazen (a brilliant historian of psychoanalysis, although he did not know German) is concerned, I had of course read all his major books (*Brother animal: The story of Freud and Tausk, Freud and his followers*, and his two books on Erik Erikson and Helene Deutsch), and I later promoted the publication of and wrote an introduction to both *Meeting Freud's family* (1993; see Conci, 1997) and *How Freud worked. First-hand accounts of patients* (1995; see Conci, 1998b). (As Roazen's books are well known in the field of the history of psychoanalysis, I will not list them all in the References.) Together with my Italian friends Michele Ranchetti, Carlo Bonomi, and Marco Bacciagaluppi—who also became Roazen's own friends—we were able in 1975 to have the Turin publisher Einaudi eventually publish in Italian his most well-known book, *Freud and his followers* (1998).

Even more important was my first meeting with Andrea Sabbadini and his wife Laura Forti (before going to London, she had edited an anthology on alternative British psychiatry [Forti, 1975], and he an anthology of papers on time in psychoanalysis [Sabbadini, 1979]), who gradually became very good friends, and we often spent time with them in the Dolomites—hiking in the summer and skiing in the winter. When Andrea in 1998 became the editor-in-chief of *Psychoanalysis and History*, he invited me to join the editorial board, and I participated in various of his successful European Film Festivals (in 2009 also with my daughter Anna, about to turn nineteen).

But back to the IAHP. It should be noted that, after London in 1990, I participated in most of its meetings (Berlin, 1994; Paris, 1996; London, 1998; Versailles, 2000; Barcelona, 2002), enjoying both the high level of competence and commitment of its participants and the very good personal and scientific contacts and encounters that took place. For all this I am still very thankful to Alain de Mijolla—and to his collaborators, for example Michelle Moreau-Ricaud and Nicolas Gougoulis.

But in 1990 I participated in three more scientific events that had important consequences for the rest of my professional life. These took place in Heidelberg, Stockbridge (Massachusetts) and Lavarone (Trento). On March 23 and 24, I was in Heidelberg with Marco Bacciagaluppi (whom I had first met in Bologna, in January) for the congress organized by Rainer Funk (Tübingen) to celebrate the tenth anniversary of Erich Fromm's death, at which Michael Maccoby gave a paper on his complex relationship with Fromm (which the historian Lawrence Friedman talks about in detail in his 2014 biography of Fromm). A psychiatrist and a psychoanalyst trained in Milan and New York City, Marco Bacciagaluppi at the time represented for me the major source of information on a whole series of authors whose work we did not encounter at the SPP—not only Fromm, but also Fairbairn, Guntrip, Ferenczi, and Bowlby. Marco had also trained with Galli, Benedetti, and Cremerius in the 1960s, but was not a member of the group that had founded the SPP, as he had instead gone his own way, joining the American Academy of Psychoanalysis—as Paolo Migone had done in the 1980s. In the 1960s and 1970s, Marco and his wife (Maria Mazza Bacciagaluppi) had spent much of their free time translating into Italian a series of books by Silvano Arieti (1914–1981), after he had trained with him in the 1960s—belonging to the same class of candidates as Arieti's nephew Jules Bemporad (1937–2011). In 1994 both Bacciagaluppi and Bemporad supported my admission to the American Academy of Psychoanalysis as a Psychiatric Associate. Having had an English mother, Marco had on the shelves of his office (close to Milan Central Station) more English-language than Italian books, and he let me borrow these. He has also published many more papers in English than in

Italian and, being very generous, has spent much time correcting and giving me feedback on many of the papers I have written in English.

On the afternoon of April 13, 1996, in Florence— after Stephen Mitchell had given an important paper on the therapeutic action of psychoanalysis—I participated with Marco in the meeting at which a new network of Italian psychotherapeutic institutes was founded, the Organizzazione Psicoanalisti Italiani, Federazione e Registro (OPIFR), of which he became the first president. Starting with the fall of 1999 in Venice, OPIFER has regularly organized in Italy a whole series of joint meetings with the American Academy. Among the numerous contacts that I owe to Marco, that with Mauricio Cortina (Washington DC) is the first that comes to mind—in the early 1990s, when he was still director of the Washington School of Psychiatry, he invited me to give a paper there on my work on Sullivan. Our many years of close contact and collaboration have also resulted in an interview I conducted with Marco (via email, directly in English) in the summer of 2005 (see Conci and Bacciagaluppi, 2006) and in him asking me to write the foreword of his 2012 book *Paradigms in psychoanalysis. An integration.*

In June 1990 I was with Pier Francesco Galli, Paolo Migone, and Maria Luisa Mantovani in Stockbridge at the Rapaport–Klein Study Group, where Pier Francesco Galli gave the paper "Psychoanalysis as the story of a crisis" (Galli, 1990) on Sunday June 10, after the business meeting. On the Saturday there had been three papers, by Sidney Blatt, Donald Spence, and Rosemarie Sand, respectively. David Rapaport's (1911–1960) work had been so important for Galli's professional evolution that he himself promoted the Italian edition of Rapaport's *Collected papers*, edited in 1967 by Merton Gill (1914– 1994)—and this made the invitation Galli received to present a paper there a central event of his professional life. This important contact allowed the group from *Psicoterapia e Scienze Umane* to create a regular connection with the Rapaport–Klein Study group, starting with a first international meeting held at the end of June 1991 in Bologna, at which the Bologna group hosted— among others—Merton Gill, Robert Holt, Morris Eagle, and Frank Sulloway.

I was also there, and I had the chance to talk about my book on Sullivan with Merton Gill, given that, in his 1982 book *Analysis of transference. Theory and technique,* he had eventually given much credit to Sullivan for his concept of the analyst as a participant observer. I was also able to talk about Freud's letters to Silberstein with Robert Holt—whose paper on the unconscious background of Freud's professional choice I had translated for the meeting and for the journal itself. Incidentally, its first English version came out in the *Psychoanalytic Review* only in 2013. I am mentioning the contact with the Rapaport–Klein Study Group because it also represented one of the topics that Arthur Lynch and I discussed when we talked for the second time about the table of contents of this book (New York City, May 2016). In the meantime, Robert Holt has been able to conclude the huge and very challenging project of editing and publishing the letters he exchanged with Rapaport between 1948 and 1960 (Holt, ed., 2017).

On July 7, 1990, the first of an annual series of meetings on Freud and psychoanalysis that the SPI organized together with the Province of Trento took place in Lavarone (see the above-reported letter of Freud to Fliess), Anna Maria Accerboni having invited me to collaborate in organizing it. In my paper on "Freud in Trentino-Alto Adige" (Conci, 1991), I not only talked about Freud's three vacations in Lavarone (1906, when he wrote his Gradiva book; 1907; and 1923, when he was there with Anna, before going with her to Rome for the last time), but—following Jones' biography—I also made a detailed list of all Freud's trips and vacations in our region, that is, the Italian (then Austrian-Hungarian) region in which he did most of his traveling. As an aside, when Bob Holt visited me in Trento in the spring of 1992, he wanted me to take him and his wife not only to Lavarone, but also to San Cristoforo, the spot on Lake Caldonazzo where the Secret Committee had gathered in August 1923 to discuss Freud's cancer of the jaw, before visiting him in Lavarone.

Not being a member of the SPI, I had no more invitations to join the scientific committee of the Lavarone Meetings over the following years. As Francesco Marchioro (Bolzano) had also been excluded from this initiative, we started organizing a series of international meetings in Bolzano and Collalbo/Klobenstein. We held them in this alpine village half an hour north of Bolzano at the same hotel where, in September 1911, Freud had celebrated his silver wedding anniversary with his whole family—and where, in the summer of 1922, Ferenczi and Rank had worked on their joint book on psychoanalytic technique (Ferenczi and Rank, 1927). I will return to this important collaboration below.

One of the major turning points of my professional life took place the following summer, at the VIth Scientific Conference of the IFPS organized in Stockholm on August 14–17, 1991 by the Swedish Society for Holistic Psychotherapy and Psychoanalysis; this was chaired by Jan Stensson and was on the topic "Male and female themes in psychoanalysis." Strangely enough, I had been informed about the conference not by my Milan teachers and supervisors, but by the SPP's secretary, Annamaria Pozzoli, who had rightly thought that such an international congress would greatly interest me. The conference took place at the Grand Hotel, where I also stayed, and the weather was gorgeous—typical August Stockholm weather. And it was in Stockholm that I first met another group of colleagues who kept accompanying me in the following years and with whom I am still working closely: Carlo Bonomi (Florence), Henri Zvi Lothane, and Valerie Tate Angel (the latter two from New York City).

Looking at the program, I soon discovered that there was a Candidates Award, offered by Tess Forrest, the widow of the White analyst Joseph Barnett (1926–1988). Having recently been the editor of the Italian edition of Freud's letters to Eduard Silberstein (see above), I decided to work on a paper with the title "Male and female themes in the young S. Freud's letters to E. Silberstein"—whose title on publication became "The young Freud's letters to Eduard Silberstein—Early traces of some psychoanalytic concepts," the first paper of this anthology. The paper not only won the Award, but also ended up being published in the very first issue of the *International Forum of Psychoanalysis*, published in 1992 (Conci, 1992a). Jan Stensson was editor-in-chief, with Arne Jemstedt, Christer Sjödin, and Ulla-Brit Parment as his major collaborators, and Mona Serenius as the managing editor of Scandinavian Universities Press. I will later describe how this very important step ended up changing my whole professional life.

But before dealing with how my work for the IFPS's journal became more important than my work at the university, let me tell you more about the latter. On September 11, 1991 I began working as an assistant professor of psychiatry at the Medical School of Brescia, collaborating directly with the full professor, Augusto Ermentini (1927–2014). I had overcome the competition to fill this post that had taken place the year before on the basis of both the quality and number of my publications and the result of an oral exam.

What I liked about Ermentini—whom I had originally met when he was one of my professors at the Psychotherapy School of Cremona, mentioned earlier in this chapter—was his eclectic orientation. On the one hand, Ermentini was one of the first collaborators of the first Italian neuropsychiatrist to become a full professor of psychiatry in an Italian university, Carlo Lorenzo Cazzullo (1915–2010); on the other hand, he had also worked with the very good director of a state mental hospital in Reggio Emilia, Virginio Porta (1904–1984). In addition, he had always been interested in not only clinical psychology, with particular regard to the Rorschach test, but also forensic and intercultural psychiatry. He had also taught at the above-mentioned University of Trento in the 1960s. And last but not least, he had spent a couple of years in Geneva studying with Julián de Ajuriaguerra (1911–1993), where he had also come in contact with psychoanalysis, with particular regard to Raymond de Saussure (1894–1971), the son of the linguist Ferdinand de Saussure, an analysand of Freud's, and one of the founders of the European Psychoanalytic Federation. Given such a background, you can understand how much I liked talking and collaborating with him. During the time he had taught at the University of Trento, he had also collaborated with the Trento neuropsychiatrist Beppino Disertori (1907–1992), who had such good international connections as to be able to promote the Italian edition of Henri Ellenberger's (1905–1993) *magnum opus, The discovery of the unconscious* (1970) (see Conci, 1995b).

Augusto Ermentini and I agreed that I would conduct analytically oriented clinical discussion groups with the psychiatric residents, whose training was one of our main tasks, and make them familiar with how psychoanalysis could help them deal with patients, both diagnostically and therapeutically. As far as my research work was concerned, Augusto Ermentini valued my interest in the history of psychiatry and psychoanalysis, and was happy that I would introduce such a point of view into the residency program he chaired. Out of this came also a research project on the history of psychiatry in Brescia. Although I worked in Brescia only part time, that is, only two full days a week, I also did some supervisory work with the nursing team that cared for a group of chronic psychotic patients.

I enjoyed working in Brescia until Professor Ermentini started increasingly to hand over to his successor, Emilio Sacchetti (born 1946), a colleague whose interests were more confined to the psychopharmacological aspects of psychiatry and with whom I found it really hard to collaborate. In fact, his generation of university psychiatrists tended to lose the overall perspective typical of Augusto Ermentini's generation and ended up specializing in subspecialties of psychiatry, such as epidemiological psychiatry, social psychiatry. psychopharmacological psychiatry, etc.; this also meant that psychiatry began to lose the fascination it had had for me, as an intellectual challenge in connection with its interdisciplinary status—which was now about to be lost. This is why in November 1997 I went to Munich as a guest professor at the Department of Psychosomatic Medicine and Psychotherapy, chaired by Michael Ermann, to take a rest and look around for an alternative to my position in Brescia. Since I did not find any, in April 2000 I gave up my position of assistant professor of psychiatry, a very rare event indeed in the Italian university system; this was also brought about by the fact that, since April 1999, I had become a psychoanalyst working inside the German *Kassensystem*, or health insurance system.

A further happy memory is of the whole series of international scientific conferences I organized together with Francesco Marchioro in Bolzano and Collalbo/ Klobenstein. The first took place in Bolzano at the end of November 1993, and we were able to invite a very good international group of psychoanalysts and historians to discuss Freud's "Totem and taboo," seventy years after its original publication. Here is the list of our invited speakers, based on the order of their papers: Leonardo Ancona, Michele Ranchetti, Berthold Rothschild, Aldo Carotenuto (1933–2005), Mechthild Zeul (Madrid), David Meghnagi (Rome), Karl Stockreiter (Vienna), and Conrad Stein (1924–2010). We were also able to collect the papers into a volume that we edited together (Conci and Marchioro, 1995). The second of our conferences, held in Bolzano in November 1995, on the 100th anniversary of Freud's "Irma dream," presented papers by Maria Bacchetta (Buenos Aires), Carlo Bonomi, Aldo Carotenuto, Ernst Falzeder (Salzburg), Giampaolo Lai and Mauro Mancia (1929–2007), the philosopher Pier Aldo Rovatti (Trieste), Karl Stockreiter, Silvia Vegetti Finzi (Pavia), and Hans-Jörg Walter (Innsbruck). Two years later, at the end of November 1997, the third conference took place, "Il divano, l'immaginario e la cura—Freud-Goethe—Der Divan, das Imaginäre und die Behandlung" [The couch, the imaginary and the treatment—Freud and Goethe], to which we were able to invite some of the previous speakers as well as Enzo Morpurgo and Valeria Egidi, Elisabeth

Schlebrügge (Vienna), Henry Zvi Lothane, philosopher Mario Perniola (1941–2018), Wolfgang Schmidbauer (Munich), Susan Herrera (Buenos Aires), writer Stefano Zecchi (Milan), and Günther Zeillinger (Innsbruck).

Starting in 1996, we also organized every two years a Freudian Week in Collalbo/Klobenstien during the third week of September, centered around a weekend workshop with famous Italian and German analysts (1996: Carotenuto and Schmidbauer; 1998: Pagliarani and Schmidbauer). I remember participating in the workshop run by Gino Pagliarani (1922–2001) and also writing a paper about his work, taking the workshop as a starting point (Conci, 2008a). Wolfgang Schmidbauer, a German pioneer of the large topic of the so-called *Helfersyndrom* (Schmidabuer, 1977), and his wife Gudrun Brockhaus, are still very good friends, whom we regularly see in Munich. The high quality and success of all these initiatives had to do with the positive climate that we were able to create, both among the speakers and between them and the audience, a climate of reciprocal listening and serious and honest exchange.

This was also the style of the already-mentioned psychoanalyst Elvio Fachinelli, a native of Luserna (near Lavarone), who studied medicine in Pavia and trained in Milan with Cesare Musatti (1897–1979), and whose original contributions to contemporary psychoanalysis Francesco Marchioro and I tried to assess through the publication of an anthology we dedicated to him in 1998 (Conci and Marchioro, 1998). Fachinelli's proposals for a less hierarchical and more socially committed psychoanalysis have recently also been rediscovered by the historian Dagmar Herzog (2016).

Let me now go back to my participation in the life of the IFPS, the result of which was my involvement in the production of its journal. At the end of August 1992, I was in Munich, where Michael Ermann had organized a further international conference under the title "Psychoanalysis between conformity and opposition," inaugurated on Wednesday August 26 at the famous *Neue Pinakothek*. Born in 1943, Michael Ermann was a *Kriegskind*, a "child of the war," as he himself discovered many years later, when it became possible for German people to look into the problem of how much they themselves had suffered under the Nazi regime and during World War II. In fact, this is one of the many topics we dealt with in the interview that we finished working on in February 2017 for publication in the *International Forum* (Conci and Ermann, in press).

After having graduated from medical school in Freiburg, he did his analytic training in Stuttgart with Friedrich Beese (1921–2012), and at the same time carried out clinical and conceptual research in psychosomatic medicine, the field of his *Habilitationsarbeit*. In 1985, he moved to Munich and started working at the Ludwig-Maximilans-Universität, as the chair of the Center for Psychosomatic Medicine and Psychotherapy of the *Psychiatrische Klinik* originally inaugurated by Emil Kraepelin (1856–1926) in 1907; and in 1987 he was elected as president of the German Psychoanalytic Society (DPG). One of the reasons why I have progressively felt closer and closer to him has been the way in which he was able to carry out the very sophisticated plan of, on the one hand helping the DPG to elaborate its Nazi past and move in the direction of the IPA, and, on the other, continuing to collaborate with the IFPS—of whose executive council he was a member from the early 1980s until 2016.

Of course, I did not know all these things back in 1992, but I rapidly realized that I had a good feeling about him and his work. Not to mention the fact that on Thursday evening August 27, there was a bus excursion to Lake Starnberg, with a boat tour and a buffet—and you already know what a magical attraction Lake Starnberg had exercised upon me as a teenager. The conference was very well organized, with papers and contributions by Friedrich Beese (Stuttgart), Maria Lindqvist (Helsinki), Hannes Friedrich (Göttingen), Jochen Kemper (Rio de Janeiro), János Harmatta, Bien Filet (Amsterdam), Arne Jemstedt, Caroline and Alan Grey (New York), Horst Petri and Jürgen Körner (Berlin), Rainer Danzinger (Salzburg) and Raoul Schindler (Vienna), and Carola Mann and Jörg Bose (New York). Several groups discussing the main papers had also been organized—a good way for people to get to know each other. Last but not least, during a visit to the above-mentioned *Psychiatrische Klinik* I met the Italian psychiatrist Gianni Minelli, who was to become one of my best friends after I moved to Munich in 1997.

Two years later, in May 1994, the IFPS met in Florence for the IXth Forum, organized by the local Istituto di Psicoterapia Analitica, with the title "Psychoanalysis at the threshold of the XXIst century." The plenary speakers were Michele Ranchetti, Jay Greenberg (New York), Maria Lindqvist, Ciro Elia, Gion Condrau (Zurich), Frank Lachmann (New York), Daniel Stern (Geneva), Ulla-Britt Parment, Carlo Bonomi, Valerie Tate Angel, Michael Ermann, Christopher Bollas, and Jan Stensson. In Florence I gave a paper with the title "Psychoanalysis in Italy: A reappraisal" (Conci, 1994), in which I dealt for the first time with the life and work of Gaetano Benedetti. But even more important was the fact that Jan Stensson asked me to collaborate with the new journal, in the role of assistant editor, which I was very happy about. What united us at the time—besides a feeling of reciprocal esteem—was our peripheral position, Jan as a Swede and I as an Italian, in the context of international psychoanalysis, and our readiness to produce an international journal in English in order to overcome this and move towards the center of mainstream psychoanalysis. This is how my name has been associated with the journal since Volume 3 (1994), Issue 2, in which my Florence paper also came out.

Even more important was the IFPS's VIIIth Scientific Conference, organized by Maarit Arppo (Helsinki) in Athens in May 1996, under the title "Myth lives within us." Together with Maarit (a very open and generous colleague), I chaired a history of psychoanalysis panel, in which I gave the paper on Freud's self-analysis (Conci, 1998a) republished in this book as Chapter 3, and in which Henry Zvi Lothane, Carlo Bonomi, and Antero Kiianmaa (Finland) presented a paper. At this time, Carlo Bonomi was also working with Patrick Mahony and Jan Stensson as editor of the book *Behind the scenes. Freud in correspondence*, in which they also published my paper "Why did Freud choose medical school?" (Conci, 1996b), reproduced here as Chapter 2. Indeed, our journal's editorial board worked very hard at the time to create as many valid international connections as possible. For example, at the beginning of 1996 we had organized a weekend workshop with Stephen Mitchell, his wife Margaret Black, and Emmanuel Ghent (1925–2003) in New York City, with the aim of developing the best possible climate of collaboration among us all (Conci, 1996a).

As far as my personal life is concerned, a dramatic, exciting, and crucial change occurred in Athens: I met a colleague from Vienna with whom I fell in love—probably also as an attempt to try to find a new direction in which to move in my life. My relationship with Claudia had gradually dried up and the only level that functioned well enough was our parental relationship toward Anna. Although I had a whole series of patients in Trento with whom I was happy to work, it was impossible to develop professionally because of the lack of an analytic community to work with. In Brescia, Ermentini was about to retire and Sacchetti to become his successor, which meant that my university career there was about to end too. The

Milan ASP, of which I had just become a member, was for me not attractive enough to leave Trento and move to Milan, and at the same time, I felt too old (I was then forty-one years old) to move somewhere else in Italy, so that I could, for example, start a new training with the SPI. So the best way out seemed to be to fall in love with a Viennese colleague, with whom I had many interests in common, for example the history of psychoanalysis—and whom of course I also valued very much, both as a person and as the mother of a young boy.

But, as you can imagine, as falling in love is actually not a good way out of one's problems, I eventually started a second analysis. From December 1996 to September 1998 I lay three times a week on the couch of Dr. N., in Verona. The sessions took place on Mondays at 7.30 am, and on Tuesdays at 7.30 am and at 4.40 pm. On Mondays I got up in Trento at 5.30 am, took the train to Verona at 6.15, arrived there around 7.15, and then took a bus to his office. After the session, I took the train back to Trento, and at 10 am I was then able to start working with my patients. After the Tuesday morning sessions I went on to Brescia, to work at the University, and returned to Verona for the week's third session. I worked in Brescia until the end of October 1997, and then, from November 1997, when I started going to Munich, I went to Verona on Tuesdays by train twice in the same day. In the meantime, I had also left the apartment in which I lived with Claudia and Anna, and had found a large apartment in the old center of Trento—Via Belenzani 41—to which I moved in November 1996, a very good location where I could both live and work.

I assumed that Dr. N. would also be able to help me because of his own life story: he had come to Italy from Argentina, where he had been born as the child of Italian parents, had done his studies and had undergone his analytic training, reaching the point of becoming a training analyst of the Argentinian Psychoanalytic Association, and he now worked in Verona. In other words, he was familiar enough with both separation and migration, exactly the problems I was struggling with at the time. And so it was! Through Dr. N.'s help, I was able to both contact a lawyer to help me with the painful process of separation and divorce, and to apply to the University of Brescia for a research project that would allow me to spend two years as a guest professor at the University of Munich—at the above-mentioned center of my friend Michael Ermann. In the meantime, my Viennese colleague and I were trying to work on our own relationship, but of course it was not at all easy.

When I started writing all the pages I have written so far it was Monday August, 14, 2017, and I was then able to spend a part of my summer vacation, in Italy, writing every single day, until today, Tuesday September 5. My original idea was to write an "Introduction" to this anthology of my papers, which I had originally proposed to Arnold Richards during the 2016 Meeting of the American Psychoanalytic Association—on January 11, 2016. Being on vacation with me, my wife Doris read every single page I wrote, and we gradually came to the conclusion that what I was writing could not be thought of as an "Introduction" to the book; instead we ended up thinking of it in terms of an "Afterword." Any reader who, after reading my papers, wanted to know more about their author would have the chance to do so through this Afterword. This was our conclusion. What had motivated me to write an "Introduction" was the need I felt to explain to the reader, through an acquaintance with my personal and professional life, how all the book's papers belong together. But it got out of hand, or maybe I really immersed myself rather deeply into it. In fact, before moving to Munich—or better still, before starting going back and forth between Trento and Munich—psychoanalysis was "a way of life" for me, that is, my way of finding and developing myself. After the fall of 1997, however, it gradually also became only a profession.

Last but not least, the psychological dimension out of which emerged the pages I have written is a process of mourning. On July 23, 2017, my third analyst, Dr. L., suddenly died in Munich—relatively suddenly, since he had spent the last couple of years of his life struggling with cancer. Doris and I were in Buenos Aires for the 50th Congress of the IPA and could not get back in time for the funeral. By writing these pages, I have been able to keep talking with him, formulating some of the things we discovered together about my life. At the same time, I gradually had the feeling that it was a good thing to come out of this private dimension and try to revisit my life in terms of sharing it with a larger group of colleagues and readers.

This will now allow me to revisit in a much briefer way the almost twenty years that have elapsed, since the day—Wednesday November 5, 1997—when I got on the train to Munich to start working there as a guest professor. If I look at that first week of November 1997 in my diary, I see the first two and a half days were spent working in my office in Trento and going to Verona for the three above-mentioned sessions; then going by train to Munich on the Wednesday evening, and arriving there around 10.30 pm after about a five-hour train ride; meeting Michael Ermann and his team for the first time on the Thursday morning and holding the first meeting of my workshop on the history of psychoanalysis in the evening; and working on the preparation of my workshop and on my book on Sullivan on the Friday, while sitting in the *Psychiatrische Klinik* and starting to interact with the team.

At the end of May, I had been able to find a very pleasant apartment in one of the nicest streets of Munich, Königinstrasse, the street where the US Consulate is located, right in front of the Englischer Garten, where I soon started jogging in the morning—with a great sense of relief at this new kind of routine. I soon discovered that going back and forth every week by train between Trento and Munich was not so stressful, and that Munich really had the potential to allow me to make a "new start" in my life. Of course, this arrangement allowed me not only to finance my life, but also to regularly see Anna—at the time we spent Monday evenings learning to play tennis, with a tennis coach. The Schengen Agreements were also starting to change the world as we knew it: since that same November 1997 passports were no longer needed for travel from Italy to Austria and from Austria to Germany. And in January 2002 Italian Liras, Austrian Schillings, and German Marks were all replaced by the Euro!

During my first year as a guest professor in Munich, I worked as much as I could on my German, so that I could increasingly enjoy the workshop on the history of psychoanalysis that I was holding for the candidates of the Munich Akademie für Psychoanalyse und Psychoanalyse. In addition, I was working on two projects: finishing my book on Sullivan, and translating into Italian an important book on the history of psychiatry, Erwin Ackerknecht's (1916–1988) *Kurze Geschichte der Psychiatrie* (see Ackerknecht, 1959). History of medicine as a university discipline was born in Germany and, at variance with Italy, was taught in almost all medical schools. If I had been able to bring back to Italy a specific competence in this field, a new university position might have opened up for me, but this was not the case. I discovered that there were not in the whole country more than about fifteen people teaching history of medicine in our medical schools. What I was able to do was become a member of the Italian Society for the History of Medicine, after presenting my work on Ackerknecht at the yearly conference held in Florence in May 1999 (see my Introduction to the book: Conci, 1999). But after formally giving up my position as an assistant professor of psychiatry in Brescia in April 2000, and still being interested in teaching at a university level, I was able to propose to the University of Trento the creation of an introductory course to psychoanalysis in form of a chapter of the history of medicine—and so we called the course "History of medicine." I held this course in the winter semester for nine consecutive years, from October 2002 until March 2010, teaching about twenty students a year.

From February 1997 I had begun attending the yearly *Symposia zur Geschichte der Psychoanalyse* organized at the University of Tübingen by the historian of medicine Gerhard Fichtner (1932–2012), a famous Freud scholar and a world expert on Freud's letters— and on the problem of deciphering his handwriting. At this important meeting on the history of psychoanalysis, I was, for eleven consecutive years, to meet most of the German-speaking colleagues working in this field, until the 2007 symposium, at which I myself gave the paper "Gaetano Benedetti in seiner Korrespondenz" (see Conci, 2008b). Furthermore, since its inception, I had subscribed to the journal for the history of psychoanalysis *Luzifer-Amor*, founded by the Tübingen publisher Gerd Kimmerle in 1988, and currently edited by Ludger Hermanns and Michael Schröter (both Berlin); in this, I have published several papers, for example a review of the biography of Henry Loewenfeld (1900–1985) written by Thomas Müller (Conci, 2000b). By coming to Germany, I had realized my dream of becoming a member of this, for me, very interesting scientific community of German-speaking historians of psychoanalysis, a regular member of which was also the above-mentioned Ernst Federn, together with his wife Hilde. In Italy there was not at the time, and is currently still not, a comparable community, given the fact that my Italian colleagues are relatively far from the linguistic and cultural roots of psychoanalysis, and that Freud's discipline became popular in Italy only in the 1970s.

Coming to Munich meant for me of course also the possibility of continuing to work on myself analytically, after I had finished—or better, interrupted—my work with Dr. N. in Verona in September 1998, after more than 200 sessions working together. I was very thankful to him for the work done; it had helped me to take the initiative for both separation and divorce, and to try to open up a new phase of my life, one that I connected to the possibility of working in Munich for two years as a part-time guest professor. And in September 1998, when I decided to interrupt the analytic work with Dr. N., I was sure that I could make it and create a new life for myself in Munich. For example, in January 1998 I had started to attend as a *Gast*—a guest—the monthly meetings of the Münchner Arbeitsgruppe, the Munich Working Party, of the DPG. But, if I am to find my way in Munich—I thought—I had better have a good analyst to help me.

In addition, while my father was still alive (he died on February 8, 2003), our relationship never became good enough that I was able to feel supported by him—his priority was always his firm, and we had two different visions of the world. In addition, the relationship with my brothers, who since the late 1980s had worked with him in the family firm, was not easy. From this point of view, I kept struggling with the feeling of being a member of a family with which I could identify to only a limited extent, and this was still for me very troubling. Not to mention the help I needed to be able to maintain a good relationship with Anna. Last but not least, the longer I stayed in Munich, the more I realized that it was not at all easy for me, as a foreigner, to feel really at home there. That this would be the definitive direction I would take became clear only at the beginning of December 1998, when—after having put together a whole series of documents concerning my medical, psychiatric, and psychoanalytic training—I was able to pass the exam through which I became a so-called *Kassenpsychoanalytiker*, a psychoanalyst whose treatments are covered by the German insurance system and not directly by patients themselves. This system is unique and allows a wider variety of people than anywhere else in the world to become analytic patients. My admission to practice as an analyst inside the so-called *kassenärtzliches System* was also connected to the fact that there was a great shortage of analysts capable of working in their mother tongue with the many Italian patients living in Munich.

This is why, before leaving Munich for the 1998 Christmas vacation, I had had my first meeting with Dr. L.; he was a North American colleague who had gone to London after his university studies in the USA in order to train at the Tavistock Clinic, where he had worked in a particularly intensive way with Donald Meltzer (1922–2004). Being a foreigner, and being neither a medical doctor nor a psychologist, he had not become a training analyst of the institute of which he was a member, the Munich

Akademie für Psychoanalyse und Psychotherapie, but he had as supervisees many of the institute's colleagues, who often turned to him also for a second or a third analysis. He had spent many years introducing a series of colleagues within and outside Munich to the work and legacy of Wilfred Bion, and was also an expert in the methodology of baby observation, in which he trained various groups of postgraduate colleagues. But particularly important for me was not only his originality and independence of mind, but even more the facts that he came from the New York area and that he had successfully found his way in Germany—where he had come after he had married a German artist.

As you can imagine, one important topic of our work was what combination of *Schicksal* and *Zufall*—necessity and chance—had brought me to Munich. I told him about my summers at the Starnbergersee and about the time I had spent in the New York City area as an exchange student. And I also told him about the family problems I still struggled with and about the complex development of my analytic identity. Through our work, I was able eventually to complete and bring to fruition all the work done in the first two analyses, and thus on the one hand become a more relaxed, mature, and happy person, while on the other hand developing the still missing part of my analytic identity.

As far as my personal life is concerned, I met Doris in July 2004 and we have had a very good relationship ever since, to the point that in July 2016 we eventually got married, in Salzburg—her native town, where she still lives and works as a medical doctor. From a professional point of view, in 2002 I became a member of the DPG, and in 2010 a member of the IPA—becoming also a member of the SPI in 2012. Such a development was of course also made possible by the lucky combination of events that I will describe below, but it mainly depended on the level of personal and professional maturation that I had been able to realize by working with Dr. L. The relationship we gradually created became my home, and I eventually ended up feeling at home with myself, with the consequence that I was much more able to help my own patients feel at home with themselves, and that, last but not least, I could myself feel everywhere at home—including in Germany, which I have not found such an easy country to live in. As I must already have written above, this was also the content of the paper I gave in May 2016 in Stuttgart, that is, "The analytic relationship as a home" (Conci, 2016c)

But here one more word is necessary. The way in which Dr. L. took care of me made me really feel at home, since he was able to share with me so many dimensions of my life and work. He was not only my analyst, but also my supervisor; and not only analyst and supervisor, but also advisor on a whole series of scientific projects. This was of course a very gradual development, but this is how far we came. In fact, after seeing each other for years twice a week, face to face, we came down to once a week, and then—in the last couple of years of his struggle with cancer—to two times a month. I saw him for the last time on Wednesday July 12, 2017 (the tenth session of the year, and our 674th session altogether), a session in which I presented to and discussed with him the paper I had written for Buenos Aires (Conci, 2017). In other words, I not only believe that we should undergo a personal analysis every five years (as Freud himself wrote), but that we should do this more often. If we spend thirty hours or more every week working with our patients, we should have the chance to spend one hour a week talking about ourselves and/or our work with a competent colleague. This is the model which I developed with Dr. L. in the more than eighteen years of our work together; this was our "analytic atelier," to use a word introduced into our field by Meltzer (1994). Last but not least, as a group analyst he himself had worked in many German institutions helping them to make sense of their work and try to plan their future. He wrote an article about this experience that he was able to publish in German, and that I, as co-editor-in-chief of the *International Forum*, asked him to translate into English for our journal, hoping to be able to publish it the third monographic issue on "German themes in psychoanalysis." This was one of his last professional projects (Lazar, in press).

It was not at all easy to find patients in Trento who were ready to work analytically three or four times a week. As the reader knows, psychoanalysis is a product of the Enlightenment, but its development was possible only in a series of advanced European capitals (like Vienna and Budapest, Berlin and London), and at a time in medical history when the chapter of anatomically based diseases had been closed, and Freud could become a pioneer in the exploration of the new category of the "functional diseases." For psychoanalysis to prosper, specific cultural, financial, and historical premises had to be satisfied, which was never the case for the people living in Trentino-Alto Adige. On the other hand, I succeeded often enough in helping the patients who consulted me in Trento between 1988 and 2000 to understand the way of working of analytic psychotherapy that I was able to motivate several of them to work with me three times a week on the couch. When I started working in Munich as a *kassenärtzlicher Psychoanalytiker* in April 1999, I was very happy finally to have the chance to work with more patients three times and with some patients four times a week.

In addition to this I had—through the Munich DPG Working Party, since the beginning of 1998—been able to see how my Munich colleagues worked, share with them a discussion of the papers presented by various speakers at our monthly meetings, and feel supported in my goal of further developing my professional identity as a psychoanalyst. The same is true for the colleagues with whom—since the spring of 1999—I have shared my Munich office (Heidi Spanl, Utz Palussek-Spanl, and Tobias von Geiso), and for the two colleagues (Giulietta Tibone and Giulia Oliveri) with whom we later created our own Italian *Intervisionsgruppe*—the German word for "peer supervision group." At the time, in order to become members of the DPG, guests had to attend the monthly meetings of the group for two years, and then present to and discuss with the group an analytic treatment conducted at a frequency of three times a week. On the basis of the above-mentioned "atelier concept," Dr. L. was ready to spend a part of our sessions supervising my work with Donato, a young Italian university student who was suffering from a chronic depressive syndrome caused by a severe narcissistic personality disorder. As an aside, the possibility of combining analysis and supervision had originally been introduced by Sándor Ferenczi and the Budapest School, and it is a pity that we have lost sight of it—as Howard Bacal (2016) has recently claimed.

Donato was the youngest child of parents in their forties who had loved him, but whose older age and whose psychological limitations had not allowed them to educate him properly, so that he had developed what we can call a "false self syndrome." He was also the first member of his family who had come so far as to study at university, and he had chosen to do this in Munich. In fact, Germany at the time offered a series of advantages (not only in terms of better housing) to university students, and a practically oriented young man like Donato had heard about these (including the possibility of undertaking psychotherapy covered by his student insurance) and had decided to emigrate. Since he had not had the chance to trust his parents to be able to see him as a child to be educated and to guide him in life, it took him several years not only to trust me, but also to develop a good contact with himself. For his simple-minded parents, to love him had meant to give him enough (or more than enough) to eat, which had made of him a rather fat boy, whom his school friends teased, making it even harder for him to love himself enough. In the treatment with me, Donato had the chance not only to better understand what had happened to him in his relationship with his parents and his immediate social environment, but also to get in touch with and express all the anger and negative feelings that had developed inside him. How often did he—especially in the first phase of treatment—hit the wall of my office with his fist while lying on my couch! If he allowed me to help him, giving up his illusion of self-sufficiency, would I have be able to do it? And would he be able to tolerate it?

After several years of work, Donato was eventually able to decide to do this, to for example discuss all aspects of his life with me, before and not after having taken his own decisions. Such a turning point could not have been brought about without working three times a week on the couch with him—in fact, for several months we met four times a week. Instead of feeling a victim or, on the other hand, excluding others from his life, he was now able to both take up his responsibilities and constructively interact with me—and with his friends and colleagues at work. Donato finished his university studies in Munich (for further details, see Conci, 2010c) and has been working as a successful sports journalist for many years—at least once a year he comes to my office for a session, in which we both revisit and renew our relationship.

But let me now go back to my membership paper for the DPG. After presenting to and discussing with the Munich DPG Working Party, in the spring of 2002, the first two years of Donato's treatment, I was accepted as a member of the group. In May 2002 in Berlin, at the yearly national congress of the DPG, the decision was ratified by the executive committee and by the general assembly of the DPG and I became its first Italian full member. An important role in this important professional event was played by Gaetano Benedetti having been my group and individual supervisor in Milan, where he had been since the 1970s a training analyst and since the 1980s an honorary member of the DPG. In fact, his very first contact with the DPG went back to the late 1950s, with his visits and papers given to the DPG that had helped it come out of its international isolation (see below and Conci, 2008a). Also for this reason, as I turned sixty years old, I proposed to the then president of the DPG, Ingo Focke, the creation of a yearly Benedetti Candidates Award, personally financing it with 1,000 Euros. The DPG's executive committee accepted my proposal, and the Award was given for the first time in May 2016, at the yearly congress of the DPG held in Stuttgart.

But let me now go back to my involvement in and work for the already-mentioned *International Forum of Psychoanalysis*. After having been invited by the founding editor, Jan Stensson, to join the editorial board in May 1994 (see above), my involvement in the journal kept growing steadily over the following years—I have described this in a paper I gave at the XVIIIth IFPS Forum held in Kaunas (Lithuania) in September 2014 (Conci, 2016a). When Jan Stensson left the board in August 2004 at the XIIIth Forum held in Belo Horizonte (Brazil), he had not only been able to create a very good work methodology and climate among us, but had also had the chance to celebrate with us the journal becoming—through the help of David Tuckett—part of the PEP-Disk. Over the following years, this contributed greatly to making of our journal not just the journal of the IFPS, but increasingly an internationally well-known psychoanalytic journal, to whose editorial board belong not only Christopher Bollas and Henry Zvi Lothane, but also André Haynal, Franco Borgogno, and Michael Buchholz (Göttingen). As far as our work methodology is concerned, this was shaped by Jan Stensson's extraordinary capacity to listen and to create a dialogical dimension with all of us, which usually made of our editorial meetings not just the instrument through which we selected the papers we received, but a way for all of us to professionally and personally grow and expand our horizons.

On the other hand, I do not believe that I could have become the co-editor-in-chief of the journal, back in 2007, if I had not in the meantime become a member of the DPG, that is, if I had not been able to place myself in the middle between Northern and Southern Europe—in line with the above-described cultural dimension of my native town. As a high school student, I had read enough of Karl Marx to remember how crucial it is to conquer Germany if the revolution is to win in the rest of the world as well. At the same time, I am very lucky to have had, since the fall of 2014, Grigoris Maniadakis at my side as a co-editor-in-chief; we share the same passion and the same diligence, and spend at least one hour a day working for the journal and writing to each other, all year round.

Furthermore, having regularly participated since 2007 in the yearly meetings of the International Council of Editors of Psychoanalytic Journals (ICEPJ), held in New York City during the yearly congresses of the American Psychoanalytic Association, I have since January 2017 been Werner Bohleber's (Frankfurt) successor as European co-chair of the ICEPJ, currently chaired by Ahron Friedberg. In fact, I so much enjoy working in this field that since 2013 I have been regularly receiving papers to evaluate from the *International Journal of Psychoanalysis*. I have also been a member of the editorial board of *Contemporary Psychoanalysis* since 2006, and of the Italian *Rivista di Psicoanalisi* since 2013. In the meantime, thanks to the very good organizational support of our publisher, Taylor and Francis, the yearly downloads of the papers we publish have kept increasing, being almost 15,000 in the year 2016.

Of course, my own increasing contacts with the IPA, SPI, and American Psychoanalytic Association also contributed to making of our journal a relevant point of reference for international scientific exchange, dialogue, and debate. The first IPA congress I participated in was the Amsterdam Congress of July 1993, at which Theodore Jacobs gave the innovative paper on countertransference that provoked such a negative reaction from André Green (1927–2012) and that was reevoked last July 2017 in Buenos Aires, when Jacobs inaugurated the congress with his plenary talk. Jacqueline Amati Mehler was at the time the IPA secretary and signed my participation form. Claudia and I ended up being in the same hotel as Amati Mehler's new group, the Italian Psychoanalytic Association, which had just split from the SPI, and to which my Florence professor of psychiatry, Adolfo Pazzagli, also belonged. One of my best memories of that congress concerns the Argentinian colleague Jorge Ahumada, who took time off to talk with me and introduce me to the IPA family, after having realized that I was probably there for the first time. He was a close collaborator of Horacio Etchegoyen (1919–2016), who in Amsterdam became the successor of Joseph Sandler (1927–1998). But my friend Henry Zvi Lothane was also there, giving a paper on his work on the Schreber Case (Lothane, 1992), and we were able to plan to go to Cerisy-la-Salle (in Normandy, close to the Abbey of Mont St. Michel) a couple of weeks later for a weekly workshop on the topic of his book—in which Jacques Schotte and Jim Grotstein (1925–2015) also participated. Such a unique experience!

Several years went by before I attended an IPA

Congress again, that one being in Nice in 2001. There I met Stefano Bolognini for the first time, and a series of Italian colleagues with whom I have kept in touch ever since (Paola Golinelli and Maria Vittoria Costantini from Padua; Anna Ferruta from Milan; Fausto Petrella from Pavia; and Franco Borgogno from Turin). The interview with Stefano Bolognini included in this anthology took place in the summer of 2005 (Conci and Bolognini, 2006). But Nice is also important in the history of the DPG as the first group of its members became IPA members there (Ingo Focke, Bernd Guttmann, and their wives, among others, for a total of about fifteen colleagues; see below). Starting with the Berlin IPA Congress of 2007, I have regularly attended them all, giving a paper at every one (Chicago, 2009; Mexico City, 2011; Prague, 2013; Boston, 2015; Buenos Aires, 2017). In Chicago and Mexico City I organized a panel on migration and psychoanalysis together with Hediaty Utari-Witt (Munich), with Ilany Kogan (Tel Aviv) and Andrea Sabbadini respectively as chairs; Ilany Kogan also chaired the presentation of my paper in Prague, in a panel on trauma at which also Maya Nadig (Bremen) gave a paper.

In Boston I had the good luck to be invited by Montana Katz (New York) to participate in a pre-congress workshop on the field concept that she had organized in Cambridge, out of which a good book was produced, *Advances in contemporary analytic field theory*, in which my contribution was included (see Conci, 2016d, and Chapter 9 of this book). But in Boston I was also involved in a panel I had organized with Henry Zvi Lothane and Sandra Buechler (New York) to revisit the work of Harry Stack Sullivan, at the moment in time when the IPA was eventually able to acknowledge the psychoanalytic nature of his point of view—and admit the White Institute as a member society. Last but not least, again with Sandra Buechler I organized a panel on field theory and intimacy in Buenos Aires in July 2017, with Stella Yardino (Montevideo) as chair. As I have already written at the beginning of this Afterword, I enjoy our international analytic congresses as they make me feel closer to my father and to the young boy who, out of love for his father, used to know by heart all the dates and places of the Winter Olympics (1948, St. Moritz; 1952, Oslo; 1956, Cortina; 1960 Squaw Valley; 1964, Innsbruck ...).

Of course, my familiarity with the SPI gradually increased through a series of congresses, starting with the one held in Trieste in June 2002, during which Anna Maria Accerboni and the family of Edoardo Weiss placed a commemorative stone on the wall of the house in which he had lived and practiced in the 1920s. At the following congress, held by the SPI in Siena in 2006, I remember meeting Luca Di Donna (San Francisco), and spending a whole evening with Giovanni Foresti and Giuseppe Civitarese (both Pavia) in the Piazza del Palio. IPA president Cláudio Eizirik (Porto Alegre, Brazil) was also there—Doris and I accompanied him to the Munich *Alte Pinakothek* in May 2008 as he was visiting Munich to participate in an IFPS conference organized by Michael Ermann. In 2008 Doris accompanied me to the SPI congress held in Rome, where we were hosted by our friend Barbara Piovano; and in 2010 we were together in Taormina (Catania), where the two main papers of the national congress were given by Fernando Riolo (Palermo) and Antonino Ferro (Pavia). In fact, Doris and I had hosted Antonino Ferro in Munich in October 2007, when we had been able to invite him to give a workshop at the Munich Akademie für Psychoanalyse und Psychotherapie—of which I had become a member in 2004. In 2011 we were able to do the same with Stefano Bolognini, then president of the SPI (2009–2013).

But let me now briefly come to my contacts with the American Psychoanalytic Association, in whose national meetings, held in mid-January at the New York Waldorf Hotel, I had started to participate in 2007, together with Christer Sjödin, in connection with the yearly meeting of the above-mentioned ICEPJ. This regular participation was made easier by the fact that Doris always accompanied me and with her I could share not only a series of friends (for example, Henry Zvi Lothane and Sandra Buechler, Valerie Tate Angel and Edith Gould, Eva Papiasvili and Linda Mayers), but also regular visits to the Tuesday Clinical Meetings at the White Institute, where Doris herself had the chance to get to know and love seeing Miltiades Zaphiropoulos (1914–2015). There I was able both to renew the relationship to the White community that I had been able to create back in 1988 (through Stephen Mitchell, and Earl Witenberg, 1917–2002), and also introduce both Antonino Ferro and Stefano Bolognini to the White colleagues through specific workshops I organized there in January 2010 and January 2011, with the help of Seth Aronson and Sandra Buechler.

Since 2015, together with Sandra Buechler, I have been holding a Discussion Group on "The initial interview. Comparing Freud, Sullivan and Ogden" at the Winter Meeting of the American Psychoanalytic Association; and since 2016 I have also chaired the

Discussion Group on "Freud as a Letter writer," which
I inherited from Henry Zvi Lothane, and through which
(together with Endre Koritar, Vancouver) I am presently
dealing with the correspondence between Freud and
Ferenczi. Last but not least, going at least once a year to
the USA also allowed me to eventually realize the English
translation of my book on Sullivan (with the first edition
in 2010, and the second in 2012), which was reviewed in
several journals (*Psychoanalytic Quarterly, Journal of the
American Psychoanalytic Association, American Journal
of Psychoanalysis, Contemporary Psychoanalysis,
Psychoanalytic Review*, and *History of Psychiatry*), the
most comprehensive and sympathetic reviews having
been written by Jane Tillman (2012) for the *Journal of
the American Psychoanalytic Association*, and Janet
Rivkin Zuckermann (2013) for the *American Journal of
Psychoanalysis*.

At this point, it is of course high time for me to tell
you how, in June 2010, I eventually became an IPA
member. I kept on, as you can imagine, enjoying working
with as many patients as possible three times a week on
the couch, and I also started working four times a week
with several patients. Such work became, for example,
necessary with a patient whom I called Penelope when
I eventually presented her treatment in Chicago in 2009
(see Conci, 2010c). But before telling you about her, let
me give you the institutional frame within which this
further development of my professional career became
possible. I have described it in the Editorials I wrote for
the two monographic issues of the *International Forum of
Psychoanalysis* I edited with the title "German themes in
psychoanalysis" (Conci, 2013, 2015a), and it is one of the
important topics that I dealt with in my interviews with
Horst Kächele (Conci, Erhardt, and Kächele, 2013) and
Michael Ermann (Conci and Ermann, in press). Let me
tell the story behind this.

Under the Nazi regime (1933–1945), the DPG, founded
by Karl Abraham, was dissolved and its Jewish members
forced to emigrate; the surviving German members were
offered the chance to join a psychotherapy institute chaired
by the cousin of Feldmarschall Göring – the Göring
Institute, an eclectic psychotherapy institute in which
Freudians, Jungians, and Adlerians worked together.
When the IPA met again in Zurich in the summer of 1949,
the two main former DPG analysts who had survived the
war, Harald Schultz-Hencke (1892–1953) and Carl Müller-
Braunschweig (1881–1958), approached the international
community with two completely different attitudes. The

former was eager to inform his colleagues of the IPA about the progresses made by psychoanalysis in Germany under Hitler, whereas the latter assumed that the best thing he could do was try to understand how psychoanalysis had in the meantime developed outside of Germany. This is the main reason why the IPA decided against readmitting the former DPG immediately. As Schultz-Hencke, who had already criticized Freud's libido theory in the 1920s, was not in any way ready to resign from the DPG, Müller-Braunschweig founded a new group, the DPV, which was easily accepted by the IPA as a member society in 1951, leaving the group around Schultz-Hencke, and therefore the whole DPG, outside it.

This exile lasted until 2009, when the DPG was readmitted into the IPA as a society, but under the condition that its members would be individually examined by a DPG/IPA commission to which they would have to present a treatment conducted four times a week. This is the door that opened up for me and for all the members, and through which the above-mentioned first group of about fifteen DPG members became members of the IPA in 2001, in Nice. Of course, it was a very long process of reorientation of the whole society, which was started by Michael Ermann during his presidency (1987–1995), continued by his successor Jürgen Körner (1995–2001), and brought to fruition by Franz Wellendorf (2001–2011). Franz Wellendorf's successor Ingo Focke (2011–2017)—one of the main protagonists of this whole complex process—described it in 2010 (Focke, 2010), also from the point of view of how it affected the whole society. At the time of writing (September 2017), the DPG has about 900 members, about 200 of which are also IPA members. The healing of this deep and very painful split of the German analytic community would of course not have been possible without the assistance and advice of Otto Kernberg and Anne-Marie Sandler—and all the members of the advisory committee, including John Kafka (Washington DC) and André Haynal.

But back to my patient Penelope. For her, the high frequency of treatment was indicated by how much she had been mistreated by her parents, and how she had reacted to their mistreatment, that is, by placing the fault upon herself, by considering herself unworthy of their love, and by deeply hating herself for all this. This is what I understood better and better through the supervision of the case with Michael Ermann. But, since in such cases, as we have learned from Fairbairn, the tie to a bad object is better than no object tie at all, it takes much time and patience to help such patients change their sense of identity and the quality of their object relations. From this dynamic comes the name "Penelope" I chose for her: the good things that we were able to create in our sessions kept apparently getting lost between one session and the next—until Penelope eventually started to trust me and to allow me to help her even when I was not physically there.

The same is true for the patient whose treatment I presented to the DPG commission chaired by Franz Wellendorf on Friday June 11, 2010, in Berlin—a case I regularly discussed per Skype with "Dr. W." who works in London. Only through analytic therapy with me had this patient, Carla, a doctoral student in her thirties, been able to realize how little free room her parents had given her in terms of her education. Her only sister had emigrated to the USA, without my patient having been able to see the connection between the behaviors of her parents and her sister. Indeed, she had even sided with her parents and lost contact with her sister. Only through a reactivation of this problematic and unhappy family climate in the relationship she developed with her husband did Carla have the chance to understand how her own family climate had influenced her and predisposed her to such a masochistic relationship. Even though she had been able to distance herself from this man, and separate from him, she had been looking for a therapy because she neither understood why she had chosen this type of man, nor felt free to divorce him—as opposed to keeping taking care of him. Only once she had been able to understand through our analytic work how much she had idealized her father as a child, and how much her father had behaved possessively with her, was Carla able to both find a new relationship with her parents and eventually go back to Italy. Although we were not yet finished with our work, I recommended her to a colleague in Italy, with whose help she was able to start a new life—in her own country and with a, for her, healthier man as a partner. But back to the IPA exam, you can imagine how happy I was to eventually become a full IPA member, almost twenty-seven years after the beginning of my personal analysis—in September 1983, in Trento.

As you can see, there is a common denominator between the three patients I have spoken about here—Donato, Penelope, and Carla. All of them migrated from Italy to Germany, since the environment from which they came gave them insufficient room and chances for a healthy and normal development. But only once they had arrived in Germany did they understand that the problem was not the environment, but the way in which they had introjected it, that is, the way in which their native environment had become a part of them. This is why they contacted me, and such an awareness made it easier for them to profit from our work. Indeed, not only did I have the chance to do similar work with Dr. L., but he also wrote a very nice paper about this kind of therapeutic work (Lazar, 2001), which I was later able to confirm through my own work (see, for example, Conci, 2015b). Since I started working in Munich as *a kassenärtzlicher Psychoanalytiker*, I have actually worked mostly with Italian patients in our common mother language—I am, to date, the only Italian male, MD, psychiatrist, and psychoanalyst working in this context in Munich. As many readers will know, the importance of working analytically in the patient's mother tongue has been confirmed by Jacqueline Amati Mehler, Simona Argentieri, and Jorge Canestri in their classic book *The Babel of the unconscious. Mother tongue and foreign languages in the psychoanalytic dimension*, whose German edition Hediaty Utari-Witt and I promoted in 2010, and which I presented to German readers (Conci, 2010b; see also Conci, 2012d). Of course, this is a topic of extreme relevance in today's world, in which migration and the search for a new home play such a central and universal role everywhere.

As you can see, after several years of familiarization with not only German culture, language, and society, but also the ways in which psychoanalysis is organized and practiced in Germany, I have been able to find the way—with help from Doris, who usually looks at and corrects the most important things I write—of also becoming scientifically active in such a hard and sophisticated language as German. And this has also made me very happy. For example, in 2011 I introduced to German readers the German editions of two important books, Ilany Kogan's *The struggle against mourning* and Stefano Bolognini's *Secret passages* (Conci, 2011a, 2011b). In addition in 2016, together with Wolfgang Mertens (Munich), I edited an anthology on Freud's most important followers (Ferenczi, Klein, Winnicott, Bion, etc.), with chapters on their life and work written by a series of German-speaking colleagues—a book meant to fill a void in the German handbooks on this topic (see Conci and Mertens, 2016). Last but not least, together with Harald Kamm, Martin Ehl, and Ingo Focke, I was able to invite Angela Rosenfeld, the daughter of Herbert Rosenfeld (1910–1986), herself a group analyst, to give a talk on her father in his native Nuremberg, where the DPG has had an institute since 1987. This was October 2014, and she herself had been to Nuremberg only a few times before, our invitation—the first of its kind—becoming a very significant event in both her life and the life of the institute (Conci and Kamm, 2016; Rosenfeld, 2016).

As far as my personal life is concerned, I am very happy with the fact that my daughter Anna is close to finishing her university studies in cultural anthropology in Bologna, and that she is even considering the possibility of working in the future as a cultural anthropologist in the psychiatric field. In the fall of 2014, I reduced my weekly trips back to Trento to two trips a month, enough to allow me not only to keep seeing a series of patients there, but also to regularly visit my eighty-eight-year-old mother and meet my brothers, with whom I still share the ownership of our father's firm. I usually go back and forth by car, the 330 km long highway trip taking about three and a half to four hours—through a beautiful alpine landscape and the towns of Rosenheim, Kufstein, Innsbruck, Brixen, and Bolzano. Fortunately, Doris spends every weekend with me and we can be together not only in Munich, Trento, and Salzburg, but also in our weekend travel destinations—to best enjoy our free time and the good relationship we have with each other. From Doris's point of view Austria still has the best hospitals, Germany has the best working conditions for me, and Italy still offers the best quality of life—and we, in present-day Europe without borders and with the Euro at our disposal, can enjoy them all. I am very happy about having been able to create for myself a new life in Munich without giving up my Italian identity, and at the same time succeeding in keeping alive the "American identity" I discovered in myself forty-five years ago. This is what allowed me to write this same Afterword directly in English—a language in which I feel at home and which allows me, at the same time, to better reflect upon myself.

Since 1999 no other Italian MD has tried to become a *kassenärtzlicher Psychoanalytiker* in Munich, for an Italian population of more than 30,000 people. In Munich I work with a fascinating variety of Italian patients, and I receive several requests for treatment every week. In addition, being the only full member of the SPI working in the Trentino-Alto Adige region, I was in September 2017 asked to formally represent the SPI across the whole region. What I have been able to do in my life was to train as a psychoanalyst in various European towns without leaving the alpine region extending from Trento to Munich in which I grew up and which I love—unlike the few colleagues of previous generations from this area who, after training either in Milan or Munich, never brought psychoanalysis back to their native communities.

Looking at my life from this point of view, I even have the possibility of seeing myself as being as unique as my father apparently considered me to potentially be for his firm, to which he succeeded in keeping me bound to an extent beyond my own imagination—as if he thought that I would have really had an important contribution to make to it. In fact, as I only gradually discovered, neither an outsider nor my brothers were interested in buying my part of the firm, and this was for many years the main reason why I continued to be involved in it. Only recently have I found the time and motivation to have a more active and creative relationship to this part of my life—and also a better relationship to my "internal father." Although I was not able—in either Italy or Germany—to follow the university career to which I aspired, I feel very happy with the work I have done since 1994 and which I still keep doing with the *International Forum of Psychoanalysis*. In fact, I still hope to be able to contribute to increasing the international dialogue that our discipline and profession should increasingly center around and profit from. Last but not least, I am very happy about my choice to become a psychoanalyst and about the way in which this choice has allowed me to profit from my assets and transform my limitations into a very useful way to help my fellow human beings—and to have a very good, rich, and interesting life. I am of course sorry not to have had a "normal" family of my own, to have met Doris only when I was almost fifty, and not to have had any children with her, but I know I can be happy enough with what I have—including the fact that my heart keeps physically functioning very well!

Before closing this long and complex autobiographical work, I would like to inform readers who are still with me about a series of further positive events and scientific achievements that I experienced between 2005 and 2007. In August 2005, I went to Basel (Bâle) with Doris and with my mother, where we visited Gaetano Benedetti at his home in Riehen to congratulate him on his eighty-fifth birthday. After telling him about my work on Freud's letters and how much I appreciated the correspondence I had received from him, I was able to convince Benedetti to give me his complete correspondence, contained in about forty large folders—which Doris and I put into my car and brought back to Trento. Although I have not yet read everything, I have already published several papers on Benedetti's life and work (see, for example, Conci, 2008b), the last of which was for a book published by his best collaborator, Maurizio Peciccia (Perugia) in 2016 (see Conci, 2016b).

The more I got to know Gaetano Benedetti through his letters, the more I understood what an important role he played for more than sixty years as a bridge in the international analytic community, creating a whole series of connections and contacts, and doing it in a way that it became for me an important model of practical action. Born in Catania in 1920, Benedetti had graduated from medical school in his home town and then moved to Zurich, where he became a very close collaborator of Eugen Bleuler's son Manfred (1903–1994). In 1956 he founded with Christian Müller (see above) the International Symposia on the Psychotherapy of Schizophrenia, whose 2017 meeting took place in Liverpool (UK), and then started going regularly to Italy, Germany, and many other countries worldwide to teach and supervise. When I started working as a psychoanalyst in Munich, he even wrote me a moving letter of congratulations, in which he said that the emigration of both of us was a loss for Italy, but a gain for Europe.

In August 2006 Doris accompanied me to Baden-Baden, where the Ferenczi movement was holding an important international conference, and we had the chance to stay in the hotel where Georg Groddeck (1866–1934) had established his private *Heilanstalt*, the private hospital in which Ferenczi and his wife Gisela spent more than one vacation in the 1920s. There we were able to eventually join the group of colleagues who had been organizing a series of International Ferenczi Conferences since 1991 (see Aron and Harris, 1993) and I started actively collaborating with them. As a member of the International Sándor Ferenczi Network coordinated by Carlo Bonomi, I am presently collaborating in the organization of the next Ferenczi International Conference, taking place in Florence at the beginning of May 2018.

In the fall of the same year, 2006, I was able to co-organize in Trento one of the very few Italian conferences to celebrate Freud's 150th birthday anniversary, at which I gave a paper in which I tried to summarize my work in the field of the history of psychoanalysis (Conci, 2008c). With Maria Luisa Martini we were able to produce a very nice volume by the title *Freud e il Novecento*, in which we collected all the papers presented at the conference (Conci and Martini, 2008).

In the spring 2007, I had the good luck to be awarded in Trento, by a representative of the Austrian Consulate in Milan, the great distinction of the *Österreichische Ehrenkreuz für Wissenschaft und Kunst Ersten Ranges*, the Austrian Honorary Cross for Science and Art of First Order, for my work in translating and promoting Freud's work both in Italy and internationally. Of course my work was nowhere near comparable to that of other recipients of such an honor, such as Viktor Frankl (1905–1997) or Eric Kandel, but—as Doris says—the awarding committee certainly did not make a mistake in attributing to me a very special passion for psychoanalysis and its promotion.

In fact, this whole *Selbstdarstellung* centers around this very topic, that is, around the way in which psychoanalysis has helped me to understand myself since my adolescence; around all the things I have gained from it in terms of my personal growth and maturation; around the many ways in which I have tried to illuminate it with my research and promote it with my practical work; and—last but not least—around the complex way in which I have developed my clinical and institutional identity as a psychoanalyst.

Such a concept luckily coincides with the concept of psychoanalysis recently formulated by my publisher Arnold Richards, and this has allowed me to think that he might appreciate the work I have put into my own "autobiographical study"—to borrow the title of Freud's 1924 work. I am referring here to Arnold Richards' concept of psychoanalysis as *"Bildung,"* that is, to Freud's own commitment to this educational ideal as a basic ingredient of his Jewish identity and of psychoanalysis (see Richards, 2014), and to his definition of psychoanalysis itself as "a kind of Jewish liberation philosophy" (Richards, 2014, p. 1001). Furthermore, through the recent publication of André Haynal's fascinating autobiographical volume *Encounters with the irrational. My story*, my publisher seems to be ready to catch up with the German tradition of the "psychoanalytic autobiography," which allowed my colleague and friend Ludger Hermanns to edit between 1992 and 2017 eleven volumes under the title *Psychoanalyse in Selbstdarstellungen* (Hermans, 1992–2017). Volume XI (2017) contains the *Selbstdarstellung* of Shmuel Erlich, whose original English version represents the opening chapter of the *Festschrift* edited by Mira Erlich-Ginor in honor of her husband—and has also now been published by International Psychoanalytic Books (Erlich, 2017).

It took me more than four weeks to write this Afterword. Today is September 12, 2017, and yesterday I resumed working with my patients in Munich, after the usual summer vacation Doris and I take at the spa resort of Montegrotto Terme, near Padua. It took me more than four weeks to deal with a writing process that on the one hand I am happy I got involved in, but, on the other hand, consumed much more time and energy than I had anticipated. Such a writing process actually represents a return to the origins and one of the essential dimensions of psychoanalysis, as Patrick Mahony defined it in his fascinating book *Freud as a writer*. According to him, Freud's self-analysis "was literally a writing cure," and "psychoanalysis had its beginning as a talking and writing cure" (Mahony, 1987, p. 161). This is also why I hope that at least a few readers will have been able to read this Afterword through to the end. And to profit from it, as I myself did in writing it.

P.S.: While working at the final linguistic revision of this Afterword, at the beginning of January 2019, I discovered—following feedback from my language editor, Carrie Walker—that my old friend Marco, my medical school colleague, whose family name I did not make the reader familiar with, belongs to the group of colleagues who took care of *The collected works of D. W. Winnicott*. I am referring here to the twelve volumes edited by Leslie Caldwell and Helen Taylor Robinson in 2017, each one of which is accompanied by a corresponding Introduction. My old friend Marco Armellini is the author of the Introduction to Volume 10, *Therapeutic consultations in child psychiatry*. In fact, the Italian colleagues Vincenzo Bonaminio (with whom Marco trained in Rome as a child psychotherapist), Anna Ferruta, and Paolo Fabozzi also played an important role in this enterprise. This fact permits me to now make the following two comments. First, both Marco Armellini and I have reached one of the goals that must have brought us together at the time of medical school—that of making a name for ourselves in the field of international psychoanalysis. In the second place, giving the significant Italian contribution to Winnicott's *Collected works*, I can allow myself to say that both this book (which I wrote directly in English) and the contribution given to international psychoanalysis by the Italian generation to which I belong well reflect our original desire to participate in the international dialogue in our field in a way that had not been possible for the previous generations. If this is the case, I am sure that we can be proud of this.

GENERAL REFERENCES

Ackerknecht, E.H. (1959). *A Short History of Psychiatry*. New York: Hafner. (Original German edition, 1957. Italian edition, 1999).

Amati Mehler, J., Argentieri, S., & Canestri, J. (1993). *The Babel of the Unconscious. Mother Tongue and Foreign Languages in the Psychoanalytic Dimension*. Madison, CT: International Universities Press.

Armellini, M. (2017). Introduction to Volume 10, *Therapeutic Consultations in Child Psychiatry* (pp. 3–21). In L. Caldwell and H. Taylor Robinson (Eds.), *The Collected Works of D.W. Winnicott*. Oxford: Oxford University Press.

Aron, L., & Harris, A. (Eds.) (1993). *The Legacy of Sándor Ferenczi*. Hillsdale, NJ: Analytic Press.

Bacal, H. (2016). The Budapest school's concept of supervision: Michael Balint's legacy to the development of psychoanalytic specificity theory. In A.W. Rachmann (Ed.), *The Budapest School of Psychoanalysis* (pp. 143–160). London: Routledge.

Balint, M. (1955). *The Doctor, his Patient and the Illness*. London: Tavistock.

Benedetti, G. (1961). Prefazione all'edizione italiana [Preface to the Italian edition]. In H.S. Sullivan, *La moderna concezione della psichiatria* (pp. vii–xxvii). Milan: Feltrinelli. (Original English edition, 1940).

Boehlich, W. (Ed.) (1990). *The Letters of Sigmund Freud to Eduard Silberstein 1871–1881*. Cambridge, MA: Belknap Press. (Original German edition, 1989).

Brecht, K., Friedrich, V., Hermanns, L.M., Juelich, D.H, & Kaminer, I.J. (Eds.) (1993). *"Here life goes on in a most peculiar way . . .". Psychoanalysis before and after 1933*. Giessen: Psychosozial-Verlag. (Original German edition, 1985).

Caviglia, G., & Lingiardi, V. (2014). The fortunes of the relational model in Italy. *Psychoanalyic Dialogues* 24:578–589.

Cederna, C. (1971). *Pinelli. Una finestra sulla strage* [Pinelli. A window on the slaughter]. Milan: Feltrinelli.

Chrzanowski, G. (1993). History of the International Federation of Psychoanalytic Societies. *International Forum of Psychoanalysis* 2:168–170.

Cremerius, J. (1985). *Il mestiere dell'analista* [The analyst's profession]. Turin: Bollati Boringhieri.

——— (1987). Alla ricerca di tracce perdute. Il "Movimento psicoanalitico" e la miseria dell'istituzione psicoanalitica [Looking for lost traces. The "psychoanalytic movement" and the misery of the psychoanalytic institution]. *Psicoterapia e Scienze Umane* 21(3):3–34.

Erlich, S.H. (2017). Migration and homecoming: A psychoanalytic autobiography. In Erlich-Ginor, M. (Ed.), *Not Knowing, Knowing, not Knowing. Festschrift Celebrating the Life and Work of Shmuel Erlich* (pp. 3–40). New York: International Psychoanalytic Books.

Ellenberger, H.F. (1970). *The Discovery of the Unconscious*. New York: Basic Books.

Ermann, M. (1990). Wandlungen der Psychotherapie und Psychoanalyse im Spannungsfeld des Nationalsozialismus [Transformations of psychotherapy and psychoanalysis in the tension field of National Socialism]. Paper given on April 20, 1990, Lindau.

Federn, E. (1990). *Witnessing Psychoanalysis. From Vienna Back to Vienna via Buchenwald and the USA*. London: Karnac.

Ferenczi, S., & Rank, O. (1927). *The Development of Psycho-analysis*. New York: Nervous and Mental Diseases Publishing Company. (Original German edition, 1924).

Focke, I. (2010). Der Weg der DPG in die IPV. Wunsch und Ambivalenz [The way of the DPG to the IPA. Desire and ambivalence]. *Psyche* 64:1187–1205.

Foot, J. (2015). *The Man who Closed the Asylums. Franco Basaglia and the Revolution in Mental Health Care*. London: Verso.

Forti, L. (Ed.) (1975). *L'altra pazzia* [The other madness]. Milan: Feltrinelli.

Freud, S. (1924). An autobiographical study. *Standard Edition* 20, pp. 3–76.

Friedman, L.J. (2014). *The Lives of Erich Fromm, Love's Prophet*. New York: Columbia.

Fromm, E. (1959). *Sigmund Freud's Mission. An Analysis of his Personality and Influence*. London: Allen & Unwin.

Furlan, P.M. (2006). The IXth ISPS Symposium in Turin, Italy, in September 1988. In Y.O. Alanen, A.-L. Silver, and M. González de Chávez (Eds.), *Fifty Years of the Humanistic Treatment of psychoses. In Honor of the History of the International Society for the Treatment of Schizophrenia and Other Psychoses, 1956–2006* (pp. 123–144). Madrid: Paradox.

Galli, P.F. (1990). Psychoanalysis, the story of a crisis. Paper given at the Rapaport–Klein Study Group, June 10, 1990, Stockbridge, MA, USA.

Gill, M.M. (1982). *Analysis of Transference. Theory and Technique*. New York: International Universities Press.

Greenberg, J.R, & Mitchell, S.A. (1983). *Object Relations in Psychoanalytic Theory*. Cambridge, MA: Harvard University Press.

Haynal, A.E. (2017). *Encounters with the Irrational. My Story, with an Interview by Judit Mészàros*. New York: International Psychoanalytic Books.

Hermanns, L.M.(Ed.)(1992–2017). *Psychoanalyse in Selbstdarstellungen* [Psychoanalysis in autobiographies]. Tübingen: Diskord (Vols 1–4); Frankfurt: Brandes & Apsel (Vols 5–11).

Herzog, D. (2016). *Cold War Freud: Psychoanalysis in an Age of Catastrophes*. Cambridge, MA: Cambridge University Press.

Holt, R.R. (2013). Freud's professional choice and the unconscious: reverberations of Goethe's "On nature". *Psychoanalytic Review* 100:239–266.

Holt, R.R. (Ed.) (2017). *The Rapaport/Holt Correspondence, 1948–1960*. New York: International Psychoanalytic Books.

Illich, I. (1971). *Deschooling Society*. New York: Harper & Row.

———— (1976). *Limits to Medicine*. New York: Harper & Row.

Jervis, G. (1975). *Manuale critico di psichiatria* [Critical handbook of psychiatry]. Milan: Feltrinelli.

Jervis, G. (1977). *Il buon rieducatore. Scritti sugli usi della psichiatria e della psicoanalisi* [The good re-educator. Papers on the uses of psychiatry and psychoanalysis]. Milan: Feltrinelli.

Jones, E. (1953–1955–1957). *The Life and Work of Sigmund Freud. Three Volumes.* London: Hogarth Press.

Kernberg, O.F. (1986). Institutional problems of psychoanalytic education. *Journal of the American Psychoanalytic Association* 34:799–834.

Kovel, J. (1980). The American mental health industry. In D. Ingleby (Ed.), *Critical Psychiatry. The Politics of Mental Health* (pp. 72–101). London: Pantheon Books.

Kurzweil, E. (1989). *The Freudians. A Comparative Perspective.* New Haven, CT: Yale University Press.

Lazar, R.A. (2001). "Fremde in einem fremden Land", oder "Es führt kein Weg zurück." Psychoanalytisch-psychotherapeutische Behandlung von Immigranten ["Foreign in a foreign country", or "There is no way back". Psychoanalytic-psychotherapeutic treatment of immigrants]. In K. Bell, A. Holder, P. Janssen, & J. Van de Sande (Eds.), *Migration und Verfolgung. Psychoanalytische Perspektiven* [Migration and persecution. Psychoanalytic perspectives] (pp. 103–123). Giessen: Psychosozial-Verlag.

——— (In press). Like a phoenix from the ashes – or "sack cloth and ashes?" – The reconstitution of psychoanalytic institutions in since 1945 and its consequences. *International Forum of Psychoanalysis.* (Original German edition, 2016).

Lothane, H.Z. (1992). *In Defense of Schreber. Soul Murder and Psychiatry.* Hillsdale, NJ: Analytic Press.

Mahony, P.J. (1987). *Freud as a Writer. Expanded Edition.* New Haven, CT: Yale University Press.

Masson, J.M. (Ed.) (1985). *The Complete Letters of Sigmund Freud to Wilhelm Fliess.* Cambridge, MA: Belknap Press.

McLuhan, M. (1964). *Understanding Media. The Extensions of Man.* New York: McGraw-Hill.

Meltzer, D. (1994). Towards an atelier system. In *Curiosity: Collected Papers of Donald Meltzer* (A. Hahn, Ed.) (pp. 285–289). London: Karnac.

Mitchell, S.A. (1988). *Relational Concepts in Psychoanalysis. An Integration.* Cambridge, MA: Harvard University Press.

——— (1993). *Hope and Dread in Psychoanalysis.* New York: Basic Books.

Müller C. (2016). *Erlebte Psychiatrie 1946–1986* [The psychiatry I lived 1946–1986] (B. Küchenhoff, Ed.). Bâle: Schwabe.

Omodei Zorini, E. (2009). In ricordo di Teresa Piacentini Corsi [In memory of Teresa Piacentini Corsi]. *Setting* No. 28:9–16.

Pinkus, L. (2012). *Un arameo errante. La mia vita* [A wandering Aramean. My life]. Trento: Il Margine.

Racamier, P.-C. (1972). *Le psychanalyst sans divan* [The psychoanalyst without couch]. Paris: Payot.

Rapaport, D. (1967). *Collected Papers of D. Rapaport* (M.M. Gill, Ed.). New York: Basic Books.

Richards, A.D. (2014). Freud's Jewish identity and psychoanalysis as a science. *Journal of the American Psychoanalytic Association* 62:987–1003.

Riesman, D., Glazer, N., & R. Denney (1950). *The Lonely Crowd*. New Haven, CT: Yale University Press.

Rivkin Zuckermann, J. (2013). Review of the book by Marco Conci "Sullivan revisited – Life and work". *American Journal of Psychoanalysis* 73:100–104.

Roazen, P. (1975). *Freud and his Followers*. New York, Knopf. (Italian edition, 1998).

——— (1990). *Encountering Freud. The Politics and the Histories of Psychoanalysis*. New Brunswick, NJ: Transaction.

Rosenfeld, A. (2016). My father, Herbert Rosenfeld. *International Forum of Psychoanalysis* 25:220–228.

Sabbadini, A. (Ed.) (1979). *Il tempo in psicoanalisi* [Time in psychoanalysis]. Milan: Feltrinelli.

Sartre, J.-P. (1938). *La nausée* [Nausea]. Paris: Gallimard.

Scheff, T.J. (1966). *Being Mentally Ill. A Sociological Theory*. Chicago, Aldine.

Schmidabuer, W. (1977). *Die hilflosen Helfer. Über die seelische Problematik der helfenden Berufe* [Helpers who cannot help. On the psychic problems of the helping professions]. Hamburg: Rowohlt.

Schwing, G. (1954). *A Way to the Soul of the Mentally Ill*. New Haven, CT: International Universities Press. (Original Swiss edition, 1940, Italian edition, 1988).

Slater, P. (1970). *The Pursuit of Loneliness: American Culture at the Breaking Point*. Boston: Beacon Press.

Sullivan, H.S. (1940). *Conceptions of Modern Psychiatry*. Washington DC: W.A. White Psychiatric Foundation.

——— (1953). *The Interpersonal Theory of Psychiatry*. New York: Norton.

——— (1954). *The Psychiatric Interview*. New York: Norton.

——— (1956). *Clinical Studies in Psychiatry*. New York: Norton.

Tillman, J.G. (2012). A major figure: H.S. Sullivan revisited – Life and work – Harry Stack Sullivan's relevance for contemporary psychiatry, psychotherapy and psychoanalysis. By Marco Conci. *Journal of the American Psychoanalytic Association* 60:615–618.

Wright Mills, C. (1951). *White Collar: The American Middle Classes*. Oxford: Oxford University Press.

PERSONAL REFERENCES

Conci, M. (1987). Review of the book by R. Jacoby "The repression of psychoanalysis. Otto Fenichel and the political Freudians", Basic Books 1984. *Psicoterapia e Scienze Umane* 21(2):103–111.

———— (1988). Prologo [Prologue]. In G. Schwing, *La pazzia e l'amore. Un cammino verso l'anima del malato di mente* (pp. 9–12). Pisa: Del Cerro. (English edition, 1954. Original Swiss edition, 1940. English edition, 1954).

———— (1990a). Review of the book by S.A. Mitchell "Relational concepts in psychoanalysis. An integration", Harvard University Press 1988. *Psicoterapia e Scienze Umane*, 24(1):24–130.

———— (1990b). S. Freud studente a Trieste nelle lettere ad E. Silberstein [S. Freud student in Trieste in his letters to E. Silberstein]. *Psicoterapia e Scienze Umane* 24(4):45–60.

———— (1990c). Review of the book by E. Kurzweil "The Freudians. A comparative perspective", Yale University Press 1989. And of the book by P. Federn "Witnessing psychoanalysis", Karnac Books 1990. *Psicoterapia e Scienze Umane* 24(4):137–142.

———— (1991). Freud in Trentino-Alto Adige. In A.M. Accerboni (Ed.), *Freud e il Trentino. Otium e scrittura a Lavarone* [Freud in Trentino. Vacation and writing in Lavarone] (pp. 25–32). Trento: Edizioni di UCT.

———— (1992a). The young Freud's letters to Eduard Silberstein. Early traces of some psychoanalytic concepts. *International Forum of Psychoanalysis* 1:37–43.

———— (1992b). Review of the book by P. Roazen "Encountering Freud. The politics and the histories of psychoanalysis", Transaction Publishers 1990. *Psicoterapia e Scienze Umane* 26(3):138–141.

———— (1993a). Prefazione all'edizione italiana [Preface to the Italian edition]. In H.S. Sullivan, *Scritti sulla schizofrenia* (pp. v–ix). Milan: Feltrinelli. (Original American edition, 1962).

———— (1993b). Presentazione [Introduction]. In S.A. Mitchell, *Gli orientamenti relazionali in psicoanalisi. Per un modello integrato* (pp. ix–xv). Turin: Bollati Boringhieri. (Original American edition, 1988).

———— (1994). Psychoanalysis in Italy: A reappraisal. *International Forum of Psychoanalysis* 3:117–126.

———— (1995a). Presentazione [Introduction]. In S.A. Mitchell, *Speranza e timore in psicoanalisi* (pp. 9–10). Turin: Bollati Boringhieri. (Original American edition, 1994).

———— (1995b). Disertori neuropsichiatra alla luce del carteggio con H. Ellenberger [The neuro-psychiatrist Beppino Disertori in the light of his correspondence with H. Ellenberger]. In Trento Townhall (Ed.), *Sotto il segno dell'uomo: Beppino Disertori. Atti del convegno di studio: Trento, Palazzo Geremia, 11.2.1995* [Under the sign of man: Beppino Disertori. Proceedings of the conference : Trento, Geremia Palace, February 11, 1995] (pp. 47–60). Trento: Comune di Trento.

———— (1996a). The "good life" and the vulnerability of the human being. Psychoanalytic perspectives. A small group seminar in New York City. *International Forum of Psychoanalysis* 5:70–71.

———— (1996b). Why did Freud choose medical school? *International Forum of Psychoanalysis* 5:123–132.

———— (1997). Presentazione [Introduction]. In P. Roazen, *I miei incontri con la famiglia di Freud* (pp. 7–19). Rome: Erre Emme.

(Original Americal edition, 1993).

—— (1998a). Freud's self-analysis – an interpersonally grounded process. *International Forum of Psychoanalysis* 7:77–84.

—— (1998b). Presentazione [Introduction]. In P. Roazen, *Freud al lavoro. I pazienti raccontano* (pp. 6–8). Bolsena, Viterbo: Massari Editore. (Original American edition, 1995).

—— (1999). Introduzione [Introduction]. In E.H. Ackerknecht, *Breve storia della psichiatria* (pp. 1–20). Bolsena, Viterbo: Massari. (English edition, 1968. Original German edition, 1958. English edition, 1968).

—— (2000a). *Sullivan rivisitato. La sua rilevanza per la psichiatria, psicoterapia e pisconalisi.* Bolsena, VT: Massari Editore. (Second English edition: *Sullivan Revisited – Life and Work.* Trento: Tangram Edizioni Scientifiche, 2012).

—— (2000b). Review of the book by T. Müller *"Von Charlottenburg zum Central Park West. Henry Loewenfeld und die Psychoanalyse in Berlin, Prag und New York"*, Edition Déjà-vu. *Luzifer-Amor* No. 26:153–158.

—— (2006). Seminari a Milano [Workshops in Milan]. In ASP (Ed.), *La parola come cura. La psicoterapia delle psicosi nell'incontro con Gaetano Benedetti* [Word as cure. The psychotherapy of psychosis in the encounter with Gaetano Benedetti] (pp. 226–247). Milan: Angeli.

—— (2008a). Un seminario con Pagliarani: Collalbo 1998 [A workshop with Pagliarani: Collalbo 1998]. *L'Educazione Sentimentale* No. 10:24–41.

—— (2008b). Gaetano Benedetti in his correspondence. *International Forum of Psychoanalysis* 17:112–129.

—— (2008c). Coltivare una passione, la storia della psicoanalisi [Cultivating a passion, the history of psychoanalysis]. In M. Conci and M.L. Martini (Eds.), *Freud e il Novecento* [Freud and the 20th century] (pp. 138–167). Rome: Borla.

—— (2010a). Introduzione [Introduction]. In C. Bartocci (Ed.), *Gaetano Benedetti. Una vita accanto alla sofferenza mentale. Seminari clinico-teorici (1973–1996)* [Gaetano Benedetti. A life taking care of human suffering. Clinical-theoretical workshops (1973–1996)] (pp. 13–19). Milan: Angeli.

—— (2010b). Geleitwort [Foreword]. In J. Amati Mehler, S. Argentieri, & J. Canestri, *Das Babel des Unbewussten. Muttersprache und Fremdsprachen in der psychoanalytischen Dimension* (pp. 13–26). Giessen: Psychosozial-Verlag. (Original Italian edition, 1990. English edition, 1993).

—— (2010c). Der Fall Penelope. Migration und Identität am Beispiel meiner Arbeit mit italienischen Patienten in München [The case of Penelope. Migration and identity in my work with Italian patients in Munich]. *Forum der Psychoanalyse* 26:151–173. (English version in preparation for the *International Forum of Psychoanalysis*).

—— (2010d). An advantage of globalization: Working with Italian patients abroad in their mother language. *International Forum of Psychoanalysis* 19:98–109.

—— (2011a). Vorwort [Preface]. In I. Kogan, *Mit der Trauer kämpfen* (pp. 9–16). Stuttgart: Klett-Cotta. (Original English edition, 2007).

—— (2011b). Geleitwort [Foreword]. In S. Bolognini, *Verborgene Wege. Die Beziehung zwischen Analytiker und Patient* (pp. 7–16). Giessen: Psychosozial-Verlag. (Original Italian edition, 2008. English edition, 2011).

────── (2012). Foreword. In M. Bacciagaluppi, *Paradigms in Psychoanalysis. An Integration* (pp. xiii–xvi). London: Karnac.

────── (2013). Editorial – German themes in psychoanalysis. Part One. *International Forum of Psychoanalysis* 22:195–198.

────── (2014). Le radici della svolta relazionale in psicoanalisi. Da Sullivan a Mitchell attraverso l'ASP, ossia il punto di vista di Benedetti e Cremerius [The roots of the Relational Turn. From Sullivan to Mitchell through the ASP, i.e., the point of view of Benedetti and Cremerius]. *Setting* No. 33–34:105–139.

────── (2015a). Editorial – German themes in psychoanalysis. Part Two. *International Forum of Psychoanalysis* 24:57–59.

────── (2015b). "I started becoming myself here in Munich . . .". Migration, psychoanalysis and identity. *Revue Roumaine de Psychanalyse* 7:129–144.

────── (2016a). My relationship to IFP in the context of the original construction of our identity as a journal. *International Forum of Psychoanalysis* 25:112–118.

────── (2016b). Postfazione [Afterword]. In M. Peciccia, *I semi di psiche* [The seeds of psyche] (pp. 143–178). Rome: Fioriti.

────── (2016c). Die analytische Beziehung als Heimat [The analytic relationship as home]. Paper given May 7, 2016, Stuttgart.

────── (2016d). "Analytic field theory: a dialogical approach, a pluralistic perspective, and the attempt at a new definition". In S.M. Katz, R. Cassorla, and G. Civitarese (Eds.), *Advances in Contemporary Analytic Field Theory* (pp. 113–127). London: Routledge.

────── (2016e). Le lettere del giovane Freud ad Emil Fluss (1872–1874) [The young Freud's letters to Emil Fluss (1872–1874)]. *Rivista di Psicoanalisi* 62:1057–1084.

────── (2017). A peculiar obstacle to intimacy: The patient who grew-up calling his mother by her first name – The interpersonal field and the analytic process. Paper given July 28, 2017, Buenos Aires.

Conci, M., & Bacciagaluppi, M. (2006). Marco Conci interviews Marco Bacciagaluppi. *International Forum of Psychoanalysis* 15:34–43.

Conci, M., & Bolognini, S. (2006). Marco Conci interviews Stefano Bolognini. *International Forum of Psychoanalysis* 15:44–57.

Conci, M., & Cortelletti, P. (1988). Dal manicomio al territorio: il caso di Mario. Direttive per la riabilitazione [From the mental hospital to the territory: The case of Mario. Guiding principles of rehabilitation]. In G. Di Giorgi, P. Michielin, B. Milani, and T. Zorzi (Eds.), *La riabilitazione degli psicotici* [The rehabilitation of psychothic patients] (pp. 175–181). Padua: Piccin.

Conci, M., & Dell'Oro, A. (1985). Saverio e noi: vicissitudini terapeutiche nell'incontro con un paziente psicotico [Saverio and us: Therapeutic vicissitudes in the encounter with a psychotic patient]. *Fogli di Informazione* Nos 111–112–113:14–19.

Conci, M., & Ermann, M. (in press). Marco Conci interviews Michael Ermann. *International Forum of Psychoanalysis*.

Conci, M., & Kamm, H. (2016). Editorial – Freud, Emma Ekstein, and Ferenczi – Herbert Rosenfeld's life and his work as a supervisor in Italy and Germany – Psychoanalysis as an intergenerational and international research work. *International Forum of Psychoanalysis* 25:201.

Conci, M., & Marchioro, F. (1995). Premessa-Vorwort [Foreword]. In M. Conci and F. Marchioro (Eds.), *Totem e tabu. Psicoanalisi e religione. Atti del convegno di Bolzano, 26–28 novembre 1993*

[Totem and taboo. Psychoanalysis and religion. Papers of the conference, Bolzano, November 26–28, 1993] (pp. iii–v). Lecce: Media 2000.

Conci, M., & Marchioro, F. (Eds.) (1998). Introduzione [Introduction]. In M. Conci and F. Marchioro (Eds.), *Elvio Fachinelli. Intorno al '68. Un'antologia di testi* [Elvio Fachinelli. About the year 68. An anthology of texts] (pp. 7–51). Bolsena, Viterbo: Massari.

Conci, M., & Martini, M.L. (Eds.) (2008). *Freud e il Novecento* [Freud and the twentieth century]. Rome: Borla.

Conci, M., & Mertens, W. (2016). Einleitung [Introduction]. In M. Conci and W. Mertens (Eds.), *Psychoanalyse im 20. Jahrhundert. Freuds Nachfolger und ihr Beitrag zur modernen Psychoanalyse* [Psychoanalysis in the 20th century. Freud's followers and their contribution to modern psychoanalysis] (pp. 13–19). Stuttgart: Kohlhammer.

Conci, M., & Pinkus, L. (1989). I primi pionieristici scritti di H.S. Sullivan sulla psicoterapia della schizofrenia [H.S. Sullivan's first pioneering papers on the psychotherapy of schizophrenia]. *Psicoterapia e Scienze Umane* 23(2):69–82.

Conci, M., Dazzi, S., & Mantovani, M.L. (Eds.) (1997a). *La tradizioone interpersonale in psichiatria, psicoterapia e psicoanalisi* [The interpersonal tradition in psychiatry, psychotherapy and psychoanalysis]. Rome: Erre Emme.

Conci, M., Erhardt, I., & Kächele, H. (2013), Marco Conci and Ingrid Erhardt interview Horst Kächele. *International Forum of Psychoanalysis* 22:228–243.

COMMENTARIES TO THE AFTERWORD

COMMENTARY BY
SANDRA BUECHLER, PHD

When Marco Conci sent me his Afterword, I read it immediately, eager to know more about my friend's life. But beyond this curiosity, I quickly understood that this is a unique document. It describes the ways in which personal experiences can focus our theoretical interests. Reading this remarkable piece of work delineates the development of one analyst's voice, and the ways personal and professional events can intertwine.

Marco Conci's Afterword is a model of courageous writing. His willingness to reveal his life experience, and its effect on the trajectory of his career, is inspirational. All clinicians, whether new to the field or advanced in their own careers, could profit from his example of open, scrupulous self-examination.

While other analysts have commented on the impact of life experiences on their professional investments (for example, see Anna Orenstein's autobiographical work *My mother's eyes* (2004), or Steven Kuchuck's collection *Clinical implications of the psychoanalyst's life experience: When the personal becomes professional*; 2014) none, to my knowledge, has offered us the painstaking detail this Afterword provides. This Afterword will serve as a model of an analyst's courageous self-scrutiny.

The cultivation of courage in the aspiring analyst has long been of great interest to me (Buechler, 2004, 2008, 2012, 2017). How do we nurture this capacity during training? Elsewhere I have suggested that being an analyst requires what I call "rash timidity" (2004, p. 67). I have adapted this phrase from an idea in Aristotle's *Nicomachean ethics* (fourth century BC). There, Aristotle defined courage as the observance of the mean between excessive fear and excessive rashness. I suggested that conducting an analysis often requires courage, in this sense. Each analyst forges his or her own style of measured spontaneity. We are pressured from within ourselves and from the patient, pulled in various directions, and yet we need to maintain a centered, therapeutic purpose. Continuing with this work, while understanding its pitfalls, can take tremendous courage.

In writing this professional memoir, Marco Conci has shown the courage of the truly dedicated analyst. With a clear sense of purpose, he prioritizes finding his truth about the relationship between his theoretical interests and his personal life story. As analysts we are often required to put therapeutic purpose ahead of our pride, or any other consideration. Elsewhere (Buechler, 2004, 2012) I have illustrated the "inconvenient truths" the courageous analyst needs to be ready to discover, about him- or herself. Dr. Conci's courage is evident in his willingness to examine and share the development of his analytic identity. He also demonstrates his capacity to make his own thought processes transparent, which I see as an extremely important ability in the analyst. Sometimes the analyst does his best work by inviting the patient into his own mind. In this Afterword, Dr. Conci opens up his mind, for the reader's benefit.

I see the analyst's task as similar to the sculptor's, in a sense. The sculptor can be understood as finding the sculpture in the marble. Similarly, the training analyst/supervisor/teacher finds the analyst in the candidate, and the clinician finds the richly complicated human being in the patient. This book reveals the process of creation of an analyst from raw materials, to a particular, fully formulated professional self.

On a more personal level, I wish I had read this Afterword earlier in my own career. I think it might have helped me reflect on the personal meaning of my own professional path. I hope it is widely read by those considering going into the field and clinicians at all phases of their careers.

New York City, October 2017

REFERENCES

Aristotle (Fourth century BC). *The Nicomachean Ethics* (H. Rackham, Trans.). Ware, Hertfordshire: Wordsworth Editions.

Buechler, S. (2004). *Clinical Values: Emotions That Guide Psychoanalytic Treatment.* New York: Analytic Press.

Buechler, S. (2008). *Making a Difference in Patients' Lives.* New York: Routledge

Buechler, S. (2012). *Still Practicing: The Heartaches and Joys of a Clinical Career.* New York: Routledge.

Buechler, S. (2017). *Psychoanalytic Reflections: Training and Practice.* New York: International Psychoanalytic Books.

Kuchuck, S. (2014) *Clinical Implications of the Psychoanalyst's Life Experience: When the Personal Becomes Professional.* New York: Routledge.

Orenstein, A. (2004). *My Mother's Eyes.* Cincinnati, OH: Emmis Books.

COMMENTARY BY
FRANK M. LACHMANN, PHD

When I agreed to write about Marco Conci's Afterword, it was out of friendship. But I read it with admiration and fascination. Marco is so modest and unassuming that I would never have suspected the personal but especially the worldwide accomplishments he details in this autobiographical essay.

It also turned out to be a beautiful illustration of Heinz Kohut's concept, the bipolar self. The two poles refer to the balance (and in cases of pathology, the imbalance) between ideals and ambitions. Marco's ideal is a vision of a worldwide psychoanalytic fellowship, a universal family of psychoanalysts. This ideal drew and continues to draw him into active participation and leadership in national and international psychoanalytic organizations that can further and bring to fruition his vision. Such a vision would be meaningless if Marco did not also have the skills, talents, interests, and drive to fuel his ambitions. In turn, this enables him to meet and live up to his ideals. According to Kohut, this balance would lead Marco to feel confidence and steadfastness about his life goals. What is particularly remarkable is that Marco had to "construct" his trajectory very much on his own, without his family as the interpersonal world to provide support and encouragement. And all this was accomplished under such a modest demeanor.

Looked at from a more personal level, Marco clearly felt in some ways like an outsider in his family. He tried to be the son his father wanted, but his father's expectations of him were rather limiting. They seemed to close off choices, rather than open up vistas. Marco thereupon embarked upon an initially solitary journey in which he devoted his life to opening vistas not only for himself, but also for the whole field of psychoanalysis, as well as for those fortunate enough to become his patients. In addition, in effect, Marco turned the entire psychoanalytic field into a family, a brotherhood into which he fitted, one that would not only welcome him, but also appreciate his many gifts and contributions.

Translating the contributions of analysts from one language into another is felt by many analysts to be a thankless and not very glamorous task. It is a lot of work, and the translator makes someone else famous while remaining in relative obscurity. However, for the field of psychoanalysis itself, translations are a real necessity. To grow as a profession we must apprise ourselves of work being done in other parts of the world. Marco, the historian, came to the rescue. Translating analytic contributions from various countries became key to furthering his vision. He became a phenomenal translator, to the benefit of the Italian analysts who could now read German, English, and American works, but in the other direction as well. Marco contributed to making the work of Italian analysts available to the non-Italian-speaking world.

Through his work as a translator, Marco enlarged the vista of psychoanalysis on a worldwide basis. He gave birth to a perspective that went beyond the borders of Trento— way beyond Italy, and way beyond Europe. Marco created a home for himself in the whole psychoanalytic world, literally and figuratively. In doing so, he contributed to breaking down barriers that inevitably arise among adherents to different psychoanalytic theories. Some of these differences are based on institutional loyalties, some on misunderstandings, and some on different cultural sensitivities.

Imagine what it must have meant for Marco, the Italian, writing about the quintessential American analyst Harry Stack Sullivan, who could not be as distinct from a European as an analyst can be. But the need to understand interpersonal relationships was crucially as important to Marco as Freud's one-person theory that focused on unconscious motivations. What a bridge he built!

Of particular interest to me was an unusual aspect of Marco's style. Probably when a historian cites a name, it is natural to follow the name with the years of birth and death of that person. I have not seen such references in psychoanalytic publications. It struck me that Marco's teachers, supervisors, and mentors, and the writers whom he cited, were all identified by their years of birth and death. And it seemed to me that many of them were dead by now. Marco's colleagues and the people in his generation were not so identified. What do I make of this? I think that in Marco we have the continuity of a psychoanalytic tradition of scholarship, and thus a sense of continuity in the evolution of our field. These luminaries of Marco's past may have died, but their contributions live on, through their impact on him, with respect for their ideas. In fact, the whole Afterword can be read, not as an end commentary to his papers, but as a transition to the riches of the past, to a future that requires their acknowledgment, and on a path to the creativity that may yet lie ahead. Marco has made sure that we do not forget what we have learned in the past—in psychoanalysis all over the world—so that we will not be condemned to repeat it.

In reading Marco's Afterword, I thought about Robert Kennedy's dictum: Some people look at things as they are and ask "Why?" I look at things that have never been and ask, "Why not?" Marco has taught us to look at things as they are and ask "What, when, where and how?" It is an attitude of inquiry rather than judgment. Marco exemplifies a crucial nonjudgmental stance as a historian and analyst. We try to understand the way things became as they are now, and out of that understanding can emerge a new perspective. Our field is full of people who ask, "Why not?" Some of these questions lead to growth in the field, but sometimes they lead to antagonism between different theoretical factions. In making connections with interpersonal theorists, field theorists, and family theorists, Marco has created a common ground rather than a battlefield. And overall, by finding his personal entry into these different analytic perspectives, he has enriched his and our world.

Marco has played an important role in enabling Italian-speaking patients in Germany to have an analysis in their native tongue. Living in New York, but having been born in Germany, I also wanted an analyst who spoke my native tongue, when I entered analysis. I did not want to have to translate my childhood experience from German into English. I believed that something always gets lost in translation. I remember the session in which I first switched from associating in English to in German. I knew my analyst understood German—although his grammar was not so good—but it was important for me to recapture my experience in the language in which I recorded my memories. One of the benefits of a bilingual analysis for us immigrants is that it promotes the integration of rather diverse experiences into a sense of self. Experiences remembered in both languages can then be integrated, rather than experiences in one language being privileged at the expense of the other.

When I came across my name in Marco's Afterword, I was happy to see that my dates of birth and death were not listed. So, according to Marco, I will continue to be around and be part of the field in which Marco Conci is vigilantly keeping track of our past, thereby making sure we have a future direction toward which to grow.

New York City, December 2017

ILLUSTRATIONS

1. With my parents, Burchiello, September 1975.

2. Trieste, December 1989.

3. With Stephen and Margaret Mitchell, Rome, April 1991.

4. With Merton Gill, Bologna, June 1991.

5. With Goldy and Paul Parin, Bologna, December 1991.

6. With Gaetano Benedetti, Milan, February 1992.

7.With Robert Holt, Trento, May 1992.

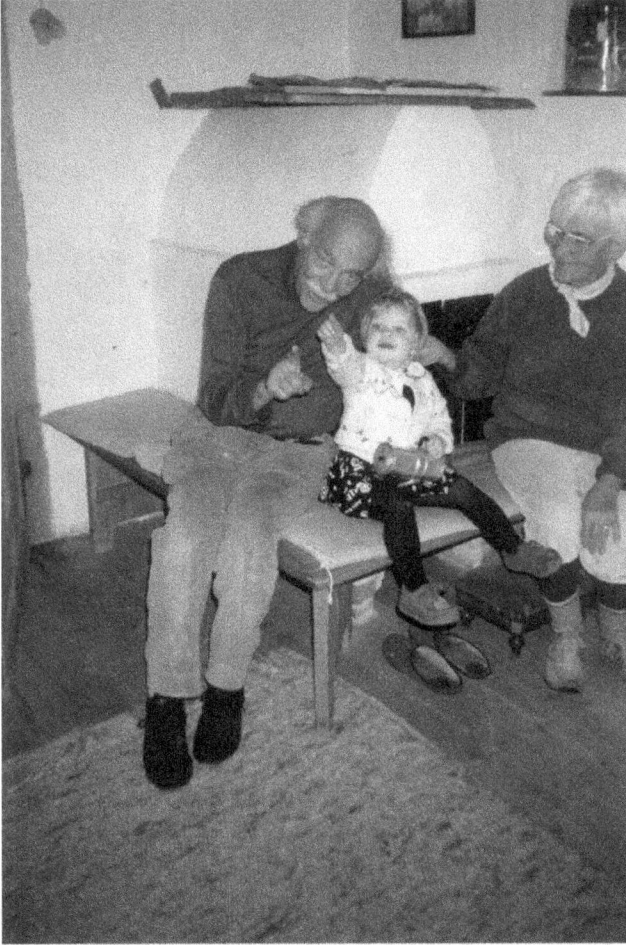

8. My daughter Anna with Johannes and Annemarie Cremerius, September 1992.

9. With Stephen Mitchell and the Editorial Board of IFP, New York City, January 1996.

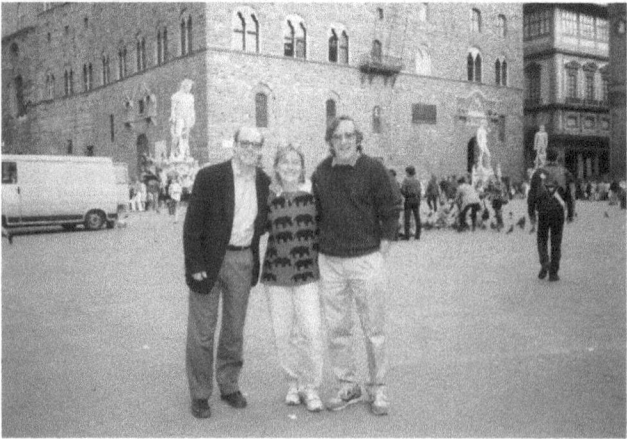

10. With Margaret and Stephen Mitchell, Florence, April 1996.

11. With Stephen Mitchell and Marianne Horney Eckardt, IFPS New York Forum, May 2000.

12. With Arnold Richards and Arthur Lynch, New York City, January 2016.

from coming in touch with a variety of authors and analytic traditions.

Franco Borgogno, University of Turin, Italian Psychoanalytic Society, and Recipient of the Sigourney Award

Every fractured field needs a capacious thinker, generous in spirit, who relaxes rigidities, heals splits, and includes the previously excluded. In this valuable anthology, Marco Conci creates a true international psychoanalysis, forging a historical arc that reverses prior disappearances. Cataloging psychoanalytic theory across continental boundaries, he demonstrates an ethic of inclusion through his long-standing *fine disregard* for geographical, parochial, and continental customs. Anyone who aspires to a broadly defined, nonprejudicial psychoanalytic awareness should read this book—it is our new global standard.

Andrea Celenza, American Psychoanalytical Association

Marco Conci has a double gift. On the one hand, he explains to us the most important points of view and the major preoccupations of Freud, Sullivan, Mitchell, and Bion, from the perspective of the historian and on the basis of a personal selection of a whole series of sources. On the other hand, his analytic competence allows him to show us the roots, the contradictions and the value of the various analytic concepts and hypothesis he deals with. His ambition and his capacity to connect and let these two perspectives interact with each other is convincing and makes his book into an important document.

Michael Ermann, German Psychoanalytic Society

Marco Conci, more than anyone else, is responsible for introducing both interpersonal and relational psychoanalysis to the European continent. Just as he did in his ground-breaking biography of Harry Stack Sullivan, here he focuses on Stephen Mitchell's contributions and how these are closely linked with Sullivan's revolutionary theorizing. Dr. Conci illustrates in great detail, partly stemming from a close personal relationship with Mitchell, how relational psychoanalysis evolved and what are its essential features. How Dr. Conci's scholarly interests and curiosities have directly led to a profound expansion of psychoanalytic theorizing in Europe is a must-read for anyone with any interest in psychoanalytic scholarship.

Irwin Hirsch, New York University Postdoctoral Program in Psychoanalysis and Psychotherapy, William Alanson White Institute

A fascinating and masterfully written account of the history of psychoanalysis—full of exciting encounters and vibrant ideas, throbbing with life. The power and glamour of Marco Conci's book spring from his deep insight into the profoundly "dialogical nature" and the international character of psychoanalysis. Bridging the divides between various schools, Conci skillfully navigates us through the history of psychoanalysis and will largely help historians of psychoanalysis and everyone interested in psychoanalysis to understand the "multiple voices" of psychoanalysis in the past, present, and in the future. This is psychoanalytic historiography at its best.

Galina Hristeva, Recipient of the 2011 IPA-Sacerdoti Prize

Marco Conci has written a valuable book for anyone interested in psychoanalysis. He offers a comprehensive view of the minds and psychoanalytic approaches of critical figures in the profession, providing biographical, social, and historical context. The book is beautifully woven together with personal and professional aspects of the author's experience. This is an excellent and wonderfully readable book in and about comparative, international psychoanalysis.

Montana S. Katz, National Psychological Association for Psychoanalysis

Internationally acclaimed historian of Harry Stack Sullivan, Marco Conci now gives us a most informative and readable history of international voices in psychoanalysis, adding an interesting autobiographical note.

Henry Zvi Lothane, Icahn School of Medicine at Mount Sinai

Marco Conci is both en route and at home in the various cultures and communities of psychoanalysis, tirelessly creating connections and promoting contacts, notwithstanding our Babylonian language confusion. His own Italian-German-American biography, openly unfolded before us, together with his scholarly achievements, offer a welcome evidence that a universal, cosmopolitan psychoanalysis is possible.

Ulrike May, German Psychoanalytic Association

Psychoanalysis goes through an ongoing process of revision and further development of Freud's original concepts. Marco Conci's unique and very well researched anthology represents mandatory reading for the knowledge of some of the most important lines of development which, starting from Freud and going through Sullivan and Bion, include the present debate on the analytic field concept.

His deep knowledge of Sullivan and Bion in particular allows us to come to new and surprising insights into the thinking of these two pioneers of contemporary psychoanalysis and represents an important contribution to an urgently needed comparative psychoanalysis.

Such an achievement was made possible not only by his historical competence, but also by his work of many years as co-editor-in-chief of the *International Forum of Psychoanalysis*. This allowed him not only to gain a unique knowledge of a variety of analytic developments in a variety of countries, but also to come into a lively contact and exchange with many colleagues around the world.

Wolfgang Mertens, Munich Akademie für Psychoanalyse und Psychotherapie, LMU Munich University

Marco Conci's "personal journey" in the field of psychoanalysis shows not only his well-known talent as a historian (detailed descriptions of events and circumstances, places, exact dates, etc.), but also another important aspect: when he discusses Stephen Mitchell's contribution to psychoanalysis, Conci always emphasizes that Mitchell's "relational" approach has to be seen not as a separate psychoanalytic school, alternative to traditional psychoanalysis. Over and over again, Conci clearly argues that the field must not be dichotomized, and that schools of thought that may seem far from each other can, instead, be seen as parts of a whole, in the tradition of authors such as Leo Rangell, Fred Pine, and John Gedo, among others. He also shows that it is impossible to fully understand the history of psychoanalytic theory without analyzing the influence of political, economical, sociological, and affective factors.

Paolo Migone, co-editor of Psicoterapia e Scienze Umane, co-chair of the Rapaport–Klein Study Group

Marco Conci's brilliance is in translating the international, historical conversation that defines our contemporary practice of psychoanalysis. This collection of essays passionately presents the conceptual steps in a practicing clinician's developing thought while, at the same time, presenting Conci, the man, deeply aware of time and timelessness, the particularities of place, and the necessary theoretical steps toward psychoanalytic universality, applicable in clinical method.

Ian Miller, New York University Postdoctoral Program in Psychoanalysis and Psychotherapy, Dublin Trinity

College

In this unique anthology of papers, Marco Conci convincingly shows how much we could all profit from giving more room and consideration to the history of our field.

Claudio Neri, Italian Psychoanalytic Society

Reading Marco Conci's book makes us understand the usefulness of an accurate vision of the history characterizing the birth and the development of psychoanalytic theories and models. The author shows us their interrelationships with the life of the authors of these models and their relations within groups and institutions. Furthermore, Conci has created a sense of continuity among facts that at a first impression might have looked as being marginal, but which, after his reconstruction, have assumed a new and different profile, thus allowing us to get a more complete vision of the international psychoanalytic scene. The author's familiarity with a series of theories outside the analytic main stream makes this book particularly precious.

Of particular interest is also the close and clear relationship between the author himself, his life, his encounters, his critical work, and his thought. Psychoanalysis is such a unique discipline that all the authors writing about it also write about themselves, as Marco does through his references to his personal and professional life, and the original and innovative way in which he connects them to the development of his thought.

Anna Nicolò, President of the
Italian Psychoanalytic Society

Marco Conci takes readers on a masterful potentially transformative dialogical journey through the history of psychoanalysis, where the person and the work are intimately connected, bridging traditional irreconcilables and presenting Freud, Sullivan, Mitchell, and Bion as dialogical partners in a common enterprise, reflecting multiple visions of human experience. In this superbly researched anthology of previously published and unpublished papers, letters, interviews, meetings, and any other kind of interaction, Conci centers upon the ways in which the lives and personalities of Freud, Sullivan, Mitchell, and Bion influenced their clinical priorities, sensibilities and theories.

Not only may personal communications (traced, as in Freud's case, to early adolescence) contain the germs of conception of later formulations of theories, they

also provide clues to understanding theories, in their
evolutionary depth and mutual interconnectedness.

In this way of presenting, talking about and
understanding history of psychoanalysis, the author
emphasizes (and illustrates) the dialogical dimension of
the founding and evolution of psychoanalysis as the field,
and a dialogical discipline and experience.

In addition, mindful the importance of multilingual
and multicultural milieu, from the birth of psychoanalysis
(and its founder) onwards, instrumental in Freud's
facility with translation between multiple symbolic codes
on the first place, ultimately informing his discovery of
the unconscious, Conci is among the pioneers of the
multilayered multitheoretical and multi-institutional
dialogue across the psychoanalytic cultures and
geographies. This includes dialogue between the tradition
and innovation fermenting on the margins, penetrating
the walls of any form of theoretical and institutional
parochialism, exclusion, and isolation.

Fortified by his own personal and professional life
transforming journey across the borders of international
psychoanalysis, Conci's transformative way of writing
about the history of psychoanalysis ultimately leads to
a fuller understanding and appreciation of the present
psychoanalytic theory and clinical practice, as it fuels the
creative ferment of its emergent future.

Eva D. Papiasvili, American Psychoanalytic Association,
co-chair for North America (USA, Canada, Japan) of
the IPA Inter-Regional Encyclopedic Dictionary of
Psychoanalysis, Czech Psychoanalytical Society

Through this anthology Marco Conci introduces us to the
life, personality, and work of important authors congenial
to him such as Sullivan, Mitchell, and Bion, given his
awareness that the variety of today's analytic languages
represents a crucial way for accessing and representing
the complexity of psychic life. This is what also allows
him to find the key of Freud's creativity in his multilingual
cultural and relational background.

In fact, Freud's letters to his school-friend Eduard
Silberstein represent the first topic of this anthology,
together with Freud's later letters to his family members,
his colleagues, and his pupils, whose importance has in
the last years become more clear to us through the work
of a whole series of researchers, including the author of
this book.

But Marco Conci's research is both unique and
precious since it has accompanied his own training as a
psychoanalyst, his work as a translator of English and

German analytic texts, and his research work in the history of psychoanalysis. Such a work, including his personal contacts with various analytic communities, accompanied him from the very beginning of his fascination with our field, and long before he eventually became a member of the IPA.

From this point of view, I do not find it surprising that the author, coming from an ancient town at the border between the Italian and the German cultural and linguistic areas, after such a long process of "initiation," ended up working in the language of his ancestors—and of Freud himself.

Mariella Pierri, Italian Psychoanalytic Society,
Department of Psychiatry, University of Padua

With indefatigable industry and an unquenchable passion for the historian's craft, Marco Conci leads the reader on a grand tour of authors who have shaped his own thinking as they have much of international psychoanalysis. One may say of Conci what Didier Anzieu has said of Freud: that he is "not a man of a single culture but of the interlocking of cultures," and his expertly conducted quartet shows why "it is not possible to become a psychoanalyst without the ability to surpass (while retaining) one's culture of origin and to combine different cultural references."

Peter L. Rudnytsky, University of Florida and Chicago
Psychoanalytic Institute

Marco Conci is a scholarly historian of psychoanalytic institutions and biographer of the intellectual and professional lives of analysts, combining in his work a variety of theoretical orientations and clinical traditions.

This voluminous collection of articles and interviews, erudite chapters introducing them, and a concluding rich *Selbstdarstellung* on his own trajectory as an analyst and a researcher in the international field provides us with a wide-ranging exploration of many aspects of the history of the psychoanalytic movement and its "multiple voices": from the early days of Freud's correspondence with his adolescence friends to the contributions of such contemporary analysts as Stephen Mitchell, Horst Kächele, and Stefano Bolognini, via such controversial authors as Sullivan and Bion.

Readers of Conci's important book will (re)discover here the pleasure of engaging with psychoanalytic ideas, old and new, with the authors who have developed them, and with the complex, pluralistic, and often surprising connections they entertain with one another.

Andrea Sabbadini, British Psychoanalytical Society

Marco Conci's characteristic scholarship is evident in this book. His interest in encompassing the variations in psychoanalytic thought across the international scene is an important project that has the potential to reduce the Balkanization of psychoanalysis that persists to some extent even today. His personal narrative of Steven Mitchell's influence on Italian psychoanalysis is probably unknown to many and offers us an insider view of how Mitchell's work interfaced with that of other theories on the Italian scene.

Joyce Slochower, New York University Postdoctoral Program in Psychoanalysis and Psychotherapy

Once, at the beginning of our friendship, Marco Conci asked me about what he called my "itinerary" in psychoanalysis. This has remained for me a fruitful way for thinking about psychoanalysis ever since. I am happy that, through this fascinating anthology of his papers, many colleagues will now have the chance to get to know his own unique personal and scientific itinerary.

Most of the papers originally came out in the *International Forum of Psychoanalysis*, which I founded in 1992, and to whose relevance in our field Marco Conci also gave an important contribution.

Jan Stensson, International Forum of Psychoanalysis

Marco Conci presents an amazing application of the talking cure method: integrating the psychoanalytic traditions by means of historical reflection and narrative transformation. There is a lot to learn from it.

Herbert Will, German Psychoanalytic Society